Illustrator® cs Bible

Illustrator® cs Bible

Ted Alspach and Jennifer Alspach

Wiley Publishing, Inc.

Illustrator® cs Bible

Published by
Wiley Publishing, Inc.
111 River Street
Hoboken, NJ 07030
www.wiley.com

Copyright © 2004 by Wiley Publishing, Inc., Indianapolis, Indiana

Published simultaneously in Canada

ISBN: 0-7645-3906-X

Manufactured in the United States of America

10 9 8 7 6 5 4 3 2 1

1B/SR/RQ/QT/IN

For general information on our other products and services or to obtain technical support, please contact our Customer Care Department within the U.S. at (800) 762-2974, outside the U.S. at (317) 572-3993 or fax (317) 572-4002.

Wiley also publishes its books in a variety of electronic formats. Some content that appears in print may not be available in electronic books.

Library of Congress Control Number: 2003105855

About the Authors

Ted Alspach is the author of many books on desktop publishing and graphics, as well as hundreds of articles on related topics, including *Illustrator 7 Studio Secrets*, *Illustrator 7 Bible*, *Photoshop Complete*, *Kai's Power Tools Studio Secrets*, and *Illustrator Filter Finesse*. He is a contributing editor to *Adobe Magazine*.

Jennifer Alspach has authored many books on computer related subjects including *Teach Yourself Photoshop 5.0/5.5*, and *Photoshop and Illustrator Synergy Studio Secrets*. Her illustrations have appeared in various publications, including *Adobe Magazine*. In addition, Jennifer regularly speaks at various seminars, Macworld Expo's, and user groups all over the country. Other works by Jennifer include co-authoring *Photoshop Studio Secrets 5/e*, and illustrating *Macworld Illustrator Bible*.

Credits

Acquisitions Editor
Tom Heine

Project Editors
Maureen Spears

Technical Editor
Dennis Cohen

Copy Editor
Beth Taylor

Project Coordinator
Ryan Steffen

Graphics and Production Specialists
Beth Brooks
Amanda Carter
Jennifer Click
Sean Decker
Lauren Goddard
Joyce Haughey
Michael Kruzil
Clint Lahnen
Kristin McMullan
Mary Gillot Virgin

Quality Control Technicians
Laura Albert
John Tyler Connoley
John Greenough
Andy Hollandbeck
Susan Moritz
Carl William Pierce
Dwight Ramsey

Proofreading and Indexing
TECHBOOKS Production Services

Special Help
Jerelin Charles
Martin V. Minner
Amanda Peterson

To the furry creatures who allow us to share their lives:

Murphy — Equus stubbornis
Toulouse — Felis monstrositis
Yote — Canis lazyis
Static — Felis obnoxious
Sage — Felis affectionis

— TA

In Memory of Linus and Pyro who shared their
wonderful furry lives with us for many years.

—JA

Preface

You are holding in your hands the biggest, most thorough, and most helpful guide to Adobe Illustrator you'll find anywhere.

Gives you a bit of a rush, doesn't it?

The *Illustrator Bible* is the book we wrote because we couldn't find the book we wanted about Adobe Illustrator. Now we have it, and believe it or not, we're constantly using our own book as a reference. We'd love to tell the world, "sure, we know that," without putting them on hold while we search the index for the "Reset Tracking to 0" Mac key command (⌘+Shift+X, by the way). There's just too much about Illustrator for any one person to keep in his or her head at one time; now, this latest edition of the book gathers all the Illustrator information you can't remember and makes it more available and easier to follow than the plot twists on your favorite soap opera.

If you're at your local bookstore looking at the different Illustrator books to choose from, don't just pick this one because it weighs the most (sorry about that . . . we get more thank-you letters from chiropractors who've stayed in business because of this monstrosity . . .) or because it works great as a booster seat for your two-year-old nephew. Instead, take a look-see through these pages, which are stuffed to overflowing with in-depth Illustrator information that you just won't find anywhere else.

What's New in This Edition

Illustrator cs has added many very cool new features as well as revamping some of the old standby tools. In this edition, you'll find complete coverage of the new functions and features and extensive explanations on how these new features work. For a complete listing of new features, see Appendix A.

Is This the Illustrator Book for You?

We've been to bookstores. We've seen the other Illustrator books out there. Some of them are quite good. Some of them are fairly awful. But none of them can match the *Illustrator cs Bible* for thoroughness, usefulness, or completeness. We've left no vector-based stone unturned.

Here are more reasons the *Illustrator cs Bible* is the best overall book on Illustrator:

✦ **The most complete coverage of Illustrator.** This book isn't big because we wanted to hog all of the retail book space to ourselves (of course, that's not a bad idea) but because we've tried to include every possible thing you'd ever want to know about Illustrator. From learning the basics of drawing to creating outstanding special effects with vectors and rasters, it's all here.

✦ **Fun, original, different artwork to illustrate the techniques and capabilities of Illustrator.** When we say different, we're not talking about the type of "art" where there's a naked guy in a room sitting on a stool reciting the first few lines of the Declaration of Independence over and over and over again (that's supposedly "performance art," heh), but instead, we mean that each technique is created with a different piece of artwork. Some of it is simple and some of it is complex, with each piece showing not only a particular feature but other Illustrator capabilities as well.

✦ **Clean artwork without those annoying jaggies.** This is vector software. When you think of vectors, you probably think of smooth, flowing paths that don't look like someone filled in a bunch of squares on a sheet of graph paper. So instead of using screen shots for paths shown in this book, each path was painstakingly drawn in Illustrator. We think you'll appreciate the difference.

✦ **Top-notch technical prowess.** Once again, the *Illustrator cs Bible* has gotten the best possible people to do a technical review of the book. Previous editions were technically reviewed by Eric Gibson, the lead technical support engineer for Illustrator, and Andrei Herasimchuk, who designed and implemented the Illustrator 7 interface and was behind such useful new features as the visible transformation origin point. This edition was tech-edited by Sandra Alves who currently works at Adobe Systems, Inc. as a UI designer for Adobe Photoshop.

✦ **Perfect for teaching.** If you know Illustrator inside and out, you'll find the *Illustrator cs Bible* the best teaching tool available for Illustrator, with examples and explanations that complement a teaching environment perfectly. Many computer training companies teaching Illustrator use this book, as do schools and universities.

✦ **Real-world examples and advice.** Illustrator doesn't exist in a vacuum. Instead, it is often used in conjunction with other programs, in a variety of different environments and situations. Some people use Illustrator to create logos, others create full-page advertisements, and still others create entire billboards with Illustrator. Throughout this book, we present various real-world situations and examples that truly add to your understanding of each topic.

You don't need to be an artist or a computer geek to learn Illustrator with this book. No matter what your level of Illustrator experience — from the person who calls tech support for help getting the #$@&#!! shrink-wrap off the box to the person who puts the frustrated party on hold at Adobe — you'll undoubtedly find new things to try, and learn more about Illustrator along the way.

How to Get the Most Out of This Book

You may want to be aware of a few matters before you dive too deeply into the mysteries of vector-based graphics, Adobe style:

✦ **Versions.** When you see the word Illustrator, it refers to all versions of Illustrator. When we stick a number after the word Illustrator, it's relevant to that version only. Version numbers in the software industry change faster than time slots for *Frasier*, so version cs.0 may become version CS.0.1, CS.1, CS.2, or some other number before you know it. When we're talking about version CS, we'll be referring to CS.*x*, where *x* is any number at all. When Adobe releases version cs or the next major upgrade, look for a new version of this book to help you through it.

✦ **Menu and keyboard commands.** To indicate that you need to choose a command from a menu, we write something like MenuName ➪ Command. For example, File ➪ Save. If a command is nested in a submenu, it is presented as MenuName ➪ Submenu ➪ Command, as in Filter ➪ Distort ➪ Roughen. If a command has a keyboard command, we mention that as well for both Macintosh and Windows versions. For example, Save uses "Command+S" on the Mac, which we'll present as ⌘+S (⌘ corresponds to the ⌘ symbol on your keyboard. The other Mac keys are spelled out — Option, Shift, Control, and so forth.). Save uses "Ctrl+S" in Windows (corresponds to the Ctrl key on the Windows keyboard). So, both platforms are specified by saying, "to save a document, press ⌘+S (Ctrl+S). Notice that the Mac convention is stated first, and that the Windows convention follows it in parentheses.

✦ **This is not a novel.** As much as we'd like you to discover plot intricacies, subtle characterizations, and moral fabric woven into the story, none of those things exist in this book (if they do, be sure to let us know about them). You can use this book in two really good ways:

1. Look up what interests you in the Contents or the Index, and refer to that section. Rinse and repeat as necessary.

2. Slowly, calmly work your way through the entire book, trying out examples (the funky Steps that are almost everywhere) and techniques as you run across them. The book is designed to be read this way, each chapter building on the previous chapter.

✦ **Have fun.** This book is a pretty straightforward, serious tome, although we have managed to include many bad puns ("rotate the image as far as you're inclined to") and terrible jokes: How many FreeHand users does it take to draw a light bulb? Three. One at the computer, one on hold to Macromedia tech support, and the other back at the computer store, trying to exchange the software for Illustrator. Of course, we show you how to draw a realistic-looking light bulb in Chapter 11, "Using Path Blends, Compound Paths, and Masks."

What's a Computer Book without Icons?

Nonexistent, for the most part. We've included several icons throughout this edition that may make reading this book a little more enjoyable and helpful.

Tip   These icons indicate some sort of power-user secret you absolutely need to know to be able to illustrate with the big kids.

Note   Did you know that the third edition of this book was the best-selling book on Illustrator 7? Interesting tidbits such as this one are noted by this icon. Sort of like having Cliff from *Cheers* rambling on about something every few pages. Slightly interesting, but they won't increase your Illustrator skills. Just something we thought you might want to know.

Caution   Danger Will Robinson!!! If Robby the Robot used Illustrator, he'd be reading about all the nasty things that can happen and how to avoid them.

New Feature   These icons indicate what's brand new in version cs of Illustrator. Kind of like finding a prize in your cereal box.

Cross-Reference   These icons point you to other places in the book where you can find more information on a given topic. If you're bored, you can play a game of jumping from one cross reference to another and see if you can make it back to where you started.

What's Inside the Book

Here's a brief rundown on what to expect in the *Illustrator cs Bible*:

- ✦ **Part I: Illustrator Basics.** This section has us pointing out all the funky elements of the cool Illustrator interface (can you say palettes a plenty) and how to work with documents (you know, the open, close, and save stuff). It also covers the basics of drawing, painting, and working with objects. You learn how to color things, how to uncolor things, and how to delete those things when you don't like their color.

- ✦ **Part II: Putting Illustrator to Work.** This section puts you to work learning about type and how to fine-tune those paths and objects you drew in Part I. It also gives you a chance to bend and distort paths. Part II also contains a healthy dose of the hard stuff — such as compound paths, masks, blends, patterns, and type.

✦ **Part III: Mastering Illustrator.** This is the section that contains the nitty-gritty — and we don't mean the dirt band. Hot topics such as using Illustrator styles, effects, filters, and techniques for creating fantastic graphics are presented. This section includes several newer features such as transparency and working with raster images. We even show you how to customize Illustrator to work better and faster.

✦ **Part IV: Getting Art Out of Illustrator.** This section describes the ways to get stuff out of Illustrator. Artwork can leave to go to the print world, or go on an all-expenses paid trip to the Web.

✦ **Appendixes.** The three appendixes contain information on what's new in Illustrator cs, shortcuts, and Illustrator resources.

Help Make Illustrator Better

Okay, you know by now that we just love Illustrator. But the program can always be made more user-friendly, more functional, and just plain better. If you have such an idea, please send an e-mail to suggestions@adobe.com.

Adobe does listen to its users, and the more readers that ask for a feature, the more likely that feature will get into a future version of Illustrator. The Illustrator product managers, including me, are eager for any and all suggestions.

— *Ted and Jennifer Alspach*

Acknowledgments

Whew. As we write these acknowledgments, we're just about finished with the total revamping of this gigantic book. And while we're just plain exhausted, we know we'd be much more tired if it were not for the help and support of several key people. This list is by no means exhaustive, but the individuals named here are the ones most responsible for getting this book out the door.

Tom Heine at Wiley Publishing is always a great support to have on our side. Thanks to Maureen Spears, who led the project to its glorious completion.

We also acknowledge all the great artists who contributed images for the color insert sections including Joe Jones, Brian Warchesik, Jason McQuitty, Martin Mendelsberg, Corey Gray and Shane Duerksen.

Contents at a Glance

Contents

Part II: Putting Illustrator to Work   271

Chapter 7: Using Illustrator to Organize Objects 273

Part III: Mastering Illustrator — 511

Chapter 12: Working with Graphic Styles, Filters, and Effects 513

Part IV: Getting Art Out of Illustrator   621

Chapter 15: Understanding PostScript and Printing 623

Illustrator Basics

Understanding Illustrator's Desktop

Not too long ago, commercial artists and illustrators worked by hand, not on computers. You might find it hard to believe, but they spent hours and hours with T-squares, rulers, French curves, and type galleys from their local typesetters.

Now, of course, most artists and artist wannabes spend hours and hours with their computers, mouses (or should that be mice?), digitizing tablets, monitors, and onscreen type that they set themselves. Some traditional artists are still out there, but more and more make the transition to the digital world every day.

After the complete of that transition, computer artists usually come face-to-face with Illustrator, the industry-standard, graphics-creation software for both print and the Web. The following is a typical example of how people get to know Illustrator.

Picasso Meets Illustrator: Getting Started

Illustrator arrives and the enthusiastic artist-to-be — we'll call him Picasso — opens the box, pops in the CD-ROM, and installs the product, while glancing at the quick reference card and thumbing through the manual. A few minutes later Picasso launches Illustrator and is faced with a clean, brand-new, empty document. A world of possibilities awaits, only a few mouse clicks away. But Picasso is a little intimidated by all that white space, just as many budding young writers wince at a new word processing document with the lone insertion point blinking away.

So, Picasso decides he'll "play" with the software before designing anything "for real." He chooses the rectangle tool first, clicks, drags, and voilà! A rectangle appears on the screen! His confidence soars. He may try the other shape tools next, but sooner or later Picasso starts playing with some of the software's other features. Eventually, he eyes the dreaded Pen tool. And thus starts his downward spiral into terror.

Confusion ensues. Hours of staring at an Illustrator document and wondering "Why?" take up the majority of his time. Picasso doesn't really understand fills and strokes, he doesn't understand stacking order and layers, and he certainly doesn't understand Bézier curves.

Even Picasso's painting-factory boss can't help him much with Illustrator; questions result in a knowing nod and the customary tilt and swivel of his head toward the Illustrator manual. Picasso goes through the tutorial three times, but whenever he strays one iota from the set-in-stone printed steps, nothing works. Picasso becomes convinced that the Pen tool is Satan's pitchfork in disguise. Patterns make about as much sense as differential equations. Then he encounters things such as effects that can be edited later (huh?), miter limits for strokes (yeah, right), and the difference between targeting a group or all the objects in that group (huh? again). All are subjects that might as well have been written about in a third-century Chinese dialect, such as the hard-to-find *Chinese Book of Patterns*.

Picasso had never used or seen software as *different* as Illustrator.

Ah, but you have an advantage over Picasso. You have this book. The following sections in this chapter take you through the interface and common editing commands that help you construct better illustrations. The other areas focused on will be the basic Illustrator functions, from setting up a new document to understanding exactly what paths are and how Illustrator uses them.

Getting started with Illustrator

The first step in getting started is to install the software, which is slightly different depending on whether you're using a Macintosh or a Windows computer. Once the software is installed, you can launch Illustrator in one of the following ways:

✦ Double-click Illustrator's application icon.

✦ Double-click an Illustrator document, which automatically launches Illustrator.

✦ In Windows, choose Start ➪ Programs ➪ Adobe Illustrator. In Macintosh, select the Illustrator icon from the Dock.

Quitting Illustrator

Having learned how to open the program, it's time to learn how to close it. You can end your Illustrator session at any time by choosing File ⇨ Quit (or Exit). This action closes the current document, and exits the application. If you have not previously saved your document, Illustrator prompts you to do so before exiting the application. You can also close Illustrator as follows:

✦ **Mac OSX:** Click and hold the Illustrator icon in the Dock, and then click Quit, or Control-click the Dock icon and then click Quit. You can also choose Illustrator ⇨ Quit. You also have the option of pressing Ctrl, clicking the Illustrator icon in the dock, and choose Quit or Command+Q.

✦ **Windows:** Right-click Illustrator's taskbar icon and click Close, or press Alt + F4 and click Close from the pop-up menu. You can also close Illustrator by right-click the taskbar icon and pick Close, or by pressing Ctrl+Q.

Note   For Mac OS X, the Quit menu item is under the Illustrator menu.

If you run into a situation in which the Quit function doesn't work, or is unavailable, you can try one of the following options:

✦ **Mac OSX:** Press the Option key at the same time you press ⌘ and click the dock. Choose Force Quit. Alternatively, you can press Command+Option+Esc to bring up the Force Quit menu and choose Illustrator from the list. Note that this causes you to lose any unsaved work. There is no need to restart your computer after force quitting. You do need to restart Illustrator, however, if you wish to continue working in Illustrator.

✦ **Windows:** Press Ctrl+Alt+Delete to enable the Task Manager, which you can use to "force" Illustrator to quit. Note that this can cause you to lose any unsaved work and may make your system unstable; if you do this, you'll be better off if you take the time to restart your computer before running Illustrator again (or before opening any other software applications, for that matter).

Working with Illustrator's Interface

Understanding the interface is the first step in learning Illustrator. Adobe has kept its products looking consistent so that using all of its programs together is easy. The tools, palettes, and menus are pretty similar when using Illustrator, Photoshop, and InDesign.

Illustrator's interface holds many elements that let you work in optimum productivity. Once you understand the interface, the creation process is much easier. When looking at Illustrator, you'll find the following:

✦ **Document window:** The Document window appears when you open an existing document or start a new document. The artboard and pasteboard are housed within the Document window. You create your illustrations using these two elements.

✦ **Toolbox:** The toolbox houses the tools you need to create amazing artwork. The tools are set as icons that represent what the tool looks like.

✦ **Palettes:** You can move the palettes around (floating) to any location. You can also close or open palettes, as needed.

✦ **Menu:** The menus are across the top of the screen (Mac) or window (Windows) and access many of Illustrator's powerful commands.

✦ **Status bar:** The Status bar runs along the bottom-left edge of the Illustrator document window. Here you can set the zoom level and see what the tool currently being used is.

✦ **Artboard:** The artboard is the part of the work area that contains the art you want to print. It is shown as a thin black rectangle.

Working in the document window

The document window is where you perform all your work. It contains two main elements: the artboard and the page, or pasteboard. The page is always centered in the artboard, as shown in Figure 1-1. The palettes have been hidden so that you can see the whole document window. You can move the printable area represented by the dashed lines using the Page tool. More detail on the Page tool is covered in this chapter.

Illustrator windows act like windows in most other programs. You use the title bar at the top of the window to move the window around your screen. On the title bar is the name of the document. If you have not yet saved your document, the name of the document is Untitled-1, with the number changing for each new document you create. (Hint: Save it as soon as you create it!) Next to the title of the document is the current viewing percentage relative to actual size.

The scroll bars on the right side of the window let you see what is above and below the current viewing area.

 Cross-Reference See "Using the scroll bars to view your document" later in this chapter for more on scrollbars.

Three vital buttons help you close, minimize, and maximize the various windows you open in Illustrator. You find these buttons on the upper-left corner in OS X, and on the upper-right corner in Windows. Although these three buttons are self-explanatory, their functions are listed as follows:

✦ **Minimize:** When you click this button in Windows, Illustrator replaces the document window with an icon on the application window, and a Restore button appears. This Restore button allows you to return the document window to its former size and position. Similiarly, in OS X, the document changes to an icon in the dock.

✦ **Maximize/Zoom:** In Windows, the Maximize button makes the document window expand to its largest size in the application window. For Macs, the Zoom button allows you to toggle the window between its current and its maximum size.

✦ **Close:** This button closes your window entirely. If you have not yet saved your file, clicking the Close button generates a dialog box that allows you to save the file. You can open multiple document windows simultaneously and have the title of each window appear at the bottom of the Window menu, where a checkmark indicates the currently active document window.

Menus

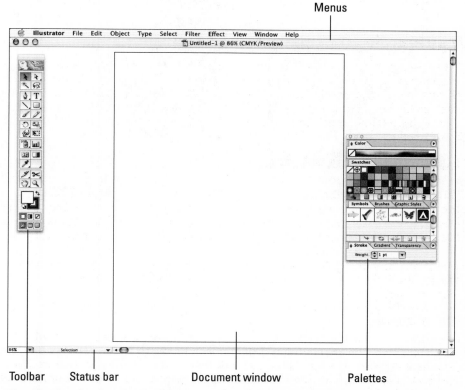

Toolbar   Status bar   Document window   Palettes

Figure 1-1: The document window contains the page, surrounded by the artboard.

In addition to these buttons, the Windows version of Illustrator offers three options that help you quickly access your files. The Cascade, Tile, and Arrange Icons commands are all accessible via the Window menu:

✦ **Cascade:** When you have multiple files open, this command lines up all of the title bars in a staggered (stairstep) arrangement going down and to the right.

✦ **Tile:** With multiple files open, this command tiles the windows next to one another to fill the application window.

✦ **Arrange Icons:** This command takes your open files and arranges them into neat rows. Figure 1-2 shows two document windows opened next to each other.

Figure 1-2: Multiple document windows can be tiled next to each other.

The artboard

The artboard is the area in which the art will be printed. Its size is determined by what you enter. The area of the artboard doesn't have to be the same as the printed document. The artboard is visible by black lines and shows the largest area in which you can print. The actual printed page is displayed as a dotted line. To set the size, orientation, and units for the artboard, use Document Setup. Open

Document Setup by choosing File ➪ Document Setup. To change the page size, use the Print Setup dialog box and choose Page. To access the Print dialog box, choose File ➪ Print.

If you don't want to see the artboard, choose View ➪ Hide Artboard. Doing this hides the dotted line. To show the artboard again, choose View ➪ Show Artboard.

If you are taking your Illustrator artwork into another application, such as Photoshop or InDesign, the size of the artboard is irrelevant; your entire illustration appears in most other software applications even if that artwork is larger than the artboard.

The work area

When using Illustrator, the worst thing that can happen is for you to lose an illustration on which you are working. "Where'd it all go?" you cry, perhaps adding a few vulgarities. This can happen very easily in Illustrator. Just click a few times on the gray parts of the scroll bars at the bottom of the document window. Each time you click, you move about half the width (or height) of your window, and three clicks later, your page and everything on it is no longer in front of you. Instead, you see the work area's scratch area, usually a vast expanse of white nothingness.

The work area measures 227.5×227.5 inches, which works out to about 360 square feet of drawing space. At actual size, you see only a very small section of the artboard. A little letter-size document looks extremely tiny on a work area this big. If you get lost in the work area, a quick way back is to choose View ➪ Actual Size. Doing this puts your page in the center of the window at 100-percent view, at which time you can see at least part of your drawing. To see the whole page quickly, choose View ➪ Fit in Window, which resizes the view down to where you can see the entire page.

This discussion assumes, of course, that you have actually drawn artwork on the defined page. Illustrator used to get frantic calls from people who chose Fit in Window, which immediately resulted in the disappearance of all their artwork. It took a while to figure out that these artists had drawn their artwork way off on the side of the work area.

The Page tool

The Page tool, shown in Figure 1-4 and which you access via the Hand tool (see Figure 1-3), changes how much of your document prints; it does this by moving the printable area of the document without moving any of the printable objects in the document. Clicking and dragging the lower-left corner of the page relocates the printable area of the page to the place where you release the mouse button.

Cross-Reference

The Hand tool is located in the Illustrator's toolbox. For more on the toolbox, see the next section.

Figure 1-3: Hand tool houses the Page tool in its toolbox slot.

Figure 1-4: You access the Page tool by clicking the Hand tool and then selecting the tool from the flyout menu that appears.

 Tip   Double-clicking the Page tool slot resets the printable-area dotted line to its original position on the page.

The Page tool is useful when your document is larger than the biggest image area your printer can print. The tool enables you to tile several pages to create one large page out of several sheets of paper. *Tiling* is the process in which an image is assembled by using several pieces of paper arranged in a grid formation. A portion of the image prints on each page, and when you fit the pages together you can view the image in its entirety. Tiling is really only good for rough laser prints, because a you need to manually trim a quarter inch around the edge of each paper.

 Cross-Reference   To learn more about how to print and all that process entails, see Chapter 16.

The toolbox

The toolbox appears on top of your document window, covering up part of your document window in the upper-left corner. The toolbox (see Figure 1-5) has no close box. To close it, you must choose Window ➪ Tools. You make the Toolbox visible by placing a checkmark next to the Window menu's Tools menu item. You hide the Toolbox by clicking the checkmarked item, so that no checkmark appears next to the Tools menu item. The tools are discussed throughout the book in the chapters that use those tools.

 Tip   To hides *all* palettes, not just the toolbox, press the Tab key.

Figure 1-5: The toolbox in its default state

Tip You can show and hide all the palettes *except* the toolbox by pressing Shift+Tab.

To choose a tool, click the tool you want to use in its slot within the toolbox and release the mouse button. Doing this highlights it on the toolbox. You can also choose tools by pressing a key on the keyboard. For example, pressing P selects the Pen tool. You can only inactivate a tool by selecting another one.

Many tools have additional *pop-up tools* called flyouts, which are tools that appear only when you click and hold down the mouse on the default tool. Illustrator denotes the default tools that have pop-up tools with a little triangle in the lower-right corner of the tool. To select a pop-up tool, click and hold a tool with a triangle until the pop-up tools appear; and then drag to the pop-up tool you want. The new pop-up tool replaces the default tool in that tool slot. Figure 1-6 shows all the pop-up tools for each toolslot.

Tip You can browse through the tools on any flyouts by pressing Option (Alt) and then clicking a toolslot. Each click displays the next tool.

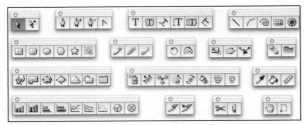

Figure 1-6: All of the flyout tools in Illustrator

Tip   You can customize the tool shortcuts under the Keyboard Shortcuts dialog box found under the Edit menu. In this dialog box, simply select the tool you want to change and enter the new shortcut letter, number, or symbol. You can also do this in Adobe Photoshop and Adobe InDesign.

Any tool with a pop-up option also has a tearoff tab on the right side of the flyout. You can make the flyout a free-floating palette by clicking this tearout tab. In Figure 1-7, you see an example of the Symbol tool becoming a floating palette after you click its flyout tab. Use this feature if you find that you are constantly switching between tools in that tearoff. Then you won't have to click+hold and drag to the next tool.

Figure 1-7: You can make your tearout tools into free-floating palettes.

Tool Tips

What if you forget what the function of a specific tool is or you can't tell the difference between the various tools in Illustrator? No problem! Illustrator comes equipped with a handy Tool Tips feature that identifies tools quickly and easily. When you have the Tool Tips activated, you simply move your cursor over the element you want to identify, and a yellow text box pops up and tells you its name. For example, when you place your cursor over the Type tool (see Figure 1-8), a box appears with the words Type Tool (T). The letter within the parentheses indicates the keyboard shortcut for the tool. In this example, if you press T, you activate the Type tool without clicking it. Illustrator provides Tool Tips for every tool in the toolbox as well as for the palette controls.

Figure 1-8: When you have the Tool Tips feature activated, you can place your cursor over a tool to see what it is.

Illustrator provides Tool Tips by default. However, if you find them annoying, or if you know the tips well enough not to need the Tool Tips, you can disable them in the General screen of the Preference dialog box. To open the Preference dialog box, simply choose Illustrator (Edit) ➪ Preferences ➪ General and deselect the Tool Tips option.

Palettes

All palettes include either a button for toggling between the Minimize and Maximize sizes of the palette (Windows) or a Zoom button for zooming in and out of the palette (Macintosh OS). A Close button usually appears in the upper corner of the palette that you can use to hide the palette. This button can toggle between displaying only the palette title tab or the entire palette.

Illustrator has over two dozen palettes, all of which can remain open while you work on your document (providing you can still see your document through all those palettes). Technically speaking, a palette is a window. Everything on the Mac and in Windows is a window except the desktop. Movable *modeless* windows (palettes) are variations on windows. The big difference between a modeless window and a dialog box is that you don't have to close the modeless window to perform other tasks. Therefore, you can work with the features on one palette without having to close another palette.

Unlike windows, palettes are never really active. Instead, the one you are working in is in the front. If the palette has editable text fields, Illustrator highlights the active one or makes the text cursor blink. To bring a palette to the forefront — that is, bring it into focus — simply click it anywhere.

Palettes are like regular windows in many ways. They have a title bar that you can click and drag to move the palette. The title bar also has buttons for minimizing (Windows) or zooming (Macintosh OS) and closing the palette. Each palette also has a tab with the name of the palette within it.

Note You can use the title tab to toggle between the minimized state (showing only the title tab and the maximized state (showing the entire palette) by double-clicking the title tab.

Occasionally, a palette has a handle, which looks like a triangle with two lines (see Figure 1-9), on the lower-right corner. You can use this handle for changing the palette's size by clicking and dragging the corner containing the handle.

Tip For some palettes, a double arrow icon appears to the left of the title name. Clicking this icon toggles the palette size among several different sizes.

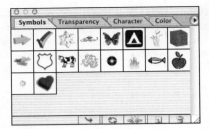

Figure 1-9: You can resize a palette that has a triangle with two lines on its lower-right corner.

Linking together and tearing apart palettes

You can place palettes together in different combinations by *tabbing* and *docking* them. Each palette (except for the toolbox) has a tab on it. Clicking the tab of a palette brings it to the front. Dragging a tab from one palette to another moves that palette into another palette. Dragging a tab out of a palette makes the palette separate from the previous palette. Figure 1-10 includes a set of palettes that have been tabbed together.

Note By default, Illustrator tabs certain palettes together. You can drag them apart and tab others together to suit your method of working.

Figure 1-10: A palette contains a number of tabs.

You can dock palettes together by dragging the tab of one palette to the bottom of another palette. When the bottom of the other palette darkens, releasing the mouse button "docks" the moved palette to the bottom of the other one. Then, when you move the other palette, the docked palette moves with it. To separate a palette from the others, click and drag the tab away from the original palette.

Working with palettes

Palettes are even more powerful when you can control when you can reveal or hide them. Under the Window menu you can choose which palettes show and which ones hide. Simply check next to a palette to show it, and uncheck next to the palette to hide it. Some palettes use a keyboard shortcut to access them, others you have to access through the Window menu. To see the shortcuts, look to the right of the palette name. Under the Window menu, you can see what palettes are visible by the checkmark next to them.

Understanding the palettes

The palettes are discussed throughout the books in various chapters. The palettes are listed as they appear under the Windows menu. The palettes are:

✦ **Actions:** Use this palette to record a sequence of events to play at any time.

✦ **Align:** This palette lets you align objects (Shift + F7).

✦ **Appearance:** Use this palette to check the attributes of a selected object (Shift + F6).

✦ **Attributes:** Use this palette to view the overprinting and any URL's associated with the selected object (F11).

✦ **Brushes:** Use this palette to select a brush type (F5).

✦ **Color:** This palette lets you apply color to your illustrations (F6).

✦ **Document Info:** Shows information on the document like color mode, artboard dimensions and other options.

✦ **Flattener Preview:** Use this to see certain areas of flattened artwork. You can also adjust the flattener options here.

✦ **Gradient:** This palette is used for changing and applying gradients (F9).

✦ **Graphic Styles:** This palette lists the default graphic styles, as well as lets you save graphic styles (Shift + F5).

✦ **Info:** Displays the info on the selected object like for measuring objects or distance (F8).

✦ **Layers:** Lets you put objects on different layers for easier organization (F7).

✦ **Links:** This lists the placed objects that are linked to the document.

✦ **Magic Wand:** Lets you adjust the settings for the Magic Wand tool.

✦ **Navigator:** Use this to quickly move around a large document.

✦ **Pathfinder:** Use this to combine, split, divide, and more to multiple paths (Shift + F9).

✦ **Stroke:** This palette lets you adjust the width and style of the stroke (F10).

✦ **SVG Interactivity:** Use this palette to set options for Scalable Vector Graphics.

✦ **Swatches:** This palette houses preset colors, gradients, and patterns.

✦ **Symbols:** This palette houses preset symbols and lets you define new symbols (Shift + F11).

✦ **Tools:** This palette contains all of Illustrator's tools.

✦ **Transform:** This palette lets you move, scale, and apply other transformations (Shift + F8).

✦ **Transparency:** Use this palette to adjust the opacity of objects (Shift + F10).

✦ **Type:** Use this palette to adjust a variety of type options such as Character (cmd-T), Character Styles, Glyphs, OpenType (cmd-shift-option-T), Paragraph (cmd-opt-T), Paragraph Styles, and Tabs (cmd-shift-T).

✦ **Variables:** This palette is used for data-driven graphics to set the options.

Using Illustrator's menus

Although Adobe places more emphasis on Illustrator's palettes and other elements, such as its toolbox, you may still find some important and useful features in Illustrator's menus.

Menus are one of the most common interface elements for all software packages. Over time, Adobe has pushed a lot of its functionality to the palettes and other interface elements rather than the menus, but menus are still important and offer another way to work with the program. Some general rules apply to Illustrator menus:

✦ To select a menu item, pull down the menu, highlight the menu item you want, and release or click the mouse button (Macintosh) or click that item (Windows). If the cursor is not on that item but is still highlighted, the command will not take effect.

✦ Whenever an ellipsis appears (three little dots that look like this...), choosing that menu item brings up a dialog box where you must verify the current information by clicking an OK button or by entering more information and then clicking OK. If the option has no ellipsis, the action you select takes place right away.

✦ When you see a key command listed on the right side of the menu — usually the Command (⌘) symbol and a character for Macintosh or Ctrl plus a character for Windows, but sometimes the ⌘ symbol (Ctrl) or another modifier key plus a character — you can type that key command instead of using the mouse to pull down this menu. Using key commands for menu items works just like clicking the menu bar and pulling down to that item.

✦ If you see a little triangle next to a menu item, it means the menu possesses a submenu. You can choose items in the submenu by pulling over to the menu and then pulling up or down to select the menu item needed. Submenus usually appear on the right side of the menu, but due to space limitations on your monitor, submenus may appear on the left side for certain menus.

Palette menus

Not only does the main document window have menus; so do palettes. You can find a variety of features and options to meet your creative needs. To open these menus, simply find and click the round button with the arrow in the middle, located on the top-right corner of most palettes. Figure 1-11 gives an example of the options you have available when you access the Character palette's menu. These options and features change with each palette.

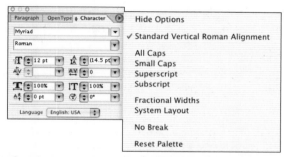

Figure 1-11: You can find a multitude of options by accessing the palette menu.

Context-sensitive menus

Illustrator provides context-sensitive menus that appear right under your cursor as you're working. To access them, press Control and then click (right-click) anywhere in the document window, and a context-sensitive menu appears. These menus contain commands that relate to the type of work you're doing and the specific tool you have. Figure 1-12 shows a context-sensitive menu that appears in a document when a rectangle shape is created and selected. This menu would look different if some other object were selected.

Figure 1-12: When you right click the document window, Illustrator reveals a context-sensitive menu.

Tips for Using Menus Effectively

If you can never remember what is on which menu and you are constantly holding down the mouse button while slowly running along the menu bar, reading every menu item and looking for a certain command, you have a disease. Every year millions of people become afflicted with Menu Bar Scanning Syndrome (MBSS), defined as "the pathological need of users to continually search and hunt for special menu items for which that they just can't remember the locations."

MBSS is deadly not only because it wastes time, but also because the user is forced to read every single menu and pop-up menu. Sure, in the File menu you *know* that Document Setup is where to go to change the size of the page, but as you work your way over, things begin to get a little fuzzy. By the time you get to the Filter menu, your mind is mush. You see the Distort category and figure that all the submenu items are legal functions. If you can manage to get to the Windows menu, thewordswouldjustruntogether, making no sense whatsoever.

Although MBSS wastes valuable production time, costing companies billions of dollars a year—don't be surprised if the next time you flip to *60 Minutes*, Steve Kroft is doing an inside investigation into the mysteries of MBSS—it is a fairly easily treated disease. You can help prevent MBSS by doing one of two things:

✦ **Memorize what is in each menu.** This is the hardest thing to do, but a few hours spent memorizing each menu item and where it goes eventually prevents countless MBSS-related searches.

✦ **Use the menus as little as possible.** Instead, memorize key commands. Most of the menu items have them, so you only need to go up to the menu bar when a menu item doesn't have a key command. If you set your own keyboard commands using the Keyboard Shortcuts command (choose Edit ➪ Keyboard Shortcuts), you can set a keyboard command for *every* menu item in Illustrator.

Typing keyboard commands

Keyboard commands are shortcuts for common activities that you perform in Illustrator. These shortcuts typically use the ⌘ (Ctrl) key in combination with other keys.

Many of the Illustrator menu items have keyboard shortcuts listed next to their names. Pressing the key combination does the same thing as choosing that menu item from the menu. Some menu items do not have keyboard commands; usually, you have to choose those items from the menu.

On a Macintosh, you commonly use the ⌘ key along with the Option key (located handily next to the ⌘ key) and the Shift key. You use the Control key only to simu- late the right mouse button that Windows users have (OS X also has multi-button mouse support, but the standard Macintosh mouse has but one button). By default, no keyboard commands use the Control key, although you can assign them if you wish. You hold down these keys while you press another key or click the mouse to perform a specific function.

On a Windows system, you use the Ctrl key along with the Alt and Shift keys. If you press certain combinations of these keys while pressing another key or clicking the mouse, the related function activates.

Mousing Around in Illustrator

Illustrator requires the use of a mouse for selecting items, pulling down menus, moving objects, and clicking buttons. Learning to use the mouse efficiently requires patience, practice, and persistence. In most programs, you can master using the mouse quickly, but you may find using the mouse with Illustrator's Pen tool difficult at first. If you're unfamiliar with using a mouse, a fun way to get used to working with one is by playing a mouse-driven game. After several hours of play (providing you don't get fired by your employer or kicked out of the house by your irritated spouse), you'll become Master of Your Mousepad, King of Your Klicker, and so on.

You use the mouse to perform five basic functions in Illustrator:

✦ **Pointing:** Move the cursor around the screen by moving the mouse around your mousepad.

✦ **Clicking:** Press and release the mouse button in one step. You click to select points, paths, and objects, and to make windows active. (Windows users: "Clicking" means clicking with the left mouse button, unless you've reconfigured your mouse.)

✦ **Dragging:** Press the mouse button and keep pressing it while you move the mouse. You drag the cursor to choose items from menus, select contiguous characters of text, move objects, and create marquees.

✦ **Double-clicking:** Quickly press and release the mouse button twice in the same location. You double-click to select a word of text, select a text field with a value in it, access a dialog box for a tool, and run Illustrator (by double-clicking its icon).

✦ **Control+clicking (right-clicking):** This displays a context-sensitive menu when you press Control and click the Mac (Windows users only need to press the right mouse button).

The cursor is the little icon (usually an arrow) that moves in the same direction as the mouse. If the cursor seems to be moving in the opposite direction from the mouse, check that the mouse isn't upside down, or, heaven forbid, that you aren't upside down yourself. In Illustrator, the cursor often takes the form of a tool that you are using. When the computer is busy doing whatever a computer does when it is busy, an ugly little watch or a spiraling circle (Macintosh) or hourglass (Windows) takes its place.

Keyboard commands are as important to an Illustrator artist as the mouse is; with a little practice, you can learn them quickly. Besides, many of the default keyboard commands are the same from program to program, which makes you an instant expert in software that you haven't used yet! Good examples of this are the Cut/Copy/Paste, Select All; and Save commands:

✦ **Cut/Copy/Paste:** You activate these by pressing ⌘+X, ⌘ +C, or ⌘+V, (Ctrl+X, C, V).

✦ **Select All:** You call select everything in a document by pressing ⌘+A (Ctrl+A).

✦ **Save:** You can quickly save your work by pressing ⌘+S (Ctrl+S).

Using the status bar

The status bar, located on the lower-left of your document window, has a Zoom pop-up list and a button that displays useful and otherwise difficult to find information. To change the item shown in the status bar, click the triangle and drag up to a different item. Although the default for this button displays the tool that you are currently using, you can change the information to display one of the following instead:

✦ **Current Tool:** Select this to show the selected tool's name.

✦ **Date and Time:** Use this to show the current date and time.

✦ **Number of Undos:** This is a handy option that shows the number of queued undos and redos.

✦ **Document Color Profile:** This shows the current Color Profile.

Navigating Around Your Document

Being able to move through a document easily is a key skill in Illustrator. Rarely can you fit an entire illustration in the document window at a sufficient magnification to see much of the image's detail. Usually you are zooming in, zooming out, or moving off to the side, above, or below to focus on certain areas of the document.

Understanding the Zoom tool

The most basic navigational concept in Illustrator is the ability to zoom to different magnification levels. Illustrator's magnification levels work like a magnifying glass. In the real world, you use a magnifying glass to see details that aren't readily visible without it. In the Illustrator world, you use the different magnification levels to see details that aren't readily visible at the 100-percent view.

Changing the magnification levels of Illustrator does not affect the illustration. If you zoom in to 200 percent and print, the illustration still prints at the size as it would if the view were 100 percent. It does *not* print twice as large. Figure 1-13 shows the same Illustrator document at 100 and 200 percent magnification.

Figure 1-13: An Illustrator document at 100 percent (left) and 200 percent (right) magnifications

In Illustrator, 100-percent magnification means that the artwork you see on the screen has the same physical dimensions when it prints. If you place a printout next to the onscreen image at 100 percent magnification, it appears at exactly the same size, depending on your monitor resolution (the higher the resolution, the smaller the document looks onscreen).

 Tip   For those of you who plan to use Illustrator with Photoshop, remember that in Photoshop, 100-percent view is different. In Photoshop, each pixel onscreen is equal to one pixel in the image. Unless the pixels per inch (ppi) of the image match those of the screen (and they would if Web graphics were being designed), the 100-percent view tends to be larger than the printed dimensions of the image.

Using the Zoom tool

Perhaps the easiest way to control the magnification of your artwork is with the Zoom tool. This tool (which looks like a magnifying glass and is located in the right column of the toolbox) can magnify a certain area of artwork and then return to the standard view.

To use the Zoom tool to magnify an area, select it in the toolbox by clicking it once. The Zoom cursor takes the place of the Arrow cursor (or whatever tool was previously selected). It looks like a magnifying glass with a plus sign in it. Clicking any spot in the illustration enlarges the illustration to the next magnification level, with the place you clicked centered on your screen. The highest magnification level is 6,400 percent — which, as all you math aficionados know, is 64 times (not 6,400 times!) bigger than the original. Where you click with the Zoom tool is very important:

- ✦ **Clicking the center of the window:** This enlarges the illustration to the next magnification level.

- ✦ **Clicking the edges (top, bottom, left, and right) of the window:** This makes the edges that you did not click (and possibly some or all of your artwork) disappear as the magnification increases.

- ✦ **Clicking the upper-right corner:** This hides mostly the lower-left edges and so forth.

If you are interested in seeing a particular part of the document close up, click that part at each magnification level to ensure that it remains in the window.

If you zoom in too far, you can use the Zoom tool to zoom out again. To zoom out, press the Option (Alt) key when you have the Zoom tool active (releasing the Option (Alt) key restores the Zoom In tool). Clicking with the Zoom Out tool reduces the magnification level to the next lowest level. You can zoom out to 3.13 percent (1/32 actual size). To access the Zoom out, hold the Option (Alt) key to see the minus sign indicating that you are zooming out.

When you use the Zoom tool, you magnify everything in the document, not just the illustration. You magnify all paths, objects, the artboard, and the Page Setup boundaries equally. However, the way certain objects appear (the thickness of path selections, points, handles, gridlines, guides, and Illustrator user interface (UI) components such as palettes and windows) does not change when you zoom in.

If you need to zoom in to see a specific area in the document window, use the Zoom tool to draw a marquee by clicking and dragging diagonally around the objects that you want to magnify. The area thus magnifies as much as possible so that everything inside the box just fits in the window that you have open, as shown in Figure 1-14. If you drag a box as you press and hold the Option (Alt) key to zoom out you do the same thing as if you had just clicked to zoom out.

Tip   To move a zoom marquee around while you're drawing it, press and hold the spacebar after you've begun drawing the marquee but before you release the mouse button. When you release the spacebar, you can continue to change the size of the marquee by dragging. A marquee is where you drag diagonally across to create a rectangle. Marquees are discussed in the "Using the Zoom tool" section in this chapter.

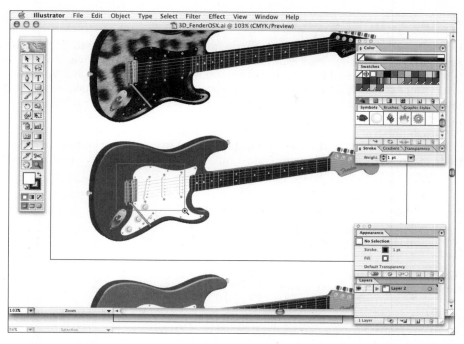

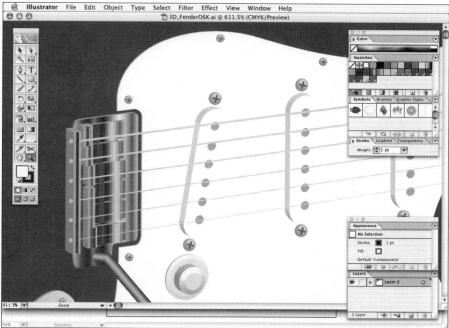

Figure 1-14: Zooming into a certain area in the original image (top) results in the magnification and placement of the image as shown on the bottom.

Other zooming techniques

You also can zoom in and out by using commands in the View menu. Choose View ➪ Zoom In (➪ cmd(Ctrl)++) to zoom in one level at a time until the magnification level is 6,400 percent. The Zoom In menu item zooms from the center out. Choose View ➪ Zoom Out (➪ cmd(Ctrl)+-) to zoom out one level at a time until the magnification level is 3.13 percent.

Although Illustrator can zoom to any level, it uses 23 default zoom levels when you click the Zoom tool or when you access the Zoom In and Zoom Out menu items (or their respective keyboard commands). Table 1-1 lists each of the default Zoom In and Zoom Out default levels.

Table 1-1
Zoom In and Zoom Out Default Levels

Zoom Out	Ratio	Zoom In	Ratio
100%	1:1	100%	1:1
66.67%	2:3	150%	3:2
50%	1:2	200%	2:1
33.33%	1:3	300%	3:1
25%	1:4	400%	4:1
16.67%	1:6	600%	6:1
12.5%	1:8	800%	8:1
8.33%	1:12	1,200%	12:1
6.25%	1:16	1,600%	16:1
4.17%	1:24	2,400%	24:1
3.13%	1:32	3,200%	32:1
		4,800%	48:1
		6,400%	64:1

Zooming to Actual Size

You can use different methods to automatically zoom to 100-percent view. The first method is to double-click the Zoom tool slot in the toolbox. This action changes the view to 100 percent instantly:

✦ **Using the Zoom feature in the Status bar:** To do this, simply click the drop down arrow in the left corner of the Status bar, and select 100%.

✦ **Using the View menu:** This is the best way to zoom to 100-percent magnification because it not only changes the image size to 100 percent, but also centers the page in the document window. Simply choose View ➪ Actual Size. The keyboard shortcut is ⌘ (Ctrl)+1.

Zooming to Fit in Window size

Fit in Window instantly changes the magnification level of the document so that the entire artboard (not necessarily the artwork, if it isn't located on the page) fits in the window and is centered in it. You can choose from two different methods to change the document view to the Fit in Window size:

✦ **Use the View menu:** One way to automatically change to the Fit in Window view is to choose View ➪ Fit in Window ➪ cmd (Ctrl)+0.

✦ **Use the Hand tool slot:** Simply double-click the Hand tool slot.

Tip

You can quickly go to 3.13 percent by Command (Ctrl)+double-clicking the Zoom tool slot in the toolbox.

Zooming to a specific magnification

If you'd like to view a document at a specific zoom level, double-click the view area at the bottom-left corner of the active document window (shown in Figure 1-15); type the magnification you want to zoom to, and press Enter or Return.

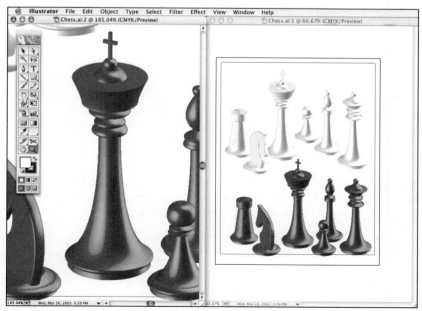

Figure 1-15: When you enter the exact zoom value in the field at the lower-left corner of the document window, you can zoom in or out quickly.

When you specify a magnification, you do not change the document. Rather, you change how you view the document. For this reason, you can never undo any type of magnification-level change. Choosing Edit ⇨ Undo after zooming undoes the last change you made to the document before you changed the magnification level, *not* the magnification-level change.

Zooming with the Navigator palette

Of course, being able to zoom in very closely to your artwork does have a pitfall. The more you zoom in on an illustration, the less of that illustration you see at one time. The Navigator palette (shown in Figure 1-16), which you access by choosing Window ⇨ Navigator, helps you out by letting you see the entire illustration as well as the portion into which you're zoomed (indicated by a red viewing rectangle). You have several options within the Navigator palette for changing your view:

✦ **The red rectangle:** You can stay zoomed in and move easily to another section by dragging the red rectangle (which actually scrolls), in the center of the Navigator palette, to another area.

✦ **The pop-up menu:** You access this menu by clicking circular icon with a left-pointing arrow located on the upper-right corner of the palette. The Navigator palette's pop-up menu includes a View Artboard Only option. This option sets the thumbnail in the Navigator palette to show only the extent of the artboard. If this option isn't set, the thumbnail shows all objects included in the document.

✦ **The magnification level box:** You can type an exact magnification level in the box in the lower-left corner of the Navigator palette.

✦ **The slider:** Located at the bottom of the Navigator palette is a slider giving you yet another way to zoom in and out by dragging the slider to the left or right.

✦ **The Zoom In and Zoom Out tools:** The Zoom In and Zoom Out tools look like little triangles and big triangles on either side of the slider triangle. You can zoom in and out a preset amount (using the same amounts used by the Zoom In and Zoom Out tools and menu items) by pressing the Zoom In or Zoom Out icons. These buttons are located on either side of the triangle slider.

Caution   The Navigator palette can slow down Illustrator if your artwork contains many patterns, gradients, and gradient mesh objects. To avoid this slowdown, you can close the Navigator palette by choosing Window ⇨ Navigator.

Figure 1-16: The Navigator palette shows a snapshot of the document.

Using the scroll bars to view your document

Sometimes, after you zoom in to a high magnification, part of the drawing that you want to see is outside the window area. Instead of zooming in and out repeatedly, you can use one of three different scrolling techniques to move around inside the document. All techniques use the scroll bars on the right side and bottom edges of the document window. The right scroll bar controls where you are vertically in the document. The bottom scroll bar controls where you are horizontally in the document window.

The scroll bars contain three elements: up and down arrows, a gray area, or bar, and a *thumb*, as called the *elevator box*, which is the blue oval (on a Mac) or gray square (in Windows) that rides along the scroll bar. The gray area of the right scroll bar is proportionate to the vertical size of the work area (the space around the artboard). If the little elevator box is at the top of the scroll bar, you are viewing the top edge of the work area. If it is centered, you are viewing the vertical center of the work area. The techniques are as follows:

✦ **Using the up and down arrows:** When you click the up arrow, you display what is above the window's boundaries by pushing everything in the window down in little increments. Clicking the down arrow displays what is below the window's boundaries by pushing the document up in little increments.

✦ **Using the thumbs:** Dragging the thumb up displays what is above the window's boundaries proportionately by whatever distance you drag it. Dragging the thumb down displays what is below the window's boundaries proportionately by whatever distance you drag it.

✦ **Using the gray bar:** Clicking the gray bar above the thumb and between the arrows displays what is above the window's boundaries in big chunks. Clicking the gray bar below thumb, between the arrows, displays what is below the window's boundaries in big chunks.

Caution   Be careful not to drag too far or you will be previewing beyond the top of the artboard.

Note   In OS X, if you want to specify how far Illustrator scrolls when you click the gray bar, you can set this in the System Preferences. Also, on a Mac, the default is for the up and down arrows to be together. You can change this in your system's preferences for General to place the scroll bars together or at the top and bottom.

Scrolling with the Hand tool

The Hand tool improves on the scroll bars. The Hand tool — which looks like a hand — is located at the bottom of the first column of tools just above the color options.

Instead of being limited to horizontal and vertical movement only, you can use the Hand tool to scroll in any direction, including diagonally. The Hand tool is especially useful for finding your way around a document when you're viewing it at a high magnification level. The higher the magnification level, the more you're likely to use the Hand tool.

To use the Hand tool, select it from the Hand tool slot in the toolbox.

Tip   To quickly access the Hand tool, press H, or press and hold the spacebar. Clicking and dragging the page moves the document around inside the document window while the spacebar is held down. If you release the spacebar, you return to the previous tool. This works for all tools, but the Type tool works a little differently. If you're currently using the Type tool in a text area, press ⌘+spacebar (Ctrl+spacebar) to access the Zoom tool, and release ⌘ (Ctrl) while keeping the spacebar pressed to gain access to the Hand tool.

When you click in the document, be sure to click the side that you want to see. Clicking at the top of the document and dragging down enables you to scroll down through almost an entire document at a height of one window. Clicking in the center and dragging enables you to scroll through only half a window's size at a time. If the window of the document does not take up the entire screen space, you can continue to drag right off the window into the empty screen space. Just be sure to click first within the document that you want to scroll.

Note   Be warned that Illustrator doesn't include support for a scrolling mouse except in Mac OS X. A scrolling mouse includes a wheel button between the two buttons (if it's a two-button mouse typical with Windows) that you can use to quickly scroll around a page. The scrolling wheel has no effect on an Illustrator document.

The best thing about the Hand tool is that it works live. As you drag, the document moves under "your Hand." If you don't like where it is going, you can drag it back, still live. The second best thing is that accessing it requires only one keystroke, a press of the spacebar.

Note   You cannot use Undo to reverse scrolling that you have done with the scroll bars and the Hand tool.

Scrolling with the Navigator palette

Use the red viewing rectangle in the Navigator palette to scroll quickly to another location within a document. Clicking and dragging within the red rectangle moves the viewing area around "live," whereas clicking outside the rectangle "snaps" the view to a new location.

Tip   You can change the red rectangle to another color by choosing the Palette Options in the Navigator palette pop-up menu.

Cross-Reference   For more on the features of the Navigator palette, see the section "Zooming with the Navigator palette" earlier in this chapter.

Opening a new window

So now you've learned how to zoom and pan around the document window, and you probably have many different sections of your artwork that you want to focus on. Illustrator lets you create a number of windows for the current artwork using the Window ➪ New Window option.

This option creates a new window that is the same size as the current window. You can then zoom and pan within this new window while maintaining the previous window. You can then place these windows side by side to see the artwork from two unique perspectives. Illustrator gives each new window a different reference number, which appears in the title bar.

Working in Outline mode versus Preview mode

In the old days, everyone worked in Outline mode (previously called Artwork mode). In Outline mode you see only the "guts" of the artwork—the paths without the fills and strokes applied. To see what the illustration looked like with the fills and strokes applied, you had to switch to Preview mode. Usually the preview was not quite what you had in mind, but to make changes, you had to switch back to Outline, and then to Preview again to check, and so forth. Many users of Illustrator from that time refer to it as the golden age, with not a little trace of sarcasm.

Today, Illustrator enables you to edit your work in both Outline and Preview modes, each shown in Figure 1-17. You can print a document from either mode. Saving the document while you are in Outline mode does not affect anything in the document, but the next time you open it, it displays in Outline mode. The same thing applies to Preview mode: Whatever mode you are in is saved with the artwork.

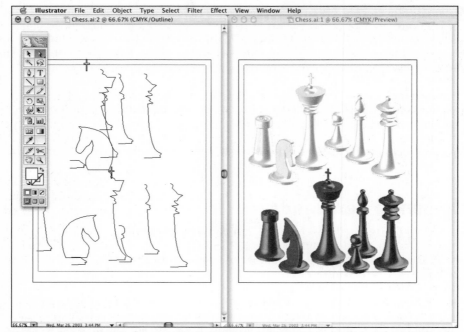

Figure 1-17: Artwork shown in both Outline mode (left) and Preview mode (right)

You cannot undo a Preview or Outline mode change (going from Preview to Outline, for example). If you make a Preview or Outline mode change and then close your document, Illustrator asks you if you want to save changes, which in this case would refer only to the view change.

The current view mode is always displayed in the title bar next to the document name.

Outline mode

You may find working with a drawing in Outline mode significantly faster than working with it in Preview mode (discussed in the next section). In more complex drawings, the difference between Outline mode and Preview mode is significant, especially if you are working on a very slow computer. The speed that you gain is even greater when the artwork contains gradients, patterns, placed artwork, and blends. Outline mode is much closer to what the printer sees — as paths. *Paths* define the edges of the objects with which you are working.

Cross-Reference   For more on paths, see Chapter 3. To learn how to edit and select paths, see Chapter 5.

Getting used to Outline mode can take some time. Eventually, your brain can learn to know what the drawing looks like from seeing just the outlines, which show all of the paths. The one big advantage of Outline mode is that you can see every path that isn't directly overlapping another path. In Preview mode, many paths can be hidden. In Outline mode, invisible masks are normally visible as paths, and you can select paths that were hidden by the fills of other objects. To select paths in Outline mode, you must click the paths directly or draw a marquee across them.

To change the current document to Outline mode, choose View ➪ Outline. In Outline mode, the illustration disappears and is replaced onscreen by outlines of all the filled and stroked paths. Text that has yet to be converted into outlines looks fine, although it is always black. When you are in Outline mode, the View menu only gives you an option to switch to Preview mode.

Note You can change how a placed image displays in Outline mode by selecting or deselecting the Show Placed Image option in the Document Setup dialog box. To display the Document Setup dialog box, choose File ➪ Document Setup. A placed image displays as a box if you check the Show Placed Images option. If you leave this option unchecked, the image displays only black-and-white surrounded by a box.

Preview mode

In Preview mode, you can see which objects overlap, which objects are in front and in back, where gradations begin and end, and how patterns are set up. In other words, the document looks just the way it will look when you print it.

Note In Preview mode, the color you see on the screen only marginally represents what the actual output will be because of the differences between the way computer monitors work (red, green, and blue colors — the more of each color, the brighter each pixel appears) and the way printing works (cyan, magenta, yellow, and black colors — the more of each color, the darker each area appears). Monitor manufacturers make a number of calibration tools that decrease the difference between what you see on the monitor and the actual output. You can also use software solutions. One software solution, CIE calibration, is built into Adobe Illustrator (choose Edit ➪ Color Settings). OS X users can use ColorSync.

Choosing View ➪ Preview changes the view to Preview mode. When in Preview mode, the View menu only gives you the option to switch to Outline mode.

The biggest disadvantage of the Preview mode is that the Illustrator begins to draw and fill in the various parts of your image, which can take some time, especially if your computer is slow. When you change the image, the screen redraws. You can stop screen redraw by pressing ⌘+Y (Ctrl+Y) at any time. This feature is useful if you want to make a small change but don't want to wait for the redraw. Of course, pressing ⌘+Y (Ctrl+Y) dumps you into Outline mode, but the redraw happens pretty much instantaneously.

Another disadvantage of Preview mode is being unable to select the path you want to change in the image. Sometimes so much stuff appears on your screen, you don't know what to click! This problem can become more complicated when you include fills in the mix, because the strokes on those paths are also visible. Instead of selecting a path by clicking it, you can select entire paths by clicking the insides of those paths in a filled area.

Note   The option that enables you to select an entire path by clicking in a filled area is called *Area Select*, activated by a checkbox (turned on by default) in the General Preferences dialog box. You can access this dialog box by choosing Edit ➪ Preferences ➪ General.

Cross-Reference   For more on paths, see Chapter 3. To learn how to edit and select paths, see Chapter 5.

Overprint Preview mode

Drawing in Illustrator often results in one or more objects overlapping each other, meaning that the colors of these objects overlap as well. When you print these objects, the top color blocks, or *knocks out,* anything below it. The advantage of using this feature is that your illustration becomes cheaper and easier for a printer to generate. To see how your overprint will look after you've set the Overprint feature, you can view it in Overprint Preview mode by choosing View ➪ Overprint Preview.

Cross-Reference   For more on color and overprinting, see Chapters 6 and 15.

Pixel Preview mode

Because most Web-page graphics are pixel-based, this mode is specifically for graphics that designers want to place on Web pages. This mode lets you view images before converting them to a Web graphics format. Choose View ➪ Pixel Preview, and Illustrator places a checkmark next to the Pixel Preview option and then shows a raster form of your image (see Figure 1-18).

Cross-Reference   For more on creating Web graphics, see Chapter 16.

Combining Outline and Preview modes

Using the Layers palette, you can easily combine Outline mode with either Preview or Preview Selection mode. You can force individual layers to display in Preview mode while other layers remain in Outline mode. This feature can be useful when you have a layer with a placed image, gradients, or patterns (or all three) that would normally slow down screen redraw and your workflow. You can place those images on their own layer and set that layer to Outline mode. To combine Outline and Preview mode in your document, place the object that you want in outline on its own layer and make that layer outline mode by pressing ⌘ (Ctrl) and clicking the eyeball icon for that layer. Then leave the rest of the layers in Preview mode.

Cross-Reference   For a complete discussion on layers, see Chapter 7.

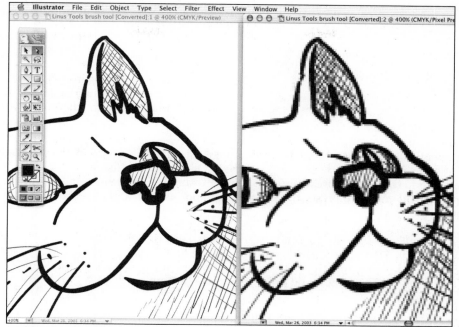

Figure 1-18: With Illustrator's Pixel Preview option, you can view an image in Preview mode (left) as well as Pixel Preview mode (right).

Using custom views

Illustrator has a special feature called custom views that enables you to save special views of an illustration. Custom views contain view information, including magnification, location, and whether the illustration is in Outline or Preview mode. If you have various layers or layer sets in Preview mode and others in Outline mode, custom views can also save that information. Custom views, however, do not record whether templates, rulers, page tiling, edges, or guides are shown or hidden.

To create a new view, set up the document in the way that you would like to save the view. Then choose View ➪ New View and name the view in the New View dialog box, shown in Figure 1-19. Each new view name appears at the bottom of the View menu. No default keyboard shortcuts exist for these views, but you can create your own shortcuts by using the Keyboard Shortcuts dialog box, available under the Edit menu. You can create up to 25 custom views. Custom views are saved with a document as long as you save it using the Illustrator format.

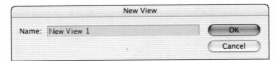

Figure 1-19: This simple dialog box lets you name the new view.

If you find yourself continually going to a certain part of a document, zooming in or out, and changing back and forth between Preview and Outline mode, that document is a prime candidate for creating custom views. Custom views are helpful for showing clients artwork that you created in Illustrator. Instead of fumbling around in the client's presence, you can, for example, show the detail in a logo instantly if you have preset the zoom factor and position and have saved the image in a custom view.

After you create a view, you can edit the view name or delete the view by choosing View ⇨ Edit Views option. Doing this opens the Edit Views dialog box, shown in Figure 1-20. To rename the view, select it and type the new name in the Name field. To delete a view, select it and press the Delete button.

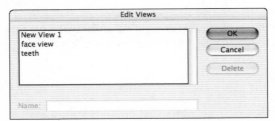

Figure 1-20: You can use the Edit Views dialog box to rename or delete custom views.

Using screen modes

So you've been working on an illustration for an important client (actually they all are important) and the client scheduled an appointment to see your progress, but the best part of the work is hidden behind the palettes and the toolbox. You can turn off the palettes and the toolbox in the Window menu or you can press the F key to switch between the different screen modes.

Illustrator uses three different screen modes represented by the three icon buttons at the bottom of the toolbox. They are Standard Screen Mode, Full Screen Mode with Menu Bar, and Full Screen Mode. You can toggle among these modes using the F keyboard shortcut. Figure 1-21 shows artwork in Full Screen Mode with Menu Bar.

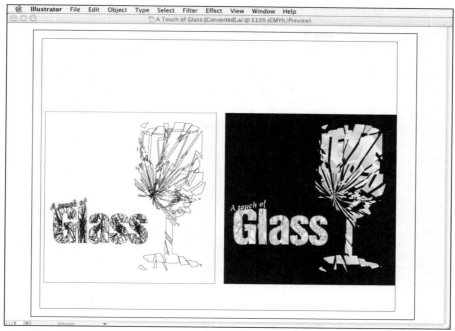

Figure 1-21: Full Screen Mode with Menu Bar maximizes the document window to fill the entire screen, eliminating all interface elements except for the menu bar.

Using the Edit Commands

In most software, including Illustrator, many basic functions of the Edit menu work the same way. If you've used the Edit menu in Photoshop or Microsoft Word (see Figure 1-22), for example, you should have no trouble using the same functions in Illustrator, because the menu options are located in the same place in each program.

Using the Clear command

The most simplistic Edit command is Clear. In Illustrator it works almost exactly like the Delete (Backspace) key on the keyboard. When something is selected, choosing Clear deletes or gets rid of what is selected.

You're probably asking yourself, "If the Delete (Backspace) key does the same thing, why do we need Clear?" or "Why didn't they just call the Clear command Delete (Backspace)?" Ah, the makers of Illustrator are a step ahead of you in this respect. Note that we said "almost" the same way; there actually is a subtle yet important difference in what the Clear command does and what the Delete (Backspace) key does, due to Illustrator's abundant use of palettes.

Figure 1-22: The various commands under the Edit menu help you to quickly cut, copy, and paste objects from place to place, as well as help you undo and redo previously applied commands.

If you are working on a palette and have just typed a value in an editable text field, the Delete (Backspace) key deletes the last character typed. If you tabbed down or up to an editable text field, highlighting text or dragged across text in an editable text field, highlighting text, then the Delete (Backspace) key deletes the highlighted characters. In all three situations, the Clear command deletes anything that is selected in the document.

Cutting, copying, and pasting

The Cut, Copy, and Paste commands in Illustrator are very handy. Copying and cutting selected objects places them on the clipboard, which is a temporary holding place for objects that have been cut or copied. After you place an object on the clipboard, you can paste it in the center of the same document, the same location as the cut or copied object, or another document in Illustrator, InDesign, or Photoshop.

Choosing Cut from the Edit menu deletes the selected objects and copies them to the clipboard, where they are stored until you cut or copy another object or until you shut down or restart your computer. Quitting Illustrator does not remove objects from the clipboard. Cut is not available when no object is selected.

Choosing Copy from the Edit menu works like Cut, but it doesn't delete the selected objects. Instead, it just copies them to the Clipboard, at which time you can choose Paste and slap another copy onto your document.

Choosing Paste from the Edit menu places any objects on the Clipboard into the center of the document window. If you select text with the Type tool, or copy text from another application to the Clipboard, you must select either a Rectangle type, Area type, Path type, or point type area with the Type tool. Paste is not available if nothing is in the clipboard.

Cross-Reference

The Type tool is located in the toolbox. For more information on the toolbox, see the section "The Toolbox" earlier in this chapter.

Note

Alternatively, you can use the Paste in Front (⌘/Ctrl+F) and Paste in Back (⌘/Ctrl+B) options to position the object you are pasting relative to other objects.

Now, the really cool part: Just because you've pasted the object somewhere doesn't mean it isn't in the clipboard anymore. It is! You can paste again and again, and keep on pasting until you get bored or until your page is an indecipherable mess, whichever comes first. The most important rule to remember about Cut, Copy, and Paste is that whatever is currently in the clipboard will be replaced by anything that subsequently gets cut or copied to the Clipboard.

Cut, Copy, and Paste also work with text that you type in a document. Using the Type tools, you can select type, cut or copy it, and then paste it. When you're pasting type, it will go wherever your blinking text cursor is located. If you have type selected (highlighted) and you choose Paste, the type that was selected is replaced by whatever you had on the Clipboard.

You can cut or copy as much or as little of an illustration as you choose; you are only limited by your hard disk space (which is only used if you run out of RAM). A good rule of thumb is that, if you ever get a message saying you can't cut or copy because you are out of hard disk space, it's time to start throwing out stuff on your hard drive that you don't need. Or, simply get a bigger hard drive.

Thanks to the Adobe PostScript capability on the clipboard, Illustrator can copy paths to other Adobe software, including InDesign, and Photoshop. Paths created in those packages (with the exception of InDesign) can be pasted into Illustrator. With Photoshop, you have the option of pasting your clipboard contents as rasterized pixels instead of as paths.

You have the ability to drag Illustrator artwork from an Illustrator document right into a Photoshop document. In addition, because Adobe lets you move things in both directions, you can drag a Photoshop selection from any Photoshop document right into an Illustrator document.

Undoing and redoing

You can keep undoing in Illustrator until you run out of either computer memory or patience. After you undo, you can redo by choosing Redo, which is found right below Undo in the Edit menu. And, guess what — you can redo everything you've undone.

Choosing Undo from the Edit menu undoes the last activity that was performed on the document. Successive undos undo more and more activities, until the document is at the point where it was opened or created or you have run out of memory.

Choosing Redo from the Edit menu redoes the last undo. You can continue to redo undos until you are back to the point where you started undoing or you perform another activity, at which time you can no longer redo any previous undos.

If you undo a couple of times and then do something, you won't be able to redo. You have to undo the last thing you did and then actually do everything again. In other words, all the steps that you undid are gone. It's fine to use the Undo feature to go back and check out what you did, but after you have used multiple undos, don't do anything if you want to redo back to where you started undoing from. Got that?

Summary

In this chapter, you learned:

- ✦ Illustrator may seem difficult to learn at first, but with this book and a bit of dedication, you can master it.
- ✦ Illustrator has many keyboard shortcuts that increase productivity.
- ✦ Adobe has kept the interface similar through its products.
- ✦ The document window, toolbox, palettes, menu, and status bar look the same in many Adobe applications.
- ✦ You can view Illustrator documents at virtually any magnification level without actually changing them.
- ✦ Use the Hand tool to scroll around your document.
- ✦ Illustrator's Outline mode lets you see paths without their strokes and fills.
- ✦ Cut, Copy, and Paste are under the Edit menu with Undo and Redo.
- ✦ Illustrator provides virtually unlimited undos and redos.

✦   ✦   ✦

Working with Illustrator Documents

When you create an illustration in Illustrator, you are actually creating a document, which you can place on the Web, send to a printer, or simply save on your computer. This chapter covers how to set up and change a document, how to open and save files as well as how to export and place files. You'll also find out the difference between pixel-based documents and vector-based documents. For more on pixels versus vectors, see Chapter 4. Figure 2-1 shows the Illustrator startup screen.

Figure 2-1: Illustrator's startup screen

Setting Up a New Document

If you have Illustrator already up and running, you can create a new document by choosing New from the File menu or by pressing ⌘+N (in Windows, Ctrl+N). This new document now becomes the active document. An *active document* means that the document is in front of any other documents.

The New Document dialog box lets you enter the name, size, units, Artboard in width and height, orientation, and color mode. Figure 2-2 shows the New Document dialog box. Although the default dimensions in the New Document dialog box are for Letter size, you can set the new document to any size you want:

✦ **Name:** Allows you to give your new document a name.

✦ **Size:** Allows you to choose standard preset dimensions, such as Letter, or Legal, for your document.

✦ **Units:** You can also select up the units you prefer to work in. Most artists choose points, but some still prefer working in picas, inches, millimeters, centimeters, or pixels.

Figure 2-2: The New Document dialog box

✦ **Width and Height:** Instead of selecting a preset size, you can specify exact dimensions in Width and Height boxes.

✦ **Orientation:** You can also choose the orientation of the page. The orientation options are portrait (meant to be viewed vertically) or landscape (meant to be viewed horizontally).

✦ **Color Mode:** Finally, you can choose from CMYK and RGB color modes.

Chapter 6 covers CMYK and RGB color modes in greater detail.

Hidden in the Page Setup dialog is an added option that sets which way the paper feeds when OS X users select the landscape orientation. This option affects what falls within the printable area of the page. For example, with a color inkjet such as the Epson 780, useful for color samples), the "top" and "bottom" margins on a legal size page are different.

The document window initially shows up at Fit in Window size. In the title bar at the top of the window, you see Untitled Art 1 <100%> or whatever percent the document is displayed at. As soon as you save the document, the title bar contains the name of the document.

You cannot change the way that some of the palettes or presets appear when you first start Illustrator. For example, the Selection tool is always selected in the toolbox. Another unchangeable item is the initial paint style with which you begin drawing: a fill of white and a stroke of 1-point black. The character attributes are always the same: 12-point Myriad, auto leading, flush left alignment. In addition, the initial layer color is always light blue — a color that is just dark enough so that it doesn't conflict with cyan.

See Chapter 15 for more on changing the startup file.

Modify the Setup of a Document

To change almost anything about the document structure and how you work with that document, after you've created it, you need to go to the Document Setup dialog box (see Figure 2-3) by choosing File ⇨ Document Setup or pressing ⌘+Option+P (in Windows, Alt+Ctrl+P). As with the New Document dialog box, you can change the size of the Artboard, the page orientation, the ruler units, and whether you want to view the file in Outline mode.

At the top of this dialog box is a pop-up (Mac) drop-down (Windows) menu that includes options for Artboard, Type, and Transparency.

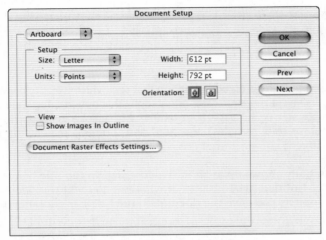

Figure 2-3: The Document Setup dialog box

The Document Raster Effect Settings affect a raster-based effect applied to a vector-based object. These effects are listed under the effects menu in the bottom section as well as the glows, shadow, and feather effects. In the Document Raster Effects Settings, you set the resolution of the document for these effects.

For more on Effects, see Chapter 12.

See Chapter 7 for more on layers and templates.

Understanding Artboard options

In Illustrator, the Artboard defines the maximum drawing area that you can print. The Artboard is useful as a guide to where objects on a page belong. In older versions of Illustrator, the maximum printable size was 11 x 17 inches; with Version 6, it increased to 227 x 227 inches or 358 square feet (provided that you can find a printer that prints that big).

Cross-Reference See Chapter 1 for more on the Artboard and pasteboard.

Illustrator's separation setup ignores the Artboard and places crop marks around the entire imageable area. The *imageable area*, according to this dialog box, is only the area where artwork exists. It may be within the Artboard, but it also may extend onto the Pasteboard. When you export an illustration to another program, such as QuarkXPress or InDesign, the Artboard is ignored entirely.

Choosing Artboard measurement units

You can view a document in points, picas, inches, centimeters, millimeters, or pixels. The measurement units affect the numbers on the rulers and the locations of the hash marks on those same rulers. The measurement system also changes the way measurements display in the Info palette and in all dialog boxes where you enter a measurement other than a percentage.

You change the measurement system in one of two ways:

✦ **Using the Units & Undo Preferences dialog box:** You use this method if you want to change all documents. To do so, choose Illustrator (Windows) ⇨ Preferences ⇨ Units & Undo.

✦ **Using the Document Setup dialog box:** You use this method for the currenly active document. You open this box by choosing File ⇨ Document Setup, or by pressing Option+⌘+P (in Windows, Alt+Ctrl+P).

Choosing the Artboard size

Choose the size of the Artboard by selecting one of the following preset sizes in the Size pop-up menu:

✦ **Custom:** Any size you type into the Width and Height fields of the Document Setup dialog box automatically changes the Size pop-up to Custom.

✦ **640 x 480:** Makes your Artboard 640 x 480 pixels

✦ **800 x 600:** Makes your Artboard 800 by 600 pixels

✦ **468 x 60:** Makes your Artboard 468 x 60 pixels

✦ **Letter:** 8.5×11 inches

✦ **Legal:** 8.5×14 inches

✦ **Tabloid:** 11×17 inches

✦ **A4:** 8.268×11.693 inches (21×29.7 centimeters)

✦ **A3:** 11.693×16.535 inches (29.7×42 centimeters)

✦ **B5:** 7.165×10 inches (18.2×25.4 centimeters)

✦ **B4:** 10.118×14.331 inches (55.7×36.4 centimeters)

Note   A4, A3, B5, and B4 are European paper sizes.

Setting Artboard orientation

You define the orientation of your Artboard by choosing one of the two Orientation pages. On the left is Portrait orientation, and on the right is Landscape orientation:

✦ **Portrait orientation:** You use this when the lesser of the two dimensions goes across the page from left to right, and when the greater of the two dimensions goes from top to bottom. You can also think of portrait orientation the vertical view.

✦ **Landscape orientation:** You use this when the greater of the two dimensions goes across the page from left to right, and when the lesser of the two dimensions goes from top to bottom. You can also think of landscape orientation as the horizontal view.

Creating a New Document in the Dark Ages

Creating a new document hasn't always been easy. Back in the days of Illustrator 88, and even Illustrator 3, creating new illustrations was rather annoying. Choosing New Document brought up a dialog box that politely, yet sternly, asked you to choose a template to trace in Illustrator. However, most of the time you didn't want a template, so you had to click the little None button in the dialog box. If you pressed Return, Illustrator would attempt to open a template.

Illustrator 3 was a little more flexible. You could create a new document without having to deal with the dialog box that asked you to choose a template. You could either press ⌘+Option+N (in Windows, Ctrl+Alt+N) or hold down the Option (Alt) key when you chose File ➪ New. If you forgot about the Option (Alt) key, you had another chance. Pressing ⌘+N (Ctrl+N) when you were in the dialog box would send the box away and create a new document with no template—as long as you didn't have Directory Assistance, Super Boomerang, or any other utilities that created a new open folder when you pressed ⌘+N (Ctrl+N).

Adobe slowly realized that you didn't want or need a template to do everything, and now, fortunately, template-forcing is a thing of the past.

Now, you can choose New from Template from the File menu. Another option is to place the image on a layer and make that layer a template.

Understanding the Show Image In Outline option

The last option you can check or leave unchecked in the Document Setup dialog box, when you're setting Artboard options, is the Show Images In Outline option. Checking this box displays all placed EPS images in Outline mode. The placed image shows up in the file as a grayscale image. Fear not, the color is still there. You can see the color image by looking at the Navigator palette. Using this option allows for quicker redraw time when working with large placed image files.

Cross-Reference   For more on the Outline option, see Chapter 1.

Changing Type options

Under the Document Setup dialog box, you can change the Type options, as shown in Figure 2-4. Choose Type from the Artboard pop-up (Mac) drop-down (Windows) menu. The following options are available under the Type options:

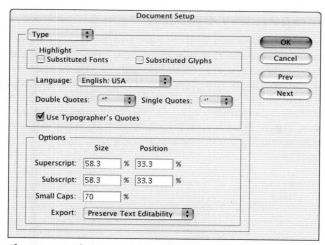

Figure 2-4: The Type options found in the Document Setup dialog box

✦**Highlight:** The options here are to check the Substituted Fonts or Substituted Glyphs in the document. This shows the fonts and glyphs that have used a substitute because the current system does not have the actual font or glyph for that particular document.

✦ **Language:** Choose a desired language from the menu. You can choose from a variety of languages from English, French, Finnish, and so on, but you have to have the language set up on your system to be able to use that language. All computers are set up and you choose the language you are using.

✦ **Double Quotes:** Choose the style from the pop-up menu. There are a variety of quotes to choose from. Some users like the "curly" quotes rather than the straight ones.

✦ **Single Quotes:** Choose the style from the pop-up menu. The choices of single quotes are the same as the double quotes.

✦ **Use Typographer's Quotes:** Check or uncheck this option.

✦ **Options:** Choose the Size and Position for Super and Subscripts and Small Caps percentage size from original.

✦ **Export:** In this pop-up menu choose from Preserve Text Editability and Preserve Text Appearance. In this case, you can either choose to be able to edit the text (but it may not look like you intended), or let the text look like it should (but make it so you can't edit it).

Type, the Type options, and the Type panel of the Document Setup dialog box are covered in more detail in Chapter 8.

Working with Transparency options

Transparency options refer to making a transparent background screen. Many users like to use a transparent grid to see the opacity of their objects. On a white background, the opacity isn't easy to see. Just as in Photoshop, you can see a checkered grid that shows the opacity of the objects in front. The Flattener settings let you pick a resolution for the object when you change it to a rasterized (pixel) object when it is flattened. The Transparency options are also found under Document Setup as shown in Figure 2-5. Choose Transparency from the pop-up (Mac) drop-down (Windows) menu for the following options:

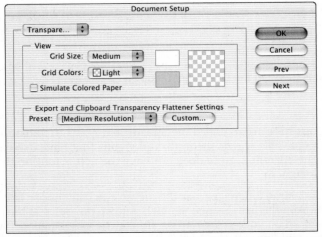

Figure 2-5: The Transparency options found in the Document Setup dialog box

✦ **View:** In this area, you can change your grid size to small, medium, or large. You can customize your own grid color. The Simulate Colored Paper checkbox makes the Artboard color match the grid color you have chosen.

✦ **Export and Clipboard Transparency Flattener Settings:** Select a preset (high, medium or low resolution) from a pop-up (Mac) drop-down (Windows) menu or choose a Custom setting.

The Transparency options are covered in Chapters 6 and 12.

Opening and Closing Illustrator Files

You can open any Illustrator file from any version of Illustrator in Illustrator CS. Regardless of which Preview options you select, Illustrator CS can still open the file. When you choose File ➪ Open or press ⌘+O (Ctrl+O), the Open dialog box appears and asks you to find an Illustrator file. Find the file and double-click it to have it open into a document window on the screen.

Using supported file formats

Not only can Illustrator open Illustrator files; it can also open rasterized files, PDF files and a wide range of other formats. The following lists the files Illustrator can open and the warnings on opening certain file types:

✦ **EPS:** Can be opened or placed. You can embed or link placed files. Many Photoshop files are saved as an EPS.

✦ **Adobe PDF:** Can be opened or placed. You can embed or link placed files.

✦ **Photoshop:** Can be opened, placed, or dragged and dropped in Versions 2.5 and up. You can embed or link placed files. Use a linked placed file when you add a Photoshop file that you want to update in Illustrator if you change it in Photoshop.

✦ **SVG/SVGZ:** Not all types are supported. May have altered information when brought in to Illustrator. You'll find SVG/SVGZ (Scalable Vector Graphics) in Web-based images.

✦ **PICT:** Can be opened or placed. You can embed or link placed files. PICT is used in many Macintosh graphics.

✦ **WMF/EMF:** Can be dragged and dropped from Microsoft Office. Placed files are embedded.

✦ **DXF/DWG:** Illustrator supports Versions 13, 14, and 2000only. Placed files are embedded. This format is used to save AutoCAD graphics.

✦ **FreeHand:** Illustrator supports Versions 5 and up. Placed files will be embedded.

✦ **CorelDRAW:** Illustrator supports Versions 5.0 and up. Placed files will be embedded.

✦ **CGM:** Illustrator supports Versions 1 and up. Placed files will be embedded.

✦ **Raster formats:** Illustrator supports Amiga IFF, BMP, Filmstrip, GIF 89a, Kodak Photo CD, JPEG, PCX, Pixar, PNG, TIFF, and TGA.

✦ **Text formats:** Illustrator supports plain text, MS RTF, MS Works 97 and up, Vertical Japanese text in RTF and Word are imported horizontally. Placed files are embedded.

How to close an Illustrator file

To close the active Illustrator file, choose File ➪ Close, or press ⌘+W (Ctrl+W). The active document is the one that is in front of all other documents and has a title bar with lines on it (Mac) and text in black. Inactive documents don't display any lines in their title bar, and the text in the title bar is gray. Closing an Illustrator document does not close Illustrator; it continues running until you choose Quit (Windows: Exit).

If you saved the file prior to closing it, the file just disappears. If you have modified the file since the last time you saved it, a box appears, asking whether you want to save changes before closing. If you press Return or Enter to save the file, the file is updated. If you have not saved the file at all, the Save As dialog box appears so that you can name the file, choose a location for it, and choose Preview and Compatibility options for the file. If you click the Don't Save button (or press the D key while the dialog box is showing), then any changes that you made to the document since you last saved it (or if you have never saved it, all the changes you made since you created it) are lost. Clicking Cancel, or pressing ⌘+period (Ctrl+period) or pressing Esc, takes you back to the drawing, where you can continue to work on it.

Saving Files

You might find controlling how files are saved in Illustrator a little daunting at first. Although you have many different options for saving file types, you need to follow one basic rule: Save as an EPS with a color preview if you are going to take the file into other applications. This type of file is not the smallest file type, but it is compatible with most software.

Opening files in Illustrator is fairly simple. Illustrator can open and manipulate files that were created in Illustrator, Photoshop, and many other applications. Illustrator can open raster files, but they will be pixel-based.

Files you place in Illustrator can be almost any raster file format. You usually can't place PostScript files that you print to disk in Illustrator, although you can open PostScript Level 1 files in Illustrator.

When Should I Save?

You really can't save too often. Whenever I put off saving for "just a few minutes," that's when the application aborts or unexpectedly quits. Depending on your work habits, you may need to save more frequently than other people do. Here are some golden rules about when to save:

✦ **Save as soon as you create a new file.** Get it out of the way. The toughest part of saving is deciding how and where you are going to save the file and naming it. If you get those things out of the way in the beginning, pressing ⌘+S (Ctrl+S) later is fairly painless.

✦ **Save before you print.** It is just a good idea in case your program quits when you print.

✦ **Save before you switch to another application.** This is another good idea in case you forget you still have the application running or another application forces you to restart such as loading new programs. This is more of an issue with older versions of Windows and OS. You don't really need to do this with Windows XP, Windows 2000, and OSX.

✦ **Save right after you do something that you never want to have to do again.** For example, you would want to save after getting the kerning "just right" on a logo or matching all of the colors in your gradients so that they meet seamlessly.

✦ **Save after you use a filter that takes more than a few seconds to complete.**

✦ **Save before you create a new document or go to another document.**

✦ **Save at least every 15 minutes.** This is just a basic rule of thumb; that way you are sure to have the latest version and in case of a power outage or a blown USB port that can shut your system down immediately.

Other important file issues: Illustrator opens pixel files as a new Illustrator document with the pixels inside. You can open arbitrary PostScript Level 1 files with the built-in PostScript Interpreter. You can also export Illustrator files directly into pixel formats through the Export dialog box only because it's not an option in the Save dialog box.

Saving and backing up Illustrator documents are the most important Illustrator activities you can do. These activities make your life less stressful and help you sleep better. Saving often prevents damage to your computer by keeping you from picking it up and sending it flying across the room when you've lost something that you've been working on for the last couple of hours.

The amount of space that a saved Illustrator file takes up on a hard drive depends on the complexity of the drawing and the Preview option (if any) that you've selected. Tiny Illustrator files take up the smallest amount, about 10K or so. The biggest illustrations are limited only by your storage space, but they can regularly exceed 2MB. As a practice, when you are working on a drawing, save it to the hard drive, not to a removable media or a removable cartridge. Hard drives are faster and much more reliable. If you need to place a file on a floppy disk, Zip, or CD, or removable cartridge, copy it there by dragging the icon of the file from the hard drive to the disk or cartridge. Because Illustrator uses virtual memory (the hard drive as RAM), you may want to keep additional hard drive space available, especially if you plan on working with lots of embedded images.

You should only save the file to another disk if you run out of room on the hard drive. To ensure that you never run out of room, always keep at least 10 percent of the hard drive space free. Having a full hard drive can cause problems more serious than being unable to save a file. For example, a full hard drive can mean being able to save a file, or being unable to run multiple programs. A simple e-mail can easily shut down Illustrator when you have a lack of hard drive space.

To save a file, choose File ⇨ Save, or press ⌘+S (Ctrl+S). If you have previously saved the file, updating the existing file with the changes that you have made takes just a fraction of a second. If you have not yet saved the file, the Save As dialog box shown in Figure 2-6 appears. Illustrator files are best saved as an .ai file. If you are using the file in other (non-Adobe) applications, use the .eps file format.

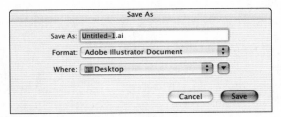

Figure 2-6: The Save As dialog box

When saving files, remember the following tips and tricks:

✦ **Decide how you are going to save the file.** Choose the correct Preview and Compatibility options for the file.

For more information, see the descriptions in the "Illustrator EPS Preview Options" and "Compatibility Options" sections, later in this chapter.

✦ **Decide where to save the file.** Make sure that the name of the folder where you want to save the file is at the top of the file-list window. Saving your working files in a location other than the Illustrator folder is a good habit. Otherwise, you can have trouble figuring out which files are yours, which files are tutorial files, and so on.

✦ **Name the file something distinctive.** If you look for a file six months from now, you may not recognize it. Avoid using Untitled Art 1, Untitled Art 2, and so on. Such names are non-descriptive and, besides, you can too easily replace the file at a later date with a file of the same name. For the same reasons, do not use Document 1, Document 2, and so on. Also avoid using Test1 (if I had a nickel for every Test1 or Test2 I've seen on people's hard drives, I'd have . . . well, I'd have a lot of nickels), stuff, #$*&!! (insert your favorite four-letter word here), picture, drawing, or your first name. A filename can't contain a slash, but other than that, there are no limitations.

The formatting choices for saving an Illustrator file are:

✦ **Adobe Illustrator Document:** For use when passing between users who have the Adobe Illustrator

✦ **Illustrator EPS (eps):** For use when sending or passing files between users who may not have Illustrator, but can place or open the files in another program such as InDesign or Photoshop

✦ **Illustrator Template (ait):** For use in creating templates that you can use as guides for future drawings

✦ **Illustrator PDF (pdf):** For use in sending the file to anyone who has or can download Adobe Reader or Acrobat 6.0 Standard or Professional

✦ **SVG Compressed (svgz):** For use when creating a Web page

✦ **SVG (svg):** For use when creating a Web page

Using the Save As command

You activate the Save As command by pressing ⌘+Shift+S (Ctrl+Shift+S). By using this command, you can save multiple versions of the document at different stages of progress. If you choose Save As and do not rename the file or change the save location, Illustrator prompts you to replace the existing file. If you choose Replace, Illustrator erases the file that you saved before and replaces it with the new file that you are saving. Most disk and trash-recovery utilities cannot recover a file that you delete this way.

The Save As command is also useful for changing the Preview and Compatibility options. If you have saved in Omit Header Preview and want to change to Color Preview, choose File ➪ Save As — don't change the file name or file location — and choose Color from the Preview pop-up menu.

For more on the Preview and Compatibility options, see the "Illustrator EPS Preview Options" and "Compatibility Options" sections later in this chapter.

Understanding the Save a Copy command

The Save a Copy command that you activate by pressing ⌘+Option+S (Ctrl+Alt+S), saves a copy of your document at its current state without affecting your document or its name. Here's the scoop: Let's say that you've designed a fairly nice logo for Dr. Whittles, which you've named Whittles Logo. Dr. Whittles is pretty conservative, but his patients aren't. You need to show him both a basic logo and the same logo but spruced up. After you've created the basic logo, you can Save a Copy as Basic Logo and continue working on Whittles Logo. The next time you press ⌘+S (Ctrl+S), Illustrator saves your changes to Whittles Logo, and the Basic Logo isn't affected by any of your changes.

Reverting to the last saved version

Choosing File ➪ Revert is an option that automatically closes the document and opens the last saved version of it. This option is grayed out if you have not yet saved the file. When you select it, a dialog box appears, asking you to confirm that you actually do want to revert to the last saved version of the document.

Caution   You cannot undo a Revert action, and you cannot redo anything you've done up to that point with the document.

Saving for Web option

Saving an Illustrator file for the Web is an easy step that ensures Illustrator properly saves your file for Web usage. Choose File ➪ Save for Web or press ⌘+Shift+Option+S (Control+Shift+Alt+S) to access the Save for Web dialog box shown in Figure 2-7.

The tabs you see in the Save for Web dialog box are: Original, Optimized, 2-Up, and 4-Up. The first tab, Original, shows the file in its original state. The second tab, Optimized, shows the file in the optimized settings you chose at the right of the Save for Web dialog box. The third and fourth tabs, 2-Up and 4-Up, respectively, show the figure in the original state along with 1 or 3 of the other default options so you can decide which option best suits your needs.

Cross-Reference   More on the Save for Web dialog box will be presented in Chapter 16.

Understanding file types and options

You can save and export Illustrator files in several ways. Actually, you can save in and export them to almost 30 different formats, although it makes no sense to save in or export to some formats.

Saving an Illustrator file with the wrong options can dramatically affect whether you can place or open that file in other software, as well as what features Illustrator includes with the file when Illustrator reopens it. For example, saving the file as anything but EPS makes it virtually useless to every piece of software but Illustrator (although InDesign, Photoshop, and a few other Adobe products can read Illustrator's native format). Saving a document as an older version of Illustrator may alter the document if the older version is missing features you used in your document.

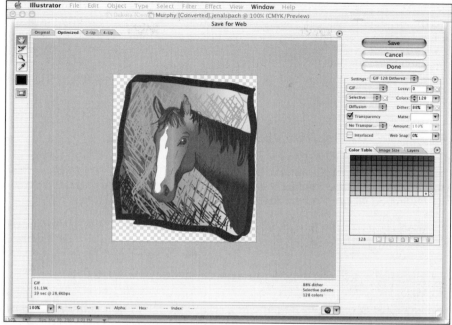

Figure 2-7: The Save for Web dialog box

As a rule, unless you're going to take your Illustrator document into another program, you can save it as an Adobe Illustrator (ai) file without any problems. Doing this keeps the file size down and makes saving and opening the file much quicker.

Compatibility options

Most software packages are forward compatible for one major version, but Illustrator is novel in that you can open an Illustrator 1.1 file in the CS version of the software, even though more than 12 years have passed between those product versions. Figure 2-8 shows the Illustrator Options dialog box. This dialog box automatically appears when you click the Save button in the Save dialog box. In the Illustrator Options dialog box, the Embed Fonts (for other applications) option is automatically checked insuring that the fonts with permissions will be embedded as part of the file. If you uncheck this option, and send the file to a printer that doesn't have the font, the printer won't print the fonts correctly.

The only reason to save illustrations in older versions of Illustrator is to exchange files with clients who haven't upgraded from an old version. The following list provides information about saving files in each version:

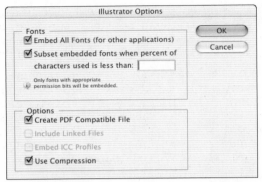

Figure 2-8: The Illustrator Options dialog box with the Embed All Fonts option already selected

✦**Illustrator 10:** Saves the file with transparency, color profiles, and embedded fonts.

✦ **Illustrator 9:** Saves the file with transparency and color profiles.

✦ **Illustrator 8:** Saves the file in a cross-platform (Mac and Windows) Illustrator 8 format. Illustrator 8 added support for EMF file format, and drag-and-drop to Microsoft Office products (Windows), Japanese format FreeHand files, and DXF file formats.

✦ **Illustrator 7:** Saves the file in a cross-platform (Mac and Windows) Illustrator 7 format. Illustrator 7 supports several bitmap file formats that Illustrator 6 cannot. In addition, RGB color is not supported in previous versions of Illustrator.

✦ **Illustrator 6:** Saves the file in the Illustrator 6 format. The major file structure difference between Illustrator 6 and Illustrator 5.x is Illustrator 6's capability to import almost any type of raster image. Illlustrator 5.x only supports EPS images. Other, not-so-obvious changes have to do with advanced object labels that plug-in developers use to achieve all sorts of effects.

✦ **Illustrator 5:** Saves the file in the Illustrator 5 format, which includes both Illustrator 5.0 and 5.5. The features that Adobe added to Version 5.5 do not affect file content. Therefore, files created in Version 5.5 have the same structure as files created in Version 5.0.

✦ **Illustrator 4:** Saves the file in the Illustrator 4 format, which is a version that is available only for Windows users. Saving a file in the Illustrator 4 format ensures that Illustrator 4 for Windows opens that Illustrator file. The Illustrator 4 format does not support gradients, views, layers, and custom artboard sizes. Technically, there is really no difference between the Illustrator 3 and 4 formats.

✦ **Illustrator 3:** Saves the file in the Illustrator 3 format. In fact, you can use the Illustrator 3 format for a lot of cheating — doing things that Illustrator normally doesn't enable you to do. For example, technically, you can't place gradients or masks into patterns. But if you save a gradient as an Illustrator 3 file and reopen it in Illustrator 7, the gradient becomes a blend, which you can use in a pattern (although Illustrator's Expand feature is quicker for this sort of thing).

✦ **Illustrator 88:** Saves the file in the Illustrator 88 format, which, for about 4 years (1988 to 1991), was the Illustrator standard. Much clipart was created and saved in the Illustrator 88 format. The main problem with saving in this format is that type changes occurred between Illustrator 88 and Illustrator 3. Illustrator 88 cannot handle type on a curve (called path type, which it turns into individual segments), and it doesn't deal correctly with compound paths (type converted to outlines are made up of several compound paths, one for each character).

✦ **Illustrator 1.1:** Saves the file in the oldest of Adobe Illustrator formats, version 1.1. Saving in the Illustrator 1.1 format is useful when you want to take files into older versions of FreeHand and many other older drawing programs. Illustrator 1.1 format doesn't support custom colors or masks.

Saving as Illustrator EPS

If you do have to place your Illustrator document in another program, such as QuarkXPress, you need to save the file as Illustrator EPS. First choose File ⇨ Save As to save the file as an EPS. After you select the Illustrator EPS option in the Save As dialog box and name the file, clicking the Save button brings up yet another dialog box, shown in Figure 2-9.

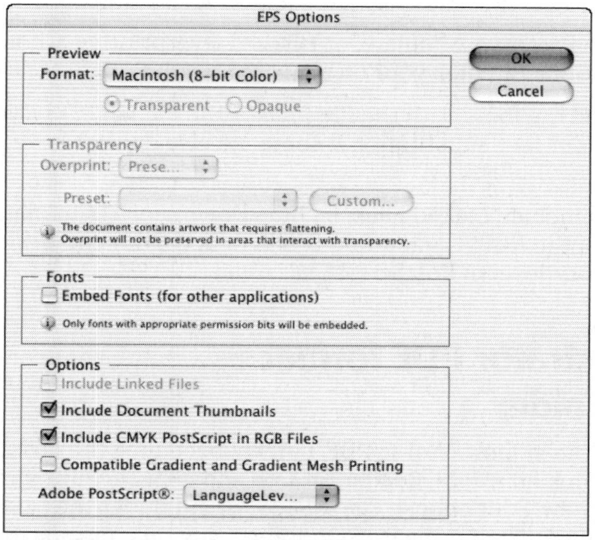

Figure 2-9: The EPS Options dialog box

The following Preview options in Illustrator CS affect the way that other software programs see Illustrator files when you save them as Illustrator EPS files:

✦ **None:** Lets most software programs recognize the Illustrator document as an EPS file, but instead of viewing it in their software, you see a box with an X in it. Usually, this box is the same size as the illustration and includes any stray anchor points or control handles. The file prints fine from other software.

✦ **TIFF (Black & White):** Saves the file with a preview for IBM systems. Page-layout or other software for PCs that can import EPS files can preview illustrations that you save with this option.

✦ **TIFF (8-bit Color):** Saves the file with a color preview for IBM systems Page-layout and other software programs display this file in 8-bit color (256 colors) when you place it in a document. An Illustrator file that you save with a color preview takes up more file space than a file saved with any other option.

✦ **Macintosh (Black & White):** Saves the EPS file with a PICT file preview as part of the EPS file. A PICT image is embedded within the EPS file (technically, a PICT resource); you do not have two separate files. Page-layout and other software programs display this illustration in a black-and-white preview with no shades of gray in it. This file may take up substantially more space than the Include EPSF Header file requires because of the PICT file. The larger the illustration measures, the more storage space the PICT file uses.

✦ **Macintosh (8-bit Color):** Saves the file with a color preview that is an embedded PICT image. Page-layout and other software programs display this file in 8-bit color (256 colors) when you place it in a document. An Illustrator file that you save with a color preview takes up more file space than a file saved with any other option.

✦ **Transparency:** You can Preserve, Simulate, or Discard Overprinting. Choose from a preset of resolutions or enter your own custom resolution.

✦ **Fonts:** Choose to embed the fonts with the file (makes the file larger) so you don't have to worry about font substitution if someone else doesn't have your font.

✦ **Options:** These let you include Linked Files, Include Document Thumbnails, Include CMYK PostScript in RGB, Compatible Gradient and Gradient Mesh printing, and choose your level of PostScript.

Saving files in Illustrator PDF format for Acrobat 6 and older

Another choice for saving a file in Illustrator is PDF, quickly becoming the format of choice because anyone can load Adobe Reader for free and view the file, and Mac OS X users can use Preview. First choose File ➪ Save As and under the Save As menu, choose Illustrator PDF. The Adobe PDF Options dialog box appears, as shown in Figure 2-10.

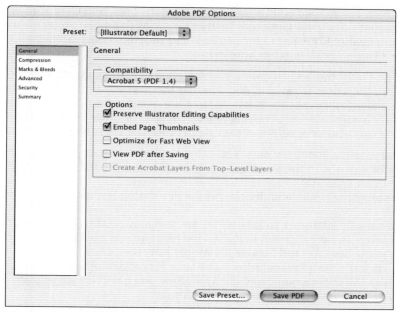

Figure 2-10: The Adobe PDF Options dialog box

Six different areas are under this dialog box for which you can set options. The following lists the areas and their options:

✦ **General:** Under this category, you can set the Compatibility ranging from Acrobat 6 (PDF 1.5) to Acrobat 4 (PDF 1.3). If a user has an older version of Acrobat, you many need to save backwards compatibility so they can read the file. The options you can check or uncheck are Preserve Illustrator Editing Capabilities, Embed Page Thumbnails, Optimize for Fast Web View, View PDF after Saving, and Create Acrobat Layers from Top-Level Layers.

✦ **Compression:** In this area, you can change compression settings for Color Bitmap Images, Grayscale Bitmap Images, and Monochrome Bitmap Images. You also have a checkbox that determines whether to compress text and line art. This makes for a smaller file when emailing or uploading files to other users.

✦ **Marks & Bleeds:** In this area, you set the Printer's Marks (Trim marks, Registration Marks, Color Bars, Page Information), Printer Mark Type, Trim Mark Weight, and how far to offset it from the artwork. The Bleeds for the top, bottom, left, and right of the page are set here. Use this to set how you want to trim the drawings once you get them back from the printer, or register the multiple color pages together.

✦ **Advanced:** The Advanced PDF settings are Color, Fonts, and Overprint and Transparency Flattener Options. Use these options to Embed Fonts for use in other applications, Embed Color profiles, and set your Transparency and Overprinting abilities in other applications.

✦ **Security:** Under the Security area, you set whether the document requires a password for a user to open it, and whether the password restricts editing. You also set the Security Permissions, and the Acrobat Permissions (printing allowed, changes allowed, copying of text, images, or other content, and enabling text access of screen reader devices for the visually impaired).

✦ **Summary:** In the Summary area, you can see all of the other options that Illustrator saves with the file. You can also add a warning to this summary.

You can save all of the options under the Adobe PDF dialog box as presets.

If you have a specific customer to save a PDF for, you may want to keep the settings for that customer. To save a preset in the Adobe PDF Options dialog box (To get to this, choose File ➪ Save As, and choose Illustrator PDF; then click Save.) enter your options and click the Save Preset button. The Save Preset dialog box appears. Type a name, such as the client's name and click OK. Now you have this preset saved anytime you need to save a file in that specific format.

Saving files in SVG

Scalable Vector Graphics, or SVG is the format chosen by the Web support industry. The format is based on XML (Extensible Markup Language), so utilizing vector-based images for the Web is even easier because you are using the most common format in the Web industry. Figure 2-11 shows the SVG dialog box with its options.

Choose File ➪ Save As. In the Save As dialog box, choose SVG from the pop-up format menu.

The SVG Options are:

✦ **Fonts Subsetting:** Includes the characters that are actually used, rather than the entire font set. You can choose None, Only Glyphs used, Common English, Common English and Glyphs used, Common Roman, Common Roman and Glyphs used, and All Glyphs.

✦ **Images Location:** (Embed or Link) If you choose to Embed, the file size is larger because it includes the placed image as part of the file. If you choose Link, it looks for the file on the system and access it that way (smaller file size).

✦ **Preserve Illustrator Editing Capabilities:** Lets you choose to keep the editing capabilities in Illustrator. That way you can use Illustrator to do any edits on the file.

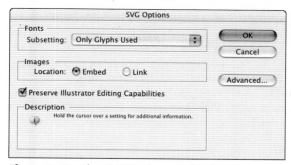

Figure 2-11: The SVG Options dialog box

Cross-Reference

The more advanced options are the CSS Properties, Decimal Places, Encoding, Optimize for Adobe SVG Viewer, Include Extended Syntax for Variable Data, and Include Slicing Data. These options are covered in depth in Chapter 16.

Using the Export Command

Adobe Illustrator allows you to export to several different file formats. Most of the export formats are bitmap formats, such as TIFF and JPEG. You can also export in PDF format so that you can read Illustrator documents with Adobe Acrobat Reader. When you choose the Export option, the following list shows the available formats with the extension in parentheses:

✦ **BMP (bmp):** This is the standard Windows format. In BMP format, you choose the color model, Resolution, Anti-alias (jaggy edges), File format, Depth (number of colors or gray), and Compression.

✦ **Targa (tga):** You use this format for systems that use the Truevision video board.

✦ **Illustrator Legacy (ai):** Using this for older versions of native Illustrator makes the older versions readable in Illustrator CS. It's not a good idea to use this format, because the text looks different and changes everything that is newer such as the Flare and makes it so you can't edit it.

✦ **Illustrator Legacy EPS (eps):** Like Illustrator Legacy (ai), except that you can place the files in other programs such as InDesign. Also not a good idea to use as explained previously.

✦ **PNG (png):** This is the alternative to GIF. Use this for lossless compression. Not all Web browsers support PNG though.

✦ **AutoCAD Drawing (dwg):** This is the standard format for vector drawings created in AutoCAD.

✦ **AutoCAD Interchange File (dxf):** This is the tagged data of the information in an AutoCAD file.

✦ **Enhanced Metafile (emf):** Windows users use this format for exporting vector data.

✦ **Macromedia Flash (swf):** Macromedia Flash Player uses this format for animated Web graphics. Figure 2-12 shows some of the options you can choose in the Macromedia Flash (SWF) Formation Options dialog box.

Cross-Reference For more on the various options in the Macromedia Flash (SWF) Formation Options dialog box, see Chapter 16.

✦ **JPEG (jpg):** You use this format mainly to show photographs on the Web.

✦ **Macintosh PICT (pct):** You use this format with Macintosh graphics and page layout programs for transferring files.

✦ **Photoshop (psd):** You use this format for taking the file into Photoshop by saving it as a raster image in the Photoshop format.

✦ **TIFF (tif):** You use this format to move files between different programs and different **computer platforms.**

✦ **Text Format (txt):** Use this format to export text into a plain text format.

✦ **Window Metafile (wmf):** You mainly use this on Windows applications for 16-bit color. WMF is supported by most Windows layout and drawing applications.

When you choose a format type, a specific dialog box that relates to that particular format appears.

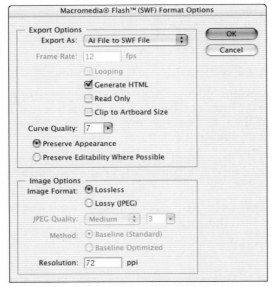

Figure 2-12: The Macromedia Flash export dialog box

Placing Art

If you look closely in the File menu, you'll find the Place command snuggled between the Revert and the Save for Web commands. At first glance, the Place command seems misplaced, but when you realize that you use it to select and place external files into an Illustrator document, you'll understand that the command is right where it needs to be. You can think of the Place command as an Import feature.

Files that you can place or import into Illustrator are EPS (Encapsulated PostScript), TIFF (Tagged Image File Format), and most other bitmap file formats. Generally, the quality of placed art is as good as the original; if the original file was bitmapped (created or saved in a paint program), the quality lessens as you scale up (enlarge) the file, and the quality increases as you scale down (reduce) the file. If the file was in PostScript outline format (created in Illustrator or FreeHand, EPS only), the quality stays consistent as you change it in size. To place files:

1. **Choose File ➪ Place.** A standard Open dialog box appears. Figure 2-13 shows the Mac Place dialog box.

2. **Navigate to the folder containing the file.** You can click the drop-down arrows on the From field to navigate to your file.

3. **Select the files that you want to place.** Only files that you can place appear in the file window. Because you can also place text files, be sure that the file you've chosen is indeed an image document.

Figure 2-13: The Place dialog box

4. **Choose how you want to place the art.** The three options are:

- **Link:** Normally, the option is unselected. Illustrator places the art within the Illustrator file. You generally do not want to select this option, because it prevents the two files from being separated; if you have one but not the other, you are out of luck. However, there are several good reasons to link the file. First, placed art can be huge and may make your Illustrator file too large. Second, if you need to make changes to a placed art file included in an Illustrator file that you have saved with a preview, you must replace the placed art in the preview file with the new version. Preview shows the actual placed image and Outline shows a box with an X through it. If you link the placed art instead of including it, the art is automatically updated when you make changes. And finally you can share placed art that you've linked across multiple files. For example, you can place a business letterhead or logo in all your company files.

- **Template:** The template option makes your placed file a template. When you make a placed file a template, it automatically locks in on a template layer in the Layers palette and dims the image so that you can use it to trace over.

- **Replace:** You may want to replace placed art with new versions or completely different artwork. Illustrator has made this process painless. If you select placed artwork, a dialog box appears asking if you want to replace current artwork or place new artwork, not changing the selected artwork. Use this to keep a certain size or transformation that you used in another placed image. Simply choose Replace and the selected image replaces the existing one transformation and all.

5. **Click the Place button at the bottom of the Place dialog box.** After you place art into Illustrator, you can transform it (move, scale, rotate, reflect, and shear it) in any way.

Caution   Be careful when importing artwork other than EPS images into Illustrator, as TIFF and most other bitmap formats increase the size of your document dramatically. The reason for this is that the image information for TIFFs and other formats is stored within the Illustrator document and is not linked to the document in the way Placed EPS images are. Making the issue even stickier, duplicating TIFFs within Illustrator increases the document size by the size of that TIFF once again.

Tip   The really cool part about changing placed art this way is that if you have placed transformed artwork, the artwork you exchange with it via the Place Art command will have the exact same transformation attributes! For example, if you scale down placed artwork to 50% and rotate it 45°, artwork that you exchange also scales down 50% and rotates 45°.

Placing and Tracing: The Real Advantage of Placed Images

A good reason to place art is to use it to trace an already created image. Creating artwork in Illustrator is often much easier when you start by tracing an object, whether it's a logo, a floor plan, or your cousin Fred's disproportionate profile. Even the best artists use some form of template when they draw to keep proportions consistent, to get angles just right, and for other reasons that help them to achieve the best possible result. For example, you can make a horse graphic in Illustrator by tracing a picture of a real horse.

Tracing is even easier when the placed image is dimmed, as shown in the figure below. You can dim placed art by checking the Dim Images To checkbox in the Layer Options dialog box on the Layers palette. You then enter a percentage by which you want to dim your image. If you dim placed art, a ghost of the image appears instead of the solid image. Dimming placed art does not affect its printed output. When you use a dimmed placed art, it is easier to see to trace over. You can also use the Transparency palette to dim the placed image.

Scanned and dimmed art ready for you to trace

You can trace templates manually or automatically. Tracing manually consists of using the Pencil and Pen tools to tediously trace the edges of a template — often a very time-consuming task. You can choose to automatically trace by using the Auto Trace tool speeds up the process, but, unfortunately, the results may not be of the quality you desire. For more on tracing, see Chapter 7.

Placing Photoshop Art in Illustrator: Understanding Vectors and Pixels

The main use of the Place command is to import raster-based images into Illustrator. These can be photographic image used within your design or images that you can trace, but this raises a critical question whose answer will help you understand how images created with a paint program like Photoshop differ from Illustrator — what is the difference between raster and vector images?

In its original version, Illustrator was a pure vector piece of software. But since Version 8, the border has been crossed, and Illustrator is just this side of the pixel border. What does this mean? It means that you can do things to pixels in Illustrator that you can't do in Photoshop. (Ah, now I've got your attention!) For example, you can use Photoshop filters in Illustrator, but you cannot apply these filters to vector images. Because Photoshop filters work only on pixel-based images, you can rasterize — that is convert your paths into a pixel-based image — or simply use the Effects menu to get some amazing Effects.

Cross-Reference   For more on the Effects menu and Filters, see Chapter 13.

You can move between Photoshop and Illustrator in one of three ways: You can:

✦ Place the raster image using the File ⇨ Place menu.

✦ Use the clipboard to transfer images.

✦ Drag and drop your art between the two programs.

But before you get into the ins and outs of moving Photoshop art to Illustrator, and vice versa, you first need to understand the difference between vectors and pixels.

The essence of Illustrator is the ability to manipulate outlines. When you think vectors, think Illustrator's paths. Illustrator's paths consist of *outlines*, which you can resize and transform into any imaginable shape and fill with various colors and gradients. You can stretch vector-based images and they won't look any worse — unless you scale blends and gradients too large. This means that when you create a curve in Illustrator, it's really a curve — not a jagged mass of pixels.

When you think pixels, think Photoshop's little teeny-tiny squares of color — squares that don't ever change position and that you don't add or delete. The only characteristic you change about pixels is their color. Pixels can only be square, and they take up space regardless of whether they're empty (filled with white or another background color) or filled (filled with a foreground color). Pixels exist on an immobile grid. Enlarging a pixel-based image results in giant, ugly squares of color.

Okay, I'm not a pixel person. If I were to reincarnate as an electronic drawing tool, it wouldn't be as a Painter piece of chalk, but instead as Illustrator's Pen tool or Direct Selection tool. I'm a believer in vectors. Some say it's an obsession, but I'm too busy staring at control handles to pay attention to that nonsense.

Fortunately, my mind is not so closed that I ignore the importance of pixels or their place in our electronic graphics society. So I'm glad there are pixels in Illustrator.

Placing raster images

Even with its pixel capabilities, Illustrator is no Photoshop. There are tools and features in Photoshop that are invaluable for adjusting pixel-based artwork. Adobe recognizes this, so it has provided several methods for moving pixels to Photoshop from Illustrator and from Photoshop to Illustrator.

The most rudimentary way, which has existed for several versions of both software packages, is to save art in a format the other program can read and then to open or place the art in the other program. To place Illustrator art into Photoshop, save the art in Illustrator format and then open the art in Photoshop. To place Photoshop art into Illustrator, save in Photoshop as a format that Illustrator can read, such as TIFF, and then in Illustrator choose File ➪ Place and select the file.

Using the Clipboard

The next way is through Adobe's wonderful PostScript on the Clipboard process, which allows for transferring artwork between Adobe software by simply copying in one program and pasting in another. To place Illustrator art in Photoshop, copy the art in Illustrator, switch to Photoshop, and paste the art in any open document. To place Photoshop art in Illustrator, copy the art in Photoshop, switch to Illustrator, and paste the art in any open document. This process works best for smaller files.

Dragging and dropping

The easiest way to move art between these programs is to drag it from one program to the other. To drag art from Illustrator to Photoshop, select the art in Illustrator and drag it out of the Illustrator window onto a Photoshop window. To drag art from Photoshop to Illustrator, select the art in Photoshop and drag it out of the Photoshop window onto an Illustrator window.

Tip   You must have a window from the "to" application showing when you start dragging for drag-and-drop to work between programs.

To place paths from Photoshop into Illustrator, select the paths in Photoshop with the Path Selection tool, copy the paths, and then paste them in Illustrator.

Working with Document and File Information

All files have information that is recorded when you save a file. You can see most of the information on a file by looking at the Document Info option. You can use this information to see the graphic styles, patterns, gradients, custom colors, fonts, and placed art. This is helpful to know what the file consists of when saving it or choosing an option to save or export. Another option is to save the document information as its own file.

There is a difference between Document Info and File Info. The Document Info is a palette found under the Window menu. The File Info is found under the File menu and you can make additions to the information.

Looking at Document Information

You find general file information in the Document Info palette. You can use the Document Info feature in any document by choosing Window ➪ Document Info. A palette (shown in Figure 2-14) appears with the arrowhead pop-up menu at the top.

Figure 2-14: The Object information listed for this particular document

✦ **Document:** Lists the Color Space, Color Profile, Ruler Units, Artboard dimensions, Output resolution, Split long paths (off or on), Show placed images (off or on), Use printer's default screen (off or on), as well as the name of the file and if there is a URL saved with the file

✦ **Objects:** Lists the Paths, Compound Paths, Clipping Masks, Opacity Masks, Transparent Groups, Transparent Objects, Styled Objects, Gradient Meshes, Symbol Instances, Symbol Instance Sets, Blends, RGB Objects, CMYK Objects, Grayscale Objects, Spot Color Objects, Pattern Objects, Gradient Objects, Brushed Objects, Fonts, Linked Images, Embedded Images, and Non-Native Art Objects

✦ **Graphic Styles:** Lists the Graphic styles used by name

✦ **Brushes:** Lists the Brushes used by name

✦ **Spot Color Objects:** Lists any objects that have a Spot color applied by name

✦ **Pattern Objects:** Lists any objects with a pattern by name

✦ **Gradient Objects:** Lists any objects with a Gradient by name

✦ **Fonts:** Lists all fonts used

✦ **Linked Images:** Lists any images that are linked by Location, Name, Type, Bits per channel, channels, Size, Dimensions, and Resolution

✦ **Embedded Images:** Lists any images that are embedded by Type, Bits per channel, Channels, Size, Dimensions, and Resolution

✦ **Font Details:** Lists more information such as PostScript name, Language, and Font type

In the Document info palette is a triangle on the right that offers more options. In this palette's pop-up menu you can check or uncheck options. If you check the Selection Only option in this pop-up menu, the palette will contain only information about the document's selected objects.

Saving Document Info

In the Document Info palettes pop-up menu options is an option to save the info. The last option in the Document Info palette's pop-up menu is the Save option. Choosing Save brings up a Save Document Info As dialog box shown in Figure 2-15. Here you choose the location of the file and all of the document's information is saved as a text file.

```
Document Info - Sun Mar 30 20:27:39 2003


-------------------------------------------------------------------------------
Document:

Name: Polywhirl:Jen's stuff:Book stuff:AI 11 Bible:*IllustratorBIBLEart:Mesh_card_6.ai

URL:

Color Space: CMYK Color
Color Profile: none
Ruler units: points
Artboard dimensions: 792 pt x 835 pt
Output resolution: 800
Split long paths: OFF
Show placed images: OFF
Use printer's default screen: ON

-------------------------------------------------------------------------------
Objects:

Paths: 172 (947 points)
Compound Paths: 2
Compound Shapes: 15
Clipping Masks: NONE
Opacity Masks: NONE
Transparent Groups: NONE
Transparent Objects: 26
Styled Objects: NONE
Gradient Meshes: 70
Symbol Instances: NONE
Symbol Instance Sets: NONE
Blends: 17

RGB Objects: NONE
CMYK Objects: 252
Grayscale Objects: 2

Spot Color Objects: NONE
Pattern Objects: 1
Gradient Objects: 2
Brushed Objects: 7

Fonts: NONE
Linked Images: NONE
Embedded Images: NONE
Non-Native Art Objects: NONE

-------------------------------------------------------------------------------
Graphic Styles:
```

Figure 2-15: The file opened in a text editing program lists all of the document and file information.

Finding File Info

To access File Info, choose File ➪ File Info. The File Info dialog box has three areas of information. Those areas are: Description (shown in Figure 2-16), Origin (shown in Figure 2-17), and Advanced (shown in Figure 2-18). Here you can enter the information you want to be saved with the file.

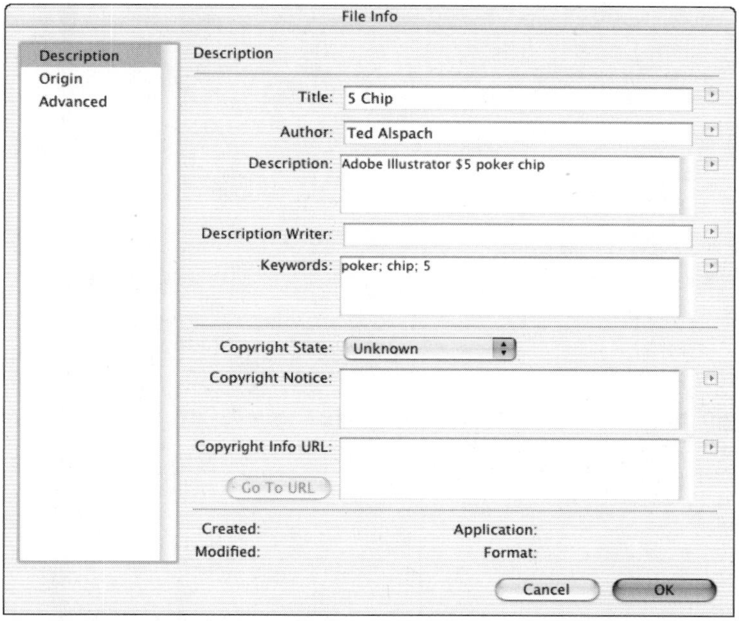

Figure 2-16: Description information lets you enter the Title, Author, Description, Description Writer, Keywords, Copyright State (Unknown, copyrighted, or Public Domain), Copyright Notice, Copyright Info URL, Created, Modified, Application, and Format.

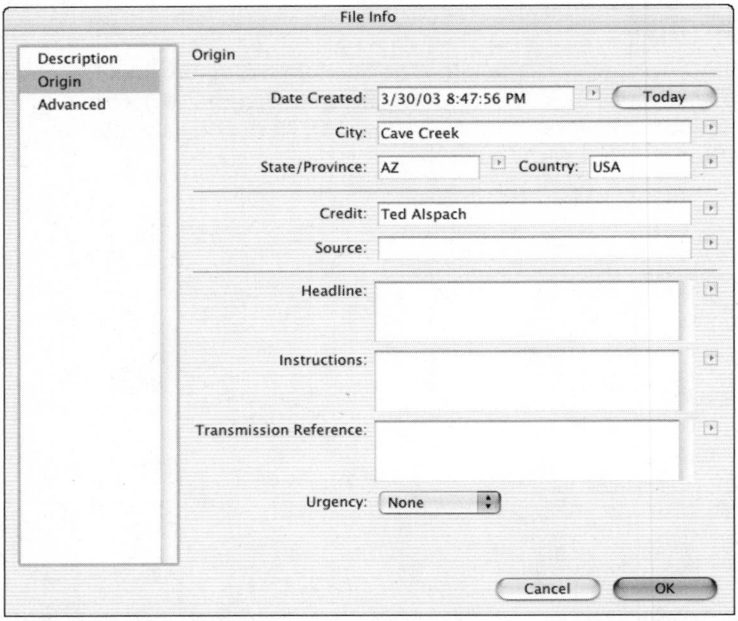

Figure 2-17: Origin information lets you enter the Date Created, City, State/Province, Country, Credit, Source, Headline, Instructions, Transmission Reference, and Urgency.

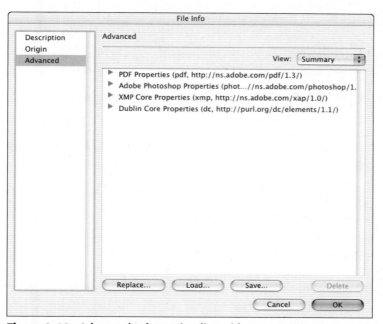

Figure 2-18: Advanced Information lists either a source or summary. The Source lists the PostScript Information, and the Summary lists the properties of the file.

Summary

Understanding Illustrator's documents is one of the basic yet most important areas of Illustrator. The main thing to keep in mind is to save and save often.

✦ Use ⌘+N (Ctrl+N) or File ➪ New to set up a New document with Artboard dimensions and units.

✦ You can change the document setup at anytime by accessing the Document Setup dialog box. Access this box quickly by choosing File ➪ Document Setup or ⌘+Shift+P (Ctrl+Shift+P).

✦ You can open a variety of files in Illustrator with the Place command.

✦ Illustrator files are best saved as an .ai file. If you are using the file in other (non-Adobe) applications, use the .eps file format.

✦ You can also export Illustrator files into a variety of formats. Keep in mind that if you want to retain editing capabilities, save a version as an Illustrator file as well.

✦ Many artist and graphic designers use a scanned image placed in Illustrator to trace over as a starting point. Dimming this image helps you to trace it better.

✦ There is a difference between Document Info and File Info. The Document Info is a palette found under the Window menu. The File Info is found under the File menu, and you can make additions to the information.

✦   ✦   ✦

Understanding Drawing and Painting Techniques

In This Chapter

Working with paths

Understanding anchor points and control handles

Drawing paths with Illustrator Pencil and Pen tools

Using the miscellaneous line tools

Using the Paintbrush tool

In this chapter you will learn about *paths*, which are the underlying lines that make up the various objects. You'll also learn to use Illustrator's drawing tools, including the Pen, Pencil, and Paintbrush tools to create these paths. You'll also learn about the techniques behind many cool effects that you can create using these tools.

Working with Paths

The most basic element in Illustrator is a path. A *path* is what Illustrator calls the black line segment that appears when you draw a line. When you select a path, its anchor points appear. A path must have at least two *anchor points*, which appear as small squares along the path, and which control which way the path goes. Paths look different in Preview and Outline modes. In Preview mode, you actually see the line weight, dashed style, color, and any effects applied to that line. In Outline mode, you simply see a thin line. Without two anchor points, you cannot draw a path as shown in Figure 3-1. Conceptually, there is no limit to the number of anchor points or segments that you can have in any one path. Depending on the type of anchor points that are on either end of a line segment, you can make a segment straight or curved. A single anchor point will never print anything.

Cross-Reference For more on viewing modes, see Chapter 1. For more on selecting paths, see Chapter 5.

Figure 3-1: This whole illustration is created with paths consisting of two anchor points with a line segment between them.

Types of paths

Now that you know what a path is, you should learn that there are various types of paths. There are three major types of paths:

✦ **Open paths:** Two distinct end points, with any number of anchor points in between. An example of this is a simple line that you draw with the Pencil tool.

✦ **Closed paths:** Continuous paths, with no end points and no start or end — a closed path just continues around and around. An example of this is a shape that you create with one of Illustrator's shape tools, such as a rectangle or circle.

✦ **Compound paths:** Two or more open or closed paths

Cross-Reference

For more on creating shapes in Illustrator, see Chapter 4. For a detailed look at compound paths, see Chapter 11.

Bézier curves

If you don't know much about geometry (or maybe don't remember much — it was eighth grade, after all), you may find the very concept of creating curves by using math frightening. But most of the curve creation in Illustrator takes place behind the scenes in the PostScript language code you almost never see.

PostScript curves are based on Bézier curves (pronounced bez-ee-ay), which were created by Pierre Bézier in the early 1970s as a way of controlling mechanical cutting devices, commonly known as Numerical Control. Bézier worked for Renault (the car manufacturer) in France, and his mission was to streamline the process by which machines were controlled.

"PostScript curves are based on Bezier curves, which were created by Pierre Bezier in the early 70s as part of his method, called Numerical Control, for controlling mechanical cutting devices."

A mathematician and engineer, Bézier developed a method for creating curves using four points for every curved segment. He placed two points at either end of the segment — in Illustrator, these correspond to the anchor points — and made two points float around the curve segment to control the curve's shape — these are control handles in Illustrator. Using these four points, you can create any curve; using multiple sets of these curves, you can create any possible shape. John Warnock and Chuck Geschke, of Adobe, decided that Bézier curves were the best method for creating curves in a page description language, and suddenly those curves became a fundamental part of high-end graphic design.

Bézier curves are anything but intuitive, and, in fact, they represent the most significant stumbling block for beginners learning Illustrator. After you've mastered the concept and use of these curves, everything about Illustrator suddenly becomes easier and friendlier. Don't try to ignore them, because they won't go away. You'll find it easier in the long run to try to understand how they work.

Understanding anchor points

As stated earlier, paths consist of a series of points and the line segments between these points. These points are commonly called anchor points because they anchor the path; paths always pass through or end at anchor points.

Anchor points consist of control handles and control handle lines. *Control handles*, which appears as small squares along the path, determine how tightly or loosely the curve bends at each anchor point. Control handle lines run on a tangent along the path and are attached to the path by the control handle. They determine the direction of the curved path. The next section discusses control handles and control handle lines in more detail. Anchor points, control handles, and control handle lines do not appear on the printed output of your artwork. In fact, they appear only in Illustrator and Photoshop, never on artwork imported into other applications.

There are two classes of anchor points:

✦ **Smooth points:** These are anchor points that have a curved path flowing smoothly through them. Most of the time you don't know where a smooth point is unless you select the path. Smooth points keep the path from changing direction abruptly. There are two linked control handles on every smooth point.

✦ **Corner points:** A class of anchor points in which the path changes direction noticeably at those specific points. There are three different corner points:

 • **Straight corner points:** Anchor points where two straight line segments meet at a distinct angle. There are no control handles on this type of anchor point.

 • **Curved corner points:** Points where two curved line segments meet and abruptly change direction. There are two independent control handles on each curved corner point. Each handle controls a curve and you can change only one side if you'd like.

 • **Combination corner points:** The meeting places for straight and curved line segments. There is one independent control handle on a combination corner point. The one control handle controls the curve.

Figure 3-2 shows the different types of anchor points in Illustrator.

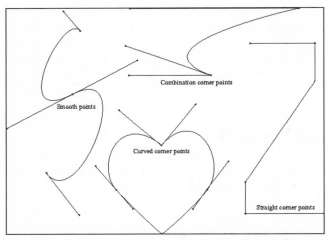

Figure 3-2: The different types of anchor points in Illustrator

Control handles and control handle lines

If an anchor point has a control handle coming out of it, the next segment will be curved. No control handle, no curve. Couldn't be simpler.

As stated before, control handles are connected to anchor points with control handle lines. Figure 3-3 shows what happens when an anchor point with no control handle and an anchor point with a control handle are connected to another anchor point. Figure 3-4 shows the anchor points, control handles, and the control handle lines on a path.

The basic concept to remember about control handles is that they act as magnets by pulling the curve toward them. This presents an interesting problem because there are usually two control handles per curved line segment. Just as you might suspect, the control handle exerts the greatest amount of force on the half of the curved segment nearest to it. If there is only one control handle, the segment curves more on the side of the segment with the control handle than on the side with no control handle.

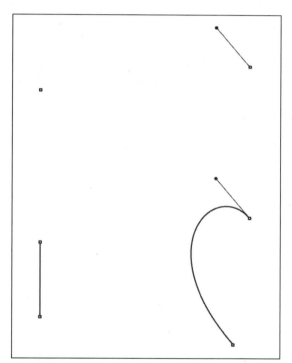

Figure 3-3: An anchor point without a control handle (top left) and an anchor point with a control handle bottom left) are connected to new anchor points, esulting in a straight line segment (top right) and a curved line segment (bottom right).

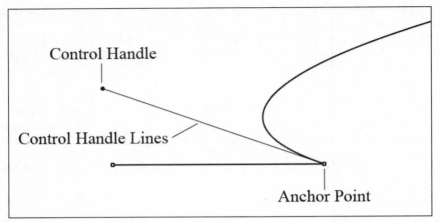

Figure 3-4: Anchor points, control handles, and control handle lines along a path

The greater the distance between a control handle and its corresponding anchor point, the farther the curve (on that end of the curve segment) pulls away from an imaginary straight segment between the two points (see Figure 3-5). If the control handles on either end of the segment are on different sides of the curved segment, the curved segment takes on the shape of an S, as the bottom path in Figure 3-6 shows. If the control handles on the ends of the curved segment are on the same side, the curve takes on the shape of a U.

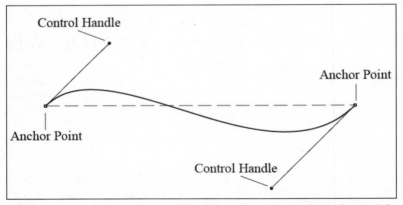

Figure 3-5: Control handles pull the line segment away from the straight line that would normally exist between them. The bottom path is an S shape because the control handles are pulling in opposite directions.

Figure 3-6: Control handle lines run tangent to the path where the path meets the anchor point.

Regardless of whether the anchor point is a smooth point, a curved corner point, or a combination corner point, control handle lines coming out of an anchor point are always tangent to the curved segment where it touches the anchor point. Tangent refers to the touching of the control handle line to the curved segment as it crosses the anchor point (see Figure 3-6).

Tip   To adjust the curves without moving the control handles, click the curve and drag it. Keep in mind that you're changing both control handles at once, and it can make adjusting hard to control the curve.

Understanding how fills and strokes relate to paths

If paths are the basic concept behind Illustrator, you might be wondering where the colors and patterns fit in. You apply all colors and patterns to Illustrator paths using fills and strokes. Basically, a fill is a color or pattern that appears within a path, and a stroke is a special style that you apply along a path.

Cross-Reference   For more on applying fills and strokes to shapes, see Chapter 4. To create fills and strokes, see Chapter 9.

To quickly review Chapter 1, when you work in Illustrator in Outline mode (View ➪ Outline), only paths are visible. In Preview mode (View ➪ Preview), fills and strokes applied to paths are visible. Unless a path is selected in Preview mode, that path (anchor points and line segments) isn't visible. You can toggle between Outline and Preview mode by pressing ⌘+Y (Ctrl+Y). Figure 3-7 shows closed paths with different fills in both Outline and Preview modes.

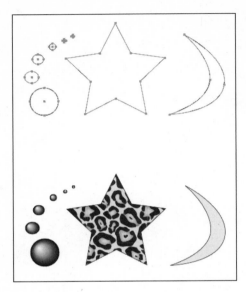

Figure 3-7: Closed paths with different fills: The top row is how they appear in Outline mode, while the bottom row shows what they look like in Preview mode. You toggle between Outline and Preview modes using the same keyboard shortcut.

You can also fill open paths. The fill goes straight across the two end points of the path to enclose the object. Figure 3-8 displays different types of filled open paths. Filling an open path is usually not desirable, although in some circumstances doing so may be necessary. Since the fill goes from the endpoints of the path, if you have an irregular shaped path, the fill can look strange. If you are looking to get a cool pair of sunglasses, use a filled path for an unusual look.

Caution   Filled two-dimensional line mistake: If you have a straight line with a fill (you don't actually see the fill and it was an error to fill the line), can cause problems when you go to print. In PostScript, when you specify a fill, but only have two dimensions to an object (a straight line), it prints (rasterizes) at one "device pixel." At 100% onscreen, the filled line looks exactly like a 1-point stroked line (72 dpi = 1 device pixel = ½ inch and 1 point = ½ inch). When you zoom in to 200%, the stroked line scales by 200%, but the filled line stays the same (1 device pixel or ½ inch). When you print this line to a laser printer, one device pixel is as tiny as ⅟₃₀₀ or ⅟₆₀₀ inch. By the time you print to a typical Imagesetter printer, one device pixel becomes ⅟₂₅₇₀ inch, making it too small to be visible in most situations. The key to fixing it is to make sure any paths that you don't want filled, you check to make sure it has no fill before sending it to print.

Cross-Reference   For more about printing, see Chapter 15.

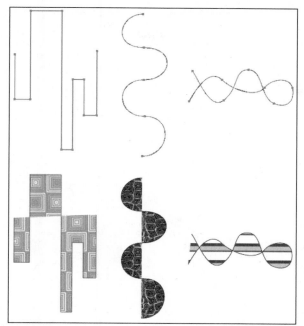

Figure 3-8: Open paths with different fills: The top row is how they appear in Outline mode, while the bottom row shows how they appear in Preview mode.

Besides filling paths, you can also stroke paths with a tint of any color or a pattern. These strokes can be any weight (thickness), and the width of the stroke is equally distributed over each side of the path. Open paths have ends on the strokes; these ends can be cropped, rounded, or extended past the end of the stroke by half the width of the stroke. Several different paths with strokes are shown in Figure 3-9.

Cross-Reference For more on Stroke weight, color, and attributes, see Chapter 4.

A single point is also considered a path; however, single points in Illustrator have no printable qualities. This isn't readily noticeable, because you can assign a fill or stroke color to a single point, although you can't see it in Preview mode or when you print it. When the document is color separated, it causes a separation of the color to print, even if nothing else on that page uses that same color, and the separation appears blank. If you think that you may have individual anchor points floating around your illustration, you can select all of them at once by choosing Select ➪ Object ➪ Stray Points and then deleting them.

Figure 3-9: Various paths with different strokes applied to them

Fills and strokes in Illustrator can be colors or an opaque white, which knocks out any color underneath. Fills and strokes may also be transparent. Transparency in Illustrator is commonly referred to as a fill, stroke, or none.

 Cross-Reference   For more on Transparency, see Chapter 12.

Drawing Paths with Illustrator Tools

The most effective (and challenging) way to create paths is to draw them with one of the drawing tools. The Pen, Paintbrush, and Pencil tools are the most common drawing instruments, but Illustrator has a Brushes palette as well with three key brushes — the Art Brush, the Scatter Brush, and the Pattern Brush. If you are look-ing for the Calligraphic option, you find it as a brush option that you can choose in the Brush palette. The Smooth tool and the Erase tool are two more helpful tools. They are located in the Pencil tool's pop-up menu. These two tools cut editing time drastically by letting you clean up lines and fix errors with the stroke of a brush.

You can use a variety of tools within Illustrator to draw paths. The three main tools are the Pen, Pencil, and Paintbrush. Although the Pen is the most difficult of the three, using it often yields the best results. The Pencil by far is the easiest but requires some editing to smooth the bumpy lines. The Paintbrush tool combined with a tablet can create some amazing hand-drawn looks in your art.

Each tool has its place, and you'll use all three to achieve the most productivity. So practice using all of the tools and find which one works best for whatever you may be working on. Figure 3-10 shows an illustration created using all three tools.

Figure 3-10: In this illustration the horses, grass, trees, and hill were created using the Paintbrush, Pencil, and Pen tools.

Here's a rundown of keys you can press while using any of the creation tools:

✦ **Tilde (~):** It duplicates here as well, but *don't* do it with spirals. The mess is usually disastrous on all but the least wound spirals.

✦ **Shift:** This keeps the spiral aligned to the constrain angle. Actually, it keeps the protruding line segment of the spiral aligned to a 45° variant of the Constrain Angle.

✦ **Option (Alt):** Pressing this key makes the spiral grow by adding or removing line segments (winds) to the spiral's outermost edge. Dragging away from the origin (where you initially clicked) adds segments; dragging toward the origin removes segments.

✦ **⌘ (Ctrl):** Pressing the ⌘ (Ctrl) key while dragging changes the decay of the spiral. Dragging away from the origin decreases the decay %, making the space between winds larger toward the outer edge of the spiral. Dragging toward the origin increases the decay %, making the space between winds similar from inside to outside. A decay of 100% results in a perfect circle. The decay can never be less than 5%.

✦ **Spacebar:** Pressing the Spacebar lets you move the spiral around the screen.

Using the Pencil tool

When you want to draw rough edges or realistic illustrations that don't look "computery," for example map drawing with beautiful bumpy edges, the Pencil tool is the tool to use. The Pencil tool, housed with the tools that edit it — the Smooth and Eraser tools — draws a freeform stroked path wherever you drag the cursor. However, instead of creating a closed path that is a certain width, the result is a single path that approximately follows the route you've taken with the cursor. The Pencil tool has the unique capability to make the lines you draw look...well... good.

Actually, part of the Pencil tool's charm is also its biggest draw back. Unlike the Pen tool — which creates precise, super-straight lines, but which is difficult to control — the Pencil tool is much easier to use, but it draws lines that are far from perfect. This is because the Pencil tool creates smooth points and corner anchor points, only. When you select it, the Pencil tool's anchor point has two control handles. If you remember the earlier discussion on anchor points, you'll know this means you can neither draw a smooth anchor point — although at first glance, you may think you can — nor a straight-corner point with the Pencil tool. This makes the construction of precise objects nearly impossible.

Before you use the Pencil tool for the first time, it's a good idea to change the Paint Style attributes to a fill of None and a stroke of Black, 1 point. Show the Color palette by choosing Window ➪ Color. Click the Fill square; then click the None (red slash) box to make sure the fill is None. Select the stroke (outlined rectangle) and click the black to make sure the stroke has a black stroke. In the Stroke palette, choose 1 point from the weight pop-up menu. Having a fill other than None while drawing with the Pencil tool often results in bizarre-looking shapes. Set the Stroke weight (found in the Stroke palette) to 1 point, the Stroke color to black (at the bottom of the Toolbox) with no fill by choosing the None option in the Color palette. You can also get the resulting path to follow your cursor-drawn line exactly by lowering the curve-fitting tolerance.

To use the Pencil tool, follow these steps:

1. **Double-click the Pencil tool.** The Pencil tool is the fifth tool down in the second column of the Toolbox and is housed with the Smooth tool and the Erase tool, which help smooth and edit Pencil tool paths. The Pencil tool, obviously, has a pencil for its icon. Double-clicking this icon causes the Pencil Tool Preference dialog box to open. Figure 3-11 shows the Pencil Tool Preferences dialog box.

Cross-Reference

For more on the Erase and Smooth tools, see the sections "Working with the Smooth tool" and "Erasing with the Erase tool," covered later in this chapter.

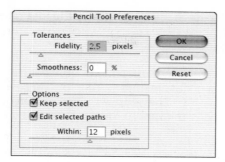

Figure 3-11: In the Pencil Tool Preferences dialog box, you can change the fidelity and smoothness for the Pencil tool.

2. **Adjust the options in the Pencil Tool Preference dialog box.** The options are as follows:

   - **Fidelity:** The Fidelity setting controls the distance (measured in pixels) in which curves may stray from the original dotted line that you draw with the mouse. A low fidelity value results in sharper angles; a high fidelity value results in smoother curves. The lowest Fidelity number is .5 and the highest 20 pixels.

   Note

   As stated previously, although you think you can create them at first glance, you cannot create smooth anchor points. You may find this especially deceiving when you set the Fidelity option to a high number so that all the anchor points look like they are smooth points. This is **not** the case. In fact, most anchor points created with the Pencil tool — with the exception of end points — are curved corner points, which are anchor points with two independent control handles shooting out. If the Fidelity setting is high enough, you'll get smooth points.

   - **Smoothness:** Measured as a percentage, the Smoothness determines how well the Pencil controls the bumpiness or irregularity of the line. A low smoothness value results in a course, angular path, while a high smoothness value results in a much smoother path with fewer anchor points.

   - **Keep selected:** The Keep selected option keeps the last path you drew selected in case you want to edit or do any changes right after drawing the path.

   - **Edit selected paths:** If you check this option, you can edit the path with the Pencil tool. If you don't check this option, you can still edit, but you have to use the Selection tools.

   - **Within pixels:** The Within pixels option sets how close your drawing has to match the existing path to be editable (works only when Edit selected paths is checked).

3. **Click OK.** Illustrator applies your preferences.

4. **To use the Pencil tool, select it from the toolbox.** Again, the tool is in the Toolbox and looks like a pencil.

5. **Click in the document window**.

6. **Begin dragging the mouse.** The Pencil tool resembles a little pencil when you are drawing. As you drag, a series of dots follows the cursor. These dots show the approximate location of the path you have drawn. The location of a path drawn with the Pencil tool is directly relevant to the direction and speed that the cursor is moving.

Tip

Pressing the Caps Lock key (engaging it) changes the cursor from the pencil shape to crosshairs, which looks suspiciously like the crosshairs from the Paintbrush tool. The line of points comes from the dot in the center of the crosshairs. Use the crosshairs if you want to see exactly the point where the drawing starts from. I like to use this when tracing over a scanned image and want to match exactly over the existing lines. If you like to use the crosshairs cursors all the time but get really mad every time you start typing because you forget to take off the Caps Lock key, you've got short-term memory problems. Fortunately, you can set your cursors to always be crosshairs style just by going to General Preferences by pressing ⌘+K (Ctrl+K) and checking the Use Precise Cursors checkbox. When this option is checked, the Caps Lock key changes the cursor back to the regular tool.

7. **Release the mouse button.** The path of dots is transformed into a path with anchor points, all having control handle lines and control handles shooting off from them. The faster you draw with the Pencil tool, the fewer points that are created; the slower you draw, the more points that are used to define the path.

8. **Create anything you'd like.** I created clumps of grass in this example by sketching their outline using the mouse (see Figure 3-12).

Tip

You can repeat the item you just drew quickly and easily. Using a Selection tool (see Chapter 5 for more on the Selection tools), click the objects you drew and press Option (Alt). Next, drag the items side by side to make more of those objects. I repeated this process until I had enough clumps to resemble a grassy area (Figure 3-12).

Figure 3-12: Clumps of grass created with the Pencil tool

Tip You can instantly transform a swooping, uneven, jagged line that looks terrible as you draw into a beautifully curved piece of artwork reminiscent of lines drawn traditionally with a French curve using the Smooth tool.

Drawing open paths and closed paths

You can draw both open and closed paths with the Pen and Pencil tools. Paths in Illustrator may cross themselves. When these paths cross, the fills may look a little unusual. Strokes look normal; they just overlap where paths cross.

 Cross-Reference For more on paths, see the section "Types of paths" earlier in this chapter.

To create an open path, draw a path with the Pencil or Pen tools, but make sure that the beginning and end of the path are two separate points at different locations. Open paths with fills may look a little bizarre because Illustrator automatically fills-in between the end points on the path, even if the imaginary line between the end points crosses the path. Figure 3-13 shows both open and closed paths drawn with the Pencil tool.

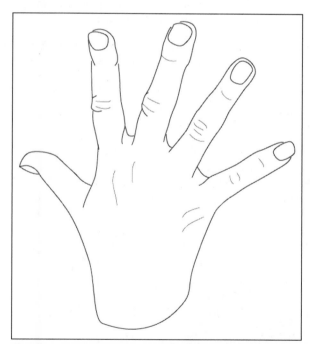

Figure 3-13: Handy drawing created by the Pencil tool

How the Fidelity and Smoothness options affect a line

Because drawing nice-looking paths with the Pencil tool and a mouse is just a tad difficult and frustrating ("Really?" you ask sarcastically), Illustrator provides a way to determine how rough or smooth your path will be before you draw it.

Normally, paths that appear from the dotted lines created with the Pencil tool are fairly similar to those dotted lines in direction and curves and such. When lines are being drawn, though, human error can cause all sorts of little bumps and *skiddles*—little round, misshaped sections resembling a small fruit-flavored candy—to appear, making the path look lumpy. In some cases, as in map creation, lumpy is good. More often than not, though, lumpy is an undesirable state for your illustrations.

The smoothness—or jaggedness—of the resulting paths drawn with the Pencil tool depends on the Fidelity and Smoothness options in the Pencil Tool Preferences dialog box, which determines how jagged or smooth each section appears from the dotted line to the path. As stated before, a low Fidelity value results in sharper angles; and a high Fidelity value results in smoother curves, while a low smoothness value results in a course, angular path, and a high Smoothness value results in a much smoother path with fewer anchor points. The figure below shows a portrait done with the Pencil tool set to a tolerance of .5 pixels (left) and 6 pixels (right).

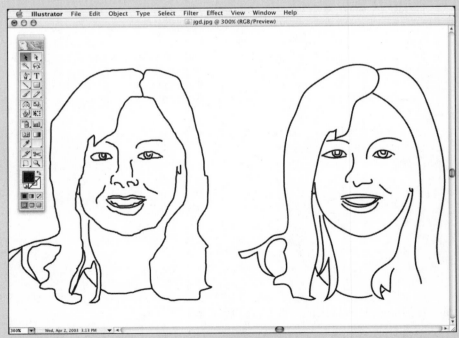

A portrait done with the Pencil tool and a fidelity tolerance set to .5 on the left and 6 on the right

At a Fidelity setting of .5, paths appear jagged and rough. Also, many more anchor points are present, although there are still no straight corner points. A setting of .5 is great for creating some photorealistic illustrations of complex, detailed objects, such as tree leaves and textures. When the setting is this low, the resulting path follows the dotted line as closely as possible.

When the Fidelity option is set to 20, paths created with the Pencil tool appear extremely smooth. Illustrator uses the smallest number of anchor points, and the curve of the line appears to be very graceful. Because so few anchor points are used, much detail is lost, and the path wavers from the original dotted line of the Pencil tool by a significant amount. Even though it appears that all the anchor points are smooth points, they are actually curved corner points with two independent control handles.

To create a closed path, end your path at the same place that you started the path. While drawing, press the Option (Alt) key. When the pencil cursor is directly over the location where the line begins, a little circle appears to the lower right of the pencil. This change means that the path is a closed path if you release the mouse button when that particular cursor is showing.

Connecting Pencil paths

You can quickly connect the Pencil drawn paths you draw in Illustrator by using the Option (Alt) key. While drawing with the Pencil tool, press the Option (Alt) key and when you release the mouse button, a line automatically connects the beginning anchor point to the ending anchor point resulting in a closed path. You can try to draw back to the beginning line, but they won't connect. You can also draw the paths close to one another; select the two endpoints, and press ⌘+J (Ctrl+J) to join the paths.

Adding to an existing open path

To continue drawing on an existing path (which could have been drawn with the Pen tool or the Pencil tool), the existing path must first be an open path with two distinct End Points. After you pass your drawing tool over one end of the path with the Pencil tool, the pencil cursor changes. The little x beside the pencil disappears. This action means that if you click and drag, you can now extend the path with the Pencil tool. If the Caps Lock key is engaged, the cursor changes from an X (crosshairs) to a +.

So far, all the points in paths drawn with the Pencil tool have been curved corner points. This changes when you add to an existing path with the Pencil tool. The point that connects the existing path to the newly drawn path is a smooth point. No matter which way you drag, the point is always a smooth point.

If you drag to the other open end of the existing path, you have the opportunity to make the path into a closed path by pressing the Option (Alt) key. This point will also be a smooth point.

You can add on only to end points on an existing path. Anchor points that are within paths cannot be connected to new (or existing, for that matter) segments. If you attempt to draw from an anchor point that is not an end point, you create an end point for the path you are drawing that is overlapping but not connected to the anchor point you clicked above.

Working with the Smooth tool

The Smooth tool came into being in version 8. This extremely cool editing tool makes changing any path a breeze. The Smooth tool works on any path regardless of what tool created it. You can apply the Smooth tool in one of two ways:

- ✦ **Using the Toolbox:** Select the path you want to edit, click the Smooth tool found in the Pencil tool's pop-up tools, and drag your mouse over a selected path to smooth out the line.

- ✦ **While using other tools:** You can also access the Smooth tool while using the Pencil tool by pressing the Option (Alt) key. You'll see the tool changes to the Smooth tool while you keep the key pressed.

You can set the sensitivity of the Smooth tool, just like the Pencil tools, in the Type and Auto Trace Preferences dialog box, which you access by choosing Illustrator (Edit) ⇨ Preferences. A lower setting for Auto Trace Tolerance results in more mouse movement being recorded and more anchor points. At a higher setting, fewer anchor points are used and the path is smoother. Figure 3-14 shows a path before and after using the Smooth tool. As you can see, the top path has more anchor points than the smoothed bottom path.

Double clicking on the Smooth tool opens a dialog box where, just as with the Pencil tool, you can set Fidelity and Smoothness values.

Cross-Reference   For more on the Fidelity and Smoothness values, see the section "Using the Pencil tool" earlier in this chapter.

Erasing with the Erase tool

You find the Erase tool with the Pencil tool in the toolbox. Like the Smooth tool, the Erase tool works on any path, no matter how you created it. The Erase tool does what you'd think; it erases a path at the point where you have dragged the Erase tool over the path as shown in Figure 3-15. You can use the Erase tool to cut a path by first selecting the path, and then dragging across a section. Illustrator removes the section you drag over. You can use the Erase tool to cut a line as you would use the Scissor tool. If you just click one time on the path, Illustrator cuts the path exactly in that spot. Unlike Photoshop's clunky eraser-looking tool, this is much more refined and easier to use.

Figure 3-14: The top illustration is pretty bumpy. The same illustration below had the Smooth tool applied to it. Notice the smoothness especially in the eye area.

Figure 3-15: The selected path is being erased using the Erase tool.

Drawing with the Pen tool

The Pen tool is the most powerful tool in Illustrator's arsenal because you are dealing more directly with Bézier curves than with any other tool. It's one thing to adjust paths, anchor points, and control handles with the Direct Selection tool, but using the Pen tool to create paths out of nothing is dumbfounding.

During the first several months of using Illustrator, you might find yourself avoiding the Pen tool like the plague. Then you slowly worked up to where you can draw straight lines with it comfortably and, finally, curved segments. Even after you draw curved segments for a while, you may still not understand how the tool worked, and may miss out on a lot of its capabilities because of that lack of knowledge. While practicing with the Pen tool, you begin to understand the four types of anchor points — smooth points, straight corner points, curved corner points, and combination corner points — and discover that understanding how anchor points work is the key to using the Pen tool. The first click of the Pen tool produces one anchor point. The second click (usually in a different location) creates a second anchor point that is joined to the first anchor point by a line segment. Clicking without dragging produces a straight corner point.

Although it is a little frustrating and confusing to use, the Pen tool is the most important tool to learn. It saves you so much time and effort because, with it, you can draw the most accurately and smoothly with fewer edits. Once you master this tool, you will use it for most of your drawing and tracing needs.

Unfortunately, the Pen tool does not do all the work; you do have to perform some of the labor involved in creating curves and straight lines. Drawing with the Pen tool isn't just placing anchor points.

Here are some things to consider when you're drawing with the Pen tool:

✦ **The first obstacle is to figure out where the heck those anchor points are going to go**. Two drawings with the same number of anchor points can look totally different, depending on anchor point placement. You have to think ahead to determine what the path will look like before you draw it. You should always locate points where you want a change in the path. That change can be a different curve or a corner. The three changes to look for are:

  • A corner of any type

  • The point where a curve changes from clockwise to counterclockwise or vice versa

  • The point where a curve changes intensity: from tight to loose or loose to tight (by far, the hardest change to judge)

✦ **The second obstacle is to decide what type of anchor point you want to use.** Remember, there are four different anchor points to choose from when drawing with the Pen tool — Smooth, Straight Corner, Curved Corner and Combination Corner. If the path is smoothly curving, you use a smooth point. If there is a corner, use one of the corner points.

✦ **The third obstacle arises when you decide that the anchor point should be anything but a straight corner point because all the other anchor points have control handles.** The obstacle is figuring out how to drag the control handles, how far to drag them, and in which direction to drag them.

Drawing straight lines with the Pen tool

The easiest way to start learning to use the Pen tool is by drawing straight lines. The lightning bolt in Figure 3-16 was created entirely with straight lines. The great thing about straight lines drawn with the Pen tool is that there are no control handles to worry about or fuss over.

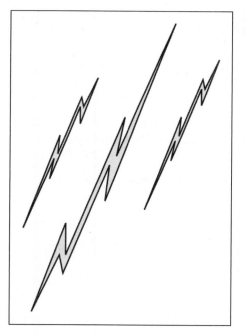

Figure 3-16: Straight lines drawn with the Pen tool

The simplest straight line is a line drawn with only two anchor points. To draw straight lines:

1. **Select the Pen tool.** This tool is located on the third row of the first column in the Toolbox and looks like an old-fashioned ink pen tip.

2. **Click and release where you want the first end point to appear.** This becomes the beginning of your line.

3. **Click and release where you want the second end point (the end of the line) to appear.** A line appears between the two points. Too easy, isn't it?

Tip   Hold down the Shift key to keep the line constrained to a 45° angle (0, 45, 90, and so on).

4. **To draw another separate line, first click the Pen tool in the toolbox or hold down the ⌘ (Ctrl) key and click.** Either action tells Illustrator that you are done drawing the first line.

5. **Clicking and releasing again in one spot and then another draws a second line with two end points.** Be careful not to drag when clicking the Pen tool to form straight lines. If you drag the mouse, you create a smooth point and the path will curve.

Paths drawn with the Pen tool, like the Pencil tool, may cross themselves. The only strange result you may see involves the fills for objects whose paths cross. In open paths created with the Pen tool, fills may look unusual because of the imaginary line between the two end points and any paths that the imaginary line crosses.

Closing paths with the Pen tool

If you want to create a closed path (one with no end points), return to the first anchor point in that segment and click. As the Pen tool crosses over the beginning anchor point, the cursor changes to a pen with a circle in the lower-right corner. After you have created a closed path, you don't need to click the Pen tool again. Instead, the next click of the Pen tool in the document automatically begins a new path.

You must have at least three anchor points to create a closed path with straight lines. You can change the identity of one of these points to a different type of anchor point by curving one of the segments and giving the closed path some substance.

Drawing curves with the Pen tool

Initially, you may find the whole process of drawing curves with the Pen tool rather disorienting. You actually have to think differently to grasp what the Pen tool is doing. To draw a curve, you need to drag with the Pen tool, rather than click and release when you draw straight lines. This section gives two sets of instructions for creating two basic curve shapes: the bump and the S shape.

The most basic of curves is the bump (a curved segment between just two points). A bump was used to create a path to fill the horses' rears (previously shown in

Figure 3-10). Use the following steps to create the bump that is illustrated in Figure 3-17.

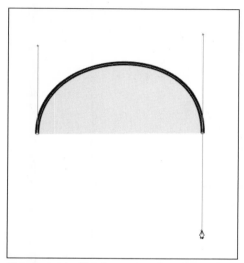

Figure 3-17: The four steps for creating a basic bump curve

1. **Click with the Pen tool and drag up about ½ inch.** You'll see an anchor point and a control handle line extending from it as you drag.

2. **Release the mouse button.** When you do so, you see the anchor point and a line extending to where you dragged with a control handle at its end.

3. **Position the cursor about 1 inch to the right of the place you first clicked.**

4. **Click with the mouse and drag down about ½ inch.** As you drag, you see a curve forming that resembles a bump.

5. **Release the mouse.** The curve fills with the current Fill color. You also see the control handle you just dragged.

Before you try to draw another curve, remember that the Pen tool is still in a mode that continues the current path; it does not start a new one. To start a new path, choose Deselect (Select ➪ Deselect), or press ⌘+Shift+A (Ctrl+Shift+A). Alternatively, you can hold down ⌘ (Ctrl) and click an empty area on-screen. The next time you use the Pen tool, you can draw a separate path.

To create an S shape, one more set of steps is needed. The steps for creating the S shape are described as follows and illustrated in Figure 3-18.

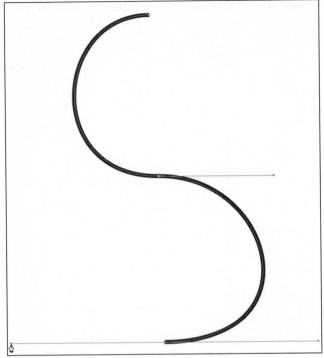

Figure 3-18: The results of creating a basic S curve

1. **Click and drag with the Pen tool about ½ inch to the left.**

2. **Release the mouse button.** You should see the anchor point and the control handle that you just drew with a control handle Line between them.

3. **Position the cursor about 1 inch below where you first clicked.**

4. **Click and drag to the right about ½ inch.**

5. **Release the mouse button.**

6. **Position the cursor about 1 inch below the last point you clicked.**

7. **Click and drag to the left, about ½ inch.** Now you have an S shape. To make the S look more like a real S, change the fill to None and the stroke to Black, 1 point.

For more on changing strokes and fills, see Chapter 6.

All the anchor points created in these two examples are smooth points. You draw the control handles in the direction of the next curve that you want to draw. The lengths of the control handle lines on either side of the anchor point are equal. However, you do not have to make the lengths of the control handle lines on either side of the smooth point the same. Instead, you can make a smooth point have both long and short control handle lines coming out of it. The length of the control handle line affects the curve, as shown on the S curve in Figure 3-19.

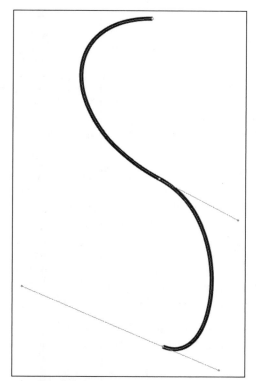

Figure 3-19: The length of the control handle lines controls the shape of the curve.

To create a smooth point with two control handle lines of different lengths:

1. **First create a smooth point along a path.** See the last set of steps to learn how to do so.

2. **Select the newly created smooth point with the Direct Selection tool.** For more on using these tools, see Chapter 5.

3. **Click and drag the control handle again.**

4. **Adjust the angle for both control handle lines and the length for the new control handle line that you are dragging.** Note that as you are dragging out this control handle line, the other control handle line wobbles to the angle that you are dragging. This happens because on any smooth point the control handle lines must be at the same angle, and as you drag out the new control handle line, you are changing the angle for both control handle lines simultaneously.

Closing curved paths with the Pen tool

The majority of the paths you draw with the Pen tool will be closed paths, not the open ones we've drawn so far. Like open curved paths, any closed curved path must have at least two anchor points, just as paths with straight corner points need three distinct points to create a closed path.

When the Pen tool is placed over the starting point of the path you've drawn, a little circle appears to the right of the pen shape. This indicates that the path will become a closed path if you click this anchor point.

Of course, to ensure that the initial anchor point remains a smooth point, you need to click and drag on the initial anchor point. Simply clicking produces a combination corner point, which only has one control handle associated with it.

Working with curved corner points

Curved corner points are points where two different, usually distinct, curved segments meet at an anchor point. Because the two curves meet this way, a smooth point does not provide the means for their joining correctly. Instead, a smooth point would make the two different curves blend into each other smoothly.

The main difference between a curved corner point and a smooth point is that a smooth point has two linked control handles on their ends; a curved corner point has two independent control handles. As the name indicates, control handles and their associated control handle lines move independently of each other, enabling two different, distinct types of curves to come from the same anchor point.

To create a curved corner point, create a smooth point in a path and then press Option (Alt) and drag the control handle you just drew. As you do this, you are creating the control handles independently. The next segment will curve as controlled by the newly split control handle, not by the original combined one.

Tip   When creating curved corner points, you can press the Option (Alt) key to create independent points all the time, not just when starting a new segment.

Practicing with the Pen tool

To give yourself some practice on using the Pen tool, you might try the following steps to create a sample illustration. Once you have your illustration looking more or less like the sample illustration that follows, you'll have a handle on the Pen tool. The weeds in the upper-right corner were created with the Pen tool. The weeds are composed entirely of straight lines that were duplicated in clumps, just as the long and short grasses were. To create a clump of weeds, follow these steps.

1. Change the Paint Style to a fill of Black and a stroke of None.

2. Using the Pen tool, click (don't drag!) at the top of the weeds. Then click lower at the bottom right of the weeds. Click to the left and click back at the start point to complete the weeds.

3. When the last weeds in the clump have been finished, click the first anchor point to close the path.

4. Repeat Step 2 to create additional weeds, making clumps of them similar to the one in the figure.

5. With the Selection tool, press Option (Alt) and then drag the clumps a few times to copy the existing weeds to create a mass of weeds as shown in the figure below.

A group of weeds drawn with the Pen tool

Tip When drawing straight lines with the Pen tool, never drag with the mouse while pressing the button. Doing so results in at least one curved segment.

The Pen tool draws both curved and straight precise lines. After you use the tips given in these pages and practice a little, you can master the tool. In the process, you will understand Illustrator much better than is possible otherwise.

Combination corner points

A combination corner point is a point where a curved segment and a straight segment meet each other. At this corner point, there is one control handle coming from the anchor point from the side where the curved segment is located and, on the other side, there is no control handle, indicating a straight segment.

To create a combination corner point with the Pen tool, draw a few curved segments and then go back to the last anchor point. There should be two linked control handles displayed at this point. Simply click once on the anchor point and one of the two control handles disappears. The next segment then starts out straight.

Tip   You can change existing smooth and curved corner points into combination corner points simply by dragging one of the control handles into the anchor points.

Using basic Pen tool drawing techniques

Now that you've gained some experience with the Pen tool, you'll benefit by living by the Pen Rules. The Pen Rules are laws to live by — or, at least, to draw by.

The rules are:

✦ **Remember not to drag where you want to place the next point; instead, go just one-third of that distance.** You must determine where you want to locate the next anchor point before you can determine the length of the control handle line you are dragging. Dragging by one-third is always a good approximation to make. You might run into trouble when the control handle line is more than half or less than one-quarter of the next segment. If your control handle line is too long or too short, chances are the line will curve erratically.

✦ **Don't get the outside of the curve and the outside of the shape you are drawing confused — they may well be two different things.** Remember that control handle lines are always tangent to the curved segment they are guiding. Tangent? Well, a simpler way of putting this rule is a line that touches the curve but does not cross or intersect the curve. If your control handle lies inside the curve you are drawing, it becomes too short and overpowered by the next anchor point. Control handles pull the curve toward themselves; this makes them naturally curve out toward the control handle lines. If you fight this natural pull, your illustrations can look loopy and silly.

✦ **Drag the control handle in the direction that you want the curve to travel at that anchor point.** The control handle pulls the curve toward itself by its very nature. If you drag backward toward the preceding segment, you create little curved spikes that stick out from the anchor points. This commandment applies only to Smooth Points. If the anchor point is a curved corner point, you must make the initial drag in the direction the curve was traveling and the next drag (an Option (Alt)+drag) in the direction that you want the curve to travel. If the anchor point is a Combination Curve Point and the next segment is straight, make the dragging motion in the direction that the curve was traveling. Next, click and release the anchor point. If the Combination Curve Point's next segment is curved, click and release the first click, and the second click should be dragged in the direction of the next curve.

✦ **Use as few anchor points as possible**. If your illustration calls for smooth, flowing curves, use very few anchor points. If, on the other hand, you want your illustration rough and gritty, use more anchor points. The fewer anchor points there are, the smoother the final result. When there are only a few anchor points on a path, changing its shape is easier and faster. More anchor points mean a bigger file and longer printing times, as well. If you're not sure if you need more anchor points, don't add them. You can always add them later with the Add anchor point tool.

 Cross-Reference   For more on the Add anchor point tool, see Chapter 5.

✦ **Place anchor points at the beginning of each "different" curve.** You should use anchor points as transitional points, where the curve either changes direction or increases or decreases in size dramatically. If it looks as though the curve changes from one type of curve to another, the location to place an anchor point is in the middle of that transitional section.

✦ **Do not overcompensate for a previously misdrawn curve.** If you really messed up on the last anchor point you've drawn, don't panic and try to undo the mistake by dragging in the wrong direction or by dragging the control handle out to some ridiculous length. Doing either of these two things may temporarily fix the preceding curve but usually wrecks the next curve, causing you to have to overcompensate yet again.

Using the various line tools

In addition to the Pencil and Pen tools, Illustrator includes several unique tools that you can use to create specialized types of lines. From straight lines with the Line Segment tool to spiral lines using the Spiral tool, these line tools fall into the convenience category. Housed with the Line Segment tool, these tools include the Line Segment, Arc, Spiral, Rectangular Grid and Polar Grid tools.

Using the Line Segment tool

Now that you've learned how to create straight lines to hard way with the Pen tool, here's an easy way—use the Line Segment tool. After using the Line Segment tool, using the Pencil or Paintbrush tool to draw straight lines is just plain ridiculous. Any amount of caffeine in your system results in a jittery line with either tool. Using this tool is a breeze. Simply click and drag the line where you want it to go (see Figure 3-20). Holding the Shift key while drawing a line constrains the line to 45-degree increments. If you press the Option (Alt) key while drawing a line your starting point begins in the middle of the line.

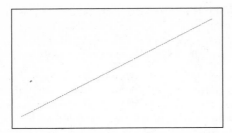

Figure 3-20: A line segment being drawn

Double-clicking the Line Segment tool, or clicking one time on the Artboard, brings up the Line Segment tool dialog box (see Figure 3-21). In this dialog box, you can set the length, angle, and whether to fill the line with the defaulted Fill color. You can use the Pen tool to draw straight lines, but when you have a tool specifically made for lines, use it.

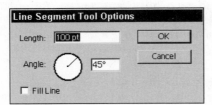

Figure 3-21: The Line Segment Tool Options dialog box lets you set the angle of the line.

Tip

Pen versus the Line Segment tool: The Pen tool can also draw straight lines and constrained lines, so why use the Line Segment tool at all? Well, if you need to draw straight lines quickly and accurately, use the Line Segment tool. One small slip of the Pen tool, and you have a curved line. In addition, you can guess at a precise length and angle using the Line Segment tool because you actually see the line rubberbanding from the original point, and with the Pen tool, you don't have this visual.

Working with the Arc Segment tool

Arcs are now easily drawn using the Arc tool. The old-fashioned way used to be to draw an oval and remove the sections you don't need via the Direct Selection tool or Scissor tool. Figure 3-22 shows an Arc drawn with the Arc tool.

The Arc tool is housed with the Line Segment tool. You can have an arc that sweeps inward or outward depending on your settings. Double-clicking the Arc tool accesses the Arc Segment tool options (see Figure 3-23). The Arc Segment Tool Options are:

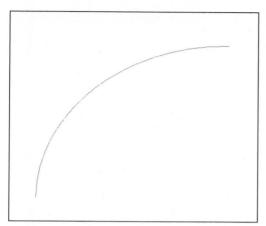

Figure 3-22: An arc

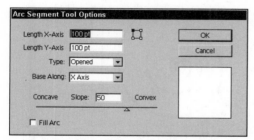

Figure 3-23: The Arc Segment Tool Options
dialog box includes a preview of the arc.

✦ **Length X-Axis:** Enter the value for the length of the slope along the X-Axis.

✦ **Length Y-Axis:** Enter the value for the length of the slope along the Y-Axis.

✦ **Type:** Choose whether you want the arc to be an open or closed path.

✦ **Base Along:** Here is where you choose the direction of the slope, either along an X- or Y-axis.

✦ **Slope:** Dragging the slider to the left results in a concave slope. Dragging the slider to the right results in a convex slope.

✦ **Fill Arc:** Checking this option fills the inside of the arc with the default color.

In the Arc Segment Tool Options dialog box, you also get to see a nice preview of the arc before clicking OK.

Tip When dragging out an arc, pressing the F or the X key toggles the arc between convex and concave. Press the Spacebar while you draw to move the whole arc. This is true with all shapes that you draw in Illustrator.

Creating spirals with the Spiral tool

If there's one really good thing to say about being able to draw spirals with the Spiral tool in Illustrator, it's that it was hellish to create spirals before a Spiral tool (or filter) existed. If there's another good thing to say, I haven't quite figured it out yet.

The Spiral tool (located with the Line Segment tool) makes spirals — all sorts of spirals. What would you use a spiral for? Well, you can use the Spiral tool to create a simulated record. Of course, the path was exceedingly long and refused to print on most Imagesetters. Other than that, you can use them to simulate nature patterns, such as snails, shells, an eddy or a whirlpool. Figure 3-24 shows several spirals manufactured with the Spiral tool.

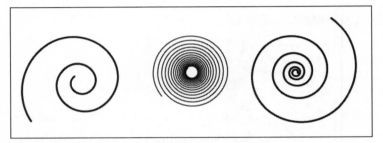

Figure 3-24: Spirals created with the Spiral tool

Tip Spirals beg to be stroked, not filled. Putting just a fill on a spiral makes it look lumpy and not quite round.

If you click in your document with the Spiral tool, the Spiral dialog box (see Figure 3-25) appears, and you can enter specific values for a spiral. Handy for all those times your client or boss wants that 82.5% decay spiral.

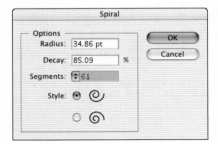

Figure 3-25: The Spiral dialog box

Making grid lines using the Rectangular Grid tool

You can easily creating a grid using the Grid tool, which is housed with the Line Segment tool. For example, you could use a grid to create a perspective drawing. Use the Skew tool to give an angled view. You can create a unique Rubik's cube. You can also create nice grid paper or use the Grid tool to create a data chart. Figure 3-26 shows a grid used to create a unique business card.

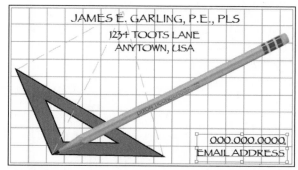

Figure 3-26: A business card created using the Grid tool

Here are the keys you can press while creating grids to make life easier:

✦ **Up or Down arrow:** Increases or decreases the number of horizontal lines.

✦ **Left or Right arrow:** Increases or decreases the number of vertical lines.

✦ **Shift key:** Creates a perfect square grid.

✦ **Option (Alt) key:** Creates a grid from a central point.

Double-clicking the Grid tool accesses the Grid Options dialog box (see Figure 3-27). Under the Grid Options you can choose to skew the Grid. That is, make the lines closer to the top or bottom, and left or right. The Options you can change are:

✦ **Default size:** Enter the width and height in points.

✦ **Horizontal Dividers:** Enter how many dividers and how much they will be skewed.

✦ **Vertical Dividers:** Enter the number of dividers and how much they will be skewed.

✦ **Use Outside Rectangle As Frame:** Uses a rectangle to frame the grid.

✦ **Fill Grid:** Checking this fills the grid with the set default fill color.

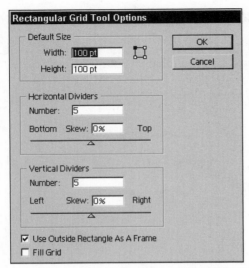

Figure 3-27: The Rectangular Grid Tool Options dialog box lets you specify dividers.

Understanding the Polar Grid tool

The Polar Grid tool is found with the Line Segment tool. A Polar Grid is also referred to as a radar grid. You would recognize it as a dartboard, or a bulls-eye. The Polar Grid dialog box lets you set the same options as found in the Rectangular Grid options, except the dividers are radial and concentric instead of horizontal and vertical:

✦ **Default size:** Enter the width and height in points.

✦ **Concentric Dividers:** Enter how many dividers and how much they will be skewed.

✦ **Radial Dividers:** Enter the number of dividers and how much they will be skewed.

✦ **Create Compound Path from Ellipses:** Uses ellipses to create a compound path.

✦ **Fill Grid:** Checking this fills the polar grid with the set default fill color.

Here are the keys you can press while creating grids to make life easier:

✦ **Up or Down arrow:** Increases or decreases the number of concentric circles.

✦ **Left or Right arrow:** Increases or decreases the number of radial lines.

✦ **Shift key:** Creates a perfect round polar grid.

✦ **Option (Alt) key:** Creates a polar grid from a central point.

Figure 3-28 shows a nice shadowed bull's-eye drawing created with the Polar Grid tool.

Figure 3-28: A bull's-eye with shadow

Understanding Paintbrush types

The Paintbrush tool draws a stroked path. This makes life so much easier when it comes to editing. The Paintbrush tool is similar to paintbrush-type tools in painting programs. The Paintbrush has a certain width, and you can paint with this Paintbrush at this width anywhere in your document. The big difference between paint programs' paintbrushes and Illustrator's Paintbrush tool is that when you finish drawing with Illustrator's Paintbrush tool, you create a stroked path.

To use the Paintbrush tool, choose the tool, then choose the brush from the Brush palette, and start drawing. A freeform path appears wherever you drag. That's all there is to it, kinda. Figure 3-29 shows a drawing that was created with the Paintbrush tool set to a variable width with a pressure-sensitive stylus.

Figure 3-29: A drawing of a horse created with the Paintbrush tool using a pressure-sensitive tablet and stylus

Drawing with the Paintbrush tool is a bit more complicated than I just explained. The most important consideration is the width of the paintbrush stroke. The paintbrush stroke can be as narrow as 0 points and as wide as 1,296 points (that's 18 inches to you and me).

Although 0 is the smallest width, a paintbrush stroke drawn with a width of 0 points actually has a width bigger than 0 points. To change the paintbrush stroke width (the default is 9 points), double-click the brush in the Brush palette (not the toolbox) and enter a number in the Diameter text field. Remember that you are actually changing that default brush.

A mouse is not an intuitive drawing tool, and not being able to draw in the first place makes it even more difficult to draw with the Paintbrush tool. So, if artists have trouble with the mouse, what's the point of having the Paintbrush tool at all? Well, instead of a mouse, you can use several types of alternative drawing devices. The best of these is a pressure-sensitive tablet. Trackballs with locking buttons are also good for drawing with the Paintbrush tool (this allows more control over the direction and speed of the Paintbrush).

Tip

When you're drawing with any of the tools in Illustrator, dragging off the edge of the window causes the window to scroll, which creates a frightening effect for the uninitiated. If you don't want the window to remain where it scrolled to, don't let go of the mouse button; instead, drag in the opposite direction until the window returns to the original position.

To help you draw more precisely, you have the option of changing the cursor shape from the cute little brush into crosshairs. Press the Caps Lock key (to engage it), and the cursor changes into cross hairs with a dot in the center. Press the Caps Lock key again (to release it), and the cursor returns to the brush shape. The dot at the center of the cross hairs is the center of any paintbrush stroke drawn with the Paintbrush tool. Normally, when the cursor is in the shape of a paintbrush, the tip is the center of the paintbrush stroke. Some people find it easier to draw when the paintbrush cursor is replaced with the precise crosshairs.

Using Brushes

If you want to create a totally new brush, choose New Brush from the Brushes palette pop-up menu and select the type of new brush you want to make. You can choose from Calligraphic, Scatter, Art, and Pattern brushes (see Figure 3-30). The Brushes palette includes samples of each of these brush types. Calligraphic brushes make strokes similar to a calligraphic pen. Scatter brushes scatter an object along the brushed path. The Art brush takes an object and stretches it along the brush path length. The Pattern brush uses repeated tiles along the brush path.

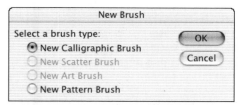

Figure 3-30: The New Brush dialog box will let you choose to create one of four different brush types.

Using the Calligraphic Brush

A Calligraphic Brush was made to simulate the actual calligraphic pen tip. You set the angle and size and draw to your heart's content. You can also create a perfectly round brush in the Calligraphic Brush dialog box by not entering an angle and by keeping the Roundness at 100%.

The Calligraphic Brush Options (shown in Figure 3-31) are as follows:

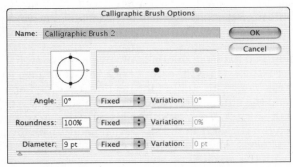

Figure 3-31: The Calligraphic Brush Options

✦ **Name:** This option lets you give your new brush a name or rename an existing brush (maximum of 30 characters).

✦ **Angle:** You can set the angle of the Calligraphic paintbrush. The angle you should choose depends on what is going to be drawn. To mimic hand-drawn lettering in a calligraphic style, the angle should be set to 45° (or if you're left-handed, it should be set to –45°).

✦ **Roundness:** This does what you'd think it does. It sets the roundness of the brush. The higher you make the value, the rounder the brush.

✦ **Diameter:** The diameter option sets the maximum diameter of the brush.

✦ **Variation:** If you choose the Random option from the Angle or Roundness pop-up (Mac) drop-down (Windows) menu, you then enter a value for Variation. The Variation for the Angle value is in a degree that you want to vary from the original setting. The Variation for the Roundness is set in percentages. A slider sets the Variation for the Diameter or you can enter a number. The Diameter Variation goes from your original value up to the Variation value. This is a great way to simulate a hand-drawn look if you don't have a pressure sensitive tablet.

Defining a Calligraphic Brush

You can use a Calligraphic Brush many ways. You can choose an existing brush and get started. If you load additional brush libraries, you'll find quite a variety of brushes to choose from. You can also create your own brush from an existing one or from scratch. To create a new brush, use an existing style that you like, but that you want to alter. To create a brush like this, choose Duplicate Brush from the Brush palette pop-up menu. You first have to select the brush you want to duplicate. To edit that duplicated brush, double-click the duplicate brush, or select Brush Options from the pop-up menu. In the Brush Options dialog box, change the brush to your specifications.

Variable widths and pressure-sensitive tablets

If you have a pressure-sensitive tablet — some call them a Wacom (pronounced "walk 'em") tablet because a large majority tend to be made by Wacom — you can select the Pressure option beside the Diameter field in the Brush Options dialog box (accessed by double-clicking on a brush in the Brushes palette). If you don't have a pressure-sensitive tablet, the Pressure option is grayed out (unselectable).

Note A pressure-sensitive tablet is a flat, rectangular device over which you pass a special stylus. The more pressure exerted by the stylus on the tablet, the wider a paintbrush stroke becomes, providing that you select the Pressure option in the Calligraphic dialog box. When using the Pressure option, try to set the Variation different from the original specified diameter to see the difference when you press harder or lighter.

Creating with the Scatter Brush

The Scatter Brush copies and scatters a predefined object along a path. You have some default Scatter Brushes to choose from such as dot rings, black spider, taro leaves, ink splash, bubble confetti, and blue balloon. Figure 3-32 shows an example of each default Scatter Brush.

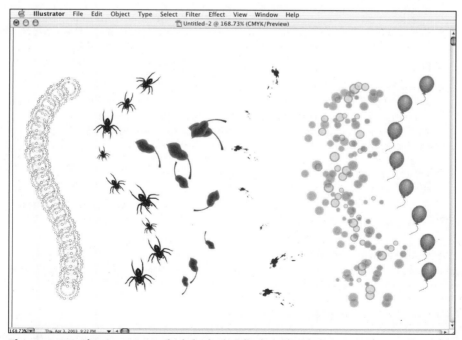

Figure 3-32: The Scatter Brush defaults applied to a path

The Scatter Brush Options (see Figure 3-33) are:

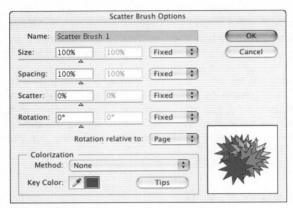

Figure 3-33: The Scatter Brush Options

✦ **Name:** You can name your brush with up to 30 characters.

✦ **Size:** In the size area, you have two pop-up options: Fixed and Random. If you choose Fixed, then the size slider will only display the left options. The fixed size lets you enter a percentage so that all of the scattered images will be the exact same size. If you choose Random, the pop-up displays two sliders. With the Random option you can set up large and small scattered-images by changing the sliders for each. If you want really big images and small images that vary in size, then drag the sliders in opposite directions.

✦ **Spacing:** This option adjusts the space between each object.

✦ **Scatter:** The Scatter option adjusts how the objects follow the original path on each side of the path. If you set a high amount, the objects are farther away from the original path.

✦ **Rotation:** This option adjusts how much the object will rotate from its original position.

✦ **Rotation relative to:** This option gives you two choices from a pop-up menu. The Page option rotates objects according to the page setup. The Path option rotates objects tangent to the path.

✦ **Colorization:** There are four Colorization choices: None, Tints, Tints and Shades, and Hue Shift. For more on colorization and colorization tips, see "Understanding colorization tips," later in this chapter.

Working with the Art Brush

The Art Brush, like the Scatter Brush, uses an object along a path. The difference is that the Art Brush stretches the object to the length of the path rather than repeat and scatter the object. Illustrator centers the object evenly over the path and then stretches it. You can choose from the default Art Brushes or create an object of your own to use. Figure 3-34 shows the five default Art Brushes: Marker, Tapered Stroke, Arrow, Paintbrush, and Type.

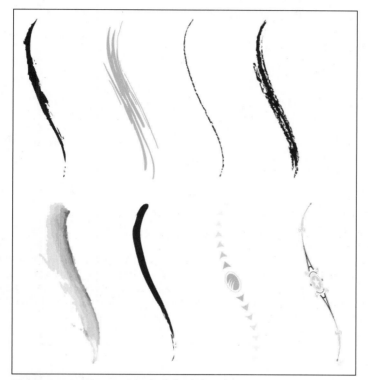

Figure 3-34: The Art Brush default brushes

The Art Brush Options (see Figure 3-35) are:

✦ **Name:** You can name your new Art Brush or rename an existing Art Brush with up to 30 characters.

✦ **Direction:** This option lets you choose from four directions. The directions are relative to how you drag the paintbrush.

✦ **Size:** This option scales the art when it is stretched. You can choose Proportional to keep the object in proportion.

✦ **Flip:** The Flip option lets you flip your object along or across the path.

✦ **Colorization:** There are four Colorization choices: None, Tints, Tints and Shades, and Hue Shift. For more on colorization and colorization tips, see "Understanding colorization tips," later in this chapter.

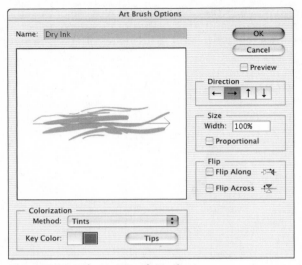

Figure 3-35: The Art Brush Options

Creating tiles using the Pattern Brush

The Pattern Brush repeats a tiled object along a path. The Pattern Brush can have tiles to display the sides, inner corner, outer corner, beginning, and end. If you think of a Pattern Brush as you would a regular Pattern tile, but keep in mind the corners, you'll have no problem creating your own interesting Pattern Brushes. I like to take apart an existing pattern to see how it was created. To do this, select the Pattern Brush in the Brushes palette and drag it to an open area on your document. You'll see the individual tiles. Figure 3-36 shows all of the default Pattern Brushes.

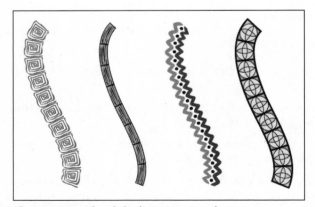

Figure 3-36: The default Pattern Brushes

The Pattern Brush Options (see Figure 3-37) are:

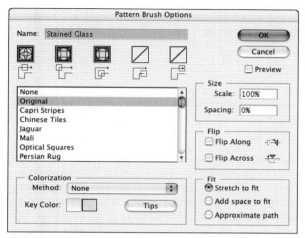

Figure 3-37: The Pattern Brush Options

- ✦ **Name:** Enter a new name or change an existing name (up to 30 characters).

- ✦ **Tile button:** This is where you choose which of the five tiles you want to create.

- ✦ **Size:** This option lets you enter the size in proportion and the space between the tiles.

- ✦ **Flip:** This option lets you flip the pattern along or across the path.

- ✦ **Fit:** In this option, you can choose Stretch to Fit, Add Space to Fit, or Approximate Path. Stretch lengthens or shortens a tile to fit your object. Add Space adds a blank space between the tiles to fit the path proportionately. Approximate Path makes the tile fit as close to the original path without altering the tiles.

- ✦ **Colorization:** There are four Colorization choices: None, Tints, Tints and Shades, and Hue Shift.

Cross-Reference

For more on colorization and colorization tips, see "Understanding colorization tips," later in this chapter.

Making a custom brush

You can create a brush two ways. If you like another brush, but not all aspects of it, you can duplicate that brush and edit its options to make it as you like. To edit a brush, double-click the brush, or choose Show Options from the pop-up menu or click the Brush Options icon at the bottom of the Brushes palette. You can also create a brush by choosing New Brush from the pop-up menu or to click the New Brush icon at the bottom of the Brushes palette. Doing this brings up a dialog box asking you to choose the type of brush you want to create. You can create a Calligraphic Brush by filling in the text fields of the Calligraphic Brush dialog box. To create any of the other brushes, you have to have your art drawn first and then choose New Brush.

Brush options

With each brush you have brush options to choose from. The Calligraphic, Scatter, Art, and Pattern brushes are your brush choices and each brush has different options to choose from.

To create your own Scatter Brush design, first create the object that you want to use. Next, select all of the parts of the object that you want as a brush and choose New Brush from the Brushes palette pop-up menu. Then choose the type of brush you want to create. The Brush Options dialog box displays, and you see your new design there. Now all you have to do is set the rest of the options and you are ready to use this new brush.

Understanding colorization tips

The Colorization Tips button in the Art, Scatter, and Pattern Brush dialogs displays a dialog box explaining the different colorization options. Figure 3-38 shows the Colorization Tips dialog box, which has four areas of colorization — None, Tints, Tints and Shades, and Hue Shift.

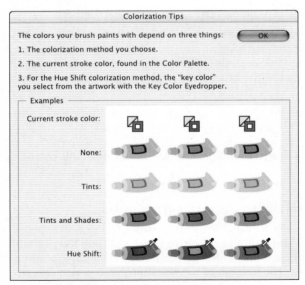

Figure 3-38: The Colorization Tips dialog box

To see how the Colorization options work, first create four copies of a brush. For example, use the red arrow brush. Then draw four red arrows. The first arrow uses the default of None. For the next three arrows change the Stroke color (you won't see anything happen yet). On the second arrow, double-click one of the copy arrow brushes you made and select Tint. Apply to stroke when asked in the dialog box. The color should change at this point. Select the third arrow and double-click a different copy of the arrow brush and select Tints and Shades. Select the last arrow and double-click the last copy and select Hue Shift. All of the arrows should look different.

Checking out the Brush Libraries

The Brush Library that displays when you choose the Brush palette is the default Library. You have additional Libraries from which to choose. Adobe has really come up with some cool brushes for our creative pleasure. The Brush Libraries are found under the Window menu, as shown in Figure 3-39. Figure 3-40 the Brush Libraries found under the Brush palette pop-up menu.

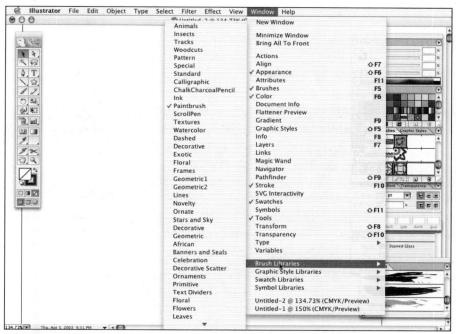

Figure 3-39: The Brush Libraries submenu under the Window menu

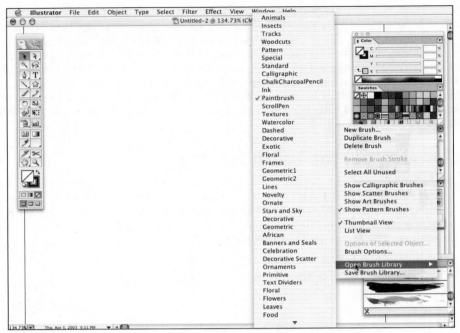

Figure 3-40: The Brush Libraries found in the Brush palette pop-up menu

Guest Artist How-to: Creating Brush People

The Art Brush in Illustrator has many uses. One way you may not think to use this great brush is to create crowds of people or things. The traditional way to create a crowd of people would be to draw a person, then copy and paste that person and transform the person to make them larger or smaller. Drawing this way is fine. However, it can be time consuming.

Create a crowd easily using the Art Brush. Make people by drawing them or using Auto Trace only one time and then make them into an Art Brush. Simply use long strokes for bigger people, and smaller strokes for smaller people. You can quickly create a crowd of people without copying and pasting and doing many transformations. By dragging your person or any object over the Brushes palette, you launch the Brushes dialog box.

Using Auto Trace can cut the time in drawing a person down considerably. You can scan a few photographs of full length people and convert them to paths the Auto Trace tool. Edit these paths to delete any path that isn't relative to the person using the Direct Selection tool. I like to Group the figure just to keep all of the parts together. Or for you more traditional artists, draw the person using the Pen tool. Remember that when you fill the shapes with color, you cannot use gradients, gradient mesh, or blends. Don't let that stop you from trying this. You can create pretty cool-looking people using solid fills varying the color to create shadows and highlights.

To create a person Art Brush:

1. Select the person and choose New Brush from the Brushes palette (Figure 1). The New Brush dialog box will pop up.

Figure 1: Dragging the person over the Brushes palette opens the New Brush dialog box.

Continued

Continued

2. Choose the Art Brush as your type of brush.

3. In the Art Brush Option dialog box, be sure to check the Proportional box or your people will be out of sorts.

4. Choose the direction in which you best draw. I tend to draw from top to bottom, so I choose the last arrow direction (Figure 2).

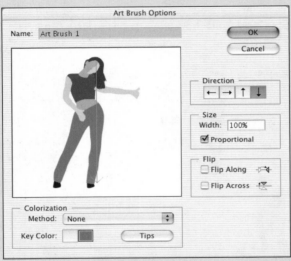

Figure 2: Choose the options for this brush in the Art Brush Options dialog box.

5. When you click OK you can start using the paintbrush with this new brush. Now you can paint a crowd of people by the stroke of a brush. The longer strokes make larger people, and smaller strokes make smaller people (Figure 3).

Figure 3: Big and small people are a breeze.

To vary the colors, you can double-click the people brush and choose Tints and Shades as your Colorization method. When you do this, don't let it apply it to the existing strokes so you can get varying colors. I would recommend that you create more than one person, especially if you are going for a crowd look, as shown in Figure 4.

Continued

Continued

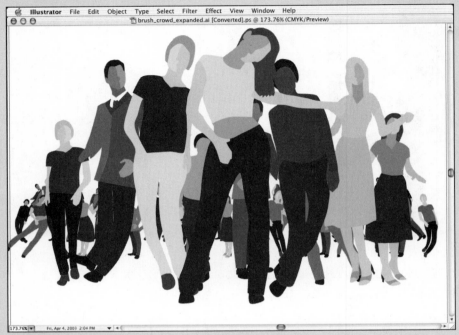

Figure 4: A crowd of people created using the Art Brush

You can create lines in any fashion. The Pen tool can create perfectly straight lines, and you can vary the lengths to be more accurate. Then you simply have to select the lines and click on your person brush to convert the lines to the Art Brush. This method opens the door to tons of fun! Curve your lines for dancing people. Try using a spiral or a star shape. Your options are limitless. To add more fun with the color, select one of the lines and choose the Expand function. Doing this will turn the person back into paths. Then you can apply any of the color features to vary the look of the crowd. Don't limit yourself to people with this tip. You can use this to create a forest or a city of buildings or to help rabbits multiply.

Summary

✦ There are four anchor point types: straight corner points, combination corner points, smooth points, and curved corner points.

✦ Edit curves with the control handles.

✦ Curves are based on the Bézier principle.

✦ Use the Pencil tool to create paths quickly.

✦ Use the Smooth and Erase tools to edit your paths.

✦ Although the Pen tool is the most difficult to learn, it yields the smoothest results.

✦ The Paintbrush tool creates a free-formed stroked path.

✦ A pressure-sensitive tablet can mimic hand drawing.

✦ The Line Segment tool can create straight lines. Other tools with the Line Segment tool let you create arcs, grids, polar grids, and spirals.

✦ The Scatter Brush repeats objects along a path rotated and sized differently.

✦ The Art Brush stretches an object to the length of the path.

✦ The Pattern Brush repeats a pattern on a path.

✦ Create a new brush in the Brushes palette.

✦   ✦   ✦

Creating Objects, Graphs, and Symbols

Technically, the name of this section should really be "Placing, Sizing, and Colorizing Preformatted Open and Closed Paths," but if it were, no one would read it — and this is an important chapter because it introduces many concepts that are built upon in later chapters.

In this chapter, you learn how to create objects such as rectangles, ellipses, stars, and polygons. In addition, you find out how to create and enhance graphs, add touches of light with the Flare tool, and create really cool repeating effects with the Symbolism tools.

Making Basic Shapes

Drawing the most basic shapes — rectangles, ellipses, polygons, and stars — is precisely what a computer is for. Try drawing a perfect ellipse by hand. Troublesome, isn't it? How about a square that doesn't have ink bubbles or splotches at the corners? A nine-point star? Drawing these objects and then coloring them in Illustrator is so easy and so basic that after a few weeks of using Illustrator, you'll never be able to draw a shape by hand again without wincing, maybe even shuddering.

Illustrator exemplifies the true power of object-oriented drawing programming. No matter what you draw, you can adjust and move each piece of the drawing independently until it's just right. Don't like the sun so high in your background? Pull it down and tuck it in just a bit behind those mountains. Is the tree too small for the house in your illustration? Scale it up a bit. This feature is great not only for artists, but also for your pesky client (or boss) who demands that everything be moved except that darned tree.

And after you create the shape, you can move, rotate, scale, and manipulate in any way you like. Figure 4-1 shows an illustration drawn one way and then modified in a matter of seconds by moving existing elements.

Figure 4-1: A basic square becomes a more interesting shape.

Here are some general things to remember when you're drawing basic shapes:

✦ **Creating common shapes:** You can draw common objects (or shapes) in Illustrator including squares and rectangles, rectangles with rounded corners, circles and ellipses, polygons, and stars. Tools for creating these objects are found as pop-up tools in the toolbox under the Rectangle tool. You basically use all of these tools in the same manner. So after you learn how to use the Rectangle tool later in this chapter, you'll know how to use the other tools.

Cross-Reference
To learn the basic way to use a shape tool, see the section "Drawing rectangles using the Rectangle tool." For more on paths see Chapter 3 and for more on selecting objects, see Chapter 5.

✦ **Lines and points that appear when you select on object:** After you draw a shape, a white outlined closed path in black appears with blue points indicating the anchor points. The edge of the path has thin blue lines surrounding it. These blue lines indicate that the object is currently selected. When you select another object, the object appears as a black outline.

Tip

Note that the closed path appears in black unless you've changed the default line and fill color. For more on changing the fill or line color, see "Filling and Stroking Shapes" later in this chapter. Also, the anchor points only appear as blue points if you are in Preview mode, the default viewing mode. To learn more about the various view modes in Illustrator, see Chapter 1.

✦ **Changing an object's shape:** The initial click you make with any of the shape tools is called the origin point. While you drag a shape, the origin point never moves, but the rest of the shape is fluid, changing shape as you drag in different directions and to different distances with your mouse. Dragging horizontally with almost no vertical movement results in a long, flat shape. Dragging vertically with very little horizontal movement creates a shape that is tall and thin. Dragging at a 45° angle (diagonally) results in a proportional shape.

✦ **Entering exact dimensions in a shape's dialog box:** If you click a tool without dragging it, the shape's dialog box appears. The center of the shape is now where you clicked (normally, the corner of the shape is where you click). Unlike manually drawing (dragging) centered shapes, the dimensions you enter are the actual dimensions of the shape. The dimension is *not* doubled as it is when you drag a centered shape.

Cross-Reference

For the exact steps on entering dimensions in the shape's dialog box, see the section "Defining properties with the Rectangle dialog box" later in this chapter.

✦ **Changing units of measure:** When you first run Illustrator, all measurements are set to points. Therefore, the values inside the various shape dialog boxes appear in so many points (12 points in a pica). To change the units of measure to something else (for example, millimeters or inches), see Chapter 7.

✦ **Moving shapes while you draw them:** While drawing a shape, you may realize that you want to move it. In Illustrator, you can move any shape by holding down the spacebar while you depress your mouse button and dragging your shape to a new location. When you let up on the spacebar, you can continue to draw your object.

✦ **Deleting shapes:** Getting rid of the shape you've drawn is even easier than creating it — you simply delete it by pressing the Delete or Backspace key.

✦ **Tool information:** If you click a tool picture Illustrator gives you some information about that particular tool. For example, if you click the Symbol Shifter and you get a little "i" in a conversation cloud saying: Hold down the Shift key to bring symbol instances forward. Hold down the Shift+Option (Shift+Alt) to send symbol instances backward.

Note Traditional bitmap paint applications do not have the capability to move sections of a drawing (with the exception of the use of layers in software such as Photoshop and Painter). After you move a section of an image in a bitmap program, a *hole* appears in the place where the section used to be. And if the new location already has information, Illustrator deletes this information, replacing it with your the new image.

Drawing shapes from their centers

When you draw a shape, Illustrator starts from the corner, and you have to move your mouse down and to the left, or up and to the right, to form your shape. However, you often place shapes on top of or under other objects, and you may need to have an even amount of space between your shape and the object it surrounds. Instead of drawing a shape from a corner, you can draw one from its center. Drawing from the corner forces you to eyeball the space around the object, while drawing from the center of the other object ensures that space surrounding the object is the same.

To draw a shape from its center, hold down the Option (Alt) key and then click and drag. The origin point is now the center of the shape. The farther you drag in one direction, the farther the edges of the shape go out in the opposite direction. Drawing from the center of a shape lets you draw something twice as big as the same shape drawn from a corner. As long as you press the Option (Alt) key, the shape continues draw from its center. If you release the Option (Alt) key before you release the mouse button, the origin of the shape changes back to a corner. You can press and release the Option (Alt) key at any time while drawing, toggling back and forth between drawing from a corner and drawing from a center. You can do this when drawing rectangles and ellipses only.

Drawing a symmetric shape (circles and squares)

You can force Illustrator to create symmetric shapes by holding down the Shift key as you draw a shape. For example, when you press the Shift key while drawing a rectangle, the rectangle constrains to a square. Likewise, you can draw a perfect circle by holding down the Shift key as you draw an ellipse. You can do this for all of the Shape tools as well as the Line and Pencil tools.

Cross-Reference For more on drawing rectangles, see the next section. For more on drawing ellipses, see the section "Drawing ellipses" later in this chapter. You can also create a square using the Polygon dialog box. To learn how to do so, see the section "Creating polygons."

You can also use the Rectangle (or Ellipse) dialog box to draw a perfect square (or circle) by entering equal values for the width and height. Simply click without dragging to get the dialog box to appear.

Tip To draw shapes from their centers and to make them symmetric at the same time, draw the shape while holding down the Option (Alt) and Shift keys. Make sure that both keys are still pressed when you release the mouse button.

Tip

Because circles can be a difficult task when you need to have the top, bottom, left, and right edges of the circle at a specific location, consider tracing circular objects. For easier tracing of circles, change the Constrain Angle value. You do this by choosing Illustrator (Edit) ➪ Preferences ➪ General and changing the Constrain Angle to 45°. Now you can place the cursor on the top, bottom, or sides of the circle, and drag horizontally or vertically for a perfect fit.

Drawing shapes at an angle

Usually, when you draw a shape with a tool, it appears to orient itself with the document and the document window. For example, the bottom of a rectangle aligns parallel to the bottom of the document window.

But what if you want to draw shapes that are all angled at 45° on the page? Well, one possibility is to rotate them after you draw them by using the Transform Each command or the Rotate tool. Better yet, you can set up your document so that every new shape automatically angles.

Creating Drop Shadows for Shapes

A useful way to add depth to an object, such as a rectangle, is with a drop shadow. You can use this technique on any type of object or text. To create a drop shadow for a shape, follow these steps.

1. **Draw a shape.** Using the shape's tool, draw a shape to the size you want it. This example uses a rectangle.

2. **Change the Fill color of the shape to the shadow color you want.** You do this by clicking the Fill square in the toolbox, and then choosing your color in the Color palette. The example uses 100% Black.

Cross-Reference

For more on palettes in general, see Chapter 1. For more on fills, see Chapter 9.

3. **Change the Stroke color of the shape to the shadow color you want.** You do this by clicking the Stroke icon in the toolbox and then choosing that color in the Color palette.

4. **Choose the Selection tool and drag the rectangle object up and to the right just a little while holding down the Option (Alt) key.** This creates a copy of the original shape. The farther you drag, the greater the depth of the drop shadow. After you release the mouse button, you should have two overlapping shapes.

5. **Change the Fill color of the top shape to a color other than the shadow color.** You do this by clicking the Fill square in the toolbox, and then clicking the desired color in the Color palette. The example uses 50% gray. The following figure shows a drop shadow for a rectangle.

Continued

Continued

A basic drop shadow box

You can create drop shadows manually in this manner, but Illustrator also includes a Drop Shadow filter and effect in the Filter ⇨ Stylize and Effect ⇨ Stylize menus. These features offer many more options for creating drop shadows automatically. You can learn to use these features in Chapter 13.

The angle of a shape depends on the Constrain Angle value. Usually, the Constrain Angle is 0°, where all shapes appear to align evenly with the borders of the document. To change the Constrain Angle, choose Illustrator (Edit) ⇨ Preferences ⇨ General and enter a new value in the Constrain Angle text field inside the General Preferences dialog box.

When you finish drawing these angled shapes, make sure that you change the Constrain Angle setting back to 0°, or you create all new shapes at the altered Constrain Angle.

Tip Constrain Angle affects shapes and other objects created in Illustrator, such as type. In addition, dragging objects while pressing the Shift key constrains them to the current Constrain Angle or to a 45° or 90° variation of it. The Constrain Angle is much easier to see if you turn on Grids (choose View ⇨ Show Grid or press ⌘+" (Ctrl+")). When the grid option is turned on, it is always aligned with the Constrain Angle.

Drawing rectangles using the Rectangle tool

The most basic shape you can draw is a rectangle. Although the following steps explain how to draw a simple rectangle, you basically use them for all the other shape tools in Illustrator.

1. **Select the Rectangle tool.** You can do this by clicking it in the toolbox or by pressing the letter M on the keyboard. You find the Rectangle tool in the second column of the Toolbox on the fourth row from the top.

2. **Click your mouse on the Artboard and hold down the mouse button.** This sets the origin point of the rectangle.

3. **Drag your mouse diagonally to the size you desire**. You can draw rectangles from any corner by clicking and dragging in the direction opposite of where you want that corner to be. For example, to draw a rectangle from the lower-right corner, click and drag up and to the left. As long as you have the Rectangle tool selected, dragging with it in the document window produces a new rectangle.

4. **Release the mouse button.** Illustrator creates a rectangle as shown in Figure 4-2. The farther the distance from the initial click until the point where you release the mouse button, the larger the rectangle.

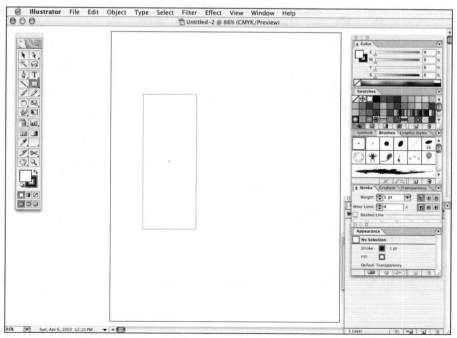

Figure 4-2: Click and drag to the opposite corner to draw a quick rectangle.

Defining properties with the Rectangle dialog box

If you want to create a rectangle with exact dimensions, all you have to do is open the Rectangle dialog box and enter the dimensions. The steps that follow also apply to the other basic shape tools in Illustrator. To draw a rectangle of an exact size, follow these steps:

1. **Click the Rectangle tool once and release where you want to place the upper-left corner.** The Rectangle dialog box, shown in Figure 4-3, appears.

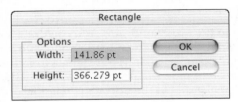

Figure 4-3: Use the Rectangle dialog box to specify the exact dimensions of a rectangle.

2. **Type in the width and height.** When the Rectangle dialog box appears, values are usually already inside the text fields. These numbers correspond to the size of the rectangle you last drew. To create another rectangle of the same size, just click OK (or press Return or Enter). To make the rectangle a different size, replace the values with your own measurements. If a text field is highlighted, typing replaces the text in the text field and deletes what had been highlighted.

Tip   To highlight the next field in a dialog box, press the Tab key. You can also highlight the preceding field in a dialog box by pressing Shift+Tab. If you'd like to highlight any text field instantly, double-click the value or click the label next to that value.

3. **Click OK.** The rectangle draws itself, becoming precisely the size that you specified. To get out of the Rectangle dialog box without drawing a rectangle, click the Cancel button, or just press ⌘+Period (Esc). Anything you type in that dialog box is then forgotten. The next time the dialog box is opened, it still has the size of the previously drawn rectangle inside it.

Rectangles whose sizes are specified in the Rectangle dialog box are always drawn from the upper-left corner. The largest rectangle you can draw is about 19 feet by 19 feet. It's a wonder you can get anything done at all with these limitations!

Cross-Reference   To learn how to draw rounded rectangles using the Corner Radius property of the Rectangle dialog box, see "Drawing rounded rectangles and squares." For more on drawing rectangles from the center rather than from the upper-left corner, see "Drawing shapes from their centers."

Drawing rounded rectangles and squares

Sometimes straight corners just aren't good enough. That's when it's time to create a rectangle with rounded corners. Why? Maybe you want your rectangles to look less "computery." A tiny bit of corner rounding (2 or 3 points) may be just what you need.

Before we get into how to actually draw rounded rectangles, it helps to understand how Illustrator sets the roundness of your corners. It performs this feat in one of three ways:

✦ **Using most recently drawn rounded corner rectangle**: Illustrator sets the Corner Radius value using the dimensions of the most recently drawn rounded-corner rectangle and places this value in the General Preferences dialog box. In other words, after you draw a rectangle using the Rounded Rectangle tool, Illustrator saves those dimensions for the next time that you draw a rounded rectangle.

✦ **Using the General Preferences dialog box.** What if you don't want to use the radius of the last rounded rectangle? Why, you use the value in the General Preferences dialog box, of course! To do so, choose Illustrator (Edit) ➪ Preferences ➪ General or press ⌘+K (Ctrl+K). All rounded rectangles are now drawn with this new corner radius until you change this value.

✦ **Using the Rounded Rectangle dialog box:** Changing the value in the Corner Radius field not only changes the current rounded rectangle's Corner Radius value but also changes the radius in the General Preferences box. Illustrator uses this corner radius for all subsequently drawn rounded rectangles until you change the radius value again. You learn how to access the Rounded Rectangle dialog box next.

Now that you understand how Illustrator works when you draw rounded rectangles, the next step is to learn how to draw one. You can create a rounded rectangle in one of two ways. You can either accept the current radius and draw, or you can change the current radius and draw.

To draw a rounded rectangle with the current radius, use the Rounded Rectangle tool:

1. **Choose the Rounded Rectangle tool.** You do this by clicking the Rectangle tool in the toolbox until a pop-up tool appears. Next, drag your mouse to the right to select the Rounded Rectangle tool.

2. **Click and drag with the Rounded Rectangle tool as if you were drawing a standard rectangle.** The only difference is that this rectangle has rounded corners. The point at which you clicked is where the corner would be — if there were a corner. Of course, with rounded corners, there is no real corner, so the computer uses an imaginary point called the origin point, as its onscreen corner reference.

Alternatively, you can specify a Corner Radius value in the Rounded Rectangle dialog box by following these steps:

1. **Click the Rounded Rectangle tool as before.**

2. **Click the Artboard with the Rounded Rectangle tool.** The Rounded Rectangle box appears, shown in Figure 4-4.

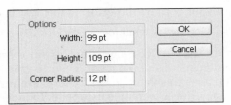

Figure 4-4: The Rounded Rectangle dialog box includes a third field for defining the corner radius.

3. **Specify a value in the Corner Radius field.** The third text field is for the size of the corner radius. This option makes the corners of the rectangle curved, although leaving the setting at a value of 0 keeps the corners straight. The corner radius in Illustrator is the length from that imaginary corner (the origin point) to where the curve begins, as shown in Figure 4-5. The larger the value you enter in the Corner Radius field of the Rectangle dialog box, the farther the rectangle starts from the imaginary corner, the bigger the curve. For example, if you set the corner radius at 1 inch, the edge of the rectangle starts curving 1 inch from where a real corner would normally appear.

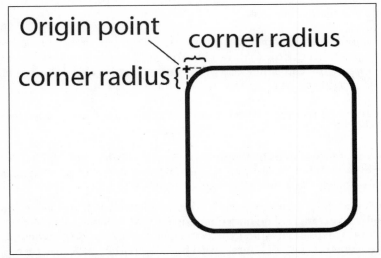

Figure 4-5: The corner radius defines the roundness of the corner.

4. Click OK. Illustrator applies your changes.

5. Click and drag with this tool as if you were drawing a standard rectangle. Your rounded rectangle appears.

Tip

If the corner radius is more than half the length of either the length or width of the rectangle, the rectangle may appear to have perfectly round ends on at least two sides. If the corner radius is more than half the length of either the length or width of the rectangle, then the rectangle becomes an ellipse!

Cross-Reference

Need to draw a rounded rectangle from the center, or create a rounded square? Use the Rounded Rectangle tool, and follow the instructions in the section "Drawing shapes from their centers, or "Drawing a symmetric shape."

How the Corner Radius Really Works

For all you geometry buffs, the whole corner radius business works this way: The width of any circle is called the *diameter* of that circle. Half the diameter is the *radius* of the circle (see the figure that follows).

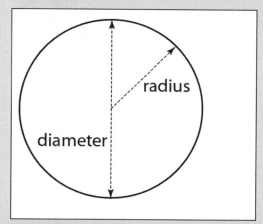

The diameter and radius of a circle

If you create a circle with a radius of 1 inch, the circle actually has a diameter of 2 inches. Put this 2-inch circle into the corner of the rectangle, as in the preceding figure, and the curve of the circle matches the curve of the rounded rectangle that has a corner radius of 1 inch.

To realistically determine the way a round corner will look, use the method that measures the distance from the imaginary corner to the place where the curve starts.

You are limited to a maximum of a 4,320-point corner radius, which works out to 5 feet. The largest rectangle you can create has a 10-foot length. So a 10-foot square with a 5-foot radius is another circle. (Those clever engineers...)

Using the round corners filter to round straight corners

If you have an existing rectangle with straight corners and you want to make the corners round, neither of the methods presented in the section "Drawing rounded rectangles and squares" are going to help you. Instead, you must choose Effects ⇨ Stylize ⇨ Round Corners and enter the value of the corner radius you want for the existing rectangle in the dialog box that appears. Using this filter allows you to change straight-corner rectangles to rounded-corner rectangles. However this effect is not recommended for changing rounded-corner rectangles to straight-corner rectangles because it usually results in an unsightly distortion.

Furthermore, this filter cannot change corners that you have rounded with either the Rounded Rectangle tool or through previous use of the Round Corners dialog box. Using this dialog box affects corners that are not round. Figure 4-6 shows the Round Corners filter applied to various rectangles and the results.

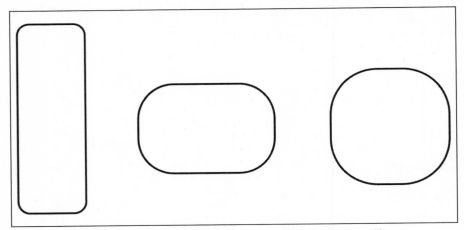

Figure 4-6: Rounded corners on rectangles using the round corner filter

Rounding corners backward

What if you want your corners to round inward instead of out? Initially, it would seem that you are out of luck, because Illustrator doesn't provide any way for you to enter a negative value for a corner radius. However, you can manipulate the corners manually. The following steps explain how to create a reverse rounded-corner rectangle:

1. **Draw a rounded rectangle to the dimensions that you desire.** For more on drawing rounded rectangles, see the section "Drawing rounded rectangles and squares" previously presented in this chapter.

2. **Select the topmost point on the left side of the rounded rectangle by dragging the Direct Selection tool (hollow arrow) overtop of the top leftmost point.** One Control Handle appears, sticking out to the left.

3. **Click and drag the control handle down below the Anchor Point while pressing the Shift key.** The Shift key makes sure that the Control Handle line is perfectly vertical and then release the mouse button.

4. **Select the second point from the top on the left side by dragging the Direct Selection tool overtop of the left top point.** A Control Handle appears, sticking straight up out of this Anchor Point.

5. **Click and drag the control handle to the left, pressing the Shift key.** Make sure that the Control Handle line is perfectly horizontal and then release the mouse button.

6. **Repeat these steps for each of the corners.** After you get the hang of it, the points start flying into position almost by themselves. Figure 4-7 shows an example of a rectangle with backward rounded corners.

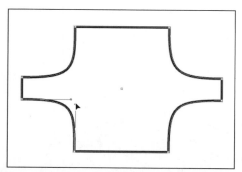

Figure 4-7: The final product of creating backward rounded corners on a rectangle

Drawing ellipses

Drawing an ellipse is harder than drawing a rectangle because the point of origin is outside the ellipse. With a rectangle, the point of origin corresponds to a corner of the rectangle, which also happens to be an anchor point. The ellipse is circumscribed within the rectangle. Figure 4-8 shows that the top edge of the ellipse is at the midpoint of the dragged rectangle.

Follow these steps to create an ellipse, which are similar to those for drawing a rectangle:

1. **Choose the Ellipse tool housed with the Rectangle tool by clicking the Rectangle tool and choosing the Ellipse tool.**

2. **Click and drag diagonally.** The outline of an ellipse forms.

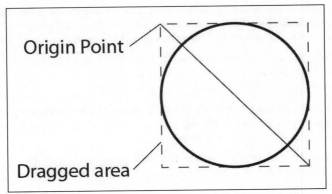

Figure 4-8: The curves of an ellipse extend beyond the boundaries of the dragged area.

3. **Release the mouse button.** The ellipse appears onscreen. Ellipses, like rectangles, have four anchor points, but the anchor points on an ellipse are at the top, bottom, left, and right of the ellipse. Only rectangles and ellipses were used to create the illustration in Figure 4-9. Through a creative use of fills, the illustration comes alive. Likewise, you can enter exact values in the Ellipse dialog box instead.

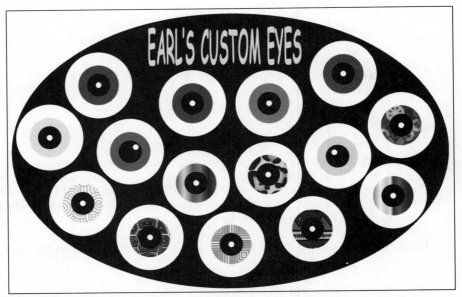

Figure 4-9: Earl's Custom Eyes was drawn using the Ellipse tool.

Cross-Reference Learn more about fills in the section "Filling and Stroking Shapes," later in this chapter. For the general steps of drawing a rectangle, see the section "Drawing a rectangle using the Rectangle tool." For the steps on entering exact values, see the section "Defining properties with the Rectangle dialog box." Both were covered earlier in this chapter.

Tip Instead of drawing an ellipse from its "corner" — a difficult task when you need to have the top, bottom, left, and right edges of the oval at a specific location — consider tracing elliptical objects. Clicking and dragging on the edge of an existing elliptical object results in a close-to-perfect match.

Creating polygons

Although creating more and more ovals, rectangles, and rounded rectangles is loads of fun, sooner or later you're going to get bored. Dare I say that you can create more interesting shapes automatically by using some of the additional shape tools that come with Illustrator. Most of these tools are located in the Rectangle tool slot in the toolbox (see Figure 4-10).

Figure 4-10: The Rectangle tool slot and the tools housed with it

To create a polygon, you first want to specify the number of sides for your polygon and then you can draw it following these steps:

1. **Select the Polygon tool.** This tool is located to the right of the Ellipse tool in the Rectangle tool slot.

2. **Click one time on the Artboard with the Polygon tool.** You want to do this before you draw the polygon. Clicking the Artboard brings up the Polygon dialog box (shown in Figure 4-11).

3. **Specify values for the polygon.** The Polygon dialog box has the following option, both of which you must specify:

   • **Radius:** The distance from the center of the polygon to one of the vertices of the polygon. For even-sided shapes (4, 6, 8, 10 and so on sides), the radius is half the width of the object, from one corner to the opposite corner. For odd-sided shapes, the radius is the distance from the center of the polygon to any of the vertices. Its diameter would be twice that value.

   • **Sides:** The number of sides that you want for the polygon.

4. **Click OK.**

5. **Click and drag in a document.** As you drag, the polygon grows from the bottom-right edge and get larger and larger.

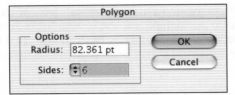

Figure 4-11: The Polygon tool dialog box

While drawing a polygon, you can change the number of sides on the fly without re-opening the Polygon dialog box. To increase or decrease the number of sides, click the up or down arrow. Figure 4-12 shows different polygons drawn with the Polygon tool.

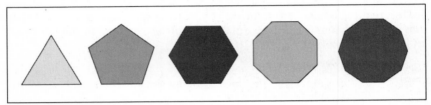

Figure 4-12: Polygons drawn with the Polygon tool

All polygons you create with the Polygon tool are equilateral polygons, meaning that they have sides of equal length. For this reason, every four-sided object you create is a square and each six-sided object is a perfect hexagon. You may find the square capabilities of the Polygon tool useful; it can save you a step when you want to draw a square at an angle. You can't do this with the Rectangle tool unless you change the Constrain Angle in General Preferences prior to drawing the square or use the Rotate tool on the square after you draw it.

If you press the Shift key while dragging your mouse, the polygon you're creating is upright. It aligns to the current Constrain Angle (usually 0°). Therefore, if you're creating a triangle and you press Shift, the triangle has one side that is perfectly horizontal (the bottom) unless you have a different Constrain Angle, in which case that edge of the triangle aligns to that angle.

Cross-Reference   For more on changing the Constrain Angle, see the section "Drawing shapes at an angle."

Note   Press the spacebar to move your polygon around when dragging with the Polygon tool. You can do this at any time during the creation of a Polygon. When you release the spacebar, the tool functions as before.

Possibly the more versatile function of the Polygon (and the Star and Spiral tools) is the wonderful Spaz function that comes from using the tilde (~) key. When you press the tilde key and draw, you see several shapes appear rapidly. As Figure 4-13 shows, Spazzing can create all sorts of interesting designs.

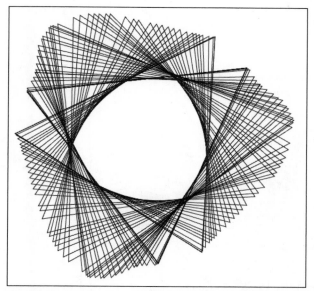

Figure 4-13: Spazzing a triangle results in a Spirographic drawing.

Seeing stars

To create stars, choose the Star tool from its hiding place next to the Polygon tool in the Rectangle tool slot and drag in the document. As you drag, a star is created. Several stars are shown in Figure 4-14.

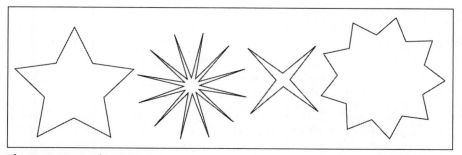

Figure 4-14: Seeing stars

Turning Regular Stars into Something Spectacular

Of course, all the stars you create with the Star tool consist of regular-looking stars. However, using the steps that follow, you can turn an "ordinary" star into something spectacular. For example, you can use these stars to jazz up text for a more eye-catching look for an advertisement. Another good idea for using spectacular stars is for seals or official looking approvals. For a more dramatic looking starburst, follow these steps.

1. Create a star with more than 30 points. Make it look something like the one shown in Figure A.

Figure A: Start with a simple star.

2. Choose Effects ➪ Distort & Transform ➪ Roughen. This displays the Roughen dialog box (Figure B).

3. In the Roughen dialog box, change the Size to 5% and the Detail to 0. Keeping the Detail at 0 won't let Roughen add any anchor points. Applying the Roughen effect randomly makes some star points longer than others.

4. Choose the Corner radio button (so we don't have curves on our starburst) and click OK. You can also check the Preview checkbox; each time you check and uncheck it, a new random preview results; clicking OK uses the Roughen preview you see onscreen (Figure C).

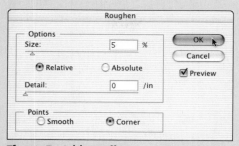

Figure B: Add an effect.

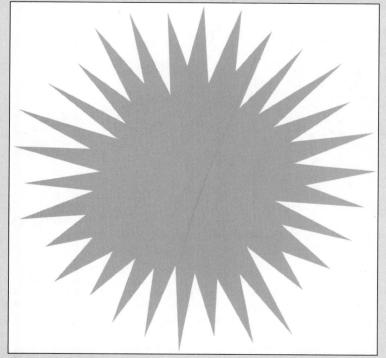

Figure C: Apply your changes.

5. Add any extras, like a drop shadow, text, and so on. My end result is shown in Figure D.

Continued

Continued

Figure D: And there you have it! A work of art!

Stars have several of the same controls as polygons when you're drawing them:
Pressing the Shift key aligns the star to the constrain angle, the Spacebar moves the
star around, and the tilde (~) key makes lots of duplicates. Figure 4-15 shows a star
with the tilde held down, then filled with various colors. The up and down arrows
work a bit differently in that instead of adding and removing edges, they add and
remove entire points. So, in a way, they're actually adding two edges. Stars have to
have an even number of sides or they're not really stars; they're the pointy lumps
you doodled during your Poly Sci classes as a sophomore.

The Star tool adds two additional keys for other functions. Pressing the Option (Alt)
key positions the inner points relative to the outer points to produce a regular-
shaped star. Adobe refers to them as fixed stars. In case it's keeping you up at night,
the Option (Alt) key has no effect on stars with three or four points.

Stars can come in all shapes, not just the fixed and standard shapes. You create
these shapes by pressing the ⌘ (Ctrl) key when you drag the mouse. When you

hold down the ⌘ (Ctrl) key, only the outer points are extended; the interior points remain fixed in place. Using this feature allows you build stars with long, thin points.

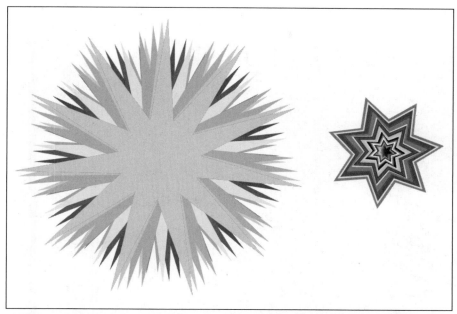

Figure 4-15: You create wild stars by pressing the tilde (~) key while dragging the mouse.

You can also specifically design a star by clicking with the Star tool to display the Star dialog box (see Figure 4-16), where you can enter the number of points and both the first and second radius of the points.

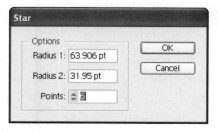

Figure 4-16: The Star dialog lets you specify both inner and outer radius values.

Working with the Flare Tool

The Flare tool came into being in Version 10 of Illustrator and is more than a welcome addition to Illustrator's amazing tools. Housed with the Rectangle tool, the

Flare tool is used to create a flare. Seems simple, but what exactly is a flare? A *flare* is a highlight or reflections from a light source. Figure 4-17 shows a basic flare on a black background.

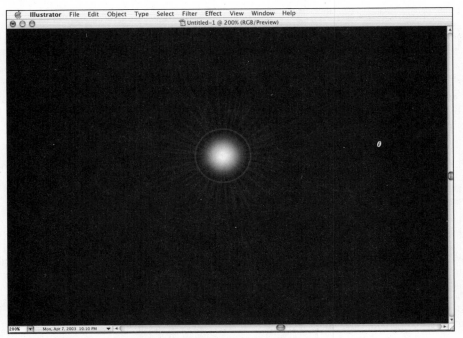

Figure 4-17: The Flare tool applied to a black background

Understanding Flare options

With most tools, there are options. To access the Flare tool options, double-click the Flare tool. Figure 4-18 shows the Flare Tool Options dialog box.

In the Flare Tool Options dialog box, you can choose from many options. The options are:

✦ **Center:** Sets the diameter, opacity, and brightness of the center of the flare.

✦ **Halo:** Sets the percentage of the halo's fade outwards and fuzziness. A low fuzziness results in a clean, crisp halo.

✦ **Rays:** Sets the number of rays, longest ray length, and fuzziness of rays. If you don't want rays, enter 0 for the number of rays.

✦ **Rings:** Set the distance of the path between the halo's center and the center of the farthest ring, the number of rings, the size of the largest ring, and the ring direction.

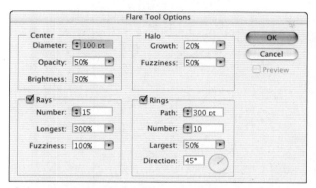

Figure 4-18: The Flare Tool Options dialog box

After you create a flare, you can always edit it by selecting the flare first; then with the Flare tool, drag your mouse to change the direction or length. If you expand the object, the flare changes to a blended object. That way you can change the number of blend steps or colors if necessary.

The Flare tool is perfect for making a nighttime sky of stars (see Figure 4-19). You can use any backdrop with your graphic illustration. For variation, drag small, medium and large flares for depth to the stars. Dragging a small amount outwards creates a small flare; a little larger drag creates a medium flare; a big drag outwards creates a large flare.

Using a flare to add highlight

The best use of flares is to add a highlight to an object. For example, you can drag out a flare on the corner of an object to simulate the light reflecting off of it (see Figure 4-20 for an example). You simply click and drag the mouse to place the center of the flare, then click to set the size of the center, halo, and rotate the ray angle.

You can use keyboard commands while drawing to modify the flare:

✦ **Shift key:** Constrains the rays of the flare to 45 degree increments.

✦ **Up Arrow:** Adds rings. Each time you press the Up Arrow key, you add rings as you are drawing the flare. Keep pressing for lots of rings.

✦ **Down Arrow:** Deletes rings. Each time you press the Down Arrow key, it takes away rings as you are drawing the flare.

✦ **⌘ (Ctrl):** Press this button while dragging to hold the center of the flare constant.

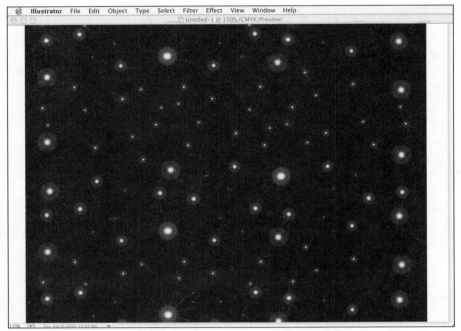

Figure 4-19: Lots of stars in the sky

Figure 4-20: Flares highlight the alien spaceship.

Editing a flare

After you have drawn the flare, it is not set in stone. Maybe you don't like how far the flare is going out, or maybe you'd like to see additional rings. You can always go back in and edit the flare to remove rings, change the distance, and so on. You have two ways to edit a flare:

✦ **Using the Flare tool:** Select the flare you want to edit. Using the Flare tool, drag the end point to a new length or direction. This is shown in Figure 4-21.

✦ **Flare Tool Options dialog box:** Select the flare you want to edit. Double-click the Flare tool to open the Flare Tool Options dialog box. Change the values in the dialog box to edit the flare.

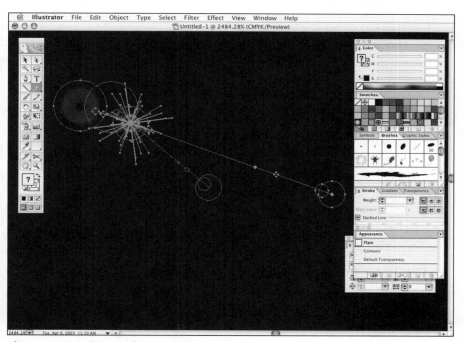

Figure 4-21: Editing a flare with the Flare tool

Filling and Stroking Shapes

One of the most powerful features of Illustrator is its ability to color objects. In Adobe Illustrator, you can color both the fill and the stroke of the paths you have created. The *fill* is the internal portion of a shape, while the *stroke* is the internal portion of a shape.

Fills

The *fill* of an object is the color inside the shape. If a path is closed (a condition where there are no endpoints and the object's path is connected from end to end), the fill exists only on the inside of the path. If the path is open, or has two endpoints, the fill exists between an imaginary line drawn from endpoint to endpoint and the path itself. Fills in open paths can provide some very interesting results when the path crosses itself, or the imaginary line crosses the path. Figure 4-22 shows an example of fills in open and closed paths and how the paths appear in Outline mode. For text, the fill is the color of the text. Fills do not appear in Outline mode, only in Preview mode. Depending on the complexity of the path and the type of fill, Illustrator may refuse to preview the fill and may automatically switch to Outline mode.

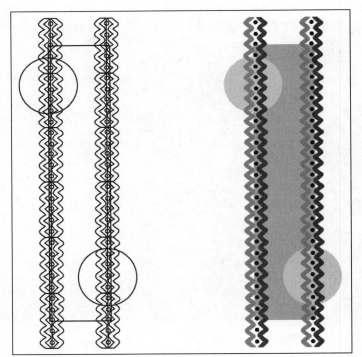

Figure 4-22: Open and closed paths in Outline (left) and Preview (right) modes

For more on the various View modes in Illustrator, see Chapter 1. For more information on fills see Chapter 9.

Besides White and Black, the Fill color options include the following:

✦ **Process Colors:** A process color is made up of four inks: Cyan, Magenta, Yellow, and Black, also known as CMYK. The printer prints using these four colors to create your illustration.

✦ **Spot Colors:** Spot color is created using inks that have been premixed. A Spot color uses its own printing plate rather than the standard CMYK plates.

✦ **Patterns:** A pattern consists of created artwork that is repeated or tiled next to each other to fill a space.

✦ **Gradients:** A gradient blends two or more colors together for a smooth transformation between colors.

✦ **Gradient Meshes:** A Gradient Mesh changes the object by adding blended lines to accommodate the changes in colors.

✦ **None:** This is where the fill is transparent. This option lets you see behind a path to what is underneath it when the stroke of an object is the visible part.

Strokes

A *stroke* is defined as the outline or the path of an object. Any object you draw can have a stroke applied to it including shapes, lines, paths and even text. The stroke of an object is made up of three parts: color, weight, and attributes. Strokes appear where there are paths or around the edges of type. Like fills, any one path or object may have only one type of stroke on it; the color, weight, and style of the stroke are consistent throughout the length of the path or the entire text object. Individual characters in a text object can have different strokes only if you select them with the Type tool after you apply the Stroke attributes.

Cross-Reference You can learn more about applying strokes to text in Chapter 8.

Stroke color

Besides White and Black, the Stroke color options are the same as those for fills, except that you cannot apply gradients and gradient meshes to a stroke. To apply a Stroke color, simply select the Stroke color at the bottom of the Toolbox, or press the X key, and then select the color to use from the Color palette or from the Swatches palette.

Stroke weight

The weight of a stroke is how thick it is. On a path, Illustrator centers the stroke on that path, with half the thickness of the stroke on one side of the path and half the thickness on the other side of the path. So a 1-point stroke has ½ point on each side of the path.

You set Stroke weight in the Stroke palette's Weight menu or by typing in a value in the Weight text field. Figure 4-23 shows the Stroke palette. You can also use the up and down arrows on the left of the text box to incrementally change the Stroke weight.

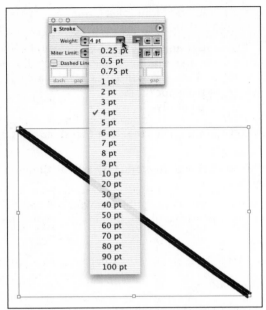

Figure 4-23: Choose from a preset Stroke weight in the pop-up menu, or enter your own value in the Weight text box.

Tip

Use mathematical operations in the Stroke weight palette! You can mathematically change the current Stroke weight by adding, subtracting, multiplying, or dividing by any value. Just place the appropriate symbol (+ for add, - for subtract, * for multiply, and / for divide) after the current value, and then the number by which you want to perform the operation. Use this when you are asked to increase the Stroke weight by, say, 2 times the current value.

Strokes have upper and lower limits. You can never create strokes wider than 1,000 points. A stroke with a weight of 0.001 can exist in Illustrator, although the recommendation is that you not choose such a value. Instead, set the stroke to None. If you do set a weight to 0.001, the path has a stroke as thick as 1 device pixel of the output device. For a 300-dpi laser printer, that translates to a healthy quarter-point thick. For a typical 1270-dpi imagesetter, that translates to about ½₇ the point, or a fourth of a quarter point; much too small to use for most purposes. Because a stroke of 0.001 changes to match the output device (it appears 1 pixel thick, or as a 1-point stroke onscreen), the potential changes in thickness can drastically change the way an image looks. Be very careful if you choose to venture into this area of Illustrator.

Stroke attributes

The attributes of a stroke consists of several parts, including the cap style, join style, miter limit, and dash pattern. Figures 4-24 and 4-25 give some examples of these attributes:

✦ **Cap style:** The way that the ends of a stroke look. This style can be either butt cap, rounded cap, or projected cap. Caps apply only to End Points on open paths. You can choose a Cap style for a closed path (with no End Points), but nothing happens; if the path is cut into an open path, that Cap style goes into effect.

- **Butt Caps:** Chop the stroke off perpendicularly at the end of the path.

- **_Rounded Caps:** Smooth, rounded ends that resemble a half-circle. These caps protrude from the End Point ½ the Stroke weight.

- **Projected Caps:** Project from the endpoint ½ the Stroke weight and appear perpendicular to the direction of the path at its End Point.

✦ **Join style:** The join style is the manner in which the corner points on paths appear when you stroke them. You can apply one of three different Join types to paths:

- **Mitered Joins:** Cause the outer edges of the stroke to meet at a point. This Join type is the only one affected by the miter limit.

- **Rounded Joins:** Round off the outside edge of corners.

- **Beveled Joins**: Are cropped off before the angle can reach a corner.

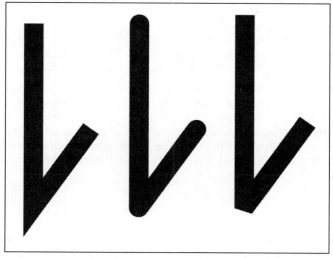

Figure 4-24: The three different cap and join styles: Butt Cap/Miter Join (left), Rounded Cap/Rounded Join (middle), and Projected Cap/Bevel Join (right)

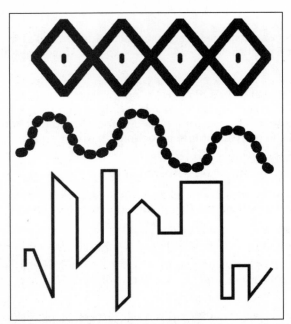

Figure 4-25: A sampling of the different cap styles, join styles, miter limits, and dash patterns for strokes. The top stroke has a thick stroke with a projected cap and a bevel join. The middle stroke uses a rounded cap and rounded join with a dash pattern set close together to resemble a string of beads. The bottom stroke is a butt cap and a miter join.

Joins only affect Corner points, including Straight Corner points, Curved Corner points, and Combination Corner points. In all cases, Join types only affect outside corners. Inside corners always appear mitered.

✦ **Miter Limit:** The Miter Limit option controls how far a corner can extend past the edge of the path. This is important for tight corners of paths with large Weights, as the place where the outside edges meets in a corner can be really far away from the original edges of the paths. The number in the Miter Limit controls how many times the width of the stroke the Miter can extend beyond the point. The default is 4, which is good for the majority of applications.

✦ **Dash pattern:** Usually, the dash pattern for a stroke is solid, but you can create various dash patterns for different effects. The bottom of the Stroke palette controls if and how dashed strokes should appear. Checking the Dashed Line box allows you to enter different values for up to three dash and gap lengths. Figure 4-26 shows different stroked paths with their Dashed Line settings.

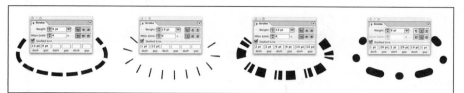

Figure 4-26: Dashed lines and their settings

Combining Strokes with Fills

Many times, paths in Illustrator require both fills and strokes. When you give both a fill and a stroke to a single path, the stroke knocks out the fill at the edges of the path by one-half the weight of the stroke. Figure 4-27 demonstrates this.

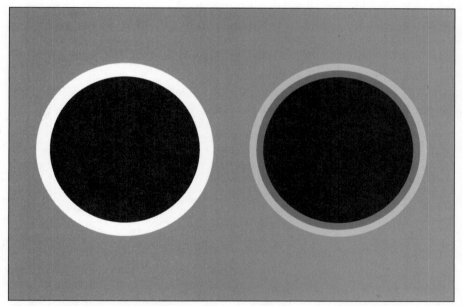

Figure 4-27: A stroke knocks out a fill by one-half the weight of the stroke, as shown on the right circle.

> **Tip** If knocking out the fill of a path hides part of the pattern that you want to be seen, you can correct this problem by copying the path and pasting it in front, removing the front-most path's stroke. Be warned though that the filled path, on top of the stroked path, knocks out the "inner" half of the stroke.

Applying Fills and Strokes

The toolbox contains two icons — one for fill and one for stroke, located in the Paint Style section of the toolbox (see Figure 4-28).

By default, the fill is set to White and the stroke is set to 1-point Black. In fact, at any time you can reset to the default fill and stroke by clicking the Default Fill and Stroke icon in the lower-left corner of the Paint Style section.

You can quickly swap between the colors in the fill and Stroke icons by clicking the Swap Fill and Stroke icon located in the upper-right of the Paint Style section.

When you first start Illustrator, the Fill icon is in front of the Stroke icon. This means that any changes made in the Color or Swatch palettes affect the fill. When the Fill icon is in front of the Stroke icon, the fill is said to be in *focus*. You can change the focus to the stroke by clicking the Stroke icon. Figure 4-29 shows the focus on the stroke and the focus on the fill. When the focus is on the stroke, changes made in the Color or Swatch palettes affect the stroke, not the fill.

Figure 4-28: The Paint Style section of the toolbox

The Paint Style section

Figure 4-29: Focus on the stroke and fill

Fill

Stroke

Tip You can quickly reset the fill and stroke colors to their default by pressing the D key. You can quickly change the focus from the Stroke to the Fill icon, by pressing Shift–X.

The Fill and Stroke icons change in appearance to match the current fill and stroke. For example, if you have a green fill and an orange stroke, the Fill icon is green and the Stroke icon is orange, and you obviously slept through the color-coordination lectures in your design classes. The Fill icon displays a gradient or pattern if that is the current fill.

You use the three icons at the bottom of the Paint Style section to determine the type of fill or stroke:

✦ **Color:** You use this icon when you want to have a solid color or pattern for the fill or stroke. Press the comma key (, or <) on the keyboard to quickly activate the color icon.

✦ **Gradient:** Use this icon when the fill contains a gradient. You cannot color a stroke with gradients; clicking this icon when the Stroke icon is in focus changes the fill to gradient and changes the focus to fill as well. Press the period key (. or >) to quickly activate the gradient icon.

✦ **None**: This creates an empty fill or no stroke. Fills of None are entirely transparent. Strokes of None are neither colored nor have any Stroke weight. Press the forward slash key (/) to quickly activate the None icon.

Oddly enough, you don't need to use the color and gradient icons to determine the type of fill when switching between color and gradient; you can simply click the appropriate swatch in the Swatches palette to change the fill type. There is, however, no swatch for None, so to change the fill or stroke to None you must either click the icon or press the forward slash (/) key. Get used to the forward slash key; it saves you loads of time when you want to change colors for objects. You can quickly combine pressing the X and / keys to change focus and apply None to the stroke or fill.

Creating and Embellishing Graphs and Charts

Graphs are most useful when they show numerical information that normally takes several paragraphs to explain or that you can't easily express in words. You can easily overlook a significant difference between two numbers until you use a graph to represent them. The Graphs feature is one of the most underused features in Illustrator. Most people use graph programs such as Microsoft Excel to design their graphs. You just wouldn't think Illustrator can do graphs with accuracy, but it can and with more than just the boring graph visuals as well.

One of the most exciting things about graphs in Illustrator is their fluidity. Not only can you create graphs easily, but you can also change them easily. In addition, if the data that you used to create a graph changes, you can enter the new data and have it show up in the graph instantaneously.

For more on graph types, see the section "Choosing Graph type" later in this chapter.

All the graph tools work in a manner similar to that of the shape creation tools. For example, when you select he Graph tool, you can click and drag to set the size of the graph, or you can display the tool's dialog box (in this case, the Graph Size dialog box) by clicking the Artboard without dragging to enter the size information.

The Graph Data dialog box (see Figure 4-30) looks like a simply spreadsheet with rows and columns. Using this dialog box, you can enter data to graph. Once you enter the data, press the Apply button (it looks like a checkmark) and Illustrator updates your graph.

For more on working with the shape tools, see "Making Basic Shapes," earlier in this chapter. For the basic steps of using a shape tool, see the section "Drawing rectangles using the Rectangle tool." For more on accessing a tool's dialog box, see the section "Defining properties with the Rectangle dialog box."

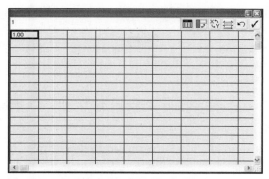

Figure 4-30: The Graph Data dialog box resembles a simple spreadsheet.

Caution

Make sure that the graph is never ungrouped (a graph always has all of its elements grouped together, meaning that you can select them with the Selection tool as a whole rather than individual pieces), at least not until you finish making all graph data and graph style changes. If you ungroup the graph, you cannot use any of the graph options to change the ex-graph because Illustrator views it as just a set of paths and text.

Cross-Reference

For more on grouping and ungrouping, see Chapter 7.

Importing Microsoft Excel graph data

You can import graph data in tab-delimited text files such as those exported by Microsoft Excel. Tab-delimited files are text and numbers that are separated by tabs and returns. To import data from another file, click the Import button while you are in the Graph Data dialog box (it is the leftmost icon at the top of the dialog box).

Because Illustrator is not really a graphing or spreadsheet program, many of the usual controls for arranging data in such programs are not available, including inserting rows and columns and creating formulas.

The Cut, Copy, and Paste functions work within the Graph Data dialog box, so you can move and duplicate information on a very basic level.

One very useful feature in the Graph Data dialog box is the Transpose row/column button. This function switches the x and y axes of the data, thus rotating everything that you have entered.

Making and editing graphs

Follow the steps below to create a basic graph. The type of graph in this example is a grouped column graph, which you commonly use to compare quantities over time or between different categories.

1. **Select the Graph tool.** The tool is located in midway down the Toolbox and looks like a bar graph.

2. **Click and drag to form a rectangular area.** You do this as you would when using the Rectangle tool. The size of the rectangle that you create becomes the size of the graph.

For more on creating rectangles, see the section "Drawing rectangles using the Rectangle tool" earlier in this chapter.

3. **Release the mouse button.** As soon as you do so, an untitled floating window appears, containing a simple worksheet. This floating window is the Graph Data dialog box.

4. **Enter your data into the Graph Data dialog box.** Information that you enter in the worksheet becomes formatted in graph form. The top row in the worksheet area should contain the labels for comparison within the same set. The items in the top row appear as legends outside the graph area. In the leftmost column, you can enter labels that appear at the bottom of the grouped column graph as categories. In the remaining cells, enter the pertinent information as shown in Figure 4-31.

To get the labels on the legends to read numbers only, you must place quotation marks (" ")around each of the numbers. If you do not use quotation marks, Illustrator considers the numbers as data, not labels.

	First Qu...	Second ...	Third Q...	Fourth ...			
Cat Toys	50.00	35.00	40.00	85.00			
Dog Toys	80.00	75.00	60.00	95.00			
Fish Toys	5.00	2.00	1.00	3.00			
Bird Toys	10.00	15.00	8.00	6.00			

Figure 4-31: The Graph data with the applied information

5. **Close the window.** This signals Illustrator to use the data that you entered in the graph. The graph appears, and it should look something like the one in Figure 4-32.

6. **Change your Graph styles.** After you create the graph, you can change the Graph styles to see which graph shows my information the best.

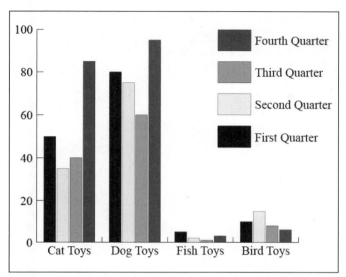

Figure 4-32: The final graph shown in Grouped Column Graph

You can change the numbers and the text in the Graph Data dialog box at any time by selecting the graph and Object ➪ Graphs ➪ Data. Illustrator recreates the graph to reflect the changes you make. If you have moved some of the graph objects around, they may revert to their original locations when Illustrator recreates the graph. If a number does not have quotation marks around it, Illustrator assumes that you want to enter the number as a value in the graph.

Customizing graphs

When a graph is selected, you can use the Object ➪ Graph ➪ Type menu to open the Graph Type dialog box (see Figure 4-33). Using this dialog box, you can quickly change between the different graph types while keeping the same data. Choosing a different graph type and clicking OK changes the tool to represent the type of graph you selected. You can choose from nine graph types; the column graph is the default.

The Graph Type dialog includes several different options for controlling the look of the graph including the following:

✦ **Type:** Separate icon buttons are available for each of the graph types including Column, Stacked Column, Bar, Stacked Bar, Line, Area, Scatter, Pie and Radar.

✦ **Value Axis:** On Left Side, On Right Side, On Both Sides, display the vertical values on the left side (the default), the right side or both sides.

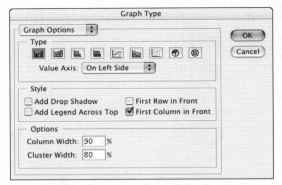

Figure 4-33: The Graph Type dialog box lets you choose the type of graph to use.

✦ **Style:** Under these options you can add a drop shadow, or add a legend across the top of the graph. You can also opt to place the first row in front, or the first column in front (for when the columns or rows stack closely together.

✦ **Options:** These options are specific to the graph you select. The default graph (grouped column graph) has the options to set the column and cluster width in percentage. Each type of graph has its own customization options.

Tip   To make visually striking graphs, use a combination of graph types. Simply use the Group Selection tool to select all the objects that are one legend type and then choose Object ➪ Graph ➪ Type and enter the new graph type for that legend.

In the Graph options pop-up menu in the Graph Type dialog box there are other options such as Value Axis, and Category Axis. The Value Axis and Category Axis options are:

✦ **Tick Values**: (Value Axis) Set the minimum, maximum, and divisions as well as the checkbox to override calculated values.

✦ **Tick Marks**: (Value Axis) Set the length and how many ticks are drawn per division.

✦ **Add Labels**: (Value Axis) Set a prefix and/or a suffix for labels.

✦ **Tick Marks**: (Category Axix) Set the length and how many are drawn per division as well as a checkbox to draw tick marks between labels.

Choosing a graph type

You can choose from nine different types of graphs in Illustrator. Each type gives a specific kind of information to the reader. Certain graphs are better for comparisons, others for growth, and so on. The following sections describe the graphs, explain how to create them, and tell how you can use them.

Grouped-Column graphs

You primarily use grouped-column graphs to show how something changes over time. Often, they are referred to as bar graphs because the columns that make up the graphs resemble bars.

The real strength of a grouped-column graph is that it provides for the direct comparison of different types of statistics in the same graph.

Both column and cluster width are two customizable options for grouped-column graphs and stacked-column graphs. Column width refers to the width of individual columns, with 100% being wide enough to abut other columns in the cluster. Cluster width refers to how much of the available cluster space is taken up by the columns in the cluster. At 80% (the default), 20% of the available space is empty, leaving room between clusters.

You can widen columns and clusters to 1000% of their size and condense them to 1% of the width of the original column or cluster.

Stacked-Column graphs

Stacked-column graphs are good graphs for presenting the total of a category and the contributing portions of each category as shown in Figure 4-34.

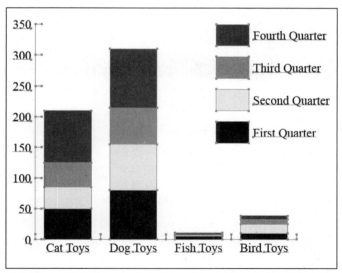

Figure 4-34: The applied data in a Stacked Column Graph

This graph shows the same amount of information as the grouped-column graph, but the information is organized differently. The stacked-column graph is designed to display the total of all the legends, and the grouped-column graph is designed to aid comparison of all individual legends in each category.

Line graphs

Line graphs (also known as line charts) show trends over time. They are especially useful for determining progress and identifying radical changes as shown in Figure 4-35.

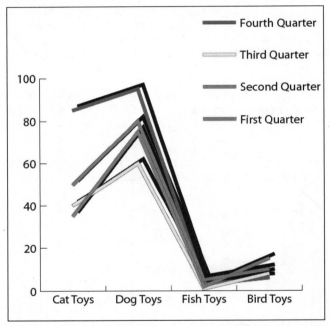

Figure 4-35: The applied data in a Line Graph. The example adds a drop shadow, First Column in Front, Connect Data Points, and Draw Filled Lines (3 pt).

The Line graph of the Graph Type dialog box (Object ➪ Graph ➪ Type) has several unique options, including:

✦ **The Mark Data Points option:** This forces data points to appear as squares. If this box is not checked, the data points are visible only as direction changes in lines between the data points.

✦ **The Connect Data Points option**: If you check this option, Illustrator draws lines between each pair of data points.

✦ **The Draw Filled Lines option and the corresponding text box for line width:** This creates a line that is filled with the data point legend color and that is outlined with Black.

✦ **The Edge-to-Edge lines option:** This stretches the lines out to the left and right edges of the graph. Although the result is technically incorrect, you can achieve better visual impact by using this feature.

Area graphs

On first glance, area graphs may appear to be just like filled line graphs. Like line graphs, area graphs show data points that are connected, but area graphs (see Figure 4-36) are stacked one on top of the other to show the total area of the legend subject in the graph. In the Area Graphs you can add style to the graph by choosing: Add Drop Shadow, Add Legend Across Top, First Row in Front, and First Column in Front.

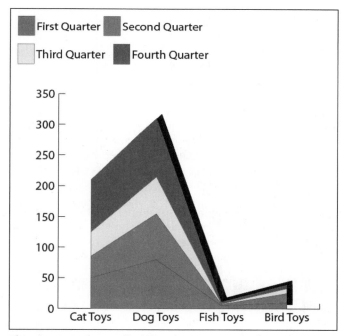

Figure 4-36: The applied data in an Area Graph

Pie graphs

Pie graphs are great for comparing percentages of the portions of a whole, as shown in Figure 4-37. The higher the percentage for a certain activity, the larger its wedge. Some of the options for Pie Graphs are: Add Drop Shadow, Add Legend Across Top, First Row in Front, First Column in Front, Legend, Sort, and Position.

When you create pie graphs, you can remove the individual wedges from the central pie with the Group Selection tool to achieve an exploding pie effect.

The Legends in Wedges option is the only option in the Graph Type dialog box that is specifically for pie graphs. If you select this option, the name of each wedge centers within that wedge. Illustrator doesn't do a very good job of placing the legend names, many times overlapping neighboring names. In addition, the letters in the legend names are black, which can make reading some of the names difficult or impossible.

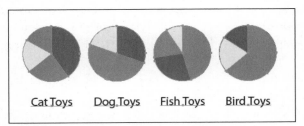

Figure 4-37: The applied data in a pie graph

Scatter graphs and Radar graphs

Scatter graphs, which are primarily used for scientific charting purposes, are quite different from all the other types of graphs. Each data point is given a location according to its x-y coordinates instead of by category and label. The points are connected, as are the points in line graphs, but the line created by the data point locations can cross itself and does not go in any specific direction. Scatter graphs have the same customization options as line graphs.

A Radar (or Web) graph compares values set at a certain point. This type of graph is viewed as a circle graph. Categories are spread around the circle and the data with higher values extend further from the center.

Utilizing marker and columns graphics

The most exciting part about the graphing functions in Illustrator is the capability to give column, line, and area graphs special icons to indicate values on the graphs.

On line and area graphs, marker designs are available for use in place of the standard markers. For each value in the graph, you place the marker design to add visual impact to the graph.

Column designs are created for grouped-column graphs and stacked-column graphs. The strength of using column designs is most evident in grouped-column graphs, where images are placed side-by-side (see Figure 4-39).

To use this feature, follow these steps:

1. **Create the graphic object(s) in Illustrator.**
2. **Select the object(s) that you want to use as a column design.** See Chapter 5 for more on selecting objects.
3. **Group the selected objects.** You do this by pressing ⌘+G (Ctrl+G). For more on grouping objects, see Chapter 7.
4. **Choose Object ⇨ Graph ⇨ Design.** The Graph Design dialog box appears as shown in Figure 4-38.
5. **Click the New Design.** This makes the selected object appear in the window.

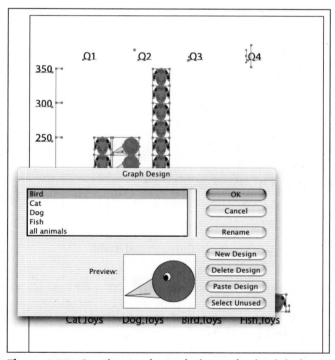

Figure 4-38: Creating a column design and using it in four different grouped-column graphs

6. **Click the Rename button.** Name the design and click the OK button. Do this for all of the designs.

7. **Back in the graph, select the first column using the Group Selection tool.**

8. **Click a second time to select all columns with that color.**

9. **Choose Object ⇨ Graph ⇨ Column and select the design from the list.** Choose the column design type. Repeat this step for each legend, as shown in Figure 4-39.

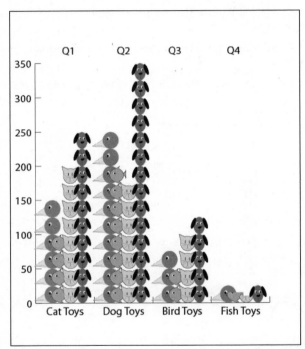

Figure 4-39: The final graph includes the designed icons.

You can combine column-design types by selecting a different type for each legend.

Manually designing a chart

You can take the graph information and choose Object ⇨ Ungroup. Doing this changes the graph data into a drawing that you can edit manually. Simply select the column and change the color, angle, anything you'd like to custom design it to fit your needs. Figure 4-40 shows a business card that was designed using an ungrouped graph.

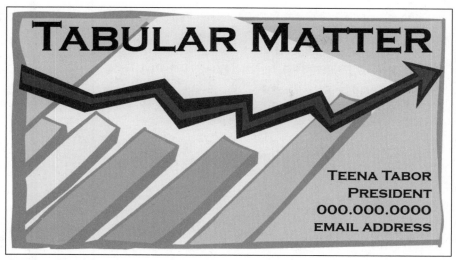

Figure 4-40: A business card created from a chart

Creating flowcharts, diagrams, and site maps

Illustrator is a great program to use to create a flowchart for a company's organization. Using the Rectangle tool and some effects, you can make a clean organization chart.

To create an organization flow chart, whether it is for a business or simply a family tree, follow these steps:

1. **Draw a rectangle.** See the section "Drawing rectangles with the Rectangle tool" for more on using this tool.

2. **Enter a name inside.** For more on entering text into graphics, see Chapter 8.

3. **Make copies of your rectangle.** Using the Option (Alt) key while dragging with the Selection tool, you can make copies of the first rectangle. Create as many rectangles as you need, then using the Type tool, edit the names appropriately.

Figure 4-41 shows a family tree flow chart.

You can use the same principle for the organizational flow chart to create a sitemap for Web sites. The main difference is that you'll organize the sitemap from left to right rather than top to bottom as in an organizational chart. The point is to show the smoothest way that information flows.

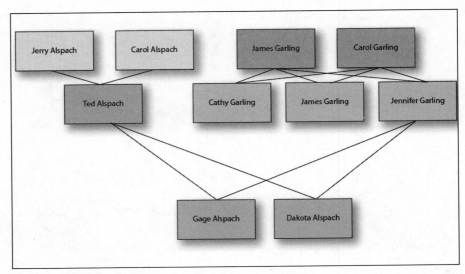

Figure 4-41: A family tree

Using Symbols

Since the addition of the Symbol tools in Illustrator 10, the world has never been the same. Small children can now, with ease, make a sensible drawing using the Symbol Sprayer tool. Adults and professionals alike can create amazing designs with very little effort. Illustrator has included a bunch of symbols to use with the Symbol Sprayer tool. If you'd like to, create your own and add it to the Symbol palette.

Spraying with the Symbol Sprayer tool

To start using the Symbol Sprayer tool, follow these steps:

1. **Choose a Symbol from the Symbol palette**. Figure 4-42 shows the Symbol palette, which you access by choosing Window ⇨ Symbols or Shift + F11.

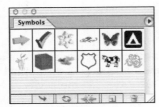

Figure 4-42: The Symbol palette

2. **Choose the Symbol Sprayer tool.** This tool is located midway down the left column of the Toolbox next to the Graph tool. It has the icon that looks like a spray can.

3. **Start spraying away.** The longer you hold the mouse button down, the more symbols are sprayed in that area. Figure 4-43 shows a bunch of butterflies sprayed on a page.

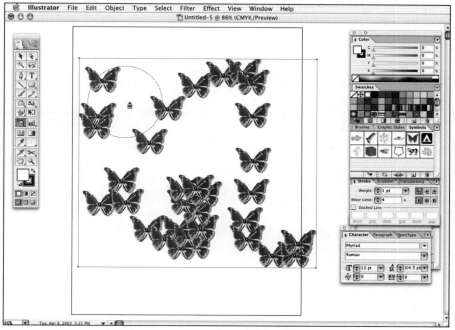

Figure 4-43: The butterfly symbol sprayed on the Artboard

To change the size of the sprayer or any other areas, double-click the Symbol Sprayer tool to access the Symbolism Tools Options dialog, as shown in Figure 4-44.

When you have a group of symbols, you can then alter them to look different. Editing the Symbol tools is done in the Symbolism Tools Options dialog box. These options are:

✦ **Diameter:** Sets the diameter of the brush in points.

✦ **Method:** Sets User Defined, Average, or Random. Only available when Symbol Sprayer tool is *not* selected. User Defined method lets you manually scrunch, size, spin, screen, stain, and style the symbols. Average method scrunches, sizes, spins, screens, stains, and styles the symbols by averaging the spaces between symbols. The Random method randomly scrunches, sizes, spins, screens, stains, and styles the symbols.

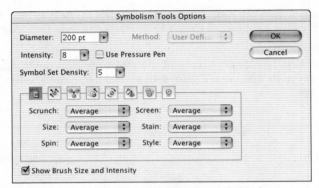

Figure 4-44: Symbolism Tools Options dialog box

✦ **Intensity:** This determines how many instances Illustrator sets when you use the mouse. *Instances* is the term for the number of symbols Illustrator sprays.

✦ **Use Pressure Pen:** Check this box if you are using a pressure sensitive tablet. The harder you press, the more symbols appear. The lighter you press, fewer symbols appear.

✦ **Symbol Set Density:** Set the density of the symbol set for the tools. Density determines how close together the symbols are.

✦ **Scrunch, Size, Spin, Screen, Stain, and Style:** The Symbol Sprayer tool first must be selected to access theses options. Choose either User Defined, or Average. User Defined method lets you manually scrunch, size, spin, screen, stain, and style the symbols. Average method scrunches, sizes, spins, screens, stains, and styles the symbols by averaging the spaces between symbols. The Random method randomly scrunches, sizes, spins, screens, stains, and styles the symbols.

✦ **Show Brush Size and Intensity:** Check this to see the actual size and intensity of the brush when using the Symbolism tools.

Making a new symbol

If you don't like the default images available in the Symbol palette, you can create your own. It's as simple as making your own symbol and adding it to the palette. You can either create a new symbol or use an existing symbol as a base.

For an existing symbol, follow these steps:

1. **Select the existing symbol in the Symbol palette.** You can access the Symbol palette by choosing Window ➪ Symbols or Shift + F11.

2. **Choose Place Symbol Instance from the pop-up menu.** You find this option by clicking the right pointing triangle in a circle on the upper right side of the

Symbol palette. Alternatively, you can simply drag the symbol from the palette to the page, as shown in Figure 4-45.

Figure 4-45: Place a symbol instance by dragging the symbol from the palette to the Artboard.

3. **With the symbol selected choose Object ⇨ Expand**. This turns the object back into editable strokes and fills.

4. **Alter the object to your liking.**

5. **Turn it back into a symbol by choosing New Symbol from the Symbols palette pop-up menu**. Alternatively, you can drag the new symbol over the Symbols palette as shown in Figure 4-46.

Figure 4-46: Create a new symbol from an existing one and either drag it to the Symbol palette or choose New Symbol from the pop-up.

You can also totally create your own new symbol. Follow the steps below to create a new symbol.

1. **Open or create something to make into a symbol.** This example uses the people that were turned into an Art Brush at the end of Chapter 3.

2. **Group the objects to become a new symbol.** You do this by pressing ⌘+G (Ctrl+G). For more on grouping objects, see Chapter 7.

3. **Drag the group atop the Symbol palette.** It magically appears in the palette, as shown in Figure 4-47. You can also choose New Symbol from the pop-up menu. You find the New Symbol option by clicking the right pointing triangle in a circle on the upper-right side of the Symbol palette.

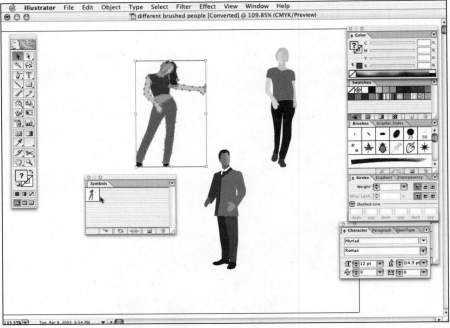

Figure 4-47: Drag the new symbol on top of the Symbol palette or choose New Symbol from the pop-up menu.

4. **Do this for as many symbols as you want.**

5. **Delete the original objects.** Simply select the object and press the Delete key.

6. **Click the Symbol Sprayer tool in the Toolbox.**

7. **Press and hold down the mouse button as you drag out your new symbol(s).** The results are shown in Figure 4-48.

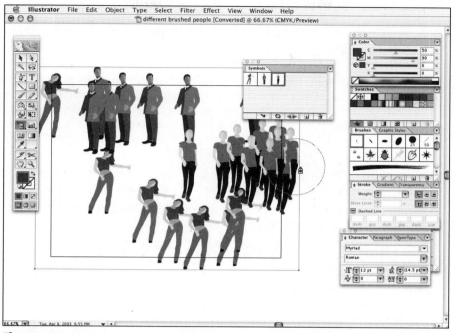

Figure 4-48: Spray out a group of new symbols as I did with these people.

Using the Symbol tool

Illustrator gives you a lot of ways to edit your symbols after you've sprayed them on your Artboard. These Symbol tools change the spacing between the objects, their size, color, transparency, style and direction. Located eight tools down on the left side of the toolbox, you access these tools by simply clicking and dragging to the tool you want.

To apply the effects of these tools, click the tool and then click the Artboard. Generally speaking, the longer you hold down the mouse, the more Illustrator applies the effect. For example, the longer you wait to release the mouse after clicking with the Symbol Scruncher tool, the more your image pull together. If you hold down the Option (Alt) key while clicking one of these tools, it decreases the effect of the tool. For example, pressing the Option (Alt) key while clicking the Symbol Scruncher tool pulls symbols apart. The available tools are as follows:

✦ **Symbol Scruncher tool:** This tool changes the location of the symbols by pulling them together. The Symbol Scruncher tool changes the density distribution of the sprayed symbols.

✦ **Symbol Sizer tool:** This tool increases the size of the symbols.

✦ **Symbol Spinner tool:** You use this tool to move symbols to a new location. Simply, choose the Symbol Spinner tool and drag the symbols in the direction you want them to go.

✦ **Symbol Stainer tool:** The Symbol Stainer tool could possibly be the coolest Symbol tool of all. Use this tool to change the color of the symbols based on the Fill Swatch in the toolbox. Keep changing the color to make the symbols look totally different. The longer you hold overtop of the symbol, the more color is infused. If you are in-between symbols, you'll get a mixture of the two colors.

✦ **Symbol Screener tool:** This tool changes the transparency of the symbols. The longer you apply this tool, the more the transparency.

✦ **Symbol Styler tool:** Use the Symbol Styler tool to apply a certain Style to a symbol. Choose the Style from the Styles palette; then apply it to the symbol.

✦ **Symbol Shifter tool:** Employ the Symbol Shifter tool to totally move the symbols in the direction you drag. To change the stacking order with the Symbol Shifter tool, pres the Shift key and click the symbol to bring it forward. To send a symbol backwards, hold the Option (Alt) key while pressing the Shift key and clicking the symbol.

Summary

✦ Even the most basic shapes, such as the rectangle and ellipse, can create some pretty cool artwork.

✦ The Flare tool can quickly add a highlight or create art on its own.

✦ There are a variety of graph styles to choose from in Illustrator.

✦ You can always go back in and edit a graph's data so long as you don't ungroup the graph.

✦ Add pizazz to your graphs using custom column graphics.

✦ The Symbol Sprayer tool creates a bunch of objects quickly and efficiently.

✦ Use the other Symbolism tools to alter the objects for variety.

✦ Change any of the Symbol tool options to create just what you want.

✦ Alter the transparency, sizes, colors, and positions of the symbols at any time.

✦   ✦   ✦

Learning How to Select and Edit

In Chapter 3, you learned how to create paths, and in Chapter 4, you learned how to create various objects; now you need to know how to change them. This chapter explains how to select what you want to change and how to change it.

After you've created, traced, or even legitimately borrowed someone else's artwork, there's always that period where you look at the artwork and you realize that it's not quite right. That's where this chapter comes in. No, I won't do your finishing for you, but I'll show you how to take advantage of Illustrator's many tools to get the best end result, from slight control-handle manipulations to massive scalings and rotations, to dramatic effects created with the Pathfinder palette.

The focus of this chapter is modifying individual paths and the points on those paths by cutting them, combining them, and adjusting them.

Learning How to Select a Path for Editing

The key to editing a path is learning how to select that path. Maybe you don't want the whole path, just a section, or maybe only a point. This section explains the selection tools and how to use them. In the Selection tool area (top of the toolbox), four selection tools are visible.

Selection methods

If there is one group of tools in Illustrator you absolutely must have, it is the set of five selection tools (one of them is a pop-up tool). As in most applications, to alter something (move, scale, and so on), you must first select it. When you draw a new path or when you paste in Illustrator, the program automatically selects the object you're working on. However, as soon as you draw another path, Illustrator deselects the preceding object and Illustrator automatically selects the new path. The selection tools let you select paths and perform additional manipulations on them. Illustrator's five selection tools are the Selection tool, the Direct Selection tool, the Group Selection tool, the Magic Wand tool, and the Lasso tool, as shown in Figure 5-1:

   Figure 5-1: The five selection tools

The following gives a list of these tools and what they do. You can either click them in the Toolbox to select them (they're all housed together with the Selection tool), or you can press a keyboard shortcut to active them.

✦ **Selection tool:** This tool, which looks like an arrow head pointing diagonally up, allows you to select an object, path, or an bunch of paths at one time. You can press V to activate it.

✦ **Direct Selection tool:** You use this tool, which looks like a diagonally pointing white arrow, to select parts of an object or path. It's more designed to select items on which you want to perform detailed work.

✦ **Group Selection tool:** As its name suggests, this tool, which looks like a white arrow with a plus sign, allows you to select hierarchal groups of objects. Each click allows you to increase a wider range of objects around the core object.

✦ **Magic Wand tool:** You use this tool, which looks like a magician's wand, to select groups of objects whose colored pixels are similar in color. Because this tool detects drastic changes in color, you shouldn't use it for objects with subtle color differences.

✦ **Lasso tool:** This tool, which — you guessed — looks like a lasso, lets you draw around the objects that you want to choose. You generally use this tool for unevenly shaped objects. Because this tool detects large differences in contrast, you use this tool if your object contrasts sharply with surrounding objects.

The specific function of each tool is discussed in greater detail later in the chapter. Before this discussion, however, you need to know that there are different categories of selecting, depending on what you want to select. These categories are: Intrapath, Path, Group, IntraGroup and Selecting All.

Intrapath selecting

Intrapath selecting means that you select at least one point or segment within a path — usually with the Direct Selection tool — to adjust individual points, segments, and series of points as shown in Figure 5-2. Note that the Anchor points appear as solid squares and that unselected points are hollow squares. Intrapath selecting also allows you to use most of the functions in the Object menu, such as hiding, locking, or grouping. But these options lock, hide, or group the entire path.

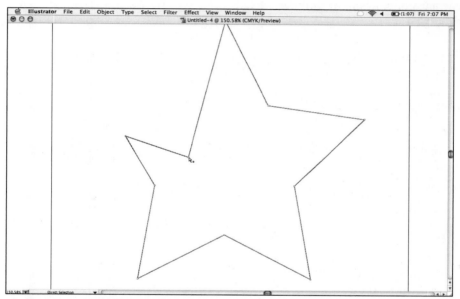

Figure 5-2: Intrapath selection on paths

Note   Although you may select just a portion of the path, many features affect the entire path, not just the selected points. For example, most of the attributes available in the Object menu (including Pathfinder, Masking, and Compound Paths) affect the entire path even when only a point or segment is selected.

Path selecting

Path selecting means that all points and segments on a path are selected. When you click a path using the Group Selection tool or the Selection tool, Illustrator automatically selects the entire path. Drawing a marquee (a dotted rectangle indicating a selection) entirely around a path with the Direct Selection tool also selects the entire path. All the capabilities from Intrapath selecting are available, such as the entire Object menu and the Arrange menu and most of the functions in the Filter menu. After you select a path, the entire path is affected by moving, transforming, cutting, copying and pasting, and deleting. An example of Path selecting is shown in Figure 5-3.

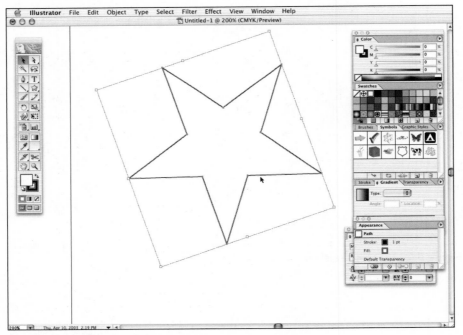

Figure 5-3: Path selection

Group selecting

You can select and affect a series of grouped paths as if it were a single object by using Group selecting. All paths in the group are affected in the same way as paths that you select with Path selecting. The Selection tool selects entire grouped paths at once. If you use the Group Selection tool instead, you need a series of clicks to select a group of paths. Figure 5-4 shows what you can accomplish with Group selecting.

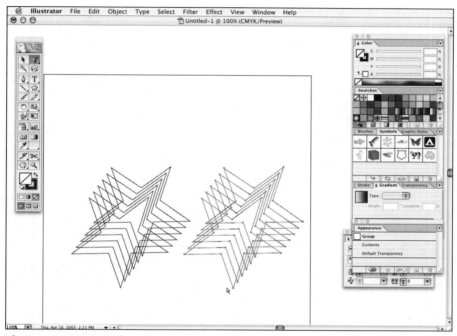

Figure 5-4: Group selection

IntraGroup selecting

You can select and affect groups of paths within other groups by using IntraGroup selecting. All paths in the group are affected in the same way as paths that you select with Path selection. Use the Group Selection tool to select a group of paths at once. Each successive click the same path selects another set of grouped paths that the initial path is within. IntraGroup selecting is demonstrated in Figure 5-5.

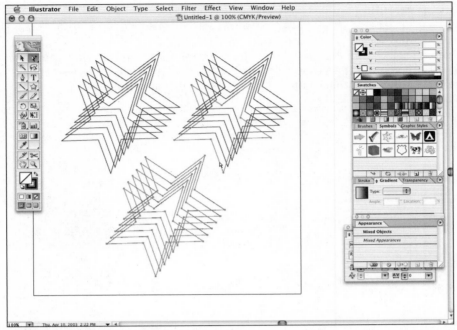

Figure 5-5: IntraGroup selection

Selecting All

To select everything in your document that hasn't been hidden or locked, choose
Select ➪ Select All, or press ⌘+A (Ctrl+A). This selects all the points and segments
on every path that hasn't been locked in the document. You can also select everything in the document by drawing a marquee around all the paths with any selection tool.

Normally, after you select something new, everything that you have previously
selected becomes deselected. To continue to select additional points, paths, or segments, you must hold down the Shift key while clicking.

The Shift key normally works as a toggle when used with a selection tool, selecting
anything that is not selected and deselecting anything that is currently selected.
Each selection tool works with the Shift key a little differently, as described in the
following sections.

Tip

To deselect everything that is selected, click a part of the document that is empty (where you can see the Pasteboard or Artboard) without using the Shift key. You also can deselect everything by choosing Select ⇨ Deselect All, or by pressing ⌘+Shift+A (Ctrl+Shift+A). Another choice under the Select menu is to Reselect. This option enables you to select the last thing selected.

You can use the selection tools for manually moving selected points, segments, and paths. You use automatic or computer-assisted manipulations when you type in specific values in the Transform palette, for example. The next few sections cover the selection tools and their functions.

Deciding which selection tool to use

After the brief overview of the selection tools, you'll need to choose which one works best in which cases. For specific path editing, use the Selection, Direct Selection, Group selection, or Bounding box tools. For selecting areas or colored sections, use the Magic Wand or Lasso tools. The next sections describe the functions of the tools.

Using the Selection tool

The Selection tool selects entire paths or complete groups at one time. You can't select just one point or a few points on a path with the Selection tool. Instead, the entire path on which that point lies is selected (all the anchor points turn black). Drawing a marquee (clicking and dragging as a box forms behind the cursor) around parts of paths or entire paths also selects entire paths.

Bounding Box and the Selection tool

Illustrator has a Bounding Box that you can access when you use the Selection tool. This Bounding Box (see Figure 5-6) enables you to move or scale the selected objects by simply dragging the control handles. When you select an object, a Bounding Box appears around the whole object or around all the objects in a selected group. This Bounding Box has handles on the four corners as well as handles at the midpoint of each side of the box. These handles enable you to scale the object any way you like. By holding down the Shift key and dragging one of the corner handles, you can easily scale the selected object proportionately. You can also rotate the object using the Bounding Box. Look for the curved arrow to indicate rotation. You can enable or disable the Bounding Box by choosing Show Bounding Box/Hide Bounding Box or by pressing ⌘-Shift-B (Ctrl-Shift-B) under the View menu.

Figure 5-6: The Bounding Box is always rectangular.

Using the Direct Selection tool

To select individual points, line segments, or a series of specific points within a path, you need to use the Direct Selection tool. This tool is the only tool that enables you to select something less than an entire path. You can also draw a marquee over a portion of a path to select only those points and segments within the area of the marquee. If the marquee surrounds an entire path, the entire path is selected. You can also select individual points or a series of points on different paths by drawing a marquee around just those points. You can switch to the Direct Selection tool by pressing A on the keyboard. Press A again to choose the Group Selection tool. Another press of the A key takes you back to the Direct Selection tool.

You use the Shift key with the Direct Selection tool to select additional points or segments or to deselect previously selected points. If you press the Shift key, the Selection tool works as a toggle between selecting and deselecting points or segments. You can use the Shift key in this way to add to or subtract from the current selection.

After you select a point, or series of points, you can manipulate those selected points by moving, transforming (via the transformation tools), and applying certain filters to them. You can select and modify individual segments and series of segments in the same way you transform points.

Using the Group Selection tool

You can find the Group Selection tool as a popup tool under the Direct Selection tool. It first selects a path, then the group that the path is in, then the group that the other group with the path is in, and so on.

For the Group Selection tool to work properly, choose the first path or paths by either clicking them or drawing a marquee around them. To select the group that a particular path is in, however, requires you to click one of the initially selected paths. To select the next group also requires a click; if you drag at any point, only the paths you drag over are selected. For example, suppose that you have a line of bicycles that belong to a group and each individual bicycle is also a group and each wheel on each bicycle is a group and each spoke is a separate path. Using the Group Selection tool, you can click once on a spoke to select it and if you click it again, you select the wheel group; a third click selects the whole bicycle and the fourth click the entire line of bicycles.

Caution   Still confused about how the Shift key selects and deselects paths? The Shift key is an odd duck when used with the Group Selection tool. What happens when you click an unselected path with this tool while holding down the Shift key? The path is selected. But what happens when you click a selected path? The process deselects just one path. What makes more sense is if you click again with the Shift key, and it then deselects the entire group. Nope. This isn't what happens. The Shift key works as a toggle on the one path you are clicking—selecting it, deselecting it, and so on.

Dragging a marquee around paths with the Group Selection tool works only for the first series of clicks; dragging another marquee, even over the already-selected paths, just reselects those paths.

Tip   You can use the keyboard to jump around each of the selection tools. No matter what tool you select in the toolbox, pressing ⌘ (Ctrl) toggles to and enables the Selection tool while you keep the ⌘ (Ctrl) key held down. You can toggle between the regular Selection tool and the Direct Selection tool by pressing V for the Selection and A for Direct Selection. When you have the Direct Selection tool, press Option (Alt) and you access the Group Selection tool!

If you have selected several paths at once, clicking a selected path selects only the group that the selected path is in. If other selected paths are in different groups, those groups are not selected until you click those paths with the Group Selection tool. However, clicking multiple times on any of the paths in the selected group continues to select "up" in the group that the selected path is part of.

The Group Selection tool is the most useful when dealing with graphs and blends, but it can be used in a number of other situations to greatly enhance your control of what is and is not selected. People who are always ungrouping and regrouping paths can greatly benefit from using the Group Selection tool. In fact, proper use of this tool prevents you from ever having to ungroup and regroup objects for work-flow reasons.

Tip   You can access the Group Selection tool when the Direct Selection tool is selected by holding down the Option (Alt) key. If the Direct Selection tool is not chosen, then select it by holding down the ⌘ (Ctrl) key (you may have to press V for the Selection and A for Direct Selection).

The Group Selection tool also selects compound paths. One click selects an individual path within the compound path, and the second click selects the entire compound path.

Using the Magic Wand tool

The Magic Wand tool lets you make a selection based on the same stroke, color, stroke color, opacity, and blending mode. Choose the Magic Wand tool from the toolbox (it looks like a magic wand) or press Y. Like Photoshop's Magic Wand, you make selections with a click of the tool. To select with the Magic Wand tool, click the object that you want to select. All of the objects with the same attributes are selected.

You can set the options on the Magic Wand tool for selecting objects. Access the Magic Wand palette by double clicking on the Magic Wand tool, or choose Window ➪ Magic Wand. The options you can set are:

✦ **Fill Color:** Check the Fill color to make your Magic Wand selection based on the object's fill color.

✦ **Stroke Color:** Use the Stroke Color option to make a Magic Wand selection based on the object's stroke color.

✦ **Stroke Weight:** Choose Stroke Weight to base your Magic Wand selection on the object's stroke weight.

✦ **Opacity:** Check the Opacity option to base your Magic Wand selection on the object's opacity.

✦ **Blending Mode:** Use the Blending Mode option to make a Magic Wand selection based on the object's blending mode.

✦ **Tolerance:** Set the tolerance for the Fill Color, Stroke Color, Stroke Weight, and Opacity. You can set the tolerance in pixels between 0 and 255 (RGB objects) and 0 to 100 (CMYK objects). Setting the tolerance low will result in a selection very close in the original selected object. A higher tolerance will select more objects.

Using the Lasso tool

The Lasso tool lets you make a free form selection by dragging the mouse. Access the Lasso tool by choosing the Lasso from the toolbox (it looks like a rope) or by pressing Q. The Lasso tool selects paths and anchor points by dragging around the path or line segment.

With both the Magic Wand and Lasso tools, you can add to a selection by holding down the Shift key while clicking with either tool. Subtract from a selection by holding down the Option (Alt) key.

Selecting, moving, and deleting entire paths

Usually, the best way to select a path that is not currently selected is by clicking it with the regular Selection tool, which highlights all the points on the path and enables you to move, transform, or delete that entire path.

To select more than one path, you can use a number of different methods. The most basic method is to hold down the Shift key and click the successive paths with the Selection tool, selecting one more path with each Shift-click. Shift-clicking a selected path with the Selection tool deselects that particular path. Drawing a marquee around paths with the Selection tool selects all paths that at least partially fall into the area drawn by the marquee. When drawing a marquee, be sure to place the cursor in an area where there is nothing. Finding an empty spot may be difficult to do in Preview mode because fills from various paths may cover any white space available. Drawing a marquee with the Selection tool while depressing the Shift key selects nonselected paths and deselects currently selected paths.

To select just a portion of a path, you must use the Direct Selection tool. To select an anchor point or a line segment, simply click it. To select several individual points or paths, click the points or paths you want to select while holding down the Shift key. You can select series of points and paths by dragging a marquee across the desired paths.

Individually select points become solid squares. If these points are smooth, curved corner, or combination corner points, control handles appear from the selected anchor point.

Illustrator doesn't tell you when a straight-line segment is selected or which one is selected. The first time you click a straight-line segment, all the anchor points on the path appear as hollow squares, telling you that something on that path is selected. Selected points turn black, and curved line segments have one or more control handles and control handle lines sticking out from the ending anchor points. Straight-line segments don't do anything when selected. The inventive side of you may think that you can get around this problem by dragging the selected segments to a new location or by copying and pasting them and then undoing. However, this solution doesn't work because of Illustrator's habit of selecting all points on paths when undoing operations on those paths.

Tip   When you run into the problem of not knowing whether a straight-line segment is selected, do the following: Instead of moving, copying, or pasting, simply whack the good ol' Delete (Backspace) key and whatever disappears is what you had selected. Now when you undo, just the segments that were selected before the deletion are still selected, not the entire path.

If paths are part of either a compound path or a group, all other paths in that compound path or group are also selected.

To move a path, click the path and drag (in one motion) with the Selection tool. To move several paths, select the paths and then click an already-selected path with the regular Selection tool or the Direct Selection tool and drag.

Tip   If you have been selecting multiple paths by using the Shift key, be sure to release the Shift key before clicking and dragging on the selection. If the Shift key is still pressed, the clicked path becomes deselected and no paths move. If this does happen, just Shift-click the paths that were deselected and drag.

To delete an entire path, select it with the Selection tool and press the Delete (Backspace) key. To delete multiple paths, select them and press the Delete (Backspace) key. Remember that line segments exist only when one point is on either side of the segment. Even if the line segment is not selected, if one of its anchor points is deleted, the line segment is also deleted. A path is made up of points, and those points are connected via segments. If the points are gone, the paths disappear along with them. But if you delete all the segments, all the points can still remain.

You can duplicate portions of paths when pressing the Option (Alt) key while releasing the mouse button. Duplicating segments also duplicates the anchor points on either side of that segment.

Often, many objects need to be moved and duplicated at the same time. To duplicate paths when moving them, hold down the Option (Alt) key while the mouse button is pressed.

Using different selection options

Illustrator has several special select functions (they are found under the Select menu). You use the Select functions for selecting paths with common or specific attributes. The Select functions make mundane, repetitive tasks easy to accomplish by doing all the nasty work for you.

To access the Select functions, choose any of them from the Select menu as shown in Figure 5-7.

Tip   Since Illustrator 8, you can redo the last selection type by choosing Reselect, or by pressing ⌘+6 (Ctrl + 6) from the Select menu.

Under the Select menu are the following:

✦ **All:** Choosing this selects everything in the document.

✦ **Deselect:** Choosing this function will deselect everything in the document.

✦ **Reselect:** This function will reselect the last selection.

✦ **Inverse:** The Select Inverse function is perfect for selecting all paths that aren't selected. You can use this selection function to instantly select paths that are hidden, guides, and other unlocked objects that are hard to select.

✦ **Next Object Above:** Choosing this selects the next object above the selected object in stacking order (stacking order is the same as Layer order). See Chapter 7 for more on stacking order.

✦ **Next Object Below:** This function selects the next object below the selected object in stacking order.

✦ **Same:** Here you can choose to select the same blending mode, fill and stroke, fill color, opacity, stroke color, stroke weight, style, symbol instance, or threaded block series (see Figure 5-8). For more on threaded blocks, see Chapter 8.

Figure 5-7: The Select functions found in the Select menu

Figure 5-8: The Same options found under the Select menu

✦ **Object:** In this area, you can choose to select the all objects on the same layer, the object's direction handles, brush strokes, clipping masks, stray points, and text objects (see Figure 5-9).

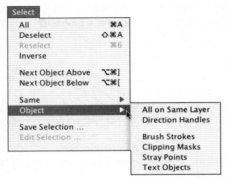

Figure 5-9: The Object options found under the Select menu

✦ **Save Selection:** Use this to save a particular selection.

✦ **Edit Selection:** Use this to edit a saved selection.

Select Same Blending Mode

Same Blending Mode (Select ⇨ Same ⇨ Blending Mode) selects objects that have the same Blending mode attributes of the currently selected object. The objects are selected regardless of their other attributes as long as the Blending Modes are the same.

Select Same Fill & Stroke

Same Fill & Stroke (Select ⇨ Same ⇨ Fill and Stroke) selects objects that have almost exactly the same paint style as the paint style of the selected object. The following information has to be the same:

✦ The Fill color (as defined in the next section)

✦ The Stroke color

✦ The Stroke weight

Some items in the object's Paint Style that don't matter (that is, they don't prevent Same Paint Style from selecting an object) are any of the Stroke style attributes and the overprinting options.

Tip

If you select more than one object, don't select objects with different paint styles. If you have different paint styles selected, the selection function does not select the. The best thing to do with Same Paint Style, as with Same Fill Color, is to select only one object.

If you have a spot color selected, the Select functions select all other occurrences of that spot color, regardless of the tint. This can be troublesome when you want to select only a certain tint value of that spot color, not all of the tint values.

Select Same Fill Color

Same Fill Color function (Select ➪ Same ➪ Fill Color) selects objects that have the same Fill color as the currently selected object. This function selects objects regardless of their Stroke color, Stroke weight, or Stroke pattern. If you select objects with different fills, Same Fill Color function won't work, but you may select two objects that have the same fill.

Same Fill Color function considers different tints of spot colors to be the same color. This function works in two ways. First, if you select one object with any tint value of a spot color, Same Fill Color selects all other objects with the same spot color, regardless of the tint. Second, you can select more than one object, no matter what tint each object contains, provided that the selected objects have the same spot color.

Cross-Reference For more on Spot colors, see Chapter 6.

Tip To be selected with Same Fill Color, process color fills have to have the same values as the original. Even single colors, such as yellow, have to be the same percentage. The Same Fill Color function considers 100% Yellow and 50% Yellow to be two separate colors.

If you use spot colors often, Select Same Fill Color is extremely useful. It enables you to instantly select all objects that are filled with the spot color, regardless of the tint, of the selected object or the tints of the selected objects.

Same Fill Color also selects objects that are filled with the same gradient, regardless of the angle or the starting or ending point of the gradient. This function does not, however, select objects that have the same pattern fill.

Select Same Opacity

Same Opacity (Select ➪ Same ➪ Opacity) selects objects that have the same Opacity value regardless of the other attributes of the object. Choosing Select ➪ Same ➪ Opacity selects all of the objects with the same opacity value of the currently selected object.

Select Same Stroke Color

Same Stroke Color (Select ➪ Same ➪ Stroke Color) selects objects that have the same Stroke color, regardless of the Stroke weight or style and regardless of the type of fill.

The color limitations that are defined in the Select Same Fill Color section, earlier in the chapter, also apply to Same Stroke Color function.

Although you can choose a pattern for a Stroke that makes the Stroke look gray, the Same Stroke Color function does not select other objects that have the same Stroke pattern.

Select Same Stroke weight

Illustrator's Same Stroke weight function (Select ⇨ Same ⇨ Stroke Weight) selects objects that have the same Stroke weight, regardless of the stroke color, the style, or the fill color.

Even if the stroke is a pattern, Illustrator selects other paths that have the same stroke weight as the patterned stroke when you apply this function.

Don't select more than one Stroke weight if you select more than one object. If you have selected different Stroke weights, Illustrator does not select any paths when you choose Select ⇨ Same ⇨ Stroke Weight. The best thing to do with the Same Stroke Weight function, as with Same Fill Color and Same Paint Style, is to select only one object.

Select Same Style

Same Style (Select ⇨ Same ⇨ Style) selects objects that have the same Style attributes. Choosing Select ⇨ Same ⇨ Style selects all of the objects with the same style attributes of the currently selected object.

Select Same Symbol Instance

Same Symbol Instance (Select ⇨ Same ⇨ Symbol Instance) selects objects that have the same Symbol Instances. Choosing Select ⇨ Same ⇨ Symbol Instance selects all of the objects with the same Symbol Instance of the currently selected object.

Select Same Link Block Series

Same Link Block Series (Select ⇨ Same ⇨ Link Block Series) selects all of the threaded text link blocks with the initial selection. If you select only one block of text, choosing Select ⇨ Same ⇨ Link Block Series selects all of the text that is linked with the currently selected text block.

Custom Paint Style Selections

Unfortunately, you cannot do multiple-type selections with any of the special selection functions. You cannot, for example, select at one time all of the objects that have the same Stroke color and Fill color, but have different Stroke weights.

The Lock Unselected command, which you activate by pressing Command+Option+Shift+2 (Ctrl+Alt+Shift+2), is the key to specifying multiple selection criteria. The following instructions describe how to perform multiple-type selections in a few steps:

1. **Select a representative object that has Stroke and Fill color that you want.**

2. **Choose Select ➪ Same ➪ Fill Color.** Illustrator selects all objects having the same Fill color as the original object, regardless of the objects' Stroke color.

3. **Press Command+Option+Shift+2 (Ctrl+Alt+Shift+2).** This locks any objects that are not selected. This step is a key step. The only objects that you can modify or select now are the ones that have the same Fill color.

4. **Choose Select ➪ Deselect , or press ⌘+Shift+A (Ctrl+Shift+A), and select the original object.** The original object now has both the Fill color and the Stroke color that you want to select.

5. **Choose Select ➪ Same ➪ Stroke Color.** Only objects that have the same Stroke and Fill colors are selected.

6. **Choose Object ➪ Unlock All, or press ⌘+Option+2 (Ctrl+alt+2) after you are done to make the other objects selectable.**

Select Masks

The Clipping Masks function (Select ➪ Object ➪ Clipping Masks) makes the process of manipulating masks much easier by showing you where masks are in the document.

Select Masks selects all the objects that are currently being used as masks. The only masks in the document that are not selected are the masks that are locked or hidden and the masks that are on layers that are locked or hidden.

Select Stray Points

The Select Stray Points function (Select ➪ Objects ➪ Stray Points) selects all isolated anchor points in the document. Individual anchor points don't print or preview. You can see them in Preview mode only when they are selected. After you cut portions of line segments, stray points often appear. These individual points often interfere with connecting other segments. You can't use this selection function enough.

You can mistakenly create stray points in various ways:

✦ Clicking once with the Pen tool creates a single anchor point.

✦ Deleting a line segment on a path that has two points by selecting the line segment with the Direct Selection tool and pressing Delete (Backspace) leaves behind the two anchor points.

    ✦ Using the Scissors tool to cut a path, and while deleting one side or another of the path, not selecting the points turns these points into stray points.

    ✦ Ungrouping an oval or rectangle in Illustrator 3.2 or older and then deleting just the frame of the shape leaves the center point in the document.

Bringing an Illustrator 4 or older document that has still-grouped rectangles or ovals into the CS version automatically deletes the center point and turns on the Show Center Point option in the Attributes palette. Choose Window ➪ Show Attributes or press F11.

Caution   Center points of objects are not stray points, and you cannot select them without selecting the object to which they belong. Center points of objects are visible when you choose the Show Center Point option in the Attributes palette. Selecting the center point of an object selects the entire object, and deleting the center point deletes the entire object.

Select Inverse

Select Inverse (Select ➪ Select ➪ Inverse) quickly selects all objects that are not currently selected while deselecting those objects that are currently selected. For example, if one object is selected and the document contains 15 other unlocked objects, the 15 objects will become selected, and the one object that was selected originally will become deselected.

Caution   Select Inverse does not cause locked or hidden objects to be selected and does not select guides unless guides are not locked. Objects on layers that are locked or hidden are not selected either.

Select Inverse is useful because selecting a few objects is usually quicker than selecting most objects. After you select the few objects, Select Inverse does all the work of selecting everything else.

When no objects are selected, Select Inverse selects all the objects, just as choosing Select ➪ Select All, or by pressing ⌘+A (Ctrl+A), would. When all objects are selected, Select Inverse deselects all the objects, just as choosing Select ➪ Deselect, or pressing ⌘+Shift+A (Ctrl+Shift+A), would.

Keeping and labeling a selection

After you have gone through any long process of selecting, you might want to save the selection, especially if you use a certain selection repeatedly. Photoshop has the ability to save selections, and now you can do the same in Illustrator. After you save a selection, you can make it reusable. To save a selection, create your selection first and then choose Select ➪ Save Selection. This will bring up the New Selection dialog box. Enter a name for your new selection and click OK. Figure 5-10 shows the New Selection dialog box. By choosing Select ➪ Edit Selection, you can change the name of the selection. You access a saved selection by choosing Select ➪ name of selection.

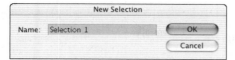

Figure 5-10: The New Selection dialog box

All on Same Layer

Select Objects on the Same Layer (Select ➪ Object ➪ All on Same Layer) selects all objects on the layer based on the currently selected object's layer.

Direction Handles

Choosing Select ➪ Object ➪ Direction Handles selects all of the direction handles on the currently selected object. This makes for easier editing of the object using its direction handles.

Brush Strokes

Select Object Brush Strokes (Select ➪ Object ➪ Brush Strokes) selects all brush strokes with the same attributes as the currently selected brush stroke.

Clipping Masks

Youc an select all clipping masks in your file by choosing Select ➪ Object ➪ Clipping Masks. Illustrator selects all unlocked and visible clipping masks, but the objects they mask are not selected.

Text Objects

Choose Select ➪ Objects ➪ Text Objects to select all text objects in your document. Illustrator selects all unlocked and unhidden objects.

Editing Paths in Illustrator

The path-editing tools are the Scissors tool; the Knife tool; and the Add Anchor Point, Delete Anchor Point, and Convert Anchor Point pop-up tools in the Pen tool slot. Clicking and holding down the Pen tool displays the Pen tool, Add Anchor Point, Delete Anchor Point, and Convert Anchor Point.

Dragging out to a path-editing tool replaces the default Pen tool with the newly selected pop-up tool. If you press the Caps Lock key at the same time that you choose a path-editing tool, the tool cursor resembles a cross hair. The cross-hair cursors enable precision positioning of cursors.

The purpose of each path-editing tool is:

✦ **Add Anchor Point tool:** You use this tool to add anchor points to an existing path. If you add an anchor point to a straight segment (one that has no control handles on either end), the anchor point becomes a straight corner point. If the segment is curved — meaning that you have at least one control handle for that segment — the new anchor point becomes a smooth point.

✦ **Delete Anchor Point tool:** This gets rid of the anchor point on which you click. Ilustrator creates a new segment between the anchor points that were on either side of the anchor point you clicked. If the anchor point on which you clicked is an end point, no new segment is drawn; instead, the next or previous anchor point on the path becomes the new end point.

✦ **Scissors tool:** You use this tool to split paths. Clicking with the Scissors tool on a closed path makes that path an open path with the End Points directly overlapping each other where the click occurred. Using the Scissors tool on an open path splits that open path into two separate open paths, each with an end point that overlaps the other open path's end point.

✦ **Knife tool:** Slices through path areas. The Knife tool is the only path-editing tool that doesn't require that you have paths selected; it works on all unlocked paths that fall under the blade. Use this to cut an object into two closed path objects.

✦ **Convert Direction Point tool:** The first is to simply change an anchor point from its current type of anchor point to a straight corner point by clicking and releasing it. You can also change the current type to Smooth by clicking and dragging on the anchor point. The second function is to move control handles individually by changing smooth points to curved corner points and by changing combination corner points and curved corner points to smooth points. (Straight corner points don't have any control handles, so using this method can't change them.)

You can add and remove anchor points in two different ways. I mentioned one method in Chapter 3, where I demonstrated how to add anchor points with the drawing tools and remove them simply by selecting them and pressing the Delete (Backspace) key.

The techniques that I cover in this chapter are unlike the methods discussed previously. Instead of adding new points that create an extension to an existing path, you learn how to add points in the middle of existing paths. Instead of deleting points and the line segments connected to them, you learn how to remove points between two anchor points and watch as a new line segment connects those two anchor points.

In Figure 5-11, the figure on the left is smoother than the one on the right that has had anchor points removed. That path will have to be altered to resemble the original path. I discuss these and other issues throughout this chapter.

Caution Figure 5-11 shows a very simple example. The Delete Anchor Point tool is most often used to remove unnecessary points from overly complicated drawings.

Figure 5-11: Adding anchor points after they've been removed does not return the shape to its original form. The figure on the left is much smoother and pleasing than the choppy figure on the right that has had anchor points removed.

Editing with anchor points

To add an anchor point to an existing path, select the Add Anchor Point tool and click a line segment of a path. You may not place an anchor point directly on top of another anchor point, but you can get pretty close. Figure 5-12 shows a path before and after several anchor points are added to it.

Tip I like to select the paths to which I am adding anchor points before I start actually adding the points. This technique ensures that I don't accidentally get the annoying message "Can't Add Anchor Point. Please use the Add Anchor Point tool on a segment of a path." It seems that if there is just one point in the middle of a path, that's where I end up clicking to add the point. After I add one point, the path becomes selected automatically.

Tip If that annoying message really bugs you, click the Don't show this message again box and instead you'll get a quiet noise alerting you that you can't add the anchor point.

Anchor points added to paths via the Add Anchor Point tool are either smooth points or straight corner points, depending on the segment where the new anchor point is added. If the segment has two straight corner points on either side of it, then the new anchor point is a straight corner point. If one of the anchor points is any type of anchor point other than a straight corner point, the new anchor point is a smooth point.

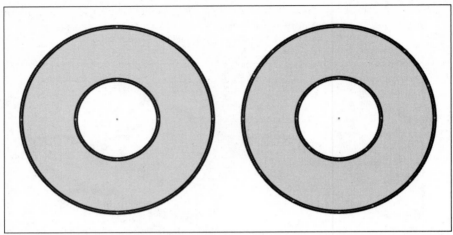

Figure 5-12: Adding anchor points to a path doesn't alter the shape of the path but allows the path to be modified more easily than if the points weren't added.

The Add Anchor Points function

The Add Anchor Points function (Object ➪ Path ➪ Add Anchor Points) adds new anchor points between every pair of existing anchor points it can find. New anchor points are always added halfway between existing anchor points.

Note   Add Anchor Points is related to the Add Anchor Point tool. This function adds anchor points the same way as the tool does, only more efficiently. Points that are added to a smooth segment are automatically smooth points; points added to a straight segment are automatically corner points.

For example, if you have one line segment with an anchor point on each end, Add Anchor Points adds one anchor point to the segment, exactly in the middle of the two anchor points. If you draw a rectangle and apply the Add Anchor Points function, Illustrator adds four new anchor points: one at the top, one at the bottom, one on the left side, and one on the right side.

Figure 5-13 shows an object that has had the Add Anchor Points function applied three times.

Tip   Want to know how many points Illustrator adds to your path when you apply the Add Anchor Points function? Each time you reapply the function, the number of anchor points doubles on a closed path and is one less than doubled on an open path.

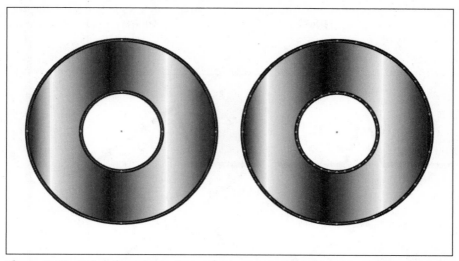

Figure 5-13: Using the Add Anchor points command doubles the number of anchor points evenly between existing points.

Adding Anchor Points is useful before using the Punk & Bloat filter and the Scribble and Tweak filter, and before using any other filter that bases its results on the number and position of anchor points.

Cross-Reference
For more on the Scribble filter, see Chapter 9, for more on effects, filters and effects, see Chapter 12.

Tip
If you need to add a large number of anchor points quickly, use the Roughen filter (found under Filter ⇨ Distort&Transform ⇨ Roughen) with a size of 0% and the detail at how many anchor points you want per inch. When you use Roughen, the anchor points are equally distributed, regardless of where the original anchor points were in the selected path (as opposed to Add Anchor Points, which places new points between existing ones, resulting in "clumping" in detailed areas).

Removing anchor points

Removing anchor points is a little trickier than adding them. Depending on where you remove the anchor point, you may adversely change the flow of the line between the two anchor points on either side of it, as shown in Figure 5-14. If the point removed had any control handles, the removal usually results in a more drastic change than if the anchor point had been a straight corner point. This situation occurs if control handles on the anchor point being removed at least half the aspect of the curve. A straight corner point affects only the location of the line, not the shape of its curve.

Figure 5-14: Removing an anchor point can drastically alter the shape of the original path.

To remove an anchor point, click an existing anchor point with the Delete Anchor Point tool. Like the Add Anchor Point tool, you can remove points without first selecting the path, but, of course, if the path is not selected, you can't see it or the points that you want to remove. If you miss and don't click an anchor point, you will get a message informing you that to remove an anchor point, you must click one.

After you remove anchor points, you cannot usually just add them back with the Add Anchor Point tool. Considering that the flow of the path changes when you remove a point, adding a point — even the correct type of point — does not give the same result as just undoing the point deletion.

If only two points are on an open path, the anchor point you click is deleted and so is the segment connecting it to the sole remaining anchor point. If there are only two points on a closed path, both line segments from the anchor point you click are deleted along with that point, leaving only one anchor point remaining.

Simplifying paths by removing anchor points

Some artwork can be unnecessarily complicated, with many more anchor points than are actually needed. These additional anchor points most often occur with artwork that has been traced by Illustrator's Auto Trace tool or using Clip Art. Unfortunately, Illustrator doesn't have a built-in method for cleaning up messy paths (the Cleanup function isn't it, unfortunately). There are, however, a few solutions you might look into:

✦ **Select the object and choose Object ➪ Path ➪ Simplify.** Doing this evenly removes anchor points.

✦ **Manually remove points via the Delete Anchor Point tool.** This takes forever, but with patience you'll get good results. Unfortunately, the tool doesn't care what happens to the paths you're deleting from, and they'll change drastically in shape with each point removal.

✦ **Pick up a copy of ILLOM Toolbox from Illom Development** (www.Illom.se/prod/). ILLOM Toolbox is designed primarily to fix artwork with too many points. It contains an amazing set of tools that can be used for that and also for other related types of work.

Removing anchor points using Simplify

Under the Path submenu of the Object menu is a wonderful command called Simplify. Use Simplify to remove anchor points. The Simplify dialog box shown in Figure 5-15 has four areas to adjust:

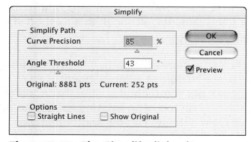

Figure 5-15: The Simplify dialog box

✦ **Curve Precision:** Adjust the Curve Precision by dragging the slider. Be sure to check the preview box first to see how much you want to keep the original curve.

✦ **Angle Threshold:** Adjusts the smoothness of the corners.

✦ **Straight Lines:** Creates straight lines between anchor points, even if they were curved in the original.

✦ **Show Original:** Check this to see the original path behind the path you are simplifying.

Figure 5-16 shows the results of applying the Simplify to an illustration with way too many anchor points.

Figure 5-16: The original path (left) had 8,881 points; the path after using Simplify (right) has 252 points.

Splitting paths

To change a single path into two separate paths that together make up a path equal in length to the original, you must use the Scissors tool. You can also split paths by selecting and deleting anchor points or line segments, although this method shortens the overall length of the two paths.

To split a path with the Scissors tool, click anywhere on a path. Initially, it doesn't seem like much happens. If you clicked in the middle of a line segment, a new anchor point appears. (Actually, two appear, but the second is directly on top of the first, so you see only one.) If you click directly on top of an existing anchor point, nothing at all seems to happen, but Illustrator actually creates another anchor point on top of the one that you clicked.

After clicking with the Scissors tool, you have separated the path into two separate sections, but it appears that there is still only one path because the two sections are both selected. To see the individual paths, deselect them by pressing ⌘+Shift+A (Ctrl+Shift+A) and select one side with the Selection tool. After you split a path, you may move one half independently of the other half, as shown in Figure 5-17.

The anchor points created with the Scissors tool either become smooth points or straight corner points, depending on the type of anchor point that is next along the path. If the line segment to the next anchor point has a control handle coming out of that anchor point that affects the line segment, the new end point becomes a smooth point. If there is no control handle for the line segment, the end point becomes a straight corner point.

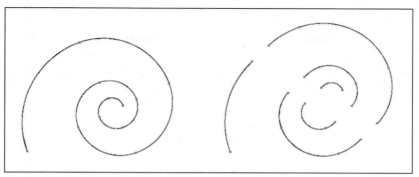

Figure 5-17: The original path (left); the path after splitting and moving the two pieces apart (right)

You cannot use the Scissors tool on a line's end point—only on segments and anchor points that are not end points.

Tired of those annoying warning boxes when you click where you shouldn't with the Scissors tool (or the Add Anchor Points tool, or the Delete Anchor Points tool, or the Convert Direction Point tool)? You can turn those warnings off by clicking a Don't show again checkbox when the warning shows up. If you want those warning boxes back, click Reset All Warning Dialogs button in the General Preferences by pressing ⌘+K (Ctrl+K).

Sectioning and repeating paths

Illustrator provides several capabilities that allow for multiple types of dividing and duplicating of paths, even paths that aren't selected. This section discusses those different features as well as the tool that makes this possible: the Knife tool.

The Knife tool

The Knife tool is located in the same area as the Scissors tool. The Knife tool divides paths into smaller sections as it slices through them. Those sections are initially selected, but they're not grouped. Figure 5-18 shows a path before and after it crosses paths with the Knife.

Pressing the Option (Alt) key when using the Knife tool cuts in a straight line rather than a curved one. The Shift key constrains the straight line to 45° angles when you also press the Option(Alt) key.

Remember that the Knife tool works on all paths that are under the existing path, selected or not.

Figure 5-18: The original path (left) and the resulting paths (right) after being dragged apart

The Slice tool

Another tool that looks like it cuts is the Slice tool. It does cut a path in sections. If you are creating artwork for the Web, this is one of the tools to use. The Slice tool slices the artwork into sections that are independent, each with its own specific information.

 For more on slicing for the Web and the Slice tool, see Chapter 17.

Reshaping paths

You can reshape paths using the Reshape tool, which is housed with the Scale tool in the toolbox. Using the Reshape tool gets results, but maybe not exact editing. The great use for the Reshape tool is to edit multiple paths at the same time.

To use the Reshape tool (see Figure 5-19) on any path, just click where you want to bend the path and drag. To use the Reshape tool on several paths at once, first select the paths with the Direct Selection or Lasso tools, then use the Reshape tool to drag-select the point(s) you want to move. You must select at least one point that is not a Straight Corner point on each path. Then drag on a Reshape-selected point; Illustrator moves all the curved points as well.

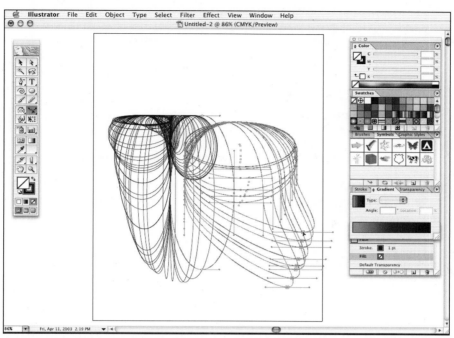

Figure 5-19: The paths being reshaped using the Reshape tool

Cleaning up a path

Cleanup removes three unwanted elements from Illustrator documents: stray points, unpainted objects, and empty text paths. Cleanup works on the entire document, regardless of what is selected. You apply this command by choosing Object ➪ Path ➪ Cleanup. The Cleanup dialog box is shown in Figure 5-20.

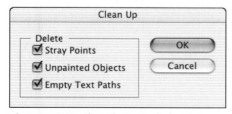

Figure 5-20: The Cleanup dialog box

Note Cleanup doesn't work on locked or hidden paths, paths turned into guides, or paths on locked or hidden layers.

The Delete options in the Cleanup dialog box are:

✦ **Stray Points:** Selects and deletes any little points flying around. These points can cause all sorts of trouble, as a point can have paint attributes but can't print. This option actually deletes the points.

Note Select All Stray Points under the Select menu only selects the points, but you have to press the Delete (Backspace) key to delete them.

✦ **Unpainted Objects:** Gets rid of any paths that are Filled and Stroked with None, and that aren't masks (masks always have fills and strokes of None).

✦ **Empty Text Paths:** Finds any text paths with no characters and deletes them.

Note Empty Text Paths is not the same as the old Revert Text Paths from Illustrator 5/5.5, which changed empty text paths back into standard paths.

If you aren't sure if your document contains these three items, run Cleanup. If none of these items are found, a dialog box appears telling you so.

Offsetting a path

Offset Path (choose Object ➪ Path ➪ Offset Path) draws a new path around the outside or inside of an existing path. The distance from the existing path is the distance that you specify in the Offset Path dialog box, which is shown in Figure 5-21. In a sense, you are creating a stroke, outlining it, and uniting it with the original all in one action. You can specify the distance the path is to be offset by entering a value in the Offset box.

A positive number in the Offset Path dialog box creates the new path outside the existing path, and a negative number creates the new path inside the existing path. When the path is closed, figuring out where Illustrator will create the new path is easy. When working with an open path, for example, a vertical line, the outside is the left side and the inside is the right side of the path.

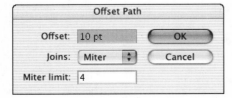

Figure 5-21: The Offset Path dialog box

The Joins option enables you to select from different types of joins at the corners of the new path. The choices are Miter, Round, and Bevel, and the result is the same effect that you get if you choose those options as the stroke style for a stroke.

The Miter Limit affects the miter size only when you select the Miter option from the Joins pop-up menu. However, the option is available when you select round and bevel joins. Just ignore the Miter Limit when you are using round or bevel joins. (You cannot use a value that is less than 1.)

Often, when you are offsetting a path, the new, resulting path overlaps itself. This creates *skiddles*, which are small, undesirable bumps in a path. If the skiddles are within a closed-path area, select the new path and choose Unite from the Pathfinder palette. If the skiddles are outside the closed-path area, choose Divide from the Pathfinder palette and then select and delete each of the skiddles.

Tip If you are thinking of using the Scale tool rather than Offset Path, the Scale tool does something totally different than Offset Path. Offset Path offsets lines around the original path equally. The Scale tool enlarges or reduces the path but does not add lines. Unless you are using a perfect square or circle, stick to Offset Path. That way, you get an even placement of the new line accurately around or inside the selected path.

Outlining a path

Outline Path creates a path around an existing path's stroke. The width of the new path is directly related to the width of the stroke.

I use Outline Path for two reasons. The first and most obvious reason is to fill a stroke with a gradient so you can view a pattern inside a stroke. The second reason is that when you transform an outlined stroke, the effect is often different from the effect that results from transforming a stroked path. Scaling an outlined stroke changes the width of the stroke in the direction of the scale. The same is true when using the Free Distort filter, which also changes the width of the stroke in the direction of the scale. This sometimes results in a nonuniform stroke. Figure 5-22 shows the difference between transforming/distorting a Stroked path and an Outlined Stroke.

Some options to consider for outlining a path are:

✦ The End and Join attributes of the stroke's style determine how the ends and joins of the resulting stroke look.

✦ Outline Path creates problems for tight corners. It causes overlaps that are similar to those generated by Offset Path.

Note Using a Dash pattern on the stroke and using Outline Path changes the stroke back to a solid line and then outlines it.

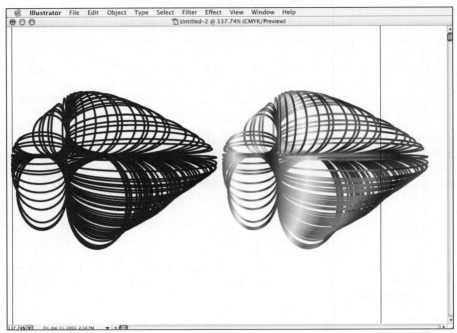

Figure 5-22: The original stroked path is to the left. The path on the right was outlined via Outline Path and then a gradient was added to the fill.

Looking under the Effects menu, you'll find a Path effect with the following options: Offset Path, Outline Object, and Outline Stroke. All of these are the same as what is found under the Object ⇨ Path menu. However, under Effects, you can always go back in and edit the options. Choosing the Path functions from under the Object menu has a more permanent result.

Cross-Reference   For more on the Effects menu see Chapter 13.

Averaging and joining

Averaging points is the process in which Illustrator determines the location of the points and figures out where the center of all the points is on a mean basis. Joining is the process in which either a line segment is drawn between two end points, or two end points are merged into a single anchor point.

Averaging and joining are done together when two end points need to change location to be one on top of the other and then merged into one point. You can perform these steps one at a time, or you can have Illustrator do both steps automatically with the Object ⇨ Path ⇨ Average menu or by pressing ⌘+Option-Shift+J (Ctrl+Alt+Shift+J).

Averaging points

To line up a series of points either horizontally or vertically, use the Average command. The Average command also works to place selected points one on top of the other. Figure 5-23 shows the different types of averaging—horizontal and vertical.

To average points horizontally, select the points to be averaged with the Direct Selection tool and choose Object ⇨ Path ⇨ Average or by pressing ⌘+Option+J (Ctrl+Alt+J). The Average dialog box (see Figure 5-24) appears, asking which type of averaging you want to do. In this case, choose Horizontal, which will move selected points only up and down.

Caution   Be sure to select the points to be averaged with the Direct Selection tool. If you select a path with either the Group Selection tool or the regular Selection tool, every point in the path will be averaged! This mistake can do quite a bit of damage when averaging both horizontally and vertically.

To average points vertically, choose the Vertical option in the Average dialog box. To average points both vertically and horizontally, choose Both. The Both option places all selected points on top of each other.

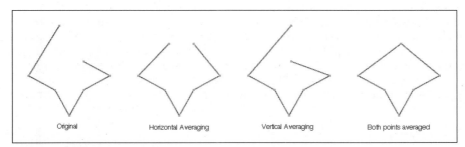

Figure 5-23: Different types of averaging

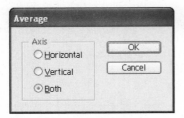

Figure 5-24: The Average dialog box lets you select Horizontal, Vertical, or Both.

When averaging points, Illustrator uses the mean method to determine the center. No, Illustrator isn't nasty to the points that it averages; rather, Illustrator adds together the coordinates of the points and then divides by the number of points. This provides the mean location of the center of the points.

If you want to average entire paths, see the Align and Distribution in Chapter 7.

Joining points

Joining is a tricky area to define. Illustrator's Join feature does two entirely different things. It joins two end points at different locations with a line segment, and it also combines two anchor points into one when they are placed one on top of the other.

To join two end points with a line segment, select just two end points in different locations (not on top of each other) with the Direct Selection tool and choose Object ➪ Path ➪ Join or by pressing ⌘+J ((Ctrl+J). Illustrator will form a line segment between the two points, resulting in a closed path as shown in Figure 5-25.

To combine two end points into a single anchor point, select the two points that are directly one over the other and choose Object ➪ Path ➪ Join or by pressing ⌘+J (Ctrl+J). The Join dialog box appears, asking what type of point you want to create when the two end points become one anchor point. If you choose smooth point, the point becomes a smooth point with two linked control handles. If you choose corner point, the point retains any control handle position that is part of it. And if no control handle is on the line, Illustrator does not place a control handle on that side of the anchor point.

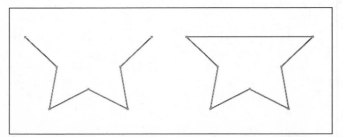

Figure 5-25: Joining two end points with a line segment

Not only can you join two separate paths, but you can also join together the end points on the same open path (overlapping end points) to create a closed path in the same way that two end points from different paths are joined.

To make sure that end points are overlapping, turn on the Snap to Point feature in General Preferences and drag one end point to the other with a selection tool. When the two points are close enough, the arrowhead cursor (normally black) becomes hollow. Release the mouse button when the arrowhead is hollow, and Illustrator places the two points one directly one above the other.

Another way to ensure that the end points are overlapping is to select them, and choose Object ➪ Path ➪ Average, or press ⌘+Option+J (Ctrl+Alt+J). Next, select the Both option in the Average dialog box.

Caution

When creating an anchor point out of two overlapping end points, make sure that the two points are precisely overlapping. If they are even the smallest distance apart, a line segment is drawn between the two points instead of transforming the two end points into a single anchor point. You can tell immediately whether the points are overlapping correctly when you select Join. If the Join dialog box appears, the points are overlapping. If it doesn't appear, and you get a warning dialog, the points are not overlapping, and it is best to undo the join.

Tip

To make the points overlap and join at once, press ⌘+Option+Shift-J (Ctrl+Alt+Shift+J). Doing this both averages and joins the selected end points. This method works only on end points. The end points are averaged both horizontally and vertically and are also joined into an anchor point that is a corner point, with control handle lines and control handles unchanged.

Joining has these limitations:

✦ Joins may not take place when one path is part of a different group than the other path. If the two paths are in the same base group (that is, not in any other groups before being grouped to the other path, even grouped by themselves), the end points can be joined.

✦ If one path is grouped to another object and the other object has not been previously grouped to the path, the end points will not join.

✦ The end points on text paths cannot be joined.

✦ The end points of guides cannot be joined.

If all the points in an open path are selected (as if the path is selected with the regular Selection tool), then choosing Object ➪ Path ➪ Join or pressing ⌘+J (Ctrl+J) automatically joins the end points. If the two end points are located directly one over the other, the Join dialog box appears, asking whether the new anchor point should be a smooth point or a corner point.

Joining is also useful for determining the location of end points when the end points are overlapping. Select the entire path, choose Object ➪ Path ➪ Join, or press ⌘+J

(Ctrl+J), and choose smooth point. These steps usually alter one of the two segments on either side of the new anchor point. Undo the join and you know the location of the overlapping end points.

Tip   If you are having trouble joining two open paths, make sure that they are not grouped. You cannot join grouped path.

Converting Anchor Points

This section deals with the Convert Anchor Point tool. The Convert Anchor Point tool only converts anchor points by adjusting control handles. The Convert Anchor Point tool works differently with each type of anchor point. The different types of anchor points are shown in Figure 5-26.

Cross-Reference   See Chapter 3 for detailed definitions of the four different types of anchor points and how they're drawn with the Pen tool.

You can use the Convert Anchor Point tool on either extended control handles or on anchor points. When there are two control handles on an anchor point, clicking either control handle with the Convert Anchor Point tool "breaks" the linked control handles (so that when the angle of one is changed, the other is changed as well), and makes them independent (the control handle's length from the anchor point and the angle can be altered individually).

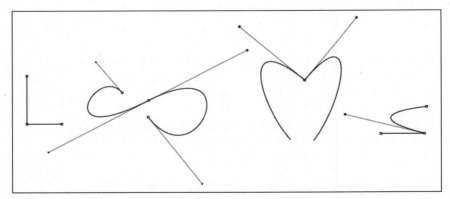

Figure 5-26: The four types of anchor points

Converting Smooth Points

Smooth points can be changed into the other three types of anchor points by using both the Direct Selection tool and the Convert Anchor Point tool as follows:

✦ To convert smooth points into combination corner points, use the Direct Selection tool or the Convert Anchor Point tool to drag one control handle into the anchor point.

✦ To convert smooth points into curved corner points, use the Convert Anchor Point tool to drag one of the control handles. After being dragged with the Convert Anchor Point tool, the two control handles become independent of each other (the movement of one will not affect the other).

The following steps show you how you can use the Direct Selection tool and the Convert Anchor Point tool to change shapes — in this case, from a circle to a rhombus or diamond shape.

1. **Draw a circle with the Ellipse tool.** Remember to keep the Shift key pressed so you end up with a perfect circle.

2. **Select the Convert Anchor Point tool.**

3. **Click each of the anchor points and release.** Doing this converts the Smooth anchor points to Corner anchor points. The rhombus or diamond shape should look like the illustration in Figure 5-27.

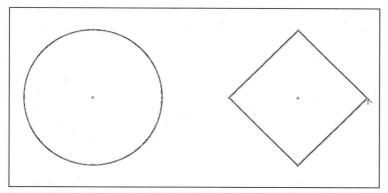

Figure 5-27: Convert the circle (left) to a diamond (right) by clicking on each anchor point with the Convert Direction Point tool.

Converting straight corner points

You can change straight corner points into one of the other three types of anchor points by using both the Convert Anchor Point tool and the Direct Selection tool as follows:

✦ To convert straight corner points into smooth points, use the Convert Anchor Point tool to click and drag on the anchor point. As you drag, linked control handles appear on both sides of the anchor point.

✦ To convert straight corner points into combination corner points, use the Convert Anchor Point tool to click and drag on the anchor point. As you drag, linked control handles appear on both sides of the anchor point. Select one of the control handles with the Convert Anchor Point tool or the Direct Selection tool and drag it toward the anchor point until it disappears.

✦ To convert straight corner points into curved corner points, use the Convert Anchor Point tool to click and drag on the anchor point. As you drag, linked control handles appear on both sides of the anchor point. Then use the Convert Anchor Point tool to drag one of the control handles. After being dragged with the Convert Anchor Point tool, the two control handles become independent of each other.

Converting combination corner points

You can change combination corner points into one of the other three types of anchor points by using both the Convert Direction Point tool and the Direct Selection tool as follows:

✦ To convert combination corner points into smooth points, use the Convert Anchor Point tool to click and drag on the anchor point. As you drag, linked control handles appear on both sides of the anchor point.

✦ To convert combination corner points into straight corner points, use the Convert Anchor Point tool to click once on the anchor point. The control handle disappears.

✦ To convert Combination Corner Points into Curved Corner Points, use the Convert Anchor Point tool to click and drag the anchor point. As you drag, linked control handles appear on both sides of the anchor point. Then use the Convert Anchor Point tool to drag one of the control handles. After being dragged with the Convert Anchor Point tool, the two control handles become independent of each other.

The following steps are another example of how you can change shapes using the Direct Selection tool and the Convert Anchor Point tool — this time, a circle into a heart.

1. **Draw a circle with the Ellipse tool.** Remember to keep the Shift key pressed so that you end up with a perfect circle.

2. **Click the lowest point on the circle with the Direct Selection tool.** For more on the selection tools, see Chapter 5.

3. **Click the right control handle of that anchor point and drag it up using your eye as a judgment for a heart shape.**

4. **With the Convert Anchor Point tool, click the left control handle of that point and drag it up which is now pointing straight down.**

5. **Click the anchor point at the top of the circle and drag it down a little.**

6. **With the Direct Selection tool, click the left control handle of the topmost point and drag it up.**

7. **Click the right control handle with the Convert Anchor Point tool and drag it down.** If you turn the Grid on by pressing ⌘+' (Ctrl+'), you'll find making adjustments such as this much easier and more precise.

8. **Adjust the anchor points and control handles until the circle looks like a heart, as shown in Figure 5-28.**

Figure 5-28: Convert a circle to a heart.

Converting curved corner points

You can change curved corner points into one of the other three types of anchor points by using both the Convert Anchor Point tool and the Direct Selection tool as follows:

✦ To convert curved corner points into smooth points, use the Convert Anchor Point tool to click and drag on the anchor point. You can then use the Direct Selection tool to adjust the angle of both control handles at once.

✦ To convert curved corner points into straight corner points, use the convert anchor point tool to click once on the anchor point. The control handles disappear.

✦ To convert curved corner points into combination corner points, use the Direct Selection tool to drag one control handle into the anchor point.

Using Illustrator's Pathfinder functions

The most powerful path functions in Illustrator are in the Pathfinder palette. They do things that would take hours to do using Illustrator's traditional tools and methods. The only drawback to the Pathfinder palette is that there are so many options that it's pretty hard to figure out which one to use for which job. Figure 5-29 shows the Pathfinder palette.

Figure 5-29: The Pathfinder palette

The Pathfinder options take over most of the mundane tasks of path editing that could otherwise take hours. Everything that the Pathfinder options do can be done manually with Illustrator tools, but the Pathfinder options do them much more quickly. Common activities such as joining two paths together correctly and breaking a path into two pieces are done in a snap.

Shape Modes and Pathfinders are the two areas in the Pathfinder palette. The Shape Modes are:

✦ Add to shape area

✦ Subtract from shape area

✦ Intersect shape areas

✦ Exclude overlapping shape areas or the symmetric difference (the union minus the union of any intersections)

The Pathfinder functions are:

✦ Divide

✦ Trim

✦ Merge

✦ Crop

✦ Outline

✦ Minus Back

The Pathfinder options change the way that two or more paths interact. The cute little symbols on each of the Pathfinder options are supposed to clue you in to what each option can do, but the pictures are small and most don't accurately depict exactly how each option works.

If you have the Show Tool tips box checked, the name of each of the Pathfinder options pops up when you hold your cursor over its option symbol. However, these names can be a little confusing. The names were undoubtedly chosen to signify what each of the Pathfinder options can do, but most of them can't be defined easily with just one word.

Tip   Now that the Pathfinder options are no longer on a pull-down menu to reapply a Pathfinder function you can use the Repeat Pathfinder function found in the Pathfinder palette's pop-up menu (see Figure 5-30) or press ⌘+4 (Ctrl+4).

Figure 5-30: The Pathfinder palette's Repeat function is found in the pop-up menu.

The Pathfinder options

To access the Pathfinder options, choose Pathfinder Options in the pop-up menu of the Pathfinder palette, previously shown in Figure 5-30. This displays the Pathfinder Options dialog box, shown in Figure 5-31, which enables you to customize the way that the Pathfinders work.

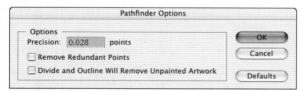

Figure 5-31: The Pathfinder Options dialog box

The options in the Pathfinder Options dialog box are as follows:

✦ **Precision:** The value in the Precision text field tells Illustrator how precisely Pathfinders should operate. The more precisely they operate, the better and more accurate the results are, but the longer the processing time is. This speed differential is most apparent when you apply Pathfinders — especially Trap (found in the pop-up (drop down) arrow of the Pathfinder palette) — to very complex objects. The default value is 0.028 points, which seems to be accurate enough for most work.

✦ **The Remove Redundant Points:** This option gets rid of overlapping points that are side by side on the same path. I can't think of why you would want overlapping points, so keeping this option checked is a good idea.

✦ **Divide & Outline Will Remove Unpainted Artwork:** If you check this option, Illustrator automatically deletes unpainted artwork. This relieves you from having to remove all those paths that Divide always seems to produce that are filled and stroked with None.

Usually, the defaults in the Pathfinder Options dialog box are the best options for most situations, except for Remove Redundant Points, which is off by default. If you change the options, be aware that the Pathfinder Options dialog box resets to the defaults when you quit Illustrator.

Adding to a shape

Add to shape area unites the selected objects if they are overlapping. A new path outlines all the previously selected objects. There are no paths where the original paths intersected. The new object takes the Paint Style attributes of the topmost object. If any objects are within other objects, those objects will be assimilated. If there are "holes" in the object, the holes will become reversed out of a compound path.

You'll find that Add to shape area is one Pathfinder option that you'll use often. Play with combining various paths for a while so you know what to expect, and you will develop a sense of when using Add to shape area is a better option than doing the same tasks manually.

Add to shape area combines two or more paths into one path, as described in the following steps.

1. **Select the objects to which you want apply the Add to shape area mode.** In the example in Figure 5-32, the artwork is a rectangle with two ellipses resembling a can shape. Pathfinders work only with paths. You have to convert type into outlined paths, and you cannot use EPS or Encapsulated PostScript images.

2. **Choose Add to shape area from the Pathfinder palette.** Any overlapping artwork is united into one path. The color of the united path is always the color of the path that was the topmost selected path before you used Add to shape area.

When you use Add to shape area, paths that don't overlap but are outside of other paths become part of a group. Illustrator draws paths between end points of open paths before it unites those paths with other paths. Compound paths remain compound paths.

Subtracting from a shape

The Subtract from shape area does the opposite of Add to shape area. The top most objects are subtracted from the bottom object. Figure 5-33 shows an object before (left) and after (right) using Subtract from shape area. The object retains the style (fill and stroke attributes) of the bottom most object.

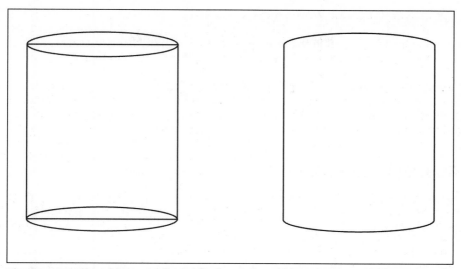

Figure 5-32: The objects on the left before using Add to shape area and on the right after using Add to shape area

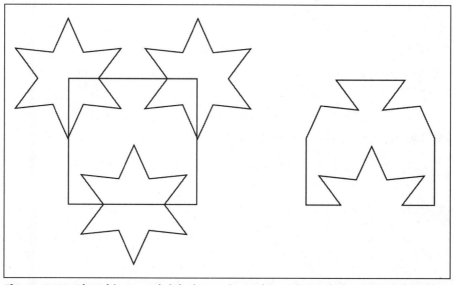

Figure 5-33: The objects on left before using Subtract from shape area and on the right after using Subtract from shape area

Intersecting and excluding shapes

Intersect and Exclude Shape Pathfinders are opposites. Using Intersect results in the opposite of what you get from using the Exclude and vice versa.

Intersect shape areas creates only the intersection of the selected paths. Any part of a selected path that does not intersect is deleted. If two paths are intersecting and selected, only the area that intersects between the two paths remains. If three or more paths are selected, all must intersect in a common area for the function to produce results. If the paths selected do not intersect at all, they all get deleted. If one selected path is contained within all the other selected paths, the result is that contained path. The resulting path has the Paint Style attributes of the topmost path.

Exclude overlapping shape areas is pretty much the opposite of Intersect. Choosing Exclude deletes the intersecting areas, grouping together the outside pieces. If you are having trouble making a compound path, use Exclude; any path within another path reverses, creating a compound path automatically.

After you select two or more paths and click the Intersect button on the Pathfinder palette, only the overlapping portions of the paths remain. If you select three paths, the only area that remains is the area where all three selected paths overlap each other.

If you use Exclude, only the areas that don't overlap remain. The color of the intersected or excluded path is always the color of the path that was the topmost selected path before you used Intersect or Exclude.

Tip By holding down the Option+ (Alt) key when clicking any of the Pathfinder Shape Modes, the objects will automatically expand.

Using the Expand button

The Expand button in the Pathfinder palette is used to ungroup the original objects you applied a pathfinder function to. The resulting paths forms a new group.

Dividing

The Divide button in the Pathfinder palette checks to see where the selected paths overlap and then creates new paths at all intersections where the paths crossed, creating new paths if necessary. Fills and strokes are kept. In the process, the Divide command also groups the pieces of the fill together. Divide also keeps selections their original colors; the illustration appears to look the same even if it previously had strokes. To keep the strokes, copy before using Divide, and then choose Edit ➪ Paste In Back or by pressing ⌘+Option+Shift+V (Ctrl+Alt+Shift+V).

Simply put, Divide divides overlaying paths into individual closed paths, as described in the following steps and Illustrated in Figure 5-34.

1. **Create the artwork that you want to divide into sections.**

2. **Create a path or paths where you want to divide the object.**

3. **Select all paths, both artwork and dividing paths and choose the Divide option in the Pathfinder palette.** Use the Direct Selection tool to move them, because the Divide command groups them automatically.

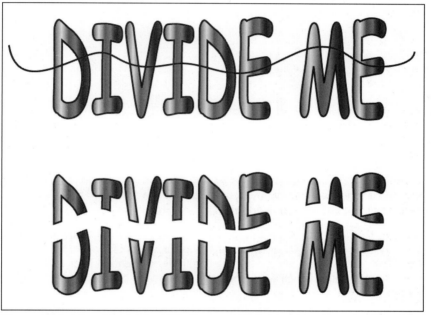

Figure 5-34: The object (above) before and (below) after separating the divided sections

Trimming

Trim removes sections of paths that are overlapped by other paths. Front most paths are the only ones that remains. This Pathfinder is very useful for cleaning up complex overlapping illustrations, although it can take a bit of time to complete. Figure 5-35 shows overlapping outlined type before (top) and after applying Trim (bottom). You can see the overlapping objects removed best in Outline mode.

Figure 5-35: In Outline mode, you can best see how trim fixed the overlapping outlined text.

Tip   I'll often use Trim if I want to use a piece of artwork for one portion of the Soft Mix Pathfinder found under Effects ➪ Pathfinder (described later). This removes overlapping paths, which would otherwise change in color when Soft Mix is applied.

Tip   By trimming your blends, you remove overlapping paths. This allows you to use Soft Mix and Hard Mix (found under Effects ➪ Pathfinder) with a blend. I trim blends to use them for shadowing or to apply highlights to objects.

Merging

Merge combines overlapping paths that have the identical fill applied to them. Even if the fill is different by as little as 1 percent, Merge creates two separate paths. This Pathfinder is much more efficient than Add to shape area for making areas of the same color into one object.

The following steps describe how to use Merge, and Figure 5-36 illustrates these steps.

1. **Create the artwork for which you want to use Merge.**

2. **Select the artwork you want to merge and choose the Merge option in the Pathfinder palette.** Illlustrator removes all overlapped paths, leaving only the paths that had nothing in front of them. All adjacent areas that contained identical colors are united.

Figure 5-36: Using Merge

Cropping

Crop works in much the same way as masks work, except that anything outside the cropped area is deleted, not just masked. Figure 5-37 shows the top original objects before and on the bottom, after using Crop. The top most object acts as the mask on the object(s) underneath.

To use the Crop command:

1. **Bring the object that you want to use as a cropper to the front.**

2. **Select all the paths you want to crop with it and the cropper itself.**

3. **Choose the Crop option in the Pathfinder palette.** Illustrator deletes everything outside the cropper. The objects that were cropped are grouped together in the shape of the crop.

Unlike masks, there is no outside shape after a crop is made. The cropper used to crop the image is deleted when Crop is chosen.

Cross-Reference For more on Masks, see Chapter 11.

Figure 5-37: The object (top) in Outline mode before crop and
after (below)

Outlining

Outline creates small sections of paths wherever paths cross and color the strokes,
using the fill of the path they were part of and giving the strokes a weight of 1 point
(Figure 5-38). Outline is useful for spot trapping as it automatically creates the sections needed that have to be chosen for overprinting, although many times the colors will be incorrect.

Outline creates smaller path pieces than Divide does; but, instead of making each
section a closed path, each path maintains its individuality, becoming separate
from adjoining paths. The result of outlining is several small stroke pieces. Instead
of maintaining the Fill color of each piece, each piece is filled with None and
stroked with the Fill color.

Figure 5-38: The original (top) before Outline and after (below) with a stroke weight added of .5 pt

Using Minus Back

Each of the Pathfinders works on the principle that one path, either the front most or backmost of the paths selected, will have all the other overlapping paths subtracted from it (Figure 5-39).

Minus Back subtracts all the selected paths behind the front most selected path from the front most selected path. With two objects, it is also quite simple. The object in the back is deleted, and the area where the object in back was placed is also deleted. Understanding Minus Back gets a little more confusing when you have more objects, but it does the same thing, all at once to all the selected paths. If the area to be subtracted is totally within the path it will subtract from, then a compound path results.

When you apply Minus Back, the color of the remaining path is the color of the front-most path before you applied it.

Trapping

The first Trap function in the Pathfinder palette is found under the pop-up menu. Trap takes some of the drudgery away from trapping. The only limitation for Trap is that it doesn't work well on extremely complex illustrations because of time and memory constraints. The other concern with Trap is that it leaves your illustrations "pseudo-uneditable" because it creates extra paths around your original trap and makes it really difficult to edit. It doesn't affect the existing paths, but if you do much editing, you'll have to delete the trap paths and retrap.

Figure 5-39: The top image shows the text on top of a shape before applying Minus Back. The bottom image shows the results of Minus Back.

For more on Trapping see Chapter 16.

Prior to trapping, I create a layer called Traps. Immediately after trapping, I move all the trap objects to the Traps layer. This keeps the traps together, in case I need to redo, adjust, or delete them.

Trap automatically creates a trap between abutting shapes of different colors. You set the amount (width) of trap in a dialog box that appears after choosing Trap.

To create a trap using the Trap option in the Pathfinder palette, follow these steps:

1. **Create and select the artwork that you want to trap.** If the artwork is overly complex, you may want to select only a small portion of the artwork before you continue.

2. **Choose the Trap option in the Pathfinder palette.**

3. **In the Trap dialog box, enter the width of the trap in the Thickness text field (the default is 0.25 points). Enter the amount that you want the height of the trap to differ from the width, which allows for different paper-stretching errors.** For example, entering the maximum, 400%, widens the horizontal thickness of the stroke to four times the amount set in the Thickness text field and leaves the vertical thickness the same.

4. **Enter a Tint reduction value that specifies how much the lighter of the two colors should be tinted on that area.** Check the Traps with Process Color checkbox to convert spot colors to process equivalents only in the resulting trap path that is generated from Trap.

5. **Check the Reverse Traps checkbox to convert any traps along the object that are filled with 100% Black but no other colors to be less black and more of the lighter abutting color.**

6. **Click OK.** Figure 5-40 shows the result of the trapping.

All traps generated by Trap result in filled paths, not strokes, and are automatically set to overprint in the Attributes palette.

Figure 5-40: The figure shows the trap darkened so you can see it.

Summary

- ✦ The first step in path editing is choosing the right tool.
- ✦ You can save selections and edit the names.
- ✦ Using Add Anchor points doesn't change the shape.
- ✦ Using Delete Anchor points changes the shape.
- ✦ Use Roughen from the Filter ➪ Distort to add anchor points evenly.
- ✦ Use Cleanup to remove any hidden, unwanted, stray anchor points.
- ✦ Reshape paths with the Reshape tool.
- ✦ Change the object's anchor points with the Convert Anchor Points tool.
- ✦ Use the Pathfinder palette's Shape modes to add, subtract, intersect, and exclude shape areas.
- ✦ Use the Pathfinder palette's Pathfinder options to divide, trim, merge, crop, outline, or minus back.
- ✦ Under the Pathfinder palette's pop-up menu is a trap function.

✦   ✦   ✦

Understanding Color, Gradients, and Mesh

This chapter covers color, gradients, and Mesh. You find color options in the Swatches palette, Color Palette, or the Color Picker. You can also apply color to fills and strokes.

Gradients allow you to apply several different colors in a specific pattern across the surface of your image. You'll learn how to use and edit the preset gradients, as well as create gradients of your own.

Mesh changes your art into a grid of meshed lines, creating a 3D color look. You have a delicate balance of color shifts and more accuracy when using the Mesh tool to add realistic shadows to your objects.

Working with the Swatches Palette

You can access the Swatches palette by choosing Window ⇨ Swatches. When you initially install Illustrator, the Swatches palette is housed with the Color palette, and you can switch between the palettes by clicking their respective tabs.

By default, the Swatches palette contains and displays several commonly used colors, patterns, and gradients. You change what displays by clicking the icons along the bottom of the palette. The following list describes each icon from left to right.

> ✦ **Show All Swatches:** This icon, which looks like three squares stacked, displays all color, gradient, and pattern swatches.

✦ **Show Color Swatches:** This icon, which looks like a solid block of color, displays only the color swatches.

✦ **Show Gradient Swatches:** This icon, which looks a block with blend of colors on it, displays only the gradient swatches.

✦ **Show Pattern Swatches:** This icon, which looks like a block divided into fourth, displays only the pattern swatches.

✦ **New Swatch:** Clicking this icon, which looks like a little piece of paper with a bent corner, creates a new swatch. You can also create a new swatch by dragging it into the Swatches palette.

✦ **Delete Swatch:** When you select a swatch and click this trashcan icon Illustrator deletes it.

You can also view the swatches in either small or large thumbnail squares, or view all the swatches in a list, with names if they have them (see Figure 6-1). You can change the view mode by selecting the appropriate option from the Swatches pop-up menu.

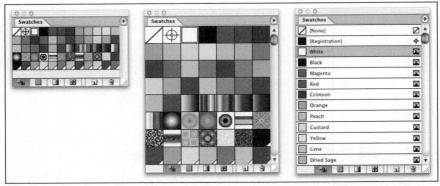

Figure 6-1: The Swatches palette displayed in Small Swatch (left), Large Swatch (middle), and List views (right)

Using the Color Swatches

You can create a new swatch based on the current paint style, which appears in the Paint Style section of the toolbox, by clicking the New Swatch icon along the bottom of the Swatches palette. If you press Option (Alt) when creating a new swatch, the New Swatch dialog box appears (see Figure 6-2). This dialog box enables you to initially name the swatch and set its color mode to either process color (CMYK) or spot color. Under the Color Mode in the New Swatch dialog box, you can set Grayscale, RGB, HSB, CMYK, or Web Safe RGB. Most default process color swatches are set up with RGB Color Mode. You can also create a new swatch by choosing

New Swatch from the Swatches palette pop-up menu, which you access by clicking the left-pointing triangle in the circle on the upper-right corner of the palette.

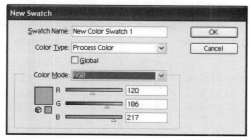

Figure 6-2: The New Swatch dialog box lets you name the new swatch.

Double-clicking a swatch displays the Swatch Options for that swatch. The Swatch Options dialog box is exactly like the New Swatch dialog box, except it includes a Preview checkbox. The Swatch Options dialog box has the following options:

✦ **Swatch name:** Lets you change the name of the swatch, which you can only view in List view mode.

✦ **Color Type:** Allows you to set the color type of the swatch to either process or spot.

✦ **Color Mode:** Lets you change the mode to CMYK, RGB, HSB, Grayscale, or Web Safe RGB.

Cross-Reference   For more on Web Safe colors, see Chapter 16.

In addition, you can select one or more swatches to edit, duplicate, or remove them from the Swatches palette. Click a swatch to select it; a frame appears on the selected swatch.

You can select more than one swatch by pressing the ⌘ (Ctrl) key and clicking additional swatches. If you press the Shift key and click additional swatches, a contiguous (connected) set of the swatches is selected, from where you initially clicked to where you Shift-clicked. You can deselect individual swatches by pressing ⌘ (Ctrl) and clicking selected swatches. You deselect all the swatches by clicking an empty area of the Swatches palette. By selecting multiple swatches, you can duplicate and delete several swatches at once.

If you want to sort the swatches manually, you can do so by selecting any number of swatches and dragging them to a new location within the Swatches palette.

Using the Swatches pop-up menu

The Swatches pop-up menu (shown in Figure 6-4) has other functions as well, some of which we've already mentioned:

✦ **New Swatch:** This option works the same as the New Swatch icon on the bottom of the Color Swatch palette. A new swatch is created from whatever you select.

✦ **Duplicate Swatch:** Duplicates the selected swatches. You can also drag a selected swatch to the New Swatch icon (the little piece of paper) to duplicate the swatch. If you press Option (Alt) while duplicating a swatch, the New Swatch dialog box appears.

✦ **Merge Swatches:** Merges two or more selected swatches by using the first selected swatch's name and color.

✦ **Delete Swatch:** To delete a swatch, select this option. You can also select the swatch and click the Trash icon A warning dialog box (see Figure 6-3) appears, asking if you want to delete the swatch selection. Click Yes to delete the swatch.

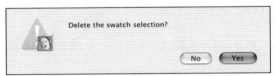

Figure 6-3: The Warning dialog box that appears when you try to delete a swatch

✦ **Select All Unused:** Selects the swatches in the Swatches palette that you aren't used in the current document. You can then delete those swatches if necessary.

✦ **Sort By Name:** Organizes the swatches (regardless of which viewing mode the swatch palette is in) alphabetically.

✦ **Sort By Kind:** Sorts the swatches to appear starting with color, then gradients, then patterns.

✦ **Show Find Field:** Opens a Find field so you can enter a specific swatch name to search for in the Swatches palette.

✦ **The View options:** You can also view the swatches in either small or large thumbnail squares, or view all the swatches in a list, with names if they have them.

✦ **Swatch Options:** Clicking this option displays the Swatch Options for the selected swatch. This dialog box was discussed in the last section.

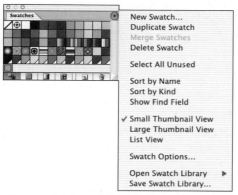

Figure 6-4: The Swatches pop-up menu

Using other swatch libraries

In addition to the standard Swatch Library palette, several other default Swatch Library palettes are accessible from the Swatch Libraries submenu of the Window menu (see Figure 6-5) or the Swatches palette pop-up menu. You can also create a new Swatch Library palette from any Illustrator document.

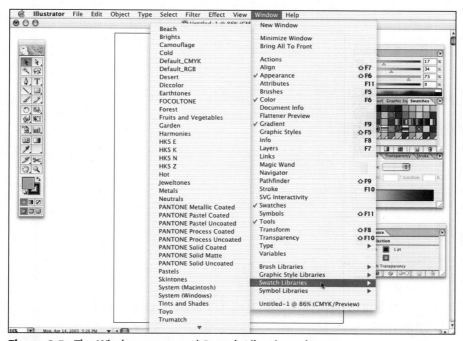

Figure 6-5: The Window menu and Swatch Libraries submenu

To view one of the other default Swatches palettes, choose it from the Swatch Libraries submenu. You cannot edit these Swatch libraries; you can only add swatches from these libraries to your main Swatches palette.

To add a swatch (or several selected swatches) to your main Swatches palette, do the following;

1. **Select the swatches you want to add.**

2. **Choose Add To Swatches from the library's pop-up menu.** Again, the left pointing triangle is in a circle located on the upper-right corner of the palette.

3. **Drag the swatches to the main Swatches palette or double-click the swatch.** Illustrator saves the main Swatches palette with your document. You can customize a palette for a specific document or edit the Adobe Illustrator Startup document's Swatches palette to use a certain set of colors in each new document you create.

Otherwise, these swatch libraries work the same way as your main Swatches palette; you can choose colors for fill and stroke, sort the swatches by Kind or Name, and view the swatches by List, Small Swatch, or Large Swatch. Figure 6-6 shows three swatch libraries.

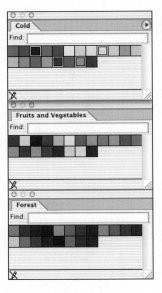

Figure 6-6: Three different swatch libraries — Cold, Fruits and Vegetables, and Forest

Using color space options in the Color Palette

The Color palette provides basic color selection via the Color Ramp along the bottom of the palette and more precise control via sliders and percentage entries in

Grayscale, RGB, CYMK, HSB, and Web Safe RGB. Most users of Illustrator use either RGB or CMYK color spaces. Heavy Web designers also use HSB, and Web Safe RGB. If you are sure you only want to work in black and white, choose Grayscale. Use the Color palette to add color to any object's stroke or fill. You can create any color to be used in an illustration by defining it in the Color palette (shown in Figure 6-7). Access the Color palette by choosing Window ➪ Color.

Figure 6-7: The Color palette

The Color palette has a pop-up menu that enables you to display options and to choose from the available color spaces. The "options" are really the color mixing sliders; I've never found a reason to hide them. In fact, the sliders take up such a small amount of space that after they're in view, you'll probably never hide them either.

The color space options let you switch between

✦ **Grayscale:** White to black with all shades of gray in between (see Figure 6-8a).

✦ **RGB:** Red, green, and blue. This color space is used by computer monitors, and it's perfect for multimedia and Web-page graphics (see Figure 6-8b). You can enter RGB values as percentages or as values from 0 to 255. Double-click to the right of the text fields to change the RGB measurement system from percentages to the numeric 0 to 255 system and back.

✦ **HSB:** Hue, Saturation, Brightness. This RGB-derived color space is best for adjusting RGB colors in brightness and saturation (see Figure 6-8c).

✦ **CMYK:** Cyan, magenta, yellow, and black. These are considered typical printing process colors, although Illustrator calls any colors process that aren't spot (see Figure 6-9a).

✦ **Web Safe RGB:** These colors are the 216 colors recognized by all graphic Web browsers on any platform (see Figure 6-9b).

✦ **Tint:** This isn't really an option in the pop-up menu, but if you select a spot color swatch (or choose a spot color with the Eyedropper tool), the color palette goes into a sort of tint color space, where you can tint the color from 100% to 0% of that color (see Figure 6-9c). The "1C" next to R isn't a percentage, it's a hex number between 00 and FF, which translates to 255 in our decimal numbering system (00 is 0%, FF is 100%, 80 is 50%, 1C is a bit over 11%).

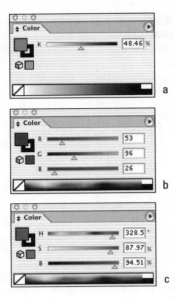

Figure 6-8: The Color palette displaying (a) Grayscale color space, (b) RGB color space, and (c) HSB color space

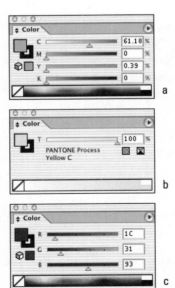

Figure 6-9: The Color palette displaying (a) CMYK color space, (b) Web Safe RGB color space, and (c) tint color space for the color Pantone Process Yellow C

As you drag a specific color's slider, the other sliders also change in color. Doing this gives you sort of a preview for what would happen if you were to drag along the sliders. The icon to the left of the sliders shows the current color and whether you're adjusting the fill (solid box) or stroke (box with a hole). Instead of dragging, you can also just simply click a different location along the slider to change its value.

Press the Shift key to adjust RGB and CMYK sliders proportionately. This is a great way to tint process colors. Shift-drag the slider with the largest value for the most control. When you release the mouse button, Illustrator makes the new color a tint of the original.

You can also change the slider values by typing in values for each of the individual color channels (Cyan is a color channel in CMYK, for instance). Press the Tab key to highlight the next text field or Shift-Tab to highlight the previous text field.

Quickly highlight the text fields by clicking to the right of the text field, or by clicking the name of the text field on the other side of the slider.

Most of Illustrator's Palettes' text fields are mathematically adept. You can add, subtract, multiply, and divide in them. This is useful when entering color percentages in the text fields of the Color palette. To add 5% to the current value, type +5 after the current value. To subtract 5%, type -5 after the current value. To divide the current value by 2, type /2 after the current value. To multiply the current value by 2, type *2 after the current value.

Press Shift-Return/Enter after entering values to rehighlight the current text field. In this way, you can type in different values without ever having to reselect the text field.

Using the Color Ramp

The Color Ramp is the bar along the bottom of the Color palette. It looks like a rainbow of colors. The Color Ramp enables you to quickly pick a color from the current color space. Resting your cursor above the Color Ramp area changes the cursor into an eyedropper.

Click any portion of the Color Ramp to select that color. Illustrator provides large rectangles of black and white to make choosing black or white easier. The Grayscale and Spot Color Ramps have large areas for both 0% and 100% to make selecting those percentages easier. You can also drag over the Color Ramp, watching the large square in the top of the Color palette (if Options are showing) to see the color you're dragging over. If Options aren't shown, look at the active Fill/Stroke icon in the toolbox to see the color you're currently positioned over (this works only when the mouse button is pressed as you pass across the Color Ramp).

When you change to a different color space, the Color Ramp along the bottom of the palette also changes to show the rainbow of colors in that particular color space.

Shift-click the Color Ramp to cycle through the color spaces; this is much faster than choosing a color space from the pop-up menu.

You can press the X key while dragging around the Color Ramp to switch between the fill and stroke focus. This way you can quickly select colors for both fill and stroke with one mouse click! If the fill is in focus, click and drag through the Color Ramp to the appropriate color. Then, with the mouse button still pressed, press the X key; you'll now be picking a color for the stroke. Want to change the fill again? Just press X while keeping down the mouse button.

Tip   Press Option (Alt) and click anywhere on a Color Ramp to affect the opposite attribute. For example, if stroke is in focus on the toolbox, pressing Option (Alt) and clicking on a Color Ramp changes the Fill color, not the stroke. Be aware, however, that Option (Alt)+clicking on a swatch in the Swatches palette does not affect the opposite attribute; this only works on a Color Ramp (and the color box in the Color palette).

Working with gamut

If you choose certain colors in the RGB or HSB color spaces, a little icon appears in the center left of the Color palette (see Figure 6-10). This icon indicates that the current color is out of gamut with CMYK color space. Therefore, the particular color you choose isn't within the range of colors that can be displayed or printed for the selected color space. This issue is only important if you plan to print the document using CMYK process colors. If you plan to use the image onscreen, such as in Web or multimedia publishing, whether the color is in gamut does not matter.

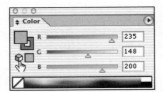

Figure 6-10: The Out of Gamut indicator appears when the current color cannot be accurately converted into CMYK values.

The best way to reset the current color to CMYK color space is to click the Out of Gamut icon. The RGB or HSB values change so that the resulting color is well within CMYK color space. Another way to change the current color to CMYK color space is to choose CMYK from the Color palette pop-up menu.

If you want to change the color space of several objects — or perhaps your entire document — to CMYK, select the objects that you want to change and choose Filter ➪ Colors ➪ Convert to CMYK. To change the whole document to a different color space, choose File ➪ Document Color Mode ➪ CMYK Color or RGB Color.

Spot colors

Spot colors are colors in Illustrator that aren't separated into process colors (cyan, magenta, yellow, and black) when printed. Instead, they are printed on a different separation. A commercial printer uses special ink (commonly Pantone) for this spot color. Spot colors are indicated in the Swatches palette in Small Thumbnail and Large Thumbnail views by a white triangle containing a black dot in the lower right of the spot color swatch. List view shows a square with a circle inside of it (a "spot") on the right edge of the swatch listing. In List viewing mode, both the color space (grayscale, RGB, or CMYK) and Process/Spot status are indicated to the right of the color chip and name.

You can use as many spot colors in an illustration as you want, though it isn't usually practical or desirable to have more than four in one document (because CMYK printing can duplicate most colors, process colors are often a better choice than four spot colors). Illustrator's default Swatch libraries (choose Window ➪ Swatch Libraries) mostly contain spot colors that you can choose among, or you can create your own. To create your own spot color:

1. **Create a new swatch with the appearance you want.** Use the color sliders to do this.

2. **Double-click the newly created swatch.** Doing this opens the Swatch Options dialog box.

3. **Change the Swatch type from Process to Spot.** Now, when you use that swatch as a fill or stroke, Illustrator considers it a spot color when it comes time to print.

Tip
You can convert any spot color to a standard CMYK color (the color, not the swatch) by selecting the spot color and then changing the color space in the Color palette to CMYK. You can even change the color space to grayscale, RGB, or HSB in this way. This only works on the selected paths; the swatch is not affected.

Applying colors with the Color palette

Now you know how the palettes work, but how do you change the color of paths to what's in the palettes? The easiest thing to do is to select the path you want to change the fill or stroke (or both) of, change the focus (if necessary) of the Fill/Stroke icons, and select a color from either the Color or Swatches palette. Press X to change the color for the other (fill or stroke).

The key here is selecting. If you have selected paths, any changes you make affects those selected paths.

When you create a new path, Illustrator uses the fill and stroke that are currently displayed in the Paint Style section of the toolbox.

To apply colors to text, you can either select an entire text area with a Selection tool, or select individual characters with a Type tool.

Tip
Selecting Type with a Selection tool can cause type paths and type areas to be filled and stroked as well as the type. You can use the Group Selection tool to deselect the associated paths, or, better yet, just use the Type tool and drag across the characters you want to select.

Transferring color from one object to another

The Eyedropper and Paint Bucket tools are lifesavers for those of us who are constantly using post-it notes to jot down what the percentages of CMYK (Cyan, Magenta, Yellow, and Black) are in one path so that we can apply those same amounts to another path. A good reason to use the Paint Bucket and Eyedropper tools is to ensure that your colors are consistent throughout an illustration. So, for example, if you used a custom color somewhere that you want to use again somewhere else, you don't try to duplicate it with a CMYK mix that may not be an exact match. With a couple of click, or keystrokes, you can easily transfer the color properties of one object to another. The tools work with paths, objects, type, and placed images.

The Eyedropper and Paint Bucket tools work similarly to the other tools in Illustrator in that their properties stay the same until you change them—in this case by clicking a new path or object with a different color. The Eyedropper tool "sucks" up color from where you click. Use this to see the breakdown of a color in the area you clicked. The Paint Bucket tool fills in an area with the active color in the Color Swatch. Just click the Paint Bucket tool on the shape you want to fill with color. To give you more control over what the tools can pick up and apply, Illustrator gives you an exhaustive list of properties to select in the Paint Bucket/Eyedropper dialog box. Double-clicking either tool brings up this dialog box (shown in Figure 6-11), where you can select or deselect options depending on what attributes you want to apply. So, for example, you can have the Eyedropper tool pick up the color and Stroke weight of a path without transferring the path's transparency properties.

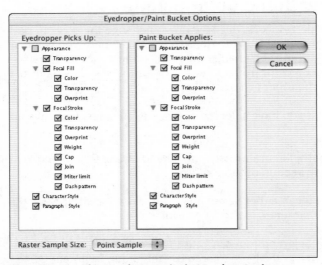

Figure 6-11: The Eyedropper/Paint Bucket Options
dialog box

Cross-Reference For more on paths, objects, and type, see Chapters 3, 4, and 8, respectively. Most of the properties listed in the Eyedropper/Paint Bucket dialog box are also discussed in these chapters.

Cross-Reference For more on placed images, see Chapter 2.

At the bottom of the Eyedropper/Paint Bucket Options dialog box is the Raster Sample Size menu. From this menu you can choose whether you suck up a Point Sample (samples the color from the point where you click), 3 x 3 Average (averages the color in an area of 3 pixels by 3 pixels), or 5 x 5 Average (averages the color in an area of 5 pixels by 5 pixels).

The Eyedropper tool

The Eyedropper tool, shown with the Paint Bucket tool in Figure 6-12, samples paint style information from a path, placed image and stores it in the Paint Style fill and stroke boxes (on the toolbox), without selecting that path. The information stays there until you change the information in the color palette, select another path with different paint style information, or click any other path or placed image with a different paint style. Pressing the Shift key when the Eyedropper tool is active allows it to do Direct Sucking. Direct Sucking is used to pull from within gradients but not from palettes or window edges.

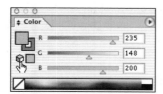

Figure 6-12: The Eyedropper/Paint Bucket Options tools

Tip If you have paths selected when you click with the Eyedropper tool, all selected objects in the document are changed to the paint style of the path that you clicked on.

The Paint Bucket tool

You use the Paint Bucket tool to apply the current paint style to both paths and 1-bit TIFF images. You can apply any attribute that is active in the Appearance palette. Using the Paint Bucket tool is a quick and painless way to apply a set style or group of attributes you like to other objects.

Holding down the Shift key when clicking a path fills the Paint Bucket tool with the current paint style and also selects that path. If the path was already selected, pressing the Shift key and clicking deselects it. Pressing the Option (Alt) key toggles from the Paint Bucket tool to the Eyedropper tool.

The Paint Bucket tool is also great to use to apply the last Appearance quickly to another object. You apply the last attributes in the Appearance palette to any object by clicking on a new object with the Paint Bucket tool.

Using Transparency

Transparency has changed the face of Illustrator. Being able to apply transparent live effects to any object in Illustrator is just plain amazing. It opens up many doors and lets in a kaleidoscope of colors to see through. Transparency is like looking through stained glass, a piece of plastic, anything you can see through. You can adjust the blending modes for a variety of effects. Blending modes are the interaction of the colors of an object with the objects underneath that object. Imagine you are playing with Plexiglas blocks in three dimensions, as shown in Figure 6-13. You can see what is behind or in front of those blocks. You can even go as far as thinking you are Superman looking through objects with X-ray vision. You can create stained glass effects, mixing color effects, and so much more. You can apply transparency to objects, groups of objects, or a whole layer.

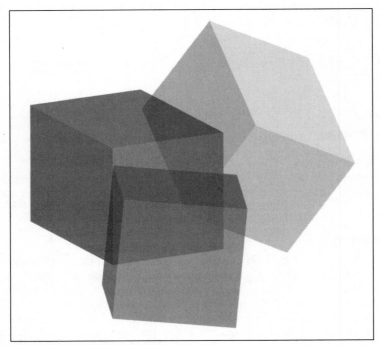

Figure 6-13: 3D transparent blocks

In Illustrator, you apply Transparency in the Transparency palette as shown in Figure 6-14. If the Transparency palette isn't showing when you start up Illustrator, choose Window ➪ Transparency. To see the options available with Transparency, click the upper-right triangle and choose Show Options. In the preview pane on the left side of the palette, you can see a thumbnail view of the current Opacity setting applied to the selected object.

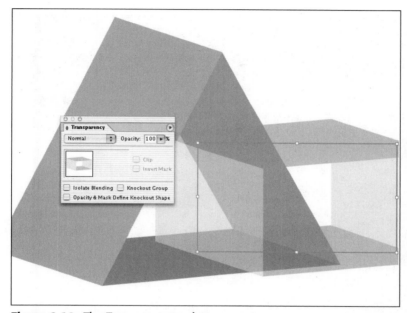

Figure 6-14: The Transparency palette

Here are the options in the Transparency palette:

✦ **Opacity:** Basically, you adjust an Opacity slider in the Transparency palette to determine how much you can see through that object.

✦ **Clip:** The Clip option gives the masks a black background.

✦ **Invert Mask:** Reverses luminosity and opacity values of the masked objects.

✦ **Isolate Blending:** Check this option to affect only the group or layer opacity.

✦ **Knockout Group:** Selecting this option means that the opacity does not affect the group or layer, just the object.

✦ **Opacity & Mask Define Knockout Shape:** Selecting this option means that you can use a Mask to delineate where Illustrator applies the transparency settings.

Cross-Reference

All of the preceding options are discussed in greater detail later in this section.

Defining transparency between objects, groups, and layers

You can apply transparency to an object, group of objects, sublayer, or the entire layer. You can also apply transparency to symbols, patterns, type, 3D objects, graphic styles, strokes, and brush strokes. To define an object's transparency, select the object first and then drag the Opacity slider in the Transparency palette to the desired opacity. Figure 6-15 shows an example of changing the top object's opacity.

Figure 6-15: The top star object's opacity was changed to 60 percent to see through the background.

Working with opacity

You adjust the transparency in the Transparency palette by dragging the Opacity slider. You access the slider by clicking the left pointing arrow on the side of the Opacity box. As mentioned previously, opacity is how see-through the object is. Applying no Opacity makes an object totally transparent. Applying any amount of opacity makes the object partially transparent. 100% opacity makes the object totally opaque, which mean you can't see through it at all. Figure 6-16 shows three shapes overlapping with varying degrees of opacity applied. If you check the Appearance palette, it shows you the amount of opacity applied to that particular object.

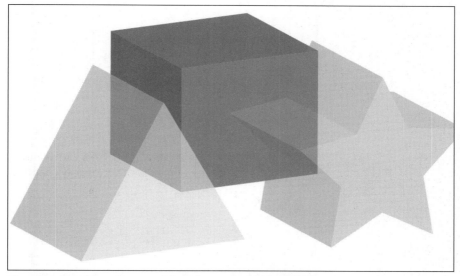

Figure 6-16: Three shapes with various opacities applied

To apply opacity to a group of objects, or to a whole layer, start with the Layers palette, do the following:

1. **In the Layers palette, click the layer you want to adjust.** This is shown in Figure 6-17.

2. **Adjust the Opacity slider or enter the Opacity value in the Transparency palette**. Figure 6-18 shows the object with a 50% opacity applied making the business card much easier to read.

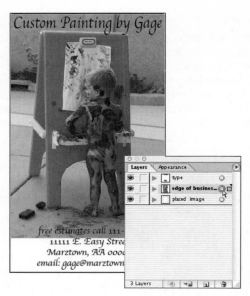

Figure 6-17: Target the layer you want to change by clicking on the radio button circle.

Figure 6-18: The business card is much easier to read with the opacity changed.

Using blending modes

Within the Transparency palette, you find 16 blending modes similar to Photoshop's blending modes. Each mode creates a different effect when applied to the same object. Blending modes can totally change the look of the opacity applied to an object. Blending modes let you choose a variety of ways the colors of the objects blend when overtop another object. You create blending modes by combining a base color (the bottom object), the blend color (of the object on top), and the resulting color from the overlapping.

Illustrator supplies a variety of blending modes in the Transparency palette. Figure 6-19 shows the list of blending modes found in the Transparency palette in the pop-up menu. The different Blending modes are:

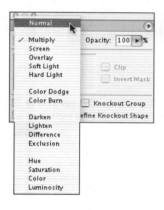

Figure 6-19: Under the pop-up in the Transparency palette, you see all of the blending modes.

✦ **Normal:** Use this for no interaction with the base color, only the blend color result.

✦ **Multiply:** This mode multiplies (2 x 2) the base color by the blend color creating a darker color.

✦ **Screen:** This multiplies the opposite color of the blend and base colors, creating a lighter color.

✦ **Overlay:** This mode either multiplies or screens depending on the base color. The base color is mixed with the blend color resulting in the lightness or darkness of the original color.With patterns or graphic styles, the highlights and shadows of the base color are kept and the blend color is mixed in to create lightness or darkness of the beginning color.

✦ **Soft Light:** This mode is like shining a softened light on the object. Blends less than 50% gray get lightened and blends greater than 50% get darkened. If the blend is 50% it is left alone.

✦ **Hard Light:** This mode is similar to soft light, but with a harsh light shining on the object. If the blend color is lighter than 50% gray the object becomes lightened. If the blend color is darker than 50% gray the object becomes darkened.

✦ **Color Dodge:** Use this to lighten and brighten up the base color.

✦ **Color Burn:** Use this to darken the base color.

✦ **Darken:** This mode uses the darker color (base or blend) as the resulting color.

✦ **Lighten:** This mode uses the lighter color (base or blend) as the resulting color.

✦ **Difference:** This mode chooses the brighter color (either base or blend) and subtracts it from the other color.

✦ **Exclusion:** This mode is similar to Difference mode, but with less contrasting values.

✦ **Hue:** Use this to create a result of the saturation of the base color and the hue of the blend color.

✦ **Saturation:** Use this mode to create a result of the hue of the base color and the saturation of the blend color.

✦ **Color:** This mode creates a result of the luminance of the base color and the hue and saturation of the blend color.

✦ **Luminosity:** This mode is the opposite of the Color mode. The result is the hue and saturation of the base color and the luminance of the blend color.

Isolating blending

Isolating blending is a necessary evil when too many objects are involved in a transparency illustration. When patterns are involved, you may lose the clarity of your artwork unless you limit how far the blending goes with the Opacity settings. In the Transparency palette, there is a checkbox for Isolate Blending. Use this to pick and choose how far you want the opacity to affect the underlying objects.

To apply a blending mode to an object:

1. **First click the popup (drop-down list) in the Transparency palette and select a choice to apply that blending mode to the selected object.**

2. **Group the objects together that you want in the blend.** To learn more on how to group objects, see Chapter 7.

3. **In the Layers palette, click the radio button to the right of the layer that contains the selected group of objects to target the group of objects you want to isolate.**

4. **Check the Isolate Blending box in the Transparency palette.**

Figure 6-20 shows a group of objects without checking isolate blending (left) and the same objects with isolate blending checked (right). For the left image, the text, its highlights and the underlying texture are all blended together making it difficult to read the text, but the right image isolates the blending so that only the text and its highlight are blended.

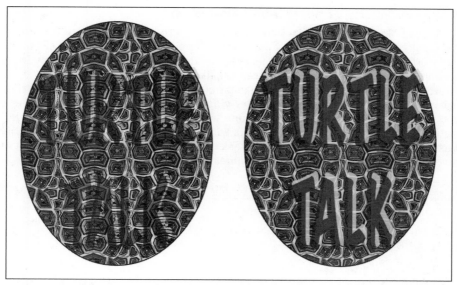

Figure 6-20: Text without Isolate Blending (left) and with Isolate Blending checked (right). The two text pieces are grouped.

Knocking out a group

Along with the Isolate Blending is the Knockout Group checkbox in the Transparency palette. Knockout Group does the opposite of Isolate Blending. Use this to disregard the group when it comes to blending modes. In Figure 6-21, Knockout Group was applied to the two pieces of text. With Knockout Group checked, you can see the pattern through the type.

Figure 6-21: Text without Knockout Group (left) and with Knockout Group checked (right). The two text pieces are grouped.

Using an Opacity, Clipping, and Invert Masks

A Clipping Mask creates a black background and crops the objects to the edges of the mask. An Opacity Mask is similar to the Clipping Masks. Instead of clipping away other objects, it clips the objects to the defined area (mask) to show transparency. The Opacity Mask in Illustrator is like the Layer Mask concept in Photoshop. Use the Opacity Mask to clip objects to the top shape and uses the Opacity Mask's luminosity to the underlying objects. Where the top mask is white, you can see the artwork underneath, and where the mask is black, it is opaque. Figure 6-22 shows a group of 3D objects with a spiky shape on top. The spiky shape was then selected to be the Opacity Mask overtop of the other objects. Invert Mask reverses the luminosity and opacity values of the selected mask.

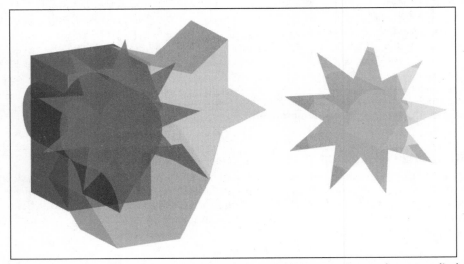

Figure 6-22: The objects before (left) and after (right) an Opacity Mask was applied to the shape on top

After applying an Opacity Mask, the original shape disappears. If you don't believe me, check Outline mode. To get the shape back, simply release the Opacity Mask. You can release the Opacity Mask under the Transparency palette pop-up menu. Choose Release Opacity Masks, and the objects return to their original state.

Cross-Reference   For more on the different viewing modes in Illustrator, see Chapter 1.

Other choices under the Transparency menu are to unlink or relink an Opacity Mask. An Opacity Mask is automatically linked to the object that it is masking. To unlink the Opacity Mask, click the link symbol between the opacity mask and the object or choose Unlink Opacity Mask in the Transparency palette pop-up menu. When you unlink the object from the mask, you can move the object(s) around under the Opacity Mask and the mask stays put. To relink the two back together, click the link between the two thumbnails or choose Link Opacity mask from the Transparency palette pop-up menu.

You can disable an Opacity Mask, and Illustrator removes the Mask from its masking task, but does not delete the objects you used to make the mask from the file. To get the mask back, choose Enable Opacity Mask from the Transparency palette pop-up menu.

You can edit Opacity Masks if you click the thumbnail of the mask. Use Illustrator's editing tools to change the mask shape. Other options in the Transparency palette for the Opacity Mask are to make the Opacity Mask act as a Clipping mask with the Clip menu command. Check this to have the mask clip the area around the selected mask (like the Clipping Mask function). Unchecking this does not clip it to the shape, but still have the Opacity mask in that shape. You can also use the Invert Mask command. Checking this inverts the dark and light, which reverses the original opacity. Figure 6-23 shows a figure with Opacity Masks with the Clip checked and unchecked.

Figure 6-23: The other options with Opacity Masks are Invert Mask (top) and Uncheck the Clip box (bottom).

Figure 6-24 shows the objects before (left) the Opacity Mask is applied and after (right). This can have some pretty cool results when using patterns in your Opacity Mask.

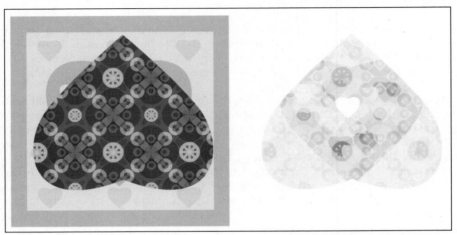

Figure 6-24: The top upside down heart is the Opacity Mask before applying (left) and after (right).

Note   When using the Make Opacity Mask function, all of the objects in the mask are automatically grouped together.

Viewing a transparency grid

Now that you are getting into this whole transparency thing, you might find it hard to see which objects have transparency applied to them. To see these transparent objects, you can enable a transparency grid. This grid shows up as a gray and white checkered pattern positioned behind all other objects.

To view the Transparency grid, choose View ⇨ Show Transparency Grid or press ⌘+Shift+D (Ctrl+Shift+D). If you want to change the look of the Transparency Grid, choose File ⇨ Document Setup and choose Transparency from the pop-up menu. You can also access the Document Setup by pressing ⌘+Option+P (Ctrl+Alt+P). Figure 6-25 shows the Document Setup for Transparency options.

Using these options, you can set the Grid Size and change the Grid Colors. A preview of the grid is also shown next to the color selection boxes. The Simulate Color Paper option shows you what your objects look like when printed on colored paper. At the bottom of the Document Setup dialog box are options for setting the Transparency Flattening settings.

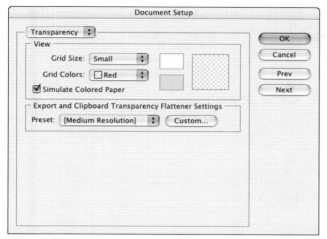

Figure 6-25: In the Document Setup, you can change the Transparency grid.

Printing and flattening

Flattening happens when Transparency is not supported by other applications. Flattening actually creates more pieces of the objects. Flattening also changes your transparency. You lose transparency and instead a color that reflects the opacity color is applied. If you have two objects overlapping and you flatten the image, where they overlap, a third object is created.

Now that you can create transparent objects, how do to you keep that transparency when printing? Illustrator automatically flattens artwork, so you'll have to change the setup:

1. **In the Print dialog box, choose the Advanced area.** In this area, you can set the Overprint and Transparency Flattener options.

2. **Set the resolution from Low to Medium to High.** These options can also be set for the entire document in the Transparency panel of the Document Setup dialog box.

Another option to flatten transparency is to select the object(s) you want to flatten and then choose Object ⇨ Flatten Transparency. In the Flatten Transparency dialog box (shown in Figure 6-26), choose your settings and then click OK. You also have the option to preview the settings by clicking the Preview box.

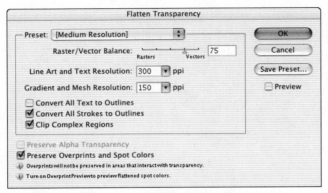

Figure 6-26: The Flatten Transparency dialog box

The options you can set in the Flatten Transparency dialog box are:

✦ **Preset**: Choose from preset transparency flattening options.

✦ **Raster/Vector Balance**: Lets you choose the amount of rasterization. Set the balance high to retain as much vector information. Set the balance lower and more objects are rasterized into pixels.

✦ **Line Art and Text Resolution**: Set the resolution of the vector objects when they are rasterized.

✦ **Gradient and Mesh Resolution**: Set the resolution of the gradients and mesh objects when they are rasterized.

✦ **Convert All Text to Outlines**: Changes all text into outlined paths.

✦ **Convert All strokes to Outlines**: Changes all of the strokes to outlined paths.

✦ **Clip Complex Regions**: Reduces the patching that happens between an object that is partially rasterized and partially vector. This option also may result in very complex paths making it hard to print.

✦ **Preserve Alpha Transparency**: Saves the opacity of flattened objects.

✦ **Preserve Overprints and Spot Colors**: Saves the Overprinting and Spot color objects.

Transparency and type

Now that you have the basics, let's delve into using transparency on objects. You can create a plethora of different effects using transparency. The following sections cover just a few of the amazing things you can do with transparency.

Transparency is not limited to objects. It is fantastic to use on type as well. Take some text and give it a three dimensional feel using Effect ➪ 3D ➪ Extrude & Bevel. Then with color, highlights, and a background added, you can use the Transparency palette to really make the text sing. Figure 6-27 shows an illustration done with text and transparency.

Figure 6-27: Text and transparency create some fantastic effects.

Separating transparent objects

Transparency isn't limited by much of anything. Use it in a brush stroke, creating fills, styles, multiple fills and more. Incorporate it in the styles palette so you can use it again and again. If you choose to flatten the transparency you'll see that Illustrator actually cuts it into sections. Figure 6-28 shows objects with transparency flattened and pulled apart so you can see the sections. To flatten a transparency, first select it; then choose Object ➪ Flatten Transparency. The Flatten Transparency dialog box appears for you to enter your settings (Figure 6-29).

Figure 6-28: Objects before (left) and with transparency flattened and pulled apart (right)

3D, Symbols, and Transparency

Transparency is not limited to basic objects. You can use transparent effects on symbols, effects, patterns, brush strokes, and 3D objects. Figure 6-29 shows three-dimensional gears with different opacity settings. Anything you can do in Illustrator can have transparency applied. The Symbol tool has a Symbol Screener tool, which applies transparency in a brush-like fashion. You can also apply Opacity to the whole group of sprayed symbols using the Transparency palette.

Cross-Reference   The Symbol Screener tool is covered in Chapter 4.

Using type with brush strokes and transparency can also result in some eye-catching effects. To create brush stroke type, follow these steps:

1. **Enter the type you want.** Don't worry about the typeface, just pick something plain.

2. **Convert the type to outlines.** You do this by pressing ⌘(Ctrl)+Shift+O.

3. **Give the outlined type a stroke color, but no fill color.** For more on stroke and fill colors, see Chapter 9.

4. **With the type selected, click one of the Art Brush presets.** Access the Art Brush presets by clicking on the Brushes tab or choosing Window ➪ Show Brushes. Then choose a preset brush.

5. **Press Option (Alt) and drag to copy the type down and to the left a bit to create a drop shadow look.**

6. **Select the back type and color the stroke a darker color and enter an Opacity value.** The example uses an Opacity value of 75%.

7. **Select the front type and enter an Opacity value.** The example uses an Opacity value of 60%.

Doing this creates almost an embossed effect. Add a background, and the text lets the background shine through. Figure 6-30 shows an example of this embossed effect.

Figure 6-29: Three-dimensional gears with different transparency effects applied

Figure 6-30: Brush strokes and symbols with transparency

Creating Gradients

The Gradient feature has no rivals. It is by far the most powerful gradient-creating mechanism available for PostScript drawing programs. Gradients in Adobe Illustrator can have 32 different colors, from end to end in a linear gradient, and from center to outside in a radial Gradient. Gradients can consist of custom colors, process colors, or just plain Black and White. The midpoint of two adjacent colors can be adjusted smoothly and easily toward either color. You can make the Gradient palette available at all times because it is a floating palette. You can access it or view it by pressing F9. And, for what they do, gradients are easier to use than blends.

Note   You can apply gradients only to the fills of paths, not to strokes or text objects. Gradients cannot be used in patterns, either.

Using preset gradients

To choose a preset gradient, select a path and make sure that the Fill box is active in the toolbox. In the Swatches palette, click the gradient swatch icon at the bottom of the palette. The four default Gradient presets appear alone in the Swatches. When you click a gradient swatch, Illustrator applies the gradient to the selected path.

Using the Gradient palette

The Gradient palette, if nothing else, is really neat looking, with all sorts of nifty little controls at your disposal for creating and modifying gradients, as shown in Figure 6-31.

Figure 6-31: The Gradient palette

The pop-up (drop-down list) at the top of the Gradient palette lets you select from Radial or Linear gradient types. Radial gradients move from a center location of an object radial outward in all directions. Linear gradients move in one direction across the object.

The bottom of the Gradient palette is where you control what colors are in the gradient and where the colors are in relation to one another.

The default gradient is black and white and moves from white on the left to black on the right. To add a new color to the bar, click below the bar where you want the new color to appear. This causes a color marker (which appears as a small square). The new color becomes a step between the left color slider and the right color slider. The Location percentage value defines how close you click to either end with 0% on the left and 100% on the right. In other words, the closer you click to the left end, the closer that color is to the left slider.

If you then click the square marker, it becomes selected. You can tell when a gradient marker is selected because the small triangle above it turns dark. When selected, you can change its color by selecting a new color in the Color palette. You can enter up to 32 color stops between the two end colors. When a color stop is selected, entering a different percentage in the text field on the right changes the color stop's position.

The diamonds above the color bar show where the midpoint between two color stops is. By moving the midpoint left or right, you alter the halfway color between two color stops. When a diamond is selected, entering a different percentage in the text field on the right changes the diamond's position.

Working with the Gradient tool

You use the Gradient tool to give a more 3D look to an object. You use the Gradient tool to change the angle and the starting and ending points for a linear gradient, as well as the location of the center and edges of a radial gradient. The tool is also used to offset the highlight on a radial gradient.

Gradients are created with the Gradient palette and applied from the Gradient or tool palette:

1. **Double-clicking the Gradient tool displays the Gradient palette.** The Gradient tool in the toolbox looks like a blended rectangle.

2. **Select a Gradient type.** Select either Radial or Linear.

3. **Enter an Angle if you choose one other than 0 degrees.** You can also enter a location for the starting color (usually 0) and the ending color (usually 100).

4. **Select at least one path that is filled with a Gradient.**

5. **Drag with the Gradient tool on the object.** Dragging on linear gradients changes the angle and the length of the gradient, as well as the start and end points. Dragging with the Gradient tool on radial gradients determines the start position and end position of the gradient. Clicking with the Gradient tool resets the highlight to a new location.

Figure 6-32 shows a gradient original (left) and after changing the angle of the gradient (right).

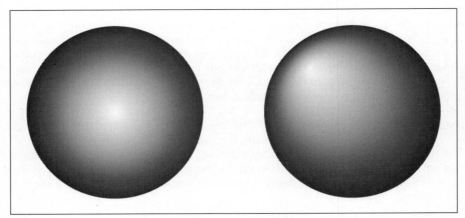

Figure 6-32: The circle on the left has a radial gradient applied to it. The circle on the right altered the highlight of the radial gradient.

Using Gradients to Create Bubbles

Gradients are great to use to create three dimensional looking objects. You can create great molecular pieces for a chemistry drawing, or bubbles for a fun illustration. Start out by drawing circles and using the Gradient tool to change the angle of the gradient. Use the Gradient tool to click where you want the highlight to be and drag where you want the darker area to be. You can create a set of random bubbles quite easily using gradients. To create bubbles follow the steps below:

1. Draw a circle using the Ellipse tool while holding down the Shift key.

2. Fill the circle with a radial gradient in a blue color. Figure A shows the Gradient palette with the settings I used for the bubbles.

Figure A: The Gradient palette with the bubble settings

3. Using the Gradient tool, change the location of the highlight by clicking once where you want it to go, as shown in Figure B.

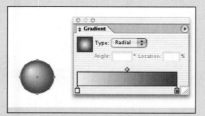

Figure B: Use the Gradient tool to change the highlight.

4. Drag the "bubble" to the Symbol palette creating a new bubble symbol.

5. Using the Symbol sprayer tool, first select the bubble in the Symbol palette and then spray out a bunch of bubbles (Figure C).

6. Using the other Symbolism tools, change the sizes, location, and transparency of the bubbles to give a more realistic look, as shown in Figure D.

Continued

Continued

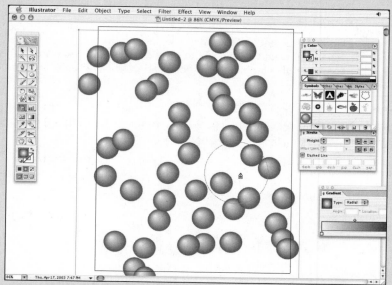

Figure C: Use the Symbol Sprayer tool to spray out a bunch of bubbles.

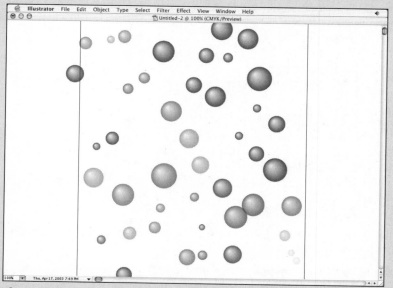

Figure D: Use the Symbolism tools to change the sizes, locations, and opacity of the bubbles.

Creating shadows, highlights, ghosting, and embossing

You can use gradients to simulate special effects by either duplicating and altering a gradient or by using the Gradient tool on similar gradients.

Ghosting is a technique where an object such as text appears lightly against a background. You can simulate ghosting by using the Gradient tool to slightly alter the starting and ending locations of the gradient.

1. **Ghosting effects are easiest to see on text, so create a rectangle and then create a large section of text on top of the rectangle.**

2. **Convert the type into outlines by choosing Type ⇨ Create Outlines.** Alternatively, you can press ⌘ (Ctrl) + Shift + O.

3. **Position the type outline in the center of the rectangle.**

4. **Select both the type and rectangle and apply a Gradient Fill to them.** For Figure 6-33, I used the Sensual Red Gradient at 90°.

Figure 6-33: Using the Gradient tool, drag from the bottom to the top of the rectangle with the type and rectangle selected.

5. **With both rectangle and type selected, drag from the bottom of the rectangle to the top with the Gradient tool to make both gradients exact as shown in Figure 6-34.**

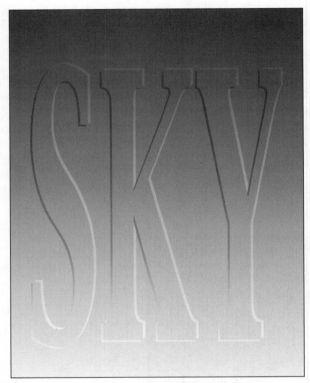

Figure 6-34: Ghosting with gradients

6. **Select and move the type slightly down on the rectangle.** The type appears to be ghosted there.

Offsetting two copies of the original graduated image creates embossed gradient images. In one offset image, the gradient is lightened; in the other, the gradient is darkened.

1. **Draw a rectangle.**

2. **Create text and convert it to outlines by choosing Type ⇨ Create Outlines.** Alternatively, you can press ⌘ (Ctrl) + Shift + O.

3. **Select Object ⇨ Ungroup.** You can also press ⌘(Ctrl) + Shift + G. This ungroups the text.

4. **Select both the type outline and the rectangle and fill them with a Gradient.** The example uses the Midday Sky gradient from the Swatches palette.

5. **Drag the Gradient tool across the rectangle keeping both objects selected.** This sets the gradient length and angle.

6. **In the Swatches palette, select the gradient used for both the rectangle and type outlines, and make two duplicates of it.** Make one duplicate lighter by selecting each color stop and moving it to the right. Make one gradient darker than the original by moving each color stop to the left.

7. **Using the Move dialog box, create a copy of the type path that's offset a few points up and to the left.**

8. **Fill the upper-left path with the lighter gradient you created.**

9. **Create another copy offset a few points down and to the right and fill with the darker one you made.**

10. **Select the middle type path and choose Object ⇨ Arrange ⇨ Bring to Front. You can also press ⌘+Shift- (Ctrl+Shift+).** The type appears embossed, as shown in Figure 6-35.

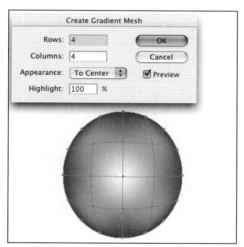

Figure 6-35: Embossed type

Tip

To make embossed images seem sunken rather than raised, make the lighter image below and to the right and the darker image above and to the left. To make the image seem further raised or recessed, increase the distance between the original path and the offset images.

Expanding gradient objects

In Illustrator, you can automatically change gradients into blends by selecting the gradient you wish to change and then by choosing Expand (Object ➪ Expand). You might want to expand a gradient into a blend to add special effects to the object with the paths rather than a gradient fill. Since you expand the object into paths, there are many more paths to change, twist, or mangle creating a lot of options for your object. Expanding the object changes the fill to a blend of paths. The Expand dialog box (see Figure 6-36) appears for you to choose to Expand the Object, fill, or stroke. You also choose whether to Expand the Gradient to a Mesh, or the number of steps in the blend.

Cross-Reference   For more on blending see Chapter 11.

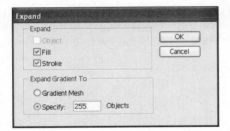

Figure 6-36: The Expand dialog box can convert a gradient into a blend.

Printing gradients

Checking the Compatible Gradient and Mesh Printing option checkbox in the Print dialog box prevents most gradient problems from occurring. Choose File ➪ Print then choose Graphics from the left side choices. When you're printing to PostScript Level 1 printers, checking this box speeds gradient printing dramatically. If your target printer is not a PostScript printer (maybe it is an Epson 785 EPX) then this checkbox is disabled. Compatible gradients bypass a high-level imaging system within Illustrator that older printers and printers without genuine Adobe PostScript (commonly referred to as "PostScript clones") cannot understand. Checking this box may cause documents to print slower on printers that would ordinarily be able to print those documents.

Adding Realism with Mesh

The Mesh tool changes a normal filled path into a multicolored object with the click of a button. You use the Mesh tool to add highlights, shading, and three-dimensional effects. Figure 6-37 shows an object created with the Mesh tool. You click and create a new color at the clicked point. The new color blends smoothly into the object's original color. The next four sections how you have to enhance highlights and color, change the highlight color, and add multiple highlights.

Figure 6-37: The Mesh tool adds more depth to the clouds.

Enhancing with highlights and color

The Mesh tool is found in the toolbox it looks like a rectangle with squiggly lines inside. The Mesh tool adds highlights or shading with the click of a mouse. To apply a mesh:

1. **Always deselect the object you want to add a point to first.**

2. **Pick the color of the highlight point in the Color palette.** If it isn't visible, choose Window ⇨ Color.

3. **Select the Mesh tool from the toolbox.**

4. **Click to set the point.**

5. **To change the highlight color, with the Direct Selection tool, select a point on the mesh and change its color values in the Color palette.**

The Mesh dialog box is accessed by choosing Object ⇨ Create Mesh, as shown in Figure 6-38. To get this dialog box, you must have something selected first or Illustrator grays the option out. In the Mesh dialog box, you can set how many mesh lines form a row and a column, whether the appearance is flat, to center, or to the edge, and the highlight intensity from 0-100%.

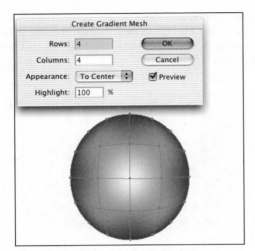

Figure 6-38: The Mesh dialog box

Adding multiple highlights

Clicking more than once on an object with the Mesh tool adds more blends to the object. Each click creates a new horizontal and vertical axis. For this reason, the tool is called a "mesh." The more clicks that are created, the more individual lines appear until the base object appears as a complex mesh of lines. Each intersection of lines is a point of color that can be changed. However, when you change a color, adjacent intersecting points aren't updated. The following steps give you an example of what happens when you add multiple highlights to an object.

1. **Create a dark colored rectangle and deselect it.**

2. **Change the color in the Color palette to a bright color.**

3. **With the Mesh tool, click in the middle of the rectangle.** A point of light appears, creating a sort of radial gradient.

4. **Deselect the rectangle, change the fill color to another bright, and click another point.** When you do this, two additional points that are somewhere between the dark background and the two bright highlights appear. Figure 6-39 shows an example of this.

Tip   If you never manually change the color of the two new points, they'll continue to update to match the color of the surrounding points. But, if you change the color of one of those points, they're no longer "smart," and remain that color regardless of the colors of the points around them.

You can create very complex Mesh objects with just a dozen or so clicks; these objects are editable, but you need to somehow keep track of which points were the originals, so that all the other ones update automatically.

Figure 6-39: The rectangle with a yellow highlight in the middle and green on three edges

Tip   You can change the background color of the object you're editing after several highlights have been added by selecting all the points on the perimeter of the original object with the Direct Selection tool. Every click with the Mesh tool adds four points to the perimeter of the object.

Summary

✦ You use the Swatches to store and apply commonly used colors.

✦ The Color palette enables you to choose colors from a Color Ramp and to mix colors using interactive sliders.

✦ You change the color space from grayscale to CMYK to RGB to HSB by selecting one from the Color pop-up menu.

✦ You can color paths and type quickly by using the Eyedropper tool (to sample colors from paths or placed images) and the Paint Bucket tool (to apply those sampled colors).

✦ Create your own gradients and save them in the Swatches palette.

✦ You can quickly turn gradients into blends by selecting the gradient and applying the Expand option.

✦ The Mesh tool makes adding shadows, highlights, and shaping a breeze, as shown in the last section of this chapter.

✦   ✦   ✦

Putting Illustrator to Work

Using Illustrator to Organize Objects

As more and more objects are added to a document, the artwork can very quickly become unmanageable. To address this problem, Illustrator includes many different features for organizing the various objects in the document. From locking or hiding objects that you don't want to accidentally move, to grouping a set of objects so they can all move together, these features are keys to success in Illustrator.

Another key way to organize objects covered in this chapter is use of the Layers palette. The Layers palette offers precise control over different objects by placing them on different layers and controlling what effects are applied to them.

Locking and Hiding Objects

All objects in Illustrator can be locked or hidden — including guides. The process of locking and hiding work is about the same, and the results are only marginally different. In a way, hiding is an "invisible lock." Locking the artwork still leaves it visible and printable. When you hide an object, it is for all intents and purposes "gone" until you show it again. Locking is great to use when you still need to see the location of the object, but don't want to accidentally move or transform it. Hiding works nicely when you need the object out of the way but not gone.

Cross-Reference　You can quickly lock and hide layers using the Show/Hide and Lock/Unlock columns in the Layer palette. For more on the Layer palette, see the section "Using the Layers palette" later in this chapter.

Locking

Locking has expanded to more than just objects. Under the Lock menu, you can choose to lock a selection, all artwork above, or other layers. To lock an object, select it and choose Object ⇨ Lock ⇨ Selection. You can also press ⌘+2 (Ctrl+2). Illustrator not only locks the object, it also deselects it. In fact, you cannot select an object once you lock it. You cannot move or change locked objects, nor can you hide them. Because you cannot select a locked object, you can't change it — in Illustrator, as in most applications, you can only modify objects when you select them.

A locked object remains locked when you save and close the document. As a result, locked objects remain locked the next time you open the document. Because locked objects are always visible, they always print. You can't tell from the printed item whether it is locked or not.

To change a locked object, choose Object ⇨ Unlock All. You can also press ⌘+Option+2 (Ctrl+Alt+2). This command unlocks (and selects) all objects. There is no way to unlock just a few objects locked with the Lock command.

Tip   A tricky way to invisibly "copyright" your illustration is to create a small text box in a far corner of the pasteboard with your copyright information in it, color the text white, and lock the text box. No one knows it is there, and it can't be easily selected. In fact, it'll even print if it is placed on top of a background in another program.

You should consider locking objects under the following circumstances:

✦ **When the document is full of complex artwork:** You can do a Select All and not have to wait forever for the selection tool to finish selecting all parts of the complex art before locking the artwork.

✦ **When you don't want to accidentally move or change certain artwork.**

✦ **When you can't easily select paths that are under other paths:** In this case, you lock the ones on top.

✦ **When you have to fit an illustration into a certain area:** In this situation, you create a box of that size and lock it so you have an instant boundary with which to work.

Hiding

Sometimes you don't want to see certain objects on your document page — perhaps because they obstruct your view of other objects or they take a long time to redraw. In these cases, it's a good idea to hide the objects in question. To do so, select them and choose Object ⇨ Hide ⇨ Selection. Alternatively, you can press ⌘+3 (Ctrl+3).

Hidden objects are invisible and unselectable; they still exist in the document, but they do not print. When a document is reopened, hidden objects reappear.

Tip

You can press Command+Option+Shift+2 (Ctrl+Alt+Shift+2) to lock all unselected objects or Command+Option+Shift+3 (Ctrl+Alt+Shift+3) to hide all unselected objects.

To show (and select) all hidden objects, choose Object ⇨ Show All. Alternatively, you can press ⌘+Option+3 (Ctrl+Alt+3). Think of it as "unhide." There is no way to show just a few of the hidden objects when using the Show All command.

Setting attributes

Choosing Window ⇨ Attributes (F11) brings up the Attributes palette. In this palette, your options are:

✦ Add notes about the document or specific objects. You can use notes to tell different things about the document such as color space, special effects used, and so on.

✦ Reverse Path direction is used when working with compound paths. Use this to reverse a path's direction when a multiple compound path isn't working.

✦ Show or hide the object's center point option lets you view the center point of a closed path or not view the center point.

✦ Change the flatness characteristics lets you alter the output DPI of the object when sending to a printer.

✦ Another useful way to "copyright" your artwork is to select all the objects and then go to the Attributes palette and enter your copyright information within the palette as shown in Figure 7-1.

✦ The Attributes palette also allows you to specify a URL (Uniform Resource Locator) for a selected object or objects.

Figure 7-1: The Attributes palette

Stacking Order

Stacking order is a crucial concept that you need to understand in the world of Adobe Illustrator. This concept is not the same as the layer concept; rather it is the forward/backward relationship between objects within each layer.

After you create the first object, Illustrator places the next object you create above the first object, or on top of it. Likewise, Illustrator places the third created object above both the first and second objects. This cycle continues indefinitely, with objects being stacked one on top of another.

A great deal of planning goes into creating an illustration so that the object you draw first is on the bottom of the pile and the last thing you draw ends up on the top. To make your life much more pleasant, Illustrator lets you move objects up and down (forward or backward) through the stack of objects. In fact, Illustrator's method of moving objects up and down is so simple and basic that it is also quite limiting. You can also move objects via the Layers palette. The Layers palette offers a wider range of moving and organizing options.

Cross-Reference   For more on layers and moving objects, see "Moving and layers" later in this chapter.

Stacking order for objects

You can change the stacking order of objects in Illustrator relative to foreground and background either all the way to the bottom or all the way to the top, or you can move objects up or down through the stacking order. Figure 7-2 shows the same illustration after various objects were moved in the stacking order. The commands for moving objects are as follows:

Figure 7-2: The stacking order changed the look of the illustration from the objects on the left to the right.

✦ **Bring to Front:** To move an object to the front, choose Object ⇨ Arrange ⇨ Bring to Front, or press ⌘+Shift+] (Ctrl+Shift+]). Illustrator moves the selected object forward so that it is in front of every other object (but only in that layer).. Bring to Front is not available when no objects are selected. Multiple-selected paths and grouped paths still retain their front/back position relative to each other.

✦ **Send to Back:** To move an object to the back, choose Object ⇨ Arrange ⇨ Send to Back, or press ⌘+Shift+[(Ctrl+Shift+[). Illustrator sends the selected object to the back so that it is behind every other object. Send to Back is not available when there are no objects selected. Multiple selected paths and grouped paths still retain their front/back position relative to each other.

✦ **Bring Forward:** To move selected objects forward one object at a time, choose Object ⇨ Arrange ⇨ Bring Forward, or press ⌘+] (Ctrl+]).

✦ **Send Backward:** To move selected objects backward one object at a time, choose Object ⇨ Arrange ⇨ Send Backward, or press ⌘+[(Ctrl+[).

Stacking order for text

Individual characters in a string of text work in a similar manner to their object cousins when it comes to front/back placement. The first character typed is placed at the bottom of the text block, and the last character typed is placed at the top, as shown in Figure 7-3. To move individual characters forward or backward, you must first choose Type ⇨ Create Outlines, or press ⌘+Shift+O (Ctrl+Shift+O), and select the outline of the character you want to arrange. The outlined text is now treated as an object. Use the same arranging commands for Object ⇨ Arrange to move the stacking order of the outlined type.

Cross-Reference

For more on text, see Chapter 8.

Figure 7-3: Text characters that overlap each other

Stacking order for strokes and fills

Try as you might, you cannot change the forward/backward relationship of strokes and fills. Strokes are always in front of fills for the same path. To get the fill to cover or overlap the stroke, you must copy the path, use the Paste in Front command (choose Edit ➪ Paste in Front or press ⌘+Option+V (Ctrl+Alt+V)), and then remove the stroke from the path you just pasted.

Cross-Reference   For more on Strokes and Fills, see Chapter 9.

Pasting objects in front of and behind selected objects

Choosing Edit ➪ Paste in Front, or pressing ⌘+Option+V (Ctrl+Alt+V), pastes any objects you have on the Clipboard on top of any selected objects, or on the top of the current layer if no objects are selected.

Choosing Edit ➪ Paste in Back, or pressing ⌘+Option+Shift+V (Ctrl+Alt+Shift+V) pastes any objects on the Clipboard behind any selected objects or on the bottom of the current layer if no objects are selected. When you paste an object in front or behind, you also are pasting the attributes of that object (their stroke and fill). You can paste an object that only has a fill or only has a stroke in front or behind other objects.

In addition, both Paste in Front and Paste in Back paste objects in the same location as the copied object, even from document to document. If the documents are different sizes, Illustrator pastes them in the same location relative to the center of each document. If the Clipboard is empty, or if type selected with a Type tool is on the Clipboard, these options are not available.

Note   Copied items in Illustrator always retain their layer name and related layer information. When you copy an item that is on layer "X-Flies" and paste that item in another document that contains an X-Flies layer, the item appears on the X-Flies layer. If the document doesn't contain that layer, Illustrator creates a new layer with that name and the item appears on that layer. This only works if you check the Paste Remembers Layers option item in the Layers palette's pop-up menu.

Creating and Deconstructing Groups

Grouping is the process of putting together a series of objects that need to remain spatially constant in relationship to each other. You generally group objects if you intend to move them, flatten them, or perform one effect on all of them at once. Your group may contain as little as one path, to an unlimited number of objects. You generally ungroup a group of objects when you no longer need the grouping.

For example, you might ungroup objects so that you can edit one of them. When you have objects that go together, say for instance a person you created, you might want to group all parts of that person to keep it neatly together. That way when you want to move the person, all pieces come as one unit. Many times you try to move a collection of objects, and you miss one or more pieces. When you group the pieces together, they move all together using the Selection tool. Ungrouping is necessary when you want to separate the objects to make them a part of another group or stand alone. When applying transformations or special effects, you'll want to ungroup so the specific object can have the effect applied.

Grouping

In any illustration, objects are much easier to manipulate if they are grouped. Group like areas together as one group and so on. Grouping similar areas is helpful for moving entire areas forward or backward as well as for doing any type of horizontal or vertical movement or transformation upon a set of objects. One example of grouping would be if you drew a tree with a bunch of apples. You would want to group the apples together so you can edit the apples all at one time, like changing the color, or size.

To group objects together, follow these simple steps:

1. **Select the items you want to group with any of the selection tools.** For a run down of the various select tools, see Chapter 5.

2. **Choose Object ➪ Group.** Alternatively, you can press ⌘+G (Ctrl+G). This command makes the separate objects stay together when you select them.

Now, when you select any object in a group with the regular Selection tool, Illustrator selects all the objects in that group and makes all the points in a path solid (selected).

Cross-Reference   The Group Selection tool is covered in Chapter 5.

Not only can you group several objects together, but you can also group groups together to form a group of groups in which there is a hierarchical series of grouped groups. In addition, groups can be grouped to individual objects or to several other objects.

After a set of objects or groups is grouped together, grouping it again produces no effect. The computer does not beep at you, display a dialog box, or otherwise indicate that the objects or groups you are attempting to group together are already grouped. Of course, it never hurts to choose Object ➪ Group again if you are not sure if they are grouped. If they weren't grouped before, they now are, and if they were grouped before, nothing unusual or unexpected happens.

Tip   If you are having trouble selecting all the objects for each type in a group, choose Object ➪ Select ➪ Same Paint Style after one object is selected. This process usually (but not always) selects all the objects of one type.

Tip   If you group several objects that are on different layers, all the objects move to the top-most layer and form a group there. This means that the perceived stacking order may change and could change the appearance of your Illustration.

Ungrouping

If you are looking to apply a specific effect to one object in the group, you'll have to ungroup the object so the whole group isn't affected. Let say in the apple tree, you want to make one apple really big and rotten looking. Ungroup the apples first, re-group the other apples (to keep them organized), and apply the effect to the one apple. To ungroup groups (separate them into standalone paths and objects), do the following:

1. **Select the group with either the Group Selection tool or the regular Selection tool.** For a run down of the various select tools, see Chapter 5.

2. **Choose Object ➪ Ungroup.** Any selected groups become ungrouped. Alternatively, you can press ⌘+Shift-G (Ctrl+Shift+G).

Ungrouping, like grouping, works on one set of groups at a time. For example, if you have two groups that are grouped together, ungrouping that group results in the two original groups. (Don't worry; I'm just as confused as you are in this area.) If you choose Ungroup again, Illustrator also ungroups those two groups. Another way to understand grouping is to think of nesting. Each operation adds or subtracts only one level of nesting.

Tip   When you absolutely do not want anything in a group grouped with anything else–and you suspect that there may be several mini-groups within the group you have selected–simply press ⌘+Shift-G (Ctrl+Shift+G) several times. You do not need to select the subgroups individually to ungroup them. To get rid of all the groups in your illustration, choose Select ➪ All, or press ⌘+A (Ctrl+A) and then proceed to ungroup by pressing ⌘+Shift-G (Ctrl+Shift+G) several times. To remove certain objects from a group or compound path, select just these objects, cut, and Paste in Front (or Paste in Back).

Layering Your Artwork

The layering feature of Illustrator provides an easy and powerful way to separate artwork into individual sections. A layer is a separate section of the document that is on its own level, above, under, or in between other layers, but never on the same level as another layer. You can view these sections separately, locked, hidden, and rearranged around each other. Figure 7-4 shows a logo illustration that has been layered and also shows the Layer palette representing the various layers.

Figure 7-4: This logo was created using a total of 10 layers to keep the illustration organized.

As you can see from this illustration, having the various elements of your illustrator helps you organize them. Each area of the illustration has its own layer. You use these layers to create the stacking order as well as keep the text on one layer for easier editing. You'll find that artists use the layers to organize the different grouped objects, shadows, borders, and backgrounds. You can also turn off and on layers to give a client different options on a logo, website, or business theme. Using the Layers palette, you can create, control, and manipulate layers to suit your needs. Another use for layers is to trace placed images.

Cross-
Reference

For more on tracing placed images, see the section "Working with Templates in Illustrator."

The biggest advantage for layers is that you can color code them to further organize your work.. By choosing Select ⇨ All, or by pressing ⌘+A (Ctrl+A), you can quickly see which objects are on which layers, just by the color of the paths and points. Using the same colors for all layers makes you miss out on half the power of layers. Use vivid, distinct colors for each layer.

Of course, having too many layers can pose problems. Layers take up RAM (Random Access Memory) and computer power. Therefore, the more layers you have, the slower your system operates. For this reason, you should only create layers only when they help you better organize an illustration. Even setting up one additional layer can dramatically ease selection and moving problems.

Tip   You can create as many layers as you want, up to the limitations of application memory. To make sure that the Adobe people were on the up-and-up about this, I created 5000 layers in one document. It worked without ever questioning my need for 5000 layers. Why would you need 5000 layers? I hope you wouldn't, but you shouldn't have any fears that you cannot create enough layers for an illustration. Of course, 5000 layers slow Illustrator to a crawl. I had to click the mouse button and hold on the menu bar for about 3 seconds before the menu appeared. Suffice it to say that the more layers you create after a certain point (several hundred), the slower Illustrator runs.

Getting started with layers

After you realize that you need to use layers, what do you do? The only way to manipulate, create, and delete layers is by using the Layers palette. If the Layers palette is not showing, choose Window ➪ Layers. Alternatively, you can press F7. When you open the Layers palette for the first time in a new document, you see only Layer 1 listed.

To create a new layer, do the following:

1. **Click the New Layer icon at the bottom of the palette.** The icon looks like a piece of paper with the corner folded over and is to the left of the Trash can icon in Figure 7-4. You can also click the triangle in the upper-right of the palette to display a pop-up menu. Clicking the first item, New Layer, displays the New Layer dialog box.

2. **Change the name of your layer.** In the Layer Options dialog box, shown in Figure 7-5, the name of the new layer, Layer 2., is highlighted. To change this name, type a new name, and it replaces the generic name.

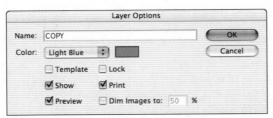

Figure 7-5: The Layers Options dialog box lets you name the layer.

Note   To create a new layer and display the Layer Options dialog box at the same time, press Option (Alt)+.

3. **Select any of the options that you want for this layer.** The options below the name in the Layers Options dialog box affect how view the layer and make it function. The options are as follows:

- **Color:** The first option is the color of the paths and points when objects on that layer are selected. Choose one of the preset colors from the pop-up menu or select the Other option to use a Custom Color. Each time you create a new layer, a different color (going in order from the list) is applied to that layer.

- **Template:** Use this option when you want to trace something, but not have it print. If you check Template, Illustrator automatically unchecks the Print option enables the Dim Placed Images option. See more on the Dim Placed Images option below.

- **Show:** This option makes the objects in the layer visible.

- **Lock:** Prevents objects on this layer from being selected and prevents any objects from being put on this layer.

Cross-Reference For more on the Lock feature, see the section "Locking and Hiding Objects."

- **Print:** Enables you to print objects that are on this layer.

- **Preview:** Makes the objects on this layer preview.

- **Dim Placed Images:** This option dims any placed images on the layer, making them 50% lighter as a default or you can enter a value.

4. **Click OK.** The new layer appears above the existing layer in the Layers palette.

If you want the objects on the new layer to appear below the objects on the existing layer, click the name of the new layer and drag it under Layer 1. To modify the existing layer, double-click it. You see the Layer Options dialog box again. Make the changes and choose the options that you want for this layer and then click OK.

Tip You can easily bypass the Layer Options dialog box when creating new layers. Clicking on the New Layer icon without pressing Option (Alt), or pressing Option (Alt) while choosing New Layer from the Layer palette pop-up menu, creates a new layer with the default naming scheme. You can always double-click that layer to access the Layer Options for that layer.

Using the Layers palette

The Layers palette, shown in Figure 7-6, is the control center where all layer-related activities take place. Most activities take place on the main section of the Layers palette, which is always visible when the Layers palette is onscreen. Other activities take place in the pop-up menu that appears when you press the triangle in the upper right of the palette.

Illustrator has wonderful options in the Layers palette. First is the capability to thin the display of layers in the palette for those illustrations with tons of layers. Second is the capability to drag to a hidden layer. Third is that Illustrator displays layers that you don't have set to print in italics so that you can see quickly what will and what will not print.

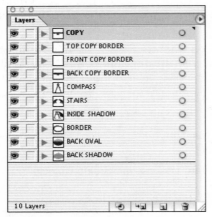

Figure 7-6: The Layers palette

Clicking the Close button in the upper-left corner (Mac) upper-right corner (Windows) closes the Layers palette. Another way to close the Layers palette is to choose Window ➪ Layers (F7). To bring the Layers palette back to the screen, choose Window ➪ Layers (F7).

Using Layer palette columns

Aside from the standard Maximize, Minimize and Close buttons at the top of the palette, the following gives an exhaustive list of the options in the Layers palette:

✦ **Show/Hide column:** The far left column controls how you view each layer is viewed. If this column has a solid eye icon, the layer is in Preview mode. The hollow eye icon means that the layer is in Outline mode. No eye indicates a hidden layer. Clicking a solid or hollow eye icon toggles it from showing to hidden. Clicking in the Show/Hide Column when no eye is present shows the layer. Pressing ⌘ (Ctrl) and clicking the eye toggles it from solid (Preview mode) to hollow (Outline mode) and back again. Pressing Option (Alt) and clicking an eye shows or hides all other layers. You also have a little icon with an overlaid square, triangle, and ellipse to indicate a template layer.

✦ **Lock/Unlock column:** The second column is the Lock/Unlock column. The lock icon indicates whether layer is locked or not. An empty column means that the layer is not locked. A lock icon means that the layer is locked from use. A grayed out eye indicates a hidden layer.

To manually activate the Lock and Hide commands and to learn about their various uses, see the section "Locking and Hiding Objects."

✦ **Layer Names:** The column in the center of the palette lists the names of all the layers in the document. When no documents are open, no layers are listed. If one layer is highlighted and has a triangle in the corner, that layer is active. All new objects are created on the active layer. You can select a range of layers by pressing Shift-clicking each layer. Pressing ⌘ (Ctrl) allows you to select or deselect additional layers.

The layer at the top of the column is the layer that is on top of all the other layers. The layer at the bottom of the column is the layer that is at the bottom of all the other layers. To move a layer, or layers, click it and drag it up or down. As you drag, a dark horizontal line indicates where the layer(s) are placed when you release the mouse button.

Press Option+Click the eye icon to turn all layers off except the selected layer(Alt+Click].

Press ⌘+Option+Click the eye icon to turn all layers into Outline mode except the selected layer (Ctrl+Alt+Click).

You can undo all layer changes as they happen by choosing Edit ⇨ Undo, or by pressing ⌘+Z (Ctrl+Z) right afterward.

✦ **Object status:** To the right of the layer's name is the object status of the layer. If a square appears in that column, at least one object on that layer is selected.

Using the Layers palette icons

There are four icons along the bottom of the Layers palette that make layer manipulation very easy. The first icon (a rectangle and a circle) is the Make/Release Clipping Mask icon. The second icon (an arrow pointing to a little piece of paper with the corner turned over) is the Create New Sublayer icon. The third icon (a little piece of paper with the corner turned over) is the New Layer icon. The fourth icon is the Trash icon:

✦ **The Make/Release Clipping Mask icon:** This icon lets you create a clipping mask in the layer. The topmost object in the layer acts as the masking shape. The difference between using Make/Release Clipping Mask from the Layers palette rather than choosing Object ⇨ Clipping Mask ⇨ Make is that the objects won't be grouped when using the Layers palette.

For more on Clipping Masks, see Chapter 11.

✦ **The Create New Sublayer icon:** You use this icon to add sublayers. To do so, select the layer and choose the Create New Sublayer icon or choose Create New Sublayer from the pop-up menu in the Layers palette. You can have many sublayers inside a layer as you want. To see the sublayers, click the triangle to the left of the layer name. You can also drag change a layer into a sublayer by dragging it under the layer you want it to go to. Figure 7-7 shows the sublayers within a layer. You'll notice a sublayer is indicated by <> brackets and it is indented to the right. Some sublayers have a triangle indicating that there are more sublayers within that sublayer. The sublayers also tell you what is in that layer, for example <path>, or <compound path>, and so on.

✦ **The New Layer icon:** clicking this icon creates a new layer instantly, without the New Layer dialog box appearing. If you press Option (Alt) and click the New Layer icon, Illustrator creates a new layer by way of the New Layer dialog box. Dragging a layer or layers to the New Layer icon duplicates those layers and everything on them.

✦ **The Trash icon:** Clicking the Trash icon deletes the selected layers. If there is art on a layer that is about to be deleted, a dialog box appears to make sure that you really want to delete that layer. Option(Alt]+clicking the Trash icon deletes selected layers without a warning dialog box, whether or not art is on the selected layers. You can also drag a layer or layers to the Trash icon; Illustrator deletes the layers without a warning dialog box.

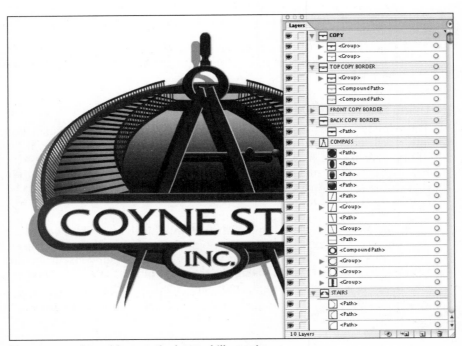

Figure 7-7: The sublayers of a layered illustration

Moving and layers

By selecting an object, you enable it to be moved to another layer. A selected object shows up on its layer with a blue square in the upper-right corner of that layer. Dragging that square to another layer moves the selected object to that layer. Figure 7-8 shows a selection marker being dragged to another layer. You can only drag to a layer that is not hidden or locked. Only one object at a time can be moved to another layer.

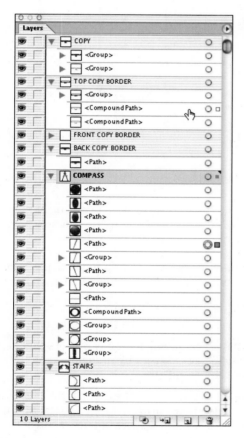

Figure 7-8: The selected object is being moved to another layer.

Using the Layers palette pop-up menu

Clicking the triangle in the upper-right of the Layers palette displays a pop-up menu that shows the different options that are available relative to the selected layers (see Figure 7-9).

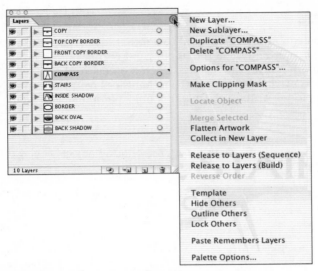

Figure 7-9: The Layers palette pop-up menu

The options are explained as follows:

✦ **New Layer:** Creates a new layer at the top of the list. When you select this option, the Layer Options dialog box appears. When you create a new layer, Illustrator automatically assigns the next color in the color list.

Tip

If you press the Option (Alt) key before you click the pop-up menu triangle, the first menu item reads New Layer Above First Layer, or New Layer Above whatever the name of the active layer is.

✦ **New Sublayer:** Creates a new sublayer underneath the selected layer.

✦ **Duplicate Layer:** Duplicates selected layers, along with any objects that are on those layers. You can also duplicate select layers by dragging them to the New Layer icon at the bottom of the Layers palette.

✦ **Delete Layers:** Deletes the layer and any artwork on the layer. If the layer you want to delete contains artwork, a dialog box warns you that you are about to delete it. If one or more objects are selected, the Layers palette menu says "Delete Selection". If you select several layers, the entry reads Delete Layers, and all selected layers are deleted. You can undo layer deletions.

✦ **Options for Layer 1:** This option is called Layer Options for whatever the name of the active layer is. The menu item reads Layers Options if you select more than one layer. Selecting Layer Options displays the Layer Options dialog box, in which you can choose a number of different options. If more than one layer is selected, the layer options affect all selected layers.

✦ **Make/Release Clipping Mask:** Creates a clipping mask in the layer. The topmost object in the layer acts as the masking shape.

✦ **Locate Object:** Use this to find where an object is located in the Layers palette. Choose an object in the document, and then choose this option to see where it is in the Layers palette.

✦ **Merge Selected:** This option combines selected layers into one. Merge Layers does two important things: First, it places art that you want on the same layer together in one step. Second, it eliminates all those empty layers automatically. When you've finished an illustration, if you know you won't need separate layers anymore, it's a great idea to go ahead and select all your layers and Merge them into one.

✦ **Flatten Artwork:** This option takes all of your layers and combines them as one layer.

✦ **Collect in New Layer:** This option moves the selected objects to a new layer.

✦ **Release to Layers (Sequence):** Use this option to move the selected objects to individual layers.

✦ **Release to Layers (Build):** Use this option to move the selected objects to layers in a cumulative sequence. You mainly use this option to create cumulative animation sequences.

✦ **Reverse:** Use this to reverse the stacking order of the selected layers. The layers must be in consecutive order.

✦ **Template:** You use this option to make your selection a template.

✦ **Hide Others:** Hides all the layers but the selected ones

✦ **Outline All Layers/Preview All Layers:** This option changes all unselected layers to Outline view or changes all unselected layers to Preview view

✦ **Lock All Layers/Unlock All Layers:** This option locks all layers but the selected ones or unlocks all layers but the selected ones.

✦ **Paste Remembers Layers:** Causes Illustrator to paste all objects on the layer from which you copied them, regardless of which layer is currently active. Unchecking this menu item causes objects on the Clipboard to be pasted on the current layer.

✦ **Palette Options:** Use this option to change the Row Size, Thumbnail views, and whether to Show Layers Only.

Tip   Double-clicking on a layer name brings up the Layer options dialog box.

Working with Templates in Illustrator

It's often much easier to create artwork in Illustrator by starting with something to trace, whether it's a logo, a floor plan, or your cousin Fred's disproportionate profile. Even the best artists use some form of template when they draw to keep proportions consistent, to get angles just right, and for other reasons that help them to achieve the best possible result.

This section discusses different methods and techniques for tracing different types of artwork within Illustrator. The general process it the same. First you place an image — the image that you eventually want to trace — on a layer, which is your template layer. Next, you use the template layer to trace your image. You can then decide whether you want to quickly and less accurately trace your image using the Auto Trace tool or accurately and slowly trace your image manually.

Don't think of these methods as cheating, but instead, as a way to quickly create better and more accurate artwork. Okay, it's cheating just a little bit. . . .

Placing a template on a layer

You can create a template in Illustrator by placing any image into a "template" layer. That image can then be used for tracing or as a guide for creating or adjusting artwork. Any layer in Illustrator can be used as a template layer; however, only raster images can be used as templates.

To create a template layer:

1. **Double-click the layer you want to modify.** The Layer Options dialog box appears. For more about the various options in this dialog box, see the section "Getting started with layers."

2. **In the Layer Options dialog box, check the Template option.** By default the Dim Images checkbox is checked, and all other options are grayed out.

3. **Enter a value in the Dim Images text field.** The lower the percent value, the lighter the image appears in Illustrator.

4. **Click OK to apply the change.** Illustrator creates a template layer from the image you selected.

Note   Paths that you place on Template layers do not show when they're selected. Instead, an icon appears in the Layers palette view column to indicate that the current layer is a template layer. Template layers do not print. For more on the columns in the Layer palette, see the section Using Layer palette columns.

Cross-Reference   For more on how to rasterize your artwork, see Chapter 2.

Tip   You can make any vector artwork into a template by rasterizing it and then setting that layer into a template layer.

Figure 7-10 shows an image before and after dimming.

Placed images work well as templates because their resolution is independent of the Illustrator document. You can scale placed images up or down, changing their onscreen resolution as you change their size. For example, if you scale a 72-dpi (dots-per-inch) image down to one-fourth of its imported size (making the dpi of the placed image 4 x 72-dpi, or 288-dpi), you may zoom in on the image in Illustrator at 400%. At 400%, the placed image still has a 72-dpi resolution because one-fourth of 288-dpi is 72-dpi. The more you increase the placed image's dpi by scaling it down, the more you can zoom in to see the details of the image. If the placed image's dpi is already higher than 72, you can zoom in to a certain amount and retain quite a bit of detail automatically.

Another plus: A placed image template is a full-color template that keeps all the shading and colors and enables you to see all the fine details easily. That way you can trace all of the tiny details that the color brings out.

Figure 7-10: The original image (left) and after dimming (right)

Using a template to trace an image

Now that you've got your template (placed image) all set up, you're ready to trace it — or so you would think. There are lots of different ways to go about tracing, and I've included the "best of the best" techniques in this section to help you muddle through this mess.

Tracing and organizing objects

When creating any artwork from a traced image, use the Layers palette to organize your drawn objects. You can put the line art on one layer, the filled shapes on another layer, and type on a different layer. This organization makes your life easier when it comes to editing the illustration. By turning some layers into outlines, you can work with a less complicated image. You can use layers for more than just dimming images for tracing. One of the unsung features of Illustrator's layers is the capability to show some layers in Preview mode and others in Outline mode (see the figure below for an example).

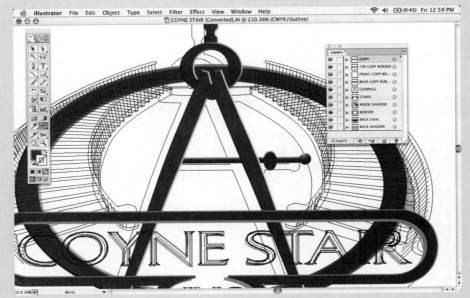

Notice in the Layers palette that some eye icons are in outline mode, showing you that the layer is in outline mode.

This is great for tracing because you can set the layer you're working on to Outline mode so objects you create aren't blocking out the template below. Just make sure your active "drawing" layer is above the template layer.

You can trace templates in two ways: manually and automatically. Manually tracing consists of using the Pencil and Pen tools to tediously trace the edges of a template — often a very time-consuming task. You manually trace an image when you have a lot of time on your hands, and when you want to retain every single detail of the traced image. As an alternatively, you can use the Auto Trace tool to speed up the process. Unfortunately, automatic tracing may result in less than desirable quality. Obviously, you use this technique when time is more important than detail.

You generally use automatic tracing for more basic forms and manual tracing for complex detail. A combination of manual and automatic tracing works quite nicely when you are drawing fairly basic illustrations, especially those composed of type and straight lines. You automatically trace the basic shapes first and then use the path editing tools to add or remove anchor points and move paths so that the image has a consistent look. After fixing the traced section, use the Pen and Pencil tools to draw in the intricate shapes. Use auto tracing to trace clear cut black and white logos or simple illustrations. Manual tracing works best for more detailed intricate designs.

Automatically tracing placed images

You can use the Auto Trace tool for basic tracing of placed images, both black and white and full color. However, the results obtained by using this tool are usually less than satisfactory, and may require a great deal of time-consuming cleanup. To trace an image automatically, follow these steps:

1. **Click and hold the Blend tool.** The Blend tool is halfway down in the Toolbox. The Blend tool has a square transforming into a circle. When you hold the tool, a flyout menu appears.

Cross-Reference To learn more about the Blend tool, see Chapter 11.

2. **Click the Auto Trace tool.** The Auto Trace tool looks like a curved line that fades to white. The Auto Trace tool is housed with the Blend tool.

3. **Click the edge of a colored area of a placed image.** The Auto Trace tool attempts to trace the edge of a solid area and applies the current Paint Style to it.

Tip Always use the Auto Trace tool from the outside in. Doing this ensures that bigger paths around the outside don't overlap the inside paths.

The default settings for Auto Trace are just general, basic, middle of the road settings. You can change the settings to create more lines and points for more accuracy or fewer lines and points for a more simple type of drawing. You can change the Auto Trace Tolerance setting in the Type & Auto Tracing preferences dialog box by pressing ⌘+K (Ctrl+K) and choosing Type & Auto Tracing from the pop-up menu (see Figure 7-11) directly affects the Auto Trace tool — the higher the number, the less precise the tracing. An Auto Trace Tolerance setting of 2 or 3 and a Tracing Gap setting of 2 works pretty well for automatically tracing templates, but neither setting enables the Auto Trace tool to follow the ridges created from the template's diagonal and curved edges.

Manual tracing

Most designers prefer manually tracing templates. Using the Pen and Pencil tools provides illustrators with a level of precision not found with the Auto Trace tool. Furthermore, illustrators may add detail, remove oddities, and change curves, angles, and the like to their satisfaction. Remember, an image that you automatically trace yields an image with a more final appearance with less editability. You'll also find using a pressure-sensitive tablet makes for really nice, accurate tracing. The Pencil tool is great to use when creating more bumpy lines as in map drawing. The Pen tool is fantastic for creating smoother, more accurate lines.

Cross-Reference For more on using the Pen and Pencil tools, see Chapter 3.

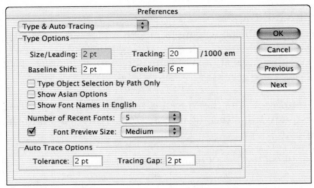

Figure 7-11: The Type & Auto Trace panel of the Preferences dialog box

Using Align and Distribute

The Align palette (see Figure 7-12) contains several buttons for aligning and distributing objects with a simple click of a button. Align treats paths, type objects, and groups as single objects, allowing for quite a bit of flexibility when aligning and distributing. Aligning objects moves them to line up along a specified area (horizontal left, horizontal middle, horizontal right, vertical top, vertical middle, and vertical bottom). Select the objects first; then choose an alignment (Figure 7-13). Distribute takes the selected objects and evenly move them a specified amount from each other (vertical distribute top, vertical distribute center, vertical distribute bottom, horizontal distribute left, horizontal distribute middle, and horizontal distribute right). Use distribute to evenly place windows in a building (Figure 7-14).

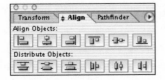

Figure 7-12: The Align palette

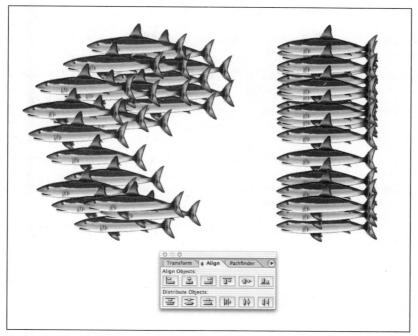

Figure 7-13: Objects before alignment (left) and after aligning along the left (right)

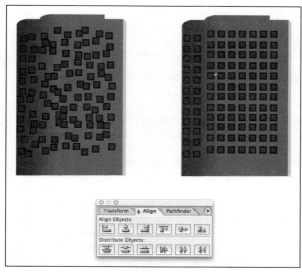

Figure 7-14: Windows before distributing (left) and after (right)

To use the Align palette, follow these steps:

1. **Select the objects you want to align and/or distribute.** See Chapter 5 for more on selecting objects.

2. **Click the appropriate button in the palette.** The palette has two areas: Align Objects, and Distribute Objects:

   - **The Align area:** In order from left to right, the icons in this area include: Horizontal Align Left, Horizontal Align Center, Horizontal Align Right, Vertical Align Top, Vertical Align Center, and Vertical Align Bottom.

   - **The Distribute areas:** In order from left to right, this area includes: Vertical Distribute Top, Vertical Distribute Center, Vertical Distribute Bottom, Horizontal Distribute Left, Horizontal Distribute Center, and Horizontal Distribute Right.

Tip Each click in the palette counts as a change in Illustrator, which means that if you click 20 times, you'll need to undo 20 times to get back to where you started.

Measuring an Image

So you're drawing the blueprints for that new civic center downtown, and your boss wants everything to scale. Wouldn't it be great if Illustrator helped you with your gargantuan task? But, wait! It does! You can measure objects or distances between objects in Illustrator in several ways:

✦ Using the Measure tool

✦ Using the Transform palette

✦ Using the rulers along the side of the document window

✦ Placing objects whose dimensions are known against the edges

✦ Using Offset Paths

✦ Eyeballing it (popular since the first artist painted his recollections of the preceding day's battle with the saber-toothed animals of his time)

Different methods of measuring for different needs. For example: you'll want to use the Measure tool to check the accuracy between objects or the size of the objects. When using the Transform palette, you can enter in exact measurements of scaling, moving, rotating, shear, and reflecting. The rulers let you drag out guidelines for keeping your objects accurately proportionate. Using the rulers again to place an object up against the 0/0 edge for more accurate placing and drawing objects. Offset path lets you specify an exact amount that the path will duplicate and offset from the original path. The last option is fine as long as accuracy isn't a condition of your illustration.

The default unit of measure for all these methods of measurements listed above is in points–unless, of course, you want to change this to something like inches or centimeters and know how to change it. Before we discuss the various ways to measure, we start with a discussion of how to change units.

Changing the measurement units

When you first use Illustrator, you are faced with points. That's great for type and numbering star tips, but when was the last time your art director said, "I'd like you to design a 360 x 288-point ad and make the logo at least 144 points high." (Or your grandmother said to you, "Gosh, you must be at least 5,600 points tall, maybe taller. You've grown at least 100 points since I last saw you. Does your mother let you wear that to school?!")

Points don't work for everything, so Adobe lets us change the measurement units to picas, inches, centimeters, or millimeters. The way to choose this is to temporarily indicate a different unit of measurement each time you enter a value, by appending a character or two to the end of your numerical value.

Centimeters and Points/Picas units of measure have been available since Version 7 of Illustrator. In the metric system, there are 100 centimeters in a meter and 10 millimeters in a centimeter. The other system, which is much more significant to Illustrator users, is the pica/point system. When the pica measurement system is selected in the Units and Display Performance Preferences, measurements are displayed using the common (common to typesetters and designers, anyway) system of picas followed by points. So a distance of 3 picas and 6 points is displayed as 3p6. Such a measurement is displayed as 42 points using the point system.

You can change to a different unit of measure in one of three ways:

✦ **Using the Preference menu:** Before you bring up a dialog box, choose Illustrator (Edit) ➪ Preferences ➪ Units & Display Performance and choose the measurement system you want in the General pop-up menu in the Units section. This permanently alters your measurement units. In other words, all dialog boxes in all new documents will now express their measurements in inches, not points.

✦ **Using the Document Setup menu:** Choose File ➪ Document Setup and choose the appropriate unit of measure in the Units pop-up (Mac) drop down (Windows) menu. This changes the units to inches in that document only.

✦ Using any dialog box: Type the appropriate unit abbreviation (see the following table) after the number in whatever dialog box you open, even if the text fields show points. Illustrator does conversions from points to inches and centimeters (and vice versa) on the fly, so after you enter a point value, the program converts the points into inches as soon as you press the Tab key. This little feature can be an excellent way for you to become more comfortable with points and picas. To get picas, enter 'p0' after the number.

Illustrator Unit Abbreviations		
Unit of Measure	*Abbreviation*	*Example*
Inches	inch, in or "	To enter 2 inches type 2 inch, 2 in, or 2"
Millimeters	mm	To enter 2 millimeters, type 2 mm
Centimeters	cm	To enter 2 centimeters, type 2 cm
Points	pt	To enter 2 points you enter 2 pt or p 2.
Picas	p	To enter 2 picas, you enter 2p.
Picas and points	p	To enter 2 picas, 6 points, type 2p6

A quick refresher on measurement units and their relations:

1"	=	6p	=	72 pt	=	25.4 mm	=	2.54 cm
.17"	=	1p	=	12 pt	=	4.2 mm	=	.42 cm
.01"	=	p1	=	1 pt	=	.35 mm	=	.035 cm
.04"	=	p2.83	=	2.83 pt	=	1 mm	=	.1 cm
.39"	=	2p4.35	=	28.35 pt	=	10 mm	=	1 cm

Using the Measure tool

The fastest way to obtain a precise, exact measurement in Illustrator is to use the Measure tool (shown in Figure 7-15). To use the tool:

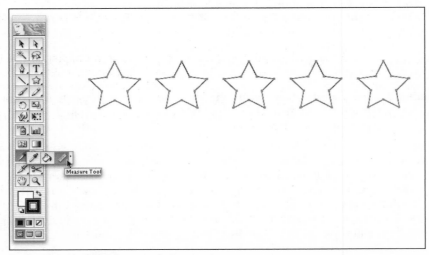

Figure 7-15: The Measure tool

1. **Click and hold the Eyedropper tool.** The Measure tool is a pop-up tool found with the Eyedropper tool and Paint Bucket tool.

2. **Click the Measure tool.** The icon looks like a ruler.

3. **Click an object where you want to begin measuring with the Measure tool.** The Info palette appears (Figure 7-16).

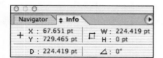

Figure 7-16: The Info palette

4. **Click where you want to end your measurement.** The Info palette shows the distance between the location first clicked and the next location clicked or the distance between where the tool was first clicked and where the mouse was released after dragging.

   Double-clicking the Measure Tool pulls up the Guides and Grid Preferences dialog box where you can set the distance between grid lines if you use the grid to help in making more accurate drawings.

Cross-Reference

To learn more about the Guides and Grid Preference dialog box, see the sections "Working with Grids" and "Using Guides" later in this chapter.

You can use the measurements you obtain with the Measure tool to move your object the distance that you want. As soon as the Measure tool measures a distance, it routes that information to the Move dialog box, shown in Figure 7-17. The next time you open the Move dialog box, it holds the values sent by the Measure tool. You open the Move dialog box either by choosing Object ⇨ Transform ⇨ Move, or by double-clicking the Selection tool. If you hold down the Shift key, you can constrain the movement of the measuring line to 45° or 90°.

Tip

Know anything about PostScript? PostScript is defined fully in Chapter 17. Well, one thing you absolutely have to know is that pages in PostScript are always measured from the lower-left corner of the page. That means moving something along the Y axis with a positive number moves it up, not down. It's a math thing. Your geometry teacher would've thought that's the way to measure things, while the rest of the world thinks it's silly.

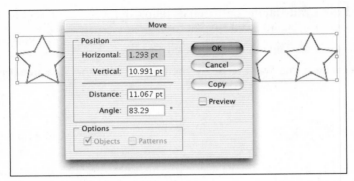

Figure 7-17: The Move dialog box

Sizing objects with the Transform palette

A great area to resize objects is the Transform palette. When you have an object selected, you can enter a new height and width in the Transform palette and immediately the object changes to match the new measurements. The Transform palette also lets you know the placement of the object via the x and y units. The Transform palette, which you open by choosing Window ➪ Show Transform, shows the height, width, and location of any selected path or paths, as illustrated in Figure 7-18.

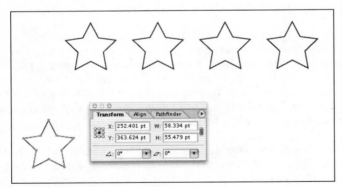

Figure 7-18: The Transform palette

The options for the Transform palette are listed as follows:

✦ **X and Y:** Show the location of the object on the page, measured (as always) from the lower-left corner.

✦ **W:** The width of the selected object (or the total width of the selected objects when more than one is selected).

✦ **H**: The height or total height of the selected object or objects.

✦ **The Rotate option:** Located on the bottom left of the palette, you use this option to rotate an object by entering a value in degrees.

✦ **The Shear option:** Located on the bottom right; you can enter a value to slant the object along a horizontal or vertical axis.

To change the objects size, select the object first, then in the Transform palette enter a new value for the Height and Width. If you want the object to move, then enter a new X and Y value in the Transform palette.

Using rulers

You can toggle rulers on and off by choosing View ➪ Show/Hide Rulers, or by pressing ⌘+R (Ctrl+R). Normally, the rulers measure up and across from the document's lower-left corner; however, you can alter this orientation by dragging the ruler origin (where the zeros are) from its position in the upper-left corner, between where the two rulers meet. Because rulers take up valuable onscreen real estate, it's usually a good idea to leave them turned off unless you are constantly measuring things or you want to display your illustration at a higher magnification. Rulers are easy to show and hide–just press ⌘+R (Ctrl+R) when you want to see them and press ⌘+R (Ctrl+R) again to lose them. To reset the rulers to their original location, double-click in the origin box of the rulers.

Tip   If you change the ruler origin to the middle of the document page, try to move it back to a corner when you are finished. When you zoom in, rulers may be the only indicator of your location within the document.

One of the rulers' nicest features is the display of dotted lines that correspond to the cursor's position. And yet, at times, measuring with rulers works no better than eyeballing; although the process requires precision, you are limited by the rulers' hash marks in pinpointing the cursor's exact position. The rulers are best suited for measuring when the document is at a very high zoom level.

Measuring with objects

Using objects to compare distances can be more effective than using either the Measure tool or the rulers, especially when you need to place objects precisely–for example, when you want several objects to be the same distance from one another.

If you place a circle adjacent to an object (so that the objects' edges touch), you know that the second object is placed correctly when it's aligned to the circle's other side. (A circle is the object most commonly used because the diameter is constant.)

You can use other objects for measuring, including these:

✦ **Squares:** When you need to measure horizontal and vertical distances

✦ **Rectangles:** When the horizontal and vertical distances are different

✦ **Lines:** When the distance applies to only one direction

To enable better precision, turn the measuring object into a guide.

Guides are discussed in more detail in the section "Using Guides," later in this chapter.

Using Offset Path (for equidistant measuring)

There may be times when you want to place several objects the same distance from a central object. You may find that using any of the previously mentioned measuring techniques time-consuming and even inaccurate, especially when you deal with complex images. However, Illustrator's Offset Path dialog box enables you to automatically align objects equidistantly from a central object.

To use an Offset Path to measure objects that are equally spaced apart, follow these steps:

1. **Select the central object.** See Chapter 5 for more on selecting objects.

2. **Choose Object ⇨ Path ⇨ Offset Path.** The Offset Path dialog box (shown in Figure 7-19) opens.

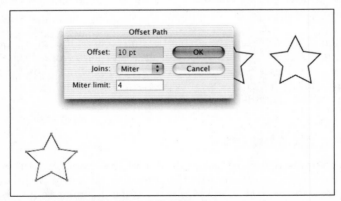

Figure 7-19: The Offset Path dialog box

3. **Enter the desired distance in the Offset text field.** You can enter a distance in points, millimeters, or inches. See the section "Changing the measurement" for more on entering the correct unit of measure.

Cross-Reference

For detailed coverage on the Offset Path dialog box and its settings, see Chapter 5.

4. **Click OK.** Illustrator creates the new Offset Path.

5. **Check your Offset Path.** Check the corner areas for overlapping areas, which appear as loops. If you find any overlaps, open the Pathfinder palette by choosing Window ⇨ Pathfinder and use the Unite function to eliminate these unsightly aberrations.

6. **Change the new path into a guide.** For more information, see the section "Creating guides" later in this chapter.

7. **Align your objects to this guide.**

Working with Grids

Nothing I've found is more useful on a day-to-day basis than the Grid feature. Grids act as a framework for your artwork, providing an easy method for aligning and positioning images. Figure 7-20 shows an Illustrator document that has grids turned on. One advantage of using grids is the Snap to Grid feature. With this feature, you can move objects near a gridline, and Illustrator automatically snaps the object directly on the grid line.

Grids start from the origin of your document (usually the lower-left corner). If you want to change the position of the grid, you can do so by dragging the origin point (at the Origin Marker where the rulers meet) to the new starting position for the grid. You reset the grid position (and the ruler origin) by double-clicking the Origin Marker.

Please note that instead of gridlines, you might want to use guides instead. For example, you might need a few lines in different locations to set a page for a flyer advertisement. Use guides by dragging them out from the rulers to the exact locations that you want to place art and enter type. Gridlines are great for using lines that are set a specific distance apart. Use gridlines to create a perspective drawing, or placing objects a specific distance apart.

Cross-Reference

For your on using guides, see the section "Using Guides" later in the chapter.

Figure 7-20: A document with Illustrator's Grid function turned on

The following list shows the commands for displaying gridlines, and the various Snap to Grid features. To activate any of the Snap to Grid feature, you must first have your gridlines displayed:

✦ **Display grid lines:** Choose View ➪ Show Grid, or press ⌘+" (Ctrl+").

✦ **Turn off grids:** Choose View ➪ Hide Grid, or press ⌘+" (Ctrl+").

✦ **The Snap to Grid feature:** Choose View ➪ Snap to Grid, or press ⌘+Shift+" (Ctrl+Shift+"). This feature snaps the object to the nearest grid.

✦ **The Snap to Point feature:** Choose View ➪ Snap to Point, or press ⌘+Option+" (Ctrl+Alt+"). This feature snaps the dragged object to another object's point. More importantly you can see this happen. When dragging, the cursor turns from black to white when you are directly over another point.

Tip If you want to display grids in each new document, open your Adobe Illustrator Startup file in your Illustrator Plug-Ins folder and turn on grids in that document. Then save the Startup file. All new documents display grids when you first create them.

Creating grid color, style, and spacing

You can customize the way grids look by changing the Grid preferences. Choose Illustrator (Edit) ➪ Preferences ➪ Guides & Grid, and the Guides & Grid Preferences dialog box (Figure 7-21) appears. Here you can change the grid color, style, and spacing.

The various options of the Grid section of the Guides & Grid Preference dialog box are listed below:

✦ **Grid Color:** In this area, you can pick a new color from the list of colors. If you choose Other, you can use the color picker to the right of the Color area to pick a new color for your grids. Because I'm just too darn picky, I pick cyan, and then go to the color picker and lighten it substantially. The result is non-repro-blue-looking lines that make my grid resemble graph paper (which I've always thought should be called grid paper).

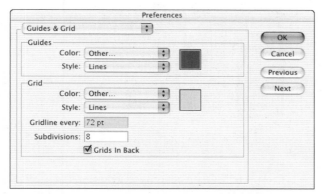

Figure 7-21: The Guides & Grid Preferences dialog box

✦ **Grid Style:** You can also choose between lines and dots as the grid style. I prefer to use lines for my grid, as dots can turn an already busy-looking page into one with all sorts of, well, dots all over the place.

✦ **Gridline every:** Enter the distance between gridlines. To change the space between the major (darker) gridlines, enter a value in the Gridline every text field.

✦ **Subdivisions:** To create subdivisions (minor) between the dark values, enter a number for how many sections should be created between the main lines. If you enter 1 as the value, no subdivisions are created. Because you're defining the number of divisions, not the number of lines, entering 2 creates one line between the two main lines. The standard 1-inch gridline with eight subdivisions creates ⅛-inch squares.

✦ **Grids In Back:** You can uncheck the Grids in Back checkbox in the Guides & Grid preferences to make your gridlines appear in front of your artwork. The box is checked by default so that the gridlines aren't running on top of your artwork.

Spinning grids

Your grid doesn't have to consist of just vertical and horizontal lines. You can rotate the grid to any angle you like by changing the Constrain Angle in General Preferences, or by pressing ⌘+K (Ctrl+K). Figure 7-22 shows a grid set at an angle of 6.275°. This is perfect for working with angled artwork; even if only a portion of the artwork is at an angle, the Constrain Angle can be set temporarily to the angle of the artwork.

Cross-Reference

For more on setting preferences see Chapter 15.

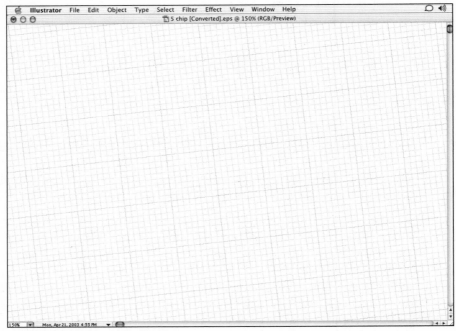

Figure 7-22: A grid rotated to 6.275°

Using Guides

Guides are teeny, tiny little people who show you around Illustrator. The more of them you make, the easier it is to use the program. (Uh huh . . . I know, let you know when the shuttle lands. . . . Sigh.)

Okay, actually, guides are dotted or solid lines that help you align artwork. Guides do not print, and they are saved with documents. In Illustrator and most desktop-publishing software, guides are straight lines extending from one edge of a document to the other. But in Illustrator, you can also turn any path into a guide.

For your on using gridlines, see the section "Working with Grids" earlier in the chapter.

For the most part, guides behave exactly like their path counterparts. As long as long as you have them unlocked, you may select them, hide them, group them, and even paint them (although paint attributes are not be visible onscreen or on a print-out until the guides are converted back into paths).

Creating guides

You can create guides in two ways: by pulling them out from the rulers and by transforming paths into guides.

To pull a guide from a ruler, first make the vertical and horizontal rulers visible by choosing View ➪ Show Rulers, or by pressing ⌘+R (Ctrl+R). To create guides that span the entire Pasteboard, click the vertical or horizontal ruler and drag out.

To transform an existing path into a guide, select the path and choose View ➪ Guides ➪ Make Guides, or press (⌘+5 (Ctrl+5).

And now a word about the Magic Rotating Guide (possibly the coolest tip you'll ever learn): When you drag a guide out from the vertical ruler, hold down Option (Alt) and the vertical guide becomes a horizontal guide. And vice versa.

Locking, unlocking, and moving guides

When you create a guide, you might want to make sure that it doesn't get moved when you are selecting and moving your objects. Locking your guide is a great way to ensure that guide doesn't get picked up and moved. Moving a guide is necessary if you create a specific guide like the outline of a business card, and you want to move it to create a different business card. Moving an unlocked guide is simple–click it and drag. If guides are locked, unlock them by choosing View ➪ Lock Guides, or by pressing ⌘+Option+; (Ctrl+Alt+;).

If you aren't sure whether the guides in your document are locked or unlocked, click and hold on the View menu. If you see a check mark next to Lock Guides, Illustrator locks the guides, and also locks all new guides. To unlock all the document's guides, choose View ➪ Lock Guide; to lock guides again, choose View ➪ Lock Guide (yes, it's a toggle).

All guides in a document have a special status of "lockedness," where all guides are either locked or unlocked. Weirdly enough, however, you can lock and unlock guides individually by selecting the guide and choosing View ➪ Guides ➪ Lock Guides, or by pressing ⌘+Option+; (Ctrl+Alt+;). You can also hide guides by choosing View ➪ Guides ➪ Hide Guides, or by pressing ⌘ +; (Ctrl+;).

Releasing guides

Now that you are getting the hang of using the Guides, you might want to delete them or release them to move. You can also release a guide if you have decided to make it into an object that you can stroke and fill. To release a guide or change it into a path, select the guide and choose View ➪ Guides ➪ Release Guides. Alternatively, you can press ⌘+Option+5 (Ctrl+Alt+5).

To release multiple guides first, make sure that the guides are unlocked; in other words, make sure that there's no check mark next to Lock Guides in the View menu. Then select the guides and choose View ➪ Guides ➪ Release Guides, or press ⌘+Option+5 (Ctrl+Alt+5).

You select multiple guides in the same way you select multiple paths: either drag a marquee around the guides or press Shift and then click each guide. For more on selecting paths, see Chapter 5.

Selecting all guides–even those that are currently paths–by dragging a marquee or Shift-clicking can be a chore. Here's another way: First, make sure that the guides are not locked (see the last section to unlock a guide). Next, choose Select ➪ All, or press ⌘+A (Ctrl+Alt). Select View ➪ Guides ➪ Release Guides, or press ⌘+Option+5 (Ctrl+Alt+5). This releases all guides and, more importantly, selects all paths that were formerly guides (all other paths and objects are deselected). Finally, choose View ➪ Make Guides, or press ⌘+5 (Ctrl+5) and all guides become guides again and are selected.

Deleting guides

Let's say you have just finished a fantastic drawing that you created with the help of many guides. Now that the image is complete you want to delete those guides. Sure, you can unlock them and select them by holding down the Shift key. Or, if you were really thinking, you could put those guides on a layer and simply Select All then Delete. Well, Illustrator has just made your life even easier. By choosing the Clear Guides option under the View menu's Guides submenu, all guides are miraculously deleted.

Changing guide preferences

In the Guides & Grid Preferences dialog box (shown in Figure 7-18), you can change the style and the color of the guides. To open the Guides & Grid Preference dialog box, choose Illustrator (Edit) ➪ Preferences ➪ Guides & Grid.

In the Guide section of this dialog box, you have the following options:

✦ **Guide Color:** Choose a color from the pop-up menu or select Other to choose a color from the color picker. With guides, I like to use a darker, more vibrant color than a watered-down cyan. No matter which color you choose, keep it different from the Grid color and make sure it contrasts with the colors you're using in your document.

✦ **Guide Style:** You can the guide style to either dots or lines; which you choose is a matter of preference. However, you may want to pick the opposite of what you've chosen for grids, to further differentiate the two.

Understanding Smart Guides

Smart Guides, which came into being in Version 8, pop-up to help you create a shape with precision, align objects with accuracy, and move and transform objects with ease. Figure 7-23 shows an example of a Smart Guide. To activate Smart Guides choose View ➪ Smart Guides, or press ⌘+U (Ctrl+U).

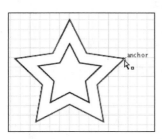

Figure 7-23: Smart Guides show you what is what in an illustration.

Checkboxes enable you to turn these options on and off in the Smart Guides & Slices Preferences dialog shown in Figure 7-21. Some of the Smart Guide display options are:

✦ **Text Label Hints:** These hints pop-up when you drag over your object. They tell you what each area is. For example, if you drag over a line, the hint pops up with the word "path." If you drag over an anchor point, the hint reads "anchor point."

✦ **Transform Tools:** When you are rotating, scaling, or shearing an object with this option checked, Smart Guides shows up to help you out.

✦ **Construction Guides:** These let you view guidelines (thin lines that pop-up when moving or copying objects) when using Smart Guides.

✦ **Object Highlighting:** When you select this option, the object to which you point highlights.

Using angles as guides

The Smart Guides & Slices Preferences dialog box (shown in Figure 7-24) lets you pick what angles display guides when you drag an object.

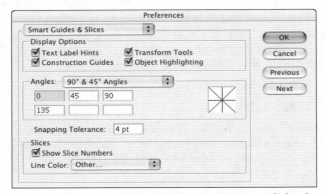

Figure 7-24: Smart Guides & Slices Preferences dialog box

You have the following options in the Angles section of the dialog box:

✦ **Angles:** You can choose presets in this drop-down menu. The preset angles are: 0, 45, 90, and 135. The angles are shown in the box to the right. When you add a custom angle, it shows up with the preset lines.

✦ **Custom Angles:** You can create a Custom Angle of your own in the boxes below the drop-down menu. To do so, simply enter the angle in one of the empty boxes.

✦ **Snapping Tolerance:** Snapping Tolerance isn't how much patience you have with a spouse before you explode. Rather, it lets you choose how close you have to have an object to another object before the first object automatically "snaps" to the second object. You set the Snapping Tolerance in points, the lower the number the closer you have to move the objects to each other. If the number is pretty high, an object snaps to another object if it's merely passing by.

Measuring for Printing

Thinking ahead to the time when your job will print is always a good thing. Two of the most important areas of printing are the placement and the sizing of your artwork within the Illustrator document. This section deals with production-oriented issues you might face while using Illustrator to create printable pieces.

Stepping

Oftentimes, you'll create something that's quite small and you'll need to have several copies of the artwork on the page at once. Setting up your artwork for optimal spacing and printing is referred to as stepping.

Illustrator doesn't do stepping automatically, but it does provide the tools you need to step your artwork.

1. **Make sure that the Transform palette is visible.** To open this palette, choose Window ➪ Show Transform.

2. **Select the finished artwork**. See Chapter 5 for more on selecting artwork.

3. **Open the Move dialog box.** You can do this by double-clicking the Selection tool, or by choosing Object ➪ Transform ➪ Move. The Move dialog box is shown in Figure 7-14. For more on the Move dialog box, see the section "Using the Measure tool," earlier in this chapter.

4. **Enter the width of the art in the Horizontal field.** This is in the Position area of the Move dialog box.

5. **Enter 0 (zero) in the Vertical field.** This is in the Position area of the Move dialog box.

6. **Click the Copy button**.

7. **Click OK.** This closes you out of the Move dialog box.

8. **Choose Object ➪ Transform ➪ Transform Again.** You can also press ⌘+D (Ctrl+D). This creates another duplicate of the artwork.

9. **Press ⌘+D (Ctrl+D).** Do this until you have the right number of pieces across the page.

10. **Select the entire row of artwork.** See Chapter 5 for more on selecting objects.

11. **Open the Move dialog box again.**

12. **Enter 0 (zero) in the Horizontal field.**

13. **Enter the height of the art in the Vertical field.**

14. **Click the Copy button.**

15. **Click OK.** This closes you out of the Move dialog box.

16. **Choose Object ➪ Transform ➪ Transform Again.** Alternatively, you can press ⌘+D (Ctrl+D). Again, this creates another duplicate of the row of artwork.

17. **Press ⌘+D (Ctrl+D).** Do this until there is the right number of pieces down the page, as shown in Figure 7-25.

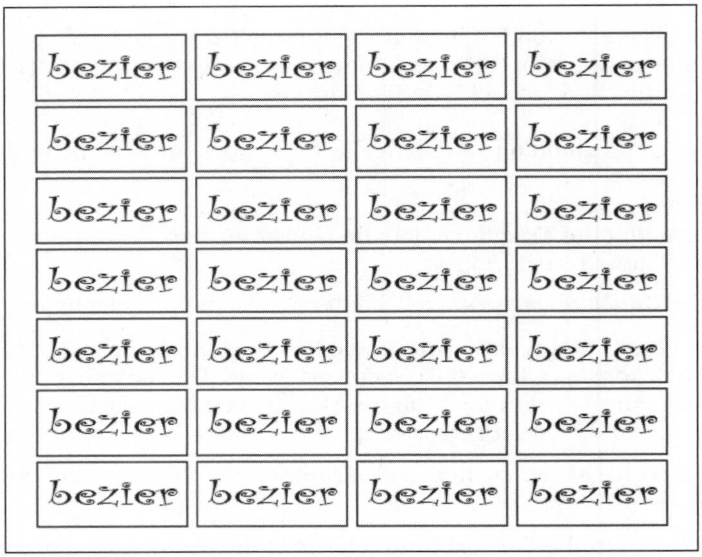

Figure 7-25: Artwork that has been stepped and repeated on a page

Creating crop marks

Crop marks are little lines that are designed to help you cut (or crop) along the edges of your illustration after the document has been printed (see Figure 7-26). Crops (that's the slang term; if you're even half cool, you won't say "crop marks") don't intrude on the edges of the artwork, but instead are offset a bit from the corners of where the edges are.

Unfortunately, you can only create one set of crop marks per document. You can make multiple crop marks by drawing them yourself or using the Crop Marks filter (Filter ➪ Create ➪ Crop Marks). However, one set of crop marks isn't enough for color separations. Black crop marks that you create by drawing may be 100% of process colors but do not contain any other spot color that you may have in your illustration. This problem is the result of a serious limitation in Illustrator: The program does not allow you to choose "registration" as a color, which would print on every color plate. Crop marks created with the Crop Marks filter are 100% black.

Cross-Reference

For more on printing, see Chapter 17.

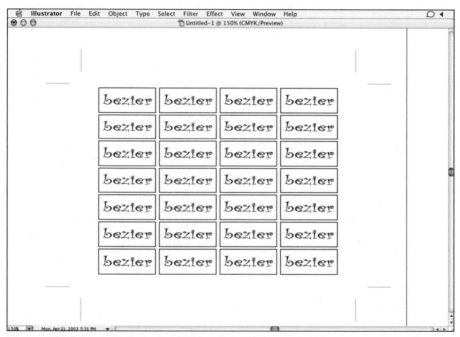

Figure 7-26: Crop marks indicate the edges of the artwork.

Here's a workaround:

1. **Choose the crop marks you created and Stroke them with 100% of all four process colors when you are printing out four-color separations.**

2. **If you are printing out spot-color separations, copy the crop marks by choosing Edit ➪ Paste in Front or Edit ➪ Paste in Back.**

3. **Color the Stroke of the crops with the spot color you are using.** Choose the Overprint Strokes option in the Attributes palette. Access the Attributes palette by choosing Window ➪ Attributes.

4. **For additional crop marks, repeat Step 2 for every additional color separation in your document.**

You can also use a rectangle to create crop marks. That way the object can have a bleed off the edge of the crop marks. For more on bleeds and printing, see Chapter 17. To transform a selected rectangle drawn with the rectangle tool into crop marks, choose Object ➪ Crop Area ➪ Make.

Tip   The rectangle can only be modified prior to becoming crop marks by moving it or resizing it via the Scale tool. If any transformation is done to the rectangle, a message appears saying that you can only make crop marks out of a single rectangle. If a rectangle is drawn with a Constrain Angle set to an angle other than 0°, 90°, 180°, or 270° (–90°), you cannot make crop marks out of that rectangle.

If you choose Object ➪ Crop Area ➪ Make when nothing is selected, crop marks appear around the edge of the single full page. If crops are set to the size of the page and you move the page with the Page tool, or if you resize the document with the Document Setup dialog box, the crop marks do not move.

To release selected crop marks, choose Object ➪ Crop Area ➪ Release. If you created the crop marks using a rectangle, that rectangle is an editable path that you can resize and change back into crop marks, delete, or modify. Any rectangle that you change back from being a set of crop marks has a fill and stroke of None.

Caution   You cannot choose Object ➪ Crop Area ➪ Release when no crop marks are in your document. In addition, Object ➪ Crop Area ➪ Release does not release crop marks made with the Filter ➪ Create ➪ Crop Marks command.

Japanese Crop Marks and crop marks

Instead of using standard crop marks, you can choose to use Japanese Crop Marks, which are different looking, yet seemingly no more functional than regular crop marks. If you check the General Preference setting Japanese Crop Marks, both regular and Japanese crop marks take on the characteristics of Japanese Crop Marks (shown in Figure 7-27).

The disadvantage to using Japanese crop marks is one of familiarity (or lack thereof). Most printers and designers (in the United States) can use the Japanese Crop Marks as well as traditional ones. However, you may experience a greater risk of cropping or measuring errors with Japanese Crop Marks because of most printers and designers are unfamiliar with them.

You can create a document that has both traditional and Japanese crop marks. To do so:

1. **Select the object on which you want traditional crop marks.**

2. **Choose Filter ➪ Create ➪ Crop Marks.** This applies the Create Crop Marks filter.

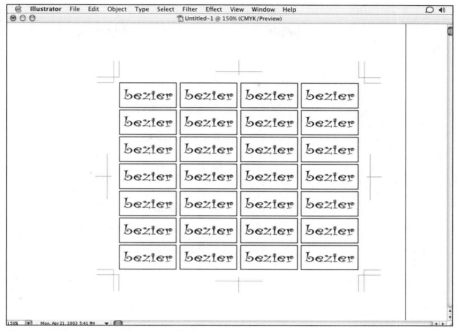

Figure 7-27: Japanese crop marks

3. **Choose Illustrator ⇨ Preferences ⇨ General.** Alternatively, you can press ⌘+K (Ctrl+K). This opens the General Preferences dialog box.

4. **Check the Japanese Crop Marks checkbox.**

5. **Select the next object**. See Chapter 5. for more on selecting objects.

6. **Reapply the filter in Step 2.** Alternatively, you can just press ⌘+Shift+E (Ctrl+E). The second set of crop marks appears as Japanese.

Summary

✦ Locking and Hiding objects can help in creating illustrations.

✦ Grouping objects keeps artwork organized.

✦ You can use layers to effectively separate different sections of your artwork.

✦ Template layers are used in Illustrator to make your drawing easier and more precise and it distinguishes them from Template documents

✦ The Auto Trace tool works with any placed image.

✦ Manual tracing usually generates better results than tracing done with the Auto Trace tool.

✦ The Measure tool provides a quick way to measure distances in your Illustrator documents.

✦ Measurements generated by the Measure tool appear in the Move dialog box the next time you open it.

✦ Guides can be created from any object by selecting the object and pressing ⌘+5 (Ctrl+5).

✦ You can quickly create document high/wide guides by dragging out from the rulers.

✦ Use the Copy button within the Move dialog box to step and repeat artwork.

✦ Use the Smart Guides feature to make editing much easier.

✦   ✦   ✦

Working with Type

Fonts are a big deal to Illustrator users. For the seasoned graphic artist, the thousands of typefaces that are available for the Mac provide a typesetting heaven on earth. For a newcomer to Illustrator and typesetting, fonts can be overwhelming. Illustrator ships with about 300 Adobe PostScript Type 1 fonts; other fonts are available for purchase at costs that range from about $2 per face to hundreds of dollars for a family.

This chapter covers creating type with various type tools and all of the different formatting available as well as cool things to do with type on a path and outlined type. New to Illustrator, Adobe incorporates the new Adobe Text Engine. This new engine supports Unicode and OpenType, so you now have the best quality of text composition.

New Feature

When accessing fonts from the Type menu or from the Character palette, the fonts now display in their actual typeface rather than the generic menu typeface. This cool new feature lets you see what the typeface looks like before choosing it. If you find this takes too much time, you can always turn off the Font Previewing off in Type & Auto Tracing preferences by choosing Illustrator ➪ Preferences ➪ Type & Auto Tracing (File ➪ Preferences ➪ Type & Auto Tracing) and unchecking the Font Preview Size box.

Understanding Fonts

Fonts come in various formats, each format having advantages and disadvantages over other formats. Fonts fall into the following categories: bitmap fonts, PostScript fonts, TrueType fonts, OpenType fonts, and Multiple Master fonts.

When installing fonts for the Macintosh, you need to place them in /Library/Application Support/Adobe/Fonts and its Illustrator CS subdirectory.

Understanding Bitmap fonts

The original fonts used for computers, bitmap fonts consist of a series of dots inside a grid pattern. They worked well both on-screen and on the dot-matrix printers that were prevalent at the time of their introduction.

Each character in a bitmap font has a certain number of square black dots that define its shape. Some bitmap fonts include different point sizes, with the smaller point sizes having fewer dots than the larger point sizes. The larger the point size of the bitmap fonts, the more detail is available, and the better the letter looks.

Problems arise when you specify a point size for which there is no corresponding bitmap font. When this happens, Illustrator uses the closest integer multiple of the requested size. For example, if you ask for 11 point text and you don't have it installed, but you do have 12 point and 22 point, Illustrator uses the 22 point size. The result is usually large, blocky-looking letters. The larger the size specified, the larger the "blocks."

Because bitmap fonts were originally designed for a computer screen, the dots in a bitmap font are set at 72 dpi (dots-per-inch). When you print a bitmap font on a laser printer, which has a resolution of at least 300 dpi, the letters look blocky, even when their sizes are supported by the typeface. A typical viewer of such a font might say, "bitmapped...too jaggy...must find outline font."

Understanding PostScript fonts

Although PostScript fonts are the most popular font format in professional publishing circles, they also are the most confusing and frustrating fonts to use because they have two parts: the screen fonts (which are really bitmap fonts) and the printer fonts.

You need the printer fonts, as their name implies, for printing. Printer fonts consist of outlined shapes that get filled with as many dots as the printer can stuff into that particular shape. Because these printer fonts are mathematical outlines and not a certain number of dots, they make characters look good at any point size. In fact, PostScript printer fonts are device independent, meaning that the quality of the type depends on the dpi of the printer (which is device dependent). The higher the dpi, the smoother the curves and diagonal lines look. If printer fonts are missing, the printer either uses the corresponding bitmap font or substitutes another font whose printer font is available (usually Courier... yuck!).

Adobe, just by coincidence, created the PostScript page description language based on outlines instead of dots, developed PostScript fonts and also created typefaces in PostScript format called Type 1 format and Type 3 format. Since the rise of desktop publishing, the font standard has been PostScript. In 1990, Apple developed a new font format called TrueType and licensed it to Microsoft.

Understanding TrueType fonts

The greatest advantage of TrueType fonts is that they have only one component — not two separate screen and printer fonts. Actually, many TrueType fonts do include screen fonts because hand-tuned screen fonts at small sizes tend to look better than filled outlines at screen resolution. The difference is that both the TrueType font and the bitmap are united.

The quality of TrueType fonts is comparable to, if not better than, that of PostScript typefaces. Apple includes TrueType fonts with every new computer it sells. Microsoft includes a boatload of fonts with Windows, Office and all of the other applications it sells and licenses. There are some potential quality advantages to TrueType fonts, such as the quadratic curves used to draw TrueType outlines and the supposedly superior hint capability.

Understanding OpenType fonts

OpenType fonts take TrueType fonts that step further by including PostScript information. It also includes a variety of features, such as ligatures and alternate glyphs that PostScript and TrueType don't offer. A glyph is the form of a character, such as a capital letter can be created with a swash making it a bit more exciting than the regular capital letter. A ligature is replacement characters for paired letters such as ff, fi, and ffl. Illustrator offers an OpenType palette for you to specify alternate characters such as ligatures. The OpenType palette is found by choosing Window ⇨ Type ⇨ OpenType. The OpenType option lets you enhance the look of your OpenType fonts.

Cross-Reference   For more on glyphs, see the subsection "Glyphs" under the section "Understanding Basic Type Menu Commands."

Adding type with Multiple Master fonts

Multiple Master fonts, again from Adobe, provide an impressive, if not somewhat complex, way to vary typestyles. Normally, a typeface may come in several weights, such as bold, regular, light, and black. But what if you want a weight that is between bold and black? Usually, you're out of luck.

The theory behind Multiple Master fonts is that a font has two extremes — black and light, for example. Multiple Master technology creates any number of in-betweens that range from one extreme to the other. Multiple Masters don't stop with weights, though. They also work to step between regular and oblique, wide and condensed, and serif or sans serif.

Multiple Master font capabilities are built into many high-end graphics applications, such as Illustrator and InDesign.

Understanding Basic Type Menu Commands

The Type menu, shown in Figure 8-1, contains all of Illustrator's type controls (with the exception of the Type tools). No longer is the Font menu a separate menu on the menu bar; it is now incorporated into a submenu in the Type menu.

You can change most of the Type options in the Character palette by choosing Window ➪ Type ➪ Character, or pressing ⌘+T (Ctrl+T). You can also change these options using the Paragraph palette by choosing Window ➪ Type ➪ Paragraph, or by pressing ⌘+Option+T (Ctrl+Alt+T).

Type is set in Illustrator in stories. A *story* is a set of continuous, linked text. When the term paragraph is mentioned, it is usually referring to the characters that are between Returns. If there are no Returns in a story, then that story is said to have one paragraph. Returns end paragraphs and begin new ones. There is always exactly one more paragraph in a story than there are Returns.

The following sections describe each of the Type menu options. In the next four sections, we discuss the first four of these commands. The rest of the options are covered throughout this chapter.

Figure 8-1: The Type menu

Font

The Font submenu of the Type menu displays the typefaces in their actual form. The Font submenu displays all the fonts that are currently installed on the computer you are using. A check mark appears next to the font that is currently selected and an indicator as to whether it is a TrueType, Type 1, or OpenType font. If no check mark appears next to any of the fonts, more than one font is currently selected. Figure 8-2 shows the Font submenu.

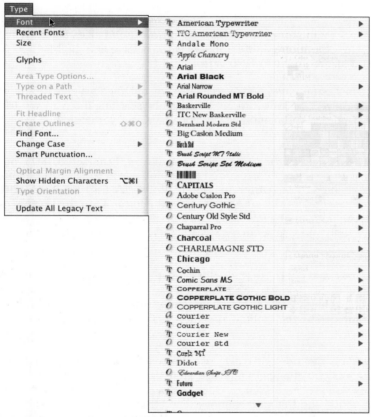

Figure 8-2: The Font submenu

Recent fonts

The Recent Fonts submenu of the Type menu displays the most recent fonts you have used in that document. The default setting for Recent Fonts is 5. You can change that number in the Type & Auto Tracing preferences dialog box. Access the type preferences by choosing Illustrator ⇨ Preferences ⇨ Type & Auto Tracing. In this dialog box, you can set the number of recent fonts from the Number of Recent Fonts pop-up. The minimum for Recent Fonts is 1 and the maximum is 15.

Size

Type ⇨ Size displays a submenu with Other and various point sizes listed. When Other is chosen, the Character palette appears with the Size field highlighted. You can type any point size from 0.1 to 1296 in this field.

Note   Type created in Illustrator may be scaled to any size, but to go beyond the size lim-its, you must convert the type into outline paths by selecting the type and using the Create Outlines command, which you activate by pressing ⌘+Shift+O (Ctrl+Shift+O).

A check mark appears next to the point size that is currently selected. If the point size currently selected does not correspond to a point size in the Size submenu, a check mark appears next to the Other menu item. Point size for type is measured from the top of the ascenders (like the top of a capital letter T) to the bottom of the descenders (like the bottom of a lowercase g). If no check mark appears next to any of the sizes, more than one size is currently selected (even if the different sizes are all Other sizes).

You can also increase and decrease the point size of type by using the keyboard shortcuts. Pressing ⌘+Shift+> (Ctrl+Shift+>) increases the point size by the amount specified in Keyboard Increments Preferences. Pressing ⌘+Shift+< (Ctrl+Shift+<) decreases the point size by the amount specified in Keyboard Increments Preferences.

Yet another way to change point size is to use the Scale tool. Using the Scale tool to change point size lets you change to any size; that size is displayed in the Character palette as soon as you are done scaling. Once again, remember that the limit in scal-ing type is 1296 points, and that you cannot exceed that limit even with the Scale tool unless the type has been converted to outlined paths.

Glyphs

A Glyph is the form of a character of text. Some fonts have multiple forms for a let-ter and the Glyphs palette is where you can choose those other options. Glyphs are also the ornamental forms, swashes, ligatures and fractions that are part of the OpenType fonts. Choosing Glyphs from the Type menu displays the Glyphs palette as show in Figure 8-3. If no type is selected, the palette displays for Entire font in the Show pop-up menu. The other choice in the Show pop-up is for Alternated for

Current Selection. Use this palette to view some of the special character fonts as Symbol or Zapf Dingbats.

Figure 8-3: The Glyphs palette

Using the Type Tools

You use the Type tools to create and later edit type. The default tool is the standard Type tool, which creates both Point type and Area type. Point type is created when you click with the Type tool, creating a point for the type to go off of. Area type is created by dragging a box that the type fills inside of. The pop-up tools on the tear-away Type palette (shown in Figure 8-4) are the Area Type tool, the Type on a path tool, the Vertical Type tool, the Vertical Area Type tool, and the Vertical Type on a path tool. Each of the type tools displays a different cursor.

Figure 8-4: The Type tools from left to right: the Type tool, the Area Type tool, the Type on a path tool, the Vertical Type tool, the Vertical Area Type tool, and the Vertical Type on a path tool.

Cross-Reference All of the tools shown in Figure 8-4 are explained in detail in the following sections.

You can select type in Illustrator with the Selection tool, in which case all the type in the story is modified. A *story* is a contiguous set of type in Point type, Rectangle type, Area type, Type on a path, or Vertical type.

You select type with a Type tool by dragging across either characters or lines — every character from the initial click until the release of the mouse button is selected. Double-clicking with a Type tool selects the entire word you clicked, including the space after it. Triple-clicking (clicking three times in the same place) selects an entire paragraph.

You can enter new type into an existing story by clicking with a Type tool where you want the new type to begin and then typing. If type is highlighted when you begin typing, the highlighted type is replaced with the new type.

The original reason for the inclusion of a vertical type capability in Illustrator was for Japanese type (commonly referred to as Kanji) compatibility. Vertical type can have a number of specialized uses as well. The following sections that discuss the different types of type blocks (Point, Rectangle, Area, and Path) address both normal (horizontal) type and vertical type capabilities.

Using the Type tool

With the Type tool, you can do everything you need to do with type. Clicking in any empty part of your document creates *Point type*, an Anchor Point to which the type aligns. Type created as Point type does not wrap automatically; instead, you must manually press the Return key and start typing the next line. Point type is usually used for creating smaller portions of type, like labels and headlines.

Clicking and dragging with the Type tool creates *Area type* — type that is bordered by a box.

As the Type tool passes over a closed path, it changes automatically into the Area Type tool. Clicking a closed path results in type that fills the shape of the area you clicked. Holding down the Option (Alt) key as you pass over a closed path changes the tool into the Type on a path tool. This intelligent switching of Type tools by Illustrator keeps you from having to choose different Type tools when you want a different kind of type.

If the Type tool crosses over an open path, it becomes the Type on a path tool. Clicking an open path places type on the path, with the baseline of the type aligning along the curves and angles of the path. Holding down the Option (Alt) key when the Type tool is over an open path changes it into the Area Type tool.

You can toggle between the Type tool and the Vertical Type tool by pressing the Shift key. In fact, pressing the Shift key with the Area Type and Type on a path tools automatically toggles those tools to their Vertical Type counterparts. This holds true even if you press Shift along with the Option (Alt) key (when toggling between Area Type and Type on a path tools).

The Area Type tool

You use the Area Type tool for filling closed or open paths with type. You can even fill compound paths in Illustrator.

Tip   You can toggle between the Area Type tool and the Type on a path tool by pressing the Option (Alt) key.

The Type on a path tool

You use the Type on a path tool for running type along any path in Illustrator. This is a great tool for placing type on the edges of a circle or wiggly lines. Figure 8-5 shows an example of text on a path.

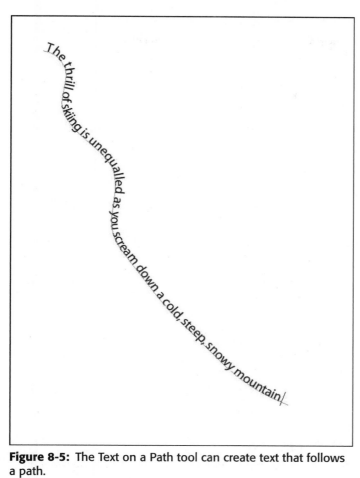

Figure 8-5: The Text on a Path tool can create text that follows a path.

The Vertical Type tools

Vertical type? I was a little confused when I first saw this tool in Version 7 (and its Area and Path counterparts). The easiest way to understand how the Vertical Type tools work is by example. Figure 8-6 shows the same line of type created with the regular Type tool and the Vertical Type tool. For the most part, the Vertical Type tool works like the regular Type tool, but instead of placing characters side by side, characters are placed from top to bottom.

Cross-Reference Because this area of Illustrator can be a little unusual, I've added a section later in this chapter that directly addresses vertical type and related issues.

Long ago and far away lived a troll.
Long ago and far away lived a troll.

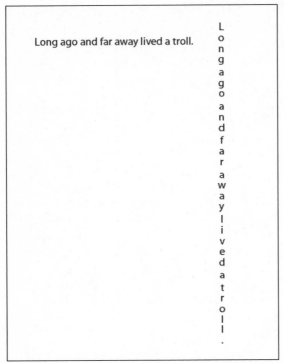

Figure 8-6: Horizontal and Vertical type

Using Point Type

To create type with a single point defining its location, use the Type tool and click a single location within the document window where there are no paths. A blinking insertion point appears, signifying that type appears where that point is located (see the top line of text in Figure 8-7). When you type on the keyboard, text appears in the document at that insertion point. You cannot enter type when you use a Selection tool (type selected with a Selection tool appears in the bottom line of of Figure 8-7).

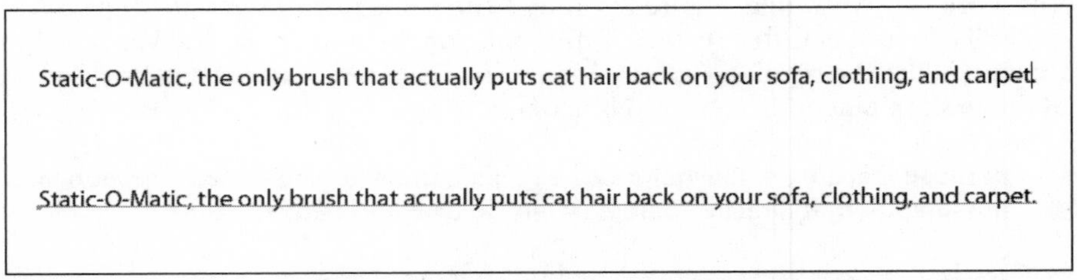

Static-O-Matic, the only brush that actually puts cat hair back on your sofa, clothing, and carpet.
Static-O-Matic, the only brush that actually puts cat hair back on your sofa, clothing, and carpet.

Figure 8-7: Point type with an insertion point at the end of the line (top) and the same line of type selected with the Selection tool (bottom).

Type the Right Way

Although at first it seems quite simple to outline characters of type using a 1-point stroke in the Stroke palette, just slapping on a stroke of a weight that seems to look good on the screen and changing the fill to None or white is technically incorrect.

The right way to outline type is only a little bit more involved. First, select the type that you want outlined and give the type a stroke that is twice the weight you want on the printed piece. Then Cop y the type by choosing Edit ➪ Copy or ⌘+C (Ctrl+C).Then choose Edit ➪ Paste In Front or ⌘+F (Ctrl+F), and give the new type a stroke of None and a fill of white. The white fill knocks out the inside half of the stroke, leaving the stroke one-half the width you specified, which is what you really want.

The following figure shows both the right way and the wrong way to outline type. The top line is the original type. The middle line is outlined the wrong way with a 2-point stroke and a fill of white. The bottom part of the figure shows "OUTLINED TYPE" outlined correctly, first with a white fill and no stroke, and then with a 4-point stroke.

OUTLINED TYPE

OUTLINED TYPE

OUTLINED TYPE

Outlining type can be tricky. The top line shows type before being outlined; the middle row is incorrect with a 1-point stroke and white fill, but the bottom row correctly has a copy with white fill and no stroke overlaid with a copy that has a 4-point stroke.

"Serif preservation," as it's known to a select few, requires a teeny bit of math, but it's worth the effort. The white area inside the stroke is exactly the size of the character when done this way, as opposed to being smaller by half the width of the stroke when done normally.

Caution   When creating Point type, remember that only a hard Return forces a new line of text to be created. If no Returns are used, text eventually runs right off the document. When importing text used as Point type, be sure that the text contains these hard Returns, or the text runs into oblivion. Hard Returns can be added after importing, but it may be difficult to do so.

Placing Area Type in a Rectangle

There are two ways to create Rectangle type (see Figure 8-8). The easiest way is by clicking and dragging the Type tool diagonally, which creates a rectangle as you drag. The blinking insertion point appears in the top row of text, with its horizontal location dependent on the text alignment choice. Choosing flush right alignment, forces the insertion point to appear in the upper-right corner; centered alignment puts the insertion point in the center of the top row; and flush left alignment, or one of the justification methods, makes the insertion point appear in the upper-left corner. Choose any alignment option in the Paragraph palette. Access this palette by choosing Window ⇨ Type ⇨ Paragraph or press ⌘+Option+P (Ctrl+Alt+P).

Sigh...please continue to hold. The next available representative will assist you as soon as possible. We appreciate your patience, please do not hang up. Your call is important to us. If you hang up and call back now, this may increase your wait. Calls are handled in the order they are received.

Please continue to hold. The next available representative will assist you as soon as possible. We appreciate your patience, please do not hang up. Your call is important to us. If you hang up and call back now, this may increase your wait. Calls are handled in the order they are received.

Please continue to hold. The next available representative will assist you as soon as possible. We appreciate your patience, please do not hang up. Your call is important to us. If you hang up and call back now, this may increase your wait. Calls are handled in the order they are received.

Figure 8-8: Area type (gray dashed line is the border of the shape)

If you press the Shift key while drawing the rectangle, the rectangle is constrained to a perfect square. There is no need to drag from upper left to lower right — you can drag from any corner to its opposite — whichever way is most convenient.

To create type in a rectangle of specific proportions, draw a rectangle with the Rectangle tool by clicking once in the document window. The Rectangle Size dialog box appears, and you can enter the information needed. Then choose the Type tool and click the edge of the rectangle. The type fills the rectangle as you type.

For more on the using the Rectangle tool, see Chapter 4.

If you use a rectangle as a type rectangle, it is always a type rectangle, even if you remove the text.

If you need to create a Rectangle type area that is a precise size but don't want to draw a rectangle first, open the Info palette by choosing Window ➪ Info, or by pressing F8. As you drag the type cursor, watch the information in the Info palette, which displays the dimensions of the type area. When the W field is the width you want, and the H field is the height you want, release the mouse button.

Working with Type Areas

For type to exist in Illustrator, you must first define a type area. You can never have type outside these areas because type is treated very differently from any other object in Illustrator.

There are different kinds of type areas:

- ✦ **Point type**: Exists around a single point clicked with the standard Type tool.
- ✦ **Area type:** Type that flows within a specific open or closed path.
- ✦ **Type on a path:** Type whose baseline is attached to a specific open or closed path.
- ✦ **Vertical type:** Type that flows vertically rather than horizontally.

Figure 8-9 shows the same sentence as Point type, Rectangle type, Area type, Type on a path, Vertical type, and Vertical Area type.

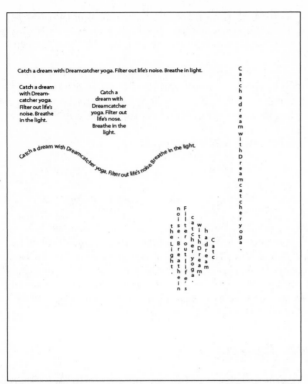

Figure 8-9: The same sentence as it appears in Point type (top row), Rectangle type (middle row, left), Area type (middle row, middle), Type on a path (third row), Vertical Type (far right, top), and Vertical Area type (far right, bottom).

Creating Area Type

The capability of placing type within any area is one of the cooler features of Illustrator, right up there with the fact that the program comes in a hip, new millennium-looking box.

To create type within an area, first create a path that confines the area of your type. You can make the path closed or open, and any size. Remember that the area of the path should be close to the size needed for the amount of text (at the point size that it needs to fit). After you create the path, choose the Area Type tool and position the type cursor over the edge of the path and click.

The type in Figure 8-10 was flowed into the outline of a word. Using text wraps, the type exists only inside the letters yet reads across all of them.

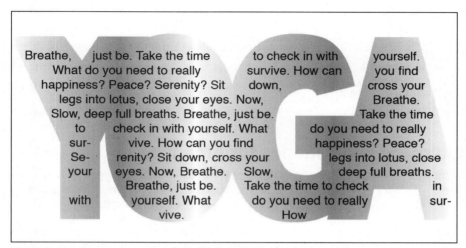

Figure 8-10: Area type created so the text flows inside the outlines

Using Area Type functions

Within area type there are options you can choose. Double-click the Area Type tool or choose Type ➪ Area Type Options to access the Area Type Options dialog box as shown in Figure 8-11. You need to have some area type selected to access these options.

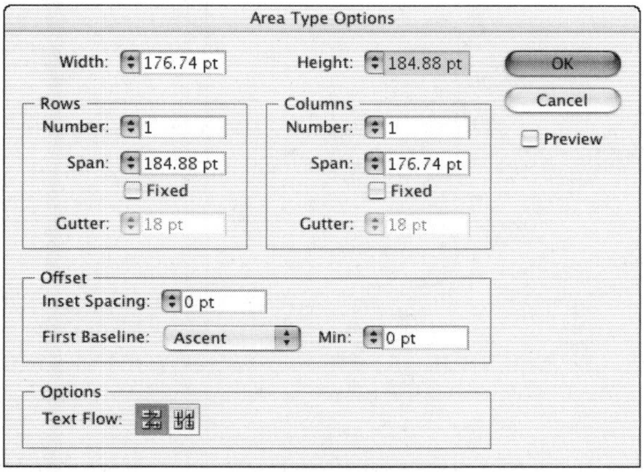

Figure 8-11: Area Type Options dialog box

The options that you can set are:

✦ **Width/Height:** Defines the area of the type

✦ **Rows/Columns:** Sets the number, size, and gutter of the horizontal rows and vertical columns

✦ **Offset:** Determines how far the text is offset from the edge of the path area

✦ **Text Flow:** Sets whether the text flows left to right top to bottom, or top to bottom left to right

Check the Preview box to see the settings you enter before hitting OK or Cancel.

Choosing good shapes for Area type

What exactly constitutes a "good" shape to be used for Area type? As a rule of thumb, gently curved shapes are better than harsh, jagged ones. Type tends to flow better into the larger lumps created by smoothly curving paths.

Try to avoid creating paths with wild or tight curves. Other designs that can cause problems are "hourglass" shapes or any closed path that has an area where the sides are almost touching. Figure 8-12 shows how type flows into a smoothly curved area and how it has trouble flowing into a sharp, spiky shape.

Try to make the top and bottom boundaries of the path have less "bumpiness" than the sides. This reduces the number of times that type jumps from one area to another.

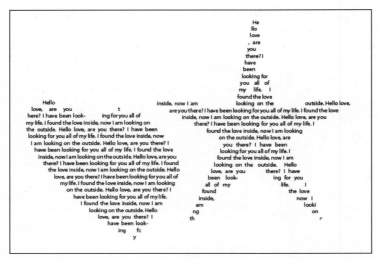

Figure 8-12: Type flows much better into a smooth curved area (left) rather than a sharp spiky area (right).

For the best results with Area type, make the type small and Force Justify it by pressing ⌘+Shift+J (Ctrl+Shift+J). This ensures that the type flows up against the edges of the path.

Outlining areas of Area type

Placing a stroke on the path surrounding Area type can be a great visual effect, but doing so and getting good results can be a bit tricky. If the stroke is thicker than 1 or 2 points, and you don't want the type to run into the edges of the stroke, there are a few things you can do. The best way to do this is to use Area Type Options and enter the value you want the text to offset away from the type. To do so, follow these steps:

1. **Create a path for your Area type with any drawing tool. For example, the Rectangle tool is a good tool to use.** For more on drawing tools, see Chapters 3 and 4.

2. **Click the shape with the Area Type tool.**

3. **Enter your type.**

4. **With the type selected, double-click the Area Type tool or choose Type ⇨ Area Type Options.** Doing this opens the Area Type Options dialog box. For more on the options in this box, see the section "Using Area Type functions."

5. **Enter the value you want to offset the type away from the edge.** You type this in the Inset Spacing area under the Offset section of the dialog box.

6. **Click the Preview button to see the result.**

7. **If you like what you see, click OK.** An example of what you might see when you finish is shown in Figure 8-13.

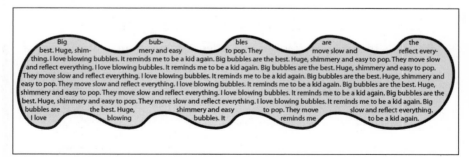

Figure 8-13: Type offset from the edges of the stroked path

Type Color and the Color of Type

There is a difference between the color of type and type color. You can paint type in Illustrator, and make it any one of millions of different shades, which determines the color we normally think of.

The color of type, on the other hand, is the way the type appears in the document and is more indicative of the light or dark attributes of the text. The actual red-green-blue colors of the type do work into this appearance, but many times the weight of the type and the tracking and kerning have a much more profound effect on color.

To easily see the color of type, unfocus your eyes as you look at your document, or turn the page upside down. This works better on a printed area than onscreen, but you can still get the gist of the way the document appears when you view it on your monitor. Dark and light areas become much more apparent when you can't read the actual words on the path. This method of unfocusing your eyes to look at a page also works well when trying to see the "look" of a page and how it was designed. Many times, unfocusing or turning the page upside down emphasizes the fact that you don't have enough white space or that all the copy seems to blend together.

Heavy type weights such as boldface, heavy, and black, make type appear darker on a page. Type kerned and tracked very tightly also seems to give the type a darker feel.

The x-height of type (the height to which the lowercase letters, such as an x, rise) is another factor that determines the color of type. Certain italic versions of typefaces can make the text seem lighter, although a few make text look darker because of the additional area that the thin strokes of the italic type covers.

With red-green-blue colors, you can make type stand out by making it appear darker, or you can make it blend into the page when you make it lighter. When you add smartly placed images near the type, your page can come alive with color.

Doing bizarre things with Area type

Probably the most overlooked rule when it comes to manipulating Area type and the paths that create the type boundaries is the simple fact that Illustrator treats the path and the type equally, unless you choose the path with the Direct Selection (or Group Selection) tool. Area type is selected when there is an underline under all the characters in the area.

When using the transformation tools, be sure that if you don't want to change any of the characteristics of the type, you select just the path. Use the Group Selection tool to click once on the deselected path, and Illustrator only selects the path, not the type. If you transform the area text when you have both selected, the transformation applies to the text as well as the path.

If you have both the type and the path selected, the transformations affect both the type and the path. Figure 8-14 shows transformations taking place to both type and the surrounding path, as opposed to transformations taking place to just the surrounding path.

Figure 8-14: The original type and path (top, left), after both the type and the path have been transformed (top right) and after only the path has been transformed (bottom)

Changing the area, not the type

Sometimes, you need to adjust the path that makes up the area of the Area type, for example when you scale a path up or down so that the text flows better. The trick here is to make sure that you select the entire path without selecting any of the characters. To do this, deselect the type and select the path with the Group Selection tool (the hollow arrow with the + sign).

Now any changes you make only affects the path, so you can scale it, rotate it, or change its Paint Style attributes without directly affecting the text within it. Figure 8-15 shows a transformed path, which allows the text inside to flow differently.

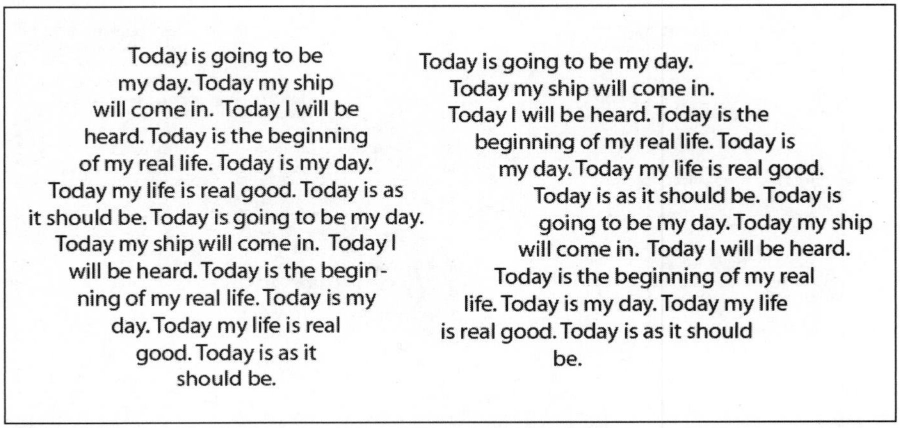

Today is going to be my day. Today my ship will come in. Today I will be heard. Today is the beginning of my real life. Today is my day. Today my life is real good. Today is as it should be. Today is going to be my day. Today my ship will come in. Today I will be heard. Today is the begin‐ning of my real life. Today is my day. Today my life is real good. Today is as it should be.

Today is going to be my day. Today my ship will come in. Today I will be heard. Today is the beginning of my real life. Today is my day. Today my life is real good. Today is as it should be. Today is going to be my day. Today my ship will come in. Today I will be heard. Today is the beginning of my real life. Today is my day. Today my life is real good. Today is as it should be.

Figure 8-15: You can edit the original area type shape (left) to change only the text flow, not the type (right).

Flowing area type into shapes

You can do all sorts of nifty things with type that you flow into areas — from unusual column designs to fascinating shapes. Using nonrectangular columns can liven up a publication quite easily. Some magazines use curved columns that are easy to read and lend a futuristic, hip look to the publication. Angled and curved columns are simple to create in Illustrator by creating the shape of the column and flowing Area type from one shape to the next.

Traditionally, forcing type into an irregular (nonrectangular) area was quite a task. The typesetter had to set several individual lines of type, each specified by the art director or client to be a certain length so that when all the text was put together, the text formed the shape (see Figure 8-16). This is probably the main reason the world has not seen too much of this, except in overly zealous art students' portfolios.

For example, you can give a report on toxic waste in New Jersey more impact by shaping the text into the form of a hypodermic needle. Or you can make a seasonal ad in the shape of a Christmas tree. Look at some of the Absolut Vodka ads to see what they've done to flow text into that all-too-familiar bottle.

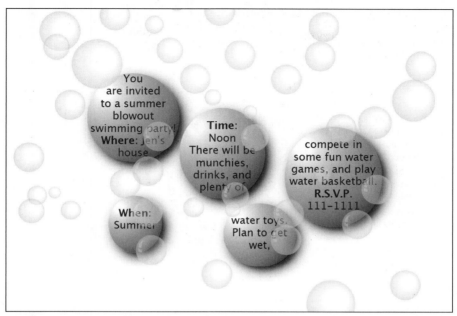

Figure 8-16: Text flowed into linked shapes

Placing Type on a Path

The unique thing about type on a path is that when the path is not visible, the type becomes the path, as shown in Figure 8-17. This can produce some really fascinating results, especially when combined with various fonts of different weights, styles, colors, and special characters.

Although using the Type on a Path tool can create some great effects, it has one glitch. You usually run into trouble when the path you're using has either corner Anchor Points or very sharp curves. Letters often crash (run into one another) when this occurs. Besides the most obvious way to avoid this problem, which is to not use paths with corner Anchor Points and sharp curves, you can sometimes kern apart the areas where the letters crash until they aren't touching anymore.

When kerning Type on a path, be sure to kern from the flush side first. For instance, if the type is flush left, start your kerning from the left side and work to the right. If you start on the wrong end, the letters you kern apart move along the path until they aren't in an area that needs kerning, but other letters instead appear there.

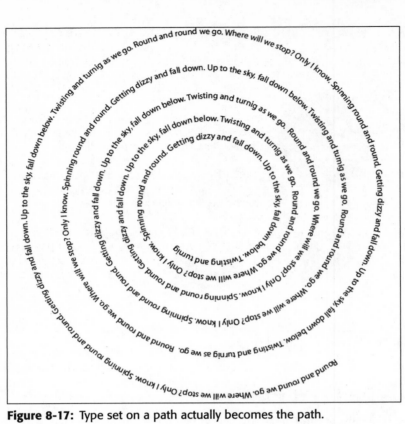

Figure 8-17: Type set on a path actually becomes the path.

Another method of fixing crashed letters is to tweak the path with the Direct Selection tool. Careful adjusting of both Anchor Points and Control Handles can easily fix crashes and letters that have huge amounts of space between them.

Cross-Reference   For more on kerning, see the section "Kerning and tracking," later in this chapter.

To create Type on a path:

1. **First create a path in your document.** It is best to create a path that doesn't cross over itself.

2. **Click the path with the Type on a path tool.** This creates an insertion point along the path. This works whether the path is a closed path or an open path.

3. **Start typing your text.** Type aligns to the insertion point; if the type is set to flush left, the left edge of the type aligns to the location where the Type on a path tool was first clicked.

4. **Click the Insertion bar (which resembles a little I-beam) with any Selection tool and dragging along the path.** This flows Type on a path along the path to which it is aligned. If you drag the I-bar to the other side of the path, the type flips over in the direction of the bar. For this reason, it is a good idea to click the topmost part of the Insertion bar before dragging.

Tip

As with other objects in Illustrator that can be moved by dragging, pressing the Option (Alt) key before releasing the mouse causes the object being dragged to duplicate instead of just move. This works with the Type I-bar, as well.

If you would like the type you are dragging to appear below the path but to not get flipped upside down and change direction, use baseline shift (found in the Character palette) to raise and lower the type to your liking.

Note

Although there are different Type tools, you only need to choose one. If you have the standard Type tool, it changes into the Area Type tool when you pass over a closed path and it changes into a Type on a path tool when the cursor passes over an open path. You can access the Vertical types versions of these tools by pressing Shift.

Typing on the top and bottom of a circle

Everyone's doing it. Peer pressure is going to make you succumb as well. If you can put type on the top and the bottom of a circle so that it runs along the same path, you are quite the designer, or so thinks the average guy on the street. The simple "Type on a Circle" shown in Figure 8-18 can be created quite easily and works quite nicely for logo design as well.

Follow these steps and with a little practice, you can create type on a circle in less than 15 seconds. Pretty impressive, even to those who understand how it's done.

1. **Draw a circle with the Ellipse tool.** You do this by holding down the Shift key to make sure it is a perfect circle.

2. **Choose the Type on a Path tool and click the top center of the circle.** The blinking insertion point appears at that point on the circle.

3. **Type the text that you want to appear at the top of the circle.**

4. **Press ⌘+Shift+C (Ctrl+Shift+C).** This centers the type at the top of the circle.

5. **Choose the Selection tool and click the top of the I-bar marker, dragging it up to the top outside center of the circle.** Before letting go of the mouse button, center the type, making sure that it is readable from left to right.

6. **Select the text with the Type tool and slowly scoot the type down below the baseline using the baseline shift field in the Character palette.** Doing this pushes the type down the baseline.

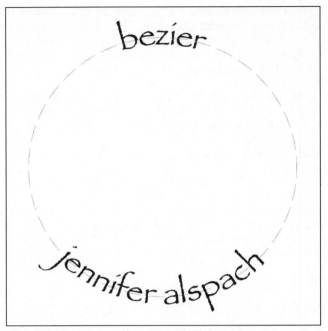

Figure 8-18: Type on the top and bottom of a circle

7. **Select the type with the Selection tool and press ⌘+C (Alt+C).** This makes a copy.

8. **Press ⌘+Option+V (Ctrl+Alt+V).** This pastes the type in front.

9. **Using the Type on a path tool, click the text to activate it, and then choose the Direct Selection tool.**

10. **With the Direct Selection tool, drag the I-bar so the text is on the bottom inside the circle.**

11. **With the Path on a Type tool, edit as desired.**

Tip   Grab the I-bar at the top with the Direct Selection tool to move type on a circle.

Coloring type that is anchored to a path

When type is anchored to a path, either as Area type or Type on a path, there are some important considerations to think of before filling and Stroking the type.

First, if you select just the type or just the path with the regular Selection tool, Illustrator selects the other (path or type) as well. Do you want to put a stroke along that path that surrounds your type? If you select the path with the regular Selection tool, the type is selected as well, and each character in the type area has the same stroke you meant to apply to the path.

For changing just the path's Paint Style attributes, be sure to use the Direct Selection tool to select the path. If an underline doesn't appear under the text, the text is not selected. To change all of the text, you must choose a Type tool, click within the text area, and then apply the Select All command by pressing (⌘+A (Ctrl+A). Only then is just the text affected.

Adding effects to type on a path

Under the Type menu, you can warp type on a path with a few default settings. Once you create type on a path, choose from the following effects: Rainbow, Skew, 3D Ribbon, Stair Step, or Gravity. To adjust the default settings, choose Type ➪ Type on a Path ➪ Type on a path options. In this dialog box, you can choose the following:

✦ **Effect:** Choose from Rainbow, Skew, 3D Ribbon, Stair Step, and Gravity. Rainbow effect places each letter's baseline along a curved path like a rainbow. Skew keeps all of the letters vertical edges strictly vertical. 3D Ribbon keeps all of the letters horizontal edges strictly horizontal. Stair Step keeps the left edge of the baseline of the letter on the path. Gravity puts the center of each letter on the baseline of the path with no rotation.

✦ **Align to Path:** This option alters the path's alignment, with the choices being ascender, descender, center, or baseline. Choosing ascender aligns the type higher on the path in line with the top of the highest part of the letter (as in an h). The descender option aligns the type lower on the path in line with the hanging part of the letter (as in a g). Choosing center aligns the type equally on the path with half being above the line and half being below the path. The baseline option aligns the base of the type (not the descender) to the path.

✦ **Spacing:** This allows you to space the path up or down from its original position.

✦ **Flip:** This option flips the type to the opposite side.

✦ **Preview:** Allows you to preview your changes before you click OK to commit to them.

Figure 8-19 shows the Type on a Path Options dialog box with the type being affected underneath.

Figure 8-19: The Type on a Path Options dialog box

Using vertical type

Vertical type is a fascinating capability in Illustrator. If you use Kanji characters, you'll find it invaluable. But even if you don't, you may find some interesting uses for setting type vertically, instead of horizontally.

There are two ways to make your type appear vertical instead of horizontal. You can create type using any of the three Vertical Type tools, or you can convert horizontal type into vertical type with Type ➪ Type Orientation ➪ Vertical. Figure 8-20 shows Rectangle type both horizontally and vertically. Note that Vertical type takes up a great deal more space than Horizontal type and flows top to bottom, right to left.

He gently reached out and touched her cheek to wake her. Mom? I had a bad dream and really need you to hold me. She shook off the remnants of sleep and took his hand quietly leading him back to his room. Soft songs soothed him back into sleep.

Figure 8-20: Vertical type (left) and the same type reoriented to horizontal (right)

Most of Illustrator's standard character and paragraph palette changes work with vertical type, but not always in ways you expect. For example, type is set on a centerline, not a baseline. The centerline runs vertically through the center of each character. The following is a list of differences in the way each major function works:

Table 8-1	
Vertical Type Functions	
Function	*Difference*
Font	Same as standard.
Size	Same as standard.
Leading	Changes the amount of space between the vertical "lines" of type, measured from centerline to centerline.

Continued

Table 8-1 *(continued)*	
Function	**Difference**
Kerning/Tracking	Changes the amount of vertical space between each character. Because very few Roman characters have both ascenders and descenders, tracking and kerning substantially can really help get rid of the excess white space between characters that makes vertical type so hard to read.
Vertical Scale	Changes the width (horizontal scale) of the characters.
Horizontal Scale	Changes the height (vertical scale) of the characters.
Baseline Shift	Moves the type left (negative values) and right (positive values) along the centerline.
Flush Left	Words are flush top.
Center	Words are vertically centered.
Flush Right	Words are flush bottom.
Justify Full Lines	Words on full (vertical) lines are justified from top to bottom.
Justify All Lines	All lines are vertically justified.
Left Indent	Top indent. Positive numbers move the text down and negative numbers move the text up.
Right Indent	Bottom indent, with numbers working like Left Indent.
First Line Indent	The rightmost line indent. Once again, positive numbers move the text down and negative numbers move the text up.
Space Before Paragraph	Paragraphs go from right to left, so this control increases the space to the right of the selected paragraph(s).
Auto Hyphenate	Hyphenates words the same way as horizontal type, but the hyphens appear at the bottom of each line.
Hang Punctuation	Punctuation hangs above and below the text area.
Tab Ruler	Appears to the right of text areas in vertical form.
Create Outlines	Same as standard.

Selecting Type

Before you can make changes to text, you must first select it. There are two ways of selecting type: You can select type areas with a Selection tool, which selects every character in the type area, or you can select characters individually or in groups with any of the Type tools.

To select the entire type area or multiple type areas, click the baseline of a line of type within the type area you want to select. Any changes made in the Type menu, Font menu, Character palette, or Paragraph palette affect every character in the selected type areas.

Note If you have blank fields in any of the palettes or no check marks next to some of the menu items (for example, you do not check any fonts), when you select type areas, Illustrator presents you with different options for each of those fields or menu items within the type area (for example, Helvetica for some characters, Times for others). Changing a blank field or unchecked menu item after you select a type area affects all characters in that area.

To select characters within a type area, you must use a type tool. As you near text that has been typed in the document, the dotted lines surrounding the cursor disappear. The hot spot of the type cursor is the place where the short horizontal bar crosses the vertical bar (see Figure 8-21). You should not use when clicking with the type cursor.

To select an individual character, drag across the character you want to select. As you select a character, its colors reverse, so that black text appears white. To select more than one character, drag left or right across multiple characters; all characters from the location you originally clicked to the current location of the cursor are highlighted. If you drag up with the cursor over straight text, you select all the characters to the left and all the characters to the right of the cursor's current location. Dragging down does the reverse. The more lines you drag up or down, the more lines you select.

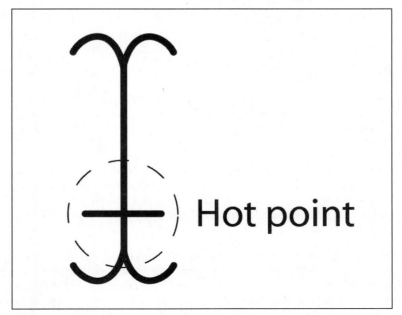

Figure 8-21: The type cursor's hot spot

To select one word at a time (and the space that follows it), double-click the word you want to select. The word and the space after it reverse. The reason that Illustrator selects the space following the word has to do with the number of times you copy, cut, and paste words from within sentences. For example, to remove the word Lazy in the phrase "The Lazy Boy," you double-click the word Lazy and press Delete. The phrase then becomes "The Boy," which only has one space where the word Lazy used to be. To select several words, double-click and drag the type cursor across the words you want to select. Illustrator selects each word you touch with the cursor , from the location you initially double-click to the current location. Dragging to the previous or next line selects additional lines, with at least a word on the first line double-clicked and one word on the dragged-to line.

For the nimble-fingered clickers, you may also click three times to select a paragraph. Triple-click anywhere inside the paragraph selects the entire paragraph, including the hard Return at the end of the paragraph (if there is one). Triple-clicking and dragging selects successive paragraphs, if you move the cursor up or down while you press the mouse button following the third click.

To select all the text within a type area with a Type tool, click once in the type area and choose Select ➪ Select All, or press ⌘+A (Ctrl+A). As in most programs, you can only select text in contiguous blocks. You have no way to select two words in two different locations of the same type area without selecting all the text between them.

You can also select type through the use of the Shift key. Click one spot (we'll call it the beginning) and then Shift-click another spot. The characters between the beginning and the Shift-click are selected. Successive Shift-clicks select characters from the beginning to the current location of the most recent Shift-click.

Editing Type

There are limited text-editing features in Illustrator. By clicking once within a type area, a blinking insertion point appears. If you begin typing, characters appear where the blinking insertion point is. The Del key (if you have one) removes the character to the right

The arrow keys on your keyboard move the blinking insertion point around in the direction of the arrow. The right arrow moves the insertion point one character to the right, and the left arrow moves the insertion point one character to the left. The up arrow moves the insertion point to the previous line; the down arrow moves the insertion point to the next line.

Pressing the ⌘ (Ctrl) key speeds up the movement of the insertion point. ⌘+right arrow (Ctrl+right arrow) or ⌘+left arrow (Ctrl+left arrow) moves the insertion point to the next or preceding word, and ⌘+down arrow (Ctrl+down arrow)or ⌘+up arrow (Ctrl+up arrow) moves the insertion point to the next or preceding paragraph.

Tip　Pressing the Shift key while moving the insertion point around with the arrows selects all the characters that the insertion point passes over. This works for the ⌘+arrow (Ctrl+arrow) movements as well.

When you select characters with a Type tool, typing anything deletes the selected characters and replaces them with what you are currently typing. Pressing the Delete key (Backspace) when characters are selected deletes all the selected characters. If you paste type by pressing ⌘+V (Ctrl+V) when you have characters selected, the selected characters are replaced with the pasted characters.

Using the Type Palettes

Illustrator offers a variety of type palettes. The Character, Paragraph, and OpenType palettes are tabbed together. The Tabs palette is on its own. There is a Glyphs palette as well. You can also create character and paragraph styles and keep them in the Character Styles or Paragraph Styles palette. You can change typeface, style, alignment, kerning, and so much more at your fingertips with the palettes.

Working with the Character palette

The easiest way to change the attributes of characters is by using the Character palette, shown in Figure 8-22. Many of the changes in the Character palette are available as options in the Type menu. As a rule, if you have more than one change to make, it is better to do it in the Character palette than the menu, if just so that everything you need is in one place. The Character palette without the options viewing lets you set the Size, Leading, Kerning, and Tracking.

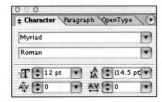

Figure 8-22: The Character palette

Character attribute changes affect only the letters that are selected, with the exception of leading (explained later), which should really be in the Paragraph palette.

Tip　You can change several character attributes by increments. The increments are set in the Keyboard Increments Preferences dialog box (choose Illustrator ➪ Preferences ➪ Keyboard Increments). You can change increments for point size, leading, baseline shift, and tracking/kerning values. Where appropriate, the key commands for each attribute change are listed in the following sections.

The Character palette expands when you show the Options as shown in Figure 8-23. Choose Show Options from the Character palette pop-up menu to display the Options section: Horizontal Scaling, Vertical Scaling, Baseline Shift, Character Rotation, and the Language. The Character palette remembers which mode the palette was in the last time it was displayed and shows that view the next time you display it.

Figure 8-23: The Character palette with options

You can use the Tab key to move across the different text fields. When in partial display palette mode, the Tab key works only in the partial palette; when you select the last field (Tracking/Kerning), the Tab key then goes back to the Font field. If you highlight a field in the lower part of the palette when the palette is closed, the Font field highlights. When the palette is in full view, tabbing past the last field highlights the Font field as well. In addition to the Tab key tabbing forward through the text fields, pressing Shift+Tab tabs backward through the text fields.

Note   Choosing Edit ➪ Undo, or pressing ⌘+Z (Ctrl+Z) does not undo items typed in the Character palette while you are still in the text field. To undo something, you must first move along (tab) to the next field and then undo, and then Shift-Tab back. Canceling (Esc) does not cancel what you have typed but instead highlights the text (if you select a Type tool).

Tip   All of the text fields in the Character palette have both pop-up (Mac) or drop-down (Windows) menus with common values in them for quick access and cute little up and down arrows to the left of each field. These arrows increase (up) and decrease (down) the values of each of the currently selected text fields. Pressing the Shift key while clicking the little arrow buttons makes the change with each press even greater.

Tip   You can use the keyboard to press these buttons. When the field is highlighted, press the Up arrow on your keyboard to press the up arrow button; press the down arrow on your keyboard to press the down arrow button. Press Shift at the same time to jump the value by a greater amount.

Changing font and style

The top field on the Character palette is the Font menu field. When you click the Font menu field triangle, the list of fonts and how they look displays. This also happens when you select Font under the Type menu.

New Feature New to Illustrator CS is the ability to see what the font looks like in the Font menu. Now when you display the Font menu from the Type menu or from the Character palette, you can see the fonts displayed before choosing the font.

Measuring type

So, you've finally mastered this whole silly point/pica concept — you know that there are 72 points in an inch, and you think that you're ready to conquer the world. And you are, as long as no one asks you to spec type.

At 72 points, the letter I is about 50 points tall. In inches that is just under ¾ inches. To get better results for specially sized capital letters, a good rule of thumb is that every 100 points is about a 1-inch capital letter. This works for most typefaces, and only for the first several inches, but it is a good start to getting capital letters that are sized pretty accurately.

Curves in capital letters are yet another wrench thrown into the equation. In many typefaces, the bottom and top of the letter O go beneath the baseline and above the ascender height of most squared letters. Serifs on certain typefaces may also cross these lines.

You measure type from the top of the ascenders (like the top of a capital T) to the bottom of the descender (like the bottom of a lowercase p). So when people tell you they want a capital I that is 1-inch high, you can't just say, "Oh, there are 72 points in an inch, so I will create a 72-point I for them."

Under the Font field, you find the font Style field. Clicking the arrow displays the styles available for the chosen font.

Tip For every text field, you can apply the information you enter, either by tabbing to the next or preceding text field or by pressing Enter or Return.

To the right of the font and style text fields, you find a little menu triangle that, when pressed, displays a list of all the typefaces installed on your system. The families are displayed in the main list, and arrows show which families have different styles. To select a font, drag the cursor over it until it is highlighted. To select a specific style of a font family, drag the cursor to the font family name and then drag to the right (if there is enough space to the right for the submenu otherwise it appears to the left) to select the style name. The fields to the menu's left are updated instantly.

Changing type size

The field below the Style field on the left is the Size field. You type in the desired point size (from 0.1 point to 1296 points in increments of ¹⁄₁₀,₀₀₀ point) and any selected characters increase or decrease to that particular point size. Next to the Size field, you find a menu triangle, which lists the standard point sizes available. Point size for type is always measured from the top of the ascenders to the bottom of the descenders. You can increase or decrease type point size from the keyboard by typing ⌘+Shift+> (Ctrl+Shift+>) to increase and ⌘+Shift+< (Ctrl+Shift+<) to decrease the point size by the increment specified in the General Preferences dialog box. Figure 8-24 shows the results of changing type size using the keyboard commands.

Figure 8-24: Original type on top, adjusted point size using the key commands on bottom

Tip   The keyboard commands for increasing and decreasing typographic attributes, such as point size, leading, baseline shift, and tracking, are more than just other ways to change those attributes. Instead, they are invaluable for making changes when the selected type has more than one different value of that attribute within it. For example, if some of the characters have a point size of 10 and some of them have a point size of 20, using the keyboard command (with an increment set to 2 points) changes the type to 12 and 22 points. This is tedious to do separately, especially if there are multiple sizes or just a few sizes scattered widely about.

Adjusting the leading

Next to the Size field, you find the Leading text field. Here you enter the desired leading value between 0.1 point and 1296 points, in increments of ⅟₁₀₀₀ point. To the right of the leading field is a pop-up menu triangle, from which you can choose common leading values. In Illustrator, leading is measured from the baseline of the current line up to the baseline of the preceding line, as shown in Figure 8-25. The distance between these two baselines is the amount of leading.

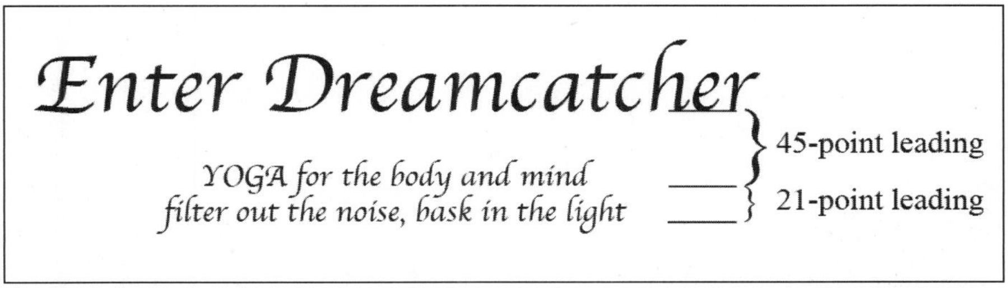

Enter Dreamcatcher

} 45-point leading

YOGA for the body and mind _____ } 21-point leading
filter out the noise, bask in the light _____ }

Figure 8-25: You measure leading from baseline to baseline. The 45-point leading was set by selecting the second line and changing the leading. The 21-point leading was set by selecting the third and fourth lines and changing the leading.

If you change the Leading field from the number that displays there by default, the Auto Leading entry in the Leading menu becomes unchecked. The Auto Leading box, when checked, makes the leading exactly 120% of the point size. This is just great when the type is 10 points because the leading is 12 points, a common point size-to-leading relationship. But as point size goes up, leading should become proportionately less, until, at around 72 points, it is less than the point size. Instead, when Auto Leading is checked, 72-point type has 86.5-point leading. That's a lot of unsightly white space.

You can set Leading increments in the General Preferences dialog box, which you access by pressing ⌘+K (Ctrl+K). Press Option+up arrow (Alt+up arrow) to increase the leading (which pushes lines farther apart) and Option+down arrow (Alt+down arrow) to decrease the leading.

Kerning and tracking

Kerning is the amount of space between any specific pair of letters. You can only change kerning values when there is a blinking insertion point between two characters.

Tracking is the amount of space between all the letters currently selected. If you select the type area with a Selection tool, it refers to all the space between all the characters in the entire type area. If you select characters with a Type tool, tracking only affects the space between the specific letters selected.

Although they are related and appear to do basically the same thing, tracking and kerning actually work quite independently of each other. They only look like they are affecting each other; altering one never actually changes the amount of the other. The Kerning field appears directly below the point size of the type, while the Tracking field appears below the leading (see Figure 8-26).

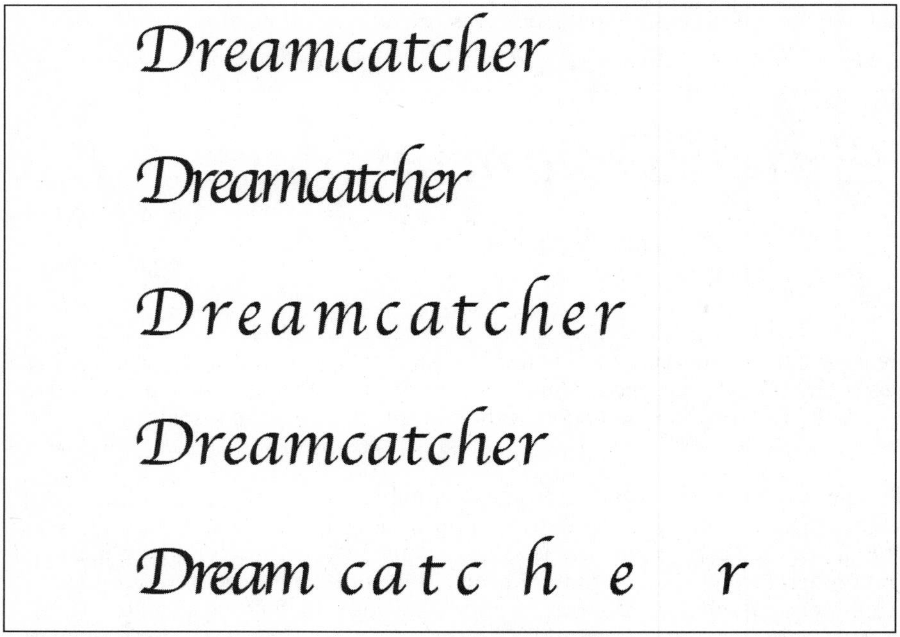

Figure 8-26: The top word is the original. The second one down is tracking set close. The third one down is tracking set apart. The fourth one down is an example of kerning set close. The last one down is kerning set farther apart.

The Kerning field often reads Auto instead of a value when you select several letters. If Auto appears in that field, the kerning built into the font is used automatically. Choosing a different value overrides the Auto setting and uses the value you type. If you select several letters, you can only choose 0, but you can enter any number if a blinking insertion point appears between the letters. Auto Kerning works by reading the kerning values of the typeface that were embedded by the type designer when the typeface was originally created. The typeface designer normally defines the space between letters; different typefaces look like they have different amounts of space between letters. There are usually a couple hundred preset kerning pairs for common Adobe typefaces, although the expert sets have quite a few more. When Auto Kerning is in effect, you can see those preset kerning values by clicking between kerned letter pairs (capital T with most vowels is a good one to check) and reading the value in the Kerning field. If you use Auto Kerning, Illustrator displays the value in parentheses. Different typefaces have different kerning pairs, and kerning pairs don't only change from typeface to typeface, but also from weight to weight and style to style.

For example, a kerning pair of the letters AV in Times New Roman Bold, when Auto Kerning is on, is set to (–129). If you type in a value of –250, that value overrides the Auto Kerning, turning it off and using your new value of –250. Figure 8-27 shows the difference between a kerning of –129 and –250.

Figure 8-27: The left letters are using Auto Kerning (–129). The right letters are using –250 kerning.

To decrease or increase the kerning or tracking by the increments specified in the Keyboard Increments Preferences dialog box, insert the Type tool between two letters and press Option+left arrow (Alt +left arrow) or Option+right arrow (Alt +right arrow). To increase or decrease the tracking or kerning by a factor of five times the amount in the General Preferences dialog box, press ⌘+Option+right arrow (Ctrl+Alt +right arrow) or ⌘+Option+left arrow (Ctrl+Alt +left arrow).

Kerning and tracking values are based on $\frac{1}{1000}$ em space. An em space is the width of two numbers (think of two zeros — they tend to be the widest-looking numbers) at that particular point size.

The values entered for tracking and kerning must be between –1000 and 10,000. A value of –1000 results in stacked letters. A value of 10,000 makes enough space between letters for 10 em spaces, or 20 numbers. That's a lot of space.

Note   Different software works with kerning and tracking differently. In programs that do offer numerical tracking, it is usually represented in some form of a fraction of an em space, but the denominator varies from software to software.

The bottom portion of the Character palette contains the Baseline Shift field, which, unlike leading, moves individual characters up and down relative to their baseline (from leading). Positive numbers move the selected characters up, and negative numbers move the characters down by the amount specified. The maximum amount of baseline shift is 1296 points in either direction. Baseline shift is especially useful for Type on a path. You can change Baseline shift via the keyboard by selecting a letter with the Type tool and pressing Option+Shift+up arrow (Alt+Shift+up arrow) to increase. Pressing Option+Shift+down arrow (Alt+Shift+down arrow) decreases the baseline shift in the increment specified in the General Preferences dialog box.

Using Vertical scale and Horizontal scale

Also in the Options section of the Character palette is the Horizontal Scale field. Horizontal scale controls the width of the type, causing it to become expanded or condensed horizontally. You can enter values from 1% to 10,000% in this field. Like most other fields in the Character palette, the values entered are absolute values, so whatever the horizontal scale is, changing it back to 100% returns the type to its original proportions.

Understanding the language barrier

If you're reading a translation of the Illustrator Bible in a language other than English, I'd like to welcome you by saying hello in your native language: "Hello." Okay, I'm probably not fooling you here; through the magic of translators who speak several languages much more fluently than I speak "westernized East Coast American English," my current language of choice, this book is translated into other languages without one iota of input from me.

If your language of choice is not English, you'll be interested in the Language option along the bottom of the Character palette. You can change to your language of choice, so that functions such as the spelling dictionary and hyphenation dictionary work for words you'll be typing.

More multinational options

The other options along the bottom of the Character palette are specifically designed for Kanji character operations, with the exception of the Direction pop-up menu, which you can use with Roman characters to achieve various effects. To even see these options you first have to choose Illustrator ⇨ Preferences ⇨ Type & Auto Tracing and check the Show Asian Options box. This reconfigures the Character palette to show the Asian options for kerning and tracking. The Character rotation option is discussed later in this chapter in the vertical type section.

Adding paragraph options

Some of the changes you make to text affect entire paragraphs at once. Paragraph attributes include alignment, indentation, space before paragraphs, hanging punctuation, hyphenation, spacing, repeated character processing, and line breaking.

You can change paragraph attributes if you first select a type area using a Selection tool, in which case, the changes affect every paragraph within the entire type area.

Welcome to the Illustrator Bible's color insert section. In this section, you not only see some pretty amazing artwork, but you also glimpse how various artists created their illustrations. Whether you create realistic illustrations, comic relief, or complicated text images, you can do so much with this powerful application.

To find contact information and biographies on the artists whose works grace this color insert, see Appendix C. Many of the artists have also contributed to this book by way of a Guest Author How-to. You find the Guest Author sections at the end of selected chapters. In these how-to sections, you learn how the artists created a specific special effect or realistic appearances in their artwork.

"A Day in the Clouds" by Joe Jones uses both Illustrator and Photoshop, as well as Ray Dream Designer and Bryce, Necessary for the 3-D modeling process. The top and side profile outlines were carefully drawn to scale from scratch to produce the hundreds of objects that compose the original aircraft models.

"A Day in the Clouds" by Joe Jones

The artist drew tens of thousands of rivets accurately and consistently. The illustration uses 28 separate texture and bump maps, which were required for all four views of just one of the B-17 Flying Fortress 3-D models. This was made possible only by utilizing Illustrator's Scatter Brushes. Because each tiny rivet had to be at least 10 pixels in the rastered texture map to create the final effect, massive high-resolution Photoshop files were necessary to export the complex layered files from Illustrator.

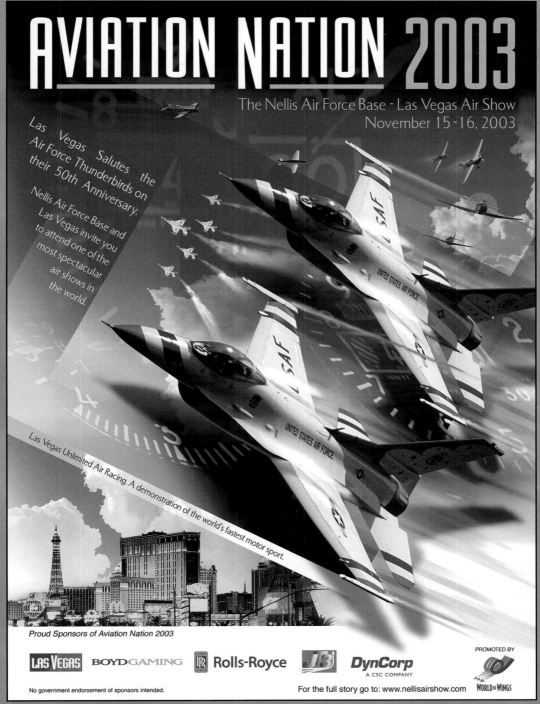

"Aviation Nation 2003" poster by Joe Jones

"Aviation Nation 2003" poster by Joe Jones, created using both Illustrator and Photoshop. This is the Air Force Thunderbirds/Nellis Air Show ad piece currently running. Basically, layout and color development for this ad were completely produced in Illustrator using multiple Layers, Transparency, and Color Modes. The art for the Air and Vertical Speed indicator instrumentation was drawn and then distorted using the transformer tool.

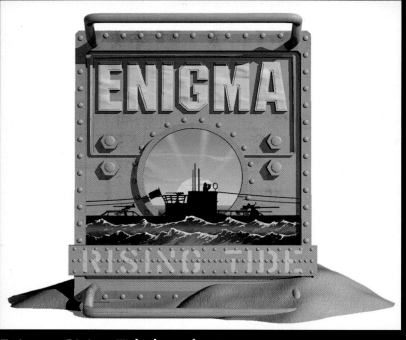

Enigma, Rising Tide logo by Joe Jones, created using both Illustrator and Photoshop. Although blending 3-D modeling and straight vector artwork is rarely done, the artist effectively uses this blending technique in this illustration. The German U-Boat, background sky, and ocean water in this logo were drawn freehand using the Pencil Tool and digital drawing tablet and utilizing multiple Layers, Transparency, and Color Modes. All elements for the 3-D modeling were also carefully produced in Illustrator.

Enigma, Rising Tide logo by Joe Jones

IAFA Logo, by Joe Jones

IAFA Logo, by Joe Jones uses both Illustrator and Photoshop. This is the new logo for the International Association for the Fantastic in the Arts. The basic layout, type design, and color development for this logo were completely produced in Illustrator using multiple Layers, Transparency, and Color Modes. All elements needed for the 3-D modeling of the structure were drawn in Illustrator.

THE INTERNATIONAL ASSOCIATION FOR THE FANTASTIC IN THE ARTS

**"Lost Girls"
by Martin
Mendelsberg**

"Lost Girls" and "Mystical Sphere" by Martin Mendelsberg, created using both Illustrator and Photoshop. Martin's amazing illustrations fully utilize Illustrator's type capabilities. Using the Hebrew typefaces he created for Masterfont, LTD, he creates feeling and emotion by mixing text, images, and color.

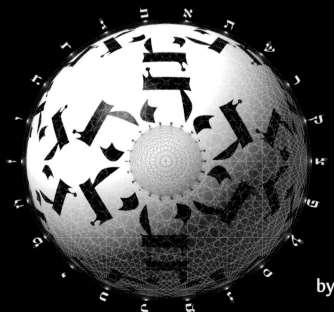

**"Mystical Sphere"
by Martin Mendelsberg**

Scribble Fill Illustrations
by Todd Macadangdang

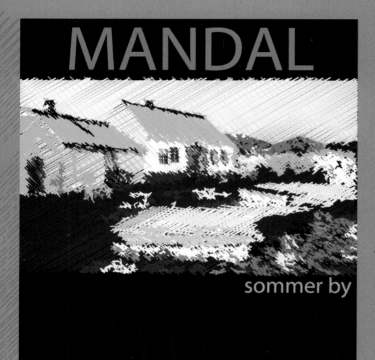

MANDAL

sommer by

Scribble Fill Illustrations by Todd Macadangdang, created using Illustrator. Todd's illustrations here fully demonstrate the power of the Scribble Fill command. The different effects of Scribble Fill are illustrated in three very different looking pieces.

RUIN DWELLERS

Speed	4
Strengh	4
Health	8

PARALLEL U424

eclipes

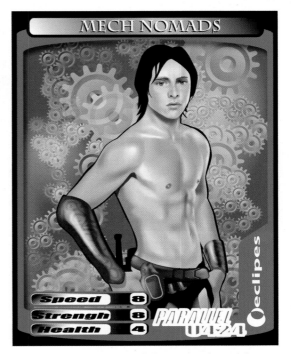

MECH NOMADS

Speed	8
Strengh	8
Health	4

PARALLEL U424

eclipes

"Mythical Cards" by Todd Macadangdang

SPACE PIRATES

Speed	8
Strengh	8
Health	4

PARALLEL U424

eclipes

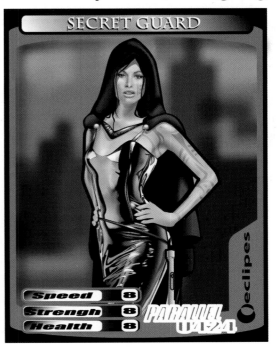

SECRET GUARD

Speed	8
Strengh	8
Health	8

PARALLEL U424

eclipes

"Mythical Cards" by Todd Macadangdang, created using Illustrator. These cards are an exercise in Gradient Mesh. Most of the cards are created fully using the Gradient Mesh tool. Todd took his time in carefully placing each gradient mesh and adding subtle nuances of color to suggest flesh, hair, and steel. To add drama to the type, he kept a strong shadow to pop out the type.

"Reluctant Wisdom" by Brian Warchesik

"Reluctant Wisdom" by Brian Warchesik, created using both Illustrator and Photoshop. For this illustration, the artist took the highly detailed areas, such as the headband and "thinker necklace," into Illustrator for two reasons. First, Illustrator allowed the artist to get a clean perspective of the pieces without the clutter of the rest of the composition to distract him. Second, Illustrator's paths gave the artist the cleanest method to render these objects, thus enhancing the crispness of their geometry.

"Elegant Bath" by Shane Duerksen

"Elegant Bath" by Shane Duerksen, created using Illustrator. In this illustration, Gradient Mesh is the ruler. The artist created the softened edges and three-dimensional color by meticulously using the Gradient Mesh tool and varying the color to make the bath pop out in realism.

**Rocky Mountain EAA
Regional Fly-In
by Joe Jones**

Rocky Mountain EAA Regional Fly In by Joe Jones, created using both Illustrator and Photoshop, as well as Ray Dream Designer and Bryce. This was the cover art that the artist created for this year's 25th Rocky Mountain EAA Regional Fly-In. The artist completely produced layout and color development in Illustrator using multiple Layers, Transparency, and Color Modes. He created the ribbon work shown in this piece using custom Calligraphic Brushes. All clouds were drawn free-hand using the Pencil Tool and digital drawing tablet. The artist created all type design in Illustrator and used the Path Type tool for the circular type elements in the top logo.

"Fantastic in the Arts" poster by Joe Jones

"Fantastic in the Arts" poster by Joe Jones, created using both Illustrator and Photoshop. This is the cover art the artist created for the 23rd Annual IAFA conference. The artist first used Illustrator to create the overall layout and type design. He then used Necessary for the 3-D modeling process. This original illustration required the artist to draw the top and side profile outlines for each of the hundreds of objects. The complex layered texture map art files that the artist created in Illustrator were then exported into Photoshop, where the artist added weathering effects, which appear in the final high-resolution texture maps.

"Tasty Waves"
by Cory Gray, created using
Illustrator. The comic shark fully
utilizes Illustrator's power. The artist
created the glint of the shark's teeth using the
Flare tool and defined the roughened outside edge
with a charcoal art brush. To achieve the softened
shadow under the text, the artist applied a Gaussian blur.

"Tasty Waves" by Cory Gray

"Do you smell smoke?" by Cory Gray, created using Illustrator. Illustrator's drawing tools flesh out the comic creatures. Some of the cool effects, such as the smoke coming from the dragon's nose and the fire's glow, were achieved using Illustrator's blur filters and effects. This illustration incorporates the use of layers to organize the pieces and characters.

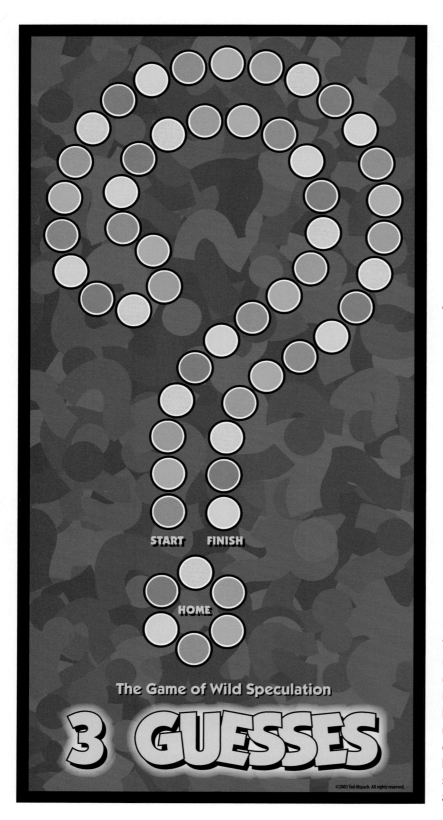

START   FINISH

HOME

The Game of Wild Speculation

3 GUESSES

"Three Guesses"
by Ted Alspach

"Three Guesses" by
Ted Alspach, created
using Illustrator. The artist
created this game board
using a variety of techniques.
He created the background
using an intricate pattern and
evenly distributed the circles.
He added a glow to the
shadow behind the type for
an eye-catching logo design.

If you use the Type tool to select one or more characters, changes you make to paragraph attributes affect the entire paragraphs of each of the selected characters.

To display the Paragraph palette (see Figure 8-28) using menu commands, choose Type ⇨ Paragraph. To display the Paragraph palette with a key command, press Option+⌘+T (Alt+Ctrl+T) and click the Paragraph tab.

Figure 8-28: The Paragraph palette

Pressing Tab moves you forward through the text fields and Shift-Tab moves you backward through the same text fields. Press Enter or Return to apply the changes that you made.

The bottom part of the Paragraph palette contains information that doesn't get changed too often, so for the most part, it doesn't need to be displayed. If you want to display it, choose Show Options from the Paragraph palette pop-up menu.

Aligning type

There are different types of paragraph alignment (see Figure 8-29). Each of them is represented by a graphical representation of what multiple lines of type look like when that particular alignment is applied. The different types of alignment are: Align Left, Centered, Align Right, Justify Last line Align Left, Justify Last line Align Center, Justify Last Line Align Right, and Justify All Lines. What these options do is listed below:

✦ **Align Left:** Moves all your text so that is lines up with the left side of your page. The most common and the default setting, experienced typesetters often refer to this option as ragged right due to the uneven right side of the text. You can also apply this type of alignment by pressing ⌘+Shift+L (Ctrl+Shift+L).

✦ **Centered:** All lines of type in the paragraph are centered relative to each other, to the point clicked, or to the location of the I-bar in Type on a path. You can also apply this type of alignment by pressing ⌘+Shift+C (Ctrl+Shift+C).

✦ **Align Right:** Use this option to create a smooth, even right side and an uneven left side (no, ragged left isn't really a correct term). You can also apply this type of alignment by pressing ⌘+Shift+R (Ctrl+Shift+R).

Figure 8-29: The different types of paragraph alignment on type inside a rectangle

✦ **Justify Last Line Align Left:** You apply this to make both the left and right sides appear smooth and even except the last line, which is, aligned left.

✦ **Justify Last Line Align Center:** Use this option to make both the left and right sides appear smooth and even except the last line, which is center, aligned.

✦ **Justify Last Line Align Right:** With this option, both the left and right sides appear smooth and even except the last line, which is aligned right.

✦ **Justify All Lines:** Commonly called Force Justify, this option is the same as Justify except that the last line of every paragraph is justified along with the other lines of the paragraph. This can create some really awful looking paragraphs, and is done mainly for artistic emphasis, not as a proper way to justify type. Justify All Lines is particularly useful for stretching a single line of type across a certain width. You can also apply this type of alignment by pressing ⌘+Shift+B (Ctrl+Shift+B).

Note   Justification works only on Area type. Illustrator does not allow you to select Justify or Justify All Lines for Type on a path or Point type.

Indenting

Paragraphs can be indented within the Paragraph palette by choosing different amounts of indentation for the left edge, right edge, and first line of each paragraph. The maximum indentation for all three fields is 1296 points and the minimum is –1296 points.

Using indents is a great way to offset type, such as quotes, that have smaller margins than the rest of the type surrounding the quote. Changing the indentation values is also useful for creating hanging indents, such as numbered or bulleted text.

To create hanging indents easily, make the Left Indent as large as the width of a bullet or a number and a space, and then make the First Line value the negative value of that. If the left indent is 2 picas, the first line is –2 picas. This creates great hanging indents every time.

Spacing before paragraphs

Illustrator lets you place additional space between paragraphs by entering a number in the Space Before Paragraphs text field. You add this measurement to the leading to determine the distance from baseline to baseline before the selected paragraphs. You can also enter a negative number to decrease space between paragraphs, if necessary. You can make values for Space Before Paragraphs between –1296 and 1296 points.

Spacing through justification

Illustrator enables you to control the spacing of letters, words, auto leading, and glyphs in text by changing the values you find in the Justification dialog box. You access this dialog box by choosing Justification option in the Paragraph palette pop-up menu (see Figure 8-30). The options you control in the Justification dialog box are:

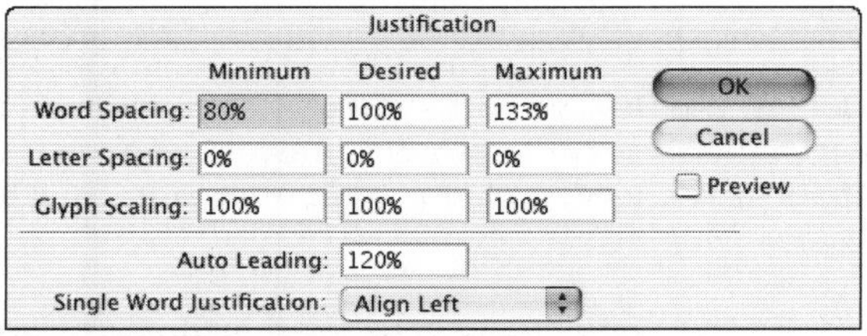

	Minimum	Desired	Maximum
Word Spacing:	80%	100%	133%
Letter Spacing:	0%	0%	0%
Glyph Scaling:	100%	100%	100%
Auto Leading:	120%		
Single Word Justification:	Align Left		

Figure 8-30: The Justification dialog box

✦ **Word Spacing**: Word spacing is the space between the words that you create by clicking the spacebar. Set Minimum, Desired, and Maximum. The word space can range from 0% to 1000%, 100% being the default with no additional space being added. The minimum is the least amount of word spacing in percentage that you want to accept. Enter the exact percentage for the Desired setting. The maximum is the most amount of spacing you accept.

✦ **Letter Spacing**: Letter spacing is the space between each letter of a word. The Letter spacing can be set from –100% to 500%. 0% means that no space is added. Set the minimum percentage of letter spacing, desired, and maximum amount of letter spacing.

✦ **Glyph Scaling**: A glyph refers to any font character. Glyph scaling lets you change the width of the character in percentage of the original. Set the minimum, desired, and maximum scaling percentages. The range of glyph scaling is from 50% to 200%. 100% is the default where no scaling occurs.

✦ **Auto Leading**: Set the Auto Leading in percentage which ranges from 0% to 500% with 120% being the default.

✦ **Single Word Justification**: When there is a single word for the last line justification, choose from the pop-up of Full Justify, Align Left, Align Center, Align Right.

Spacing affects the space between letters and words regardless of the alignment, although Justified text has even more spacing control than Flush Left, Flush Right, or Centered text.

When you choose Flush Left, Flush Right, or Centered alignment, the only text fields in the dialog box that you can change are the Desired fields for Letter Spacing and Word Spacing.

You can enter values between 0% and 1000% for Word Spacing. The Minimum must be less than or equal to the amount in the Desired box and the Maximum must be equal to or more than the amount in the Desired box. At 100%, the word space is normal; at less than 100%, the word space is reduced; and at a number greater than 100%, the word space is increased.

The values for Letter Spacing must be between 50% and 500%. The Minimum must be less than or equal to the amount in the Desired box and the Maximum must be equal to or more than the amount in the Desired box. At 0%, the letter space is normal; at less than 0%, the letter space is reduced; and at a number greater than 0%, the letter space is increased.

The Minimum and Maximum boxes in the Word Spacing, Letter Spacing, and Glyph Scaling areas are mainly used to control where the extra space goes and where it is removed from when stretching out and compressing the lines of text.

Hyphenating

Hyphenation? In a drawing program? I couldn't believe it either, but there it was staring me in the face. A nice addition to Illustrator's text-handling capabilities, hyphenation works in the background, silently hyphenating when necessary.

To use Illustrator's hyphenation, you must check the Auto Hyphenate box in the lower-left of the Paragraph palette. After you check this option for the text that is currently selected, that text hyphenates fairly well.

Hyphenation in Illustrator works from a set of hyphenation rules that you define in the Hyphenation Options dialog box (shown in Figure 8-31). View the Hyphenation dialog box by choosing Hyphenation from the Paragraph pop-up menu. Here you can specify how many letters must fall before the hyphen can appear and how many letters must fall after the hyphen. You can also limit the number of consecutive hyphens to avoid the "ladder look" of multiple hyphens.

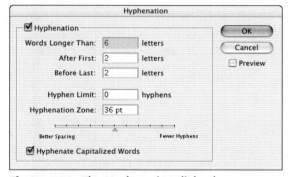

Figure 8-31: The Hyphenation dialog box

Tip

When you need to hyphenate a word at a place where Illustrator doesn't seem to want to hyphenate it, you can create a discretionary hyphen. You do this by placing the blinking insertion point where the word should break and typing ⌘+Shift+Hyphen (Ctrl+Shift+Hyphen). This causes the word to hyphenate at a certain part of the word, but only if that word needs hyphenation. If the word doesn't need hyphenation, no hyphen appears. This is much better than just typing a normal hyphen, which works temporarily; if you remove the manually hyphenated word from the edge of the line, the hyphen remains within it.

Using Every-line and Single-line composer

In Illustrator you can choose from two composition methods: Adobe Japanese Every-line composer or Adobe Japanese Single-line composer. These composer options are found in the Paragraph palette's pop-up menu. What this means is that in a paragraph, the composer checks and chooses the best breaks, hyphenation, and justification for the specific paragraph.

Every-line composer checks all of the lines in the paragraph and makes its evaluation on the paragraph as a whole. Single-line composer looks at each line of type rather than the whole paragraph to determine the best breaks, hyphenation, and justification. You can select both these options from the popup menu in the Paragraph palette.

Controlling punctuation

Roman Hanging Punctuation handles the alignment of punctuation marks for a specified paragraph. With Roman Hanging Punctuation option turned on, apostrophes, quotes, commas, period, hyphen/minus, ellipsis, are 100% out of the margin. The characters: asterisks, tildes, en dashes, em dashes, colons, semicolons are 50% out of the margin.

If you check Roman Hanging Punctuation in the Paragraph palette's popup menu, punctuation at the left edge of a Flush Left, Justified, or Justified Last Line paragraph appears outside the type area. Punctuation on the right edge of a Flush Right, Justified, or Justified Last Line paragraph also appears outside the type area. Strangely enough, Illustrator is one of the few programs that support this very hip feature.

Another choice for punctuation is Optical Margin Alignment. Optical Margin Alignment handles the punctuation marks alignment for all paragraphs inside a type area. With this option turned on, all punctuation hangs outside of the margin so the type is aligned. You can find this feature under the Type menu.

There is also the Burasagari option in the Paragraph palette popup menu. To see the Burasagari option you first must turn on Asian Options in the Type & Auto Tracing preferences. To do this, choose Illustrator ➪ Preferences ➪ Type & Auto Tracing (Edit ➪ Preferences ➪ Type & Auto Tracing). Then check the Show Asian Options box. Use this for aligning double-byte punctuation marks, which aren't affected by choosing Roman Hanging Punctuation. The Burasagari is also available in Chinese, Japanese, and Korean fonts.

Working with OpenType

You can choose Window ➪ OpenType, or press ⌘+Option+Shift+T (Ctrl+Alt+Shift+T) to access the OpenType palette. Use this palette to apply specific options to alternate characters with OpenType fonts. In the OpenType palette, the symbols at the bottom are from left to right: Standard Ligatures, Contextual Alternates, Discretionary Ligatures, Swash, Stylistic Alternates, Tiling Alternates, Ordinals, and Fractions. Figure 8-32 shows the OpenType palette. Other options you can access for Asian OpenType fonts as well.

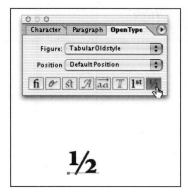

Figure 8-32: The OpenType Palette, displaying a fraction

Using the Tabs palette

You use the Tabs palette to set tabs the same way you would in your word-processing or page-layout software. To access the Tabs palette, choose Window ➪ Type ➪ Tabs or ⌘+Shift+T (Ctrl+Alt+T).

To set tabs for type, select the type and choose Window ➪ Type ➪ Tabs, or press ⌘+Shift+T (Ctrl+Alt+T). The Tabs palette appears above the type you have selected and automatically assumes the width of the type area.

To change the width of the Tabs palette, click and drag on the resize box in the lower-right corner of the palette. The Tabs palette can be made wider, but not taller. To reset the Tabs palette back to the exact size of the type area, drag the Resize box back.

Tip　The Position Palette Above Text button moves the Tabs palette to make it flush left with the type and moves it up or down so that it is right above the selected text area.

Illustrator automatically sets tabs at every half inch. These are called Auto tab stops. Once you set a tab, all the Auto tab stops to the left of the tab you have set disappear. The Auto tab stops work like left-justified tabs.

If you check the Snap option box, tab stops correspond to ruler tick marks.

The measurement system shown on the ruler is the same system that the rest of the documents use. You can change the measurement system in the Units ^ Display performance preferences dialog box. You can access this by choosing Illustrator ➪ Preferences ➪ Units & Display Performance (Edit ➪ Preferences ➪ Units & Display Performance).

To set a tab, select a tab from the four Tab Style buttons on the upper left of the Tabs palette and click the ruler below to set exactly where you want the new tab. Once the tab has been set, you can move it by dragging it along the ruler, or remove it by dragging it off the top or bottom edge of the ruler.

There are four types of tabs you can set:

✦ **Left-justified:** Make type align to the right side of the tab, with the leftmost character aligning with the tab stop.

✦ **Center-justified:** Make type align to the center of the tab, with the center character aligning with the tab stop.

✦ **Right-justified:** Make type align to the left side of the tab, with the rightmost character aligning with the tab stop.

✦ **Decimal-justified:** Make type align to the left side of the tab, with a decimal or the rightmost character aligning with the tab stop.

To change a tab from one style to another, select a tab stop and click the Tab style button to which you want to change. To deselect all tabs, click in the area to the right of the Tab position box. (If you don't click far enough away from the Tab position box, you'll end up changing the units.) It is a good idea to deselecting tabs after setting them so that whey you define a new tab style for the next tab stop, it does not change the tab stop that you just set.

Graphical tabs

Graphical tabs are tabs that flow around objects (paths) in Illustrator automatically. The following steps show you how to use graphical tabs.

1. **Create a rectangle type area.** See Chapter 4 for more on creating a Rectangle.

2. **Type in five words separated by tabs.** Yes, each word is set ½ inches apart — we'll fix that shortly!

3. **Press Return after entering the last word.**

4. **Select all the text by pressing ⌘+A (Ctrl+A).**

5. **Press ⌘+C (Ctrl+C) to copy the text.**

6. **Click the last line of type.** It should be blank.

7. **Paste your text it a few times by repeatedly pressing ⌘+V, (Ctrl+V).**

8. **Using the Pencil tool, draw a series of four straight or curved vertical lines that extend above the top and below the bottom of the type area.**

9. **Select the lines and the type area and choose Object ⇨ Text Wrap ⇨ Make Text Wrap.** The type should tab to the lines that you drew.

The results are shown in Figure 8-33. Tabs take you to the other side of text wrap objects. Play with this a little and you'll discover that this method is much more flexible than standard word processing tab stops. This works better when you turn off the lines' visibility in the Layers palette.

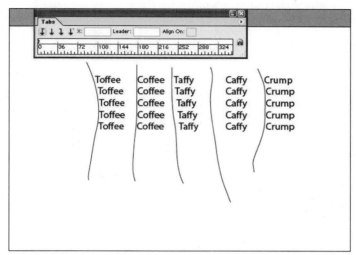

Figure 8-33: You can use lines as graphical tabs.

Using Advanced Type Functions

Illustrator has built in some more advanced type functions that go beyond the basic user. In these functions you'll find the Threading text, wrapping text, fitting head-lines, Find Font, Check Spelling, and Change Case. You find each of these functions under the Edit and Type menus.

Threading text

The Threading Text option (Type ➪ Threaded Text ➪ Make) links text from one area or rectangle to another, continuing a story from one area or rectangle to another (see Figure 8-34). Linked blocks act like groups, enabling you to use the regular Selection tool and click just one area to select all areas. (You can still select individual blocks with the Direct Selection tool.) Whenever you have more text than can fit into a text area, a tiny little red plus sign in a box appears, alerting you that there is more text in the box than you see.

To use Threaded Text, select a text area or rectangle and any other shapes, even text rectangles and areas, and choose Threaded Text. The text areas then act as if they are grouped. Text flows from the back-most shape to the front-most in any group of linked blocks, so be careful to order your boxes correctly when setting up linked text. In fact, if you send a box to the back, Illustrator starts the from that location, then goes to the next box forward, and then the next, and so on. You cannot select Threaded Text if at least one text area and one other path or text area are not selected.

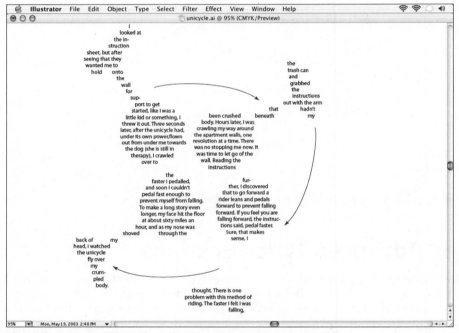

Figure 8-34: Text blocks threaded together in the order of the arrows

Unthreading text

There are various ways to unthreading text. To release the object from the text thread, choose Type ⇨ Threaded Text ⇨ Release Selection. This removes the text from the objects. To remove the thread, but leave the type in the objects, choose Type ⇨ Threaded Text ⇨ Remove Threading. You can also break the threads by double-clicking on an out port. The out port is the little box at the edge of the object that the type is flowed into. Figure 8-35 shows an out port showing the link. When the cursor is over the out port, you can see the link button.

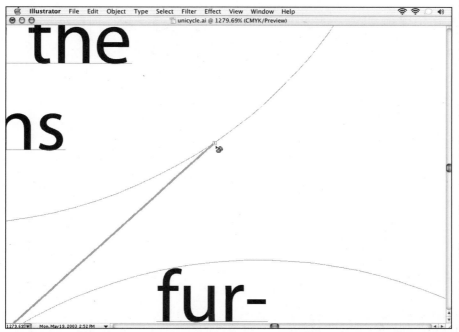

Figure 8-35: The in or out port depends on whether it is going into or out of an object.

When you double-click either the out port, or the in port, the text flows back or forward into the next object. Figure 8-36 shows the text block unthreaded, flowing the type back into the first object. The port is now a red X indicating that there is more text than can be shown.

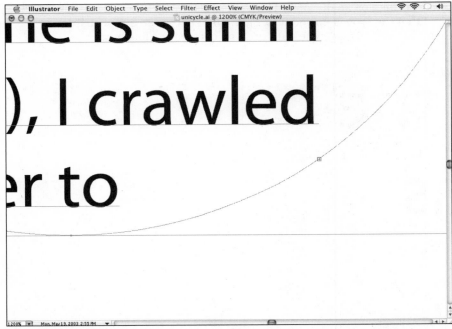

Figure 8-36: Double-clicking on a port unthreads the port to the previous object.

Wrapping with type

The Make Text Wrap option wraps text around any paths, as shown in Figure 8-37. To use Make Text Wrap, select both the type and the paths you want the type to wrap around. The paths that the type wraps around must be in front of the type for the text to wrap around the paths. Choose Object ⇨ Text Wrap ⇨ Make Text Wrap. The objects then act like a grouped object; you can use the regular Selection tool to select all objects in a Make Text Wrap area.

Make Text Wrap only works with Area type and Rectangle type (the option is dimmed for Type on a path and Point type).

I looked at the instruction sheet, but after seeing that they wanted me to hold onto the wall for support to get started, like I was a little kid or something, I threw it out. Three seconds later, after the unicycle had, under its own power, flown out from under me towards the dog (she is still in therapy), I crawled over to the trash can and grabbed the instructions out with the arm that hadn't been crushed beneath my body. Hours later, I was crawling my way around the apartment walls, one revolution at a time. There was no stopping me now. It was time to let go of the wall. Reading the instructions further, I discovered that to go forward a rider leans and pedals forward to prevent falling forward. If you feel you are falling forward, the instructions said, pedal faster. Sure, that makes sense, I thought. There is one problem with this method of riding. The faster I felt I was falling, the faster I pedalled, and soon I couldn't pedal fast enough to prevent myself from falling. To make a long story even longer, my face hit the floor at about sixty miles an hour, and as my nose was shoved through the back of my head, I watched the unicycle fly over my crumpled body.

Figure 8-37: Object with type wrapped around them

To create a text wrap:

1. **Select both the text and the object(s) to wrap the text around.**

2. **Choose Object ⇨ Text Wrap ⇨ Make Text Wrap.** This brings up the Text Wrap Options dialog box (see Figure 8-38).

3. **Set the Text Wrap Options dialog box options.** Set how far the text is offset from the path. If you choose to Invert the Wrap, the text flows inside the objects rather than around them. There are plenty of warnings that the object you want to wrap around must be on the top of the text in arrangement order.

4. **Click OK.** Illustrator applies your options.

Make Text Wrap works in levels: You can make text wrap with one type area or rectangle to a path and then make text wrap again with the same type area or rectangle to another path, and the type wraps around both paths.

Caution

Remember that Make Text Wrap only wraps around paths; regardless of how thick the stroke on your path is, the wrap does not change. Use the Text Wrap options to set the distance around the objects and the text.

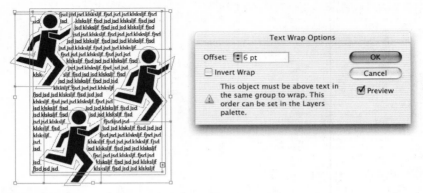

Figure 8-38: The Text Wrap Options dialog box

You can use additional objects to wrap. Just place them in front of the type area, select both the type area and the new wrapping object, and choose Type ➪ Make Text Wrap.

Note Text wrapping objects need no fill or stroke, but they do need to be closed. If you want to use an existing path and that path is not closed, simply copy the path, choose Edit ➪ Paste In Front, or press ⌘+Option+V (Ctrl+Alt+V), and change the fill and stroke to None.

Tip You can make the wrap objects anything. You can use symbols by dragging the symbol you want from the Symbol palette to the Artboard. Scale, rotate as needed and the color and Illustrator retains the styles after the text wrap.

Releasing a wrap

The Release Wrap (Choose Object ➪ Text Wrap ➪ Release Text Wrap) option releases any text wraps that are selected, all at one time. Release Text Wrap does not release wraps in the order that they were created. Because paths wrapped to type areas and rectangles do not lose or change attributes when they become wrapped paths, those paths retain their original Paint Style attributes when released.

Fitting a headline

The Type menu's Fit Headline option is designed to automatically increase the weight and width of type using Multiple Master fonts in order to fit type perfectly from the left side of a type area or rectangle to the right side of that same type area or rectangle. This also works with other fonts by changing the tracking value only to fit the headline. Another option for non Multiple Master fonts is to use Justify All Lines in the Paragraph palette, but it doesn't do as nice of a job as Fit Headline.

Finding and replacing text

Under the Edit menu are more choices for text editing. Illustrator lets you find certain text and replace with another text. Use this to replace specific letters, words, or characters. Under the Find and Replace dialog box (shown in Figure 8-39), you'll find the following options:

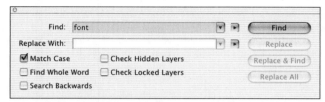

Figure 8-39 The Find and Replace dialog box

✦ **Match Case**: Selects the characters only if they have the same uppercase and lowercase attributes as the characters you type in the Find text field.

✦ **Find Whole Word**: Tells Illustrator that the characters you type in the Find area box are an entire word and not part of a word.

✦ **Search Backward**: Tells Illustrator to look before the current word for the next instance of the characters, instead of using the default, which is to look after the current word.

✦ **Check Hidden Layers**: Instructs Illustrator to look in the text in hidden layers.

✦ **Check Locked Layers**: Instructs Illustrator to look in the text in locked layers.

The following steps describe how to use these options to find and replace text.

1. **Choose Edit ⇨ Find and Replace.** The Find and Replace dialog box appears.

2. **Type in the word, phrase, or characters that you want to find in the Find text field.**

3. **Check the appropriate options described in the previous section.**

4. **Click the Find Next button to find the first occurrence of the word or characters.**

5. **In the Replace with box, type the word or characters that you want to use to replace the text that Illustrator found.**

6. **Click the Replace button to replace the selected text.** Click the Replace and Find button to change the next occurrence. If you want to change all occurrences, click the Replace All button.

Note   You do not need to select areas of type the Selection or Type tools — all that is necessary is that the document that you want to search be the open and active document.

Finding fonts

Find Font looks for certain fonts in a document and replaces them with fonts you specify.

Select type with either a selection tool or with a type tool. Then choose Type ➪ Find Font. The Find Font dialog box appears, as shown in Figure 8-40.

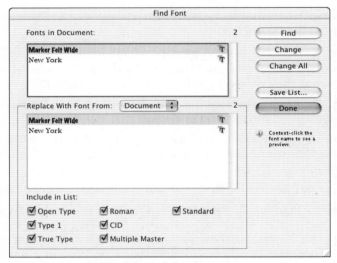

Figure 8-40: The Find Font dialog box

To change all occurrences of a certain font to another font, select the font you want to change in the top window, titled Fonts in Document. Then select a font in the Replacement Font From pop-up menu's list box and click the Change All button. To change one particular instance, click the Change button. To find the next occurrence of that font, select Find Next. The Skip button skips over the currently selected text and finds the next occurrence of that font. Keep in mind that choosing System from the Replace With Font From pop-up can take a while for Illustrator to build and display the font list, especially if you have a ton of fonts on your system.

Pressing the Save List button enables you to save your font list as a text file. After the fonts are found, you have to select type with the Type tool, no matter how it was selected before Find Font was used.

Checking spelling

Check Spelling checks all text in a document to see if it is spelled (and capitalized) correctly. To use this feature, choose Edit ➪ Check Spelling. The Check Spelling dialog box shown in Figure 8-41 appears.

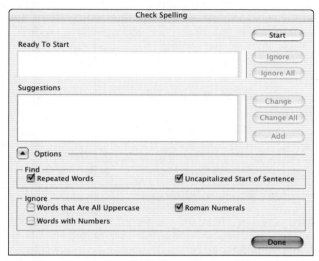

Figure 8-41: The Check Spelling dialog box

 Note Check Spelling uses a standard user dictionary as well as all foreign language and hyphenation dictionaries that are available.

If all words are spelled correctly, a congratulatory message appears telling you that your spelling is "excellent."

If you have any misspelled words or words that are not in the spelling dictionaries, those words are listed at the top of the Check Spelling dialog box in the Misspelled Words window. Selecting a word in this list displays similar words below in the Suggested Corrections window.

Some of the options you can change are to Find Repeated Words or Uncapitalized start of sentence. Other options are to Ignore Words that are all uppercase, Roman numerals, and words with numbers.

You use the Add button when you want to add the selected "misspelled" word to your custom dictionary. Clicking the Edit List button displays the Learned Words dialog box, showing you which words are currently in the user dictionary. The Learned Words dialog box enables you to add, remove, or change entries in the user dictionary.

To add a new entry to the user dictionary, follow these steps:

1. **Select the Edit List button in the Check Spelling dialog box.** This displays the Learned Words dialog box.

2. **Type in the word that you want to add to the user dictionary.**

3. **Click the Add button.** Illustrator adds the word to the list of words in the user dictionary. Capitalization is very important when adding words, so be sure to place initial caps on proper nouns and to use correct capitalization on all words that require it. If the word you are trying to add exists in the user dictionary or the main dictionary, a dialog box appears telling you that it is already a dictionary entry.

4. **Repeat Step 2 until you have added all the words you want to add.**

5. **If necessary, edit your entries.** If at any time you make a mistake, you may change the spelling of an entered word by selecting it in the window above, typing in the correct spelling, and then clicking the Change button. If you want to delete an entry that exists in the Learned Words window, select that word and click the Remove button.

6. **When you are finished, click the Done button.**

The user dictionary words are saved in a file called AI User Dictionary, which is stored in the Plug-Ins folder. The file is in text-compatible format, but the character that separates the words is indistinguishable (it appears as an open rectangle, the symbol for a symbol that is not available in that typeface), so there is no way to add words to the dictionary by using a word processor.

Caution   Be careful not to delete or remove the AI User Dictionary file when reinstalling the software or moving the files in the Plug-Ins folder. Doing so causes Illustrator to create a new user dictionary file with no words in it. There is no way to combine two different user dictionary files. You can drag the AI User Dictionary from the Plug-ins folder of the old version of Illustrator to the Plug-ins folder of the new version.

While you're checking your spelling in the Check Spelling dialog box, clicking the Change button replaces the misspelled word with the highlighted word in the Suggested Corrections list. Clicking the Change All button replaces all misspelled occurrences of that word throughout the entire document with the correctly spelled word.

Clicking the Skip button ignores that occurrence of the misspelled word. Clicking Skip All skips all occurrences of that word in the document.

Clicking the Language button uses a dictionary for the language you specify. Illustrator supplies dictionaries for the United States and the United Kingdom, both located in the Plug-In filters files.

Clicking the Done button closes the Check Spelling dialog box.

Changing case

Change Case converts selected text to one of a variety of case options. To use this filter, select type with a Type tool and then choose Type ➪ Change Case. The four submenu choices are: Uppercase, Lowercase, Title case, and Sentence case.

Type must be selected with a Type tool (characters must be highlighted) to use the Change Case feature.

The four Change Case options affect only letters, not numbers, symbols, or punctuation. The options are as follows:

✦ **UPPERCASE:** Converts all selected letters into uppercase, regardless of whether any letters were uppercase or lowercase.

✦ **lower case:** Converts all selected letters into lowercase, regardless of whether any letters were uppercase or lowercase. It also doesn't matter if the letters were originally uppercase because they were typed with the Caps Lock key engaged, or if the uppercase letters were uppercase because of a style format.

✦ **Title case:** Capitalizes the first letter of each word.

✦ **Sentence case:** Uses periods, exclamation points, and question marks as the end of the sentence to capitalize the first letter of each sentence.

Using Smart Punctuation

The Smart Punctuation filter looks for certain fonts in a document and replaces them with fonts you specify. To use this filter, select type with either a Selection tool or with a Type tool. Then choose Type ➪ Smart Punctuation. The Smart Punctuation dialog box shown in Figure 8-42 appears.

The Smart Punctuation filter works after the fact, making changes to text already in the Illustrator document. There are no settings, for example, to convert quotes to curved quotes as you are typing them. The types of punctuation to be changed are determined by a set of checkboxes in the Smart Punctuation dialog box. A checked box means that Illustrator looks for these certain instances and, if it finds them, corrects them with the proper punctuation.

The first two options are used for replacing ff, fi (or fl), and ffi (or ffl) with ligatures. Ligatures are characters that represent several characters with one character that is designed to let those characters appear nicer when placed next to each other. Most fonts have fi and fl ligatures, which look like fi and fl, respectively.

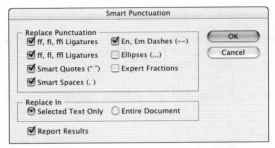

Figure 8-42: The Smart Punctuation dialog box

The remaining Smart Punctuation options work as follows:

✦ Smart Quotes replaces straight quotes (" " and ' ') with curly quotes, known as typesetter's quotes or printer's quotes (" " and ' ').

✦ Smart Spaces replaces multiple spaces after a period with one space. (In typesetting, there should only be one space following a period.)

✦ En, Em Dashes replaces hyphens (-) with en dashes (–) and double hyphens (–) with em dashes (—).

✦ Ellipses replaces three periods (...) with an ellipsis (…).

✦ Expert Fractions replaces fractions with expert fractions if you have the expert fractions for the font family you are using. Adobe sells "Expert Collection" fonts that contain these fractions. If you do not have expert fractions, your fractions remain unchanged.

Other options are Replace in Selected text only or Replace In Entire Document. Checking the Report Results box displays a dialog box when the filter is finished, telling you how many of the punctuation changes were made.

Adding rows and columns

Area Type Options divides rectangular paths (text rectangles) into even sections.

To add Rows and Columns, select a path and choose Type ➪ Area Type Options. The Area Type Options dialog box shown in Figure 8-43 appears.

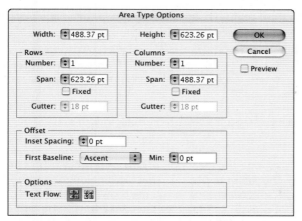

Figure 8-43: The Area Type Options dialog box

You can select any text path, open or closed, and divide it into rows and columns, with one catch: the object becomes a rectangular shape, the size of the original path's bounding box (the smallest box that can completely contain the path). There is no way to divide a nonrectangular path automatically. See the steps later in this section for a way to do this without Illustrator knowing about it. The Area Type Options dialog box has the following options:

✦ The left side of the Area Type Options dialog box determines the width of the columns. The right side determines the height of the rows. At the bottom of the dialog box is a Preview checkbox; checking this displays changes as you make them in the Area Type Options dialog box.

Note   All measurements in the Area Type Options dialog box are displayed in the current measurement system.

✦ The first text field is the Number of Rows into which the original path divides. The second text field, Height, is the height of each of the rows. The Height must be less than the Total (the fourth field) divided by the number of rows. The third text field on the left is Gutter, which is the space between rows. The Total is how high the entire rectangle is.

✦ When you decrease Row Height, the Gutter increases. Likewise, as the Gutter is increased, the Height decreases. When the Gutter is decreased, the Height increases.

✦ In the Column section, Number determines into how many columns you cut the selected path. Below that, the Width text field determines the width of the columns. The Width must be less than the Total (fourth field) divided by the number of columns. The third text field is Gutter, which is the space between columns. The Total value is how wide the entire rectangle is.

✦ As the Column Width increases, the Gutter decreases. When you decrease Column Width, the Gutter increases. Likewise, as you increase the Gutter, the Column Width decreases. When the Gutter decreases, the Column Width increases.

Remember that using the Area Type Options feature actually divides the selected rectangle into several pieces.

✦ The Text Flow options determine the direction of text as it flows from one section to the next. You may choose between text that starts along the top row and flows from left to right, and then goes to the next lowest row, flowing from left to right, and so on. The second option is to have text start in the left column, flowing from top to bottom, and then to the next column to the right, flowing from top to bottom. The third option causes text to flow from the upper-right to the upper-left to the lower-right to the lower-left. The fourth (rightmost) option flows the text from the upper-right to the lower-right to the upper-left to the lower-left.

✦ The Offset options are for Inset Spacing (from the edge of the object area) and First Baseline (either Ascent, Cap Height, Leading, x Height, or Fixed with a minimum in points).

Showing hidden characters

When you are typing, nonviewing characters such as spaces, returns, and tabs are included. Typically, you don't see these characters. You can choose to view the hidden characters by choosing Show Hidden Characters from the Type menu.

Changing type orientation

You can easily change the orientation of your type by choosing Type Orientation from the Type menu. That way if you wanted vertical type and did it as horizontal, you can change it easily without retyping it.

Updating Legacy text

Legacy text is any text created in version 10 and earlier. Because Illustrator now uses a new Adobe Text Engine, the older text must be converted to take advantage of this new type engine. The changes are character positioning with tracking, leading, and kerning, shifts in the words resulting in different hyphenation, and changes in wordflow from threaded text. The fix for this is to choose Type ➪ Update All Legacy Text. Also, when you open an older file, a dialog box pops up, asking you if you want to update all Legacy text.

Exporting and placing

To export text, select the text you want to export and choose File ➪ Export. A Save dialog box appears, which asks in what format and to where you want to save the text (shown in Figure 8-44). Then a dialog box comes up asking what platform you are saving to.

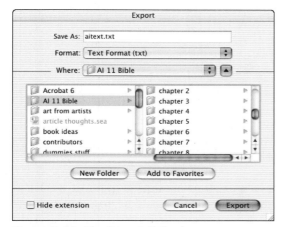

Figure 8-44: The Export dialog box

You can save text in most of the common formats, and you can import it back into Illustrator with the Place command (choose File ➪ Place when a text area is active with a Type tool). Word-processing software, page-layout software, or any other software that can read text files can open and use text that you saved in Illustrator.

Creating Outlines

After your type is set (and spelled correctly), choose Type ➪ Create Outlines, or press ⌘+Shift+O (Ctrl+Shift+O), and the type selected converts into editable paths (see Figure 8-45). To convert type to outlines, you need to select the type with a selection tool, not a type tool. Each letter is its own compound path, and you can edit each path with the Direct Selection tool.

Cross-Reference For more on the Direct Selection tool, see Chapter 5.

OpenType, and TrueType combines the screen and printer fonts into one file — if you can select any of these font types in Illustrator, you can create outlines from it. Illustrator locates the font file and uses that information to create the outlines.

Figure 8-45: Type converted into outlines can make for some cool effects.

When you convert type to outlines, you can apply gradients to its fill, as well as apply patterns to its fill that you can preview onscreen. You can apply patterns to non-outline type.

Caution   While you can undo Create Outlines, be forewarned that there is no way to convert back to type in case you made a spelling error or want to change the font or any other type attribute.

You can convert all forms of type, including Point type, Type on a path, Area type, and Rectangle type to outlines.

Tip   Creating outlines out of type is also very useful when you want to send the file to be outputted and the person doing the output does not have the font you are using. Simply use the Create Outlines option before you send the file, and it prints just fine. (This is not advised for 4-point type or smaller, as described in the "Hinting" section later in this chapter).

Working with type outlines

The process of creating editable type outlines has many uses, including distorting mild-mannered characters into grotesque letters. More practical uses for editable type outlines include making type-based logos unique, arcing type (where one side is flat and the other is curved), special effects and masking, and avoiding font compatibility problems. You can apply some of the basic effects by warping the text.

Cross-Reference   For more on warp effects see Chapter 9.

To change type from being editable text into an Illustrator path (for that is what an editable type outline really is), select the type with a selection tool, not a type tool. Choose Type ➪ Create Outlines, or press — +Shift+O (Ctrl+Shift+O), and the type changes into paths that you can edit.

After you change type into Illustrator paths using Create Outlines, the only way back is to use the Undo command (⌘+Z) (Ctrl+Z). There is no "Convert from Paths to Type" function. You cannot edit type in Outline mode. This means that if you misspell something, it remains misspelled.

Initially, when type is converted into outlines, individual characters are turned into compound paths. This ensures that holes in letters, such as in a lowercase a, b, or d, are see-through, and not just white-filled paths placed on top of the original objects.

See Chapter 11 for an in-depth discussion of compound paths.

Making letters that normally appear in your worst nightmares

After letters have been turned into outlines, there is nothing to stop you from distorting them into shapes that only resemble letters in the most simplistic sense of the word.

The results of letter distortion usually aren't all that eye pleasing, but they can be fun. Few things in life are as pleasing as taking a boring letter Q and twisting it into "the letter that time forgot." Or fiddling around with your boss' name until the letters look as evil as your boss does. Or adding pointed ears and whiskers to a random array of letters and numbers and printing out several sheets of them with the words "Mutant kittens for sale." Some samples are shown in Figure 8-46.

When modifying existing letters, use the Direct Selection tool. Select the points or segments you want to move, and drag them around to your heart's content. This can be great practice for adjusting paths, and you might accidentally stumble onto some really cool designs.

Type outlines provide you with the flexibility to manipulate letters to turn an ordinary, boring, letters-only logo into a distinct symbol embodying the company's image.

Outlines are flexible enough that there really are no limits to what can be done with something as simple as a word of type.

Figure 8-46: Creating cool effects by distorting outlined type

Masking and other effects

Standard type or type that has been converted into outlines can then be used as a mask or filled with a placed image or any objects, as shown in Figure 8-47.

For outlined words to work as a single mask, you must first change them into a compound path. Usually, individual letters of converted type are changed into individual compound paths, whether the letter has a hole in it or not. For masks to work properly, you must select the entire word or words you want to use as a mask and then choose Object ➪ Compound Path ➪ Make, or press ⌘+8 (Ctrl+8). This changes all the selected letters into one compound path.

In some third-party (non-Adobe) and shareware typefaces, making a compound path out of a series of letters can produce results where the holes are not transparent. This issue is usually one of path direction, which can be corrected by selecting the inner shape (the hole) and changing the direction with the path direction buttons on the Attributes palette.

Figure 8-47: Type masked with an image

After the words are a compound path, place them in front of the objects to be masked, select both the words and the masked objects, and then choose Object ➪ Clipping Mask ➪ Make (⌘+7) (Ctrl+7).

Avoiding font conflicts by creating outlines

If you ever give your files to a service bureau or to clients, you've probably already run into some font compatibility problems. A font-compatibility problem usually means that the place you gave your file to doesn't have a typeface that you used in your Illustrator document or that they have a different version of the same typeface with different metrics.

This is a problem that there is no great solution to, and the trouble seems to be worsening as more font manufacturers spring up — TrueType fonts being the Windows standard, and PostScript Type 1 fonts being the Mac standard. And then there are shareware typefaces, some of which resemble Adobe originals to an uncanny degree of accuracy. All this leads to a great deal of confusion and frustration for the average Illustrator user. With OS X you can use the Windows TrueType fonts and version differences are easier to avoid.

But there is a way around this problem, at least most of the time. Convert your typefaces into outlines before you send them to other people with other systems — they don't need your typefaces for the letters to print correctly. In fact, converted letters aren't really considered type anymore, just outlines.

Tip   Save your file before converting the text to outlines and then save it as a different file name after converting the text to outlines. This allows you to do text editing later on the original file, if necessary.

Hinting

Most Type 1 fonts have *hinting* built into them. Hinting is a method for adjusting type at small point sizes, especially at low resolutions. Although hinting is built into the fonts, when those fonts are converted into paths via the Create Outlines command, the hinting functionality is gone. This is part of the reason that type converted to outlines can look heavier than it does otherwise.

Creating outlines shouldn't cause that much of a problem when the type is to be output to an imagesetter, because the high resolution of the imagesetter makes up for the loss of hinting. However, very small type — 4 points or less — could be adversely affected.

Note Converting typefaces to outlines removes the hinting system that Adobe has implemented. This hinting system makes small letters on low-resolution (less than 600 dpi) devices print more accurately, controlling the placement and visibility of serifs and other small, thin strokes in characters. Type at small point sizes looks quite different on laser printers, although it retains its shape and consistency when it is output to an imagesetter or an output scanner system.

Understanding Other Type Considerations

When you're using type in Illustrator, there are a number of things to remember to get good results:

✦ Make sure that the person you are sending the Illustrator file to has the same fonts you have. It isn't enough just to have the same name of a font; you'll need the exact font that was created by the same manufacturer.

✦ Try not to mix TrueType fonts with PostScript fonts. This usually ends up confusing everyone involved.

✦ If the person you are sending Illustrator files to does not have your typeface, select the type in that font and choose Type ➪ Create Outlines, or press ⌘+Shift+O (Ctrl+Shift+O).

✦ Ttype styles may go unnoticed until after the job has printed. Be doubly sure that the person outputting the file has all the fonts in the embedded Illustrator file.

✦ If you are saving your illustration as an EPS file to be placed into another program and you are not going to open the file, you can select Include Document Fonts in the EPS Save dialog box. This forces any fonts used in the illustration to be saved with the illustration and allows the illustration to print as a placed image from within another program or to print from Illustrator as a placed EPS. The same goes for PDF files.

Summary

✦ Point type has one point as its "anchor," and the type is aligned to that point.

✦ There are four different ways to put type on a page: Point type, Rectangle type, Area type, and Type on a path.

✦ Rectangle type exists within a rectangle drawn with the Type tool.

✦ Type can be selected all at once by clicking the path (or point) of the type with the Selection tool.

✦ Individual characters, words, and paragraphs can be selected by using any of the Type tools.

✦ Area type is type that exists within the confines of any path.

✦ Type on a path is type that runs along the edge of a path.

✦ The Character palette (accessed by pressing ⌘+T (Ctrl+T)) contains all the character-specific information about selected type and can be used to change that information.

✦ Tracking and kerning remove or add space between groups or pairs of letters, respectively.

✦ The Paragraph palette (accessed by ⌘+Option+T) (Ctrl+Alt+T) contains all the paragraph-specific information about selected type and can be used to change that information.

✦ Most of the options used to control type can be found in the Type menu.

✦ Type can be set to wrap around selected paths by using the Text Wrapping feature.

✦ Type can be set to jump from text block to text block by threading text blocks together.

✦ The Tabs palette is used to set tabs for text areas.

✦ If you have both the screen font and the printer font of a Type 1 typeface, or if you have an OpenType or TrueType font installed, you can convert the font into outlines via the Create Outlines command.

✦ Once type has been changed to outlines, you may use those outlines as a mask, or fill those outlines with gradients or patterns.

✦   ✦   ✦

Using Creative Strokes and Fills with Patterns

No Illustrator book would be complete without discussing the how-to's of creating creative strokes, patterns, and textures with the Scribble effect. Sure you can create these by simply drawing them, but Illustrator makes their creation a breeze. Illustrator enables you to create a pattern and save that pattern for future use.

We all have the desire to add some texture to make flat images pop up. The Scribble effect lets you add some sketchy or computery effects to a boring drawing. Scribble lets you add a loose, free quality look to your illustrations.

Using Creative Strokes

In Chapter 3, I discuss how to apply strokes to paths, and in Chapter 4, I discuss all the attributes of a stroke and how to apply them to objects. In this chapter, you find out how to use strokes to create something spectacular.

The ability to stroke a path in Illustrator is greatly underrated. Strokes can do more than just outline shapes and vary thickness and patterns. You can create illustrations with a combination of strokes. You can easily create a filmstrip or a railroad with some Stroke attribute changes as you'll see in the upcoming examples.

In the first part of this section, I explain some of the greatest mysteries and unlock some of the deepest secrets that surround strokes. If that sounds at all boring, take a look at the figures in this chapter. I created most of them by using strokes, not filled paths. Amazin', ain't it?

You create most effects with strokes by overlaying several strokes on top of one another. By using the Appearance palette's pop-up menu to Add New stroke, you place an exact duplicate of the original path on top of itself.

Changing the weight and color of the top stroke gives the appearance of a path that is a designer, or custom, stroke. You can add strokes on top of or under the original stroke to make the pattern more complex or to add more colors or shapes.

Stroke essentials

Strokes act and work differently than fills. Remember these basic rules when using strokes:

✦ **Even distribution:** The most important thing to remember when using strokes is that you should evenly distribute stroke-weight width on both sides of a path. In other words, for a stroke with a 6-point weight, there are 3 points of the stroke on both sides of the stroke's path.

✦ **Using Patterns in strokes:** You can place patterns into strokes, and you can see the pattern on the stroke.

✦ **Gradients are not allowed:** Due to PostScript limitations, you cannot use gradients to color strokes. The work around for this is to use the Outline Path command under the Effects menu so you can edit later, then fill with a gradient. Choosing Outline stroke from the Object ⇨ Path submenu creates path outlines around the width of the stroke. When you convert a stroke into an outline, it is really an outlined path object and you can fill it with patterns and gradients (both of which appear when previewing and printing).

✦ **Consistent Stroke weight:** Stroke weight never varies on the same path.

✦ **No Stroke weight:** A stroke with a color of None has no Stroke weight.

✦ **Strokes and Pathfinder functions:** Strokes are, for the most part, ignored when combining, splitting, or modifying paths with the Pathfinder functions. Strokes are never considered when the Pathfinder functions search for the locations of the paths.

Cross-Reference

For more on applying patterns to strokes, see the section "Creating Perfect Patterns" later in this chapter. For more on Gradients, see Chapter 6. For more information on Stroke weights as they relate to path and objects, see Chapters 3 and 4. For more on the Pathfinder functions, see Chapter 11.

Using the stroke charts

The stroke charts in Figures 9-1 through 9-3 show how some of the basic stroke-dash patterns look with various options checked, at different weights, and in different combinations. The great advantage of these charts is that you can find a style similar to the one you want and then modify it to suit your situation. The charts should help you determine when to use certain types of stroke patterns because, as you can see, some patterns work better than others with curves and corners. All the paths in the charts were taken from an original shape that included a straight segment, a corner, and a curve.

The first chart (Figure 9-1) consists of thirty-two 3-point stroke paths that have a variety of dash patterns and end and join attributes. The second chart (Figure 9-2) shows eighteen 10-point stroke paths with similar attributes. These two charts show stroke effects with only one path. The area in the middle of each path in the chart describes the path.

The third chart (Figure 9-3) contains paths that have been copied on top of the original by using the Appearance palette. To access the Appearance palette, select the path and choose Add New stroke. The paths are listed in the order that they were created. The first path is described at the bottom of the list. The first path is duplicated in the Appearance palette by choosing Add New stroke from the pop-up menu, and given the Paint Style attributes of the item in the list. In the case of blended paths (the fourth one down in row 1 of Figure 9-3), you need to copy the original line, then choose Edit ⇨ Paste In Front or press ⌘+Option+V (Ctrl+Alt+V) rather than using the Appearance palette to duplicate the path. You can't blend multiple paths in the Appearance palette because Illustrator reads the paths as one path. So in the case of blends, invoke the Paste in Front option before blending. Then you can just select all paths and choose Object ⇨ Blend ⇨ Make.

Tip

To create some really great effects such as a pearl necklace, you need to blend the paths. You can blend paths from one to another. Simply select the paths and choose Object ⇨ Blend ⇨ Make. You can change the blend amount if necessary by choosing Object ⇨ Blend ⇨ Blend Options.

Cross-Reference

For more on Blends, see Chapter 12.

When you create a stroke pattern, frequently the original path is selected in the Appearance palette and copied on top of the original by using the Appearance palette's pop-up menu (select the path and choose Add New stroke) several times.

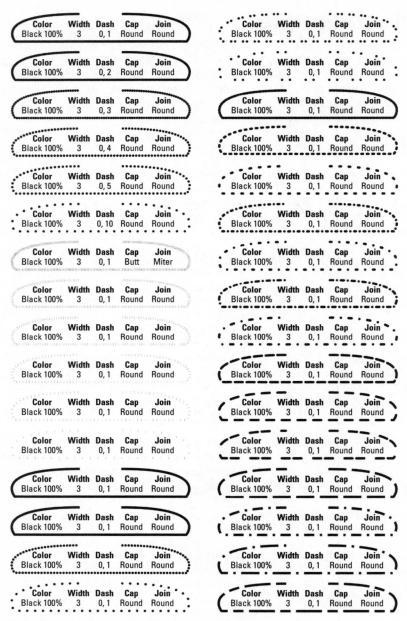

Figure 9-1: Thirty-two 3-point stroke paths

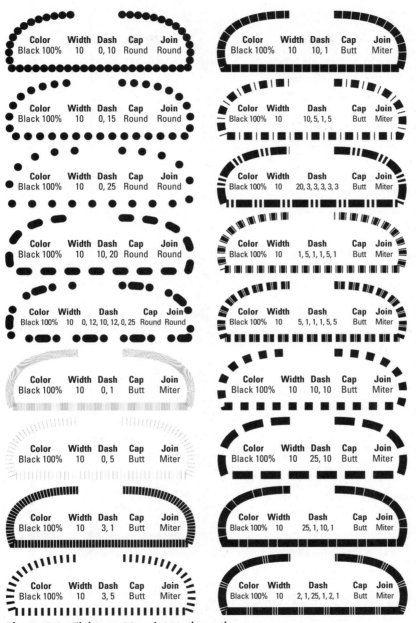

Figure 9-2: Eighteen 10-point stroke paths

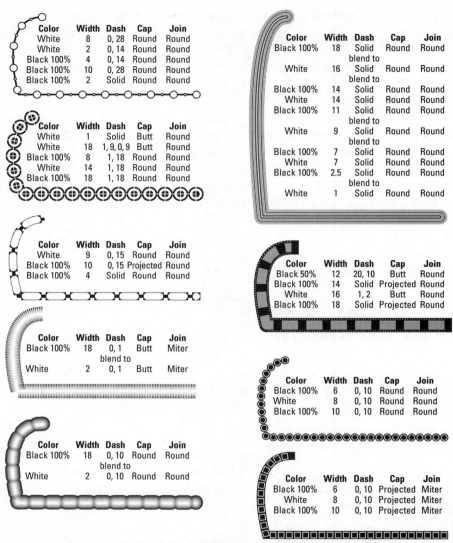

Figure 9-3: Paths that have been copied on top of the original paths

Creating parallel strokes

Do you need to create a railroad track or a race-track quickly? Creating the curvy parallel lines to make your illustration realistic is easier than you think. The following steps describe how to create a specialty stroke that looks like parallel strokes.

1. **Use the Pen tool to draw a short line.** The example uses a fill of None and a stroke path that is 18-point and black.

2. **Under the Appearance pop-up menu, choose Add New stroke.** You access the pop-up menu by clicking the left pointing arrow in the circle on the upper-right corner of the Appearance palette. The example uses a stroke with a 6-point weight and a white color.

3. **Select the path in Step 1 and choose Add New stroke from the Appearance palette pop-up menu.**

4. **Select the path in Step 2 and choose Add New stroke from the Appearance palette pop-up menu.**

5. **Select the bottom path from Step 3, change the weight of the stroke to something larger.** In the example, the Stroke weight is changed to 42 points.

6. **Select path from Step 4 and change the stroke to something larger.** In the example, this is changed to 30. In the final product (Figure 9-4), the 30-point stroke is 12 points more than the 18 points of the black stroke, or 6 points on each side. The 42-point stroke is 12 points more than the white 30-point stroke.

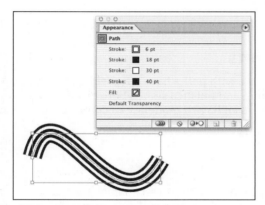

Figure 9-4: The final parallel stroke

This example is just the tip of the iceberg in creating custom strokes. Not only can you have paths that overlap, but you also can give the stroke on each path different dash patterns, joins, and caps. You can even add fills to certain paths to make the stroke different on both sides of the path. And if all of that isn't enough, you can use Outline Path to outline strokes.

Tip   When you are creating parallel strokes, determine how thick each of the visible strokes should be, multiply that number times the black and white visible strokes that you want for the base stroke, and work up from there. For example, if you want 10-point strokes, and there are four white strokes and five black strokes, make the first stroke 90-points thick and Black. Then, make the next stroke 70-point White, and then 50-point Black, 30-point White, and 10-point Black.

Knowing the secrets doesn't let you in on the really good stuff, though. Read on to learn how to apply these to achieve truly amazing effects with strokes.

Half-stroked paths

Half-stroked paths create a unique look on an object. Create a heavier stroke on one side of the path and a lighter stroke on the other. This technique gives a hand-drawn quality to your artwork. One relatively unknown technique is locking one side of the stroke as the path layers are built up. To lock half of the stroke at any level, paste in front as you normally do, choose Select ⇨ Inverse, or press ⌘+2 (Ctrl+2). Illustrator only locks the path that you just pasted (and which is currently selected).

Using the Pen tool, connect the ends of the just-pasted path and fill it with the background color and a stroke of None. This action obliterates one side of the stroke because the file of the path covers the "inside" part of the stroked path. Any strokes that you place on top of this object become visible on both sides of the path.

Cross-Reference   For more on using the Pen tool, see Chapter 3.

Creating map elements

Several effects that you can create with paths have a traveling theme, mainly because a path starts somewhere and finishes somewhere else. Railroad tracks, roads, highways, trails, and rivers all have a tendency to conform very nicely to stroke effects with paths.

Create a railroad track with a gradient

One of the trickiest traveling paths to create is a railroad track. The practical point of creating this railroad track is to illustrate how to change a stroke into a gradient. As mentioned at the beginning of the chapter, you can only do this if you convert your stroke into an outline. Then you can fill it with the gradient of your choosing. To get the real railroad-track look, some advanced cheating is necessary, as described in the following steps.

1. **Create a background shape and fill the background with a color.** This example (see Figure 9-5) uses dark green.

2. **Draw a path to represent the railroad with the Pen tool.** To learn more about drawing paths, see Chapter 3.

3. **Copy the path by choosing Edit ⇨ Copy.** Alternatively, you can press ⌘ (Ctrl)+ C. This creates a second path, like the one in Step 2, which is the second track of the railroad.

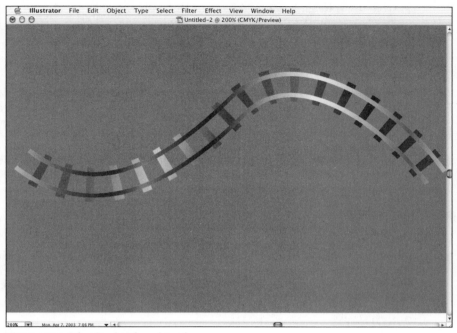

Figure 9-5: The final railroad tracks

4. **Give the paths a desired Stroke weight.** This example uses a Stroke weight of 30 points.

5. **Choose Edit ➪ Paste in Front.** Alternatively, you can press ⌘+Option+V (Ctrl+Alt+V). You'll still be pasting the original copied path from the Clipboard.

6. **Give the paths a desired Stroke weight.** The example uses a Stroke weight of 20 points giving the inner track to the train track.

7. **Select both paths and choose Object ➪ Path ➪ Outline stroke.** This changes the paths into outlined paths because strokes cannot contain gradients.

8. **Fill the paths with a metallic gradient.** For more on applying gradients, see Chapter 6. Now you have two metal tracks of your railroad.

9. **Select both paths and choose Exclude from the Pathfinder palette.** This command subtracts the inner section of the track from the two outer sections.

10. **Check the ends of the path and delete any excess paths that are not part of the tracks.** In the example, I also joined the ends on each individual track.

11. **Choose Paste in back (this pastes the original copied path from the Clipboard).** Alternatively, you can press ⌘+Option+Shift+V (Ctrl+Alt+Shift+V).

12. **Give the new path a Stroke weight that you want.** This example uses a Stroke weight of 40 points and will be the wood tracks.

13. **Choose Object ➪ Path ➪ Outline stroke.** This changes the strokes into outlined paths. Stroke and fill this path with a gradient consisting of several wood-like browns. This path is the wood that underlies the tracks.

14. **The last thing to do is to split the pieces of wood into individual railroad ties**. Select the wood path and choose Edit ➪ Paste in Front. You can also press ⌘+Option+V (Ctrl+Alt+V). This command pastes a path right on top of the wooden area.

15. **Give the stroke in Step 14 the same color as the background and give it a Dash Pattern of Dash 20, Gap 10.** The gaps are the see-through areas, showing the wood-filled path below them.

Tip

To change the color of the new path in Step 14 easily, select the new path, choose the Eyedropper tool, and click the background.

Outline Path is often used on this type of stroke design because strokes can't have gradient fills. The reason that the railroad ties were not given a dash pattern before Outline Path was applied is that Outline Path doesn't work with dash patterns.

The highway

Figure 9-6 shows a stroke design that I discovered a few years back while I was playing with Illustrator. It has the makings of a cute parlor magic trick that you can use to impress your friends. Back when you had to work in Artwork mode, that is, before Illustrator 5.0, creating designs with strokes was much more difficult. Artists couldn't see what they were drawing on-screen, so they had to envision it in their minds. Editing dashes and weights is almost a pleasure now that you can use the stroke palette and undo multiple changes.

Creating a Filmstrip stroke

As stated before, the stroke Charts can help you find a specific style, which you can then modify for your situation. As an example, the stroke in the middle of the right-hand column in the third stroke chart (Figure 9-3) is a stroke that looks like a strip of film. The following steps describe how to create this film stroke, which is a basic stroke that produces a stunning effect.

1. Draw a wavy path with the Pen tool. For more on using the Pen tool, see Chapter 3.

2. Change the stroke of the path to 18-point Black and the fill to None.

3. Choose Add New stroke from the Appearance palette pop-up menu. You access the pop-up menu by clicking the right pointing arrow in a circle on the upper right of the Appearance palette. Change the new stroke to 16-point White, and use a Dash Pattern of Dash 1, Gap 2.

4. Choose Add New stroke from the Appearance palette pop-up menu again and change the new stroke to 14-point Black, Solid.

5. Choose Add New stroke from the Appearance palette pop-up menu once more and change the new stroke to 50% Black, 12 points, with a Dash Pattern of Dash 20, Gap 10.

The figure that follows shows the final filmstrip and the Appearance palette displaying the list of strokes. You can use this procedure to create any of the strokes in the third stroke chart (Figure 9-3) by substituting the values that are listed in the chart for the stroke that you want.

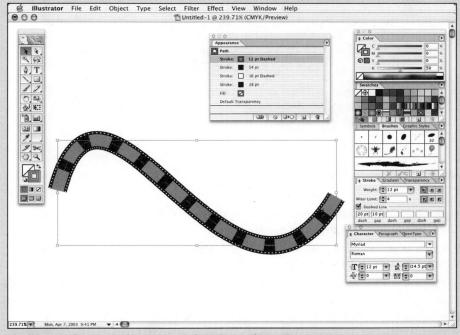

The film stroke created using a stroke pattern from Figure 9-3

After creating the railroad tracks stroke design, which I thought was pretty clever, I yearned for a similar effect — turning one path into some form of artwork. I especially liked the effect of doing several paths and several Stroke attributes in Artwork mode and then switching to Preview mode when I was finished.

Follow the steps below to create a four-lane highway by drawing just one path. These steps are described here.

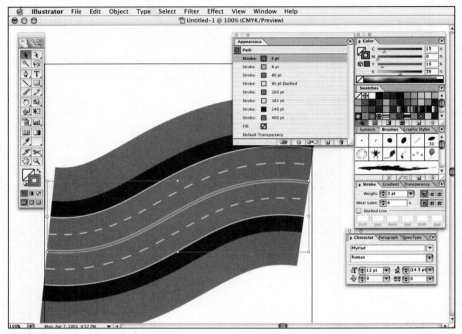

Figure 9-6: The final highway

1. **Use the Pen tool to draw a slightly wavy path from the left side of the Artboard to the right.**

2. **Change the Path to a fill of None and create a 400-point stroke that is colored green.** This path is the grass next to the highway.

3. **Choose Add New stroke from the Appearance palette pop-up menu.** Change the paint style of the stroke to Cyan 25, Yellow 25, and Black 85, with a weight of 240 points. This path is the shoulder of the highway.

4. **Choose Add New stroke from the Appearance palette pop-up menu. Change** the paint style to Cyan 5 and Black 10, with a weight of 165 points. This path is the white line at the edge of the highway.

5. **Choose Add New stroke from the Appearance palette pop-up menu.** Change the paint style to Cyan 15, Yellow 10, and Black 50, with a weight of 160 points. This path is the highway's road surface.

6. **To create the dashed white lines for passing, choose Add New stroke from the Appearance palette pop-up menu.** Change the paint style to Cyan 5 and Black 10, with a weight of 85 points, a dash of 20, and a gap of 20.

7. **Choose Add New stroke from the Appearance palette pop-up menu.** Change the paint style to Cyan 15, Yellow 10, and Black 50, with a weight of 80 points. Uncheck the Dashed line box. This path is the inner part of the highway's road surface.

8. **To create the double yellow line, choose Add New stroke from the Appearance palette pop-up menu.** Change the paint style to Cyan 15, Magenta 20, and Yellow 100, with a weight of 8 points.

9. **Choose Add New stroke from the Appearance palette pop-up menu.** Change the paint style to Cyan 15, Yellow 10, and Black 50, with a weight of 3 points. This path is the piece of highway that divides the double yellow line.

Creating Perfect Patterns

"The Perfect Pattern is one in which you cannot determine the borders of its tiles," so says the Chinese Book of Patterns. If that is true, you can use Adobe Illustrator to create perfect patterns.

The Pattern function in Illustrator is twofold. First, you can fill or stroke any path with a pattern. Second, you can edit existing patterns or create new ones from Illustrator objects. The real strength of Illustrator's pattern features is that you can create patterns as well as apply them onscreen in almost any way imaginable.

A *pattern* in Illustrator is a series of objects within a rectangle that is commonly referred to as a *pattern tile*. When you choose a pattern in the Swatches palette, Illustrator repeats the selected pattern on each of the four sides of the rectangle as well as in the four corners, as shown in Figure 9-7.

Illustrator places the pattern tiles together for you. After you apply a pattern to an object, you can use any of the transformation tools to alter it, and you can move within the object by using the Move command. You can move and transform patterns either with the object that houses the pattern or just the pattern.

Note Tile patterns can either have a background color or they can be transparent. Transparent patterns can overlay other objects, including objects filled with patterns.

Cross-Reference For more about creating objects with fills, see Chapter 4.

Using the default patterns

There are eight patterns available at all times in Illustrator. You can open other libraries from the Swatch Libraries submenu of the Window menu. Under the Swatch Libraries submenu, you have a variety of libraries from which to choose. The last option is Other Library. Through Other Library, you can bring in saved libraries as well as the sample libraries that ship with Illustrator. Figure 9-8 shows the eight default Fill patterns and their names.

To fill a path with a pattern, select that path, make sure the Fill icon is active, and click the corresponding pattern swatch in the swatches palette. Illustrator fills the path with the pattern you select.

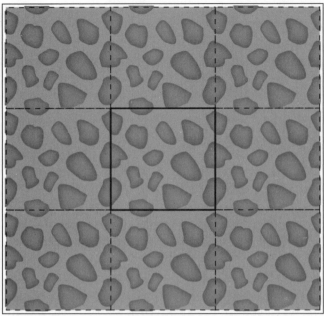

Figure 9-7: The area inside the solid rectangular outline in the center of the figure is the original pattern tile. The dotted line rectangles represent additional pattern tiles that are aligned with the original to create the pattern and fill up the object.

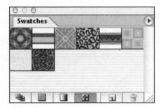

Figure 9-8: The default patterns in the Swatches palette

While there are a few different default Fill patterns, each one can take on a whole new perspective if you use the various transformation functions — move, rotate, scale, reflect, and skew — on them. The default patterns are stored in the Adobe Illustrator Startup file.

Cross-Reference For more on the move, rotate, scale, reflect and skew functions, see Chapter 10. To learn how to modify the startup file to have a specific set of patterns available every time you use Illustrator, see Chapter 15.

Caution Using patterns in a stroke can send your Postscript printer to a crashing halt. A pattern-filled object has to analyze the object's path to figure out where to put the pattern when you print it. The stroke command in PostScript is a one-shot command that follows the path with thickness and a line join attribute. With a pattern in a stroke, the PostScript interpreter must figure out where the stroke should be and then fill it with a pattern. A better solution is to apply the Outline Path filter by choosing Object ⇨ Path ⇨ Outline Path. Doing this converts the stroke into a compound path that you can fill with a pattern.

Creating custom patterns

In addition to using the patterns provided with Illustrator, you can create custom patterns by following the steps described below.

1. **Create the artwork you want to appear in the pattern tile.** This example uses a bunch of different stars created and arranged in a specific order.

2. **Select the artwork with the Selection tool.** For more on how to use the Selection tool, see Chapter 5.

3. **Drag your artwork into the Swatches palette.** A swatch with your new pattern appears on the palette.

4. **Select the object first, and then choose the new pattern you created in the Swatches palette.** This applies the new pattern to your object.

Figure 9-9 also shows the artwork applied as the fill of another shape. The pattern was scaled down dramatically when placed in the larger star shape.

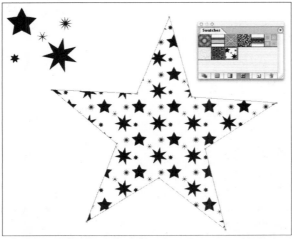

Figure 9-9: The final basic pattern tile as a pattern in a star

Why Patterns Aren't Always Seamless

For patterns to appear seamless, you cannot make the edges of the pattern noticeable. Avoiding this sounds rather easy: All you have to do is avoid placing any objects that touch the edges of a background rectangle. Well, that technique will do it, but when you use such a pattern, the lack of any objects along the borders of the tile makes the pattern look strange.

So, then, you do want objects to cross the edges of the pattern rectangle. The catch is that those objects cannot appear to be broken. Doing an illustration the wrong way can help you understand this principle:

1. Start by drawing a background rectangle with a fill of None.

2. Draw a 1-point Black stroked wavy path from left to right, overlapping both edges.

3. Draw a circle that is filled with 50% Gray and that overlaps the bottom of the rectangle.

4. Select all the objects and define the pattern. You define the pattern by dragging it to the Swatch palette. The result is the top image in the following figure.

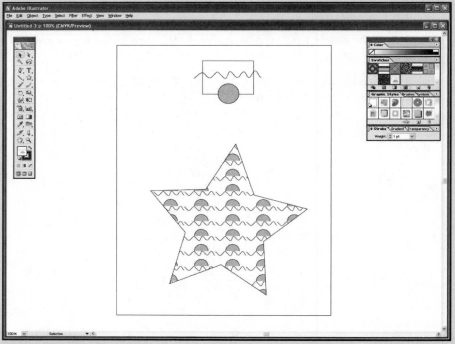

The non-seamless patterns that you create when you follow the steps (top) look funny because the seams are obvious, especially when you apply the pattern to an object (bottom).

When you fill an object with the new pattern, the edges of the pattern are very noticeable because the wavy path and the circle are both cut at the edges of the pattern boundary Therefore, it is important to watch the edges of the pattern if you are looking for a smooth, seamless pattern.

Pattern backgrounds and boundaries

Any pattern tile you create can have the color background you specify, simply by making a rectangle the size of the tile and placing it behind the objects in the pattern. When you create the pattern on top of the background rectangle, just select the entire background with the pattern objects to create the pattern.

If you don't create a background rectangle, Illustrator uses the bounding box of the selected objects to determine the size of the pattern tile. The bounding box is the smallest rectangle that completely encloses all selected objects and paths. (See Figure 9-10.)

Figure 9-10: The bounding box is the smallest rectangle that completely encloses your select objects and paths.

But what happens if you want the edge of the pattern tile to be somewhere inside the bounding box? Illustrator provides a way for you to define a boundary box to define pattern tiles that consist of objects that extend beyond the pattern edges. You create a boundary box by creating a Rectangle with the Rectangle tool, fill it with None, and make it the back-most object in the pattern tile.

Making seamless patterns

To make patterns seamless, you need to remember that objects that lie across the edge of the pattern border are cut into two sections, the outside section of which is invisible. You also need to make sure that lines that stretch from one edge of a pattern border to the other side connect to another line on the opposite edge of the boundary. The second problem is more difficult to deal with than the first one. To make a line match well from one side to the other, you usually have to move one or both of the ends up or down slightly.

Use the following steps to fix objects that get sliced apart at the edges of the pattern tile boundary.

1. **Create the boundary by drawing a rectangle (always the back-most rectangle) and then create the objects you want to use as the pattern tile.** The objects may overlap any of the edges, including the corners. The stones overlap all four sides as well as one of the corners. The background rectangle was created so that you can see the boundary clearly (Figure 9-11a). For more on creating rectangles and other shapes, see Chapter 4.

2. **Select all of the objects that you created, including the pattern boundary, and group them by pressing ⌘+G (Ctrl+G).** For more on grouping, see Chapter 7.

3. **Click the left edge of the pattern and drag to the right with the Option (Alt) key pressed until the arrow pointer is directly over the opposite edge to create a copy.** If you press the Shift key while dragging, Illustrator constrains the group to move horizontally making it easier to line up. The result is Figure 9-11b.

4. **Repeat the process in Steps 2 through 4.** Do this until all four sides have copies of the pattern up against them. The result is Figure 9-11c.

5. **Select all five sections and ungroup them by choosing Object ⇨ Ungroup.** Alternatively, you can press ⌘+Shift+G (Ctrl+G).

6. **Select the boundary rectangles on the four copied sections and delete them.** Figure 9-11d shows the boundary rectangles when you've selected they and before you've deleted them.

7. **Delete all the paths that don't cross the border of the rectangle.** In this example, you're deleting stones. Figure 9-11e shows the copied sections deleted as well as the paths that cross the border of the rectangle.

8. **Look at the corners of the rectangle to see if there are any overlaps on the other three corners.** If an object overlaps any of the corners at all, it should overlap the other three corners.

9. **Repeat Steps 6 and 7.** Move the boundary with a corner as in Step 7 so that the piece lines up perfectly, deleting the rectangle after you finish (Figure 9-11d).

10. **Look for any overlapping pieces of art in the artwork, including areas of objects that are too close for your liking.** Move any pieces of art that are not overlapping a boundary.

11. **Make the boundary and objects into a pattern.** You do this by dragging them into the Swatch palette.

12. **Apply the new pattern to a shape and check the seams to make sure that they are correct.** You apply the new pattern by selecting the shape and clicking the new pattern in the Swatch palette. In this example, the pattern is applied to a eight-pointed star, shown in Figure 9-11f. If you are even the least bit doubtful that a pattern is showing seams, zoom in to 1600% to examine and correct the questionable area.

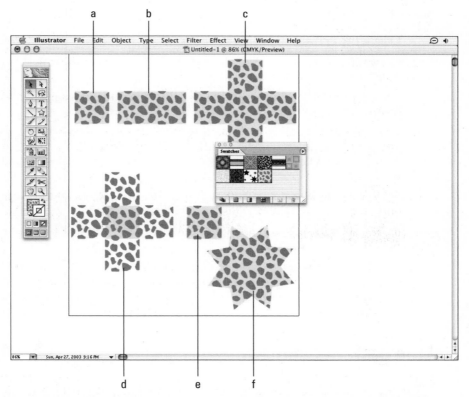

Figure 9-11: The steps for creating a seamless pattern are shown in this figure. Create an initial tile that you want for the pattern (a), create a copy of the pattern (b), place the copies of the pattern around the initial tile (c), select the initial tile and delete the rest (d), delete all paths that don't cross the border (e), and apply the new pattern to the object you want (f).

Symmetrical patterns

You can easily create symmetrical patterns in Illustrator. The key to creating them is to draw the boundary box after you create the rest of the objects, drawing outward from the center point of one of the objects.

When you create symmetrical patterns, the main difficulty is judging the space between the objects in the pattern. Objects always seem too close together or too far apart, especially in patterns that have different amounts of space between the objects horizontally and vertically. The solution is to use a square as the pattern tile boundary. This ensures that you have an equal amount of space from the center of one object to the center of the next object, both vertically and horizontally.

Using the method described in the following steps, you can visually adjust the amount of space between objects before you make the objects a pattern.

1. **Create the artwork to use in the pattern.**

2. **Draw a rectangle from the center of the object so that the object is in the upper-left corner of the rectangle.**

3. **Press Option(Alt) while dragging the object and the rectangle across and down.** Delete the extra rectangles.

4. **Using the Direct Selection tool, drag to select the objects on the right and Shift-drag the objects to change the horizontal spacing.** You Shift-drag the objects by moving them while pressing the Shift key, releasing the mouse button before the Shift key.

5. **Drag with the Direct Selection tool to select the objects on the bottom and Shift-drag up or down to adjust the vertical spacing.**

6. **Move the rectangle so that it surrounds only the initial object and delete the other three objects.**

7. **Make the objects into a pattern and fill a path with it.** You make the object into a pattern by dragging it to the Swatch palette. You fill the path by selecting the path and then selecting the newly created pattern from the Swatch palette. The pattern is the background for Figure 9-12.

Line patterns and grids

Using lines and grids for patterns is ideal because they are so easy to create. The key in both types of patterns is the size of the bounding rectangle. You use a grid to draw accurate floor plans, or even for drawing perspective scenes. Line patterns are great for creating fences or any repeating linear paths.

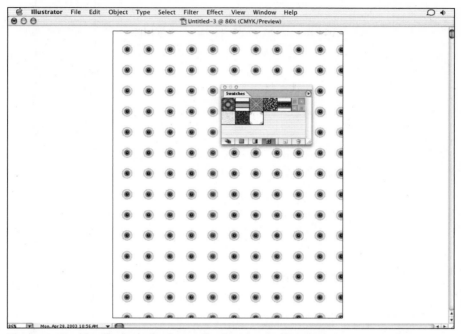

Figure 9-12: The final result of a perfectly symmetrical pattern

Creating line patterns

1. **Decide what point size you want for the lines and how far apart you want them.**

2. **Draw a rectangle making the height exactly how far apart you want the lines to be.** Makes sure you draw the rectangle with a fill and stroke of None. The result is the top image in Figure 9-13.

3. **Draw a horizontal line with a fill of None and a stroke of the point size you want from outside the left edge of the rectangle to outside the right edge of the rectangle.**

4. **Make a pattern out of the two objects.** You make a pattern by adding the top image in Figure 9-13 to the Swatch palette.

5. **Apply the pattern to the object of your choice.** You can apply a pattern by selecting the object, and then clicking the pattern in the Swatch palette. The bottom image of 9-13 shows the results.

You can use this technique with vertical lines as well. Just make the bounding rectangle's width the distance from line to line.

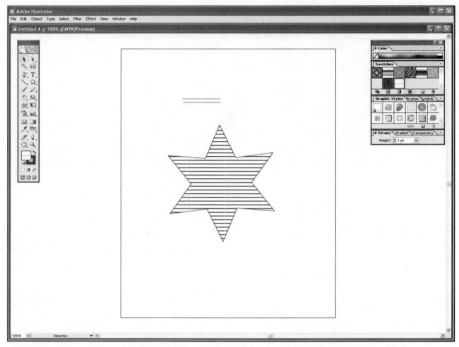

Figure 9-13: You can easily make a pattern from straight lines and apply it to any object.

Creating grid patterns

You can use a grid pattern to create graphing paper for a logo or business logo. Another good use of grid patterns is for grates or windows because you can use the transformation tools to add the perspective. Creating grids is even easier than creating evenly spaced lines:

1. **Create a rectangle that is the size of the grid holes.** For example, for a ¼-inch grid, you make the rectangle ¼ inch x ¼ inch. For more on creating rectangles, see Chapter 5.

2. **Apply a stroke to the object.** Make the stroke the weight that you want the grid lines to be.

Cross-Reference

For more on Stroke weights, and applying strokes, see Chapter 4.

3. **Make that rectangle into a pattern.** You make a pattern by adding your object to the Swatch palette. That's it. You now have a pattern grid that is as precise as possible.

Tip

If you want the space between grid lines to be an exact measurement, make the rectangle bigger by the Stroke weight. A ¼-inch grid (18 points) with 1-point grid lines requires a rectangle that is 17 points x 17 points. Remember that four of these grids combined don't equal an inch; instead, they equal 4 points more than an inch.

Diagonal-line and grid patterns

Shading effects, such as hatched lines, are easily created with a diagonal line and grid pattern. Figure 9-14 shows a close up of a horse using a diagonal line pattern rotated and scaled to show a shaded effect. You may find creating diagonal-line and grid patterns difficult if you try to make a rectangle; draw a path at an angle, and then use the rectangle with the path in it as a pattern. Joining diagonal lines at the edges of the pattern is nearly impossible.

Using this technique is also a great way to avoid making several patterns when you need line patterns that are set at different angles. Just make one horizontal line pattern and rotate the patterns within the paths.

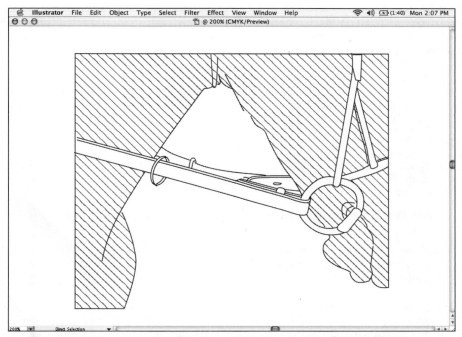

Figure 9-14: A line pattern applied to an object to create a shaded effect

A better method is as follows:

1. **Create a bounding box.** To learn how to select objects, see Chapter 5.

2. **Create line (or grids) in horizontal or vertical alignment that extends beyond the bounding box.** To learn how to create lines, see Chapter 3.

3. **Make the lines (or grids) into a pattern.** You can do this by dragging the lines (or grids) to the Swatch palette.

4. **Apply the pattern to an object.** You do this by selecting the object and clicking the pattern in the Swatch palette.

5. **Double-click the Rotate tool.** Doing this opens the Rotate dialog box.

6. **In the Rotate dialog box, enter the angle to change the lines and uncheck the Object checkbox.** The pattern rotates to the desired angle inside the path.

Transparency and patterns

Transparent patterns are great to use overtop of color, or gradients, or even other patterns. Instead of creating a bunch of specific patterns that use other patterns, use the transparent pattern option to layer overtop of other patterns. A great use of this option is to use a gradient and then use a line pattern to add a hatched shading look. To make the background of a pattern transparent, don't use a background rectangle. Only the objects in the pattern will be opaque.

A transparent pattern is great to use overtop another color or pattern. You can use the simple line pattern with a transparent background alone or over another pattern. Figure 9-15 shows an object with a transparent pattern over a regular pattern.

To make the objects in a pattern transparent, do the following:

1. **Make the background rectangle and the other objects into a compound path.** For more on creating paths, see Chapter 3. For more on creating objects, see Chapter 4.

2. **Select the compound path and make the objects into a pattern.** You create a pattern by dragging your object into the Swatch palette.

3. **If desired, apply a transform tool.** For more on transform tools, see Chapter 10. You can achieve some fascinating effects by using the transformation tools to make transformed copies of patterns on top of themselves.

Tip   When you make the bounding rectangle part of a compound path, it is no longer a rectangle and you cannot use it as the bounding rectangle. Always copy the rectangle before you make the objects and the rectangle into a compound path.

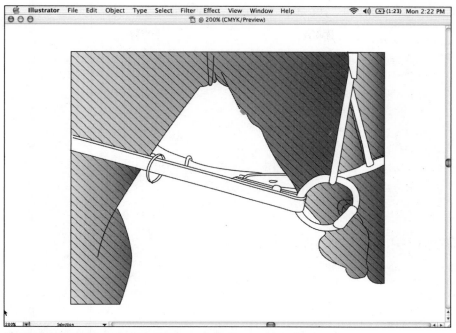

Figure 9-15: A transparent pattern applied over a gradient

Another way to achieve interesting effects is by making a copy of the object behind the original:

1. **Select the object.** For more on creating objects, see Chapter 4. To select an object, see Chapter 5.

2. **Choose Edit ⇨ Copy.** Alternatively, you can press ⌘+C (Ctrl+C). Doing this creates a copy of the object.

3. **Select the copy of the object and choose Edit ⇨ Paste in Back.** You can also press ⌘+Option+Shift+V (Ctrl+Alt+Shift+V). Doing this pastes the object in back of the original object.

4. **Change the fill in the copy of the object to a solid, a gradient, or to another Pattern**. For more on filling objects, see Chapter 4. For more on gradients, see Chapter 6.

Placing patterns and gradients into patterns

Sometimes you like a combination of patterns. Instead of placing one on top of the other, consider combining the ones you like together to create a new pattern.

Figure 9-16 shows two standard Illustrator patterns combined to make one pattern. Under normal circumstances, you cannot place gradients into patterns or patterns into other patterns. But Illustrator doesn't think of the objects as patterns or gradients, so you can place patterns and gradients into patterns.

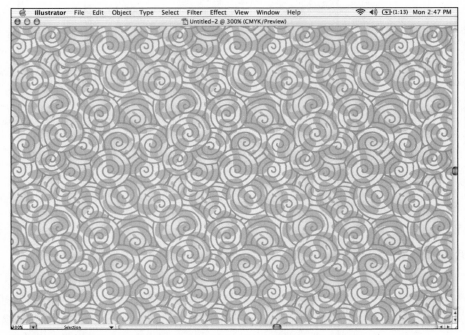

Figure 9-16: Two default patterns combined to make one pattern

Placing a pattern into a pattern

To place a pattern into another pattern:

1. **Drag the pattern that you want to place into the new pattern from the Swatches palette to your document.**

2. **Group the pattern artwork and press Option(Alt) as you drag.** This makes a copy of several squares.

3. **Draw a rectangle around the squares.** You can also add any additional artwork for the new pattern.

4. **Select the artwork and drag it to the Swatches palette.** This creates your new combined pattern swatch.

Placing a gradient into a pattern

Including gradients in patterns is not quite so simple:

1. **First, create the object in the shape of the gradient.** For more on creating objects, see Chapter 4.

2. **Fill the object with the gradient.** For more on applying a gradient, see Chapter 6.

3. **Expand the gradient with the Object ⇨ Expand command.** You can then use the blended object in any pattern.

Note   When you transform gradients into blends via Expand for placement in a pattern, check for masked areas. You cannot use masks in patterns, so you need to release the mask before you incorporate the blend into the pattern. Also, try to keep the number of blend steps to a minimum.

Transforming patterns

After you create patterns and place them within paths, you may find that they are too big or at the wrong angle for the path. Likewise, they may start in an awkward location. You can use the transformation tools and the Move command to resolve these problems.

To transform a pattern inside a path:

1. **Select the path.** For more on selecting a path, see Chapter 5.

2. **Double-click the transformation tool that corresponds to the change that you want to make to the pattern.** The transformation tool's dialog box appears (see Figure 9-17).

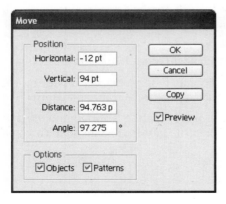

Figure 9-17: The Move dialog box (along with the other Transformation dialog boxes) will let you transform patterns independent of objects.

3. **In the Transformation dialog box, uncheck the Objects checkbox.** Doing this selects the Patterns checkbox. The Patterns and Objects checkboxes are grayed out if the selected object does not contain a pattern.

Any changes that you make in the Transformation Tool's dialog box when only the Patterns checkbox is checked affect only the pattern, not the outside shape.

If you are using any of the transformation tools manually, the pattern inside the selected object only transform with the object if you check the Transform pattern tiles option in the General Preferences dialog box.

 Cross-Reference   For more on transforming objects, see Chapter 10.

To move a pattern within a path, choose Object ➪ Transform ➪ Move (or double-click the Selection tool). The Move dialog box also contains Patterns and Objects checkboxes. If you uncheck the Objects checkbox, which selects the Patterns checkbox, only the pattern will be moved.

Summary

✦ The most attractive aspect of strokes is that you can use them together, on top of one another.

✦ The Stroke charts provided in this chapter show some of what you can do with strokes.

✦ When you stroke type, be sure to place another copy of the filled text on top of the stroked type.

✦ Use Outline Path to create filled paths out of strokes.

✦ Use fills to create half-stroked paths.

✦ Patterns are a type of fill that provides texture to any path.

✦ Illustrator supplies several default patterns. You can transform these patterns in the same ways that you can transform other Illustrator objects.

✦ You can use almost anything you create in Illustrator as a pattern, with the exception of masks, gradients, placed images, and other patterns.

✦ You construct diagonal-line patterns by creating a horizontal-line pattern and rotating it with the Rotate tool when the pattern is filling a path.

✦   ✦   ✦

Applying Transformations and Distortions

PostScript has the capability to transform any PostScript object by scaling it, rotating it, reflecting it, shearing it, and reshaping it. Illustrator takes advantage of this power and enhances it by providing you the flexibility of using transformation functions with menus, palettes, and certain tools.

In addition to transformations, Illustrator really gets fun when you work with distortions. Distortions are accomplished with a number of different filters and effects, warps and the amazing Liquify tools.

Adding a Transformation with Tools

Although there are many places to find the transformations functions, the first stop is the Transformation tools. The Transformation tools in the Illustrator toolbox address fundamental functions: rotating, reflecting, shearing, scaling, and reshaping. Before you can use any of these tools, however, you must select one or more objects including paths, points, and segments). The selected paths are the paths that are transformed.

Using the various Transformation tools, you can transform selected objects in five ways:

  ✦ Click with the Transformation tool to set an origin point and then drag from a different location. This is called a manual transformation.

✦ Click and drag in one motion to transform the object from its center point or last origin point.

✦ Press Option (Alt) and click to set the origin and then enter exact information in the tool's transformation dialog box. This method is more precise than manually transforming.

✦ Double-click a Transformation tool to set the origin in the center of the selected object; then enter information in the tool's transformation dialog box.

✦ Use the Transform palette (discussed later in this chapter).

All of the transformations have an additional option in the dialog boxes. The Copy button will make a copy of the original and transform it to your settings. The Object box when checked will apply the transformation only to the object (not the fill pattern inside). The Pattern box checked will apply the transformation to just the pattern (not the object). Not checking either of the Object or Pattern boxes applies the transformation to the object and the pattern inside.

Cross-Reference   For more on copying and transforming patterns, see the "Transforming patterns" section later in this chapter.

All the Transformation tools work on a relative basis. For example, if you scale an object 150% and then scale it again by 150%, the object becomes 225% of its original size 150% x 150% = 225%). If the object is initially scaled to 150% of its original size, and you want to return it to that original size, you must do the math and figure out what percentage you need to resize it or you could just use the Undo feature) — in this case, 66.7% 100% ÷ 150% = 66.7%). Entering 100% in the Scale dialog box leaves the selected objects unchanged.

Illustrator automatically creates a visible origin point, shown in Figure 10-1, when you use any of the Transformation tools. Because the origin is in the center of the selection, if you just drag with the Transformation tool, the origin point is visible as soon as you select the Transformation tool. If you click without dragging to set the origin, it shows up at that location until the origin is reset. Having the origin point visible as a blue cross hair makes the transformation tools much more usable and functional.

When manually transforming objects, you can make a copy of the selected object and thus leave the original untransformed by holding down the Option (Alt) key before and after releasing the mouse button. In a transformation dialog box, you can make a copy by clicking the Copy button, pressing Option (Alt) -Return, or Option (Alt)-clicking OK.

If the Patterns checkbox is available (you must have a pattern in one of the selected paths for this option not to be grayed out) in any of the Transformation dialog boxes, you can check its option box to transform your pattern along with the object. You can also transform the pattern only, leaving the object untransformed, by unchecking the Objects box.

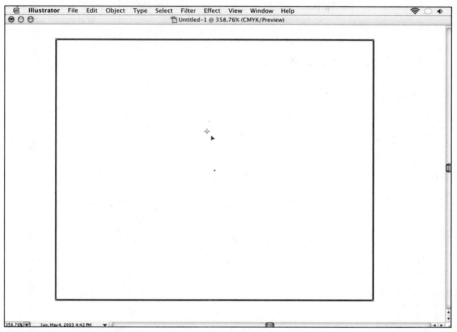

Figure 10-1: The origin point that appears when using any of the Transformation tools

Cross-Reference

You can learn more about patterns in Chapter 9.

Tip

You can manually transform just patterns and not the objects themselves) by pressing the tilde ~) key while using any of the transformation tools including the Selection tool for moving).

Manually transforming objects is fairly simple if you remember that the first place you click the point of origin), and the second place should be a fair distance apart. The farther your second click is from the point of origin, the more control you have when dragging to transform.

All the Transformation tools perform certain operations that rely on the Constrain Angle setting as a point of reference. Normally, this setting is set to 0°, which makes your Illustrator world act normally. You can change the setting by choosing Illustrator (Edit) ⇨ Preferences ⇨ General, or by pressing ⌘+K (Ctrl+K), and entering a new value.

You can access each of the Transformation dialog boxes from the Object ⇨ Transform submenu (see Figure 10-2).

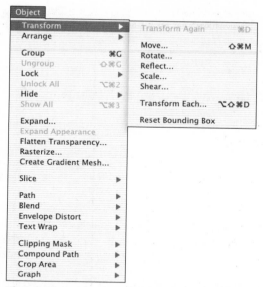

Figure 10-2: The Transform submenu under the Object menu

Note   If the bounding box is visible (View ➪ Show Bounding Box), you can use the Selection tool to rotate, scale, or move the object.

Rotating with the Rotate tool

The Rotate tool is found in the toolbox. The Rotate tool rotates selected objects within a document. Double-clicking the Rotate tool displays the Rotate dialog box, where you enter the precise angle of the selected item's rotation in the Angle box. The object rotates around its origin, which by default is located at the center of the object's bounding box. A positive number between 0 and 180 rotates the object counterclockwise that many degrees. A negative number between 0 and –180 rotates the selected object clockwise. The Rotate tool works on a standard 360° circle of rotation, although it is usually easier to type in numbers between 0 and 180 or 0 and –180, than numbers such as 270, which is the same as –90°.

Holding down the Option (Alt) key and clicking somewhere in the document also brings up the Rotate dialog box (see Figure 10-3), where you can enter the angle of rotation; however, the object now rotates around the point where the Rotate tool was clicked. This point can be on or off the selected object. Be careful because it is quite easy to rotate an object right out of your viewing area! Illustrator has many precautions; however there are no warnings that prevent you from transforming or moving an object off the Pasteboard.

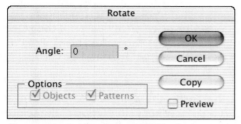

Figure 10-3: The Rotate dialog box

Click once to set the origin point from where the object's center of rotation should be and then click fairly far from the origin and drag in a circle. The selected object spins along with the cursor. To constrain the angle to 45° increments as you are dragging, hold down the Shift key. This angle is dependent on the Constrain Angle box, and is in 45° increments plus the angle in this box. You open the Constrain Angle box by choosing Illustrator (Edit) ⇨ Preferences ⇨ General or by pressing ⌘+K (Ctrl+K). Figure 10-4 shows an illustration before and after rotation.

Figure 10-4: The object before (left) and after (right) rotation

Reflecting with the Reflect tool

The Reflect tool makes a mirror image of the selected objects, reflected across an axis of reflection. You can find the Reflect tool as a popup tool under the Rotate tool. Double-clicking the Reflect tool reflects selected objects across an axis of reflection that runs through the horizontal center or vertical center of the selected objects. In the Reflect dialog box (see Figure 10-5), you can enter the axis of reflection. If you want to reflect the object through either the horizontal or vertical axis, click the appropriate button.

Note   Pressing Option (Alt) and clicking in the document window also brings up the Reflect dialog box, but the axis of reflection is now not in the center of the selected object and in the location in the document where you Option(Alt)-clicked.

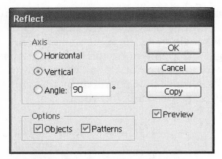

Figure 10-5: The Reflect dialog box

Manual reflecting is done by clicking once to set the origin point the center of the axis of reflection) and again somewhere along the axis of reflection. If you click and drag after setting your origin point, you can rotate the axis of reflection and see what your objects look like reflected across various axes. The Shift key constrains the axis of reflection to 90° angles relative to the Constrain Angle. Again, you open the Constrain Angle box by choosing Illustrator (Edit) ⇨ Preferences ⇨ General or by pressing ⌘+K (Ctrl+K). Holding down the Option (Alt) key during the release of the click leaves a copy of the original object. Figure 10-6 shows an illustration before and after being reflected.

Scaling with the Scale tool

The Scale tool resizes objects both uniformly and non-uniformly. You can also use the Scale tool to flip objects, but without the precision of the Reflect tool. It is impossible to keep both the size and proportions of an object constant while flipping and scaling.

Figure 10-6: The object before (left) and after (right) being reflected across the vertical axis

Double-clicking the Scale tool brings up the Scale dialog box, shown in Figure 10-7. All selected objects are scaled from its origin, which by default is located at the center of the object's bounding box. If the Uniform option is chosen, numbers typed into the text field result in proportionately scaled objects where the width and height of the object remain proportional to each other). Numbers less than 100% shrink the object; numbers greater than 100% enlarge it. When the Uniform option is chosen, you may also check the box called Scale Strokes & Effects.

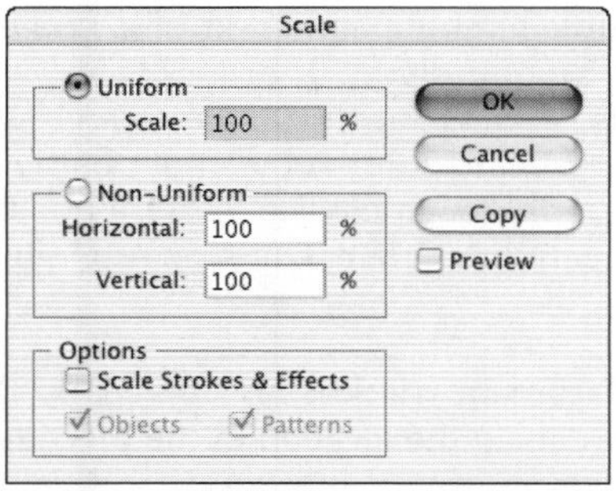

Figure 10-7: The Scale dialog box

Non-uniform scaling resizes the horizontal and vertical dimensions of the selected objects separately, distorting the image. The way non-uniform scaling works is related to the Constrain Angle box (Illustrator (Edit) ⇨ Preferences ⇨ General or ⌘+K (Ctrl+K)), where the angle set there is the horizontal scaling, and the vertical scaling is 90° from that angle.

Tip   Pressing the Option (Alt) key and clicking in the document window also brings up the Scale dialog box, but now the objects are scaled from the location in the document that was Option (Alt)-clicked.

You can achieve manual resizing by clicking your point of origin and then clicking away and dragging to scale. If you cross the horizontal or vertical axis of the point of origin, the selected object flips over in that direction. Holding down the Shift key constrains the objects to equal proportions, if you drag the cursor at approximately 45° from the point of origin. Alternatively, holding down the Shift key constrains the scaling to either horizontal or vertical scaling only if you drag the cursor along at about a 90° angle from the point of origin relative to the constrain angle.

Shearing with the Shear tool

This tool should actually be called the "Swear" tool because it causes more cursing (no, not cursoring; that's different) than any other tool, except perhaps for the mighty Pen tool. Another good name for the Shear tool — one that I have heard many people use is the "Stupid" tool because that's usually how you feel when trying to get good results from its use. It's a terrifying feeling to see the artwork you spent an hour touching up to get it just right, go zinging off the screen, seemingly all by itself.

You find the Shear tool as a pop-up tool with the Scale tool. The Shear tool is rightfully distrusted because using it manually is usually a quick lesson in futility. Essentially what it does is move all points above the origin point to the side and all points below the origin point in the opposite direction. The further the points are from the origin, the farther to the side they are moved. The effect is a slated, perspective like look to your object. Use shear to add a shadow to an object or text. Another great use of shear is to make an object or text look like it is in perspective.

Double-clicking the Shear tool brings up the Shear dialog box, shown in Figure 10-8, which is much more controllable. Double-clicking causes the origin to be in the center of the selected object. The Angle box is simple enough; in its text box, you enter the angle amount the object should shear. Any amount over 75° or less than — 75° renders the object into an indecipherable mess, because at this angle or higher the art has been "flattened into a straight line." The Shear tool reverses the positive-numbers-are-counterclockwise rule: To shear an object clockwise, enter a positive number; to shear counterclockwise, enter a negative number. The Axis Angle box is for shearing an object along a specified axis.

Tip   Pressing Option (Alt) and clicking in the document window also brings up the Shear dialog box, with the origin of the shear being the location of the preceding Option (Alt)-click.

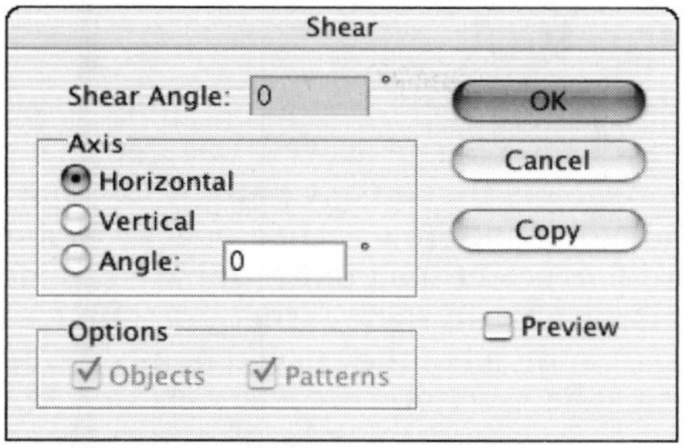

Figure 10-8: The Shear dialog box

Manual shearing is something else again because, while you click, hold, and drag with the Shear tool, you are doing two things at once. From the beginning of the second click until you release the mouse, you change the angle of shearing the distance. When you drag the mouse during the second click, you change the angle of the axis of shearing the angle. Usually, it's best to start your second click fairly far away from the point of origin. Holding down the Shift key constrains the axis of shearing to a 45° angle relative to the constraining angle. Figure 10-9 shows an illustration before and after being sheared.

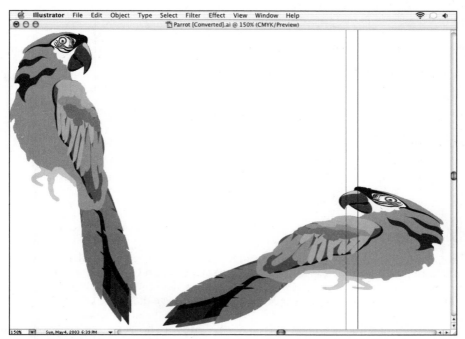

Figure 10-9: The parrot before (left) and after (right) being sheared

Reshaping with the Reshape tool

You use the Reshape tool to select one or multiple anchor points in order to change their shape. You can also select parts of paths to change as well. Located as a pop-up tool under the Scale tool, you use the Reshape tool on any path by clicking where you want to bend the path and then dragging. To use the Reshape tool on several paths at once, use the Reshape tool to select the points you want to move first. You must select at least one point that isn't a straight corner point on each path. You then drag on a Reshape-selected point; all of the curved points move as well. Figure 10-10 shows an example of the Reshape tool.

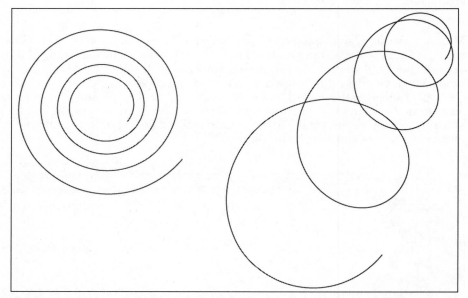

Figure 10-10: The spiral before (left) and after (right) using the Reshape tool

> **Tip**   The Reshape tool works best on curved objects such as spirals, ovals, and so on.

Moving objects

The most common way to move an object is to use a Selection tool and drag the selected points, segments, and paths from one location to another.

The precise way to move an object is to use the Move dialog box (see Figure 10-11) or the Transform palette (see the following section). Select the object you want to move and then choose Object ➪ Transform ➪ Move. The Move dialog box appears, and you can enter the appropriate values in either the horizontal or vertical text fields. If you want to move an object diagonally, enter a number in the Distance text field and then enter the angle of movement direction in the Angle text field.

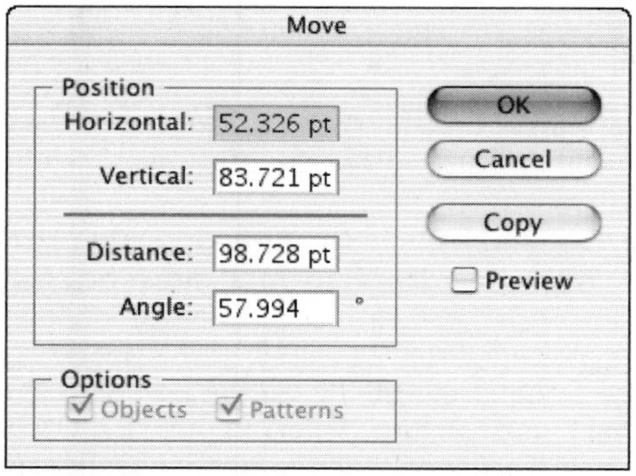

Figure 10-11: The Move dialog box

You can move any selected object (except for text selected with a Type tool) via the Move dialog box, including individual Anchor Points and line segments.

By default, the Move dialog box contains the distance and angle that you last moved an object, whether manually with a Selection tool or in the Move dialog box. If you use the Measure tool prior to using the Move dialog box, the numbers in the Move dialog box correspond to the numbers that appeared in the Info palette when you used the Measure tool.

Tip   Double-clicking the Selection tool in the toolbox displays the Move dialog box.

In the Move dialog box, positive numbers in the Horizontal text field move an object from left to right, while negative numbers move an object from right to left. Positive numbers in the Vertical text field move an object from bottom to top, while negative numbers move an object from top to bottom. Negative numbers in the Distance text field move an object in the opposite direction of the Angle text field. The Angle text field works a bit differently. Negative numbers in the Angle text field move the angle in the opposite direction from 0° so entering –45° is the same as entering 315° and entering –180° is the same as entering 180°.

The measurement system in the Move dialog box uses the Units set in the General Preferences dialog box. To use units other than those of the current measurement system, use these indicators:

✦ For inches: 1" or 1in 1 inch)

✦ For picas: 1p or 1pica 1 pica)

✦ For points: 1pt or 0p1 1 point)

✦ For picas/points: 1p1 1 pica, 1 point)

✦ For millimeters: 1mm 1 millimeter)

✦ For centimeters: 1cm 1 centimeter)

The Horizontal and Vertical text fields are linked to the Distance and Angle text fields; when you change one of the fields, Illustrator alters the others accordingly.

Pressing the Copy button duplicates selected objects in the direction and distance indicated, just as holding down Option (Alt) when dragging duplicates the selected objects.

Tip   The Move dialog box is a great place to enter everything via the keyboard. Press Tab to move from text field to text field, press Return (Enter) to push the OK button, and press ⌘+Period (Esc) to push the Cancel button. Pressing Option(Alt)-Enter or pressing Option (Alt) while clicking OK pushes the Copy button. The same is true for all of the transformation dialog boxes.

Using the Free Transform tool

Free Transform enables you to rotate, scale, reflect, and shear all with one tool. This way you can create multiple transformations at one time. The Free Transform tool is located in the Toolbox directly underneath the Scale tool.

What is unique about this tool is that you can select more than one object to change the size, shape, and placement in one step. The Free Transform tool does not replace the Free Distort filter. Using this cool tool to create distorted effects is different from using the Free Distort filter.

Cross-Reference   The Free Distort effect is covered with the other effects in Chapter 12.

At first glance they may seem the same, but they aren't. The Free Transform tool actually adds perspective, while the Free Distort effect mimics the shape, but keeps the spacing uniform. This sounds confusing, but the visual example that follows may help. The top row of objects in Figure 10-12 shows the application of the Free Transform tool to the top and bottom of the row. This gives a tree-line effect with perspective. The bottom row of trees in Figure 10-12 show the application of the Free Distort effect to the top and bottom of the row again. Note the different results.

Tip   To apply the Free Transform tool to top and bottom at the same time, hold down the Option (Alt) key. For more control, hold down the Command (Ctrl) key as you start to drag.

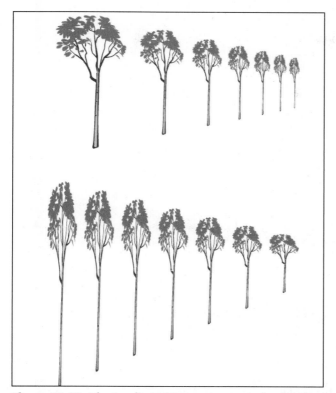

Figure 10-12: The top line of trees was created using the Free Transform tool. The bottom line of trees was created using the Free Distort effect.

Working with the Transform Palette

Imagine a palette that combines four of Illustrator's five transformation capabilities into one place. Then take a look at Figure 10-13, which shows Illustrator's Transform palette in all its glory.

The Transform palette provides a way to Move, Scale, Rotate, and Shear selected artwork. There's no reflect option (you'll need to use the tool or the Transform sub-menu option to reflect artwork). Instead of manually setting an origin point or transforming from the center by default, the Transform palette gives you nine "fixed" origin points based on the bounding box of the selected objects; the bounding box is the blue box that surrounds any selected objects. You can select these fixed origin points using the square set of points to the left of the palette. Choose an origin point before entering values in the palette, and the transformations will originate from the corner, center of a side, or the center of selected objects.

Figure 10-13: The Transform palette

The text fields in the Transform palette are as follows:

✦ **X:** This is the horizontal location of the artwork, measured from the left edge of the document or horizontal ruler origin (if it has been moved from the left edge).

✦ **Y:** This is the vertical location of the artwork, measured from the bottom edge of the document or vertical ruler origin (if it has been moved from the bottom edge).

✦ **W:** This is the width of the artwork's bounding box.

✦ **H:** This is the height of the artwork's bounding box.

✦ **Rotate:** This field lets you apply a rotation to the selected artwork.

✦ **Shear:** This field lets you apply a shear to the selected artwork.

To use the palette, type the new value you'd like to use in any field and then press Enter. If you have another value to enter, press the Tab key to go to the next text field or Shift-Tab to go back a field). Pressing Option (Alt) when you press Enter or Tab creates a duplicate of the selected artwork with the transformations you specified.

For Scaling, you can enter either absolute measurements (the size in inches, picas, and so on, that you want the artwork to be), or by percentage by adding the % symbol after your value. You can also force Illustrator to scale uniformly, regardless of whether you're using absolute measurements or percentages, by pressing ⌘ (Ctrl) when you press the Enter or Tab keys.

Okay, time for me to 'fess up. I'm not a big fan of the Transform palette, and here's why:

✦ **No Reflect option:** Couldn't we have a button enabling us to enter a negative scale value to reflect across the horizontal/vertical axis?

✦ **Transform Each option:** Transform Each is hard to get to and this would've provided an easy way to do these transformations. Transform each is found by choosing Object ⇨ Transform ⇨ Transform Each or Command (Control) + Option (Alt) + Shift + D.

✦ **No Random option:** Transformations are perfect for random values, as evidenced by Transform Each's Random check box.

✦ **No Keyboard commands to highlight the text fields:** Even the Transformation tools can be accessed by pressing the keyboard keys.

✦ **After rotating and shearing, the value reverts back to 0° instantly:** It would be nice to see how far the art has been transformed since it was created. There are a few technical issues to work out here (groups? compound paths? portions of paths? objects pasted?), but I'm sure Adobe can figure them out.

✦ **No automated repeat function:** A text field for number of duplicates would be handy. You have to pressing ⌘+D (Ctrl+D) 3 to 4 times when you want to duplicate/rotate an object around a circle at 10° increments.

✦ **No Apply at Once feature like Transform Each has.**

✦ **No floating origin point:** You have to use one of the nine presets — and there's no way to change them automatically or revert to center using the keyboard.

Okay, sure, many of the things I don't like about the Transform palette are wish-list features, not missing functionality. But if I'm going to have this palette sucking up valuable screen real estate, I want something back for it. Most of Illustrator's other palettes are worthy of taking up chunks of pixels; the Transform palette isn't.

Note

The previous comments are here for two reasons. First, because I think you should know that while I love Illustrator (my program of choice if I were ever stuck on a desert island with a computer), I don't like a few features or, at least, I feel could be improved. The second reason is to show a sample of the types of communication that Adobe and other software companies use to determine what features take priority for future implementation. If instead of listing what I don't like and would like to see in the next version of Illustrator I just said, "I don't like the transformation palette," Adobe would just shrug and ignore me. But their concern is to make the best software they can, and that means addressing their customers' needs. If you have suggestions or ideas for Adobe, make sure that you're both as concise and descriptive as possible.

Transform Each

Transform Each provides a way to do several transformations in one shot, but that's only the beginning. The unique thing about Transform Each is that each selected object is transformed independently, as opposed to having all the selected objects transformed together. Figure 10-14 shows the difference between "normal" rotating and scaling, and the Rotate and Scale functions in Transform Each.

To access the Transform Each dialog box (see Figure 10-15), choose Object ➪ Transform ➪ Transform Each. In the dialog box, use the sliders/dial or type in values for each of the transformations. The Random checkbox on the right side of the dialog box gives each object selected a random value that falls between the default (100% for Scale; 0 for Move and Rotate) and the value set by the slider/dial.

Figure 10-14: The logo original (top), with changes applied using the Transform Each dialog box (bottom, left), and with changes using the Random check box (bottom, right)

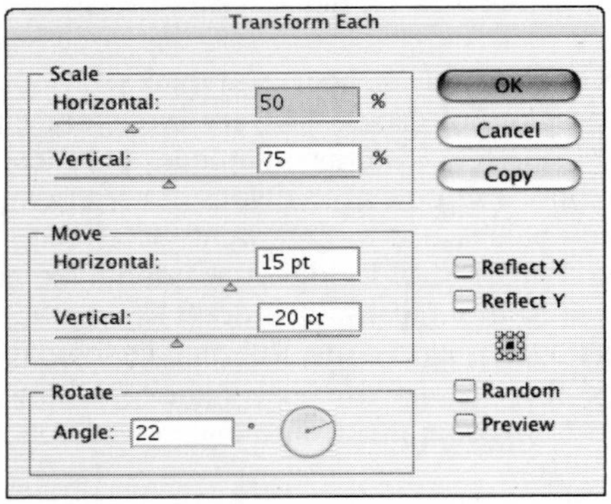

Figure 10-15: The Transform Each dialog box

In addition to controls for setting the Scale, Move, and Rotate values, the Transform Each dialog box includes checkbox to reflect the selected objects about the X or Y axes and an icon for selecting an origin point. But of all offerings, the randomize function of Transform Each is its most powerful asset. Checking the Random checkbox can turn a grid into a distinct random texture, as shown in Figure 10-16.

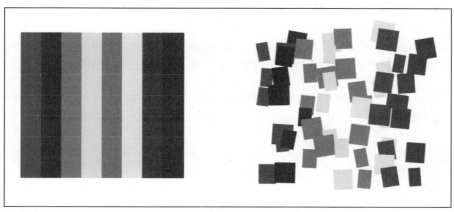

Figure 10-16: Transform Each's Random function applied to a pattern of stripes of colored squares

Using Transformations

The Transformation tools open a world of possibilities within Illustrator. The following tips and ideas should give you a head start in exploring the amazing power of transformations.

Choosing Object ⇨ Transform ⇨ Transform Again, or pressing ⌘+D (Ctrl+D) redoes the last transformation that you performed on the selected object. Transformations include Move, Rotate, Scale, Reflect, Shear, and Transform Each. Transform Again also makes a transformed copy, if you made a copy either manually or by clicking the Copy button in the prior Transformation dialog box.

Tip

Transform Again remembers the last transformation no matter what else you do, and it can apply that same transformation to other objects or reapply it to the existing transformed objects.

Creating shadows

You can create all sorts of shadows by using the Scale, Reflect, and Shear tools. To create a shadow, follow these steps.

1. **Select the path where you want to apply the shadow.** See Chapter 5 for more on the selecting paths.

2. **Click the bottom of the path once with the Reflect tool.** This action sets the origin of reflection at the base of the image.

3. **Drag the mouse down while pressing the Shift key.** The image flips over, creating a mirror image under the original.

4. **Press the Option (Alt) key while keeping the Shift key pressed before and during the release of the mouse button.** Doing this makes a copy of the image.

5. **Using the Shear tool, click the base of the reflected copy to set the origin.**

6. **Click and drag left or right at the other side of the reflection.** Doing this sets the angle of the reflection.

7. **Using the Scale tool, click once again on the base of the reflected copy to set the origin.**

8. **Click and drag up or down at the other side of the reflection.** This step sets how far away from the original object, the shadow falls.

9. **Color the shadow darker than its background.** The resulting shadow is shown in the illustrations in Figure 10-17.

Figure 10-17: A shadow created with the Transformation tools

To create a shadow for type, you must:

1. **First vertically scale a copy of the type.**

2. **Hold down the Option (Alt) key when you release the mouse button.** This makes the copy.

3. **Hold down the Shift key as you drag the mouse up or down.** This constrains the scaling to vertical. Setting the origin of the scale to the baseline of the type helps, as does using all caps or type with no descenders.

4. **Send the copy to the back by pressing ⌘+Shift+((Ctrl+Shift+().**

5. **Shear the shadow off to one side or the other, once again setting the origin at the baseline of the type.** Holding down Shift as you shear prevents the baseline of the copy from angling up or down.

If you want the shadow in front of the type to make it appear as if the light source is coming from behind the type, use the Reflect tool to flip the copy of the type across the baseline of the type.

Transforming gradients

You can transform gradients in the same way that you transform objects that are colored by gradients. All of the transformation tools affect gradients, but the best effects are achieved by scaling and shearing gradients, especially radial gradients, as shown in Figure 10-18. One of the best examples of why you want to do this is oval gradients. If you by chance need an oval shape rather than a perfect circle and want that oval to look three dimensional, you either have to use Blends or Gradient Mesh to get a nice look. Well, now you can use a gradient in a perfect circle and simply apply a transformation. Think of it this way; if you want to create that perfect olive, or M&M peanut, use this and save a lot of frustration and memory size as well.

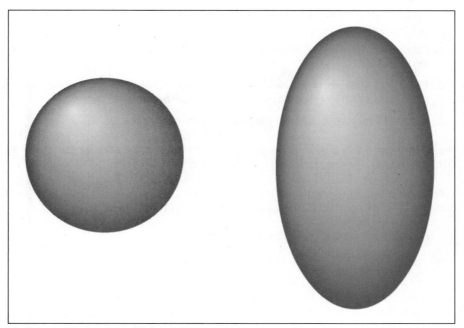

Figure 10-18: Transforming a radial gradient

Rotating into a path

Clever use of the Rotate tool can create a realistic, winding path by duplicating the same object at different rotational intervals, rotated from different origins. To create a path of objects using the Rotate tool, follow these steps.

1. **Start by creating an object of some sort.** (The illustration in Figure 10-19 uses paw prints.)

2. **Select the objects and choose the Rotate tool.** You may find it helpful to group the objects together first. Group the objects by first selecting the objects and then choose Object ➪ Group or Command (Control) + G.

For more on grouping objects, see Grouping Objects in Chapter 7.

3. **Click to set an origin to the side of the object.**

4. **Click the other side of the object and drag.** As you drag, you see the outline of the shape of the object that you are dragging.

5. **When the object is a good distance away, press the Option (Alt) key.** Doing this copies the object. Release the mouse button; then release the Option (Alt) key. A copy of the object appears.

6. **Press ⌘+D (Ctrl+D)** (Transform Again) to create another object the same distance away. Repeat this step a few times.

7. **Click with the Rotate tool on the other side of the object to set another origin.**

8. **Click and drag the outline of the object about the same distance; then press the Option (Alt) key and release the mouse button.**

9. **Use the Transform Again command a few more times.**

The farther you click from the objects to set the origin, the smaller the curve of the path of objects. Clicking right next to the objects causes them to turn sharply.

If you want a quicker way to put paw prints on a path, create the paw print and then use the Scatter Brush to apply the paw prints to a path.

For more on the Scatter Brush, see Chapter 3.

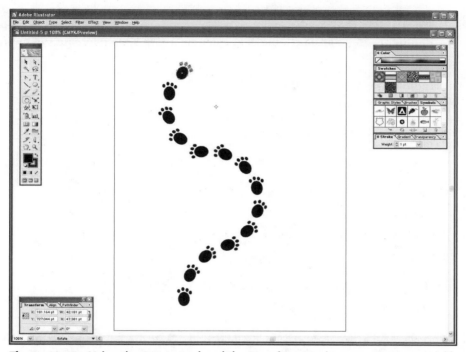

Figure 10-19: Using the Rotate tool and the Transform Again menu, you can quickly make a path of objects.

Making tiles using the Reflect tool

You can make symmetrical tiles with the Reflect tool. You can use a set of four differently positioned, yet identical, objects to create artwork with a floor-tile look. To do this, follow these steps.

1. **Create the path (or paths) that you will make into the symmetrical tile.**

2. **Group the artwork together by selecting the artwork first, then choose Object ⇨ Group or Command (Control) + G.**

3. **Take the Reflect tool and click off to the right of it to set the origin.**

4. **Click and drag on the left edge of the object and drag to the right while pressing the Shift and Option (Alt) keys.** Using the Shift key reflects the image at only 45° angles.

5. **When the object has been reflected to the right side, let go of the mouse button, still pressing the Option (Alt) key. Release the Option (Alt) key.** You now have two versions of the object.

6. **Select the original and reflected object and reflect again and also across the bottom of the objects.** You now have four objects, each mirrored a little differently, that make up a tile. You can now use this tile to create symmetrical patterns.

The resulting tile pattern is shown in Figure 10-20.

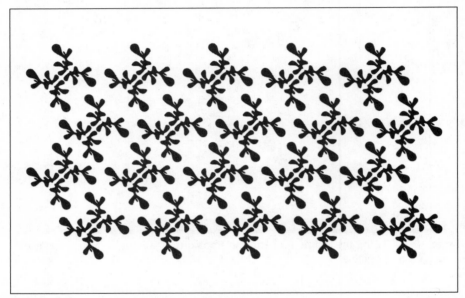

Figure 10-20: Creating tiles with the Reflect tool

Using Transformation tools on portions of paths

When using the Transformation tools, you don't need to select an entire path. Instead, try experimenting with other effects by selecting single Anchor Points, line segments, and combinations of selected anchor points and segments. Another idea is to select portions of paths on different objects.

Tip   When you're working with portions of paths, one of the most useful Transformation tool procedures is to select a Smooth Point with the Direct Selection tool and then choose a Transformation tool.

You can achieve precise control with the Rotate tool. Click the center of the anchor point and drag around the anchor point. Both Control Handles move, but the distance from the control handles to the anchor point remains the same. This task is very difficult to perform with just the Direct Selection tool, which you can also use to accomplish the same task.

You can accomplish the exact lengthening of control handle lines by using the Scale tool. Click the anchor point to set the origin and then drag out from one of the control handles. Both control handles grow from the anchor point in equal proportions.

When working on a smooth point, you can use the Reflect tool to switch lengths and angles between the two control handles.

Here are some more portion-of-path transformation ideas:

✦ Select all the points in an open path except for the end points and use all the different Transformation tools on the selected areas.

✦ Select the bottom-most or top-most anchor point in text converted to outlines, and scale, rotate, and shear for interesting effects.

✦ Select two anchor points on a rectangle and scale and skew copies into a cube.

Transforming patterns

The option in all Transformation dialog boxes and the Move dialog box to apply transformations to patterns can produce some very interesting results, as shown in Figure 10-21.

Figure 10-21: A pattern that has been scaled up inside the text and rotated

One of the most interesting effects results from using patterns that have transparent Fills. Select an object that has a pattern Fill and double-click a Transformation tool. Enter a value, check the Pattern tiles box, uncheck the Objects box, and then click Copy. A new unchanged object overlaps the original object, but the pattern in the new object has changed. If desired, use the Transform Again command by pressing ⌘+D (Ctrl+D) to create additional copies with patterns that have been transformed even more.

Tip You can transform patterns "live" by pressing the tilde (~) key while dragging with any Transformation tool (including the Selection tool for moving).

Using Liquify Tools on Objects

Illustrator has another group of tools called the liquify tools, which includes the Warp tool, the Twirl tool, the Pucker tool, the Bloat tool, the Scallop tool, the Crystallize tool, and the Wrinkle tool. These tools are found housed with the Warp tool (finger smushing a line) in the toolbox. The Liquify tools give you free-form morphing abilities unlike any other.

All of these tools work with a brush interface. You can alter the brush options and the individual tool options by double-clicking on the active tool. Figure 10-22 shows the Warp tool dialog box. In all of the Liquify tools, you can always adjust the Global Brush Dimensions and even set it to use a pressure pen.

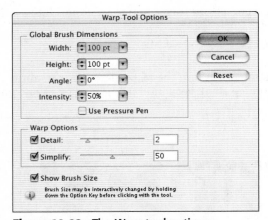

Figure 10-22: The Warp tool options

The Global Brush Dimensions section includes setting for the Width, Height, and Angle of the brush. The Intensity setting controls how hard you need to move against the path before a change shows up. Using the Warp Option settings, you can control the Detail and Simplify settings for each of the Liquify tools.

Tip   Change the brush size while applying the tools by holding down the Option key before clicking with the tool.

Warping

The Warp tool treats objects like play-doh. You stretch, drag, or pull areas of an object. Figure 10-23 shows the original object on the left and the warped one on the right. You can push out the shape by dragging outwards. Push dents in the object by dragging from the outside in.

Figure 10-23: The object before (left) and after (right) using the Warp tool

Twirling

The Twirl tool applies a spiraled effect to the object. Use this to swirl and ripple distortions on your artwork. Figure 10-24 shows the original object on the left and the swirled object on the right.

Figure 10-24: The object before (left) and after (right) using the Twirl tool

Puckering

The Pucker tool is similar to the Pucker effect. Using this tool in a brush fashion applies a pinched or pulled in look with spikes (see Figure 10-25).

Bloating

The Bloat tool, like the Pucker tool, is similar to its effect counterpart. Use this to bulge out or puff out in a brushed controlled fashion. Figure 10-26 shows the original object on the left and the bloated object on the right.

Scalloping

The Scallop tool is used to add arc shapes to your object. This tool randomly brushes the arc shapes along the area you brush over. Figure 10-27 shows the original object on the left and the scalloped object on the right.

Figure 10-25: The object before (left) and after (right) using the Pucker tool

Figure 10-26: The object before (left) and after (right) using the Bloat tool

Figure 10-27: The object before (left) and after (right) using the Scallop tool

Crystallizing

The Crystallize tool applies arcs and spikes by using a brush to the object. Click and drag outwards pushes the path out. Click and drag inward, and you push the path inward. The object does not have to be selected; simply drag the brush over-top the object you want to crystallize. Figure 10-28 shows an example of this tool.

Figure 10-28: The object before (left) and after (right) using the Crystallize tool

Wrinkling

The Wrinkle tool applies a roughened edge to your artwork, similar to the Roughen effect but applied in a brush fashion. Figure 10-29 shows the Wrinkling tool.

Figure 10-29: The object before (left) and after (right) using the Wrinkle tool

Distorting with Commands

I am calling this section distorting with commands because if you look under the Effect menu and the Filter menu, you'll find a two different Distort submenus under each. You may wonder if Adobe made an error in repeating itself, especially because both submenus include the same menu items. You can use either menu to apply the same commands. The difference is that Effects are live and editable and Filters are more permanent. Sure you can undo, but that might change what you have done afterwards. With Effects, you can go back in and edit or remove just the Effect without losing any of your other applied options.

 Cross-Reference   For more on Filters and Effects, see Chapter 12.

All Effects are the same look as Filters but fully editable via the Appearance palette. You'll find some filters and effects are exactly the same, except that using filters applies the effect permanently.

Using Free Distortions

The first of the Distortion effects is the Free Distort. This was discussed briefly with the Free Transformation tool earlier in this chapter. The big difference between the Free Transformation tool and the Free Distort command is that the Free Distort keeps the spacing relevant and doesn't use the perspective as the Free Transformation tool does.

The Free Distort command enables you to alter the shape of the selected object by dragging 4 corner points. Some may think of this as enveloping, but it is a much simpler effect. Figure 10-30 shows text that has the Free Distort command applied.

Using Pucker and Bloat

Although the Pucker and Bloat command undoubtedly has the coolest sounding name that Illustrator has to offer, this command also is one of the least practical. But Illustrator is a fun program, right? And these commands make it lots of fun.

Puckering makes objects appear to have pointy tips sticking out everywhere, and bloating creates lumps outside of objects. Puckering and bloating are inverses of each other; a negative pucker is a bloat, and a negative bloat is a pucker. If you are bewildered by these functions, stop reading right here. The following information spoils everything.

Figure 10-30: Free Distort effect applied on type

Selecting Pucker and Bloat opens the Pucker and Bloat dialog box (see Figure 10-31), where you may specify a percentage that you want the selected paths to be puckered or bloated by either typing in the amount or dragging a slider.

Pucker & Bloat		
Pucker	34 % Bloat	OK
		Cancel
		☐ Preview

Figure 10-31: The Pucker & Bloat dialog box

Bloating causes the segments between anchor points to expand outwards. The higher the percentage, the more bloated the selection. You can bloat from –200% to +200%. Using Bloat makes rounded, bubble-like extrusions appear on the surface of your object and using Pucker makes tall spikes appear on its path. When you drag toward Pucker, you can enter how much you want to pucker the drawing. Pucker amounts can range from –200% to +200%. The number of spikes is based on the number of anchor points in your drawing. Figure 10-32 shows text puckered (above) and the same text bloated (below).

Note Text is great to play with using these distortion commands because it is still fully editable. You don't have to create outlines first.

The Pucker and Bloat command moves anchor points in one direction and creates two independent direction points on either side of each anchor point. The direction points are moved in the opposite direction of the anchor points, and the direction of movement is always toward or away from the center of the object.

The distance moved is the only thing that you control when you use the Pucker and Bloat command. Entering a percentage moves the points that percentage.

Note Nothing about the Pucker and Bloat command is random. Everything about it is 100% controllable and, to some extent, predictable.

Figure 10-32: Original type (above), pucker applied to type (middle), and Bloat applied to type (below)

Roughening

Roughen adds anchor points and then moves them randomly by a percentage that you define.

Because the mangle commands work randomly, you get different results when you apply the same settings of the same command to two separate, identical objects. In fact, the results will probably never be duplicated. The Mangle command is a good reason for having the Undo command, so that you can apply the command, undo, and reapply until you achieve the desired effect.

Tip   Using the keyboard, you can continually reapply any command that works randomly and get different results. Select the object and apply the command by choosing the menu item and entering the values. If you don't like the result, press ⌘+Z (Ctrl+Z) to undo it. Press ⌘+E (Ctrl+E) to reapply the last filter and ⌘+Shift+E (Ctrl+Shift+E) reapply last effect.

One important limitation of the mangle commands is that they work on entire paths, even if only part of the path is selected. The best way to get around this limitation is to use the Scissors tool to cut the path into separate sections.

The Roughen command does two things at once. First, it adds anchor points until the selection has the number of points per inch that you defined. Second, it randomly moves all the points around, changing them into straight corner points or smooth points, whichever you specified.

Selecting Roughen opens the Roughen dialog box (see Figure 10-33), where you can enter information to roughen up the illustration — literally.

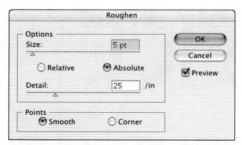

Figure 10-33: The Roughen dialog box

Three options are available:

- ✦ **Size:** How far points may move when roughed relative to the width or height (whichever is greater) of the selected path.

- ✦ **Detail:** How many points are moved. For example, if you have a 1-inch x 1-inch square, the number of points added is 36. Four inches at the top, bottom, left, and right at 10 points per inch equals 40 points. (Four points are on a rectangle, so you only need 36 more points.)

✦ **Smooth or Corner:** If you select Smooth, all the anchor points added will be smooth points. If you select Corner, all the points added will be straight corner points.

Roughen never takes away points when roughening a path.

Tip   You can use the Roughen command as a very hip version of the Add Anchor Points command. If the Size box is set at 0%, all added points are added along the existing path all at once. Instead of going to Add Anchor Points again and again, just try entering a value of 25 in the Segments/Inch field of the Roughen command. You have instant multiple Add Anchor Points. This technique is great for Tweak or anything else where you need a bunch of anchor points fast.

Tip   The Roughen command has a secret function that very few people know about: You can use it to add Anchor Points to paths. Simply enter 0% in the first text field, and the points that are added will not be moved at all. This method is especially useful as a substitute for Add Anchor Points when some of the paths in a compound path don't need as many additional anchor points as others. The Roughen command evens out the number of points for each of the paths in a compound path.

Transforming

You find the Transform command under the Distort & Transform submenu of the Effect menu. The Transform Effect is similar to the Transform palette except that you can go back in an edit as well as see the preview before applying. You also only have the Rotate option instead of Option and Shear.

Choosing Effect ⇨ Distort & Transform ⇨ Transform brings up the Transform Effect dialog box as shown in Figure 10-34. One really cool use of this is the copies box. Here you can enter a multiple number of copies as shown in this re-creation of the paper doll in Figure 10-35.

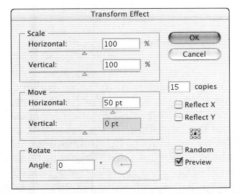

Figure 10-34: The Transform Effect dialog box

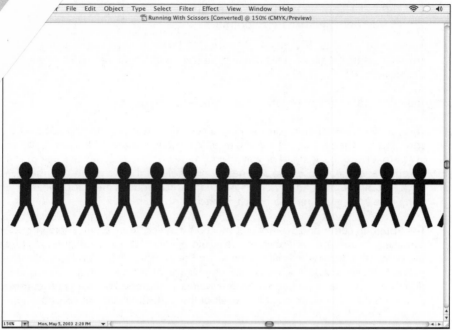

Figure 10-35: Paper dolls created using the Transform effect

Tweaking

One important thing needs to be made clear right away: The Tweak filter does one thing. Choosing Relative will apply the filter to the bounding box edges of the object. Choosing Absolute moves the points based on the absolute measurements that you enter.

Selecting Tweak displays the Tweak dialog box as shown in Figure 10-36. When the Relative option is selected, you define the amount of tweaking, including how much horizontal and vertical percentages and which points are moved (anchor points, in control points, or out control points).

Note No Anchor Points are added with the Tweak dialog box.

For Relative, horizontal and vertical percentages correspond to the movement of the selected points. If you enter 0% in either field, no movement occurs in that direction. Illustrator bases the percentage on the width or height of the shape—whichever is longer. If you check the Anchor Points option, all anchor points on the selected path move in a random distance corresponding to the amounts set in the Horizontal and Vertical text fields. If you check either In Control Points or Out Control Points, those points move the specified distance as well. The in control points are the points on one side of the anchor point. Out control points refers to the points on the other side of the anchor point.

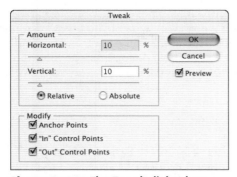

Figure 10-36: The Tweak dialog box

Selecting Tweak displays the Tweak options. Instead of specifying a distance based on percentage, the Tweak option lets you enter the distance in real measurements, such as picas or inches, in whatever unit your measurement system is currently using.

Tip   Consider using the Tweak option when you are not sure of the size of the selected artwork, or when you can determine only that you want points moved a certain portion of the whole, but cannot determine an absolute measurement.

Figure 10-37 shows an object that had the Tweak effect applied with the Relative option chosen (above) and the same values with the Absolute option chosen (below).

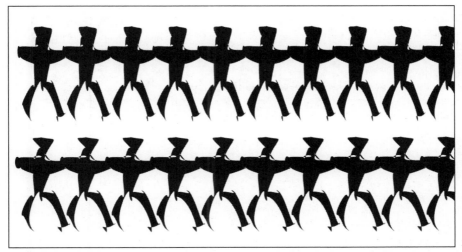

Figure 10-37: The top row was tweaked using the Relative option; the bottom row was tweaked using the Absolute option.

The percentages that you enter in the Scribble dialog box move points relative to the size of the bounding box. The bounding box is an invisible box that surrounds each object. If the bounding box is 5 inches wide and 2 inches tall, and you enter a percentage of 10% for width and height in the Scribble dialog box, the filter moves the points randomly up to 0.5 inches horizontally and 0.2 inches vertically in either direction.

Using the Twist command

The Twist command is found under the Filter ⇨ Distort ⇨ Twist or Effect ⇨ Distort &Transform ⇨ Twist. This cool command rotates or twists the selected object with more action being in the center of the object. Twist is the new name for Twirl in previous versions. In the Twist dialog box, shown in Figure 10-38, you set the amount of Twist.

You can twist paths and text (without converting to outlines), to create some really great effects. One of my favorite looks is to take a starburst of lines and twist them into a flower or spirographic shapes using the Twist and Tweak effects, as shown in Figure 10-39. The top left has no Twist applied and a 10-degree Twist is added to each consecutive one. A positive number twists the object clockwise; a negative number twists the object counterclockwise.

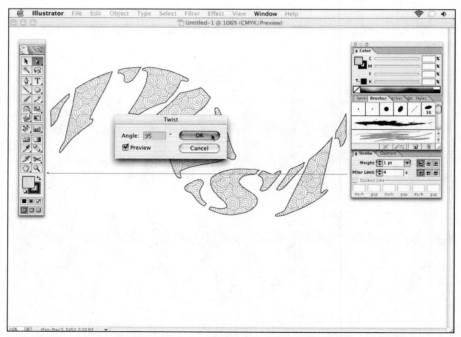

Figure 10-38: The Twist dialog box and objects twisted using the Twist command

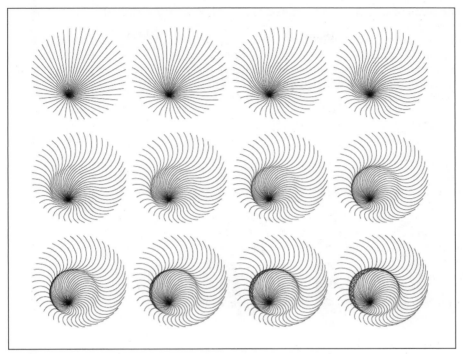

Figure 10-39: A range from 10-110 degree Twist added to this object

Working with the Zig Zag filter

The Zig Zag filter changes normally straight paths into zigzagged versions of those paths. When you first select Zig Zag, the Zig Zag dialog box appears, shown in Figure 10-40.

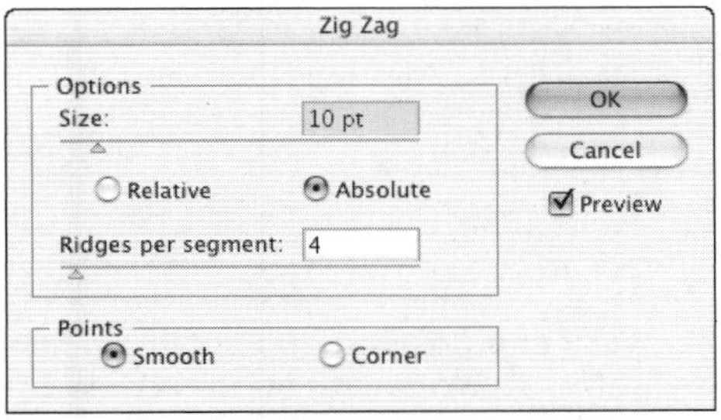

Figure 10-40: The Zig Zag dialog box

The dialog box enables you to specify various parameters of the zigzag effect, including the Amount, which is how large each zigzag is, and the number of Ridges, which is the number of zigzags. In addition, you can specify whether you want the zigzags to be curved (choose Smooth) or pointed (choose Corner). Like most of the other Illustrator filters, Zig Zag has a handy Preview checkbox. Figure 10-41 shows an example of zigzagged artwork.

Caution   Don't keep the Preview checkbox checked while you're changing values in the Zig Zag dialog box. Instead, change your settings first, and then click the Preview checkbox. This prevents massive slowdowns that can occur when the Preview checkbox is checked.

Figure 10-41: Art with Zig Zag applied to it

Using Warp Effects

Warp effects are also known as envelopes. Warp effects bend objects into a selected shape. Unlike Free Distort, you have many points to work with and a variety of preset options. Warp effects you can choose from a variety of predefined presets: Arc, Arc Lower, Arc Upper, Arch, Bulge, Shell Lower, Shell Upper, Flag, Wav, Fish, Rise, Fisheye, Inflate, Squeeze, and Twist.

You can find all these warp effects by choosing Effect ➪ Warp menu. Each of these predefined styles for Warp can also be altered into your own design in the Warp Options dialog box, as shown in Figure 10-42.

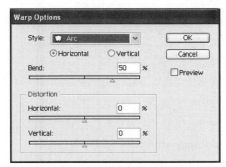

Figure 10-42: The Warp Options dialog box

In all of the preset options you have Warp Options to edit to your heart's desire. The options you can set are:

✦ **Style:** Pick from fifteen different predefined warps.

✦ **Horizontal or Vertical:** Edit this area to affect either the horizontal or vertical areas of the shape.

✦ **Bend:** Change how much of an affect is applied in percentage.

✦ **Distortion Horizontal:** This option enables you to increase or decrease the horizontal distortion in percentage.

✦ **Distortion Vertical:** This option enables you to increase or decrease the vertical distortion in percentage.

Understanding Warp types

There are 15 different Warp presets.

✦ **Arc:** Bends the shape top and bottom in an arc shape.

✦ **Arc Lower:** Bends just the lower half of the shape in an arc.

✦ **Arc Upper**: Bends just the upper half of the shape in an arc.

✦ **Arch:** Bends the upper, middle, and lower areas into an arch shape.

✦ **Bulge:** Pushes out the top and bottom of the shape.

✦ **Shell Lower:** Squeezes in the middle and bulges out the lower area of the shape.

✦ **Shell Upper:** Squeezes in the middle and bulges out the upper area of the shape.

✦ **Flag:** Pushes the shape on the top and bottom into an upper and lower curve.

✦ **Wave:** Pushes the shape on the top middle and bottom into an upper and lower curve.

✦ **Fish:** Squeezes the shape into a fish shape.

✦ **Rise:** Pushes the shape upwards from lower left to upper right.

✦ **Fisheye:** Bulges out just the center of the shape.

✦ **Inflate:** Bulges out the whole shape instead of just the center.

✦ **Squeeze:** Pushes in the left and right sides of the shape.

✦ **Twist:** Like the Twist effect, twists the object around a center.

Figure 10-43 shows one shape with all fifteen presets applied.

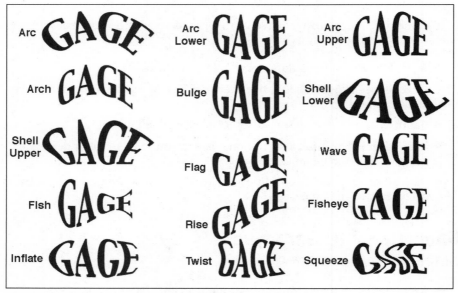

Figure 10-43: One shape, warped 15 different ways

Changing Warps

Take any one of the presets and make it your own by altering the Options as I did here in Figure 10-44. Choose any of the presets and check the Preview box to see how dragging the sliders affects your object.

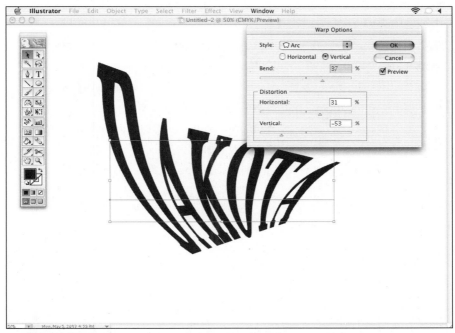

Figure 10-44: Create your own style by changing the preset options.

Summary

✦ You can transform an object multiple ways. You can use the transformation tools, the transform menu, the Transform palette, transform filters, or transform effects.

✦ Add awesome effects by using the Liquify tools in a brush-like fashion.

✦ The Distort filters work by moving points around selected paths.

✦ Pucker and Bloat create spiked and bubbled effects, respectively.

✦ Roughen can be used to intelligently add anchor points.

✦ Use either the Twist filter or with the Twirl tool to twist artwork.

✦ Twirling adds anchor points as needed when twirling.

✦ Tweak is used to move existing points and control handles randomly.

✦ Zig Zag creates even wavy or spiky paths.

✦ Warps push the object into a specific shape.

✦   ✦   ✦

Using Path Blends, Compound Paths, and Masks

Three of the more difficult areas of Illustrator to master
are masks, path blends, and compound paths. Of course,
these are also three of the more powerful functions in
Illustrator. You use a *mask* to hide portions of an image, or
mask them out. *Compound paths* consist of two or more separate paths that Illustrator treats as a single path. A *blend* is a
bunch of paths created from two original paths.

Understanding the Difference between Blends and Gradients

In Illustrator, a *blend* is a series of paths that Illustrator creates based on two other paths. The series of paths transforms
from the first path into the second path, changing Fill and
Stroke attributes as it moves. A *gradient* is a smooth blend of
colors between one or multiple objects. The big difference is
that the gradient shows up as a box rather than a series of
paths as in a blend. With a gradient, you use a palette to signify where the colors start and stop.

At first glance, blends and gradients seem to do the same
things but in different ways — so why have both? The Blend
tool, moreover, seems to be much harder to use than the
Gradient Vector tool. On the surface, it seems that you can do

more with gradients than with blends. Blends take a long time to redraw; gradients take a fraction of the time.

After all, if gradients are so much easier to use and produce so much better results, is it really necessary to have a Blend tool or a Blend function? Students, clients, and the occasional passerby have asked me this question quite often, and they seem to have a good point at first. Upon further study, however, it becomes apparent that blends are quite different from gradients, both in form and function.

You only use gradients as fills for paths. You can make gradients either linear or radial, meaning that color can change from side to side, top to bottom, or from an interior point to the outside. Every gradient can have as many distinct colors in it as you can create, limited only by RAM. Gradients are simply an easier way to create blends that change only in color, not in shape or size.

Cross-Reference   You can read about gradients in Chapter 6.

Blends, on the other hand, are series of transformed paths between two end paths. The paths between the end paths mutate from one end path into the other. All the attributes of the end paths change throughout the transformed paths, including shape, size, and all Paint Style attributes. The major benefit is that you can blend multiple colors at one time.

Blends can be incredibly flexible when it comes to creating photorealistic changes in color, if you plan ahead. Changes to blends aren't really changes at all; instead, they are deletions of the transformed objects and changes in the attributes of the end paths. If you know what you want, blending colors can take on an incredibly realistic look by changing the shapes of the blend's end paths just slightly.

But even more useful than creating realistic changes in color is blending's capability to transform shapes from one shape to another, as shown in the examples in Figure 11-1. With a bit of practice (and the information in this chapter), you can transform any illustration into another illustration. There is a limit to the complexity of the illustrations that you can transform, but the limit is due more to the time it takes to create the blends than to limitations inherent in Illustrator. Think of blends as morphing from one object into another.

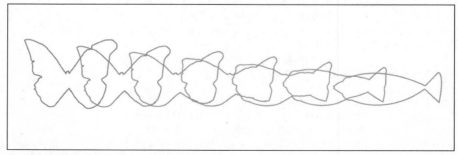

Figure 11-1: Blending to transform a shape

Because blends work on both Stroke and Fill attributes of objects, you can create some really exciting effects that aren't possible by using any other technique, electronic or traditional.

Creating Path Blends

In past versions of Illustrator, you used blends predominantly for what you use gradients for now: to blend between different colors, normally just two different colors. But some artists took it on themselves to stretch the capabilities of the Blend tool to create fantastic effects that amazed even the creators of the tool.

Originally, Adobe marketed the Blend tool (which was new to Illustrator 88) as a tool whose primary purpose was to transform shapes, not blend colors. Instead, designers used the tool for blending colors to create what were known as vignettes, or what traditional artists called gradients.

The Blend tool creates in-between steps in the area between two paths, where the paint style and shape of one path transform themselves into the paint style and shape of the second path.

Version 8 of Illustrator dramatically enhanced the Blending function. The big change is that blends are now live, or editable. This huge change enables users to change the color, shape, and location of the blend shapes. The blend instantly reblends to the new changes. Another great change is the capability to blend along a path.

Although any blend takes into account both color and shape, I treat color and shape separately in this chapter because people using the Blend tool are often trying to obtain either a color effect or a shape effect, rather than both at once.

You use the Blend tool to create blends, which are a group of paths (commonly referred to as blend steps) that change in shape and color as each intermediate path comes closer to the opposite end path. The following steps show how to create a blend.

1. **Using a shape tool, create a small (1-inch) vertical shape**. For more on creating shapes, see Chapter 4. This example uses a rectangle.

2. **With the Selection tool, press Option (Alt).** This copies the path a few inches to the side. Press Shift as you drag horizontally to constrain the movement of the path.

3. **On the left shape, change the fill and stroke to desired values.** This example uses a fill of Black and a stroke of None. For more on changing the fill and strokes on shapes, see Chapter 4.

4. **For the right rectangle, change the fill and stroke to desired values.** This example uses a fill of White and a stroke of None.

5. **Click the Blend tool by pressing the W key.** Click the top-left point of the left path and then the top-left point of the right path. This step tells Illustrator to blend between these two paths and it uses the top-left points as reference. The Blend tool cursor changes from x to + in the lower-right corner. Illustrator creates a spine between the two end paths (which are now transparent).

6. **Press ⌘-Shift-A (Ctrl+Shift+A).** This deselects all previously selected paths. The default Blend Option creates smooth color between the two shapes. The blend consists of 256 paths, including the two end paths. In the example, each path is a slightly different tint of black. Figure 11-2 shows the resulting blend.

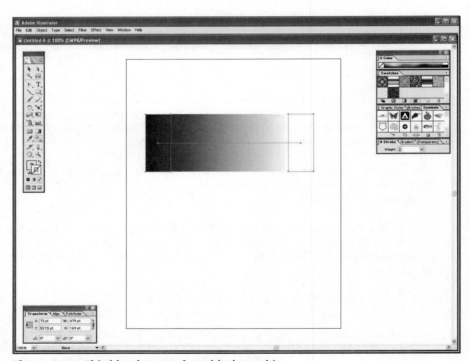

Figure 11-2: This blend moves from black to white.

Defining Linear Blends

You create color blends by making two end paths, usually identical in shape and size, giving each path different Paint Style attributes, and generating a series of steps between them with the Blend tool. The more end paths you create, the more colors you can create.

The following steps describe how to create a basic linear blend, and Figure 11-3 illustrates these steps.

Note   The examples in this chapter are easier to understand when you are working in Preview mode.

1. **Draw a curved path with the Pen tool, filling and stroking it as desired.** The examples gives the path a fill of None and a stroke of two points Black.

2. **Option(Alt) copy the path to the right, filling an stroking the copied path as desired.** The example gives the new path a stroke of two points White.

3. **With the Blend tool, click the path on the left and then the path on the right.** Alternately, you can select both objects and choose Object ⇨ Blend ⇨ Make. In Figure 11-3, the settings are on smooth color with a setting of one intermediate.

4. **Deselect all by pressing ⌘+Shift+A(Ctrl+Shift+A) to see the result.**

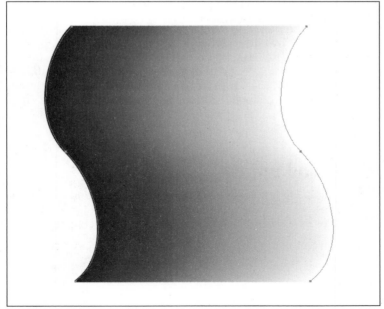

Figure 11-3: The final result is a linear blend.

You have a variety of ways to blend objects. Keep in mind a few suggestions when blending objects:

✦ You can edit blends by using the selection, rotate, or scale tools.

✦ You can perform blending with any number of objects, colors, opacities, and gradients.

✦ You cannot apply blending with mesh objects.

✦ You cannot edit the path (or *spine* as it is called) that the blend creates.

✦ The fill of the topmost object is used when blending patterns.

✦ When intermixing process and spot colors, the blend is colored with process colors.

✦ When blending with transparent objects, the topmost object's transparency is used.

✦ You can blend symbols.

✦ You can change the number of steps Illustrator uses in the Blend Options dialog box.

✦ Blends create a knockout with transparency groups. (If you don't want this, change it in the Transparency palette by unchecking the Knockout Group.)

Working with Blend Options

Adobe has enhanced the Blending functions of Illustrator by making the Blend tool easier to use, faster, and by adding a Blends submenu under the Object menu. The Blends options are Make, Release, Blend Options, Expand, Replace Spine, Reverse Spine, and Reverse Front to Back. With Illustrator's Live Blend capability, you may not need to release a blend to change it. You can use the Direct Selection tool to select the path and edit or change the color and the blend instantly updates. Live Blending is the capability to change the shape or color of a blend and update it automatically.

Using the Blend option

The Blend Options dialog box lets you change the Spacing and Orientation aspects. Select the blend you want to adjust and either double-click the Blend tool or choose Object ➪ Blend ➪ Blend Options to open the dialog box to change the settings.

Figure 11-4 shows the Blend Options dialog box. The three Spacing choices are Smooth Color, Specified Steps, and Specified Distance. The Orientation options are Align to Page and Align to Path.

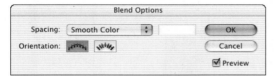

Figure 11-4: The Blend Options dialog box

The Blend Options are as follows:

✦ **Smooth Color:** This option automatically determines the best number of steps needed to make this blend look very smooth.

✦ **Specified Steps:** The Specified Step option lets you choose number of intermediate steps you want in the blend.

✦ **Specified Distance:** This option enables you to type in the distance between the steps.

✦ **Align to Page:** This option runs the blend vertically or horizontally depending on your page orientation.

✦ **Align to Path:** This option runs the blend perpendicular to the path.

Blending multiple objects

Illustrator has the capability to blend multiple objects in one step. Long gone are the days of blending, hiding, blending, hiding, and so on. Select all the objects you want to blend and choose Object ➪ Blend ➪ Make, or use the Blend tool to click all the objects you want to blend. Figure 11-5 shows a blend that uses four different shaped rectangles.

Editing a blended object

The Live Blend option lets you change the colors of a blend without having to redo the whole blend. With the Direct Selection tool select the path that you want to change the color of in the blended shape. Select a new Fill and/or Stroke color. The blend updates instantly with the new color.

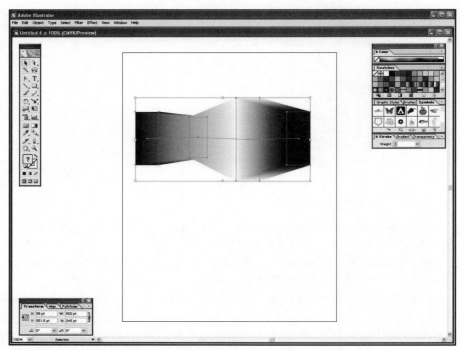

Figure 11-5: Blends can use multiple objects.

Another great aspect of Live Blends is the capability to edit the blend at any time and have it automatically update on the fly. As mentioned before, Illustrator creates a path, or spine when you create a blend. With the Direct Selection tool you can select an anchor point on the spine and move it. Doing this is easier if you are in Outline rather than Preview mode. This changes the location of that point and the blend updates accordingly.

Now you can edit lines by adding, deleting, or moving any part of your blend and it updates automatically. You can delete and add points or change the shape of a path with the Direct Selection tool. Figure 11-6 shows a figure before and after editing the blend.

Releasing a blend

If you want to redo a blend, you have to release it first. By choosing Object ➪ Blend ➪ Expand, the blend expands into a mess of shapes.

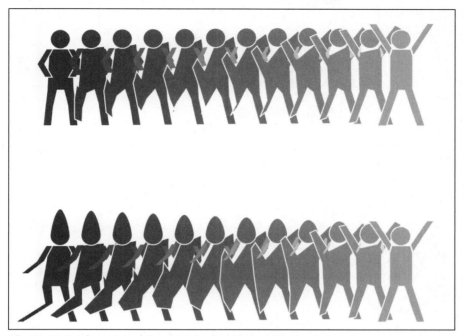

Figure 11-6: The original (top) and edited blend (bottom)

Replacing the spine

The Replace Spine option enables you to apply a blend to a selected path. Figure 11-7 shows the before and after of applying a blend to a path. To apply this effect:

1. **Select the stroked path and your blend and choose Replace Spine from the Blend submenu.** See Chapter 5 for more on selecting the path.

2. **Draw a path in the shape you want the spine of the blend to follow.**

3. **Select the blend with the spine you want to change and the path that you want to become the new spine.**

4. **Choose Object ➪ Blend ➪ Replace Spine.** The blend updates automatically.

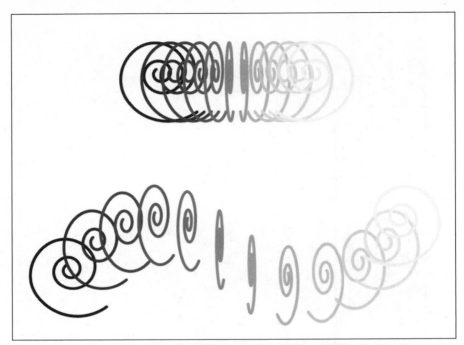

Figure 11-7: The original (top) and after applying Replace Spine (bottom)

Reversing the spine

This menu option reverses the sequence of the objects you are blending. If you have a rectangle on the right blended to a circle on the left, choosing Reverse Spine places the circle on the right and the rectangle on the left. Reversing the spine flips the position of the shapes on the spine, as shown in Figure 11-8.

Reversing front to back

The Reverse Front to Back option reverses the order in which your paths were drawn when you created your blend. If you drew a small circle and a large circle second, choosing Reverse Front to Back places the small circle underneath and the large circle on top (see Figure 11-9).

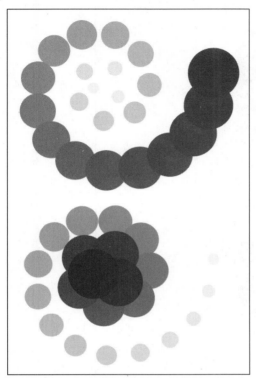

Figure 11-8: The original (top) and after applying Reversing Spine (bottom)

Expand

Choosing the Expand option lets you change any blend or gradient into filled shapes. You can then move or edit these shapes independently of the rest of the shapes.

Figure 11-9: The original (top) and after applying Reverse Front to Back (bottom)

Using nonlinear blends

You don't have to make end paths created with two end points that make up blends just horizontal or vertical. And when you create multiple color blends, you don't have to align the intermediate end paths the same way as you align the end paths. Careful setup of intermediate blends can create many interesting effects, such as circular and wavy appearances, all created with straight paths.

Note   End paths that cross usually produce undesirable effects; if carefully constructed, however, the resulting blends can be quite intriguing. Blending crossed end paths creates the appearance of a three-dimensional blend, where one of the end paths blends "up" into the other.

To create nonlinear blends, set up the end paths and either rotate them or change their orientation by using the Direct Selection tool on one of the end points. Then blend from one end path to the intermediate end paths and then to the other end path. Figure 11-10 shows an example of nonlinear blends.

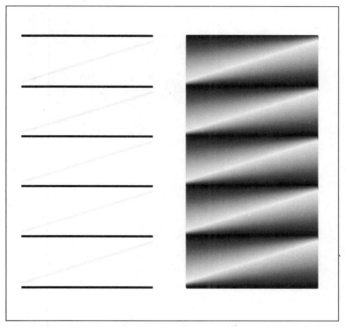

Figure 11-10: Using Blend to create a nonlinear blend. On the left are the lines before blending. On the right are the lines blended with the Blend tool (Smooth option).

Another good example of a nonlinear blend is to create a color wheel by aligning straight lines in a hexagon with differing colors and blending between them, as shown in Figure 11-11.

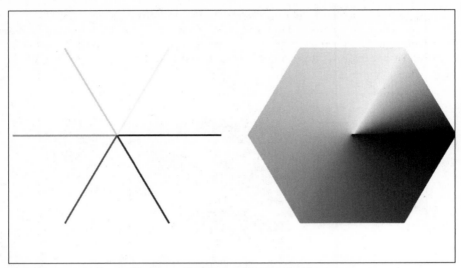

Figure 11-11: A linear blend applied in a perimeter fashion

Understanding pseudolinear blends

Very little difference is in the end product of straight-line linear blends and linear gradients. Both are very "computery" looking, but gradients are a little easier to manipulate. The important factor to remember about blends is that you don't have to make the end paths of linear blends straight lines.

If you use a smoothly curving line, the blend takes on a fluidity and life of its own, gently caressing the objects it is behind, next to, or masked by. The curves (especially if the end paths are masked off) are not always visible to the eye, and this creates an effect that is both realistic and surreal, giving depth to your illustration in a way that flat linear blends can't.

Instead of smoothly curving lines, try broken, jagged paths, which can add fierce highlights to a blend. Once again, this type of blend is even more effective when you mask off end paths. Figure 11-12 shows two examples of masked pseudolinear blends.

Figure 11-12: Masked pseudolinear blends

Finding end paths for linear blends

You can also use rectangles with fills and no strokes to achieve a linear blend effect. Figure 11-13 shows both lines and rectangles used for end paths.

Although you can use a rectangle as an end path, you should use a single line with two end points instead. In fact, lines are better than rectangles for three reasons. First, lines use half as much information as rectangles because there are two anchor points on a line while there are four on a rectangle. Second, the width of a line (Stroke weight) is much easier to change after you create the blend (just select the lines and enter a new weight in the Stroke palette) than it is to change the width of rectangles (you would have to use the Scale Each option). Third, creating a linear blend with lines (strokes) creates a thick mess of paths, but creating a linear blend with rectangles creates a thicker mess, so much so that it is difficult to select specific rectangles.

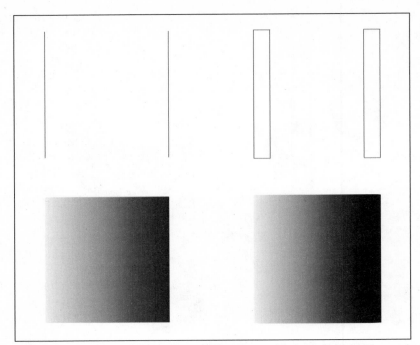

Figure 11-13: Lines (top) and rectangles (top right) in outline mode used to create the linear blends in preview mode (bottom left & right)

Tip   You can blend an open path with a closed path and vice versa with Illustrator. You can blend open or closed paths to any path by choosing Object ➪ Blend ➪ Make or using the Blend tool.

Calculating the number of steps

Whenever you create a blend, Illustrator provides a default value in the Specified Steps text field of the Blend Options dialog box that assumes that you want to print your illustration to an Imagesetter or other high-resolution device capable of printing all 256 levels of gray that PostScript allows.

The formula Illustrator uses is quite simple. It takes the largest change that any one color goes through from end path to end path and multiplies that percentage by 256. The formula looks like this:

```
256xlargest color change % = the number of steps you want to create
```

For example, using our linear blend example, the difference in tint values is 100% (100% – 0% = 100%). Multiply 100% by 256, and you get 256. Because the total number of grays must be 256 or fewer, Illustrator only creates 254. When you add this to the two ends, you have 256 tints.

In the second example, where the first line was changed to a 10% stroke, the difference in tint values is 10% (10% – 0% = 10%). 10% × 256 is 26, the number of steps Illustrator calculates.

In a process color example, if the first end path is 20% Cyan, 100% Magenta, and 40% Yellow, and the second end path is 60% Cyan, 50% Magenta, and 0% Yellow, the largest difference in any one color is Cyan (100% – 50% = 50%). The number of steps created is 128 or 50% × 256.

But, of course, not everything you create outputs on an Imagesetter. Your laser printer, for example, cannot print 256 grays unless you set the line screen extremely low. To determine how many grays your laser printer can produce, you must know both the dpi (dots-per-inch) and the line screen. In some software packages, you can specify the line screen, but unless the printer is a high-end model, it is usually difficult to specify or change the dpi. Use the following formula to find out how many grays your printer can produce:

```
(dpi/line screen) × (dpi/line screen) = number of grays
```

For a 300-dpi printer with a typical (for 300-dpi) line screen of 53, the formula looks like this:

```
(300/53) × (300/53) = 5.66 × 5.66 = 32
```

A 400-dpi printer at a line screen of 65 has the following formula:

```
(400/65) × (400/65) = 6.15 × 6.15 = 38
```

A 600-dpi printer at 75 lines per inch uses this formula:

```
(600/75) × (600/75) = 8 × 8 = 64
```

Sometimes you may want to reduce the number of blend steps in a blend from the default because either your printer can't display that many grays or the distance from one end path to another is extremely small (see the sidebar "Airbrushing and the Magic of Stroke Blends" later in this chapter).

When reducing the number of blends, start by dividing the default by two and then continue dividing by two until you have a number of steps with which you are comfortable. If you aren't sure how many steps you need, do a quick test of just that blend with different numbers of steps specified and print it out. If you are going to an Imagesetter, don't divide by two more than twice or banding can occur.

Creating radial blends

To create a radial blend, follow these steps:

1. **Make a shape about two inches in diameter.** See Chapter 4 for more on creating circles. Fill the circle. The example uses a fill of 100% Black.

2. **Make a smaller shape inside the larger shape and fill it as desired.** The example fills the smaller circle with White.

3. **Select both shapes and choose Object ⇨ Blend ⇨ Make.**

4. **To change the number of steps, choose Object ⇨ Blend ⇨ Blend Options.** When blending black to white, Illustrator automatically uses 255 steps. When blending other colors Illustrator automatically chooses the best amount.

You can create radial blends with almost any object. Figure 11-14 shows a radial blend using a star.

Caution   As with most other blends, when blending from two identically shaped end paths, always click the anchor point in the same position on each object. Figure 11-14 shows the difference between clicking the anchor points in the same position (top) and clicking on those that are not in the same position (bottom).

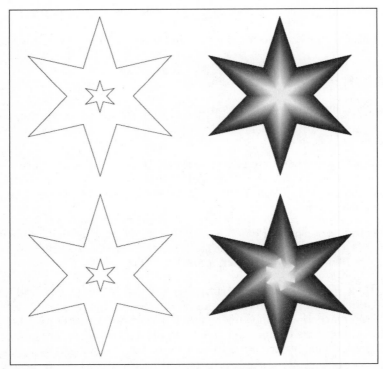

Figure 11-14: The top example was blended by choosing the same position points in the images and the bottom example was blended by choosing different position points in the images. The left side shows the image in Outline mode, and the right shows it in Preview mode.

One of the nice things about creating radial blends manually (not using the gradient feature) is that by changing the location and the size of the inner object, you can make the gradient look vastly different. The larger you make the inner object, the smaller the blended area becomes.

The Gradient feature enables you to change the highlight point on a radial Gradient without changing the source, or angle, of the highlight.

 Cross-Reference The Gradient Mesh tool enables you to create easy highlights with the click of a mouse. See Chapter 6 for more information on this tool.

Making a Color Blend

Using colors in a blend is really no different from using black and white, except for the spectacular results. The only difficulty in using colors in blends is whether the colors look good together.

Avoiding Banding

The graphic artist's worst nightmare: Smooth blends and gradations turn into large chunks of tints, and suddenly get darker or lighter instead of staying nice and smooth. *Banding*, as this nightmare is called, is an area of a blend where the difference from one tint to the next tint changes abruptly and displays a defining line showing the difference between the two tints. Individual tints appear as solid areas called bands.

Avoiding banding is easier when you know what causes it. Usually one of two factors in Illustrator is the cause: too few blend steps or too little variation in the colors of the end paths. Preventing banding due to any of these causes depends on the line screen setting and the capability of your printer to print it.

These causes pretty much make sense. Take the linear blend example earlier in this chapter. If you only have three intermediate steps between end paths, you will only have five colors in the blend, thus creating five bands. If you place each of the end paths on one side of a 17-inch span, each created blend step takes up the five points of width of the stroke, making each shade of gray five points wide. If you make the color on the left 10% Black instead of 100% Black, Illustrator only creates 26 color steps between the two end paths. So, to avoid banding, use the recommended number of steps over a short area with a great variation of color.

If you find it hard to fix the banding problem and your blend consists of process colors, try adding a small amount of an unused color (Black, for instance) to cover up the banding breaks. A 5% to 30% change over distances may provide just enough dots to hide those bands. Keeping this in mind, you have more of a chance for banding if you use the same tints for different process colors. Alter the tint values for one of the colors at one of the end paths just a little, and this alteration staggers the bands enough to remove them from sight.

See the "Calculating the number of steps" section earlier in this chapter for more information on banding.

Using multiple colors with linear blends

To create linear blends that have multiple colors, you must create intermediate end paths, one for each additional color within the blend.

1. **Create two end paths at the edges of where you want the entire blend to begin and end.** Don't worry about colors at this time.

2. **Select the two paths and choose Object ⇨ Blend ⇨ Make.** Alternatively, you can press ⌘+Option+B (Ctrl+Alt+B).

3. **Choose Object ⇨ Blend ⇨ Blend Options.** This opens the Blend Options dialog box.

4. **Choose the values you want for the blend.** Change the Smooth Options to Specified Steps. Choose your orientation and enter a number for the steps. (I entered 3 to create three evenly spaced paths between the two end paths.)

5. **Expand the newly created strokes by choosing Object ⇨ Blend ⇨ Expand.** Color each of the strokes of the paths differently, and then give them a desired weight. The example using a weight of 2 points.

6. **Select all of the paths and choose Object ⇨ Blend ⇨ Make.** Alternatively, you can press ⌘+Option+B (Ctrl+Alt+B). The result should look like the blend of colors in Figure 11-15.

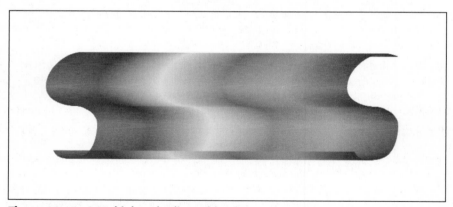

Figure 11-15: A Multiple color linear blend

Using guidelines for creating color linear blends

Although the preceding procedure should have gone smoothly with no problems, follow these guidelines when creating blends to get good results each time you print:

✦ **For linear blends, use either rectangles with only four anchor points or a basic 2-point path.** If you use a shape with any more anchor points or if you use a curved shape with any paths that aren't perfectly straight, you get extra information that isn't needed to create the blend, and printing takes much longer than usual.

✦ **When creating linear blends, use one rectangle per end path and color the fills of the paths, not the strokes.** Coloring the strokes may appear to work, but it usually results in a moiré pattern when you print. Make sure you set the stroke to None, regardless of what you have for the fill.

✦ **Don't change the number that appears in the Specified Steps text field in the Blend Options dialog box if you want smooth color.** Making the number higher creates additional paths that you can't print; making the number lower can result in banding when you print (see the "Avoiding Banding" sidebar, earlier in this chapter).

Creating Shape Blends

The difference between color blends and shape blends is in their emphasis. Color blends emphasize a color change; shape blends emphasize blending between different shapes.

You have a number of details to remember when creating the end paths that form a shape blend. You must make both paths either open or closed. If open, you can only click end points to blend between the two paths. If the shapes also change color, be sure to follow the guidelines in the earlier section related to color blends.

For the best results, both paths should have the same number of anchor points selected before blending, and you should have the selected points in a relatively similar location. Illustrator pairs up points on end paths and the segments between them so that when it creates the blend steps, the lines are in about the same position.

Complex-shape blending

Whenever a shape is complex (that is, it isn't a perfectly symmetrical shape, such as a circle or a star), you may have to perform a number of functions to create realistic and eye-pleasing effects. Figure 11-16 shows a complex-shape blend.

One function you can perform to improve the blend involves adding or removing anchor points from the end paths. Even if you select the same number of points and those points are in similar areas on each path, Illustrator may not give you an accept result. The Add Anchor Point and Delete Anchor Point tools become quite useful here. By adding points in strategic locations, you can often fool Illustrator into creating an accurate blend; otherwise, the blend steps can resemble a total disaster.

Figure 11-16: Complex shape blends

Tip   As a general rule, you disturb the composition of the graphic less if you add anchor points instead of remove them. On most paths, removing any anchor points changes the shape of the path dramatically.

Another method of getting the paths to blend more accurately involves shorten them by splitting a long, complex path into one or two smaller sections that aren't nearly as complex. You must blend each path, which you can do in one step by choosing Object ➪ Blends ➪ Make.

Creating realism with shape blends

To create a realistic effect with shape blends, the paths you use to create the blends need to resemble objects you see in life, which are generally curved rather than straight. Take a look around you and try to find a solid-colored object. Doesn't the color appear to change from one part of the object to another? Shadows and reflections are everywhere. Colors change gradually from light to dark, not in straight lines but in smooth, rounded curves.

Computer Vents

Look on the side of your monitor or on the side of a computer or hard drive case. You undoubtedly see vents or simulated vents used for design purposes running back along these items. This type of blend (changing the angle of straight lines) is the most basic of shape blends and is rather easy to create, so I add an extra tip at the end of this section to make these blends more realistic. The following steps describe the process for creating computer vents and figure below illustrates this process.

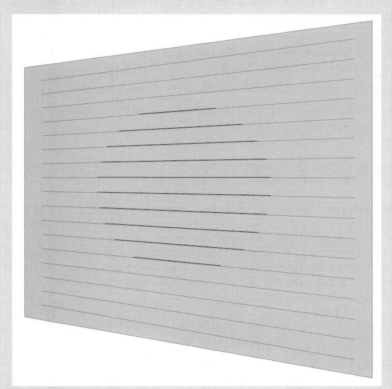

A computer vent blend

1. Using the Pen tool, draw a rectangular shape that you have distorted to appear like the side of your monitor. See Chapter 3 for more on drawing with the Pen tool.

2. Choose a fill and stroke for the rectangle. The example uses a fill of 25% Black and a stroke of 0.5-point, 50% Black.

3. Select the shape and double-click the Scale tool. This opens the Scale dialog box.

4. Enter 90% in the Uniform field of the Scale dialog box.

Continued

Continued

5. Click Copy, or press Option[Alt]-Return.

6. With the Direct Selection tool, select and delete the two vertical segments of the shape.

7. Select both of the horizontal segments and change the fill to None.

8. Blend the two paths together.

9. Choose Object ➪ Blend ➪ Blend Options to open the Blend Options dialog box. Change the Spacing to Specified Steps and the number to 15. One side of a monitor is now complete.

10. Select all the paths and copy them up 0.5-point by using the Copy button in the Move dialog box. Change the stroke to 75% gray.

11. Draw a circle over the center of the group and select the darker group and the circle.

12. Choose Object ➪ Masks ➪ Make. You now have a "real" vent in the simulated one.

You can use blends to simulate reflections and shadows. You usually create reflections with shape blends, and shadows with Stroke blends.

Figure 11-16 shows you how to simulate reflections with shape blends. This procedure is a little tricky for any artist because the environment determines a reflection. The artwork you create may be viewed in any number of environments, so the reflections have to compensate for these differences. Fortunately, unless you create a mirror angled directly at the viewer (impossible, even if you know who the viewer is in advance), you can get the person seeing the artwork to perceive reflection without really being aware of it.

The chrome-like type in the word DON'T in Figure 11-17 was created by masking shape blends designed to look like a reflective surface.

1. **Type the word or words you want to use for masking the reflective surface.** The typeface and the word itself have an impact on how an observer perceives the finished artwork. The example uses the word DON'T and the typeface Stencil. The examples also required a great deal of tracking and kerning to make all the letters touch so that the word look like one piece of material. In addition, the example uses baseline shift to move the apostrophe up several points.

2. **Choose Type ➪ Create Outlines or by pressing ⌘+Shift+O (Ctrl+Shift+O).** Choose a fill of White for the text and a stroke of Black. At this point, most of the serifs on the letters overlap.

3. **Select all the letters and choose Add to Shape Area from the Pathfinder palette.** This command gets rid of any unsightly seams between the letters. If desired, crreate a rectangle and place it behind the letters. This makes the letters of the word stand out.

4. **Using the Pencil tool, draw a horizontal line from left to right across the rectangle.** Option(Alt)-copy several of this pencil drawn path from the original down to the bottom of the rectangle. An easy way to copy the paths is to Option(Alt)-drag down just a bit and then choose Object ➪ Transform ➪ Transform Again or by pressing (⌘+D (Ctrl+D) several times. The example required the creation of five more paths.

5. **With the Direct Selection tool, randomly move around individual anchor points and direction points on each path, but try to avoid overlapping paths.** I left the third and fourth paths virtually identical and kept them close together so that there would be a swift change in color that brings out a "shine." Color the stroke of each path differently, going from dark to light to dark. In my example, I went from dark to light to dark to light and back to dark again.

6. **Blend the stroked paths together and mask them with the type outlines.** The mask you are creating is an opacity rather than a clipping mask.

Figure 11-17: Creating reflective surface type blend

In the preceding steps, you press Option(Alt) to copy the path not only because it makes things easier, but also to ensure that the end paths in the blends have the same points in the same locations. This technique is much more effective than adding or deleting points from a path.

Tip With slight transformations, you can use the same reflection blend for other objects in the same illustration and no one will be the wiser. A method that I often use is to reflect the original, scale it to 200%, and then use only a portion of the blend in the next mask.

Figure 11-18 shows how to use shape blends to create the glowing surface of a lit object, in this case a light bulb. The key to achieving this effect successfully is to draw the shape first and then use a copy of exactly the same path for the highlights. The relative locations of anchor points stay the same and the number of anchor points never changes.

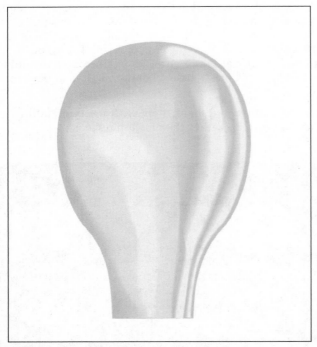

Figure 11-18: A light bulb created with blends

1. **Draw the shape you want to light.** Take your time and get it exactly the way you want it, because this path is the basis for everything else in this example. The example of the light bulb uses a fill of 30% Magenta, 80% Yellow, and a stroke of None.

2. **Option(Alt)-scale the object down just a little bit, setting the origin on the base of the bulb.** Option(Alt)-scale two more copies of the object. Use the Direct Selection tool to change the shape of the paths until they resemble the interior paths shown in Figure 11-18. These paths are the basis for blends within the illuminated object. Don't change the color of these paths.

3. **Option(Alt)-scale down three copies of the path on the left and shape them.** While your paths do not have to be exactly like the ones in the picture, be sure that each smaller path does not overlap the larger path. In the example, the color of the light bulb's paths from inside to outside is as follows: Color the

first (inside) path as 5% Magenta, 10% Yellow; the next path as 10% Magenta, 30% Yellow; and the last path as 15% Magenta, 40% Yellow. The outermost path should still be 30% Magenta, 80% Yellow.

4. **Option(Alt)-scale one copy of each of the other two outermost paths and reshape them.** In the example, the color the new paths is 5% Magenta and 10% Yellow.

5. **The paths should be in the correct top-to-bottom order, but if they are not, fix them.** To see if they are in the correct order, go to Preview mode. If the smaller paths are not visible, then send the outer paths to the back.

6. **Blend the paths together by selecting similar anchor point locations on each step.**

Blending symbols

The Blend tool can also blend symbols. Use the Symbol Sprayer tool to spray one symbol or drag the symbol from the palette. Select the symbols and blend them together. Not only can you blend like symbols, but different ones as well. Figure 11-19 shows a basic blend from a large flower symbol to a small flower symbol, and the spine was edited to an arch shape.

Cross-Reference   Chapter 4 covers the Symbol Sprayer.

In blending different symbols, the blend may be a bit distorted. Even expanding the symbol won't change the blend outcome. Figure 11-20 shows several sets of blends between different symbols.

Figure 11-19: A flower symbol sized large and small and blended

Figure 11-20: A blend between different symbols

Blending envelopes

Not only can you blend symbols, but you also can take a blend and stuff it in an envelope like shape with Warp effects. Simply select the blend and choose Effect ➪ Warp ➪ Arc and either press OK or choose another preset or create your own warp. Figure 11-21 shows three blends with three different Warp effects applied.

Cross-Reference　　Chapter 10 covers Warp effects.

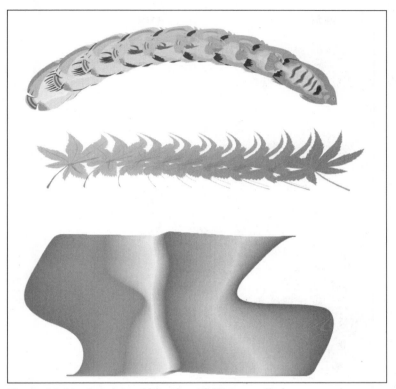

Figure 11-21: A variety of blends with Warp applied

Blending 3D objects

Another great use of blending is to blend 3D objects. You create a 3D object and then either create another one or duplicate and alter the original and choose ⌘+Option+B or by pressing Ctrl+Alt+B to blend the two together. To change anything, select one of the objects in the blend, and in the Appearance palette make your edits. Figure 11-22 shows a 3D star blended with another 3D star on a curved spine.

 For more on the Appearance palette, see Chapter 12.

 For more on 3D, see Chapter 13.

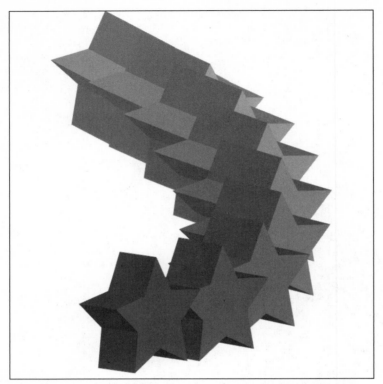

Figure 11-22: 3D stars blended together and still fully editable

Airbrushing and the Magic of Stroke Blends

Blending can create effects that are usually reserved for bitmap graphics software, such Adobe Photoshop, but without the limitation of pixels. Blending identical overlapping paths together and varying their Stroke weights and colors creates most of the effects described in this section. This technique can provide some of the best effects that Illustrator has to offer.

An important key to getting shape blends to look really good is to blend from the background color of the shape to the first blend, or to make that first blend the background color. That flows the blend smoothly into the background, so you can't tell exactly where the blend starts and stops.

Usually, the bottom-most stroke has a heavier weight than the topmost stroke, and as the color changes from bottom stroke to top stroke the colors appear to blend in from the outside.

Tip A really cool function to do with the 3D stars is to select all objects and the blend, and then go under the Layers palette and choose Release to Layers (Sequence), and then go under File and Export. Choose Macromedia Flash (swf), and then choose make AI Layers to SW Frames and this creates a File that you can open in your browser that becomes animated. It creates three files: an HTML file, a JPG file, and an SWF file. When you open the HTML file in your browser, it plays the SWF file using the JPG file.

Tubular blends

Creating tubular blends with the Blend tool is quite often easier than creating any other type of Stroke blend for one simple reason: The two paths, while identical, are not placed directly one over the other, but instead are offset just slightly, giving the tube a three-dimensional appearance. To create a tubular blend:

1. **Draw a path with the Pen tool.** Smooth curves work better than corners. The example changes the fill to None and the stroke to 50% Yellow, with a weight of 0.25 point. You can make the path may cross itself.

2. **Copy the path and Paste in Back by pressing ⌘+Option+Shift+V (Ctrl+Alt+Shift+V).** The example changes the stroke on the copy to 50% Yellow and 100% Black and a weight of 4 points.

3. **Blend the two paths together.** Create a Black rectangle and send it to the back. The result should look similar to the tube in Figure 11-23.

If you prefer the exactly-over-the-top method, you can simply omit the moving part in Step 2 of the previous procedure and blend the objects by using the Object ⇨ Blend ⇨ Make or by pressing ⌘+Option+B (Ctrl+Alt+B) command.

Note When you're creating Stroke blends, the number of steps usually doesn't need to exceed 100. If the default is more than 100, divide it by 2 (as explained in the earlier section, "Calculating the number of steps") until the number is less than 100.

In order to see the end points better on Stroke-blend end paths, draw a tiny marquee around one of the ends with the Zoom tool. If you still can't see the end points, switch to Outline mode while creating the blend. You can also choose Object ⇨ Blends ⇨ Make Command or by pressing ⌘+Option+B (Ctrl+Alt+B).

To create a Stroke blend that has more shine to it, make the stroke lighter and thinner and do not offset it as far as in the tubular blend example.

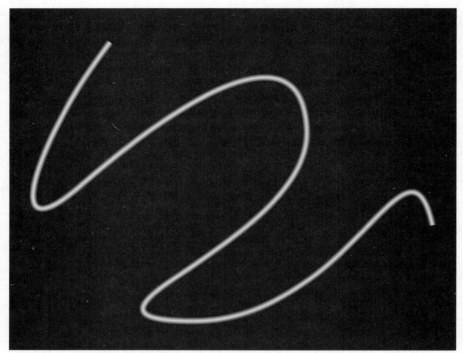

Figure 11-23: A tubular blend

To create a color Stroke blend that has more depth, make two end paths and color the bottom darker and wider and the top lighter and thinner. Then blend the paths together with one step between the end paths. Add a bit of Black (20% to 40%) to the bottom-most stroke and then blend from the bottom to the middle and from the middle to the top. The extra Black usually creates a much more realistic appearance of depth than using just two colors, and it keeps Black from being in the upper-half of the tube.

Caution   Try not to use White as your topmost path when creating tubes, because White looks bad and can also cause problems when you print. I like to use as low as 5% of the original color. The more subtle your color change, the more realistic your results. If necessary, you can always add highlights of much lighter colors after the stroke has been blended.

There are many shapes besides free-flowing tubes that benefit from the neon type of Stroke effect, including stars, spirals, and line drawings. Objects that appear in everyday life that can be created with tube-like Stroke blends include wires, rods, paper clips, hangers, antennas, pins, and needles.

Airbrushing shadows

To create a realistic shadow effect, the edges of an object must be a little fuzzy. The amount of fuzziness on the edges of the path is relative to the distance of the object from its shadow and the strength of the light source. These two areas also affect how dark the shadow is.

To make really cool shadows, you can use either Soft Mix from the Pathfinder palette, which can be used to darken areas, or the Color Adjust filter, which can be used to change the types of color in a selected area. The Drop Shadow filter creates hard-edged shadows, which are usually good only for creating text shadows quickly.

A second way to create cool shadows is to use Stroke blends. Stroke blends can allow the shadows to fade smoothly into the background with a Gaussian Blur-like effect. You can combine Stroke blends with the Soft Mix option from the Pathfinder palette for even better effects.

Cross-Reference For information on using the Soft Mix option from the Pathfinder palette to create shadows, see Chapter 6.

1. **Create a path (or copy it from an original object) for which you want to create a shadow.** At this point, you may want to hide the object from which you are creating the shadow so that it doesn't get in your way, especially if this object is right above where you want to place the shadow.

2. **Fill the shadowed path with the color you want the shadow to be and then make the stroke the same color, with a 0.5-point Stroke weight.**

3. **Copy the shadow, choose Edit ⇨ Paste in Back or press ⌘+Option+Shift+V (Ctrl+Alt+Shift+V).** Then change the Stroke color to whatever the background color is (usually White, unless something else is under the shadow). Make the Stroke weight twice the distance you want the shadow to fade out to. In my example, I made the stroke 12 points.

4. **Now blend these two paths.** Blending is easy with the Object ⇨ Blend ⇨ Make command or by pressing ⌘+Option+B (Ctrl+Alt+B). Watch for the cursor to change from an x to a +. The shadow slowly fades in from the background color to the shadow color. Show the hidden objects (you may have to bring them to the front), and your shadow effect has been created (see Figure 11-24).

Figure 11-24: Airbrushed shadows with linear blends

Creating glows

Glows are very similar to soft-edged shadows, but instead of a dark area fading into the background, a lighter area fades into the background. Using the light bulb from a previous figure, you can create a glow for that light bulb by using Stroke blending.

To create a glow behind an object:

1. **Select the edge of the object on which you want to create the glow.** In my example, I use the light bulb. Copy the edge, Paste in Back by pressing ⌘+Option+Shift+V (Ctrl+Alt+Shift+V), and press ⌘+ 2 (Ctrl+2) to lock everything that is not selected. Give the copied edge a stroke of 6% Magenta and 62% Yellow, and a Weight of 1 point.

2. **Draw a Black rectangle around the outside edge of the object and send it to the back.** Copy the edge of the light bulb and Paste in Back by pressing ⌘+Option+Shift+V (Ctrl+Alt+Shift+V) again. Change the stroke to 6% Magenta, 60% Yellow, and 100% Black and make the stroke about 40 points wide.

3. **Unlock the previous path by pressing ⌘+Option+2 (Ctrl+Alt+2).**

4. **Blend the two edge paths together to create the glow of the light bulb (see Figure 11-25).** The larger the Weight of the second copied path from Step 2, the bigger the glow.

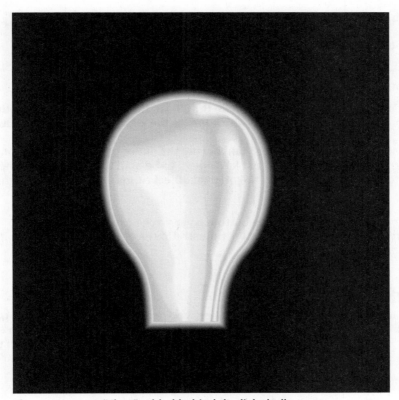

Figure 11-25: A "glow" added behind the light bulb

Note   When creating glows, make the initial glow area (around the edge of the object) lighter than the object edges if there are bright highlights in the object. Make the initial glow darker than the edges if the edges of the object are the brightest part of the object.

Softening edges

You can soften edges of objects in a manner very similar to that of creating shadows. The reason you soften edges is to remove the hard, computer-like edges from objects in your illustration. You can softening edges to an extreme measure so that the object appears out of focus, or just a tiny bit for an almost imperceptible change.

When determining how much of a distance you want to soften, look at the whole illustration, not just that one piece. Usually, the softening area is no more than one or two points (unless you are blurring the object).

To soften edges on an object:

1. **Select the object, copy it, and then hide the original object.**

2. **Choose Edit ⇨ Paste in Back or press ⌘+Option+Shift+V (Ctrl+Alt+Shift+V).**

3. **Make the stroke on the object 0.1 point, the same color as the fill.**

4. **Copy again, Paste in Back, make the stroke the color of the background, and make the Weight 2 points (which makes the softening edge 1-point thick).**

When softening objects, rather than moving the entire path in the background, try moving one anchor point out just far enough to be able to click it. Blend the two paths together and then show the original object (it may have to be brought to the front).

To blur an object, just make the bottom layer stroke extremely wide (12 to 20 points or more, depending on the size of the illustration) and blend as described in the preceding paragraphs.

Designing neon effects

To create neon effects with Stroke blends, you need to create two distinct parts. Part one is the neon tubing, which by itself is nice, but it doesn't really have a neon effect. The second part is the tubing's reflection off the background, which usually appears as a glowing area. These two separate blends give the illusion of lit neon.

Note Neon effects work much better when the background is very dark, though some interesting effects can be achieved with light backgrounds.

1. **To make the tubing, create a path to be the neon.** In Figure 11-26, I used two paths: a candle and a flame. Give the stroke of the paths a Weight of 8 and color them 100% Yellow. Make sure that the fill is set to None. Change the cap of the stroke to round and the join of the stroke to Round.

2. **Create a rectangle that is larger than the area of the path.** Send it to the back and set the fill to Black.

3. **Select the neon path, copy it, and choose Edit ⇨ Paste in Front or by pressing ⌘+Option+V (Ctrl+Alt+V).** Change the Weight of the copy to 0.5 point. Hold down the Shift key and change the color of the stroke by dragging the sliders to the left to make the color lighter. Do not make the copy White, but make it noticeably lighter than the neon color.

4. **Blend the two paths together ⌘+Option+B (Ctrl+Alt+B).** This is the neon tube part of the illustration. Hide this tube.

5. **To create the reflected area of the background, choose Edit ➪ Paste in Back or by pressing ⌘+Option+Shift+V (Ctrl+Alt+Shift+V).** This step pastes a copy of the original path behind the bottom part of the existing neon tube. Give the path a stroke of 8 and change the color to 100% Yellow and 75% Black.

6. **Copy the stroke and Paste in Back by pressing ⌘+Option+Shift+V (Ctrl+Alt+Shift+V) again, changing the color of the stroke to the same as the background and then making the weight of the stroke 20 points.**

7. **Choose Object ➪ Show All or press ⌘+Option+3 (Ctrl+Alt+3).** Your result should now look similar to Figure 11-26.

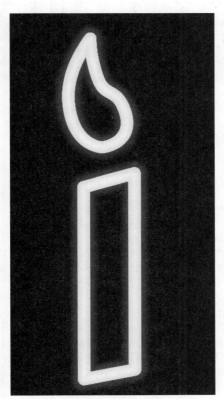

Figure 11-26: Neon candle

Tip

Try crossing paths with neon, or, for an even more realistic look, create "unlit" portions of neon by using darker shading with no reflective glow.

Backlighting

You can accomplish backlighting effects by creating a glow for an object and then placing that same object on top of the glow. By making the topmost object filled with Black or another dark color, a backlit effect is produced, as shown in Figure 11-27.

Figure 11-27: Backlighting on text

Using Compound Paths

Compound paths are one of the least understood areas of Illustrator, but after you understand a few simple guidelines and rules, manipulating and using them correctly is simple.

Compound paths are paths made up of two or more open or closed paths. Where the paths cross with fills is a transparent hole. You can specify which paths create the holes by changing the direction of the paths via the Reverse option in the Attributes palette. The general rule is that paths traveling in the opposite direction of any adjoining paths form holes.

Creating compound paths

You can create compound paths of all sorts by following the steps described here (which are also illustrated in Figure 11-28. Making sure that none of the paths are currently compound paths or grouped paths before creating a new compound path is a good idea.

1. **Create all the paths that you need for the compound path, including the outside path and the holes.**

2. **Select all the paths and choose Object ⇨ Compound Path ⇨ Make or press ⌘+8 (Ctrl+8).** Illustrator now treats the paths as one path. When you click one of the paths with the Selection tool, the other paths in the compound path are selected as well. Fill the object with any fill.

3. **Place the compound path over any other object.** (I used a placed EPS image for this example.) The inner paths act as holes that enable you to see the object underneath.

Figure 11-28: The window frame is a compound path with several holes in it.

You can select individual paths by clicking them once with the Group Selection tool. As always, you can select points and segments within each path by using the Direct Selection tool. Clicking only once with the Group Selection tool on paths that you want to select is important. Clicking those paths more than once with the Group Selection tool selects all the other paths in the compound path. To click (for moving or copying purposes) the selected individual paths after the Group Selection tool has clicked them once, click them with the Direct Selection tool.

Note Paths belonging to different groups cannot be made into a compound path unless all paths in all the groups are selected.

When you create a compound path, it takes on the Paint Style attributes of the bottom-most path of all the paths that were selected and have become part of that compound path. You can create a compound path that is only one path, though there are few reasons to do so. If the singular compound path is selected as part of a larger compound path (with either the Direct Selection tool or Group Selection tool), the path directions may be altered. If you aren't sure whether an individual path is a compound path, check the Release option in the Object ⇨ Compound Path submenu. If the Release option is available, then it is a compound path, if not, then it isn't a compound path.

Blending Between Multiple-Path Compound Paths

You can blend between multiple-path compound paths.

1. Select the Blend tool and click from one compound shape to the other shape.

2. While the initial blend between the two objects is still selected, double-click the Blend tool in the Toolbox to open the Blend Options dialog box.

3. Select the Spacing pop-up menu and choose Specified Step and enter a number. Remember that the larger the number you enter, the smoother the blend.

4. Select Preview to see the results before you close the dialog box.

For really cool results, make sure the two objects are different colors. For smoothest blends make sure you don't have a stroke color applied to your shapes.

Compound paths do not work in a hierarchical process as groups do. If a path is part of a compound path, it is part of that compound path only. If a compound path becomes part of another compound path, the paths in the original compound path are compounded only with the new compound path.

Releasing compound paths

When you want to release a compound path, select the path and choose Object ➪ Compound Path ➪ Release or press ⌘+Option+8 (Ctrl+Alt+8). The path changes into regular paths.

If any of the paths appeared as holes, they are, instead, filled with the fill of the rest of the compound path. The results may be a little confusing because these holes then seem to blend right into the outer shape of the compound paths.

If the compound path that you are releasing contains other compound paths, they are released as well because Illustrator doesn't recognize compound paths that are within other compound paths.

Understanding holes

Holes for donuts, Life Savers, and rings are quite simple to create. Just select two circles, one smaller than, and totally within, a larger circle, and choose Compound Path ➪ Make or press ⌘+8 (Ctrl+8). The inside circle is then a hole (see Figure 11-29).

A compound path considers every path within it to lie along the borders of the compound path. Path edges within an object appear to you to be on the inside of an object, but they appear to Illustrator to be just another edge of the path.

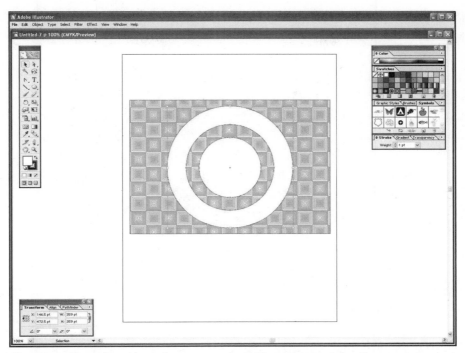

Figure 11-29: Holes appear for every path within a compound path.

With this concept in mind, you can create a compound path that has several holes, such as a slice of Swiss cheese or a snowflake. Just create the outermost paths and the paths that you want to make holes, select all the paths and then select Object ⇨ Compound Path ⇨ Make.

Tip   You aren't limited to one set of holes. You can create a compound path with a hole that has an object inside it with a hole. In that hole can be an object with a hole, and so on.

Overlapping holes

Holes, if they really are paths that are supposed to be empty areas of an object, should not overlap. If anything, you can combine multiple holes that are overlapping into one larger hole, possibly by using Add to Shape Area in the Pathfinder palette.

If holes within a compound path do overlap, the result is a solid area with the same Fill color as the rest of the object. If multiple holes overlap, the results can be quite unusual, as shown in Figure 11-30. (See "Reversing path directions," later in this chapter, to read more about multiple overlapping holes.)

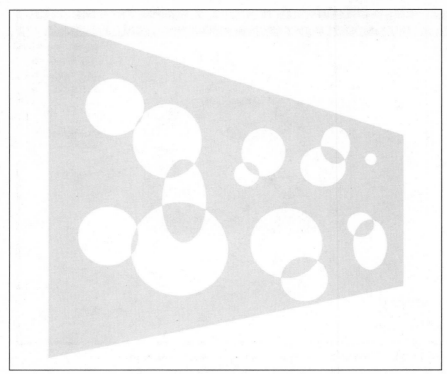

Figure 11-30: Overlapping holes in compound paths in Outline (left) and Preview (right) modes

Note

In most cases, you get the desired results with holes only if the outermost path contains all the holes. As a rule, Illustrator uses the topmost objects to "poke" holes out of the bottom-most objects. If you want holes to overlap, make sure that the holes are above the outside border.

Creating compound paths from separate sets of paths

Compound paths are very flexible. You can choose two sets of paths, each with an outline and a hole, and make them into one compound path. This technique is especially useful for making masks, but you also can use it to alleviate the repetition of creating several compound paths and selecting one of them at a time.

For example, if you have two shapes, a square and a circle, and want a round hole in each of them, you draw two smaller circles and put them into place. After you position the two shapes in the correct locations, you select them and the round paths inside each of them, and then you choose Object ➪ Compound Path ➪ Make or press ⌘+8 (Ctrl+8). Each of the objects now has a hole and they act as if they are grouped (see Figure 11-31).

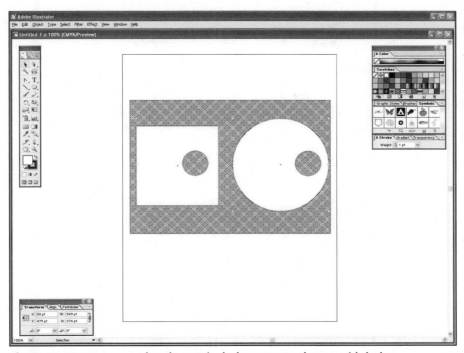

Figure 11-31: Compound paths can include separate shapes with holes.

To move separate objects that are part of the same compound path, select each object with the Group Selection tool, which selects an entire path at a time, and then move them. Remember that after they're selected, you should use the Direct Selection tool to move the selected portions of a compound path.

Working with type and compound paths

You have been using compound paths as long as you have been using computer PostScript typefaces. All PostScript typefaces are made of characters that are compound paths. Letters that have holes, such as uppercase B, D, and P and lowercase a, b, and d, benefit from being compound paths. When you place them in front of other objects, you can see through the empty areas to objects behind them that are visible in those holes.

Each character in a PostScript typeface is a compound path. When you convert characters to editable outlines in Illustrator, each character is still a compound path. If you release the compound paths, the characters with empty areas appear to fill with the same color as the rest of the character, as shown in Figure 11-32, because the holes are no longer knocked out of the letters.

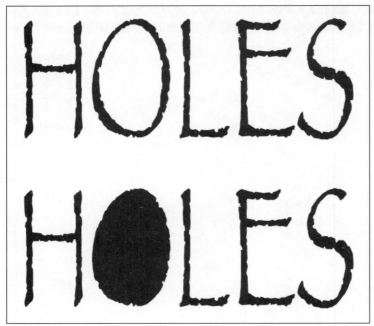

Figure 11-32: Type as it normally appears after you convert it to outlines (top) and after you release compound paths (bottom)

Note   Many times, type is used as a mask, but all the letters used in the mask need to be one compound path. Simply select all the letters and choose Object ➪ Compound Path ➪ Make or press ⌘+8 (Ctrl+8). This action creates a compound path in which all of the letters form the compound path. Usually, all the holes stay the same as they were as separate compound paths.

Any letters that overlap in a word that you make into a compound path can change path directions and thus affect the "emptiness" of some paths. If letters have to overlap, use the Pathfinder Unite feature on them first and then select all the letters and choose Object ➪ Compound Path ➪ Make or by pressing ⌘+8 (Ctrl+8).

Finding Path Directions

Each path in Illustrator has a direction. For paths that you draw with the Pen or Pencil tool, the direction of the path is the direction in which you draw the path. When Illustrator creates an ellipse or a rectangle, the direction of the path is counterclockwise.

Tip

If you're curious about which way a path travels, click any spot of the path with the Scissors tool and then choose Filter ⇨ Stylize ⇨ Add Arrowheads under the first submenu for Stylize. In the Add Arrowheads dialog box, make sure that the End button area only is selected and click OK. An arrowhead appears, going in the direction of the path. (Figure 11-33 shows several paths and arrowheads appearing for each path.) If the path is filled and not stroked, you see only half the arrowhead in Preview mode. Choose the Undo command twice (once for the arrowhead and once for the path splitting) to go back to where you started. You can also check (and reverse) the path direction in the Attributes palette.

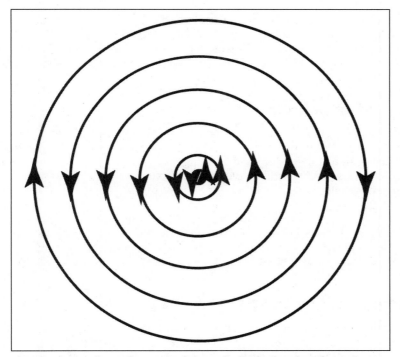

Figure 11-33: The paths on the left are individual paths. The paths on the right make up a compound path. The arrow represents the direction of the paths.

Paths have directions for one purpose (one purpose that you need to know about, anyway), and that is to determine what the solid areas of a compound path and the empty areas become. The individual paths in a compound path that create holes from solid paths go in opposite directions.

1. **Create a large circle and put a smaller circle within it.** Both circles are traveling counterclockwise.

2. **Select both of them and choose Object ➪ Compound Path ➪ Make or by pressing ⌘+8 (Ctrl+8).**

3. **The outside circle changes its direction to clockwise so that the two circles can work together to form a doughnut-like shape.**

If two smaller circles are inside a larger circle, they still punch holes in the larger circle because both of them are traveling in the same direction. But what happens when the two inside circles overlap? The area where they overlap is inside the empty area, but both holes go in the same direction. The intersection of the two holes is solid because of the winding path rule.

If you're curious about which way a path travels, click any spot of the path with the Scissors tool and then choose Filter ➪ Stylize ➪ Add Arrowheads under the first submenu for Stylize. In the Add Arrowheads dialog box, make sure that the End button area only is selected and click OK. An arrowhead appears, going in the direction of the path.

Figuring out which way to go

Understanding the Winding Numbers Rule is helpful when you are dealing with compound paths. The Winding Numbers Rule counts surrounded areas, starting with 0 (outside the outermost edge) and working its way in. Any area with an odd number is filled, and any area with an even number (such as 0, the outside of the path) is empty, or a hole.

You can apply this rule to most compound paths — although taking the time to diagram the paths you've drawn and place little numbers in them to figure out what is going to be filled and what isn't is usually more time-consuming than doing it wrong, undoing it, and doing it right.

Reversing path directions

To change the direction of a path, select just the path using the Group Selection tool and choose Window ➪ Attributes (F11). In the Attributes palette box (see Figure 11-34), click the other (not darkened) direction button.

When you change paths into compound paths, their direction may change. The strange thing about this is that the Reverse Path Direction button is usually on for objects that are traveling counterclockwise. The outermost path does not change direction from counterclockwise to clockwise until you make more than one overlapping path into a compound path. The paths that make up the holes don't change direction. They're still counterclockwise, but when you look at their Attributes, Reverse Path Direction is on.

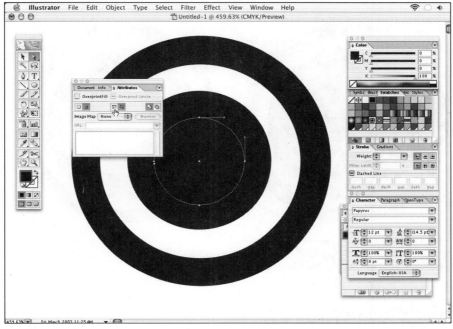

Figure 11-34: The Attributes palette

One element that is consistent when dealing with path directions is that holes must travel in the opposite direction from the outside path. As a result, if the Reverse Path Direction button is on for the holes, it is not on for the outside path. That scenario is the normal one when you create compound paths with holes. You can, if you so desire, check the Reverse Path Direction button for the outside path and uncheck it for the inside paths. The resulting image has the same holes as produced by the reverse. Figure 11-35 shows a compound path and its path directions before and after four of the paths were reversed.

Caution   Never attempt to change path direction when all paths of a compound path are selected. Clicking once on either button makes all the paths in the compound path go in the same direction at this point, which means that no holes appear.

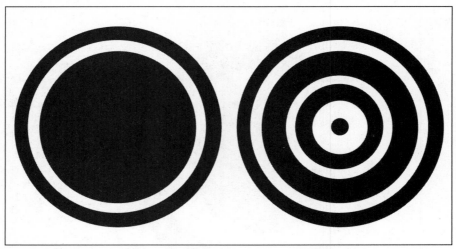

Figure 11-35: Reversing the direction of the paths in the illustration on the left fills those holes, as shown in the illustration on the right.

Faking a compound path

At times, using a compound path just doesn't work. You may need to cheat a little. Except in the most extreme circumstances, you can fake compound paths, but you need to make quite an effort.

If the background is part of a gradient, select the hole and the object that is painted with the gradient, apply the gradient, and use the Gradient tool to make the gradient spread across both objects in exactly the same way. This trick can fool even the experts.

Tip   One way to fake a compound path is by selecting the background, making a copy of it, making the hole a mask of the background area, and grouping the mask to the copy of the background.

Using Clipping Masks

In Illustrator, you use clipping masks to mask out parts of underlying objects that you don't want to see. The path that you draw in Illustrator defines the shape of the mask. Anything outside the mask is hidden from view in Preview mode and does not print.

Clipping Masks are objects that mask out everything but the paths made up by the mask (see Figure 11-36). Clipping Masks can be open, closed, or compound paths. The masking object is the object whose paths make up the mask, and this object must be in front of all the objects that are being masked.

Figure 11-36: An object, its mask, and the resulting masked object

You can make clipping masks from any path, including compound paths and text. You can use masks to view portions of multiple objects, individual objects, and placed images.

Creating masks

To create a mask, the masking object (the path that is in the shape of the mask) has to be in front of the objects that you want it to mask. You select the masking object and the objects that you want to mask. Then you choose Object ➪ Clipping Mask ➪ Make or press ⌘+7 (Ctrl+7). In Preview mode, any areas of the objects that were outside the mask vanish, but the parts of the objects that are inside the mask remain the same. Figure 11-37 shows an illustration with masks and without them.

Figure 11-37: The image on the left uses masks to hide portions of objects. The image on the right is the result of releasing those masks.

Colorizing 1-bit TIFF Images

You can color one-bit TIFF images (black and white only) in Illustrator. This effectively turns the black pixels into the color you specify. You can create an unlimited number of colors in a 1-bit image by creating additional copies and applying different masks to each one. Colorizing the 1-bit image gives you a sepia-type look. Great for logos that only want to pay to print in one color or to add an old fashioned look to an illustration.

Cross-Reference   For more on importing images, see Chapter 2.

The following steps describe how to color portions of a 1-bit image and the figure below illustrates the final product.

1. Select the imported 1-bit TIFF image and change the Fill color in the Color palette. This changes the image's color.

2. Copy the image with the Edit ⇨ Copy command and use the paint tool to paint the copy with a different color.

3. With the Rectangle tool, create a rectangle that partially covers the copied image. Then select the rectangle and the copied image and choose the Object ⇨ Clipping Mask ⇨ Make command.

4. Realign the copied image or mask with the original image.

The colorized 1-bit TIFF image

Tip   Masks are much easier to use and understand in Preview mode than in Outline mode.

If you want to mask an object that is not currently being masked, you need to select the new object and all the objects in the mask, including the masking object. You then choose Object ➪ Clipping Mask ➪ Make or press ⌘+7 (Ctrl+7). The mask then applies to the new object as well as to the objects that were previously masked. The new object, like all others being masked, must be behind the masking object.

Like compound paths, masking does not work in hierarchical levels. Each time you add an object to a mask, the old mask that didn't have that object is released, and a new mask is made that contains all of the original mask objects as well as the new object. Releasing a mask affects every object in the mask, as described in "Releasing masks," later in this chapter.

Tip   Grouping all the objects in a mask is usually a good idea, but group them only after you have created the mask. Having the objects grouped facilitates moving the mask and its objects and selecting them when you want to add other objects to the mask.

Masking raster images

There are two different ways to mask raster images. You accomplish the first method in Photoshop by creating a clipping path and saving it as an EPS image. For the second method, you use a clipping mask in Illustrator.

Each of the two methods has its strengths and weaknesses. The best solution is a combination of both methods. The main advantage to creating a clipping path in Photoshop is that you can adjust the path while viewing the image clearly at 16:1. (Viewing an image at 1600% in Illustrator displays chunky, unrecognizable blocks of color.) In this manner, you can precisely position the path over the correct pixels so that the right pixels are selected for masking. The first disadvantage to using Photoshop's clipping path is that the Path tool and path-editing controls in Photoshop are a limited version of Illustrator's Pen tool and path-editing controls, which makes it more difficult to create and edit a path. The second disadvantage to using a clipping path is that compound paths in Photoshop adhere to one of two different fill rules, which control the way holes appear for differing path directions. Illustrator is much more flexible in this respect because you are able to change the path direction of each individual path with the Reverse Path Direction check box in the Attributes palette.

The best solution is to create the clipping path in Photoshop, and then, with you select the clipping path, choose File ➪ Export ➪ Paths to Illustrator, which saves an Illustrator-compatible file with the clipping path intact. Save the Photoshop image as an EPS file and place it in Illustrator (File ➪ Place). Then open the Illustrator file (that was created by Paths to Illustrator) and copy the path to the document with the raster image. The path sizes to fit directly onto the raster image.

Using mask with other masks

You can mask objects that are masking other objects. Just make sure that you select all the objects in each mask and that, as with other objects, they are behind the path that you want to use for a masking object.

Note   You can apply a stroke or fill to a masking object. A fill and stroke of None replace any Paint Style attributes that you applied to the object prior to transforming it into a mask. But if you select the object after it is a mask, you can apply a stroke or fill to that mask. If you release the mask, the path that was the masking object continues to have a fill and stroke of None.

Releasing masks

To release a mask, first select the masking object (you may select other objects as well). Then choose Object ➪ Clipping Mask ➪ Release or press ⌘+Option-7 (Ctrl+Alt+7), and the masking object no longer is a mask.

If you aren't sure which object is the masking object or if you are having trouble selecting the masking object, choose Select ➪ Select All, or press ⌘+A (Ctrl+A), and choose Object ➪ Clipping Mask ➪ Release, or press ⌘+Option+7 (Ctrl+Alt+7). Of course, this action releases any other masks that are in the document — unless they were separate masks that were being masked by other masks.

To release all the masks in the document, even those masks that are being masked by other masks, Select All or press ⌘+A (Ctrl+A) and choose Release Mask repeatedly. Usually three Release Masks gets everything, unless you went mask-happy in that particular document. You can also use the Select ➪ Clipping Masks option to check if there are any remaining masks. If the Release menu option is enabled, then a mask still remains.

Masking and printing

As a rule, PostScript printers don't care too much for masks. They care even less for masks that mask other masks. And they really don't like masks that are compound paths.

Unfortunately, because of the way that Illustrator works, every part of every object in a mask is sent to the printer, even if you only use a tiny piece of an object. In addition, controlling where the masking object slices objects requires a great deal of computing power and memory. You can have a problem, for example, when you have more stuff to mask than the printer can handle.

More important than any other issue involved with masks and printing is the length and complexity of the masking path.

The more objects in a mask, the more complex it is. More anchor points and direction points coming off those anchor points add more complexity to the document. In other words, your printer enjoys a mask if the masking object is a rectangle and you are not making other objects.

Masking and compound paths

Creating masks from compound paths is especially useful when you are working with text and want several separate letters to mask a placed EPS image or a series of pictures that you created in Illustrator.

The reason that you need to transform separate objects into compound paths is that a masking object can only be one path. The topmost object of the selected objects becomes the masking object, and the others become objects within the mask. Creating a compound path from several paths makes the masking feature treat all the objects as one path and makes a masking object out of the entire compound path.

You can use compound paths for masking when you are working with objects that need to have holes as well as when you are working with text and other separate objects. Figure 11-38 was created by making one compound path from all of the parts of the window frame and using that compound path as a mask.

Figure 11-38: Creating a compound path out of all the parts of the window frame made this window frame a clipping mask for the background.

Tip   Cropping has two serious advantages over masking. First, unnecessary paths are deleted, and second, potential printing problems that might occur when a mask is being used are eliminated.

Masking, however, enables you to edit the artwork in the future. You can change the shape, size, whatever, of the mask and the masked objects. And you can mask raster images and non-outlined text.

Designing a filmstrip

In the first set of steps (described here and illustrated in Figure 11-39), you create the strip of film and place the beach pictures into the film. You do not use masks in this process. I make this point so that you don't think that you always have to use masks, especially when another method is easier.

1. **To create the film shape, draw a long, horizontal rectangle with the Rectangle tool and distribute five equal-sized rounded-corner rectangles inside the long rectangle.**

2. **To create the sprocket holes in the film, place a right-side-up triangle next to an upside-down triangle and continue placing triangles until you have a row of triangles across the top of the film.**

3. **After you group all the triangles together, Option(Alt)-copy them (drag the triangles with the Option (Alt) key pressed, releasing the mouse button before releasing the Option (Alt) key) to create a second row of triangles along the bottom of the film.**

4. **Select all the pieces of the film and choose Object ➪ Compound Paths ➪ Make or press ⌘+8 (Ctrl+8).** Fill the compound path with a dark purple color that is not quite black.

5. **Place one image, size it so that it just covers the hole, and Option-copy it across the remaining holes.** Select each image in turn, choose File ➪ Place, and select a different image for each square. To complete the effect, simply bring the strip of film to the front.

6. **Before you place the film into the poster, group the images and the film and rotate them slightly.** Grouping them prevents the hassle of selecting each one later if you need to move or transform them.

Figure 11-39: This filmstrip technique is easy to create by using Compound Paths.

Summary

✦ Using blends rather than gradients can produce some pretty cool realistic results.

✦ With Blend options, you can change the blend to steps, distance, or smooth color.

✦ You can blend from 3D objects to Symbols and use different objects.

✦ Compound paths are one or more paths that Illustrator treats as a single path.

✦ Compound paths give you the ability to put holes in your paths.

✦ Changing the direction of a path via the Attributes palette can change the holes in the compound path.

✦ Each character of type converted to outlines consists of a compound path.

✦ Masks are paths that overlay other Illustrator objects, showing the objects only through the masking path.

✦ When using text outlines as a mask, make sure that all the paths that make up the text outlines are a single compound path.

✦   ✦   ✦

Mastering Illustrator

Working with Graphic Styles, Filters, and Effects

Probably some of the most amazing illustrations you see in Illustrator come from using graphic styles, filters, and effects. Graphic styles can increase your production with any type of repeating symbol or set of attributes you use daily. Set as a style, you can use it over and over again.

Filters and effects are similar when you look at their menus. Those of you looking to create special effects, look no further. In this chapter, you discover the difference between filters and effects as well as when to use them.

Along with filters and effects, you see a variety of artwork that uses filters, effects, and graphic styles all combined.

Understanding how Graphic Styles Work

Graphic styles have brought Illustrator to the front of the pack in illustrating software. Graphic styles give you the ability to save all attributes of an object in a palette. You can use the Graphic Styles palette to quickly add the attributes, such as transparency, effects, strokes and fills to another object. Creating a Style is pretty darn easy. Simply create the look you want on an object, and then with your object selected, choose New Style from the Graphic Styles palette pop-up menu. That is it! Now you can use that style anytime you'd like. Seems like a breeze, but before diving head first into the Graphic Styles palette, first check out appearances.

The Appearance palette houses all of the information about a selected object. The information includes the Stroke information, Fill information, any effects from the Effect menu, and Transparency information. In this Appearance palette you can continually edit, rearrange, and delete this style information.

 Note   You can't apply graphic styles to type unless you change the type to outlines.

Using the Appearance palette

You find the Appearance palette by choosing Window ➪ Appearance. Use the Appearance palette to check out what the object is made up of. The Appearance palette shows all strokes, fills, transparency, multiple fills, and any effects or transformations applied to that selected object. Figure 12-1 shows the Appearance palette.

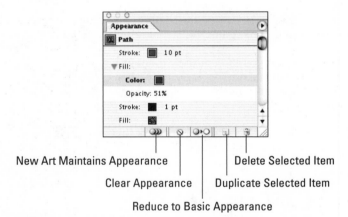

Figure 12-1: With an object selected, the Appearance palette displays the object's information.

The icons at the bottom of the Appearance palette from left to right are:

✦ New Art Maintains Appearance

✦ Clear Appearance

✦ Reduce to Basic Appearance

✦ Duplicate Selected Item

✦ Delete Selected Item

The palette area shows the sequential order of the items that make up the object. Each time you add to the object, it gets listed above the previous entry. With this stacking order, you can drag other information, such as stroke weight, above or below the other entries, creating a different look to the object.

The Appearance palette's pop-up (drop-down) menu (Figure 12-2) has a few options from which to choose. To access this menu, simply click the left-pointing arrow inside the circle located on the upper right of the palette. Under this menu, you can find the following: Add New Fill, Add New Stroke, Duplicate Item, Remove Item, Clear Appearances, Reduce to Basic Appearance, New Art Has Basic Appearance, Hide Thumbnails, and Redefine Graphic Style. Each of these items is discussed in detail later in this section.

Editing and adding strokes and fills

Editing an item is as easy as double-clicking. Double-click the item you want to edit, make your changes, and the object immediately updates to your edits. When you double-click an effect, it brings up the Effect dialog box for that particular effect. Double-clicking a transformation effect brings up the Transform dialog box (Figure 12-3).

The Appearance palette can also be used for editing. You can select a stroke or fill in the Appearance palette and do the edits in the Stroke or Fill palette.

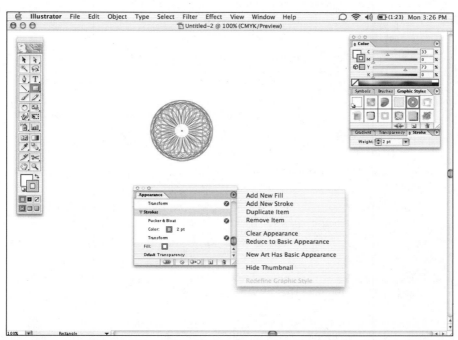

Figure 12-2: With an object selected, the Appearance palette displays the object's information.

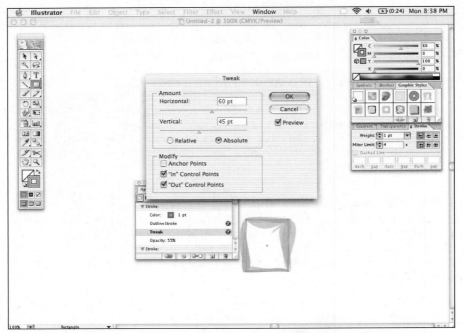

Figure 12-3: After you double-click an effect in the Appearance palette, you get the dialog box for that effect.

Cross-Reference

For more on using the Appearance palette, see Chapter 13.

To edit a stroke or a fill, click one time in the Appearance palette to select the stroke or fill and then change the color of the stroke or fill and the stroke weight.

To edit the stroke weight and color by using the Appearance palette:

1. **Select the Object first with the Selection tool.** See Chapter 5 for more on the selection tool.

2. **In the Appearance palette, select the stroke by clicking it one time.** You open the Appearance palette by choosing Window ➪ Appearance.

3. **In the color palette, choose a new color.** The color is automatically updated in the object.

4. **With the stroke still selected, change the stroke weight in the Stroke palette.** The weight of the stroke is instantly updated in the object.

Figure 12-4 shows an object in its original state and with the color and stroke weight changed. It is amazing to think just a few minor changes can give a totally different look to the object.

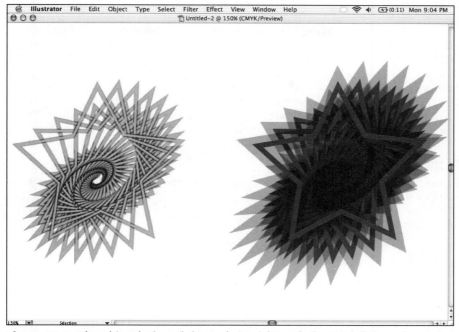

Figure 12-4: The object before (left) stroke weight and after (right) the color and stroke weight were edited

Duplicating and removing items

Under the Appearance pop-up menu is a menu item you can use to remove an item in the object's list. Click the item to select it and then choose Remove Item from the pop-up menu. The item is removed from the list and the object. Use this to edit a preset Style to make it the way you want. Another way to remove an item is to select it then click the trashcan icon at the bottom right of the Appearance palette.

You can also duplicate an object in the Appearance palette. Select the item you want to duplicate in the list in the Appearance palette and then choose Duplicate Item from the pop-up menu. This comes in handy when you want to use some of the item's attributes, but not all. Duplicate the item and then edit as you want.

Clearing an Appearance

Clearing an Appearance removes the effects as well as changes the stroke and fill to none. If there are multiple fills or strokes, all are removed to one stroke and one fill. You find this feature in the pop-up menu and in the icons at the bottom of the Appearance palette.

Reducing to Basic Appearance

Choosing Reduce to Basic Appearance from the Appearance palette pop-up menu removes all but one stroke and fill and all of the effects. The remaining stroke and fill are assigned the default attributes (the bottom most stroke and fill color and the stroke weight of the bottom most stroke). If you didn't use a stroke, Illustrator reduces the object to the original fill color only. Similarly, if you didn't use a fill, Illustrator reduces the object to the original stroke color and weight. Figure 12-5 shows the object before applying Reduce to Basic Appearance and after. The end result looks a bit bland from the original.

Setting New Art preferences

If you check the New Art Has Basic Appearance check box, all art created afterwards will have a basic appearance of a white fill and a black stroke. If you do not check the box (Figure 12-6), all art created after using a style will have the appearance of the last used style.

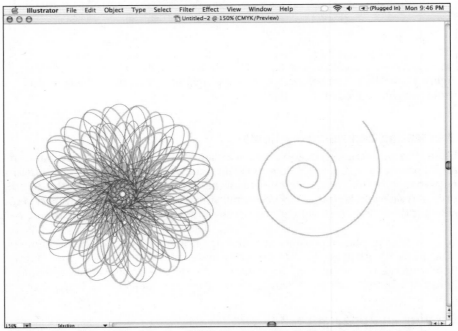

Figure 12-5: The object on the left has all of its graphic styles and attributes. The object on the right has been reduced to a basic appearance.

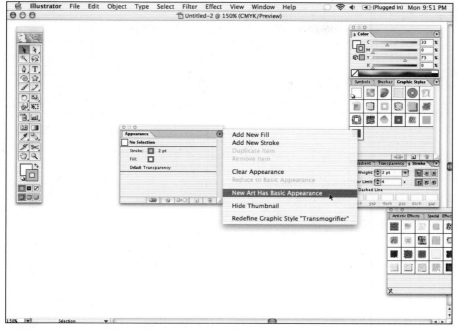

Figure 12-6: If the New Art Has Basic Appearance is not checked, all new art will have the same attributes of the last style used.

Viewing thumbnails

In the Appearance palette, you have the option to view a small thumbnail of the selected object's style. The Thumbnail appears in the upper left of the Appearance palette (Figure 12-7). If you don't want to see this little thumbnail, choose Hide Thumbnail from the Appearance palette's pop-up menu. To see the thumbnail again, choose Show Thumbnail from the menu.

Redefining graphic styles

The Redefining Graphic Style option is only available when you apply one of the preset styles from the Graphic Styles palette. When you use the Redefining Graphic Style option, your new changes overwrite the original, and any objects that use that style immediately update to your new changes.

Figure 12-7: With an object selected, the Appearance palette displays the object's information.

Working with the Graphic Styles palette

Now that you understand the Appearance palette, it is time to dive head first into the Graphic Styles palette. In this magnificent little palette are lots of creativity and amazing preset effects. The Graphic Styles palette shown in Figure 12-8 has few icons. The icons are Break Link to Graphic Style, New Graphic Style, and Delete Graphic Style. You find the guts of the palette in the pop-up menu, which you access by clicking the left-pointing arrow within the circle on the upper right of the palette. The following sections explain all of the options found in the Graphic Styles palette's pop-up menu.

Figure 12-8: The Graphic Styles palette

Creating a New Graphic Style

You use the New Style icon to make your selected object's attributes into a new style in the Graphic Styles palette. Create an object with the attributes you want, select the object, and then click this icon to make it into a style. You can also create a new style by choosing New Graphic Style from the pop-up menu in the Graphic Styles palette. To create a new style:

1. **Create an object.** See Chapter 4 for more on creating objects.

2. **Add color to the fill and/or stroke, a stroke weight, and dash pattern if desired.** For more on adding fills and strokes, see Chapter 4.

3. **Add effects from the Effects menu.** You can include transformations, twists, distortions, or anything you'd like. For more on effects, see the section "Using Effects," later in this chapter.

4. **After the object looks just right, select the whole object.**

5. **Click the New Graphic Style icon (which looks like a piece of paper with the corner turned up and is located in the middle of the icons at the bottom of the graphic styles palette) or choose New Graphic Style from the pop-up menu in the Graphic Styles palette.** This brings up the Graphic Style Options dialog box (Figure 12-9).

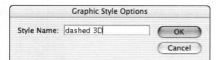

Figure 12-9: The Graphic Style Options dialog box

6. **Enter a name for the New Graphic Style and click OK.** This adds the new style to the Graphic Styles palette. The new graphic style now appears in the Graphic Styles palette.

7. **You can apply that new graphic style to any object you create.** Figure 12-10 shows an example.

Tip

Another way to create a new graphic style is to drag the object thumbnail from the Appearance palette into the Graphic Styles palette. This automatically creates a new graphic style. If you want to name it, you can either double-click it, or select it and choose Graphic Style Options from the pop-up menu.

Figure 12-10: You can apply the new graphic style to any object. The example shows a style being applied to outlined text with no stroke and no fill.

Duplicating and merging graphic styles

Under the Graphic Styles palette menu, you can duplicate a style. Select a style in the palette and choose Duplicate Graphic Style from the menu in the Graphic Styles palette. This creates a duplicate swatch at the end of the list of graphic style swatches. Use this to alter and create your own custom style. You use Duplicate Graphic Style to duplicate a default swatch so that you don't overwrite the original swatch.

To duplicate a style:

1. **Apply the graphic style to an object.** To do so, select the object and click the style in the Graphic Styles palette.

2. **Edit the duplicate in the Appearance palette.**

3. **After the edits are done, choose Redefine Graphic Style from the Appearance palette menu.** This changes the duplicated swatch in the Graphic Styles palette to match your edits.

Say you like two different styles and you want them combined as one. Use the Merge Graphic Styles command found in the Graphic Styles palette menu. To combine two or more graphic styles:

1. **Press and hold the Shift key.**

2. **Click the graphic styles you want to combine in the Graphic Styles palette.** To select non-contiguous graphic styles, press the ⌘ (Ctrl) in addition to the Shift key.

3. **Choose Merge Graphic Styles from the pop-up menu in the Graphic Styles palette.** The new combined graphic style is added to the end of the swatches in the Graphic Styles palette.

Delete graphic style

To delete a graphic style, select the graphic style in the Graphic Styles palette and choose Delete Graphic Style from the pop-up menu. Alternatively, you can click the trashcan icon at the bottom of the palette. A warning will come up that says, "Delete the Style Selection?" Click either Yes or No.

Break link to graphic style

You use the Break Line to Style option to break the graphic style from the object. The object still retains the appearance of the graphic style, but changes to the object's appearance no longer alter the graphic style's definition. A good use of this option is to find a graphic style that you like, but want to change. Fill an object with that graphic style, choose the Break Link to Graphic Style icon, and then alter the object as you want. When you have it as you like it, make it into a new style.

Other Graphic Styles palette options

Choosing Select All Unused selects all graphic styles that aren't used in the document. You can then choose to delete the unused graphic styles from the Graphic Styles palette.

Sort by Name sorts the Graphic Style swatches alphabetically.

In the Graphic Styles palette, you can choose how you view the graphic style swatches. Choosing Thumbnail shows you a swatch of the graphic style. Choosing Small List View displays a small swatch next to the name of the graphic style. The Large List View displays a larger swatch next to the name of the graphic style.

The Override Character Color menu item overrides the object's original color with the graphic style. If you want to retain the original color qualities, uncheck the Override Character Color option in the Graphic Style palette's menu.

The Graphic Style Options lets you name or rename a graphic style swatch. That is pretty much all you can do in the Graphic Style Options.

Opening and saving Graphic Style Libraries

After you create a bunch of cool styles, you'll want to save them as a Library for future use. To save a Graphic Style Library:

1. **Choose Save Graphic Style Library from the Graphic Styles pop-up menu.** This launches the Save dialog box opened to the Graphics Style folder within the Presets folder under the Illustrator installation.

2. **Enter a name for the library**.

3. **Click the Save button.** Mac is /Applications/Adobe Illustrator CS/Presets/ Graphic Styles...Windows is (usually) Program Files/Adobe/Illustrator CS/Presets/Graphic Styles.

4. **Quit Illustrator; then re-launch to see the new Library listed with the other Graphic Style Libraries.** You can open a saved Graphic Style Library by choosing Open Graphic Style Library and selecting from the list.

To open a saved Library:

1. **Choose Other Library from the Open Graphic Style Library under the Graphic Style palette pop-up menu.** This launches the Open dialog box.

2. **Choose the saved file.**

3. **Click Open.** The saved Library opens.

Using the Paintbucket/Eyedropper tools to apply styles

Any graphic styles can be applied using the Paintbucket and Eyedropper tools. To apply a graphic style quickly to another object, select the object you want to apply the graphic style to first. Choose the Eyedropper tool and click the object with the graphic style you like. This automatically applies that object's graphic style to the selected object.

For more information on applying attributes of any kind with the Paintbucket and Eyedropper tools, see Chapter 6.

Using Filters in Illustrator

If you look closely, filters are available for Photoshop and Illustrator. The filters in Illustrator have to be different from the filters in Photoshop because Illustrator deals with vector-based images and Photoshop works with bitmapped graphics. Many electronic artists use Photoshop as a staple of their graphics work. For them, the word "filter" conjures up thoughts of blurring and sharpening, as well as some of the fantastic effects that they can achieve by using filters from third parties, such as Alien Skin's Eye Candy.

The very term *filters* is based in photography terminology for special lenses that are attached to cameras to achieve special effects. Photoshop's filters are based on this concept, and they take it quite a bit further, creating controls for variety and exactness that a camera lens could never match.

Instead of just changing the appearance of objects or images, most of the filters in Illustrator perform tasks that took hours to do manually in previous versions of Illustrator. In a way, most of these filters work as intelligent macros, and they enable you to produce a variety of cool effects.

Some filters, such as the Zig Zag filter, seem to perform quite simple tasks. In reality, however, these filters are complex math-based programs that accomplish certain tasks faster than the fastest illustrator could dream of performing without them.

So why are all these functions in the Filter menu (Figure 12-11) and not just functions within the software? Because none of them are really integrated into Illustrator; instead, each filter is an individual file called a plug-in, which resides in the Plug-Ins folder. For a filter to be available, the plug-in must be in the Plug-ins folder.

Finding the Plug-Ins folder

All of the filters in Illustrator are in the Filter menu because a file with the same name as the filter is in the Plug-Ins folder. If the filter's file is not in the Plug-Ins folder, the filter will not appear in the Filter menu.

To see the list of all Illustrator's plug-ins, choose Illustrator ⇨ About Plug-Ins (Help ⇨ About Plug-Ins). In the About Plug-Ins dialog box (Figure 12-12), choose the filter you want to know about by clicking one time on it and then clicking the About button.

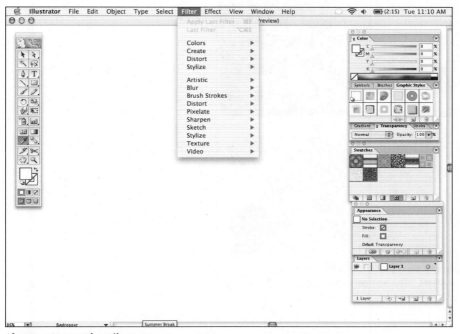

Figure 12-11: The Filter menu

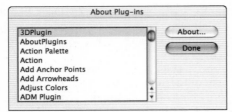

Figure 12-12: The About Plug-Ins dialog box

Color filters

The color filters in the Colors submenu of the Filter menu really take Illustrator's color capabilities to the next level in many ways. Unfortunately, they fall far short of Photoshop's color capabilities, but they're making good headway. Figure 12-13 shows an original illustration and the same illustration with a variety of color filters applied.

Figure 12-13: The top illustration is the original. The bottom illustration had various color filters applied.

Adjust Colors

Adjust Colors increases and decreases process color Fills in each color component. The percentages entered in Adjust Colors are absolute changes, meaning that a 10% decrease of Cyan when Cyan is 100% results in 90%, and a 10% decrease of Cyan when Cyan is 50% results in 40%, not 45%. If the increase makes the tint of a color greater than 100%, it stays at 100%, but other colors may still increase if they are not yet at 100%. If the decrease makes the tint of a color less than 0%, that color remains at 0%, but other colors may still decrease, as long as they are not yet at 0%. For example, a 25% increase to both Yellow and Magenta to a path with 80% Yellow and 50% Magenta results in the colors being 100% Yellow and 75% Magenta. Reapplying this filter results in 100% Yellow and 100% Magenta. Reapplying this filter at this point results in no change at all.

The Adjust Colors dialog box is shown in Figure 12-14.

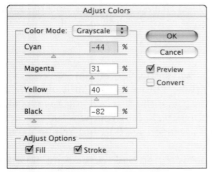

Figure 12-14: The Adjust Colors dialog box

At the bottom of the Adjust Colors dialog box are several options. The Preview check box lets you see the changes that have been applied so far. The check box automatically converts custom and Illustrator Black-based colors to process equivalents.

 Tip   You can adjust colors using any color mode, even if your selected paths are a different model. Click the Convert check boÒx and choose a different model.

 Cross-Reference   For more on color modes, see Chapter 2.

The Color Blend filters

The Blend Front to Back, Blend Horizontally, and Blend Vertically filters blend the colors of at least three objects whose ending objects are either both process tints or both Black tints. The Blend filters do not work with custom colors, patterns, or gradients. Using the Blend filters is very similar to using the Blend tool, but instead of making different shape and color blends, the Blend filters create new colors inside the between objects automatically. If the ending paths' colors are different color types, the Blend filters produce undesirable results.

The main difference between each of these filters is how each determines what the end paths are, and in what direction the blend flows.

The Convert to filters

The three Convert to filters — Convert to CMYK, Convert to Grayscale, and Convert to RGB — enable you to change the color model of selected paths with a simple menu selection. In addition to switching between Grayscale, CMYK, and RGB, the Convert to filters change custom colors to those color models as well.

The Invert Colors filter

Invert Colors works in strange and mysterious ways on selected paths. Whatever the color of the path, Invert Colors takes the first three colors in the Paint palette (Cyan, Magenta, and Yellow) and subtracts them from 100. If the original color was a shade of Red (for example, where Cyan = 0%, Magenta = 100%, and Yellow = 100%), then Invert Colors makes the new color Cyan = 100%, Magenta = 0%, and Yellow = 0%.

For CYMK colors, the percentage of Black is not affected by Invert colors. If you are working with the RGB or Grayscale images, however, the Invert Color Filter produces a photographic negative effect.

The following steps invert colors using the Invert Color filter. The example that follows is starting with a CMYK color file. Be aware that when you use these steps, slight differences may result from changing the color mode of your artwork:

1. **Select the CMYK color art you want to invert.**

2. **Choose Filter ➪ Color ➪ Convert to RGB.**

3. **Choose Filter ➪ Color ➪ Invert Colors.**

4. **Choose Filter ➪ Color ➪ Convert to CMYK.**

The Overprint Black Plug-In

Overprinting enables you to set black to print overtop any color underneath. Overprinting prevents white gaps from showing up between colors and black areas. Choosing Filter ➪ Color ➪ Overprint Black displays the Overprint Black dialog box (shown in Figure 12-15), which enables you to apply overprinting of black to selected paths. You can select a number of options, including whether to add or remove overprinting from the selected objects. Another option lets you specify the minimal amount of black (as a percentage) that the printer will use to overprint.

Caution A mistake I have made in the past is thinking that if I select an 85% Black to over-print that everything from 85% to 100% Black in my illustration will overprint. But that is not the case—you have to select each object and enter the specific value for that object.

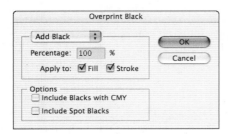

Figure 12-15: The Overprint Black dialog box

You can specify where the overprint affects Fills or Strokes or both. The other options in the Overprint Black dialog box determine whether black will overprint when combined with CMY or when part of a spot color.

The Overprint Black filter adds overprinting only to selected objects that are not currently overprinted when you select the Add Black choice from the pop-up menu in the Overprint Black dialog box, and it removes overprinting from objects that currently have overprinting when you select the Remove Black choice from the pop-up menu in the Overprint Dialog box. The Overprint Black filter does not remove overprinting when you select the Add button, even if the overprinting object does not fall within the parameters of the settings of the Overprint dialog box.

Note In the Attributes palette, the appropriate check boxes are selected when you use the filter on selected objects.

The Saturate filter

Saturate adds or subtracts equal amounts of color to the selected objects. This filter does not correspond in any way to saturation changes made by Photoshop; instead, the color added is proportional to each color in a path. Saturate works in much the same way as pressing the Shift key and dragging a triangle to the right in the Color palette. Saturate does not work with patterns or gradients.

The Saturate dialog box (shown in Figure 12-16) enables you to saturate or desaturate, depending on the direction you drag the slider. Dragging the slider to the left desaturates the selected object, reducing the intensity of the color fill. Dragging the slider to the right saturates the selected object, increasing the intensity of the color fill. The Preview check box in this dialog box is quite helpful, letting you see what is happening to the paths in real time.

Figure 12-16: The Saturate dialog box

Manipulating colors with the color filters

The color filters provide automated ways of changing colors on a variety of objects. Most of the filters work on paths that are filled with black or a process color, and some of them work on the strokes of the paths as well. The following sections describe various uses for the color filters.

Techniques for creating shadows and highlights

You can easily use color filters to create shadows and highlights for black and process-color paths. You create most shadows by simply creating a copy of the object and placing it under, and slightly offset from, the original. You can darken the copy in a number of ways, but the easiest way is to use the Adjust Colors filter. Figure 12-17 shows the four steps that you follow to create shadows and highlights.

You create highlights in the same way as you create shadows, but instead of darkening the copy, you lighten it.

1. **Create an object that has several colors in it.**

2. **Group the individual elements in the object by selecting the elements and choosing Object ⇨ Group.**

3. **Copy the object and choose Edit ⇨ Paste in Back.** Instead of choosing the Edit ⇨ Paste in Back menu path, you can press ⌘+Option+Shift+V (Ctrl+Alt+Shift+V).

4. **Offset the copy down and to the right.** Do this by selecting the object and dragging the object while holding down the Option [Alt] key. This makes a copy in the area to which you dragged.

5. **Choose Filter ⇨ Colors ⇨ Adjust Colors.** This launches the Adjust Colors dialog box. To darken the shadowed copy evenly, I added 20% to Cyan, Magenta, and Yellow, and 40% to Black.

6. **To create the highlight, choose Edit ⇨ Paste in Back and offset the copy up and to the left.** Decrease all four process colors by 40% if the background is dark or 20% if the background is light. My background is dark, so I reduced the color in the highlight by 40% of each color.

Figure 12-17: The final results of the shadows and highlights applied to an object

Creating negatives with the color filters

You can produce negative images in Illustrator almost automatically by using the Invert Colors filter. For a process color, the Invert Colors filter subtracts the tints of Cyan, Magenta, and Yellow from 100% and leaves Black as is. On an object that is Filled or Stroked with Black only, the filter subtracts the tint of Black from 100%.

To get around the way that this filter works when creating negatives:

1. **Select all the objects that you want to reverse.**
2. **Next, choose Filter ⇨ Colors ⇨ Invert Colors.**
3. **Select each path and check whether the paths have a process color Fill that contains Black.** If you find any Fills that contain Black, manually change black to the correct value.

Tip   After you check a path to see whether it is a process color that contains Black, hide that path. Using this method can help you be sure that you have checked every path, and you do not have to worry about wasting time by rechecking paths.

Create filters

Bunches of create filters were in older versions of Illustrator. Now the category is all but extinct, with only Crop Marks and Object Mosaic being the stragglers. As with most filters, you can manually perform the functions that the two create filters do, but using the filters is much easier.

Adding Crop marks

Use Crop marks to add lines to the edges of your object, showing you how much to trim the object when printed.

Crop marks are fully covered in Chapter 7.

Creating object mosaics

The Object Mosaic filter creates a series of tiles out of a placed bitmap image, as shown in Figure 12-18. Any size or color image may be used. When an image is converted through the Object Mosaic filter, it becomes a series of rectangles, each Filled with a different color.

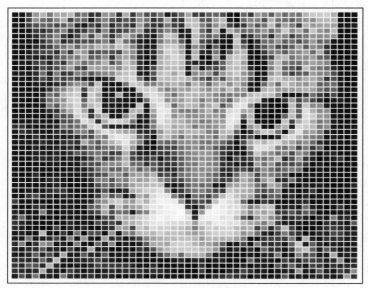

Figure 12-18: An image after applying Object Mosaic

In the Object Mosaic dialog box (see Figure 12-19), you can specify the number of tiles that the image is made up of and the space between the tiles. You also can specify a different size for the entire object mosaic.

The more rectangles, the more detail in the mosaic. Bitmapped images are mosaics of a sort, with each pixel equal to one square.

If you need to apply Object Mosaic to an illustration you created in Illustrator, you can rasterize it by using the Object ⇨ Rasterize command. Do this at a low resolution (72-dpi works great for me), and then apply Object Mosaic to the rasterized image.

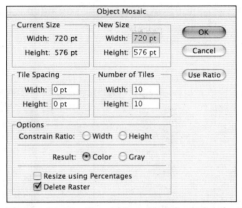

Figure 12-19: The Object Mosaic dialog box

Use the following steps to create a fairly simple and basic mosaic in Illustrator.

1. **Create a TIFF file and place it in Illustrator with the File ➪ Place command.** You do not need to use a high-resolution TIFF file. The Illustrator object mosaic looks just as good when you convert a 72-dpi TIFF file as when you convert a 300-dpi TIFF file.

2. **Choose Filter ➪ Create ➪ Object Mosaic.** The Object Mosaic dialog box appears (Figure 12-19).

3. **In the Object Mosaic dialog box, enter the size that you want the mosaic to be and also the number of tiles across and down.**

   • **Current Size:** Current Size lists the size of the selected image.

   • **New Size:** Enter the size in width and height that you want the object mosaic to be. You can keep it the same size or enter a different size in width and height.

   • **Tile Spacing:** In the Tile Spacing area, enter the space between the tiles in width and height.

   • **Number of Tiles:** Enter the number of tiles you want to use to create the Object Mosaic. Keep in mind the less tiles creates an Object mosaic with less details. The larger the number of tiles, the better the details, but it takes longer to create.

   • **Options:** Under the Options area, choose from Constrain Ratio by width or height, the result to be in color or gray, whether to resize the image with percentages, and to delete the raster.

4. **Click the Use Ratio button.** This keeps the same proportions as in the original image.

5. **Click OK when you are satisfied with the information that you have entered in the Object Mosaic dialog box.** Figure 12-20 shows the results that are produced by entering two different tile widths and heights into the Number of Tiles boxes.

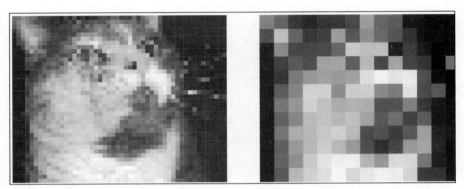

Figure 12-20: The final object mosaic

Combining Object Mosaic with Round Corners

You can create some very exciting effects with the Object Mosaic filter when you use it in conjunction with other filters. The best ones to use with it are Round Corners, all of the Distort filters, and most of the color filters, as well as the Transform Each function. In the following example, I combined the Object Mosaic filter with the Round Corners filter and the Transform Each function. See Figure 12-21.

1. **Create an object mosaic with an average number of tiles.** Use between 1,600 and 10,000 tiles, which would be from 40×40 to 100×100). I used an object mosaic with 50×63 tiles, or 3,150 tiles.

2. **Select all the mosaic tiles and choose Filter ⇨ Stylize ⇨ Round Corners.**

3. **In the Round Corners dialog box, enter a large number.** I usually enter at least ten points. As long as the tiles are not larger than 20 points wide, the Round Corners filter turns all the tiles into circles.

4. **Ungroup the tiles by choosing Object ⇨ Ungroup.**

5. **Copy all the tiles and choose Edit ⇨ Paste in Front.** You can also press ⌘+Option+V (Ctrl+Alt+V).

6. **Select all the tiles and choose Object ⇨ Transform ⇨ Transform Each.** This brings up the Transform Each dialog box.

7. **In the Move section of the dialog box, enter a number in both text fields and check the Random check box and click OK.** I entered the number 5.

8. **If you want less white space between the circles, choose Edit ⇨ Paste in Front again and then choose Object ⇨ Transform ⇨ Transform Again.** The tiles created with the Object Mosaic filter are placed on the page from top-left to bottom-right. The top-left tile is underneath all the other tiles (in the back), and the bottom-right tile is on top of all the other tiles (in the front). The tiles abut each other, so that none of them overlap.

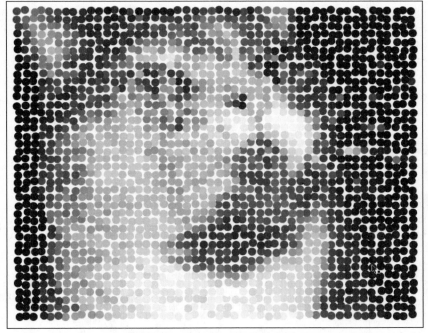

Figure 12-21: Creating a Seurat-like effect with the Object Mosaic filter

Because of the way that these tiles overlap, you can create a tiled or shingled roof quite easily, providing the original image is upside down. The section set of steps describes this process in detail.

Creating an object mosaic with no white-space overlap

The following steps describe how to make the tiles in a mosaic overlap with no white space between them. This technique can easily create a background image or a funky illustration.

1. **Create an Object Mosaic from a raster image.** Open a New document and choose File ⇨ Place. Find a pixel based (raster) image on your computer. Then choose Filter ⇨ Create ⇨ Object Mosaic. Enter your specifications and click OK.

2. **Ungroup the Object Mosaic by choosing Object ⇨ Ungroup.**

3. **Choose Object ⇨ Transform ⇨ Transform Each and enter the amount of movement for the tiles in the Move section.**

4. **Check the Random check box.**

5. **Measure one tile with the Measure tool.** The tiles that I created for the example shown in Figure 12-22 are 3.3 points across, and the move distance that I used is 3.3 points. The most white space between any two tiles is 6.6 points.

6. **Choose Object ⇨ Transform ⇨ Transform Each.** Enter the percentage that the tile must be scaled up to eliminate the white space in the Scale area. In this example, I entered 200%.

   To see the edges of the tiles more easily, place a 0.25-point 100% Black Stroke on them.

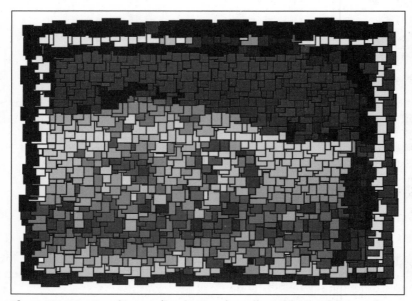

Figure 12-22: Creating overlapping random tiles with no white spacing between tiles

Distort filters

The distort filters create twists, bends, alterations ranging from small to huge changes in the object's path. The filters under Distort are: Free Distort, Pucker and Bloat, Roughen, Tweak, Twist, and Zig Zag.

Cross-Reference   For full coverage of the Distort filters, see Chapter 10.

Stylize filters

The Stylize filters are used for a variety of functions, kind of a catchall for filters that really couldn't go anywhere else. With the Add Arrowheads filter, you can place arrowheads (all sorts!) on the ends of open paths. With the Drop Shadow filter, you can add a darkened shadow to a selected path. The Round Corners filter seems better suited to the Distort submenu, but Adobe has chosen to put it here. The Round Corners filter removes Corner Points and replaces them with Smooth Points.

Add Arrowheads filter

The Add Arrowheads filter is exactly the same as the Add Arrowheads effect, but when used as a filter, you can no longer edit the arrowheads later. Using the Effects' Add Arrowheads enables you to go back in and edit later.

Cross-Reference For more on Add Arrowheads, see the Effects section later in this chapter.

Drop Shadow filter

The Drop Shadow filter makes creating drop shadows for most paths a relatively simple task.

Unlike most other filters, selecting Drop Shadow affects both Stroke and Fill. In the Drop Shadow dialog box (see Figure 12-23), you may specify the offset of the drop shadow by entering values for how far across the drop shadow should move (X) and how far up or down it should move (Y). Positive numbers move the shadow to the right and down; negative numbers move the shadow to the left and up.

Some of the other options in the Drop Shadow dialog box are:

✦ **Opacity:** Set how much you can see through the shadow.

✦ **X and Y Offset:** The general rule in drop-shadowing is that the more offset the drop shadow is, the higher the original object looks. To make an object look as if it is floating far above the page, enter high offset values.

✦ **Blur:** Lets you enter how far the blur will go outwards in pixels.

✦ **Color:** You choose this to make a colored shadow instead of black.

✦ **Darkness:** The percentage entered in Darkness is how much Black is added to the Fill and Stroke colors. Darkness does not affect any of the other custom or process colors.

✦ **Create Separate Shadows:** If you are creating a drop shadow on multiple objects, choosing this option will create a shadow for each object. If you don't choose this option, one big shadow will be created for all objects.

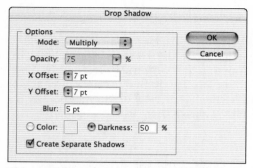

Figure 12-23: The Drop Shadow dialog box

To create a drop shadow, do the following:

1. **Create and select the artwork that you want to give a drop shadow.**

2. **Choose Filter ➪ Stylize ➪ Drop Shadow.** The Drop Shadow dialog box appears, as shown in Figure 12-23.

3. **Enter the amount that you want the drop shadow to be offset.** A positive value in the X text field puts the shadow to the right of the object; a negative value in the X text field puts the shadow to the left of the object. A positive value in the Y text field puts the shadow below the object; a negative value in the Y text field puts the shadow above the object.

4. **Enter the Opacity value.** This determines how see-through Illustrator makes the shadow.

5. **You can also set the mode for the shadow.** I chose Multiply. You can read move about the various modes in Chapter 6.

6. **Enter a value for Darkness.** The value that you enter in the Darkness field determines how much black Illustrator adds to the shadow to make it appear darker.

7. **If desired, check the Create Separate Shadow option.** If you check the Create Separate Shadow box, the shadow is grouped to the original object.

8. **Click OK.** If the shadow isn't what you want, use the Undo command by pressing ⌘+Z (Ctrl+Z), choose Filter ➪ Stylize ➪ Drop Shadow, and create a new drop shadow. Figure 12-24 shows an example of text with a drop shadow.

The Round Corners filter

You can use the Round Corners filter to create round corners just like (snap your fingers) that. This filter works on any path that has corner points, but the best results seem to be on polygons and stars.

Figure 12-24: Text with a drop shadow

 Note Round Corners replaces most corner points with two Smooth Points.

Selecting Round Corners changes all types of corner points to Smooth Points. In the Round Corners dialog box (see Figure 12-25), you specify what the radius of the Round Corners should be. The larger the number you enter for the radius, the bigger the curve.

 Note Don't apply the Round Corners filter to a rounded rectangle to make the corners more rounded. Instead of making the corners rounder, the flat sides of the rounded rectangle will curve slightly.

Figure 12-25: The Round Corners dialog box

To use the Round Corners filter, do the following:

   1. **Select the artwork that you want to convert to rounded corners.** I used type converted to outlines in the example in Figure 12-26.

Figure 12-26: The original outlined type (top), and after applying Round Corners (bottom)

2. **Choose Filter ⇨ Stylize ⇨ Round Corners.** The Round Corners dialog box appears (Figure 12-25).

3. **Enter the amount that you want the corners to be rounded.** Entering a large number usually ensures that all points become as curved as possible. (I wanted my corners rounded as much as possible, so I entered 8 pt in the dialog box.)

4. **Click OK.**

You can use the Round Corners filter to smooth out overly bumpy edges. Using the Round Corners filter with Roughen can produce very smooth, flowing areas.

Applying the Last filter

Whenever you start Illustrator, the top menu item in the Filter menu reads "Apply Last Filter," but it is grayed out. This causes some confusion initially. After you use a filter, its name appears where the menu once listed "Apply Last Filter." Thereafter, the name of the last filter that you used appears at the top of the menu. The key command for reapplying the last filter is ⌘+E (Ctrl+E).

Tip   To return to the last filter's dialog box, choose Filter⇨([Name of Last Filter), located right below the Apply Last Filter option or press ⌘+Option+E (Ctrl+Alt+E).

Using Photoshop-Compatible Filters in Illustrator

By themselves, these Photoshop filters are really neat. However, because many Illustrator users also have Photoshop, are they necessary?

For starters, these filters make things a bit easier than before Illustrator could use Photoshop filters, especially for creating features such as drop shadows and other special effects. Instead of having to allocate memory to Photoshop, you can do filter operations right in Illustrator.

Working with rasterized Illustrator artwork

Photoshop filters work only on pixel-based images. If you want to apply a Photoshop filter to your Illustrator artwork, you have to first rasterize it to turn it into a pixel-based image.

You have several ways to turn Illustrator art into pixels, but the best way is to use the Object ⇨ Rasterize command, which transforms any selected artwork into pixel-based artwork, at the resolution you specify. The following steps tell you how to do this, and Figure 12-27 shows the Rasterize dialog box.

1. **Create your artwork in Illustrator.**
2. **Select the artwork by dragging the mouse over the top of it.** You can also choose the Select ⇨ All menu command.
3. **Choose Object ⇨ Rasterize**. The Rasterize dialog box appears.
4. **Specify the resolution, choose the background, add any Options; then click OK.** Your artwork has been rasterized. Your final output determines the resolution. I chose 300 ppi so the printed piece looks nice. Choose screen (72 ppi) if your final result will be on the Web or only viewed on a computer screen. The background choices are white or transparent. The other options you can choose are Anti-aliasing options (Art Optimized, Type Optimized, or None), Create Clipping Mask, and Add space around object in points.

The rasterized art won't look different other than the path edges are gone and there is a box around the art. But now you can apply any of the Photoshop filters to this rasterized image.

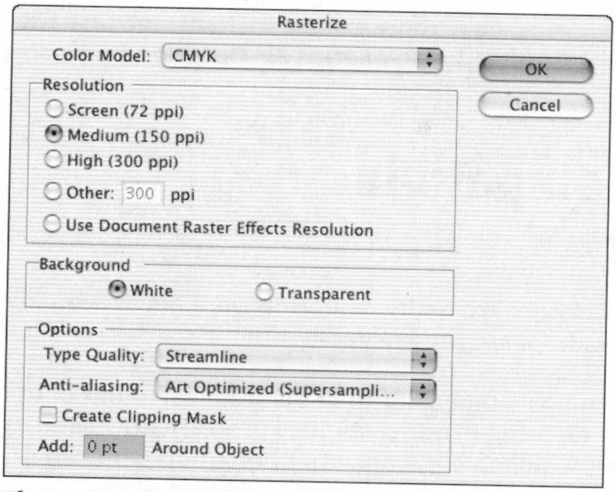

Figure 12-27: The Rasterize dialog box

As an Illustrator user, you may not be familiar with having to decide resolution as you do in Photoshop. The quick rule of thumb is that the resolution of pixel-based images should be 1½ to 2 times the line screen that the piece will be printed at. So if you'll be using a line screen of 133, your ppi should be between 199 and 266. It doesn't hurt to go higher than two times the line screen, but it is unnecessary. Because the math is easier, use double the line screen for the resolution.

Using Illustrator's Photoshop plug-ins

Illustrator includes all the Photoshop plug-ins that were originally Aldus Gallery Effects (back in the days before Adobe bought Aldus). They're separated from the vector filters and appear below the vector filters (the logic being that you won't be using them as much as Illustrator filters, so why let them get in the way). The plug-ins are primarily special-effect plug-ins.

Photoshop filters work only on pixel-based and RGB images. Before starting this exercise, be sure that you are in RGB color mode in the document by choosing File ➪ Document Color Mode ➪ RGB. The following steps describe how to apply a Photoshop filter to an image and Figure 12-28 illustrates the final result of these steps.

1. **Select the pixel-based image in Illustrator to which you want to apply the Photoshop filter.** For more on selecting images, see Chapter 5.

2. **Choose Filter ➪ Name of Photoshop filter submenu ➪ Name of filter.** For example, this could be Filter ➪ Texture ➪ Craquelure.

3. **In the Filter dialog box (if there is one), adjust the settings and values.**

4. **Click OK in the Filter dialog box to produce the effect.**

Figure 12-28: The rasterized image with a Craquelure texture filter applied to it

One big limitation of using Photoshop filters in Illustrator is that you can't make any selections within the pixel-based image. A way around this is to create a copy of the image, apply the filter, and then mask the area to which you'd like to apply that effect.

Using Effects

Effects are an intense set of commands. They apply their magic to any of the appearance attributes. Effects seem to have some of the same functions of filters. The one huge difference is that an effect is fully editable at any time. A Filter is permanent. After you apply the filter (short of undoing), it is not editable later. However, any effect you apply shows up in the Appearance palette. The Appearance palette is where you edit any of the applied effects.

To apply the last used effect quickly to another object, choose Effect ➪ Apply Last Effect or press ⌘+Shift+E (Ctrl+Shift+E). If you like the Effect, but want to change some of the parameters, choose Effect ➪ Last Effect or press ⌘+Shift+Option+E (Ctrl+Shift+Alt+E).

Effects aren't limited to vector-based objects. You can apply effects to raster images as well.

3D effects

One of the biggest new features of Illustrator cs is the inclusion of three-dimensional abilities. Because this is such a cool, new, and intense feature, it's being covered in its own chapter.

 For more on 3D, see Chapter 13.

Converting to Shape effects

The Convert To Shape effect takes any selected object and fits them into a Rectangle, Rounded Rectangle, or Ellipse. The Convert to Shape Effect puts a frame around your selected object. The frame is in one of the shapes that you choose (rectangle, rounded rectangle, or ellipse). Convert To Shape creates a new shape based on the original object's dimensions. Setting a negative value in the relative area decreases the size of the frame, and a positive number increases the size of the frame relative to the original size. To set the new size of the shape, enter the height and width values.

Distorting and transforming effects

The Distort and Transform effects include: Free Distort, Pucker & Bloat, Roughen, Transform, Tweak, Twist, and Zig Zag. You may wonder why there are Transform effects in the Effect menu when you can do transformations in the Object menu. The big reason to apply a transformation under the Effect menu is that you can go back in and edit that particular transformation at any time.

 For in depth coverage of the Distort and Transform effects, see Chapter 10.

Creating Path effects

The Path effects you can apply are: Offset Path, Outline Object, and Outline Stroke. As with the Transform options, the Path options are the same as under the Object menu. The Path effects under the Effect menu are exactly the same as under the object menu except that the effects are live and editable at any time. This means that you can go back in at any time and change any of the Path effects you have applied.

 For in depth coverage of the Path functions, see Chapter 5.

Rasterizing effects

Raster effects are the bottom half of the effects menu. These effects can only be applied to a rasterized image. To access the Rasterize effects, choose Effect ➪ Rasterize. This brings up the Rasterize dialog box (Figure 12-29).

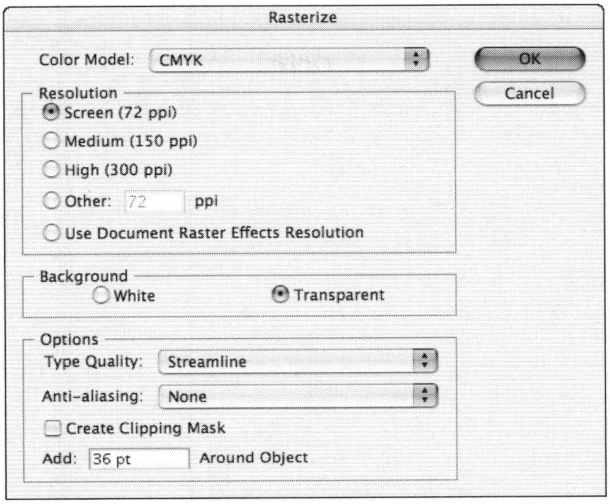

Figure 12-29: The Rasterize dialog box

In the Rasterize dialog box you can set the resolution (from low to high or set your own). Choose from white or transparent background. Set a Streamline or Outline in the Type Quality. Other options are clipping mask or adding space around the object.

This effect has the same affect as the Object ⇨ Rasterize menu command, but when applied as an effect, you can easily remove it at a later time by using the Appearance palette.

Stylizing effects

Under the Stylize effects are options you can use to embellish paths and add effects to objects. The Stylize options are: Add Arrowheads, Drop Shadow, Feather, Inner Glow, Outer Glow, Round Corners, and Scribble.

Add Arrowheads

The Add Arrowheads filter is a boon to technical artists, sign makers, and anyone else in need of a quick arrow. The number one complaint about the Add Arrowheads filter is that Illustrator offers too many arrowheads from which to choose. Some complaint!

Choosing Effect ⇨ Stylize ⇨ Add Arrowheads adds an arrowhead (or two) to any selected open path. If more than one path is selected, arrowheads are added to each open path. To use Add Arrowheads, select an open path and choose Effect ⇨ Stylize ⇨ Add Arrowheads. The Add Arrowheads dialog box appears, as shown in Figure 12-30. In this box, you can pick which of the 27 different arrowheads you want to stick on the end of your path. Scale refers to the size of the arrowhead relative to the Stroke weight of the path; you may enter any number between 1% and 1000% in this box. Choosing Start places the arrowhead at the beginning of the path (where you first clicked to draw it); choosing End places the arrowhead on the ending of the path (where you last clicked to draw it); and choosing Start and End places the same arrowhead on both the beginning and ending of the path. Reapplying this filter to the same paths continues to put arrowheads on top of arrowheads. Figure 12-31 shows customized arrowheads created in Illustrator.

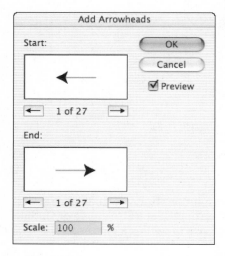

Figure 12-30: The Add Arrowheads dialog box

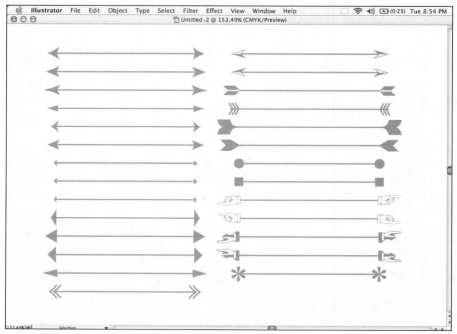

Figure 12-31: Create customized arrowheads.

Note Add Arrowheads does not work on closed paths.

Arrowheads are grouped to the paths that were selected when they were created; it is sometimes necessary to rotate the arrowhead by either ungrouping it or choosing it with the Direct Selection tool.

The size of the arrowheads is based on the width of the Stroke, but you can alter each arrowhead's dimensions in the Scale text field in the Add Arrowheads dialog box.

Creating Custom Arrowheads

Custom arrowheads can add just enough to a design to set it apart from the others. Using the various tools at your disposal, the arrowheads you create aren't limited except by your own imagination. To create a custom arrowhead, follow these steps.

1. Use the Pen or Pencil tool to create an open path. Set the width of the path to the width that you want it to be with an arrowhead attached to it. (You have to use an open path – nothing happens when you select a closed path and apply the Add Arrowheads filter. Even if you want just the arrowhead, and not the path, you still have to create a path first – you can delete the path after the arrowhead appears.)

2. Choose Effect ⇨ Stylize ⇨ Add Arrowheads. The Add Arrowheads dialog box appears. Enter the size of the arrowhead (100% = normal size). Pick the end of the path where you want the arrowhead to appear.

3. If you want the arrowhead on both ends of the path, click the Start and End option. (If you drew the path yourself with either the Pen or Freehand tool, the path direction is the direction that you drew the path – closed paths that were created with the Rectangle or Oval tools or the Create filters and were then cut usually go in a counterclockwise direction.) Pick an arrowhead from the 27 options.

4. Click OK. The path now has an arrowhead. Whenever arrowheads are created, they are grouped to the path. You have to use the Group Selection tool to select individual pieces of the arrow. Alternatively, you can choose Arrange ⇨ Ungroup or press ⌘+Shift+G (Ctrl+Shift+G).

5. To add a different arrowhead to the other end of the path, select the path with the Direct Selection tool and then choose Effect ⇨ Stylize ⇨ Add Arrowheads. Change the buttons to indicate that the new arrowhead should go at the other end of the path and select the type of arrowhead.

6. Click OK. Make sure that the arrowhead is correct. If it isn't, choose Edit ⇨ Undo (⌘+Z) [Ctrl+Z] and choose Effect ⇨ Stylize ⇨ Add Arrowheads. Then add a different arrowhead.

7. To make the arrowheads and path into one path, select the path and choose Object ⇨ Path ⇨ Outline Path. Then select both the new outlined path and the arrowheads and choose Unite from the Pathfinder palette. Now you can Fill the new arrow object with anything, including gradients, and Stroke the entire object at once.

Drop Shadow

The Drop Shadow effect is almost the same as the Drop Shadow filter, except that you can go back in and edit the Drop Shadow effect at any time. For more details on Drop Shadow, see "Drop Shadow filter" earlier in this chapter.

Feather

The Feather effect adds a fade out to the selected object. Feather fades the object to transparent over a specified number in points. To add a Feather effect to an object:

1. **Select the object to which you want to apply the Feather.**

2. **Choose Effect ⇨ Stylize ⇨ Feather.** This opens the Feather dialog box (Figure 12-32).

Figure 12-32: The Feather dialog box

3. **Enter the Feather Radius in points you want in the Feather dialog box.**

4. **Click OK to see the Feather effect (see Figure 12-33).**

Inner and Outer Glow

The Inner and Outer Glow effect creates a softened glow on the inside or outside edge of the object. Choose Effect ⇨ Stylize ⇨ Inner Glow, or Effect ⇨ Stylize ⇨ Outer Glow. In the dialog box, choose the blending mode for the glow as well as the Opacity, Blur distance, and whether the glow goes from the center or the edge. The Center option starts the glow from the center of the object. The Edge option starts the glow from the edge of the object. Figure 12-34 shows the Inner Glow dialog box with the preview option checked so you can see the results on the object.

Round Corners

The Round Corners effect does the same thing as the Round Corners filter, except that you can go back in and edit it at any time.

Cross-Reference   For more detail on the Round Corners function see the section "The Round Corner filter" earlier in this chapter.

Figure 12-33: The original (top) and faded-out text (bottom)

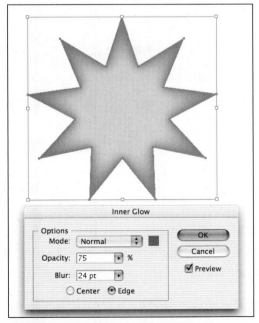

Figure 12-34: The Inner Glow dialog box

Understanding Scribble

The Scribble effect is new to Illustrator CS. It takes an illustration and adds a sketchy quality to it. You can choose from a variety of presets or create your own. The scribble effect can create a mass produced, mechanical look or a loose, flowy, childlike scrawl. The breakdown of what Scribble does is that it converts an objects stroke and fill to lines divided by transparency. The Scribble dialog box options let you alter the line style, density, looseness of the lines, and stroke width.

You find the Scribble effect under the Stylize submenu of the Effect menu. Figure 12-35 shows a portrait with two different Scribble effects applied. Within the Scribble dialog box are options you can choose to change or customize your Scribbled art or to choose from preset Scribble effects.

Figure 12-35: Two different Scribble effects result in two very different-looking portraits.

Using the Scribble presets

Under the Scribble dialog box are a variety of preset options. Figure 12-36 shows a poster softened using the Scribble effect. Figure 12-37 shows each of the standard presets applied to an original illustration (top left). The Scribble presets are:

✦ **Custom:** This option remembers the last settings you entered.

✦ **Default:** Applies 30° angled lines with varying thickness to the fill and stroke.

✦ **Childlike:** Applies 10° loopy angled lines that look very loose and as if a child had sketched them.

✦ **Dense:** Applies very tight 45° angled line with little space between lines.

✦ **Loose:** Applies very loose loopy –20° angled lines with lots of spacing between lines.

✦ **Moiré:** Applies tight –45° lines so close they actually create a moiré pattern with the fill.

✦ **Sharp:** Applies–30° angled lines tightly with little space between lines. Similar to Dense.

✦ **Sketch:** Applies –30° angled lines with a thicker stroke for the lines, but with little space between lines.

✦ **Snarl:** Applies 60° angled lines tightly together with loopy lines and a thin stroke weight.

✦ **Swash:** Applies a figure 8 loop to the object with a thinner stroke weight and a symmetrical look to the lines.

✦ **Tight:** Applies a 30° angled line with tight lines and a thin stroke weight for an even line filled area.

✦ **Zig-Zag:** Applies a –20° angled line, a thin stroke weight for an even symmetrical look to the lines in the filled area.

Figure 12-36: Using the Scribble effect gives poster art a softer edge.

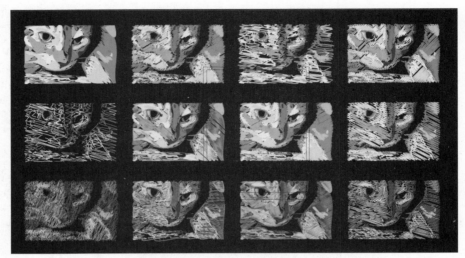

Figure 12-37: Each of the scribble presets applied to an illustration

Working with the Scribble options

Under the Scribble options dialog box there are a variety of options you can set. From Angle and Path Overlap, with a Variation setting for Path Overlap. Line Options are Stroke Width, Curviness, and Spacing, the latter two of which can have a Variation applied. You can choose from a preset value, or check the preview box and enter your own values to see immediate results. Figure 12-38 shows the Scribble Options dialog box.

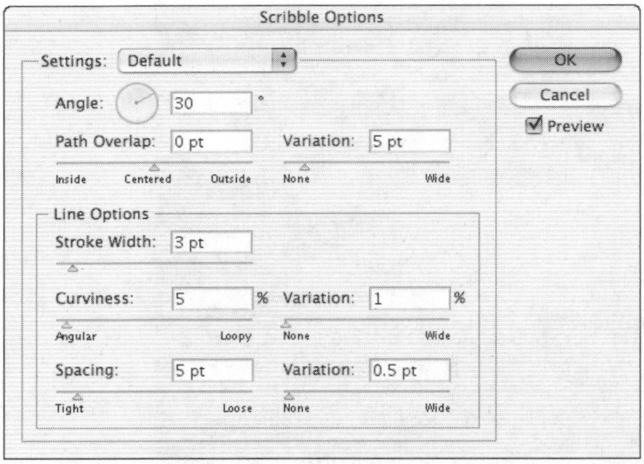

Figure 12-38: The Scribble Options dialog box

The following are the options you can set under the Scribble effect:

✦ **Path Overlap:** This sets the amount the scribble lines stay inside or go beyond the object's edge.

✦ **Variation:** Sets how the scribble line lengths differ (loopy or angled) and how close together they are set.

✦ **Stroke Width:** Sets the width of the Scribble lines.

✦ **Curviness:** Sets how far the different Scribble lines curve from each other.

✦ **Variation:** Sets a range for how much the curviness may vary from line to line.

✦ **Spacing:** Sets the spacing amount between scribble lines.

✦ **Variation:** Establishes the range in which spacing magnitudes will fall.

✦ **Preview:** Check this to see the effect before applying it.

Using SVG Filters effects

You find SVG Filters under the Effects menu. Seems odd, Filters being under Effects instead of Filters. Well, that is because these pretty cool filters are XML-based and resolution independent. A perfect fit for vectors.

Cross-Reference   For more on XML and SVG, see Chapter 16.

To access the SVG Filters choose Effect ➪ SVG Filters. You have many different SVG filters from which to choose:

✦ **Alpha:** Creates transparent fluctuations.

✦ **Bevel Shadow:** Creates a beveled shadow that is softened.

✦ **Cool Breeze:** Creates fluctuations on the top edge of the object.

✦ **Dilate:** Takes the fill outwards to the edge of the object.

✦ **Erode:** Takes away the fill from the edge of the object.

✦ **Gaussian Blur:** Adds a soft shadow by blurring the object's edge.

✦ **Pixel Play:** Uses light effects on the object.

✦ **Shadow:** Creates a harsh shadow on the object.

✦ **Static:** Uses a static fill in place of the original fill color.

✦ **Turbulence:** Creates transparent fluctuations to the object.

✦ **Woodgrain:** Creates a woodgrain effect to the object.

Warp effects

The Warp effects are also part of the Effect menu. Chapter 10 covers these effects extensively.

Creating Photoshop filter effects

You can apply a ton of Photoshop filter effects to any rasterized image. Turn your vector art into raster art and apply effects from artistic to texturizing. The Photoshop filters found under the Filter menu are identical to the ones found under the Effect menu. The only difference is that when you use the Effect menu, you can go back in and edit the Photoshop effect on the rasterized image. The main filters are: Artistic, Blur, Brush Strokes, Distort, Pixelate, Sharpen, Sketch, Stylize, Texture, and Video.

These filters are the same that you find in Photoshop, but don't have to go back and forth between the applications to access them. Use them to create more exciting rasterized artwork.

Caution Be sure you change the document colors space to RGB, or you'll find the Photoshop filter effects grayed out.

Summary

✦ Graphic Styles are where you can access saved Appearance settings.

✦ Choose from a wide range of graphic styles in the Graphic Style Libraries.

✦ Use the Appearance palette to edit an object's attributes.

✦ Filters add extra functionality to Illustrator through commands in the Filter menu.

✦ To use a filter, select the artwork you want to "filterize" and select the filter from the Filter menu.

✦ The hardest aspect about filters is knowing what they do, and when and how to use them; the filters themselves are pretty simple.

✦ You can reapply the last filter quickly by pressing Ô-E [Ctrl+E].

✦ Access the last filter's dialog box by pressing Ô-Option-E [Ctrl+Alt+E].

✦ Adjust Colors adds and subtracts various amounts of process colors from multiple colored objects.

✦ The color blend filters look at two opposite paths and blend between the two colors.

✦ Saturate increases or decreases the amount of color in selected paths.

✦ The Object Mosaic filter takes rasterized files and square streamlines them into Illustrator paths.

✦ Add Arrowheads creates arrowheads at the ends of open paths.

✦ Drop Shadow creates instant drop shadows.

✦ Round Corners changes Straight Corner Points into Smooth Points.

✦ Photoshop filters appear in the Filter menu underneath the Illustrator filters.

✦ Effects let you go back in and edit at any time.

✦ Scribble effects can add a softer, sketchy look to your illustration.

✦ Many Effects are similar to Filters, except that the Effects are fully editable and the Filters are more permanent.

✦　　✦　　✦

Creating 3D in Illustrator

Creating depth and adding perspective has been the desire of many illustrators. Now you can create three-dimensional images in Illustrator. Adding 3D to your package design, logo, or any illustration is a breeze. Take any path, type, or object and model them into a 3D form, adding lighting and rotating them in three dimensions. Use 3D to take your artwork to the next level. Imagine a logo in three dimensions on a Web site rotating around 360°. The possibilities are endless.

Using 3D inside Illustrator

New to Illustrator is the ability to create 3D inside the application. Use the Extrude command to pop a two-dimensional item into a three-dimensional world. Revolve a path into a three-dimensional object with highlights and even map artwork onto an image in 3D. Not only can you revolve and extrude, but you can rotate the object as well. Because your 3D object is an effect, you can edit it at any time.

Take any flat shape and add depth with 3D, and you still retain all of the editing abilities of the flat shape. Illustrate takes any changes you make later and incorporate them in the 3D form. Illustrator adds a preview option so you can see what the object will look like. Extrude, revolve, rotate, and map artwork all in one clean, neat dialog box.

In the past, Adobe offered Adobe Dimensions, which was a three-dimensional creation program. With Dimensions, you could extrude and revolve two-dimensional paths to create three-dimensional art. You could also add depth and lighting effects to make the object appear realistic. Most of Dimensions' capabilities are now inside Illustrator. The main difference in Illustrator is that you can't position multiple objects in 3D space. You can only position one object at a time. And Illustrator creates the 3D effect live rather than have to render as Dimensions did.

Many 3D packages are on the market, ranging from high-end software, such as 3ds max, or Maya, to low-end programs. They both handle high-end 3D into video, special effects, and movies. And video artists use them in upscale game designs and animation. The low-end 3D programs are Poser and Strata. Poser allows you to create 3D models (people and animals), down to the facial hair and realistic skin. Strata can create a model, render the 3D, and animate the 3D objects. Illustrator's 3D abilities don't quite go that far, but it has come a long way for an illustrating program. Adobe took the three-dimensional qualities of Adobe Dimensions, made a cleaner, user-friendlier interface and put it inside Illustrator.

Understanding the Three-Dimensional World

The concept of three dimensions should be more intuitive and easy for us to understand, because we are three-dimensional creatures who live in a three-dimensional world. But because most of our media are two-dimensional (reading, watching TV, working on a computer), adjusting to a three-dimensional digital world can be confusing and frustrating.

Changing from two dimensions to three dimensions

Television is a two-dimensional medium. The picture tube has height and width. Computer screens are two-dimensional. The pages of books are two-dimensional. Maps are two dimensional, even though the world is round. Most people think in two dimensions.

Most of the two-dimensional objects that we deal with may very well be replaced with three-dimensional objects. Three-dimensional life will become a reality as soon as technology makes it so. Holograms have been around for a while, and technology is making them more accurate and lifelike. Video games and virtual-reality glasses already simulate three dimensions through the use of holograms and computer-generated imagery; even Viewmasters give the three-dimensional effect.

Three-dimensional positioning

When you are trying to understand the concept of three dimensions on a computer screen, the most difficult aspect to grasp is depth. Left, right, up, and down are all simple concepts, but what about things that are closer or farther away? Maybe sometime in the future we will have to look up and down when we are driving.

Note

You are already thinking in three dimensions if you are familiar with Illustrator's Send to Back and Bring to Front commands. If you feel comfortable with stacking order and layers, then you are one step closer to working with three-dimensional positioning.

Cross-Reference For more on arranging with Send to Back and Bring to Front, see Chapter 7.

You use three different indicators to position objects in the 3D Extrude & Bevel Options dialog box:

✦ **X is the object's horizontal location.** A value greater than 0 means that the object is positioned to the right of center (0). A value less than 0 (any negative number) represents an object to the left of center.

✦ **Y defines the object's vertical position.** A Y value that is greater than 0 means that the object is above center. A Y value that is less than 0 means that the object is below center.

✦ **Z represent's the object's depth.** This variable indicates how far forward or backward the object is from the center. A value greater than 0 means that the object is behind 0, or farther away. A value less than 0 means that the object is in front of 0, or closer to you.

Figure 13-1 shows the X, Y, and Z values as you would see them initially in the 3D Extrude & Bevel Options dialog box. In the dialog box, relative X (horizontal), Y (vertical), and Z (Depth) positions of selected objects can be rotated around those axes. In a direct, straight-from-the-front view, you cannot determine an object's Z position. From the default position, which is a view of the object from above and to the right of the front, you can determine all three positions visually.

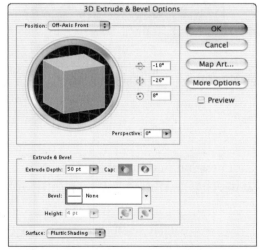

Figure 13-1: The rotational values in the 3D Extrude & Bevel Options dialog box

Extruding and Revolving 2D Objects

Illustrator's 3D Extrude command adds sides, a top, and a back to an object. When extruding an object, you can fill the object or leave a hole in the middle (extruding the path but not the Fill). Another option is to bevel the edges, which creates an amazing look for 3D text.

The Revolve command takes a path and turns it around a center axis, creating a 3D effect in a circular fashion. This is a great way to create a bottle, chess piece, or any other revolved shape. Not only can you apply light and shading to the revolved object, but you can map artwork directly on the face of the object.

Extruding flat art

Extruding is the process of giving two-dimensional art depth that is equal on every part of the artwork. Figure 13-2 shows the flat art and the same art extruded. When extruding art, you can retain the default depth (50 pt) or set the Extrude Depth slider anywhere from 0 to 2000 points.

Figure 13-2: The original flat art (left) and the extruded art (right)

To create a basic extrusion on an object:

1. **Create an object to extrude.**

2. **Select the object.** See Chapter 5 for more on selecting objects.

3. **Choose Effect ⇨ 3D ⇨ Extrude & Bevel.** Doing this brings up the 3D Extrude & Bevel Options dialog box (Figure 13-3).

4. **Click the preview box.** This let you see the default settings on your selected object.

5. **Click OK.** Illustrator applies the 3D extrusion to your object (Figure 13-4).

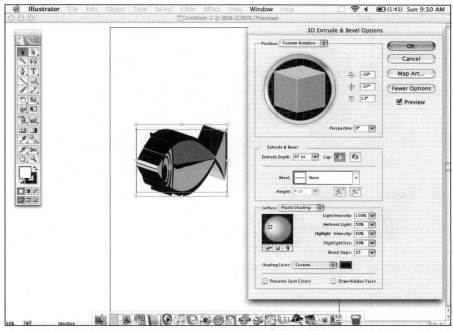

Figure 13-3: With an object selected you can see the default settings in the 3D Extrude & Bevel Options dialog box.

The options you can choose in the Extrude and Bevel dialog box are:

✦ **Extrude Depth:** This option lets you control how far in points the object's path will be extruded. Drag the slider with the Preview button on to see a live preview of the depth.

✦ **Cap:** Choose whether to have the cap turned on for a more solid look or off for a hollow look.

✦ **Rotate:** Use the Rotate option to rotate your object around an x, y, and z axis.

✦ **Views:** The view option lets you change the view around the x, y, and z axis.

✦ **Position:** The position pop-up menu lets you choose from a variety of positions for your selected object. Choose a view from the Front, Back, Left, Right, Top, Bottom, Off-axis back, Off-axis left, Off-axis right, Off-axis top, Off-axis bottom, Isometric Left, Isometric Right, Isometric Top, and Isometric Bottom. You can also drag the box around to create a custom rotation.

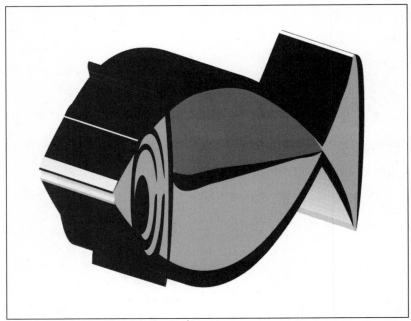

Figure 13-4: The final extruded artwork

That was just a basic extrusion. There is so much more you can do. To begin with, you can cap or uncap an object. Uncapping takes away the front and back panes making the object hollow. Capping puts a front and back pane on the object, making the object solid.

In the Position area in the top of the 3D Extrude & Bevel Options dialog box, you can rotate the object, move the view around the X, Y, and Z axis, and add perspective to the object. The default position is Off-axis front. The other options available are: Custom, Front, Back, Left, Right, Top, Bottom, Off-axis back, Off-axis left, Off-axis right, Off-axis top, Off-axis bottom, Isometric Left, Isometric Right, Isometric Top, and Isometric Bottom. Figure 13-5 shows guitars with extrusion, lighting, and altered views applied in 3D.

For more on lighting effects, see Changing the Appearance of Three-Dimensional Objects later in this chapter.

Figure 13-5: Guitars that were extruded, lighting applied, and a rotated view

Extruding a stroke

One visually appealing effect that you can achieve is to take a dashed stroked line and use Extrude to make it 3D. This technique creates a bamboo look or individual bars. To extrude a dashed line:

1. **Create an object with a dashed line Stroke, no Fill.** I used outlined text with a dashed stroke, but no fill.

2. **Choose Effect ➪ 3D ➪ Extrude & Bevel.** Doing this opens the Extrude & Bevel Options dialog box.

3. **Set the Extrude depth in points.** Alternatively, you can drag the slider, change the views by picking an option from the Position pop-up, or drag the box to a different view.

4. **Click OK to see the extruded dashed lines**. Figure 13-6 shows the resulting effect.

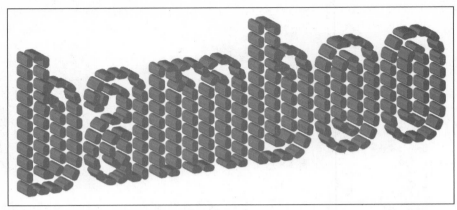

Figure 13-6: The extruded dashed stroke

Tip   Try using any of the Graphic Styles on your object before taking it into the 3D dialog boxes. You can come up with some pretty cool results.

Understanding bevels

The use of bevels can make or break your artwork. Bevels carve out an edge to your 3D object. You can use Illustrator's preset bevels, or, if you are feeling ambitious, you can create your own bevel.

To add a bevel to an object:

1. **Create an object to which you want to add 3D.**

2. **Choose Effect ⇨ 3D ⇨ Extrude & Bevel.** Doing this opens the Extrude & Bevel Options dialog box.

3. **Optionally, apply an extrusion and change the position.**

4. **Choose a bevel from the drop-down menu.**

5. **Choose the height of the bevel and whether it bevels out or bevels in.** The height option is how large or small you want the bevel to be. You set this option by dragging the Height slider to a bevel in points. The other option is whether you want to add the bevel to the outside of the object or subtract it from the inside of the object. This make this determination, you click either the Bevel In or Bevel Out button.

6. **Check the preview box to see the bevel.** Leave the Preview box unchecked until you are done with your settings; otherwise it may take a while to preview your object.

7. **Click OK to see the final results.** Figure 13-7 shows the resulting bevel along the edge of the extruded path.

Figure 13-7: Beveled art

Although the preset bevels are nice to use, you can also create your own custom bevel. To add your own bevel to the Bevel menu:

1. **Open the Bevels.ai file found in the Adobe Illustrator Plug-ins folder.**

2. **Create the path you want to be your bevel in the Bevels.ai document.**

3. **Turn that path into a symbol.** You do this by choosing Window ⇨ Symbols. Either drag the path to the Symbols palette or select the path and click the New Symbol button in the Symbols palette. Or with the path selected, choose New Symbol from the Symbol palette drop-down menu.

Cross-Reference

For information on symbols, see Chapter 4.

4. **Rename the symbol.** To rename the symbol, double-click the symbol in the Symbols palette. Enter a name in the Symbol Options dialog box and click OK.

5. **Choose File ⇨ Save.** Doing this saves the new path symbol in the Bevels.ai file.

6. **Quit Illustrator and start Illustrator again.** Now when you look at the Bevel menu in the 3D Extrude & Bevel Options dialog box, your new bevel will be listed there (Figure 13-8). Now you can apply the custom bevel as you would any other bevel.

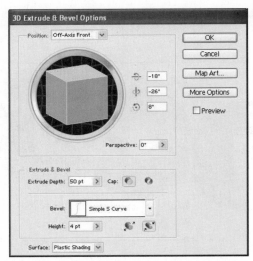

Figure 13-8: The custom bevel is listed with the other preset.

Revolving objects

Revolving, also called *lathing*, is the process of spinning a 2D object around an axis a specified number of degrees in order to create a 3D object. You can create things by revolving different objects around different axes. You can create a lamp, a chess piece, a wedge of cheese, and more.

To revolve a path:

1. **Draw a path first using any of the path tools (Pen, Pencil, Line).** See Figure 13-9. For more on the different path tools, see Chapter 3.

2. **Select the path and choose Effect ➪ 3D ➪ Revolve.** Doing this brings up the 3D Revolve Options dialog box (Figure 13-10).

3. **Click the Preview button.** You see the revolved object.

4. **Click OK.** The revolving is finished (Figure 13-11).

The default option is to revolve the path 360 degrees. You can change that to any number between 1 and 360. A number less than 360 creates an open section like a wedge taken out of a round of cheese.

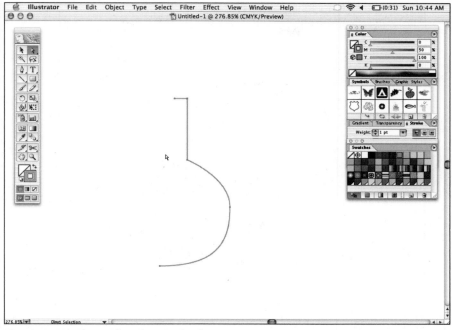

Figure 13-9: The path to be revolved

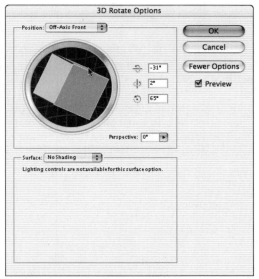

Figure 13-10: The Revolve dialog box

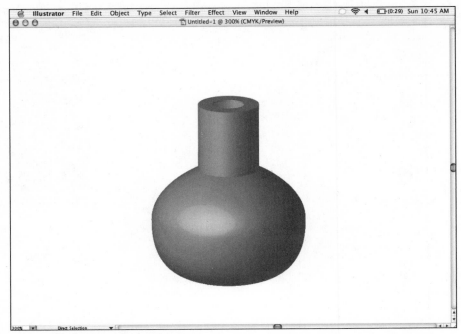

Figure 13-11: The revolved path

Rotating objects

You can use the Rotate function found under the 3D effect menu to rotate 2D and 3D objects. This rotation happens in 3D space. This is a great way to apply a sheared effect or perspective to an object that is 2D.

3D rotation is done in its own dialog box. Choose Effect ➪ 3D ➪ Rotate. This launches the Rotate dialog box, as shown in Figure 13-12. In this dialog box, you can either enter values in the text fields or click and drag the position square to the rotation you'd like. Make sure that you click the Preview button, so you can see the rotation happen live.

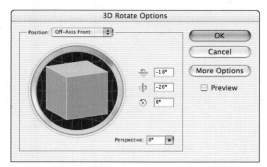

Figure 13-12: The 3D Rotate Options dialog box

Changing the Appearance of Three-Dimensional Objects

Objects created in the 3D Extrude and Bevel Options dialog box are not only colored but also lit. With lighting comes additional specifications — shading and reflectance. You control the light by its surface characteristics. If you don't see any lighting options, click the More Options button on the right side of the 3D Extrude and Bevel Options dialog box. This opens up the shading and light areas, as shown in Figure 13-13. To access the lighting options, you need to click the More Options button on the right side of the dialog box.

The Surface characteristics

The Surface properties control the look of the outside surface of the 3D object. You can create 3D objects that are just outlined, have no shading, have soft shading, or have intense, glossy shading. Your options are: Wireframe, No Shading, Diffused Shading, and Plastic Shading. Figure 13-14 shows one object in each of the surface characteristics applied to them.

✦ **Wireframe** traces the curves of the object's geometric shape and fills the shape with transparent fill (there are no lighting options with this surface characteristic).

✦ **No Shading** fills the object with the same color as the original 2D object (there are no lighting options with this surface characteristic).

✦ **Diffuse Shading adds a soft diffused light source on the object's surface.**

✦ **Plastic Shading** adds a bright shiny light as if the object were made of plastic.

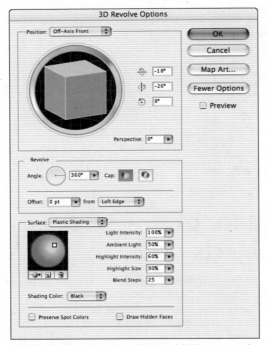

Figure 13-13: The shading and light areas of the 3D Revolve dialog box

Understanding lighting

Lighting can be a little confusing in a 3D program. Because lights in 3D are positioned an infinite distance from objects, shading for different objects is the same, no matter what the position of the objects. For example, if the lights are in the upper-left, objects on the far left will have the same lighting as objects on the far right. If the lights were positioned closer, the shading would appear differently.

A good way to think of the lights that you create is that they resemble sunlight to us earth bound creatures. Light from the sun shines on an object in New York City almost exactly the same way it shines on an object in Boston. Because the sun is so far away, the differences in the position of the sun relative to the two cities is minute. If the sun were an infinite distance away and the earth were flat, the two cities would have exactly the same sunlight.

Because there are no shadows in Illustrator's 3D Extrude & Bevel Options dialog box, objects that are between the light source and another object let light pass through them so that the light can reach the "hidden" object.

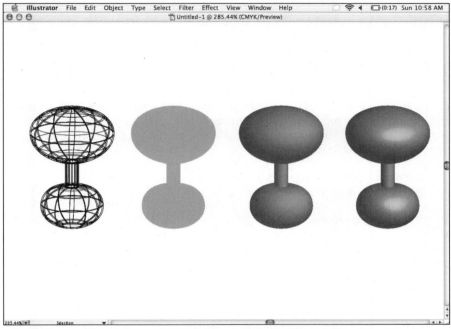

Figure 13-14: An object with all four surfaces applied from left to right (wireframe, no shading, diffuse shading, and plastic shading)

Lighting options

In the Lighting Sphere in the 3D Extrude & Bevel Options dialog box, you can set a variety of lighting choices on your object. The buttons in the Lighting Sphere are from left to right: Send selected light to back, New light, and Delete light buttons.

The lighting options for Diffuse or Plastic shading are:

✦ **Light Intensity** controls how intense the light is. The values are from 0 to 100.

✦ **Ambient Light** changes the brightness of all of the surfaces of the object. The values are from 0-100.

✦ **Blend Steps** adjust how smooth the shading flows across the object. A lower number creates a more matte look. A higher number creates a glossy shiny look.

If you are just using Plastic Shading, you can use these additional options:

✦ **Highlight Intensity** controls the reflecting light. A low number creates a matte look. A high number creates a glossy look.

✦ **Highlight Size** controls the size of the highlight on the object from 0 (none) to 100 (all).

Along with the lighting is the shading color. The default is black, but you can click the swatch and access the color picker. From the color wheel you can choose any color you wish.

Cross-Reference For more on Color, see Chapter 6.

The Surface area shows the light on a surface. You can move the light around by dragging it to a new location. By clicking the New Light icon, you can add additional lights to the surface. The active light has a box around it. Each light can have different settings applied to it.

Note The default setting is that all 3D objects must have one light. You can add as many as you'd like in addition to the default.

The trashcan icon lets you delete lights. Select a light and then click the trashcan to delete the light. The first icon is Send selected light to back. It sends that light behind the object for backlighting. Figure 13-15 shows objects with different lighting applied to them.

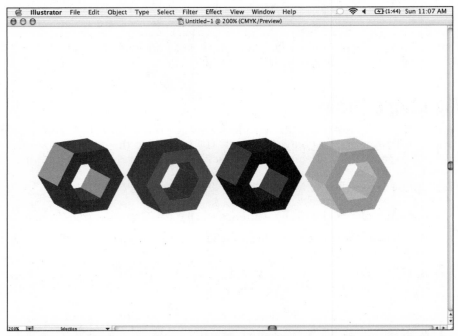

Figure 13-15: Objects with different lighting effects applied by moving the light source and changing the Light Intensity, Ambient Light, Highlight Intensity, Highlight Size, and Blend Step sliders

Spot colors are automatically changed to process colors unless you check the Preserve Spot Colors box. By checking the Draw Hidden surfaces box, you can view the back faces through transparent surfaces.

Tip If you hold down the shift key while adjusting lighting in the 3D dialog box, you see the changes update in real time.

Using the Appearance palette with 3D

The amazing Appearance palette works wonders with 3D objects. If you have an object with multiple Strokes and Fills, and 3D, try moving the 3D to different areas of the Appearance palette. Move it above a Fill, under a Stroke, and see how different the object can look. Figure 13-16 shows an object with multiple attributes. I moved the 3D section to different areas to create different looks.

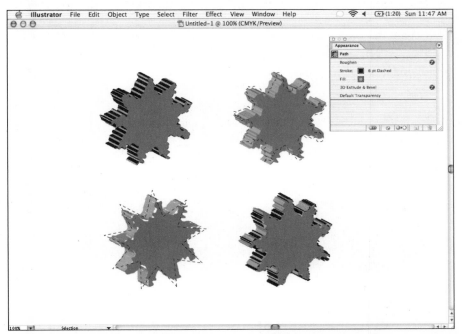

Figure 13-16: An original object (left) and after different attributes were moved in the Appearance palette (right and below left and right)

Mapping 2D art to 3D surfaces

One of the most powerful features of 3D is the ability to wrap 2D objects around 3D surfaces. This feature alone makes upgrading or buying Illustrator worth the money. The Mapping feature is a great way to add a label to a bottle or any type of package design. Now your clients can see how their product will look before printing and packaging.

The most important concept to understand when you are mapping artwork is that each 3D object usually has several different surfaces and each of those surfaces can have separate mapped artwork. The key to mapping 2D to 3D is to make the 2D object that you want to use as the map, and turn it into a symbol. Any of Illustrator's symbols can be mapped onto 3D objects. Figure 13-20 shows the final result of mapping a type on a 3D object. The following are the steps to achieve this:

1. **Create the text that you want to map onto the revolved art.**

2. **Drag the created text into the symbols palette.** Doing this makes the text a new symbol.

3. **Create the path you want to revolve.** I chose a path to indicate a bottle.

4. **Choose Effect ➪ 3D ➪ Revolve.** Doing this brings up the 3D Revolve Options dialog box (Figure 13-17).

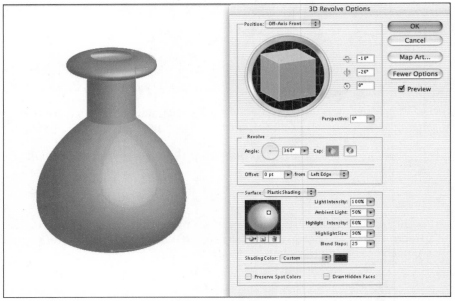

Figure 13-17: The 3D Revolve Options dialog box with the path for a bottle

5. **Press the Map art button.** This brings up the Map Art dialog box (Figure 13-18). In this dialog box, you can see the number of surfaces on the revolved object, starting with surface 1.

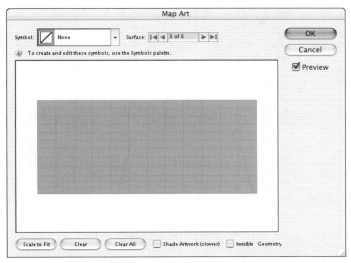

Figure 13-18: The Map Art dialog box

6. **Choose the surface you want to map.**

Note

As you choose a surface, the original will highlight in red wireframe the surface you are selecting to make it easier for you to see where the mapping will occur.

7. **When you have the surface you want to map, choose a symbol from the drop-down menu on the left.** The symbol you created will be there (Figure 13-19).

8. **When you have the art chosen for all of the surfaces, click OK.** You exit out of the Map Art dialog box.

9. **Change the rotation or axis view if you want.**

10. **Click OK.** The final results are shown in Figure 13-20.

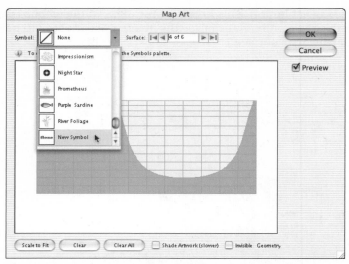

Figure 13-19: Your created symbol shows up in the list.

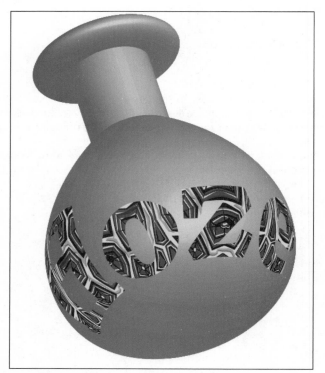

Figure 13-20: The final mapped artwork on the extruded object

When you choose a symbol to map, the symbol appears in the center of the screen with a bounding box around it. This box gives you the ability to stretch, rotate, or move the object to fit the area you want. Figure 13-21 shows a 2D symbol being rotated and stretched to fit a surface.

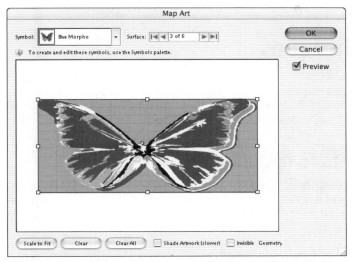

Figure 13-21: The symbol being manipulated to fit the surface

The Map Art dialog box also has a preview button in which you can see the object mapped onto the shape. One of the cool things to do is to use a cube and map artwork on all surfaces of the cube to make custom dice. Use the dice later in animation for a Web page.

Cross-Reference   For more on Web stuff, see Chapter 16.

The Map Art dialog box has several other useful features:

- ✦ **Symbol:** Choose the 2D object to map onto your shape.
- ✦ **Surface:** All the object's surfaces are listed here. Apply mapped art to one surface or as many as you'd like.
- ✦ **Scale to Fit:** Choose this option to scale the mapped artwork to fit the whole surface.
- ✦ **Clear:** Use this to remove mapped artwork from the selected surface.
- ✦ **Clear All:** Use this to remove all mapped artwork from all surfaces.

✦ **Shade Artwork (slower):** This option shows the mapped artwork along with the shade and lighting applied. A preview takes longer with this option turned on.

✦ **Invisible Geometry:** Choosing this option previews just the mapped art on the object with the object showing in wireframe.

Other 3D Techniques

Using Adobe Illustrator's 3D isn't the only way to create depth in illustrations. You can do many things in Illustrator to create the illusion of depth. Drop shadows and blended shadows help define depth, but the most useful thing that you can do is to think about how a light source would hit an object and reflect back to the viewer.

Using gradients to make bumps and dents

When you place gradients on themselves and one gradient has a different direction than another, 3D effects appear. If you remember that highlights reflect off surfaces that bounce light to your eye, that principle should help you determine the direction of the gradients.

Of course, whether an object is coming at you or going away from you should be obvious, shouldn't it? Figure 13-22 shows ten different buttons. See whether you can determine which buttons are "innies" and which buttons are "outies." To assist you further, each button is on a standard background and has a button ring. The ring makes the direction of several of the buttons quite obvious.

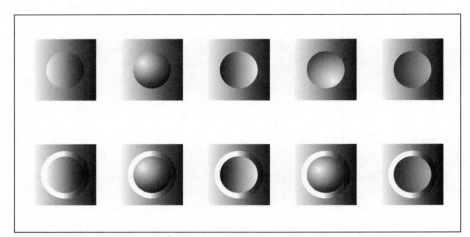

Figure 13-22: Innie and outie buttons

Perspective drawing

Another new aspect to Illustrator is the addition of perspective. The perspective option is found in the 3D Extrude & Bevel Options dialog box. This option gives your 3D object a perspective look. The perspective slider ranges from 0 to 160 degrees. The perspective is a simulated distance from the object in the actual file (see Figure 13-23).

Figure 13-23: A 3D object with perspective applied

Guest Artist-how to: Use Illustrator to Create 3D Texture Maps (Joe Jones)

Though I would never claim to be one of the best texture mappers, 3D modelers, or science-fiction illustrators around, which I certainly aspire to be, the techniques I show here seem to work pretty well for me so far.

Very early on when I was experimenting in a 3D environment, I quickly realized the key to creating 3D images was to texture map with as much detail as possible. Creating a wireframe for every little intricate component that I wanted to show in my architecture would create incredibly huge files and probably take a couple of weeks to render. Not the thing to do! For me, it was logistically impossible to model everything, so I had to quickly come up with a system to create the necessary level of detail in my Illustrations. I am currently still refining my process of creating 3D illustrations, which has already taken several years of development. Incredibly difficult, but very fun stuff though!

Being able to have full control of each step and to see it all come together in 3D is nothing less than incredible to me. I've worked on every type of graphics and illustration projects you can imagine for over 20 years now, but nothing comes close to the intimacy that I feel when working on 3D texture images. Though I'm sure a psychiatrist would claim this is a form of escapism, I say, hey, an artist has to dream!

Well, without further ado, here's a brief description of each of the steps involved:

Conceptualization

I first created a slew of small conceptual thumbnails, sketches, and studies. Figure 13-24 shows the original conceptual sketch that I worked from for this piece entitled "Port Merillia."

Figure 13-24: A Sketch of the original concept

In the business of illustration, we have a saying: Practice safe design and still use the concept!" In the end, concept is everything. Although in 3D illustration, true craftsmanship is in the model-making and texture mapping, the concept still has to pull it all together for the illustration to work. I first developed a large series of conceptual sketches (one of which is shown in Figure 13-25), and I defined the look of my architecture. Then I designed and built all the outline parts for the shape of each building as paths in Illustrator, which were later used in the modeling process in Ray Dream Studio. The actual texture mapping for each building is a process that starts in Illustrator, which I discuss in a coming section.

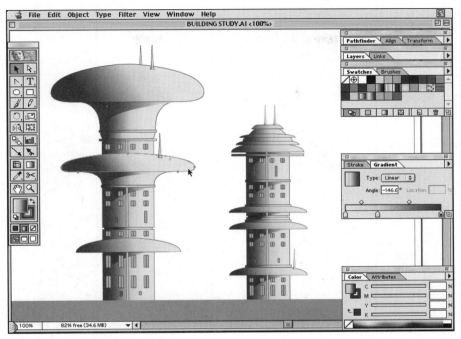

Figure 13-25: Structure study

Modeling

Yes, yes, I know, this is surely the poor boy's approach to 3D illustration. What can I say, it works and I'm still not quite ready to drop several thousand dollars on applications such as Maya or 3D Studio Max. Soon, maybe. Figure 13-26 is a conceptual vector study created in Illustrator. Here, I work on refining the scale, depth, color, and balance I want from this piece.

Figure 13-27 shows the actual wireframe model of the "Dome" element of just one structure after construction. It is now ready to be assembled with other modeled elements and texture mapped. To turn a basic shape into a 3D model, you must generate at least two separate paths — one is the shape of how it would look from the side, and the other is from the top. These paths are called *Cross Sections* and *Envelope Lines* and are essential in extruding or lathing a shape into a 3D model.

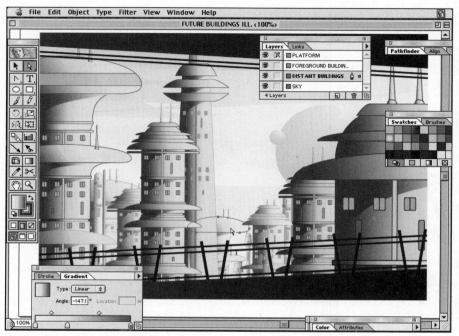

Figure 13-26: Structure study

As you look at these illustrations, remember that for every single shape in each building, I had to produce at least two precise paths in Illustrator. I created all line work for the models, as well as the artwork for the texture mapping, at the same time to ensure everything would fit and map correctly in the final steps. Very important!

Texture mapping

Figure 13-28 shows the wireframe model of the "dome" element, quickly texture mapped for a better idea of its look, smoothness, and form.

All of the custom mapping I created was based on my original sketches and more refined drawings, which had to be the first carefully laid out in Illustrator, as shown in Figure 13-29. Starting with the circular base shape for the "dome" on the first layer, I created various panels, lights, and windows on separate layers for full control of these elements in Photoshop.

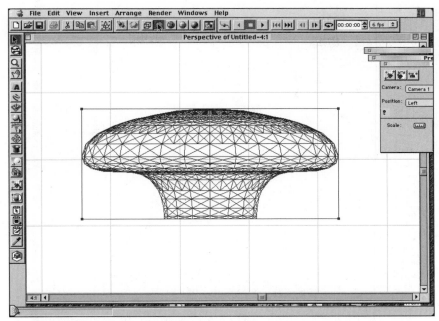

Figure 13-27: Dome wireframe

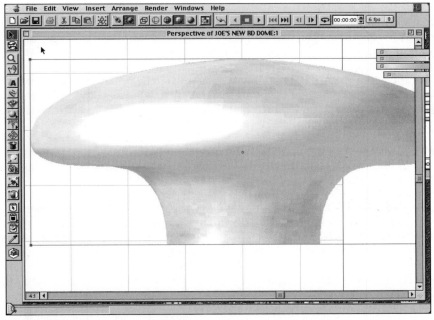

Figure 13-28: Texture-mapped dome

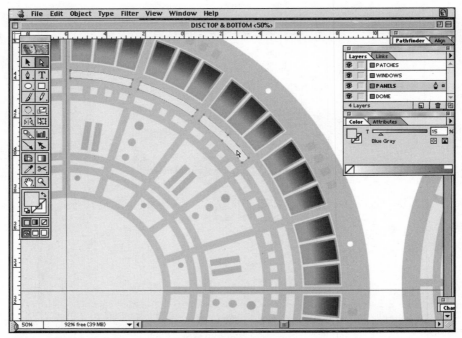

Figure 13-29: The dome texture map in Illustrator

I carefully constructed each map to proportionately match the building models that were built. To maintain their layers, I then exported these Illustrator files into Photoshop, where I added additional weathering and edge effect treatments.

Just like the "dome" map, the building map, shown in Figure 13-30, was created in a similar manner. Each element of the panels, patches, windows, and lights were set up on separate layers to be exported into Photoshop with the layers intact, to complete the final rendered map.

Figure 13-31 is the "dome" map file being brought into Photoshop. I start with some color correction and create the custom brushes that are needed for painting the weathered appearance.

As any experienced texture map artist will tell you, the appearance of weathering and signs of aging are critical to creating an illusion of reality. Figure 13-32 shows the final "dome" texture map with all of its edge effects and hand painted weathering. I worked both in Layers and Adjustment Layers in Photoshop to create this effect. When this map is applied to its model, it looks very convincing. Though the shapes in these maps are basic, this gives you some idea of the level of detail that can be created with a good texture map.

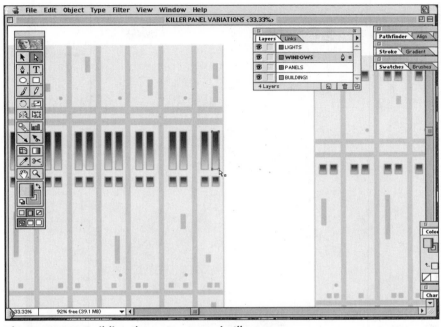

Figure 13-30: Building the texture map in Illustrator

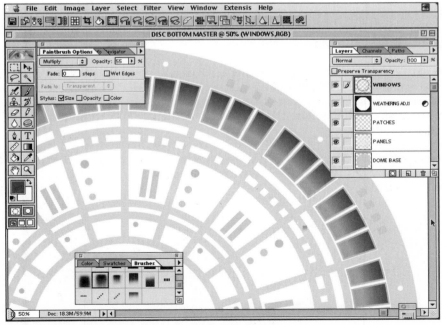

Figure 13-31: The dome texture map in Photoshop

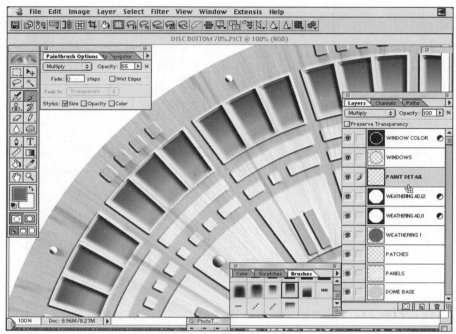

Figure 13-32: The weathered dome texture map in Photoshop

Figure 13-33 shows one of the many final building texture maps I had to create. Again, I created its edge effects and hand painted weathering in Layers and Adjustment Layers working in Photoshop.

To create certain effects, and especially the illusion of transparency and ambiance for the window and the lights, I first had to create this window mask for the "dome" in Illustrator, as shown in Figure 13-34. I then rasterized it as a grayscale file to be mapped in later. If done right, this creates a convincing effect without the pains of extensive modeling.

Figure 13-35 shows four different texture maps applied to just one structure model. Add some light and atmosphere and we're well on our way. What'd I tell you, pretty convincing, huh!

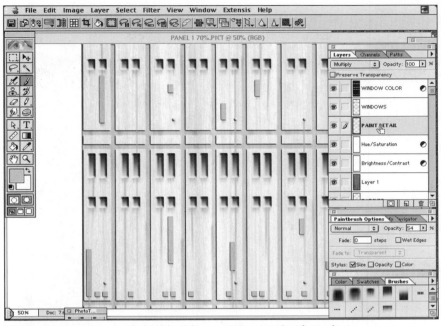

Figure 13-33: The weathered building texture map in Photoshop

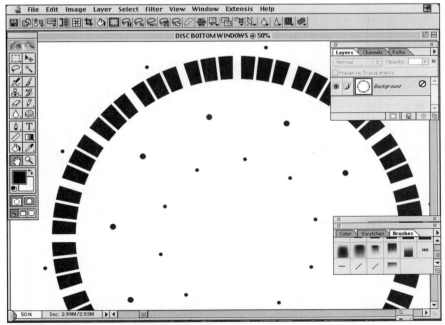

Figure 13-34: The dome window mask

Figure 13-35: The final dome texture maps

The final completed wireframe model partially rendered is shown in Figure 13-36. Of course, after all of the texture mapping is applied to all of the various models, this scene based on the original sketch needs to be built, lit, and then rendered. From there the file is brought into Photoshop, where color correction and a ton of touchup work is done. For example, the clothing for the figures is hand painted using a digital tablet. We're not in Kansas anymore!

You can view the finished image after all the final touch-ups in all its glory in the color insert pages.

Figure 13-36: A sample of the final model

Summary

✦ You can extrude or revolve 2D objects to create 3D objects.

✦ You can add multiple lights and change the color of the shading on a 3D object.

✦ Change the surface characteristics to be wireframe, no shading, diffuse shading, or plastic shading.

✦ You can map 2D artwork onto 3D objects.

✦ Layering gradients creates a 3D look.

✦   ✦   ✦

Customizing and Automating Illustrator

Along with using Illustrator to do all types of incredible artwork is the practical, real-world side of Illustrator where deadlines have to be met and there's little or no time for play. This chapter focuses on real-world applications of Illustrator and on how to get the most out of the software.

Who's Responsible?

Under the Illustrator menu on a Macintosh and under the Help menu in Windows, you'll find some useful information about the creators of Illustrator and its plug-ins.

About Illustrator displays a dialog box (see Figure 14-1) with the user information and credits for the Illustrator team. The credits list everyone who ever helped with getting Illustrator updated and created and made you aware of the large number of people who are involved in creating the software.

About Plug-Ins displays a dialog box (see Figure 14-2) that lists all the installed plug-ins. Choosing one of the items in the Plug-Ins submenu displays who made the plug-in and, occasionally, some useful or interesting information about that plug-in.

Figure 14-1: The Adobe Illustrator dialog box

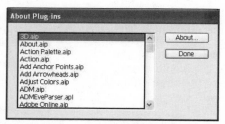

Figure 14-2: The About Plug-Ins dialog box

Customization Options

No two illustrators work the same. To accommodate the vast differences among styles, techniques, and habits, Illustrator provides many settings that each user can change to personalize the software.

Illustrator provides four major ways to change preferences:

✦ The most dramatic and difficult changes are to a small file called Adobe Illustrator Startup. The startup file changes how new documents appear and which custom colors, patterns, and gradients are available.

✦ You can also control how Illustrator works by accessing the Preferences sub-menu (choose Illustrator ⇨ Preferences on the Mac [File ⇨ Preferences on Windows]). You make most of these changes in the Preferences dialog box, which you access by choosing Illustrator ⇨ Preferences on the Mac [File ⇨ Preferences on Windows] (⌘+K) [Ctrl+K]. Within the Preferences dialog box, a number of different preference panels can be selected from the pop-up menu at the top of the dialog box. You can go through each of the preference panels one by one by clicking the Next and Previous buttons or simply by choosing a preference panel from the Preferences submenu. The preference panels are General, Type & Auto Tracing, Units & Display Performance, Guides & Grid, Smart Guides & Slices, Hyphenation, Plug-Ins & Scratch disks, Files & Clipboard, and Workgroup.

✦ A third way to make changes is by changing preferences relative to each document. You usually make these changes in the Document Setup dialog box, but a few other options are available. There is more information on document-specific preferences later in this chapter.

✦ The fourth way to customize preferences happens pretty much automatically. When you quit Illustrator, it remembers many of the current settings for the next time you run it. These settings include palette placements and values in toolbox settings.

Illustrator has a few settings that you cannot customize. These features can really get under your skin because most of them seem like things that you should be able to customize. See the "Things You Can't Customize" section later in this chapter for a list of these settings.

Modifying the Startup File

When you first run Illustrator, the program looks to the Illustrator startup file to check a number of preferences. Those preferences include window size and placement, as well as custom colors, gradients, patterns, zoom levels, tiling options, and graph designs.

Illustrator has two startup files for each color mode (RBG or CMYK). When launching Illustrator and starting a new document, you choose which color mode you want to work in.

New documents have all the attributes of the startup file. Opened documents have all the gradients, custom colors, patterns, and graph designs of the startup file. To modify the startup file:

1. Open the startup file. The startup file is called either Adobe Illustrator Startup_CMYK or Adobe Illustrator Startup_RGB and is located in the Plug-Ins folder in the Adobe Illustrator folder. The file is an Adobe Illustrator document, so double-clicking the file opens Illustrator, as well.

2. Figure 14-3 shows the Adobe Illustrator Startup_CMYK file. If you delete a pattern, custom color, or gradient from the startup file, it is gone. Kaput! The only way to get it back is to replace the startup file from the original CD-ROM.

3. To add something to the startup file, add the color, pattern, or gradient to the Swatches palette. (To add a graph design, create the graph design and apply it to a graph. Then place the graph in the startup file.)

4. To change the window size, just save the startup file with the window size that you want new documents to have.

5. To change the color swatches on the Swatches palette, add, replace, or delete color swatches while the startup file is open and then save the startup file.

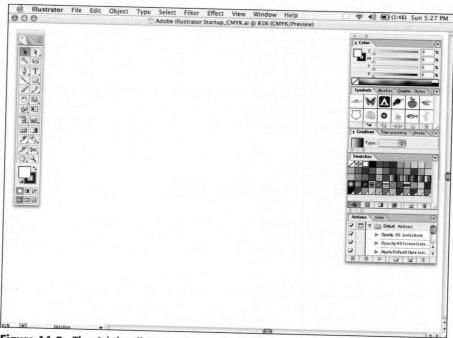

Figure 14-3: The Adobe Illustrator Startup_CMYK file

If you delete the Adobe Illustrator Startup file, most patterns, gradients, and custom colors will not be available until you create a new startup file or place the original startup file from the CD-ROM in the Plug-Ins folder.

To check whether changes that you made in the startup file will work, quit Illustrator and run the program again. You cannot tell whether the changes are in place until you quit and reopen Illustrator.

You can change both the window size of new documents and the viewing percentage. Most people like documents to fit in the window when it is created.

Changing Preferences

The General portion of the Preferences dialog box (choose Illustrator ⇨ Preferences ⇨ General for the Macintosh or File ⇨ General ⇨ Preferences for Windows or press ⌘+K or Ctrl+K) contains most of the personalized customizing options for Illustrator. The options in this box affect keyboard increments, measuring units, and the way that objects are drawn. These options are considered personalized options because they are specific to the way that each person uses the program. Few people have the same preference settings as others have (unless they never change the defaults). The General portion of the Preferences dialog box is shown in Figure 14-4.

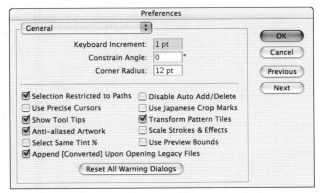

Figure 14-4: The General portion of the Preferences dialog box

Altering the Keyboard Increment option

The cursor key increment that you specify in this option controls how far an object moves when you select it and press the keyboard arrows.

I have this increment set to 0.5 point because this is the smallest amount that I usually need to move things. The default for this setting is 1 point, which many people feel is small enough. I make my increment smaller when I am working in 800% or 1600% views.

Tip   While the arrow keys move selected objects the distance that is set in the keyboard increment option. Option [Alt] + the arrow key makes a copy of the object in that direction.

Using the Constrain Angle option

The Constrain Angle option controls the angle at which all objects are aligned. Rectangles are always drawn "flat," aligning themselves to the bottom, top, and sides of the document window. When you press the Shift key, lines that you draw with the Pen tool and objects that you move will align to the Constrain Angle, or 45°, 90°, 135°, or 180°, plus or minus the constraining angle.

The Constrain Angle also affects how the four transformation tools transform objects. The Scale tool can be very hard to use when the Constrain Angle is not 0°, and the Shear tool becomes even more difficult to use than normal at different Constrain Angles. Pressing Shift when you are using the Rotate tool constrains the rotational angle to 45° increments added to the Constrain Angle.

Cross-Reference   For more on the Rotate tool and other transformational tools, see Chapter 10.

In Illustrator, 0° is a horizontal line and 90° is a vertical line. Figure 14-5 shows Illustrator angles.

If you set the Constrain Angle at 20°, objects are constrained to movements of 20°, 65°, 110°, 155°, and 200°. Constrain Angles of 90°, 180°, and –90° (270°) affect only type, patterns, gradients, and graphs; everything else works normally.

When Option[Alt]-copying objects, you can use the Shift key in conjunction with a Constrain Angle to duplicate objects at a specific angle. Option[Alt]-copy means to press the Option [Alt] key while dragging an object and then to release the mouse button before releasing the Option [Alt] key to produce a duplicate of the object at the new location.

Changing the Corner Radius option

The Corner Radius option affects the size of the curved corners on a rounded rectangle.

Cross-Reference   For a complete explanation of the corner radius and rounded rectangles, see Chapter 4.

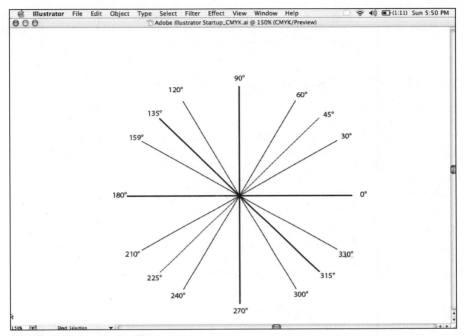

Figure 14-5: Angles in Illustrator

The corner radius value changes each time you enter a new value in the Rectangle dialog box. This dialog box appears when you click the Rectangle or Rounded Rectangle tools without dragging in a document. If, for example, you create one rounded rectangle with a rounded-corner radius of 24 points, all rounded rectangles that you create from that point forward will have a radius of 24 points. The only ways to change the corner radius are to click a Rectangle tool without dragging in a document and then enter a new value in the Rectangle dialog box or to enter a new value in the Corner Radius text field in the Preferences dialog box.

The real advantage to changing the corner radius in the Preferences dialog box is that the corner radius affects manually created (dragged with the Rounded Rectangle tool) rounded rectangles immediately. Changing the corner radius in the Rectangle dialog box requires that you know the exact dimensions of the rectangle or that you draw a rectangle by entering information in the Rectangle dialog box (clicking with the Rectangle tool without dragging) and specify the corner radius. You must then delete the original rectangle in order to draw a rounded rectangle with the correct corner radius manually.

Caution Because you can change the Corner Radius setting easily, be sure to check it before you draw a series of rounded rectangles manually. There is no easy or automatic way to change the corner radius on existing rounded rectangles.

If you use 0 point as the Corner radius setting, the corners are not rounded at all. If you click with the Rounded Rectangle tool and enter 0 point as the corner radius, the Corner Radius setting in the Preferences dialog box changes to 0 point.

Adjusting the General options

The eleven checkboxes in the General Options section of Preferences are Illustrator's version of the Battlestar Galactica ragtag fleet of unwieldy spacefaring craft. Some are quite powerful, others seem like they aren't capable of transferring millions of people across the galaxy, much less defending themselves against the evil menace of the Cylon Empire. Okay, that wasn't the best analogy. The fact is, there is no other place in Illustrator where so many totally unrelated options share the same dialog box, and I had to come up with a snazzy introduction.

Selection Restricted to Paths

With Selection Restricted to Paths checked, you have to select the object's path with a Selection tool to select the object, rather than click on the fill. If you uncheck this option, you can click on the fill with the Selection tool to select it.

The Use Precise Cursors option

Precise cursors are cursors that appear as a variation of a cross hair instead of in the shape of a tool. Figure 14-6 shows cursors that are different when the Use Precise Cursors option is on.

Tip   The Caps Lock key toggles between standard cursors and precise cursors. When the Use Precise Cursors option is checked, the Caps Lock key makes the cursors standard. When the Use Precise Cursors option is not checked, the Caps Lock key activates the precise cursors.

I usually keep this option on and rarely engage the Caps Lock key to change the cursors back to normal. In particular, I've found the precise cursor for the Brush tool to be quite useful, seeing as how the standard Brush cursor is one giant amorphous blob.

The Show Tool Tips option

This option displays little pop-up names for each of the tools if you rest your cursor above them for one second. It's a great idea to keep this option on, as not only do you see the name of the tool, but also the key to press to access that tool.

Tip   Illustrator lets you see the name of each swatch as you pass your cursor over it if you have Tool Tips active.

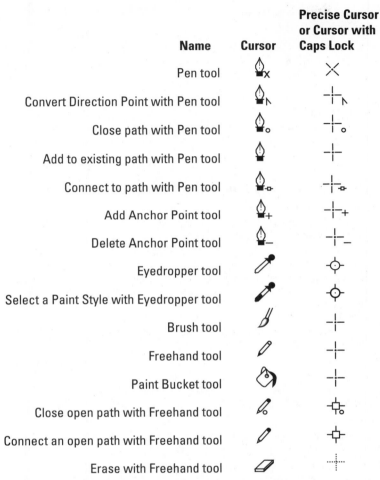

Figure 14-6: The regular cursors on the left, the precise cursors on the right

The Anti-aliased Artwork option

The Anti-aliased Artwork option turns on anti-aliasing for onscreen representation of vector objects. Curved and diagonal edges appear smooth instead of jagged (or "stair-stepped"). The resulting effect is for onscreen viewing only, and won't affect output or rasterization of your artwork.

Select Same Tint % option

This option specifies that the objects must have the same tint percentage when selecting objects with the same color. When this option isn't checked, you select a color and all tints are selected of that color.

Append [Converted] Upon Opening Legacy Files option

When you open an older version of Illustrator with Illustrator 11, you'll get a dialog box telling you "This file contains text that was created in a previous version of Illustrator. This legacy text must be updated before you edit it". Because the text engine was revamped in Illustrator 11, all old type needs to be updated. By default this option is checked so all files with legacy type or other functions such as older files before gradients and transparency will be updated when opening the file.

Disable Auto Add/Delete option

This option refers to the Pen tool's automatic add/delete feature. The default is unchecked. When the box is not checked, you can add or delete points while drawing with the Pen tool. As you are drawing a path with the Pen tool, you can click on the path to add more Anchor Points. You can also click an Anchor Point to delete it and continue to draw your path without having to switch tools. When you check this option, this new feature is turned off.

The Use Japanese Crop Marks option

When checked, the Use Japanese Crop Marks option changes the standard crop marks, usually created with Filter ➪ Create ➪ Crop Marks, to Japanese Crop Marks (see Figure 14-7).

The Transform Pattern Tiles option

Check the Transform Pattern Tiles option if you want patterns in paths to be moved, scaled, rotated, sheared, and reflected when you use the transformation tools. When this option is checked, pulling up a transformation dialog box (Move, Rotate, Scale, Reflect, or Shear) automatically checks the Pattern checkbox. When the option is not checked, the Pattern checkbox is not checked in the transformation dialog box. This option controls whether selected patterns are transformed when the transform palette is used.

Figure 14-7: Standard crop marks (top) and Japanese crop marks (bottom)

I usually check the Transform Pattern Tiles box, which sets all patterns to automatically transform and move with the objects that are being transformed and moved. This feature is especially useful when you want to create perspective in objects because the transformations of patterns can enhance the intended perspective.

The Scale Stroke & Effects option

When the Scale Stroke & Effects feature is on, it automatically increases and reduces line weights and applied effects relative to an object when you uniformly scale that object manually. For example, if a path has a Stroke weight of 1 point and you reduce the path uniformly by 50%, the Stroke weight changes to 0.5 point.

Note   Scaling objects nonuniformly (without the Shift key pressed) does not change the Stroke weight on an object, regardless of whether the Scale Line Weight feature is on or off.

The Use Preview Bounds option

When you check the Use Preview Bounds option it affects how the Info palette measures the dimension of the selected object. With the Use Preview Bounds checked, Illustrator's Info palette includes the size of the stroke width and other elements like feathered shadows in the dimensions.

Reset All Warning Boxes dialog

The Reset All Warning Boxes will put back all of those lovely warnings Illustrator has. For example, you get a warning when you try to delete a point and don't click on the point. You can turn this off by clicking the don't show this again box. When you choose to reset all warning boxes, it will be turned on again.

Changing Preferences for Type and Auto Tracing

The Type & Auto Tracing preferences enable you to customize your type options and your tracing options. There are nine type options to choose from. The Auto Trace options affect how the Auto Trace and Pencil tools work. Figure 14-8 shows the Type & Auto Tracing dialog box.

Altering Type preferences

The nine type preference options you can set are: Size/Leading, Baseline Shift, Tracking, Greeking, Selection Restricted to Path/Characters, Show Asian Options, Show Font Names in English, Number of Recent Fonts, and Font Preview Size.

The Size/Leading option

You can use the keyboard to increase and decrease type size by pressing ⌘+Shift+ > [Ctrl+Shift+>] and ⌘+Shift+ < [Ctrl+Shift+<], respectively. You can increase and decrease leading by pressing Option-_ [Alt+_] and Option-↓ [Alt+↓], respectively. In the Size/Leading text box, you specify the increment by which the size and leading change.

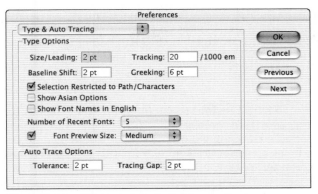

Figure 14-8: The Type & Auto Tracing preferences
dialog box

You can increase or decrease the type size and leading only until you reach the
upper and lower limits of each. The upper limit for type size and leading is 1296
points, and the lower limit for each is 0.1 point.

Tip　I keep my settings fairly high, at 10 points, because I have found that I require
large point changes, usually quite a bit more than 10 points. If I need to do fine-
tuning, I either type the exact size that I want or use the Scale tool.

The Baseline Shift option

The Baseline Shift feature moves selected type up and down on the baseline, independent of the leading. The increment specified in this box is how much the type is
moved when you press the arrow keyboard commands. To move type up one increment, press Option+Shift+_ [Alt+Shift+_]. To move type down one increment, press
Option-Shift+-↓ [Alt+Shift+-↓].

I keep the Baseline shift increment at 1 point so that I can adjust Path type better;
specifically, I like to be able to adjust the baseline shift of type on a circle.

The Tracking option

Tracking changes the amount of space between selected characters, and the setting
in this text field represents the amount of space (measured in thousandths of an em
space) that the keyboard command adds or removes. To increase tracking, you
press ⌘+right arrow[Ctrl+right arrow]; to decrease it, you press ⌘+left arrow
[Ctrl+left arrow].

To increase the tracking by five times the increment in the Type & Auto Tracing
portion of the Preferences dialog box, press Shift+Option+⌘+\ [Shift+Alt+Ctrl+\].
To decrease the tracking by five times the increment, press Shift+Option+⌘+
backspace [Shift+Alt+Ctrl+backspace].

The value in the Tracking text field also affects incremental changes in kerning. Kerning is the addition or removal of space between one pair of letters only. Kerning is done instead of tracking when a blinking insertion point is between two letters, as opposed to at least one selected character for tracking.

The Greeking option

The number that you enter in this field defines the point at which Illustrator begins to greek text (see Figure 14-9). Illustrator greeks text — turns the letters into gray bars — when the text is so small that reading it on the screen would be hard or impossible. This change reduces screen redraw time dramatically, especially when the document contains a great deal of text.

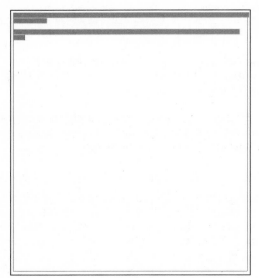

Figure 14-9: Text on screen is so small that it is greeked.

The size in this text field is relative to the viewing magnification of the document. At a limit of 6 points, 6-point type at 100%, 66%, 50%, 25%, or smaller will be greeked; but 6-point type at 150%, 200%, or larger will be readable. With the same limitations, 12-point type will be greeked at 49% and smaller, but it is readable at 50% and larger.

The Type Object Selection by Path Only option

Checking this option makes it possible to select text by clicking on the text path itself. The default is turned off allowing you to click anywhere on the type with the Selection tool to select the type.

The Show Asian options

Check the Show Asian option to be able to view and set the options for Asian fonts. The Asian fonts include Chinese, Japanese, and Korean.

The Show Font Names in English option

If you have a font from another language installed on your system (like Kanji, the Japanese character set), this option allows you to see these typefaces in the font/type menus as English words, rather than the seemingly indecipherable names that double-bit fonts turn into when they're displayed in Roman characters.

Adjusting Auto Trace options

In the Auto Trace Options you can set the Tolerance and the Tracing Gap for the Auto Trace tool. The Auto Trace setting controls the accuracy of paths that are created when tracing placed templates.

Cross-Reference

Chapter 8 discusses tracing.

The Tolerance option

The lower the Tolerance setting, the more exact the resulting path. A higher setting results in smoother, less accurate paths. You can enter a value from 0 to 10, in increments of $\frac{1}{100}$ point (two decimal places).

The Auto Trace number is relative to the number of pixels on the screen that the resulting path may vary. A tolerance of 10 means that the resulting path may vary up to 10 pixels from the location of the actual dragged or traced area.

The Tracing Gap option

When you use the Auto Trace tool to trace a placed image, the tool may encounter gaps, or white space, between solid areas. The Tracing Gap option enables you to specify that if the Auto Trace tool runs into a white-space gap of 1 or 2 pixels, it can jump over the gap and continue tracing on the other side of it.

A value of 0 prevents the Auto Trace tool from tracing over gaps. If you use a value of 1, the Auto Trace tool traces over gaps that are up to 1 pixel wide. If you use a value of 2 (the highest allowed), it traces over gaps that are 2 pixels wide. The Tracing Gap setting not only goes over gaps; it also adheres less closely to the original template.

I usually use a setting of 0 because when I trace any image in Illustrator, I examine it closely in Photoshop to make sure that it does not have any gaps. I can then be sure that the resulting paths will not be misshapen because of image-tracing inaccuracies.

Using Units & Display Performance

The Units & Display Performance preferences enable you to select the measurement system you want to use and set the performance of the Hand tool. Figure 14-10 shows the Units & Display Performance dialog box.

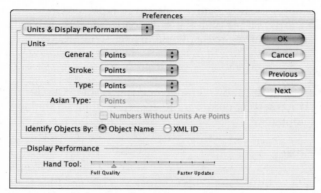

Figure 14-10: The Units & Display Performance dialog box

Changing Units settings

The General pop-up menu in the Units section changes the measurement system for the current document and all future new documents. The areas the measurement can be specified for are: General (which includes the Rulers), Stroke, Type, and Asian Type. Illustrator contains five different measurement units: inches, picas, points, millimeters, and centimeters.

✦ **General:** The General measurement area applies to the measure tool and the Rulers.

✦ **Stroke:** The Stroke measurements apply to the weight of the path's stroke.

✦ **Type:** Use the Type area to set the type measurement increments.

✦ **Asian Type:** Sets the type measurement increments for Asian type.

Caution   Changing the General units in the Units & Display Performance Preferences dialog box changes the Ruler units in the Document Setup dialog box (choose File ➪ Document Setup or press ⌘+Option+P [Ctrl+Alt+P]).

The other areas under Units that can be changed are: Numbers Without Units Are Points checkbox and Identify Objects By (Object Name or XML ID).

✦ **Numbers Without Units Are Points:** When you enter a number with no measurement indicator (I for inches, p for points, and so on) the default is points.

✦ **Identify Objects By:** In this area, choose a radio button to identify objects by name or XML ID.

Being aware of which measurement system you are working in is important. When you enter a measurement in a dialog box, any numbers that are not measurement-system-specific are applied to the current unit of measurement. For example, if you want to move something 1 inch and you open the Move dialog box (choose Object ⇨ Transform ⇨ Move or double-click the Selection tool), you need to add either the inch symbol (") or the abbreviation after you type a 1 in the dialog box if the measurement system is not inches. If the measurement system is points and picas, entering just a 1 moves the object 1 point, not 1 inch. If the measurement system is inches already, entering just the number 1 is fine.

Usually a corresponding letter or letters indicates the measurement system: in for inch, pt for points, and cm for centimeters.

I use the points/picas system for several reasons. First, using points and picas is easier because you can specify smaller increments exactly (ever try to figure out what $\frac{1}{12}$ inch is in decimals?). Second, type is measured in points, not inches. Third, points and picas are the standard in measuring systems for designers and printers.

Caution

The default measurement is points and picas, so if you ever toss your preferences file or reinstall Illustrator, be aware that you may have to change the measurement system.

Changing Display Performance

The Hand tool's viewing performance is what you are adjusting under the Display Performance area. Drag the slider to the left so you see more quality when moving around your screen. Drag the slider to the right to get a quicker update with less quality viewing. Quicker update will show a rough preview as you are dragging rather than an exact preview of your illustration as you move around.

Changing Guides and Grid preferences

The Guides & Grid section of Preferences lets you control the color and style of your guides and grids, and the spacing of your grid. Figure 14-11 illustrates the Guides & Grid dialog box. Chapter 4 has the lowdown on using these options and grids and guides.

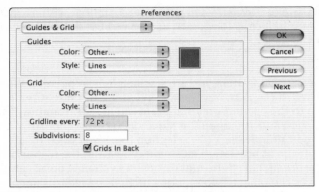

Figure 14-11: The Guides & Grid dialog box

 Tip   You can place grids in back of or in front of your image by checking or not check-ing the Grids In Back option in the Guides & Grid Preferences dialog box.

Adjusting Smart Guides & Slices

Smart Guides are helpers that show you the angle of the line and list the line as a path. You can check or uncheck four different Display Options as well as adjust the angles and snapping tolerance. The Smart Guides snap to other objects aiding you in aligning, editing, and transforming. Figure 14-12 illustrates the Smart Guides & Slices dialog box. Slices are subdivisions of a Web-based graphic and used for Web pages. For more information on Slices and the Web, see Chapter 16.

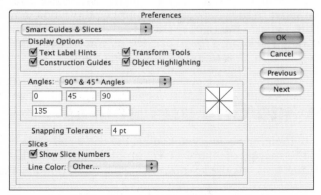

Figure 14-12: The Smart Guides & Slices dialog box

Changing Display options

The four Display Options are:

✦ **Text Label Hints:** These hints pop up when you drag your mouse cursor over your object. They tell you what each area is. For example, if you drag your mouse cursor over a line, the hint will pop up with the word "path." If you drag your mouse cursor over an Anchor Point, the hint will say "anchor point."

✦ **Transform Tools:** When you are rotating, scaling, or shearing an object with this option checked, Smart Guides shows up to help you out.

✦ **Construction Guides:** This lets you view guidelines when using Smart Guides.

✦ **Object Highlighting:** This option highlights the object that you are pointing to.

Altering Angles

The Angles you can choose in the Smart Guides & Slices dialog box let you pick what angles will display guides when you drag an object. You can choose from seven presets or create Custom Angles of your own. The six lines indicate the standard guide angles. When you add your own angled lines, a line will show up representing the particular angle you entered.

Changing Snapping Tolerance

The Snapping Tolerance enables you to choose how close you have to have an object to another object before the first object automatically "snaps" to the second object. You set the Snapping Tolerance in points and the lower the number the closer you have to move the objects to each other. The snapping tolerance default is 4 points. That means when you are within 4 points from another object, your selected object will snap to the second object. I tend to stick with the default.

Adjusting Slices

The options for Slices are: Show Slice Numbers checkbox and Line Color. The Show Slice Numbers will show the numbers for each slice if checked. The Line Color option lets you change the slice lines to a color of your choice. The default is to use a contrasting color.

Cross-Reference
Slicing is covered in Chapter 16.

Changing Hyphenation

The Hyphenation Options dialog box contains options for customizing the way Illustrator hyphenates words. At the top of the dialog box is a pop-up menu that lists various languages. Select the default language. Typically if you use Illustrator in English, you don't have to change anything. If you use a different language, you need to have that language installed on your computer. Then you can choose the language you want to use as a default. At the bottom of the dialog box is an area where you can add to the list of hyphenation exceptions. These exceptions are words that you don't want Illustrator to hyphenate under any circumstances. Figure 14-13 illustrates the Hyphenation Options dialog box.

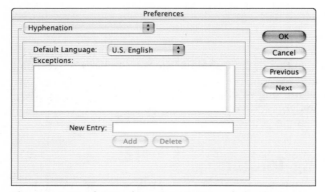

Figure 14-13: The Hyphenation Options dialog box

Adjusting the Plug-ins and Scratch Disks

The next preference item in the Preference pop-up menu is a two-trick pony, the Plug-ins & Scratch disks Preferences dialog box (see Figure 14-14). The first section in this dialog box enables you to specify a folder for plug-ins. The default is the Plug-Ins folder in the Adobe Illustrator folder.

The second section in the Plug-in & Scratch disks dialog box lets you define what drives to use as scratch disks (places where Illustrator stores information when it runs out of RAM). Typically, you should assign the fastest, largest drive to be your primary scratch disks. The settings you choose won't take effect until you restart Illustrator.

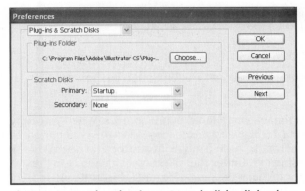

Figure 14-14: The Plug-ins & Scratch disks dialog box

Customizing the File Handling & Clipboard

The Files and Clipboard preferences let you change how the files are saved with extensions and links and how to handle the clipboard files. You set these preferences in the Files & Clipboard Preferences dialog box (Figure 14-15).

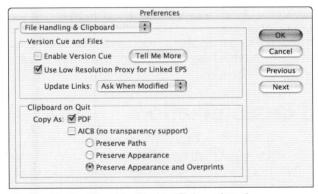

Figure 14-15: File Handling & Clipboard Preferences dialog box

The File Handling preferences are used when saving and updating files. The preferences you can choose from are:

✦ **Enable Version Cue:** Lets you see what version you are saving.

✦ **Use Low Resolution Proxy for Linked EPS:** Will put a box in for a Linked EPS to save in file space.

The Clipboard is another area that can be altered in preferences. When you copy and paste, the clipboard holds that information. Objects copied to the clipboard are PDF files by default. You can change that to AICB (Adobe Illustrator Clip Board) and you won't have any transparency support. Under the AICB you can choose to Preserve Paths, Preserve Appearance, or Preserve Appearance and Overprints. All of the AICB options will enable you to do more with editing, but also take up more file space.

Altering Placement and Toolbox Value Preferences

Most Illustrator users take many preferences for granted. But if Illustrator didn't remember certain preferences, most Illustrator users would be quite annoyed.

Palettes (including the toolbox) remain where they were when you last used Illustrator. Illustrator remembers their size and whether they were open. Values in the toolbox are still whatever you set them to last. For example, the options in the Paintbrush/Eyedropper dialog box remain the same between Illustrator sessions.

Adding Keyboard Customization

Those long-time users of Illustrator have noticed keyboard shortcut changes. While they may be frustrating, there is a method to Adobe's madness. They want to make working between programs (Illustrator and Photoshop, for instance) seamless and that means making keyboard shortcuts the same throughout their programs. If you liked a certain keyboard command, you can always customize the keyboard to what you like. Figure 14-16 shows the Keyboard Shortcuts dialog box. Choose Edit ➪ Keyboard Shortcuts to access this dialog box. In this dialog box you can change and save your own settings. Once you start to edit the Keyboard Shortcuts, the Illustrator Defaults changes to Custom and you can save your Custom settings. Next time you start Illustrator, your custom settings that are available under the Illustrator Defaults pop up.

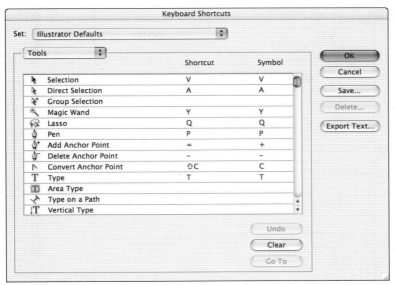

Figure 14-16: The Keyboard Shortcuts dialog box

 Note   You can't use the Command [Ctrl], Option [Alt], or Shift with keys for tool shortcuts.

Knowing What You Can't Customize

There are a few things that you cannot customize in Illustrator, and they can be annoying:

✦ Type information always defaults to 12-point Helvetica, Auto Leading, 100% Horizontal Scale, 0 Tracking, Flush Left, Hyphenation Off. There is no easy way around this set of defaults.

✦ Layers for new documents are limited to one, which is colored light blue and called Layer 1.

✦ When you create new objects, they are always 0% Black Fill and a 1-point Stroke.

✦ The Selection tool is always the active tool.

Using Actions

Adobe has brought the same technology from Photoshop into Illustrator to ease mundane repetitive tasks. The Actions palette (see Figure 14-17) is found by choosing Window ⇨ Actions. The tasks of applying color, object transformations, and text functions are easily automated using the Actions palette. Illustrator comes with some prerecorded actions and you can create your own.

Figure 14-17: The Actions palette

In the Actions palette, the box on the far left side toggles an item off or on. The next box toggles the dialog off or on. The icons underneath from left to right are: Stop, Begin Recording, Play Current Selection, Create New Set, Create New Action, and Delete Selection.

Using a Default Action

Accessing Default Actions requires little effort. To activate a Default Action click on the action to highlight it and then press the Play button.

Creating a New Action

If the numerous default actions aren't enough, you can create your own actions. To start recording a new action you need to create a new action. Click on the Create New Action icon at the bottom of the Action palette or choose New Action from the pop-up menu. Hold down the Option [Alt] key to pass up the New Action dialog box to name the action and the action set. After entering a name (I prefer to give it a name so I know what action it does), you press the Record button and start doing your action. After you are done, you can move the order or delete parts of your action.

Caution   Not everything can be recorded. If an action can't be recorded, Illustrator displays a warning box.

Creating a new set

When you create a new action, it gets put in a folder with a set of actions. You can have multiple actions in a folder, or just one. A new action needs to be a part of a set (or in a folder). It can be an existing set or a new set. Think of actions as packages. To create a new set click on the New Set icon at the bottom of the palette or select New Set from the pop-up menu.

What is recordable?

In Illustrator, not everything is recordable. As with anything, there are limits. The following actions are recordable in the Actions palette:

✦ **File:** New, Open, Close, Save, Save as, Save a Copy, Revert, Place, and Export

✦ **Edit:** Cut, Copy, Paste, Paste in Front, Paste in Back, Clear, Select All, Deselect All, and Select filters

✦ **Object:** Transform Again, Move, Scale, Rotate, Shear, Reflect, Transform Each, Arrange, Group, Ungroup, Lock, Unlock All, Hide Selection, Show All, Expand, Rasterize, Blends, Mask, Compound Path, and Cropmarks

✦ **Type:** Block, Wrap, Fit Headline, Create Outlines, Find/Change, Find Font, Change Case, Rows & Columns, Type Orientation, and Glyph Options

✦ **Filters:** Colors, Create, Distort, Stylize, and the Photoshop filters

✦ **View:** Guides-related only

✦ **Palettes:** Color, Gradient, Stroke, Character, MM Design, Paragraph, Tab Ruler, Transform, Pathfinder, Align, Swatch, Brush, Layer, and Attribute

✦ **Toolbox tools:** Ellipse, Rectangle, Polygon, Star, Spiral, Move (Selection tool), Rotate, Scale, Shear, and Reflect

✦ **Special:** Bounding-box Transform, Insert Select Path, Insert Stop, and Select Objects

Duplicating and deleting an action

You can duplicate an action when you want to modify an existing action but don't want to re-record the whole darn thing. To duplicate an action, first select an action in the Action palette and then choose Duplicate from the pop-up menu. This makes a copy of the action. To change the name of the action, double-click on the action to open the Action Options dialog box (see Figure 14-18). You can change the name of an action this way, but not the name of the action set. You can also see which Set the selected action is a part of. Assign a Function key here in the Options especially if it is an action you use repeatedly. You can also change the color of the action icon listed in the Actions palette. Deleting an action is pretty easy. Select the action you want to delete and drag it onto the trash icon at the bottom of the palette or use the pop-up menu item.

Figure 14-18: The Action Options dialog box

Starting and stopping recording

To start recording, do one of the following:

✦ Create a new action set and action.

✦ Select an existing action and click the Begin Recording icon at the bottom of the palette.

✦ Activate an action and select Start Recording in the pop-up menu.

To stop recording, do one of the following:

✦ Click the Stop Playing/Recording icon button.

✦ Select Stop Recording in the pop-up menu.

Inserting a menu item

If you have either duplicated an action or want to add to an action, you may want to insert an item into the action. To insert a menu item, activate an action, start recording, and select Insert Menu Item from the pop-up menu. This allows you to record most menu items: File, Edit, Object, Type, Filter, and guide-related Views. You don't have to use this to record a menu item.

Inserting a stop

Insert Stop enables you to stop the playback of an action at a point where you may want to make the action stop so you can add something to a certain area each time you replay it. During your recording select Insert Stop in the pop-up menu. You can have some fun with this one. You are creating your own dialog box when you insert a stop (see Figure 14-19). Put a message in this dialog box just for fun. Always allow the user to continue if they want. That way you continue on with the rest of the action after the stop. This is great for using Actions to partially do the creation, but stops so you can enter specifics in a dialog box.

Figure 14-19: The Insert Stop command lets you create your own dialog box.

Action options

The Action Options are where you can name or rename the action, move it to a set, assign a Function Key, or assign a Color to the Action. The Function key is a cool feature that lets you assign an "F" key number to an action so you can just press the F+number and your action starts.

Playback options

The Playback Options let you customize your actions even further. You can accelerate, step through, or pause your Actions, as follows:

✦ **Accelerated:** Plays the action all at once, quickly. This is great for monotonous, repetitive actions such as renaming figures or adding a tag line.

✦ **Step by step:** Plays the action one step at a time. This lets you decide whether you want to perform a step or add in-between steps.

✦ **Pause for:** Stops at each step for the specified time. This is a good choice if you want to see closely how something was recorded and would like to stop the recording at a certain spot.

Inserting a selected path

You cannot record the Pen tool or the Pencil tool, but you can record a path. Follow these steps:

1. **Draw the path.**

2. **While the path is selected, start recording.**

3. **Choose Insert Select Path from the pop-up menu.**

4. **Stop recording.**

You have just placed a path in your action.

Selecting an object

If you want to select an object to use later in your recording, you need to name and select an object or path first, as described in the following steps.

1. **Select the object or path.**

2. **Choose Show Note from the Attributes palette pop-up menu.**

3. **Enter the name you want to give the object in the bottom field and click the Actions palette to record the new setting.**

4. **When you need to select the object or path, choose Select Object in the pop-up menu (see Figure 14-20), type the name you gave it in the Attributes palette, and click OK.** The object or path is now selected.

Figure 14-20: The Set Selection dialog box can select objects by name.

Clearing, resetting, loading, replacing, and saving actions

Whew, even after creating a bunch of cool actions, you want more options. You can clear, reset, load, replace, and save actions. Now you can create, delete, load sets, and save to your heart's content. The following describes what each option does:

✦ **Clear Action:** Deletes all the action sets in the Action palette.

✦ **Reset Action:** Resets the palette to the Default Actions.

✦ **Load New or Replace Action:** Lets you navigate to a folder where the action sets are and select one. You can find a ton of prerecorded actions and action sets on the application CD.

✦ **Save Action:** After you have recorded an action you need to save it just like a file if you want to use it the next time you launch Illustrator. Select Save Action in the pop-up menu and navigate to where you want to save your action set (maybe the Action Sets folder within the application folder).

Using the Button mode

Button mode lets you play an action by clicking the button. You can only play — not record — in this mode.

Summary

✦ The different preference areas can be changed in Illustrator: Preferences, Keyboard shortcuts, and the Startup file.

✦ By changing the Adobe Illustrator Startup file, you can change the default colors, patterns, gradients, and zoom level of each new document created in Illustrator.

✦ Many preferences in Illustrator can be changed in the General panel of the Preferences dialog box.

✦ The Constrain Angle option controls the angle at which objects are drawn and moved when the Shift key is pressed.

✦ The Auto Trace option controls the behavior of the Auto Trace Tool.

✦ The General Units option controls how all measurements are controlled in Illustrator.

✦ Use the Actions palette to streamline repetitive tasks in Illustrator.

✦　　✦　　✦

Getting Art Out of Illustrator

Understanding PostScript and Printing

Up until the mid-1980s, computer graphics were, well, crusty. Blocky. Jagged. Rough. If we saw graphics that were done on computers in 1981 and printed to a black-and-white printer, we'd laugh so hard we couldn't breathe, stopping the laughter only when we realized that we actually could not breathe. Of course, in 1981, the world was gaga over the capabilities of computers and computer graphics. Those same pictures were admired, and the average person was generally amazed (the average designer, on the other hand, shuddered and prayed that this whole computer thing wouldn't catch on).

Desktop publishing was pushed to a level of professionalism in 1985 by a cute little software package called PageMaker. With PageMaker, you could do typesetting and layout on the computer screen, seeing everything on the screen just as it would eventually be printed. Well, almost. Aldus was the company that created PageMaker. In 1994, Adobe swallowed Aldus, and now PageMaker is "made" by Adobe as well.

Problems aside, PageMaker would not have been a success if the laser printer hadn't handily arrived on the scene. Even so, there were problems inherent with laser printers, too: at 300 dpi, there were 90,000 dots in every square inch. A typical 8½ x 11-inch page of type had 8.5 million dots to put down. Computers were finally powerful enough to handle this huge number of dots, but the time it took to print made computers pretty much useless for any real work.

Several systems were developed to improve the printing process, and the one standout was PostScript from Adobe Systems. Apple licensed PostScript from Adobe for use on its first LaserWriter, and a star was born. Installed on every laser printer were two things from Adobe: the PostScript page description language, and the Adobe base fonts, which included Times, Helvetica, Courier, and Symbol.

PostScript became fundamental to Apple Macintosh computers and laser printers and became the standard. To use PostScript, Apple had to pay licensing fees to Adobe for every laser printer it sold. Fonts were PostScript, and if there ever was a standard in graphics, the closest thing to it was PostScript (commonly called EPS, for Encapsulated PostScript).

Today, the majority of fonts for both Macintosh and Windows systems are TrueType fonts. However, the vast majority of typefaces used in professional work are still PostScript, and almost all graphics and desktop-publishing software can read PostScript in some form. However, technically speaking (I'm supposed to speak technically, aren't I?) there are actually a greater number of TrueType fonts available.

You can print Illustrator documents in two ways: as a composite, which is a single printout that contains all the colors and tints used; and as a series of color separations, a printout for each color. Color separations are necessary for illustrations that will be printed on a printing press.

Understanding the Benefits of PostScript

A typical graphic object in painting software is based on a certain number of pixels that are a certain color. If you make that graphic larger, the pixels get larger, giving a rough, jagged effect to the art. To prevent these jaggies, two things can be done: Make sure that enough dots-per-inch are in the image so that when the image is enlarged, the dots are too small to appear jagged. Or define graphics by mathematical equations instead of by dots.

PostScript is a mathematical solution to high-resolution imaging. Areas, or shapes, are defined, and then these shapes are either Filled or Stroked with a percentage of color. The shapes are made up of paths, and the paths are defined by a number of points along the path (Anchor Points) and controls off those points (Control Handles, sometimes called curve handles or direction points) that control the shape of the curve.

Because the anchor points and control handles have real locations on a page, mathematical processes can be used to create the shapes based on these points. The mathematical equation for Bézier curves is quite detailed (at least for someone who, like me, fears math).

PostScript is not just math, though. It is actually a programming language and, more specifically, a page description language. Like BASIC, Pascal, Forth, SmallTalk, and C, PostScript is made of lines of code that are used to describe artwork.

Fortunately, the average user never has to deal directly with PostScript code; instead, the average user uses a simplified interface, such as Illustrator. Software that has the capability to save files in PostScript or to print to a PostScript printer writes this PostScript code for you. Printers that are equipped with PostScript then take that PostScript code and convert it to dots on a printed page.

Using PostScript

That most applications can handle EPS files and that most printers can print PostScript are of great benefit to users, but the strength of PostScript is not really in its widespread use.

If you create a 1-inch closed path in Photoshop or any other pixel-based drawing software and then enlarge that same path in any application, the path begins to lose detail. A 300-dpi path at twice its original size becomes 150 dpi. Those jagged edges become more apparent than ever.

If you create a 1-inch circle in Illustrator, you can enlarge it to any size possible without losing one iota of resolution. The Illustrator circle stays perfectly smooth, even enlarged to 200% because the circle's resolution depends on the laser printer or imagesetter that prints it. Therefore, a perfect 1-inch circle has the potential to be a perfect 2-foot circle (providing you can find a printer or imagesetter that can print a 2-foot x 2-foot diameter circle).

But scaling objects is only the beginning. You can distort, stretch, rotate, skew, and flip objects created in Illustrator to your heart's content, and still the object will print to the resolution of the output device.

Note   The capital S in the middle of PostScript was a creative way to establish a trademark, considering the word "postscript" is quite common. Adobe's normally pretty conservative about that sort of thing. They didn't do "IllusTrator" or "PhotoShop" or "StreamLine" or "DimeNsions" or "PreMiere." Because PageMaker was an Aldus product, Adobe didn't change it for marketing reasons.

Here's an example: A company wants its tiny logo on a 3-foot wide poster. If you use conventional methods, the edges will become fuzzy and gross looking, pretty much unacceptable to your client. Your other conventional option is to redraw the logo at a larger size or to trace the blown-up version — a time-consuming proposition either way.

Illustrator's solution is to scan the logo, trace it either in another software tracing program or with the Auto Trace tool, touch it up, and build your design around it. Afterward, output the illustration on a printer that can handle that size poster. There is no loss of quality; instead, the enlarged version from Illustrator will often look better than the scanned original.

Prior to Printing

Before you start the printing process, you may need to change or adjust a few items. For example, you may need to change the page size and orientation, or set how certain colors will separate. This section deals with the issues you should be aware of before you press ⌘+P (Ctrl+P) to send your file to the printer.

Understanding Document Setup

Choosing File ➪ Document Setup, or pressing ⌘+Option+P (Ctrl+Alt+P), enables you to set the initial page size of an illustration via the Artboard. Bringing up the Document Setup dialog box (shown in Figure 15-1) displays a wealth of options that assist in printing. If the Artboard is smaller than the printable page, then anything entirely outside the edges of the Artboard will be cropped off when you print the illustration through Illustrator. Any objects that are partially on the Artboard will print. Anything outside the Artboard will print when you print the illustration through another application.

Cross-Reference   For more on Document setup, see Chapter 2.

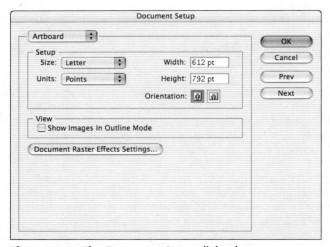

Figure 15-1: The Document Setup dialog box

Another area you can change in the Document Setup dialog box is the Show Images in Outline option, which enables you to choose whether placed images will preview. Checking this box lets you see the placed image rather than a box with an X through it.

Using Page Setup (Macintosh)

The Page Setup button is found inside the Print dialog box (Figure 15-2). Please note that the buttons differ from Mac to Windows. When you click the Page Setup button, you get a warning as shown in Figure 15-3. To access the Page Setup dialog box, click Continue. The Page Setup dialog box, shown in Figure 15-4, is used for specifying printing options when printing out a composite image.

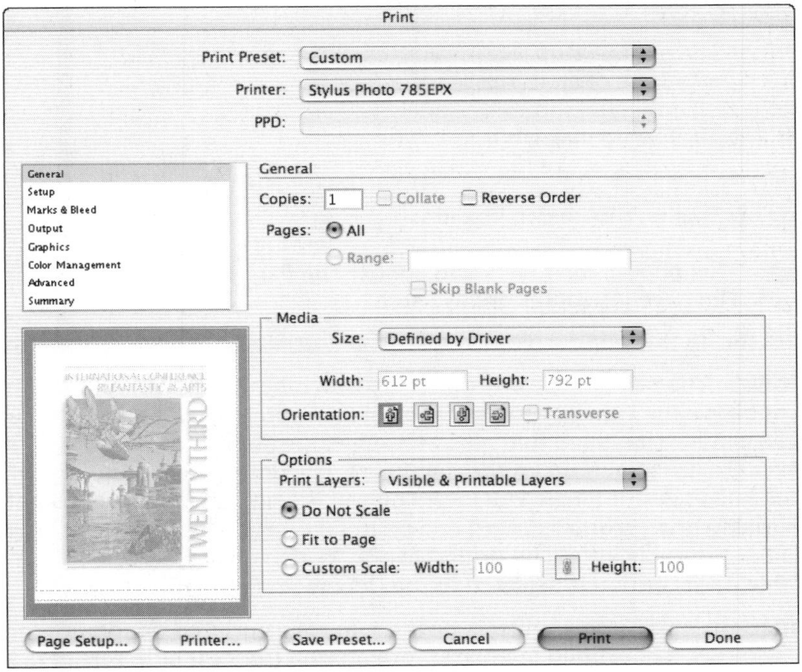

Figure 15-2: The Print dialog box

Figure 15-3: A Warning dialog box

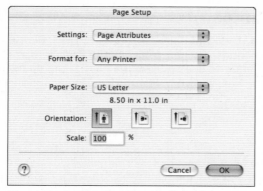

Figure 15-4: The Page Setup dialog box

The printing options on this dialog box are:

✦ **Settings:** This pop-up menu lets you choose the Page Attributes or PostScript Options. The page attributes are as listed:

✦ **Format for:** In this pop-up, you choose which printer you want to print to.

✦ **Paper Size:** You can choose any paper size, including one that your printer does not have the capacity to use. The Tabloid option is an option in a set of choices in a pop-up menu that also lists envelope sizes and positions. The size that you choose shows up on the document as a dotted-line boundary when the Tile Full Pages or Single Full Pages option is selected in the Document Setup dialog box. Another dotted-line boundary, inside the page-size boundary, is the printable area. The printable area is also displayed when the Tile Imagable Areas option is selected in the Document Setup dialog box.

✦ **Orientation:** This option controls how the image is printed on the printed page, whether it is printed in portrait orientation (longest side vertical), landscape orientation (longest side horizontal), or a Transverse orientation (rotates the page 90 degrees).

✦ **Scale:** This option controls how much the illustration is scaled when it's printed. Reducing or enlarging affects the way that the dotted-line page boundaries and imageable-areas dotted lines appear in the document. A value above 100% makes the page smaller, while a value less than 100% makes the page and its boundaries larger. This feature is helpful when you want to print everything that's on a large Artboard. If you select a reduced size in the Page Setup dialog box, the dotted lines in the document reflect the reduced size.

Working with Print Setup (Windows)

The Print Setup dialog box (accessed by clicking the Print Setup button in the Print dialog box) contains Print Setup options that are specific to your printer. Clicking the Properties button displays a plethora of options for customizing page size and other print properties.

Printing composites

A composite printout looks very much like the image that appears on the screen when you preview the document by choosing View ➪ Preview, or pressing ⌘+Y (Ctrl+Y). If you have a color printer, the image appears in color; otherwise, the colors are replaced by gray tints (see the next section, "Gray Colors").

Note　Objects that are hidden or that exist on layers that are currently hidden will not print. Objects that exist on layers that have the printing option unchecked in the Layers Option dialog box also will not print.

The final printing step is to choose File ➪ Print, or to press ⌘+P (Ctrl+P). This action opens the Print dialog box (the Mac version is shown in Figure 15-5), in which you may choose which pages to print, how many of each to print, and several other options. If you click the Cancel button, or press ⌘+period (Ctrl+period), the dialog box disappears and no pages are printed. To print, click the Print button or press Return or Enter.

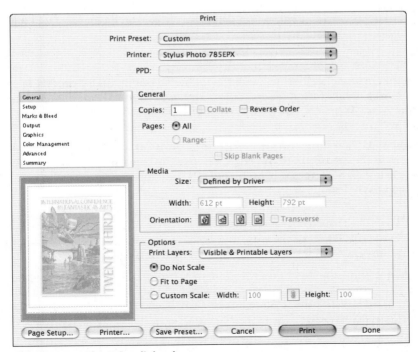

Figure 15-5: The Print dialog box

The General area of the Print dialog box and the Windows Print dialog box contain these options:

✦ **Copies:** The number that you enter here determines how many copies of each page will print. All copies of a single page are printed at one time, so if you enter 4 when you are printing a four-page document, you get four copies of page 1, then four copies of page 2, and so on.

✦ **Pages:** If you check the All button, all the pages that have art on them will print. If you enter numbers in the From and To fields, only the pages that those numbers refer to will print. (Print Range in Windows)

✦ **Media:** This handles the Size, Width, Height, and Orientation of the document.

✦ **Options:** This option determines how to print the layers and scaling options. In the Print Layers pop-up, choose from Print Visible & Printable Layers, Visible Layers, and All Layers. The Scaling Options are Do Not Scale, Fit to Page, and Custom Scale (enter a width and height).

The Setup area handles the following:

✦ **Crop Artwork to:** Choose from Artboard, Artboard Bounding Box, or Crop Area.

✦ **Placement:** Choose where you want the printing origin to start from.

✦ **Tiling:** This relates to paging. You can print Single Full Page, Tile Full Pages, or Tile Imageable Areas.

The Marks & Bleed area covers:

✦ **Marks:** Lets you check or uncheck the following options: All Printer's Marks, Trim Marks, Registration Marks, Color Bars, and Page Information. As for Printer Mark Type, choose from Roman or Japanese. You can also set the Trim Mark Weight and offset from the art.

✦ **Bleeds:** Relates to how the art bleeds or extends off the page. This is used to make sure the art prints to the edge. Choose the top, bottom, left, and right. There is a Link button that is on by default so if you change one, the rest change in synchrony.

The Output option covers:

✦ **Mode:** Controls whether the print will be a Composite (all colors together) or Separation (each color plate printed on its own page).

✦ **Emulsion:** Emulsion has to do with film or repro paper. Up (Right Reading) means that the layer is facing you, and you can read the text. Down (Right Reading) means that the layer is facing away from you, and the type is readable when facing away.

✦ **Image:** This controls whether the print will be a Negative or a Positive.

✦ **Printer Resolution:** Lets you change the printer's resolution (lines per inch/dots per inch). You can only go as high in resolution as your printer will allow. You can always go lower in resolution.

✦ **Checkboxes:** These checkboxes control whether all Spot Colors will print as Process, or Black will Overpint.

✦ **Document Ink Options:** Controls whether the ink will be printed or not or convert a spot to a process color.

The options in the Graphic area are as follows:

✦ **Paths:** The Flatness setting adjusts the lines. The curved lines are defined by lots of tiny straight lines. The more accurate to the curved path, the better the quality, and slower to print. The lower accuracy to the path, the faster it will print but not be as high a quality as you might want.

✦ **Fonts:** Controls how PostScript fonts are downloaded to the printer. Some fonts are stored in the printer, but others that aren't standard on your printer can either be held on the printer or your computer.

✦ **Options:** The other options under Graphics are setting the PostScript language and Data format for type. You can check the Compatible Gradient and Gradient Mesh printing by converting the gradient or gradient mesh to a JPEG format. This area also is where you are informed of your Document Raster Effects Resolution (choose Effect ⇨ Document Raster Settings).

The options in the Color Management area are as follows:

✦ **Source Space:** This lists the color space that the file was created in.

✦ **Print Space:** The Print Space lists the Profile (the color management profile that you want to use) and Intent (the rendering intent to use when converting colors to a profile space).

The Advanced Options are as follows:

✦ **Print as Bitmap:** Check this box to have your file print as a Bitmapped image. This is useful to see a quick printout without the quality.

✦ **Overprints:** In this area, you select whether you want to Simulate, Preserve, or Discard Overprints. You also choose the resolution from presets or custom.

The Summary area lists the summary of the whole file. All of the printing options you have chosen are listed here and any warnings are listed at the bottom.

Tip Choosing Level I PostScript options will reduce errors when printing with an older printer.

Tip When an illustration doesn't print, always choose Print Detailed Report. That way you can read exactly what the error was.

Tip Always Save before printing.

Working with gray colors

When you are printing a full-color illustration to a black-and-white printer, Illustrator substitutes gray values for colors. In this way, the program creates the illusion that each color has a separate, distinct gray value.

Of course, each color can't have its own unique gray value, so the colors have to overlap at some point. Illustrator converts each of the process colors into specific gray values when it prints to a black-and-white printer.

Magenta is the darkest process color, ranging from 0% to 73% gray. Therefore, at 100% makes magenta print at 73% gray. Cyan is second darkest, ranging from 0% to 57% gray. Yellow is extremely light, ranging from 0% to only 11% gray. Figure 15-6 shows a comparison of the four process colors at various settings and their printed results. The four bars show different values, indicated above the bars, for each process color. Within each bar is the percent of black that prints when you are printing that color at that percentage to a black-and-white printer.

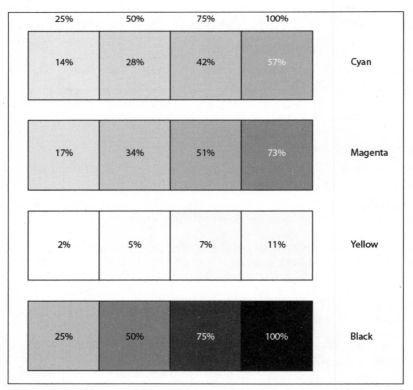

Figure 15-6: How colors appear when printed on a black-and-white laser printer

Different printers may produce different tints of gray. Lower-resolution printers, such as 300-dpi (dots-per-inch) laser printers, do not create an accurate gray tint, because they use dots that are too large to create accurate tint patterns.

Using the Separation Setup

After you choose File ➪ Print and then click the Output option on the left, the Print dialog box with the Output option appears (shown in Figure 15-7). The left side shows how the illustration is aligned on the page and which elements will print with the illustration. The right side contains all the options for how the illustration is to print on the page.

The picture on the left side initially shows the illustration on a portrait-oriented page, even if landscape was selected in Illustrator.

Understanding the printer's marks and bleeds

The various marks shown on the page are the printer mark defaults. The Trim Marks are used for cutting the image after it is printed. The Registration marks are used when printing separations, and you can line up the registration marks to ensure that the print didn't get shifted and all looks as you planned.

Figure 15-7: Output Options with separation setup

The Bleeds define how much of the illustration can be outside of the bounding box and still print. The default for bleed is 18 points, regardless of the size of the bounding box. To change the bleed, enter a distance in points in the Bleed text field. As you type the numbers, the bleed changes dynamically.

Bleed is useful when you want an illustration to go right up to the edge of the page. You need to account for bleed when you create an illustration in Illustrator so that the illustration is the correct size with X amount of bleed.

Changing printer information

To change the PPD, click the Open PPD button in the upper right of the Print dialog box. The Open a PostScript Printer Description (PPD) file window appears.

Select the PPD file that is compatible with your printer and click the Open button. Adobe Illustrator Installer places the PPD folder in the Utilities folder automatically.

Note   PPDs were created with specific printers in mind. Unpredictable and undesirable results can occur when you use a PPD for a different printer than it is intended for. If you don't have a PPD for your printer and must use a substitute, always test the substitute PPD before relying on it to perform correctly.

If your printer's PPD is not included with Illustrator, contact the dealer from whom you purchased the printer and ask for it. If you bought the printer by mail order or from a retail store, the dealer will probably not have a PPD for you and may not even know what a PPD is. In this case, contact the printer manufacturer directly. Another place to find PPDs from manufacturers is on online services such as America Online. Adobe does not have PPDs for printers other than the ones supplied with the software.

Tip   If you have two or more printers in your workplace, chances are that from time to time you will change the PPD file in the Separation Setup dialog box. To make this task easier, open the PPD folder on the hard drive, select all the PPD files that you don't use, and drag them to the trash. Having a shorter list to choose from makes finding the right PPD much easier and frees up space on the hard drive. If you get a new printer at a later date and need a different PPD, you can get it from the Illustrator floppy disk or CD-ROM.

When you choose a different PPD file, the information in the main panel changes to reflect the new selection. Certain default settings in the pop-up menus are activated at this time. You can change the settings at any time, but most of them will revert to the defaults if you choose a new PPD.

Changing page size

Under the Media area of the General Printing Options pop-up menu lists the available page sizes for the printer whose PPD is selected, not the printer selected in the

Chooser or your default Windows printer. For laser printers, few page and envelope sizes are supported. For imagesetters, many sizes are supported, and an Other option enables you to specify the size of the page that you want to print on.

Imagesetters print on rolls of paper or film. Depending on the width of the roll, you may want to print the image sideways. For example, on a Linotronic 180 or 230 imagesetter, paper and film rolls are commonly 12 inches wide. For letter-size pages, you should check the Transverse option to print the letter-size page with the short end along the length of the roll. For a tabloid page (11 x 17 inches), do not check the Transverse option because you want the long edge (17 inches) of the page to be printed along the length of the roll. If you check Transverse for a tabloid-size document, 5 of the 17 inches will be cropped off because the roll is not wide enough. As always when trying something new with printing, run a test or two before sending a large job.

Note The page size that you select in the Media pop-up menu determines the size of the page on the left side of the main panel. The measurements next to the name of the page size are not the page measurements; instead, they are the measurements of the imageable area for that page size. The imageable-area dimensions are always less than the dimensions of the page so that the margin marks can fit on the page with the illustration.

Changing the orientation

The Orientation setting controls how the illustration is placed on the page. You have two choices from the pop-up menu: Portrait and Landscape.

Selecting Portrait causes the illustration to print with the sides of the illustration along the longest sides of the page. Selecting Landscape causes the illustration to print with the top and bottom of the illustration along the longest sides of the page.

Usually, the orientation reflects the general shape of the illustration. If the illustration is taller than it is wide, you usually choose Portrait orientation. If the illustration is wider than it is tall, you usually choose Landscape orientation.

Note It doesn't matter to Illustrator whether the illustration fits on the page in one or both of these orientations. If you can't see all four edges of the bounding box, chances are the illustration will be cropped. Orientation is quite different from Transverse in the Other Page Size dialog box. Orientation changes the orientation of the illustration on the page, but Transverse changes the way that the page is put on the paper. A seemingly small difference, but an important one to understand.

Figure 15-8 shows an illustration that is placed on a page in both Portrait and Landscape orientations, with and without the Transverse option selected.

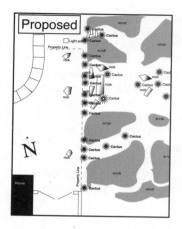
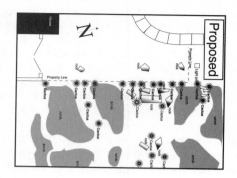
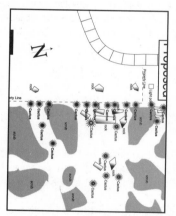
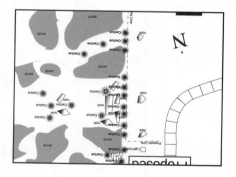

Figure 15-8: An illustration placed on a page in portrait orientation (upper left), landscape orientation (lower left), a portrait with transverse checked (upper right), and a landscape with transverse checked (lower right)

Understanding emulsion

Hang out around strippers (at a commercial printing company . . . get your mind out of the gutter), and you will hear them constantly talk about "emulsion up" and "emulsion down." What they are referring to is the black stuff on film. If you have a piece of film from a printer lying around, look at it near a light. One side is shinier than the other side. That side is the side without emulsion. When you are burning plates for presses, the emulsion side (dull side) should always be toward the plate.

In the Separation Setup dialog box, you use the Emulsion option to control which side the emulsion goes on. If you are printing negatives on film, choose Down (right reading) from the Emulsion pop-up menu. For printing on paper, just to see what the separations look like, choose Up (right reading). Always consult with your printer for the correct way to output film.

Tip   Although "wrong reading" isn't an option in the Separation Setup dialog box, you can reverse an illustration by choosing the opposite emulsion setting. In other words, Down (right reading) is also Up (wrong reading), and Up (right reading) is also Down (wrong reading).

Reversing text creates the kind of secret code illustrations that you can send to your friends. The only way to understand the illustrations is by viewing them in a mirror. This technique works best with text, of course, and I wouldn't expect to fool really smart people with this kind of code.

Thinking of the emulsion as the toner in a laser printer may help you understand this concept better. If the toner is on the top of the paper, you can read it fine, as always (Up emulsion, right reading). If the toner is on the bottom of the paper and you can read the illustration only when you place the paper in front of a light, the emulsion is Down, right reading. Thinking along these lines helped me back when I was new to the printing industry, and it should help you as well.

Changing from positive to negative to positive

You use the Image pop-up menu to switch between printing positive and negative images. Usually, you use a negative image for printing film negatives and a positive image for printing on paper. The default for this setting, regardless of the printer chosen or PPD selected, is Positive.

Working with different colors

At the lower right of the output area of the Print dialog box, a color list window displays where you can select different colors and set them to print or not print, and set Custom Colors to process separately.

The list of colors contains only the colors that are used in that particular illustration. At the top of the list of separation colors are the four process colors in italic, if they, or spot colors that contain those process colors, are used in the illustration. Below the process colors is a list of all the spot colors in the document.

Tip   If the illustration has any guides in it, their colors are reflected in the color list window. From looking at the preview of the illustration in the Output options in the Print dialog box, you can't easily determine that these blank separations will print. The best thing to do is release all guides and delete them.

By default, all process colors are set to print, and all spot colors are set to convert to process colors. Clicking the Convert To Process checkbox at the bottom of the Output options in the Print dialog box toggles between converting everything (checked) and spot colors (unchecked).

Each color in the list has its own frequency and angle. Don't change the angle or frequency for process colors because separator has automatically created the best values for the process colors at the halftone screen you've specified. Instead, make sure that any spot colors that may be printing have different angles from each other so that no patterns develop from them.

As soon as you type new values or check different options using the color list, the changes are applied.

Outputting a Color-Separated File

Color separations are necessary to print a color version of an illustration on most printing presses. Each separation creates a plate that is affixed to a round drum on a printing press. Ink that is the same color as that separation is applied to the plate, which is pressed against a sheet of paper. Because the ink adheres only to the printing areas of the plate, an image is produced on paper. Some printing presses have many different drums and can print a four-color job in one run. Other printing presses have only one or two drums, so the paper has to pass through the press four or two times, respectively, to print a four-color job.

The two types of color separation are process color separation and spot color separation. Each type has its own advantages and drawbacks, and you can use either type or a combination of both types for any print job.

Tip   You should always determine which type of separation you want before you begin to create a job electronically.

Using spot color separations

Jobs that are printed with spot colors are often referred to as two-color or three-color jobs when two or three colors are used. Although you can use any number of colors, most spot color jobs contain only a few colors.

Spot color printing is most useful when you are using two or three distinct colors in a job. For example, if I needed only black and green to create a certain illustration, I would use only black and a green custom color for all of the objects in the illustration.

There are three main reasons for using spot color separation rather than process color separation:

✦ It's cheaper. Spot color printing requires a smaller press with fewer drums. For process color separation, you usually need to use a press with four drums or run the job through a smaller press a number of times.

✦ Spot colors are cleaner, brighter, and smoother than the same colors that you create as process colors. To get a green process color, for example, you need to mix both cyan and yellow on paper. Using one spot color will result in a perfectly solid area of color.

✦ You cannot duplicate certain spot colors, especially fluorescent and metallic colors, with process colors.

Illustrator creates spot colors whenever you specify a spot color in a swatch. If you use six different spot colors and Black, you could print out seven different spot color separations.

Spot colors do have their limitations and disadvantages. The primary limitation of using only spot colors is that the number of colors is restricted to the number of color separations that you want to produce. Remember that the cost of a print job is directly related to the number of different colored inks in the job.

The cutoff point for using spot colors is usually three colors. When you use four spot colors, you limit yourself to four distinct colors and use as many colors as a process color job that can have an almost infinite number of colors. Spot color jobs of six colors are not unusual, however. Sometimes people use more than three spot colors to keep colors distinct and clear. Each of the six colors will be bright, vibrant, and distinct from its neighbors, whereas different process colors seem to fade into one another.

Note   Spot colors are often incorrectly referred to as Pantone colors. Pantone is a brand name for a color-matching system. You can select Pantone colors as custom colors and use them in Illustrator, and you can print them as either spot colors or as process colors.

Printing process color separation

Process color separation, also known as four-color separation, creates almost any color by combining cyan, magenta, yellow, and black inks. By using various combinations of different tints of each of these colors, you can reproduce many of the colors (more than 16 million of them) that the human eye can see.

Process printing uses a subtractive process. You start with bright white paper and darken the paper with various inks. Cyan, magenta, and yellow are the subtractive primaries, and black is added to create true black printing, a color that the primaries together don't do very well.

The use of process color separation is advisable when:

✦ The illustration includes color photographs.

✦ The illustration contains more than three different colors.

Learning Printing from the Experts

If you have never visited a printing company, make a point to visit one and take a tour. Most printing companies have staff members who are more than willing to explain their equipment and various printing processes. In a 30-minute tour with a knowledgeable guide, you can learn enough to save yourself hours of work, money, and misunderstandings.

When you are talking to a printing rep, find out what type of media they want your work on. Printing companies commonly use imagesetters that can output the job for you, and some companies even perform this service at no charge or for a significant discount if you have the job printed there.

Imagesetters are similar to laser printers, except that they produce images with a very high dpi, from 1,273 to 3,600, and sometimes higher. Imagesetters can print directly to RC (resin-coated) paper or to film negatives (or positives). The paper or film runs through the imagesetter and then must run through a developing process for the images and text to appear.

Most printing company salespeople can tell you when to give them negs (film negatives) and paper, and which service bureau to use if they don't have an imagesetter in-house. Many can tell you which software their clients prefer and which software packages create problems, and they can give you tips that can help you get your project through the process without problems.

A service bureau is a company that has on its premises an imagesetter and whose function is to provide the general community of desktop publishers with imagesetter output at a cost between $7 and $40 per page. Service bureaus often have color output capabilities, and offer disk-conversion and other services that are sometimes needed by desktop publishers.

Better yet, do what I did: Work at a printing company for a short period of time. The first job I had out of college, working in the prepress department of a four-color commercial printer, taught me more than I learned in four years of school. The experience instilled in me some of the most important basic skills for graphics design that I still use and need every day. Ever wonder why your printer gets so grumpy when you say your negs won't be available until two days past the promised date? Working at a printing company can give you an understanding of job scheduling, an art of prophecy and voodoo that gives ulcers to printing company managers and supervisors.

The more you know about printing and your printer, the better your print job will turn out, and the fewer hassles you will have to deal with.

How many colors?

Everyone always says that you can create as many colors as you could ever want when you are using process colors. Maybe.

In Illustrator, you can specify colors up to $\frac{1}{100}$ percent accuracy. As a result, 10,000 different shades are available for each of the four process colors. So, theoretically, $10,000^4$, or 10,000,000,000,000,000, different colors should be available, which is

10 quadrillion or 10 million billion. Any way you look at it, you have a heck of a lot of color possibilities.

Unfortunately, most imagesetters and laser printers can produce only 256 different shades for each color. This limitation of the equipment (not PostScript) drops the number of available colors to 256^4, or 4,294,967,296, which is about 4.3 billion colors — only 1 billionth of the colors that Illustrator can specify.

This limitation is fortunate for us humans, however, because the estimate is that we can detect a maximum of 100 different levels of gray, probably less. As a result, we can view only 100^4, or 100,000,000, different colors.

We can run into a problem when we preview illustrations, however. An RGB monitor (used on computers) can display up to 16.7 million colors, theoretically, if each Red, Green, and Blue pixel can be varied by 256 different intensities.

Another problem is that about 30% of the colors that you can view on an RGB monitor can't be reproduced by using cyan, magenta, yellow, and black inks on white paper. You can't create these unprintable colors in Illustrator, but you can create them in most other drawing and graphics software packages. These colors are for on-screen viewing pleasure only.

The secret to process color separation is that the four colors that make up all the different colors are themselves not visible. Each color is printed as a pattern of tiny dots, angled differently from the other three colors. The angles of each color are very important. If the angles are off even slightly, a noticeable pattern commonly known as a moiré emerges.

The colors are printed in a specific order — usually cyan, magenta, yellow, and black. Although the debate continues about the best order in which to print the four colors, black is always printed last.

To see the dots for each color, use a magnifying device to look closely at something that is preprinted and in full color. Even easier, look at the Sunday comics, which have bigger dots than most other printed pieces. The different color dots in the Sunday comics are quite visible, and their only colors are magenta, cyan, yellow, and black.

The size of the dots that produce each of these separations is also important. The smaller the dots, the smoother the colors appear. Large dots (such as those in the Sunday comics) can actually take away from the illusion of a certain unified color because the different color dots are visible.

For more information on the common dot sizes and on the relation of dot size to the quality of the illustration, see the section "Setting Up the Halftone Screen," earlier in this chapter.

Figure 15-9 shows how process colors are combined to create new colors. In the figure, the first four rows show very large dots. The top three rows are cyan, magenta, and yellow. The fourth row is all four process colors combined, and the bottom row shows how the illustration looks when you print it.

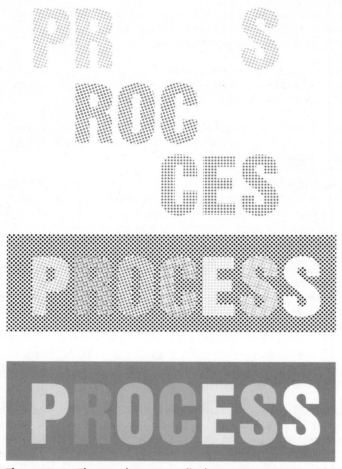

Figure 15-9: The top three rows display cyan, magenta, and yellow. The fourth row displays their combination. The fifth row displays the colors as they will print.

Process color printing is best for photographs because photographs originate from a continuous tone that is made on photographic paper from film, instead of dots on a printing press.

In Illustrator, you can convert custom colors to process colors either before or during printing. To convert custom colors to process colors before printing, select any objects that have a specific custom color and tint and click the process color icon. The color will be converted to its process color counterpart, and all selected objects will be filled with the new process color combination.

After you click the Process Color icon, if the selected objects become filled with White and the triangles for each process color are at 0%, you have selected objects that contain different colors or tints. Undo the change immediately.

To make sure that you select only objects that have the same color, select one of the objects and choose Select ➪ Same ➪ Stroke Color. Objects that have different strokes or objects with different tints of the same color will not be selected.

You can convert custom colors to process colors in the Output options in the Print dialog box and in many page layout programs.

Combining both spot and process color separations

You can couple spot colors with process colors in Illustrator simply by creating both process and named spot colors in a document.

Usually, you add spot colors to process colors for these reasons:

✦ You are using a company logo that has a specific color. By printing that color as a spot color, you make it stand out from the other coloring. In addition, color is more accurate when it comes from a specific ink rather than from a process color combination. Often, the logo is a Pantone color that doesn't reproduce true to form when you use process color separation.

✦ You need a color that you can't create by using process colors. Such colors are most often metallic or fluorescent, but they can be any number of Pantone colors or other colors that you can't match with process colors.

✦ You need a varnish for certain areas of an illustration. A varnish is a glazed type of ink that results in a shiny area wherever you use the varnish. You commonly use varnishes on titles and logos and over photographs.

✦ You need a light color over a large area. The dots that make up process colors are most noticeable in light colors, but by using a spot color to cover the area with a solid sheet of ink that has no dots, you can make the area smoother and enhance it visually.

In some circumstances, you need to use a spot color as a spot color and also use it as a process color. Normally, you can't do both, but the following steps describe one way to get around this problem:

1. **If the color doesn't exist as a swatch, create a swatch for the color.**

2. **In the Swatch Options (double-click on the swatch), set the pop-up menu to Spot Color and click OK.**

3. **Duplicate the swatch by dragging it on top of the New Swatch icon (the little piece of paper).**

4. **In the Swatch Options for the duplicated swatch, set the pop-up menu to Process Color and click OK.**

Note   You can tell which swatch is which by looking at the lower-right corner of the swatches; the spot color swatch will have a white triangle with a "spot" in it, and the process swatch will be solid.

Using Other Applications to Print

Many other software programs, particularly page-layout software programs, incorporate color-separation capabilities. These programs usually enable you to import Illustrator files that have been saved as Illustrator EPS files.

When you produce color separations from other software, make sure that any custom colors that are in the Illustrator illustration are present and accessible in the document that the illustration is placed within. Usually, you can set the custom colors to process separately or to spot separately.

Note   You cannot change the colors of an imported Illustrator EPS document in a page-layout program, so be sure that the colors are correct for the illustration while it is in Illustrator.

Understanding Trapping

Trapping is one of the most important but least understood issues in all of printing.

Traps solve alignment problems when color separations are produced. The most common problem that occurs from misalignment is the appearance of white space between different colors.

Note   Illustrator, while it does incorporate a trapping filter, is not a trap-happy piece of software. For detailed illustrations, it usually isn't worth your time to set the trapping inside Illustrator; instead, you'll want to have your printer do the work for you.

Note   The thought of trapping scares many graphic designers, not just because they don't know how to do it, but also because they aren't sure what trapping is and what purpose it serves. Understanding the concept of trapping is the hard part; trapping objects is easy (though somewhat tedious in Illustrator).

Figure 15-10 shows a spot color illustration with four colors. The top row shows each of the individual colors. The first illustration in the second row shows how the illustration prints if all the separations are aligned perfectly. The second illustration in the second row shows what happens when the colors are misaligned. The third illustration in the second row shows how the illustration looks when trapped, with black indicating where two colors overprint each other.

This example shows extreme misalignment and excessive trapping; I designed it just as a black-and-white illustration for this book. Ordinarily, the overprinting colors may appear a tiny bit darker, but they do not show as black. I used black so that you can see what parts of the illustration overlap when trapping is used. The trapping in this case is more than sufficient to cover any of the white gaps in the second illustration.

Trapping is created by spreading or choking certain colors that touch each other in an illustration. To spread a color, enlarge an object's color so that it takes up more space around the edges of the background area. To choke a color, expand the color of the background until it overlaps the edges of an object.

The major difference between a spread and a choke has to do with which object is considered the background and which object is the foreground. The foreground object is the object that traps. If the foreground object is spread, the color of the foreground object is spread until it overlaps the background by a certain amount. If the foreground object is choked, the color of the background around the foreground object is expanded until it overlaps the foreground object by a certain amount.

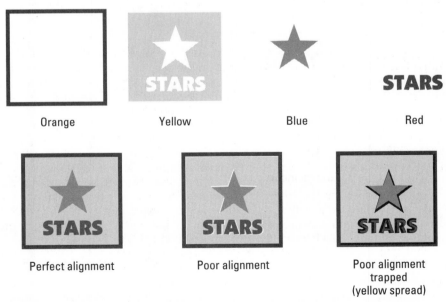

Figure 15-10: A Spot Color illustration that shows individual colors (top) and aligned, misaligned, and trapped composites

Tip   To determine whether to use a choke or a spread on an object, compare the lightness and darkness of the foreground and background objects. The general rule of thumb is that lighter colors expand or contract into darker colors.

Figure 15-11 shows the original misaligned illustration and two ways of fixing it with trapping. The middle star has been spread by 1 point, and the third star has been choked by 1 point.

Original   Blue (star shape)   Blue (star shape)
                    1-pt spread   1-pt choke

Figure 15-11: The original illustration (left), fixing the star by spreading it 1 point (middle), and fixing the star by choking it 1 point (right)

Why color separations do not properly align and require trapping

Three common reasons why color separations don't align properly are that the negatives are not the same size, the plates on the press are not aligned perfectly when printing, or the gods have decided that a piece is too perfect and needs gaps between abutting colors. Trapping is required because it is a solution for covering gaps that occur when color separations do not properly align.

Negatives can be different sizes for a number of reasons. When the film was output to an imagesetter, the film may have been too near the beginning or the end of a roll, or separations in the same job may have been printed from different rolls. The pull on the rollers, while fairly precise on all but top-of-the-line imagesetters, where it should be perfect, can pull more film through when there is less resistance (at the end of a roll of film), or less film when there is more resistance (at the beginning of a roll of film). The temperature of the film may be different if a new roll is put on in the middle of a job, causing the film to shrink (if it is cold) or expand (if it is warm).

The temperature of the processor may have risen or fallen a degree or two while the film was being processed. Once again, cooler temperatures in the chemical bays and in the air dryer as the film exits the process have an impact on the size of the film.

Film negatives usually don't change drastically in size, but they can vary up to a few points on an 11-inch page. That distance is huge when a page has several abutting colors throughout it. The change in a roll of film is almost always along the length of the roll, not along the width. The quality of the film is another factor that determines how much the film will stretch or shrink.

Most strippers are quite aware of how temperature affects the size of negatives. A common stripper trick is to walk outside with a freshly processed negative during the colder months to shrink a negative that may have enlarged slightly during processing.

Check with your service bureau staff to see how long they warm up the processor before sending jobs through it. If the answer is less than an hour, the chemicals will not be at a consistent temperature, and negatives that are sent through too early will certainly change in size throughout the length of the job. Another question to ask is how often they change their chemicals and check the density from their imagesetter. Once a week is acceptable for a good-quality service bureau, but the best ones will change chemicals and check density once a day.

The plates on a press can be misaligned by either an inexperienced press operator or a faulty press. An experienced press operator knows the press and what to do to get color plates to align properly. A faulty press is one where plates move during printing or are not positioned correctly. An experienced press operator can determine how to compensate for a faulty press.

No press is perfect, but some of the high-end presses are pretty darn close. Even on those presses, the likelihood that a job with colors that abut one another can print perfectly is not very great.

If a job doesn't have some sort of trapping in it, it probably will not print perfectly, no matter how good the negatives, press, and press operator are.

How much trap?

The amount of trap that you need in an illustration depends on many things, but the deciding factor is what your commercial printer tells you is the right amount.

The most important thing to consider is the quality of the press that the printer will use. Of course, only the printer knows which press your job will run on, so talking to the printer about trapping is imperative.

Other factors to consider include the colors of ink and types of stock used in the job. Certain inks soak into different stocks differently.

Traps range from 4\1,000 of an inch to 6\1,000 of an inch. Most traditional printers refer to traps in thousandths of inches, but Illustrator likes values in points for this sort of thing. Figure 15-12 is a chart with traps in increments of 1\1,000, from 1\1,000 of an inch to 10\1,000 of an inch, and gives their point measurements. The trapped area is represented by black to be more visible in this example.

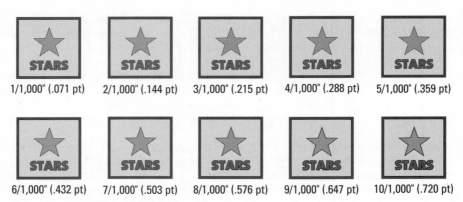

Figure 15-12: Different trap amounts

Remember that the greater the trap, the less chance that any white gaps will appear, but the trap may actually be visible. Visible traps of certain color pairs can look almost as bad as white space.

Trapping Illustrator files manually

In Illustrator, you accomplish manual (nonfilter) trapping by selecting a path's Stroke or Fill and setting it to overprint another path's Stroke or Fill. The degree to which the two paths' Fills or Strokes overlap and overprint is the amount of trap that is used.

The most basic way to create a trap on an object is by giving it a Stroke that is either the Fill color of the object (to create a spread) or the Fill color of the background (to create a choke).

Tip　Be sure to make the width of any Stroke that you use for trapping twice as wide as the intended trap, because only half of the Stroke (one side of the path) actually overprints a different color. In some circumstances, fixing a Stroke that is not wide enough initially can be difficult.

1. **Select one path of a pair of overlapping or abutting paths.** If possible, select the lighter of the two paths.

2. **Give the selected path a Stroke of the same color that the Fill is.** Change the weight to the amount of trap you'd like to use. For this example, so it could be seen easily in this book, I've used a 3-point trap.

3. **Set the overlapping Stroke to overprint.** These steps are shown in Figure 15-13.

Figure 15-13: The results of manual trapping

Trapping with Trap

For this example, I'll use the same paths from Figure 15-13 to show how Trap works.

1. **Select all pieces of art that are overlapping or abutting.**

2. **Choose Trap from the Pathfinder palette.** (You will find the Trap button when you choose Options from the Pathfinder pop-up menu.) Then enter the width into the Width text field (see Figure 15-14.)

3. **Click OK.** The object has trapping applied instantly (well, if the artwork is complex, it won't be instant. . .).

Complex trapping techniques in Illustrator

The preceding trap illustrations are extremely simplified examples of trapping methods in Illustrator. In reality, objects never seem to be a solid color, and if they are, they are never on a solid background. In addition, most illustrations contain multiple overlapping objects that have their own special trapping needs.

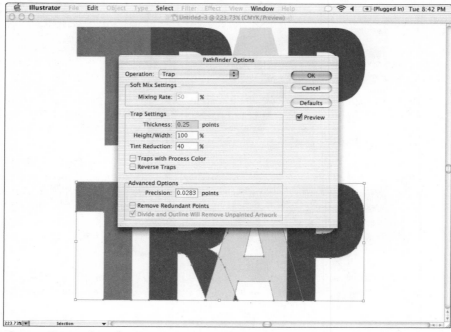

Figure 15-14: Choosing Trap from the Pathfinder palette

I consider trapping to be complex when I can't just go around selecting paths and applying trap quickly. Complex trapping involves several different techniques:

✦ Create a separate layer for trapping objects. By keeping trapping on its own layer, you make myriad options available that are not available if the trapping is intermixed with the rest of the artwork. Place the new layer above the other layers. Lock all the layers but the trapping layer so that the original artwork is not modified. You can turn trapping on and off by hiding the entire layer or turning off the Print option in the Layers Options dialog box.

✦ Use the round joins and ends options in the Stroke portion of the Stroke palette for all trapping Strokes. Round joins and ends are much less conspicuous than the harsh corners and 90-degree angles of other joins and ends, and they blend smoothly into other objects.

✦ Trap gradations by stroking them with paths that are filled with overprinting gradients. You cannot Fill Strokes with gradients, but you can Fill paths with gradients. You can make any Stroke into a path by selecting it and choosing Outline from the Pathfinder palette. After you have transformed the Stroke into a path, Fill it with the gradient and check the Overprint Fill box (in the Attributes palette) for that path.

When Trapping It Yourself Isn't Worth It

Before you spend the long amounts of time that complex trapping entails and modify your illustration beyond recognition (at least in Artwork mode), you may want to reconsider whether you should do the trapping yourself.

If you estimate that trapping your job will require several hours of work, the chances of doing it correctly dwindle significantly. If the illustration includes many crisscrossing blends and gradations or multiple placed images, you may not have the patience to get through the entire process with your sanity intact.

If you determine that you cannot do the trapping yourself, you can have it done after the fact with Luminous TrapWise or Island Trapper, or you can have a service bureau with special output devices create trapping automatically. These services will undoubtedly cost more than doing the trapping yourself, but it will get done right, which is the important thing.

Note   Whenever I start a heavy-duty trapping project, I always work on a copy of the original illustration. Wrecking the original artwork is just too easy when you add trapping.

Summary

✦ Illustrator can be interpreted as a good front-end for the PostScript page description language.

✦ Print separations from within Illustrator.

✦ Choose whether to print a composite or separations from the Print dialog box.

✦ Determine separation information in the Separation Setup dialog box.

✦ Prevent potential white strips that can appear when a printer isn't perfectly aligned with trapping.

✦ Output options under the Print dialog box lets you specify which colors print and what angle and frequency they print at.

✦   ✦   ✦

Creating Web Graphics

In concept, designing for the Web and designing for print are very similar. In this chapter, I discuss challenges that the designer faces when attempting to present ideas graphically that appeal to the eye and get the right point across. Web design encompasses more than just converting your picas to pixels.

Designing for the Web versus Designing for Print

A Web designer faces specific issues that a print designer never even thinks about. Consider these:

✦ **A print designer chooses the specific color inks and paper with which to print, giving the designer complete control over how a reader will see it.** A Web designer has no way of knowing what kind of monitor a reader is using to view his Web site — a nice yellow color on one screen may end up looking orange or green on another monitor. Monitors also display at different resolutions (older machines might be set to 640x480 or 800x600 while newer ones may be 1024x768 or higher), meaning Web designers must make their Web sites work for all of them.

✦ **A Web designer is always at the mercy of the Web browser.** In the ever-changing world we live in, there's no telling what a reader will use to view your Web site. When the Web first became popular, Netscape Navigator was the browser of choice. Microsoft's Internet Explorer has taken the world by storm and is by far the most prevalent browser out there. Recently Apple introduced a browser called Safari to run specifically on the Mac platform. Because each browser does things differently, a Web site in Explorer can look very different than the same Web site in Navigator or Safari.

✦ **A Web designer must be conscious of how long it takes an average reader to download a page or graphic.** Although high-speed broadband connections are more popular, this is still an issue and limits Web designers from using large full color images or graphics. You still need to consider how many colors to use, what file types to use, and even limits font usage.

✦ **The most alluring aspect of the Web is interactivity.** Web designers can take advantage of technologies that print designers can only dream of. Examples include having graphics change when users moves their mouse (rollovers), making images come alive with animation. Other advantages are utilizing advanced programming techniques (called scripting) to deliver customized graphics tailored specifically to the reader or displaying a greeting based on the time of day.

Tip   Sometimes a Web designer actually does know what monitor or system their viewers are using. When creating Web sites for use on intranets, which are employee accessible internal company or organization sites, designers can take advantage of that knowledge and use it to their benefit. For example, if a designer knows everyone has Windows computer running Internet Explorer, they can design just for that browser and not worry or care what the site may look like in Netscape or Safari.

Illustrator and the Web — the Basics

Illustrator is a great tool for creating Web graphics because it possesses all of the necessary production tools, supports all the standard file types, and offers superb integration with other Web applications such as Adobe Photoshop, Adobe ImageReady, Adobe GoLive, and Macromedia Flash. Even more important, because Illustrator is a vector-based application, you can easily repurpose graphics for both print and the Web, which means that you don't have to recreate your artwork for one or the other.

While in theory you could create an entire HTML Web page using only Illustrator, no one would mistake Illustrator as the only tool you need for Web design. Illustrator's strength is creating graphics for a Web page or designing Web pages for assembly on an HTML editor, such as Adobe GoLive or Macromedia Dreamweaver. Brave designers might also utilize text-based HTML editors such as BBEdit. Illustrator is also perfect for creating vector-based graphics that you import into Macromedia Flash for creating truly interactive content.

Illustrator is well equipped to handle Web graphics, and before you actually run off and start creating them, I want to discuss some of the fundamental tools and functions that you need to know. The first idea to remember is that all Web graphics are in RGB mode, so when you create a new document make sure that you choose RGB. If you forget, you can always choose File ➪ Document Color Mode ➪ RGB to change to RGB color mode (see Figure 16-1).

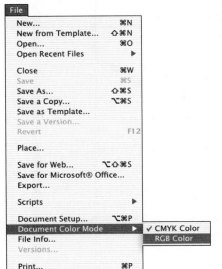

Figure 16-1: Specifying a document's color mode

Pixel preview

Sometimes you just have to face the facts: Web graphics are always displayed in pixels. Even "vector-based" Web formats like Flash and SVG end up displaying on a computer screen, which means they are viewed in pixel form. Although some monitors display at 96 of 105ppi (pixels per inch), most still display graphics at 72ppi. In either case, the resolution is *a lot* less than the 3450dpi (dots per inch) you are used to seeing from your high-end imagesetter or even the 600dpi you see on your printouts from your laser printer.

At such a low resolution, curved lines and text appear jaggy and can make your graphics look like they came from the early 1980s (Space Invaders and Asteroids come to mind). To compensate for low resolution on monitors, software programs usually employ a technique called *antialiasing*. By applying a gentle blur to the edge of your text or graphics, you eliminate the jaggedness of your image, replacing it with a smooth transition and a clean look (see Figure 16-2). Illustrator uses antialiasing to allow you to preview your graphics and text on screen beautifully. Don't worry; your printed output remains unaffected and your text will look crisp and sharp when you print from your laser printer or imagesetter.

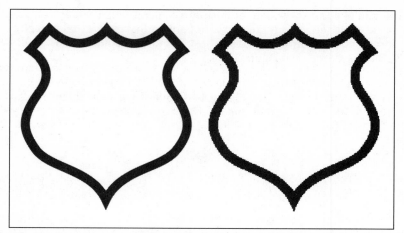

Figure 16-2: Art on a monitor with (left) and without (right) anti-aliasing

Because the delivery medium for Web graphics is a computer screen, a Web designer cares very much about antialiasing. For one reason, although soft edges on your graphic may make large text and graphics pretty on screen, they can also make small text fuzzy and unreadable (see Figure 16-3).

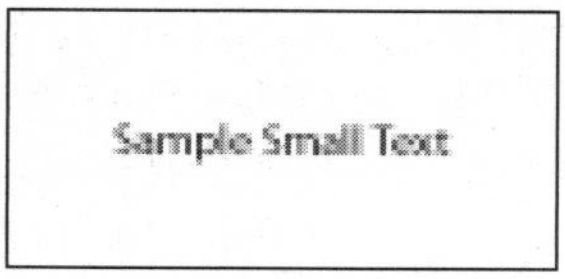

Sample Small Text

Figure 16-3: Small antialiased text can be very hard to read.

Illustrator has a special preview mode called Pixel Preview (choose View ⇨ Pixel Preview) that displays the graphics on screen as actual rasters — the exact way they would display in a Web browser. Using Pixel Preview mode lets you know exactly how antialiasing affects your graphics. Because antialiasing is based on your monitor's pixel grid (see the "Thin Black Lines versus Fat Gray Lines" sidebar), moving your art around can affect its overall appearance. The first step in creating Web graphics from Illustrator is to turn on Pixel Preview. You can tell when you're in Pixel Preview mode by looking at the title bar of your document (see Figure 16-4).

Illustrator_Bible.ai @ 100% (RGB/Pixel Preview)

Figure 16-4: The title bar indicates what Preview mode you are in.

Cross-Reference

For more on the various View modes in Illustrator, see Chapter 1.

Tip

You can turn off anti-aliasing to see how it affects your display by going into the General Preferences dialog box (Ilustrator [Edit] ➪ Preferences ➪ General) and unchecking the box for Anti-aliased Artwork. All artwork also appears anti-aliased when you're in Artwork preview mode. Disabling anti-aliasing won't make your graphics look pretty on screen, but it will slightly enhance the performance of Illustrator.

Thin Black Lines versus Fat Gray Lines

Sometimes the process of anti-aliasing produces results that are less appealing to the eye. Good examples of this are thin lines and small text. Anti-aliasing can make a thin black line look like a fat gray line, or it can make small crisp text an unreadable mush of pixels. Fortunately, Illustrator provides you with the tools to avoid these issues.

First, let's understand why these things happen. A pixel can either be on or off—you can't have a pixel that's only half-colored. By default, Illustrator always draws objects that "snap" to an invisible pixel grid. (You can turn off this feature by choosing View ➪ Snap to Pixel when you're in Pixel Preview mode). Illustrator also paints strokes on the center of a path. This means that if you select a 1 pixel stroke, Illustrator centers it on my path, effectively placing half pixel on either side of the stroke. However, because you can't fill only half a pixel with color, Illustrator uses anti-aliasing to turn that 1 pixel black line into a 2 pixel gray line. If you turn off the Snap to Pixel option, and then move the line half a pixel in either direction (via the Move dialog), you'll see the 2 pixel gray line turn into a 1 pixel black line (see Figure 1).

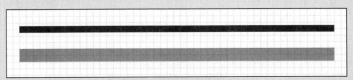

Figure 1: A 1 pixel black line snapped to the pixel grid appears as a 2 pixel black line when antialiased.

Small text actually reads better without anti-aliasing at all. Here you can use Illustrator's Effects to your advantage:

1. Type some small text.

2. Choose Effect ➪ Rasterize. This opens the Rasterize dialog box (Figure 2).

3. For the antialiasing option, choose None. This is shown in Figure 2.

4. Click OK. Figure 3 shows text with and without anti-aliasing.

Continued

Continued

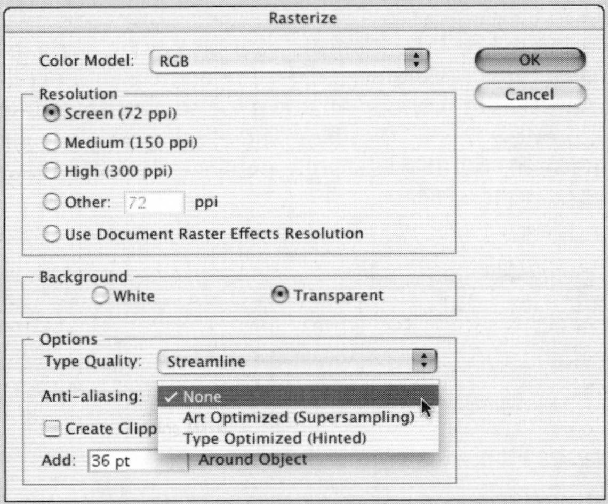

Figure 2: The Rasterize dialog box

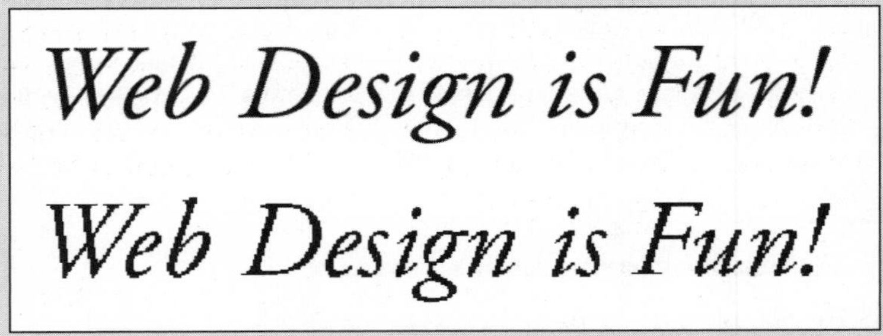

Figure 3: Text with (top) and without (bottom) anti-aliasing applied

Because applying Rasterize in this way is a Live Effect, you can still make edits to your text with the Text tool as normal, yet the text will never be antialiased (see Figure 3). You can also use this technique for thin rules and lines.

Web-safe colors

As we mentioned earlier, one of the problems that a Web designer faces is choosing a color that looks consistent no matter what computer you view the Web site on. First, I want to explore the way monitors display colors. The average monitor can display 256 different colors on the screen at any one time (VGA). So what if one of the colors that you pick isn't one of those 256 colors? In such cases, the monitor uses a process called *dithering* to simulate that color on the screen.

Dithering is a process in which different colored pixels are placed in a pattern to match the desired color. This process is similar to 4-color process printing, where dots of Cyan, Magenta, Yellow, and Black are used to simulate other colors. However, dithering can sometimes result in noticeable and ugly patterns, much like a Moiré. Besides not displaying the exact color you wanted, dithering can make text or parts of your Web site unreadable (and you thought Web design was easy, right?)

Don't worry; there's hope in the form of a *Web-safe color*, which is basically a color that you know displays correctly without dithering on any computer. Is it magic? Believe it or not, it's actually math. A Windows computer has 256 standard system colors and a Macintosh also has 256 standard colors. Only they don't both use the same 256 colors for their system palettes. When you actually match the two standard system palettes, only 216 colors are identical and the other 40 are different. This means you can safely specify 216 colors that are guaranteed to display without dithering on any computer.

Sign me up! Where do I find these Web safe colors? Illustrator has a Web safe color palette. You access this palette by going to the Swatches palette fly-out menu, choosing Open Swatch Library, and selecting Web. All colors listed in this palette are Web safe colors. You can also pick Web safe colors directly from the Color palette. To do so, choose Web Safe RGB from the palette fly-out menu (see Figure 16-5). When you drag the color sliders, Illustrator "snaps to" Web-safe colors. Clicking the color bar in the Color palette allows you choose a color that's outside of the Web safe color gamut, and if you do so, Illustrator displaying an "out-of-gamut" icon that looks like a 3D cube (see Figure 16-6). Clicking that cube "snaps" your color to the nearest Web-safe color.

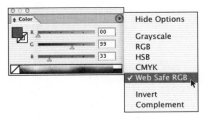

Figure 16-5: Choosing the Web-safe RGB option in the Color palette

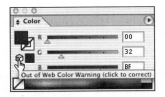

Figure 16-6: The "out-of-gamut" Web-safe color warning

Hexadecimal colors

Hexa-*what?* No, we're not trying to put a spell on you (well, other than the spell we put on you that made you buy this book). In HTML-speak, colors are usually defined by hexadecimal code, which is based on a 16 number system, where each digit is a number from 0 to F (15). Although you may not find it very intuitive to call a color "FFFF00" (red 255, green 255, blue 0), instead of yellow, Hex values allow designers to use a specific color (after all, there are plenty of shades of "yellow" out there). When you have the Color palette set to Web safe RGB mode, you can enter Hexadecimal values for a specific color. If you open the Web Safe color palette, Illustrator also displays hexadecimal codes if you mouse over the swatches (see Figure 16-7). You can also enter Hex values directly into the Find field to jump directly to a color.

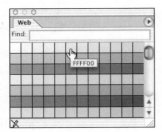

Figure 16-7: Hexadecimal values in the Web-safe color palette

Optimizing and Saving Web Graphics

So you've created your lovely graphic and now it's time to save it in a format that a Web browser can understand and display. Back in the old days (um, like five years ago) Web designers were forced to export graphics with all these different settings and then open those graphics in a Web browser to see how they looked. More often than not, they ended up repeating this process until the graphics looked just right.

The exporting process is difficult because there's an important balance between file size and file appearance. In general, the more colorful and complex a graphic is, the larger its file size. But the larger the file size, the longer it takes to download the image. The average Web surfer isn't very patient, and if it takes too long to load a page, they move on to another one. So designers are forced to find that happy medium — an image that looks good enough, but that also downloads fast enough.

Note There are two kinds of compression you can use to help make files smaller, one called *lossless*, which compresses the file without losing any data. The other is *lossy*, which throws out data that is deemed not important (by the mercy of the compression Gods). With lossy compression, you usually have control over how much information gets tossed — the more data you choose to "lose," the higher the compression rate, and the smaller the file.

Introducing the Save for Web dialog box

Several years ago, Adobe released a product called ImageReady, which gives designers a way to preview how Web graphics look with different file types, compression settings and more, as well as obtain real-time feedback on file size. This product was so monumental that Adobe built the basic ImageReady functionality, called *Save for Web*, into Photoshop, Illustrator, and GoLive as well.

Note Today, Photoshop actually includes ImageReady as a separate application (most Photoshop users aren't even aware of this) and adds specific functionality like animation. See more information on how to use Illustrator with ImageReady later on in this chapter.

To use the Save for Web interface, choose File ➪ Save for Web and you'll be presented with a dialog box that takes up nearly the entire screen. There's good reason for this, as Save for Web has many different settings and options (see Figure 16-8). The next section discusses what all these options are about. Get comfy; this is where things get busy....

Previewing Web graphics

The most notable and most important part of the Save for Web dialog is the Preview pane. You can choose to either view your art in Original mode, Optimized, 2 Up, or 4 Up (the latter of which I find the most useful), where you can view your image in up to 4 different ways at once, allowing you to easily choose the best one. The way Save for Web works is you click one preview, choose settings, click another, choose different settings, and so on and then compare the different versions. You can then pick the one you think is best (all without leaving the dialog).

Tip The Save for Web dialog honors Illustrator's Crop Marks for clip sizes. So if you want to easily export images for the Web in a particular size — even if you have other art on the page — you can draw a rectangle around the portion you want to export. You can then convert the rectangle to crops by choosing Object ➪ Crop Marks ➪ Create), and then choose Edit ➪ Save for Web.

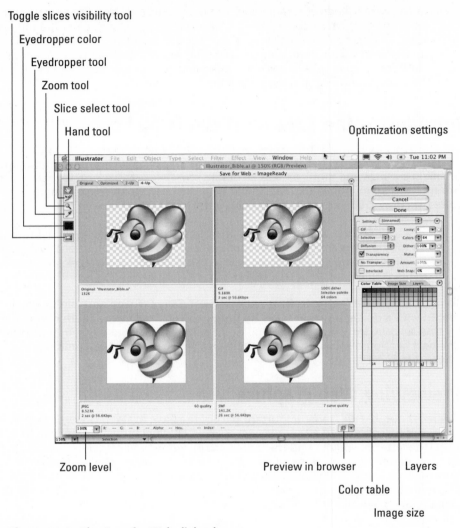

Figure 16-8: The Save for Web dialog box

Along the left side of the dialog are the four tools you'll use in Save for Web:

✦ **Hand Grabber tool:** Lets you move artwork around in the preview window.

✦ **Slice Select tool:** Allows you to choose with which slice you want to work.

Cross-Reference

For more about slices, see the section "Web Slicing," later in this chapter.

✦ **Zoom tool:** Lets you increase or decrease the magnification of your image.

✦ **Eyedropper tool:** Allows you to sample or select colors from your image (some functions in the Color Table require you to choose a color).

You also find two additional buttons here:

✦ **Eyedropper color:** This indicates the color chosen with the Eyedropper tool, or you can click on it, which brings up the Color Picker, allowing you to key in a specific color.

✦ **Slice Visibility:** Clicking this button either shows or hides the slices in your preview pane (not that art that's in them, just the slice boundaries and numbers themselves).

Located on the upper-right side of preview pane is a pop-up menu where you can choose a modem speed (see Figure 16-9). Save for Web uses this setting approximate how long it will take your graphic to load. You'll notice that each preview pane lists the settings along with estimated download times in the lower left of the preview pane (see Figure 16-10).

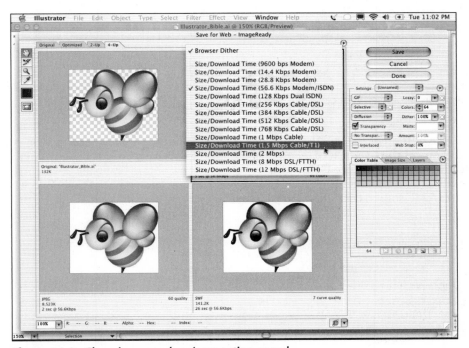

Figure 16-9: Choosing a modem/connection speed

Optimization settings and approximate download times

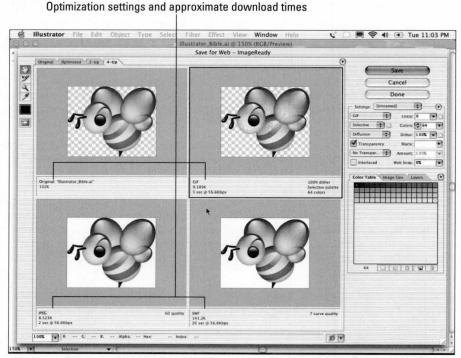

Figure 16-10: Each preview lists file-optimization settings and approximate download times in the lower-right corner of each box.

At the bottom of the palette, you have a zoom pop-up as well as feedback on colors and one of the handiest of features — a button to preview your art in an actual Web browser of choice (see Figure 16-11). Choosing this option launches a Web browser and not only displays the art but also all of the information about the file as well as the HTML source code to display it (see Figure 16-12).

Figure 16-11: Previewing art in your Web browser of choice

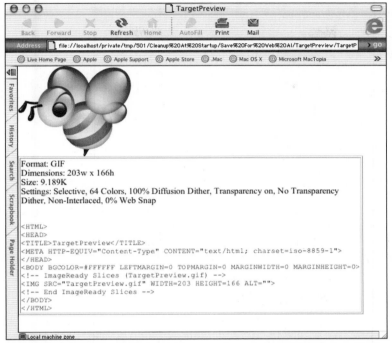

Figure 16-12: Along with a preview of your graphic, the browser displays all of the file's settings as well.

Along the right side of the Save for Web dialog are all of the settings you'd ever need (and some you'd probably never need) to customize your Web graphics to perfection. At the top are the Save, Cancel, and Done buttons (you'd use Done if you just wanted to specify Web settings but didn't want to export anything at that time). Pressing Option (Alt on Win) will turn Cancel and Done into Reset and Remember.

Directly below is where you'll set the file format options, such as choosing among GIF, JPEG, PNG, SWF, SVG, or WBMP and all of the specific settings that go with them (see Figure 16-13). You also have a Color Table palette that lets you control specific colors in your image, an Image Size palette, and a Layers palette where you can specify the output of CSS (Cascading Style Sheet) Layers (any top-level layer can be specified as a CSS layer here).

Figure 16-13: Choosing a file format

Tip

CSS stands for Cascading Style Sheets and is part of what DHTML (or Dynamic HTML, which is now part of the HTML 4.0 specification) is all about. CSS Layers gives Web developers the ability to overlap images and slices and also interactively show and hide each layer. You can learn more about CSS layers later in the chapter.

Learning the Web-graphic formats

As stated in the previous section, you have a lot of options for formats in the Save for Web dialog box (see Figure 16-13). Which one should you use? Each of these format types have advantages and disadvantages, and understanding the difference between them will help immensely as you design and build Web pages. This section thoroughly discusses each format and walks you through the various options associated with each one.

Note

Realize that there isn't one setting that's best suited for all Web graphics. Some settings are better suited for certain types of graphics. With experience, you'll come to understand and choose Web formats and settings with ease.

The GIF format

One of the most popular file formats for Web graphics, there's a never-ending controversy over how to pronounce GIF. Some say it with a soft G (as in Giraffe) while others pronounce with a hard G (as in Gift). Either way you say it, a GIF can contain a maximum of 256 colors, but more important, you can specify your image to have fewer colors to control files size. GIF uses a lossless compression algorithm and basically looks for large areas of pixels that are the same color to save file size. Lossless compress makes this format perfect for most flat color images, such as logos and text headlines.

The GIF format also has specific settings that can control how the GIF displays in a Web browser. Because GIF only supports a maximum of 256 colors, you have to choose a color-reduction algorithm, which is basically how Illustrator forces all of the colors to fit within a specific table of colors. You can go a step further by specifying exactly how many colors your GIF should contain as well, which can have a large impact on file size. If your image is just some black text, you can reduce your GIF to 4 or 16 colors (see Figure 16-14) with the same visual result — but get a huge saving in file size.

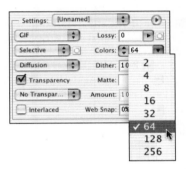

Figure 16-14: Changing the number of colors in a GIF

You can choose different dither methods as well (to get colors that aren't in the color table to appear in your GIF). Here's where the different preview panes can really help you choose the best setting for your graphic; GIF also supports transparency, so that you can choose one color as a "none" color, allowing your image to have a transparent background (necessary for placing images on colored backgrounds). The Matte setting also works in tandem with this. Anti-aliasing allows colors to blend into each other to create smoother transitions of color, but if you start off with art on a white background, you might see white pixels if you place that graphic on a non-white background. If you know what color on which you intend to display your graphic (that is, a background color), specifying that color as a Matte ensure that the graphic blends perfectly into the background.

You can also interlace a GIF, which means that the image quickly appears in a browser at a low resolution, and then improves in resolution and quality as it continues to load. This allows readers to start seeing graphics on their screen even while the page is still downloading. It's more of a psychological thing than anything else.

The JPEG format

If the GIF format is perfect for flat color images, the JPEG format (pronounced JAY-PEG) is the perfect format for photos and continuous tone graphics. JPEG was created originally to allow photographers to easily transmit photos electronically. Utilizing a lossy compression algorithm, JPEG can achieve some astonishing file savings by allowing you to compress a 10MB file to about 1MB in most cases.

Illustrator lets you set different levels of JPEG compression by either choosing options from a popup (Low, Medium, High, Maximum), or by moving a slider between 0 and 100 (see Figure 16-15). In Save for Web dialog box, these settings refer to quality, not compression, so a setting of Maximum means maximum quality (and less compression), not maximum compressions and lower quality. Because JPEG compression can result in files that have visible artifacts or look "chunky," you also have the option to apply a blur to minimize such artifacts. You can specify a blur setting of up to 2 pixels using the Blur slider (located under the Quality slider).

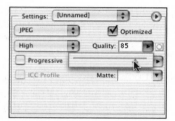

Figure 16-15: Specifying the quality of a JPEG

You can also set JPEG images to "progressive," which means that they load incrementally in a browser (similar to GIF's interlacing). You can also specify a Matte color for JPEG images (the same as we did for GIF earlier).

The PNG format

When the GIF format became popular, an issue arose with regard to the patent holder who created the compression algorithm (Unisys). To get around possible legal issues, the PNG format was born. Pronounced *ping*, the format offers similar lossless compression as GIF, but can support up to 32 bit color images and 256-level alpha channels for transparency (far more than the 256 color limit and 1 color alpha of GIF). An alpha channel is another term for the part of a file that's transparent. Save for Web allows users to save PNG images in PNG-8 and PNG-24 format, which offers support for more colors (see Figure 16-16).

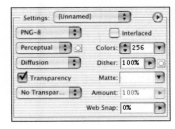

Figure 16-16: The options available for PNG-8 are similar to those available for GIF.

Because PNG can support continuous tone color, the format is great for both flat and photographic images. The additional settings you can apply to PNG images are similar to those that you can apply with GIF images. The downside is that most Web browsers, such as Microsoft's Internet Explorer, still do not properly support this standard format.

The WBMP format

You use the Wireless Bitmap format specifically for graphics that you want to display on cell phones and PDA devices. The WBMP format is 1 bit, which means that pixels can be either black or white, so you're limited in choosing between different dithering methods (Diffusion, Pattern, and Noise) and a dithering amount.

Cross-Reference Remember from the previous discussions in this chapter that dithering is a process in which different colored pixels are placed in a pattern to match the desired color. For more on this subject, see the section "Web Safe Colors," earlier in this chapter.

Output options

When you've chosen how to optimize your graphics, you can click the Save button. Doing this launches the Save Optimized As dialog box, where you can choose to save your graphics in one of three different formats. The options in the Format pop-up box are:

✦ **Image only:** Saves just the images themselves.

✦ **HTML and Images:** Saves the images and an HTML page that contains them.

✦ **HTML only:** Saves just the HTML code without the images at all.

Not all Web designers work alone. In many cases, a Web designer works hand-in-hand with a Web developer or someone who either writes code or defines how it's written. Because there are so many different ways of authoring HTML, many developers are very sensitive to how they write or how they build Web pages. Adobe certainly is aware of this because at the bottom of the Save Optimized As dialog is a pop-up menu called Settings. If you choose Other from the list (see Figure 16-17), you'll be rewarded with the Output Settings dialog, which is a dream come true for even the pickiest developer.

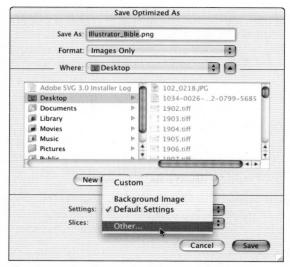

Figure 16-17: Choosing Other from the Save Optimized As dialog

There are five separate panes in the Output Settings dialog box, and each offers a wealth of options:

> ✦ **HTML:** Allows you to specify exactly how the HTML code is formulated, along with options that you can include for better integration with other Adobe products such as ImageReady and GoLive. The Always Add Alt Attribute setting includes Alt tags even where you don't specify them, which is a Section-508 (Government Accessibility) requirement (see Figure 16-18).

> ✦ **Slices:** Gives you control over how tables are coded in HTML and whether CSS layers are generated (see Figure 16-19). You can also choose exactly how each slice is named. Slicing is covered in the section "Web Slicing," later in this chapter.

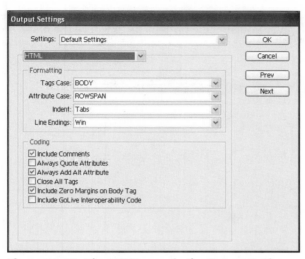

Figure 16-18: The HTML pane in the Output Settings dialog box

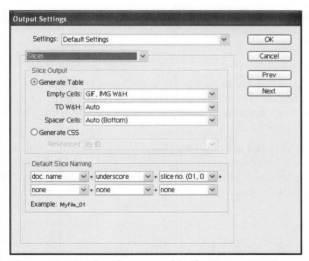

Figure 16-19: The Slices panel in the Output Settings dialog box

✦ **Image Maps:** If you've created image maps (which we'll cover later on in the chapter), this tab gives you specific options as to where the maps are stored (see Figure 16-20).

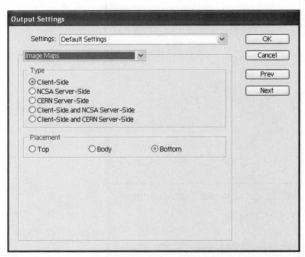

Figure 16-20: The Image Maps panel in the Output Settings dialog box

✦**Background:** HTML allows you to specify a background color or a background image for the entire page (images *tile* or repeat to fill the entire page). In this tab you can specify what color or image you want for the background of your HTML page (see Figure 16-21).

✦ **Saving Files:** Here you can specify exactly how to name your files as well as where you want to save them (see Figure 16-22). The included XMP option allows you to save metadata along with the files. XMP metadata comes from the File Info dialog found under the File menu in Illustrator.

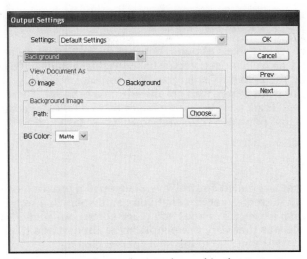

Figure 16-21: The Background panel in the Output Settings dialog box

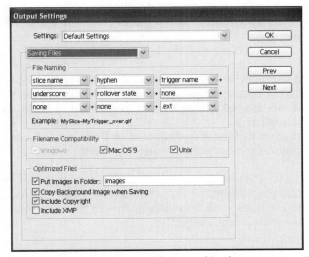

Figure 16-22: The Saving Files panel in the Output Settings dialog box

Vector Graphics for the Web

Sure, the Web is a place where pixels abound, but that doesn't mean there's no room for vectors to play as well. In fact, vector-based Web graphics have become quite popular. They add the benefit of enlarging Web graphics without getting "the jaggies" and allow you to print better Web graphics from a browser. There are other benefits as well which we'll talk about — oh we might as well talk about them now as we discuss the two most popular vector Web formats — Flash and SVG.

Flash

Once upon a time, a company called FutureWave developed a program called FutureSplash Animato that creates vectors that you can display in a Web browser. The program let you animate vector shapes and place some cool animation in a Web page. The downside was that very few people knew about it and to play the animations in a Web browser you had to install a special plug-in.

One day a company called Macromedia bought FutureWave and renamed FutureSplash to Flash. They also provided a browser plug-in for Flash to go along with their already popular Shockwave plug-in, calling it Shockwave Flash (SWF). The rest is modern day Internet history. The Flash plug-in is now installed by default in every mainstream Web browser and it has become the standard for creating interactive and engaging Web sites. Flash support is now even built-in to Apple's QuickTime video player, some cell phones and continues to expand.

> **Note** Although Flash and Illustrator do share the similarity of being vector-based programs, Illustrator isn't a competing product to Flash. Adobe did try to unseat Macromedia's hold on the Web market with LiveMotion, but by the time LiveMotion reached version 2.0, Adobe cancelled it. LiveMotion was cancelled under protest; most users thought it was superior to Flash because it was modeled after the very popular motion video product Adobe After Effects.

Although Illustrator can't do anywhere *near* the kinds of things that Macromedia Flash can do, it *can* export graphics in the SWF (Shockwave Flash) format. In fact, many designers who use Flash also use Illustrator to create their graphics and then import them into Flash to make them interactive.

To export graphics in the SWF format, choose File ⇨ Export, select Macromedia Flash (SWF) from the Format popup and click Export, which will get you the Macromedia Flash (SWF) Format Options dialog box (see Figure 16-23). For export options, you can choose from three different settings:

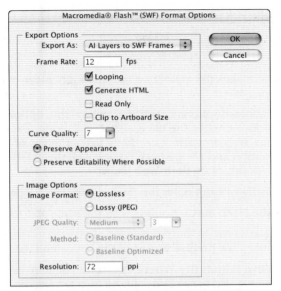

Figure 16-23: The Macromedia Flash (SWF) Format Options dialog box

✦ **AI File to SWF File:** Creates a single static SWF file from whatever is in your Illustrator file. This is perfect for when you want to display a static SWF image in your Web page.

✦ **AI Layers to SWF Frames:** Creates a single animated SWF file from the layers in your Illustrator file. Each Illustrator layer becomes its own frame, allowing you to export animations right out of Illustrator. When you select this option, you can choose a frame rate as well as whether you want the animation to loop (see the next bulleted list for more on these options).

✦ **AI Layers to SWF Files:** This final option creates separate SWF files, each one containing the contents of one layer in your Illustrator file. This is useful for designers who want to import individual art pieces into a Flash project.

Flash understands and takes advantage of Symbols, so if you define and use Symbols in your Illustrator file, they appear as Symbols when you open the SWF file in Flash. You also benefit from smaller file sizes when using Symbols in your SWF files. See Chapter 4 for more information on using Symbols in Illustrator.

Here are some of the other functions you encounter in the Macromedia Flash (SWF) Format Options dialog box:

✦ **Frame Rate:** How fast the animation plays each frame.

✦ **Looping:** Selecting this option makes the animation continuously plays over and over again.

✦ **Generate HTML:** One of the coolest options in this dialog box, this option not only creates the SWF file, but also creates the necessary HTML code that correctly displays the graphic in a Web browser. It certainly takes the guesswork and gruntwork out of the equation and allows even novice Web designers to easily incorporate cool Flash graphics on their Web pages.

✦ **Read-only:** Assures you that others can't open the SWF to edit it.

✦ **Clip to Artboard Size:** Sets the Flash movie boundary to the same size as your Illustrator artboard.

✦ **Curve Quality:** Lets you choose how precise vector paths are calculated.

✦ **Preserve Appearance/Preserve Editability Where Possible:** You can either choose to Preserve Appearance or Preserve Editability. The later option affects how SWF files display certain effects or appearances that Illustrator can apply to objects but that are not supported in Flash. In cases where Flash does not support the effect or appearance, the Preserve Appearance option rasterizes the objects so that it looks correct. However, rasterizing the object may result in a file that isn't as editable when you open it in Flash.

✦ **Image Options:** Come into play only if you have placed images or rasterized areas in your file. If you choose Lossless, your image will be saved in GIF format, or you can choose Lossy and export your images as JPEG files, where you can choose quality and resolution (similar to those options we defined for JPEG earlier).

You can also save SWF files directly from the Save for Web dialog, the benefit being that you can preview your art before you save.

For more on the Save for Web dialog box, see the section "Previewing Web Graphics," earlier in this chapter.

While the Save for Web dialog can't preview SWF animations, you can use the Preview in Browser feature to see what your animation looks like before actually saving the file.

Illustrator uses Apple's Quicktime plugin to preview SWF files in Save for Web. If you can't see a preview of your image when you choose SWF in Save for Web, make sure you have Quicktime installed.

SVG

SVG stands for "Scalable Vector Graphics" and is an open standard format that is based on XML. To view SVG files in a Web browser, a plug-in is required, although future versions of Web browsers (Explorer, Navigator, Safari, and so on) will most likely provide built-in SVG support, because the format is becoming increasingly popular. One cool aspect of SVG is that you can edit it in any text editor and change values easily, thus changing the look of your graphic.

Cross-Reference

Other benefits of SVG are covered in the section "Using Data-Driven Graphics" later in this chapter, where the XML text-based format is used to include variable content in a file.

Illustrator is actually one of the most robust tools available for creating SVG graphics. Illustrator cannot only save files in the SVG format, but it can also open SVG files — even if they weren't created in Illustrator. Similar to how Illustrator can open just about any EPS or PDF file, opening an SVG file enables you to edit just about any SVG file you can find.

You can save SVG files directly out of Illustrator by choosing File ➪ Save and picking SVG from the Format pop-up (see Figure 16-24). You can also choose to save SVG files via Save for Web, as we mentioned earlier in the chapter. Of course, the advantage to saving them from the Save for Web dialog is that you can preview the results before you save them.

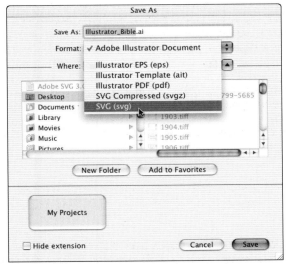

Figure 16-24: Choosing to save your file as SVG

When you save an SVG file, you can choose to embed fonts (where the font license agreement allows) and you can also choose whether to include linked images as separate links or to embed them and include them inside the SVG file. You'll also notice an option to Preserve Illustrator Editing Capabilities (see Figure 16-25). Turning this option on enables you to roundtrip the file back into Illustrator without losing any native information. Because the option adds data into the file that only Illustrator can use, it increases the file size, so turn off this option if you don't need to edit the file later. Of course, saving a copy of the file as a regular file is always a good idea so that you don't lose any work.

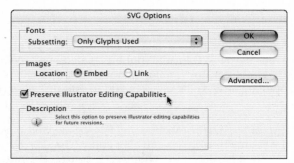

Figure 16-25: Choosing the Preserve Illustrator Editing Capabilities option

In the SVG Options dialog, you also find an Advanced button where you can specify even more details about your SVG files (see Figure 16-26). You can specify CSS Properties settings, choose how precise vectors are calculated (decimal places), and choose text encoding formats. Optimize for Adobe SVG Viewer, which installs along with Illustrator, allows you to take advantage of certain features that only the Adobe SVG Viewer plugin can offer (which is currently the standard, so using it is a safe choice). Include Extended Syntax for Variable Content is discussed in the "Data-Driven Graphics" section later in this chapter, and it allows for the inclusion of variable content in the SVG file. Include Slicing Data does exactly what it says: it includes Web-slice data in the file (I cover Web slicing later in the chapter).

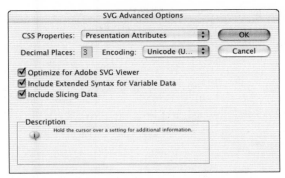

Figure 16-26: The SVG Advanced Options dialog

Applying SVG filters

SVG filters are cool because they are attributes you can apply to your art in real-time as they display in a Web browser. If you apply a drop shadow to text as an SVG filter, that text is still live and editable in your Web browser (you can select, copy, and paste it, a search engine can "see" the text), yet it has a drop shadow applied to it when it displays on the Web page. Because you can zoom in on vector graphics in a Web browser, you can enlarge the SVG text as much as you want, and the drop shadow renders each time, ensuring a nice smooth drop shadow. (You won't get "the jaggies.")

Applying an SVG Effect is similar to applying any other effect (see Figure 16-27). Make your selection and then choose Effect ➪ SVG Filter and choose one. You can't preview some of these filters in the Illustrator window, so previewing the file in your browser is a good idea. After you apply a filter, you can see it listed in the Appearance palette (see Figure 16-28) for that object or selection. Therefore, to edit or remove the effect, you use the Appearance palette.

Cross-Reference

Effects are covered in more detail in Chapter 12.

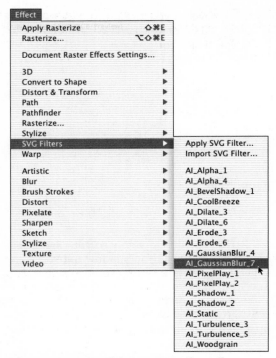

Figure 16-27: Applying an SVG Filter effect

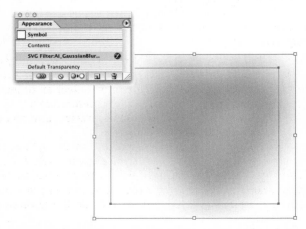

Figure 16-28: The SVG Filter effect as it appears in the Appearance palette after it's applied

Illustrator has with several SVG Filters. However, if you know SVG, you can also create your own effects by choosing Effect ⇨ SVG Filter ⇨ Apply SVG Filter and clicking the New SVG Filter icon button (see Figure 16-29). You can also import SVG filters from other Illustrator files by choosing Effect ⇨ SVG Filter ⇨ Import SVG Filter.

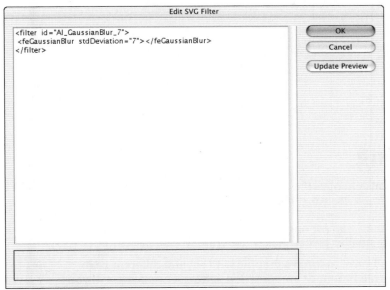

Figure 16-29: Creating your own SVG Filter effect

The SVG Interactivity Palette

In reality, SVG is Javascript-driven XML code. Illustrator allows you to add interactive options to graphics that you can save as SVG via the SVG Interactivity palette. Doing so requires the knowledge of Javascript because you must select an object, choose an event from the popup (see Figure 16-30), and write or reference a Javascript to perform a specific function (change color, animate, resize, and so on).

> **Note**
>
> The SVG format supports many levels of interactivity and animation. Although Illustrator cannot create or preview these effects directly, you can use a text editor to add these functions after you create the graphics. For more information on using SVG, check out the SVG Zone on the Web at www.adobe.com/svg or read the *Creating SVG with Adobe Illustrator cs* white paper that's on the Illustrator application CD.

Figure 16-30: Applying a Javascript event via the SVG Interactivity palette

Web Slicing

Throughout this chapter, the term slicing comes up. It refers to the process of cutting up Web graphics into smaller pieces to achieve several goals:

✦ Rather than wait for one large graphic to load in a Web page, loading several different smaller pieces makes the graphic load faster.

✦ You don't have to force a graphic with several different parts or styles to use just one file format or compression setting. For example, if you have a graphic that has some text or a logo on one side and a photo or gradation of color on another side, rather than force the entire graphic to a larger size to make sure the gradient looks good, you can split the image up into pieces and optimize the text and gradient differently, saving file size overall.

✦ You can assign links to a slice. By creating different slices, you can allow users to click different parts of a graphic, which link to different locations or pages on the Internet.

✦ You can assign rollovers to a slice. Rollovers are actually created outside of Illustrator (in ImageReady, for example), but you can still assign the slices right in Illustrator to save time in the workflow process. A rollover swaps one graphic for another when a user performs an action, such as moving the mouse over the slice. For example, you can make a graphic of a button look lit up when the user rolls the mouse over the button.

What the slicing process really does is divide your image into different pieces, which are described in HTML as a table (see Figure 16-31). Each cell of the table contains a different image, optimized as you specify with or without a link. Because a cell must be rectangular, you must make all slices rectangular as well. When the table is rendered in a Web browser, the image looks like a complete graphic.

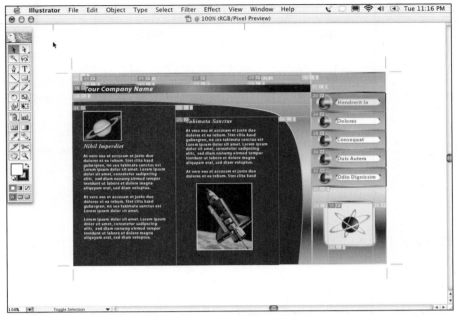

Figure 16-31: A Web graphic sliced into an HTML table

Object-based Web Slicing

Illustrator has two was of applying slices. The traditional way is to choose the Slice tool from the Toolbox and draw slices over your graphics (see Figure 16-32). Numbered slices appear on your screen as you create the slices and auto slices are created as well (*user slices* are those that you create; *auto slices* are those that are automatically created to fill the rest of the table). Slices don't print—they just indicate how the slice table is going to be created.

Figure 16-32: Drawing a slice with the Slice tool

The down side of using this method is that if you ever want to edit your art, you may also need to update or redraw the slices. Illustrator includes a second way to create slices called *object-based slicing*. By applying slices as an attribute to an object rather than just drawing a separate shape, Illustrator creates a dynamic slice that moves and resizes itself based on the shape or selection to which it is assigned. You do this by first making a selection and then choose Object ➪ Slice ➪ Make (see Figure 16-33). A slice appears, but now when you edit that object, the slice grows or shrinks to fit the updated object.

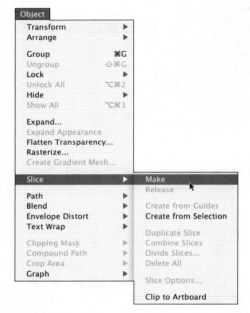

Figure 16-33: Creating a dynamic object-based slice

Working with slices

Object-based slices don't need modifying — they are basically maintenance-free slices. But if you draw slices with the Slice tool, you can edit those slices using the Slice Select tool, which allows you to move the slices as well as resize them. The Slice Select tool also allows you to select slices so that you can apply settings to them. Selecting a slice and choosing Object ➪ Slice ➪ Slice Options opens the Slice Options dialog (see Figure 16-34), where you can specify the slice name, a URL link, Alt text (for Alternative text display in Web browsers) and more. The drop-down list at the bottom of the dialog allows you to specify a background for that slice — each slice can have its own background color or image — and there's a pop-up (drop-down) menu that lets you specify the slice in one of three "states":

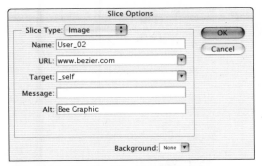

Figure 16-34: The Slice Options dialog

✦ **Image:** The contents of the slice, or table cell, is an image, GIF, JPEG, and so on, that you specify.

✦ **No Image:** The contents of the table cell is an HTML, which you can specify directly in the dialog. This is useful if the graphic you have is just a placeholder for something else, such as Quicktime video clip or a script that calls a graphic.

✦ **HTML Text:** If the contents of the slice is text, this option becomes available, and Illustrator basically codes the HTML to display text rather than an image in the table cell.

> **Tip**
>
> Specifying slice options in Illustrator can save you time down the road if you're also using Photoshop, ImageReady, or GoLive. The options that you specify in Illustrator are stored and recognized in these programs.

Other functions from the Slice submenu lets you release an object-based slice, divide a single slice into multiple slices of equal size, create slices from either guides or selections (these won't be object-based slices), and combine multiple slices into a single slice. There's also an option called Clip to Artboard, which uses the Artboard size as the table boundaries rather than the size of the art on your Artboard. This is a great feature if you need to create a table of a specific size. By setting the document Artboard size to the correct dimensions, you have one less thing to worry about (see Figure 16-35).

After you've created all of your slices, you can open Save for Web and then use the Slice Select tool to choose individual optimization settings. You can press Shift and click to select multiple slices. If you're exporting HTML directly from Illustrator, click Save. However, but if you plan to save your graphics as SVG to bring into GoLive, or if intend to take your art into ImageReady, you can click the Done button to return to Illustrator.

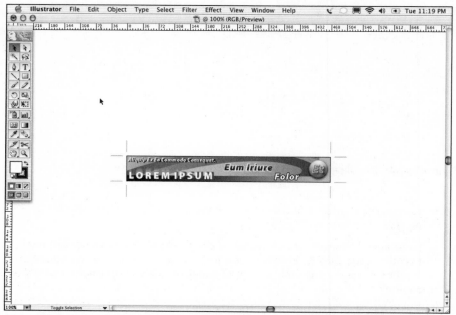

Figure 16-35: An Artboard set up to the exact size necessary for a Web ad banner

CSS Layers

In HTML there is one "layer" that you can describe, which means that text and images can't overlap each other. You can't overlap images either. When CSS Layers were added to the HTML spec, Web designers finally had the ability to specify layers of information in a single HTML page. CSS, which stands for *Cascading Style Sheets*, gives designers and developers the ability to lay out elements of a page with pixel by pixel accuracy. It allows images and text to overlap each other.

The catch is that Web browsers don't always support CSS Layers in the same way, so use this feature with caution and lots of testing. Basically, Illustrator allows all top-level layers to be described as CSS Layers. You can turn this option on in the Save for Web dialog's Layers palette (see Figure 16-36). You can then choose what state you want each layer to assume (Visible, Hidden, and so on).

Figure 16-36: Choosing to export CSS Layers from the Save for Web dialog

Getting Interactive

As we mentioned before in this chapter, adding interactivity to a Web site is a great way for designers to add interest to their site as well as add a functional element. Be it a cool animation or a navigation bar, Illustrator can help turn a static Web site into something that adds flair and value. While Illustrator isn't Flash, LiveMotion or even ImageReady, it can still hold its own when creating these kinds of elements.

Specifying an image map

Some Web sites feature a graphic that links to different pages or places depending on what part of the graphic you click. An *image map* is basically a set of coordinates (sometimes called *hotspots)* that you can apply to a Web graphic — with each coordinate taking the user to a link of your choice. Setting up an image map is really easy in Illustrator:

1. **Select an object and open the Attributes palette.** See Chapter 5 for more on selecting an object. To open the Attribute palette, choose Window ➪ Attributes.

2. **From the Image Map pop-up, choose Rectangle or Polygon**. You want to choose the latter for non-uniform shapes.

3. **Type the full link in the URL field.** This is shown in Figure 16-37. Illustrator will store each URL you use in a single file, so you don't have to repeatedly type the URL if you are using it again.

4. **Click the Browser button:** The Browser button that appears in the Attributes palette lets you quickly test your URL to make sure that it works.

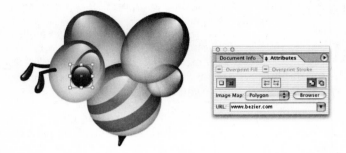

Figure 16-37: Selecting an image map and specifying a URL

> **Note**
>
> Image maps are used less these days because slicing can achieve the same functionality and also add fancy effects like rollovers. However, there are still times when image maps are useful, such as when creating non-rectangular links (remember that slices are always rectangular).

Image maps are written in several different ways, and you should speak to a Web developer or a technical contact at your Web-hosting company to find out which image map is best to use for your particular need and configuration. *Client-side* image maps reside inside the HTML code itself, and *server-side* maps reside in a separate file that links to the HTML file. You can specify these settings in the Image Maps tab of the Output Settings dialog when using Save for Web (see Figure 16-38).

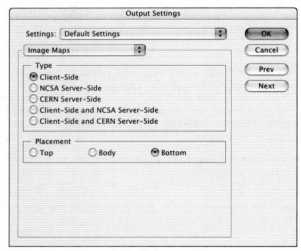

Figure 16-38: The Image Maps tab of the Output Settings dialog

Creating animations

Creating animations for the Web in Illustrator can be fun and is actually easy as well! *Animations* is basically creating multiple images and playing them consecutively to give the appearance of motion. Each image in an animation is called a *frame*. In Illustrator, you animate using each layer in your file as a frame. You can then export your file as a SWF file and choose the AI Layers to SWF Frames option at export time to create your animation.

You can create unique and interesting animations when you combine Blends along with effects like 3-D and Scribble. Animating blends are easy because Illustrator has a feature called Release to Layers that automatically places each step of a blend onto its own layer — ready for exporting as an animated SWF.

The Release to Layers command is found in the Layers palette menu and you can choose between sequence and build. A sequence is much like traditional animation in that each frame contains a single image that moves from frame to frame. A build allows you to keep art in multiple frames and is useful for animating text, where you want letters to stay on the screen while they appear. For example, the animated word "hello" would contain "H" in the first frame, "HE" in the second frame, "HEL" in the third, and so on.

When you blend effects, Illustrator actually calculates each step of the blend individually, allowing you to create some spectacular effects, such as this one with the Scribble effect:

1. **Start off by typing the letter "A" and choose Type ➪ Create Outlines to convert the text to a Bezier path.** Scale it so that it's nice and big (there's no need for you to squint at the screen).

2. **Choose Effect ➪ Stylize ➪ Scribble, and choose Sketch from the Settings popup; click OK** (see Figure 16-39).

3. **Give the "A" a color of your choice and then copy it by pressing Command-C (Control-C) and then Paste in Front by pressing Command-F (Control-F).** Doing this makes a copy of the "A" right on top of the original one.

4. **With the new "A" still selected, give it a different fill color and then marquee select with the Selection tool to select both of them.**

5. **Choose Object ➪ Blend ➪ Make** (see Figure 16-40).

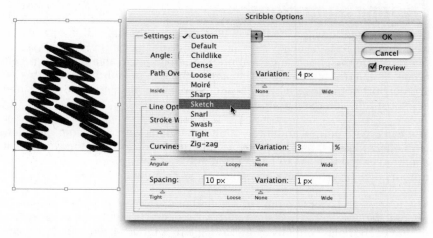

Figure 16-39: Applying a Scribble effect to the "A"

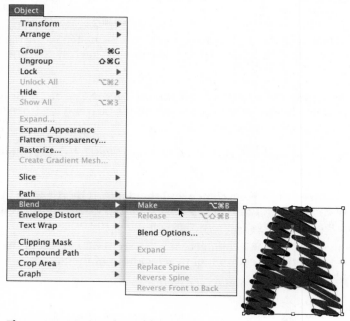

Figure 16-40: Creating a blend

6. With the blended object still selected, choose Object@@ > Blend ⇨ Blend Options and change the pop-up to Specified Steps and choose 10 for the number of steps (see Figure 16-41).

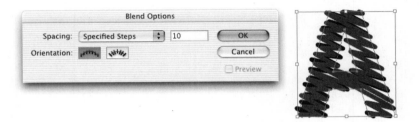

Figure 16-41: Specifying the number of blend steps

7. Now that you've created your blend, head over to the Layers palette and click on the little triangle to expose the contents of Layer 1.

8. Select the Blend layer and then choose Release to Layers — Sequence from the Layers palette flyout menu (see Figure 16-42). Notice that the Layers palette now lists many more layers — and each layer now contains one step of the blend that you created in Step 4 (see Figure 16-43).

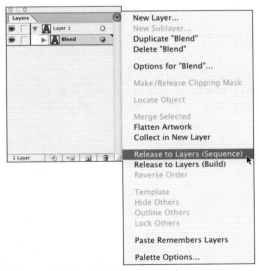

Figure 16-42: Choosing the Release to Layers (Sequence) option

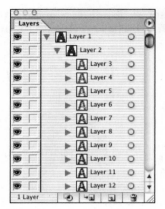

Figure 16-43: The Layers palette with all of the new layers displayed

9. **Choose File ➪ Save for Web and select SWF for the image format.** You should now only see the first frame of the animation in your preview pane (see Figure 16-44).

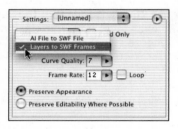

Figure 16-44: Choosing SWF as the export file format from Save for Web

10. **To see what the animation looks like, click the Preview in Browser button and if you're OK with the results** (see Figure 16-45), **go back to Save for Web and click the Save button.**

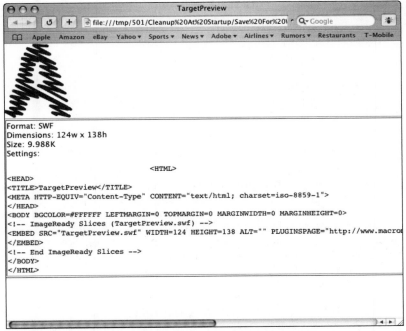

Figure 16-45: Viewing the animation in your Web browser

Adding rollovers with Adobe ImageReady

We mentioned earlier that Illustrator can't assign rollovers, but you can create your graphics and then bring those graphics into ImageReady and assign your rollovers there. This capability allows you to create your graphics with your familiar tools in Illustrator, take advantage of vector drawing tools and powerful text features, and even apply slice settings. You can quickly customize them in ImageReady.

Start out by planning your layers carefully and laying out your slices so that you can easily set up where your rollovers will go. The way you specify a rollover is to specify certain *states* for each slice. One state is for normal, one state is for mouseover, one state for click, and so on. For example, if you want a button to change color or glow for a rollover, create the normal state on one layer; then create a separate layer for the mouseover state, and so on. When you bring the file into ImageReady all you'll have to do is toggle which layer you want visible (see Figure 16-46).

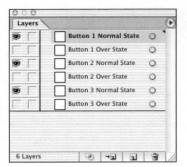

Figure 16-46: Layers set up for easy creation of rollovers in ImageReady

When you're done, choose File ➪ Export and choose Photoshop (.PSD) from the format popup. Most people don't know that you can export .PSD files directly from Illustrator. You can then choose specific options, such as preserving layer information – even live text and slices (see Figure 16-47). Makes sure you check all of these and then click Export. When you open that file in ImageReady it's ready with text, layers and slices all intact, and you can assign your rollovers, and export it to HTML (or to import into GoLive as a Smart Object).

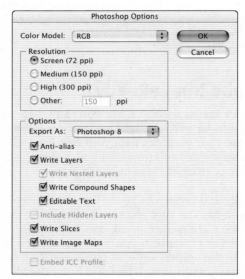

Figure 16-47: The Photoshop Export Options dialog

Using Data-Driven Graphics to Streamline Design Work

Designing a business card can be fun. It's challenging to come up with a cool and clean design that gets the message across in a readable and usable format. What isn't fun is copying that card over and over again and typing in different information for each employee in the company. Wouldn't it be great if there was some way to do all the fun stuff yourself and then let the computer too all the tedious boring stuff?

That's where Data-Driven Graphics comes into play. Sure, it's a mouthful to say, but it can save a lot of time. You start off by creating a regular Illustrator file, which you use as a base file, or template (see Figure 16-48), similar in concept to the templates discussed in Chapter 2. This template contains your design, but you tag the content as *variables*. You then have a *script* fetch data from an external file, such as a text file or any ODBC-compliant database, and the script automatically generates customized files for you, while you go search for a nice beverage to enjoy. Now that you know the basic steps for creating data-driven graphics, the rest of the sections in this chapter walk you through how to go about performing those steps.

Tip   The data-driven graphics feature was originally created for Web graphics because that medium demands instant updates and graphics that are generated on-the-fly. However, it can prove very beneficial to print workflows as well.

Figure 16-48: A sample data-driven graphics template

Variables

A variable is something that changes. In Illustrator, defining something as a variable means that "this will change." For example, when you type the name "Joe Smith" on a business card and then define it as a variable called "name," running the appropriate script replaces the words "Joe Smith" with whatever you have in the Name field of your database.

There are four different kinds of variables that you can set in Illustrator:

✦ **Text:** A text variable is simply a string of text, either point text or area text, that gets replaced with new text. The font and style applied to that text remains. Only the characters themselves change. For example, the Joe Smith case mentioned previously.

✦ **Visibility:** You can apply visibility to any kind of object in Illustrator and control whether that object is shown or hidden. For example, you can show a starburst graphic in certain cases, but not others.

✦ **Linked Image:** This kind of variable is specific to replacing linked images (any format). For example, if your business card design contains a picture of the employee, setting the image as a variable allows you to create business cards with each employee's photo on it. Because images can vary in size, there are options that allow you to control how to place images (see Replacement Options, later in this chapter).

✦ **Graph data:** Creating a graph in Illustrator is easy enough (see Chapter 4), and by defining a graph as a variable, you can replace the data of that graph to generate customized graphs automatically. For example, you can automatically generate a weather chart by retrieving the latest weather forecasts from the Internet.

The Variables palette

You define Variables in Illustrator via the Variables palette (see Figure 16-49). The palette enables you to keep tabs of all of your variables in a single location and allows you to define *data sets* as well. A data set is very much like a record in a database and stores information for a specific range of variables.

Cross-Reference   See the section "Setting Up a Data-Driven Graphics Template," later in this chapter, to see exactly how this works.

Figure 16-49: The Variables Palette, with all four kinds of variables defined

You define a visibility variable by making a selection and clicking the Make Visibility Dynamic icon. Likewise, you define other variables by making a selection and clicking the "Make Dynamic" icon. These are context sensitive (see Figure 16-50), so if you select text, the button is labeled "Make Text Dynamic," and if you select a graph, it is labeled "Make Graph Dynamic."

a   b   c

Figure 16-50: The "Make Dynamic" button changes depending on what kind of object you have selected.

Clicking the little camera icon in the upper left of the palette (see Figure 16-51) allows you to capture a data set. Data sets are stored in Illustrator as XML data and you can both import and export variables and data sets from the Variables palette fly-out menu. Because XML is a standard format, Illustrator can very easily integrate into complex workflows and back-end systems (see Figure 16-52). For more information on how Illustrator stores variables in an XML file, see the *Illustrator XML Grammar Guide*, which you can find on the Illustrator application CD.

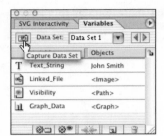

Figure 16-51: "Capturing" a data set

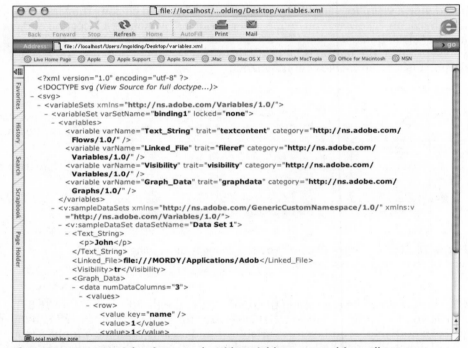

Figure 16-52: A sample of XML code with variables exported from Illustrator

Understanding scripting

A script is a list of commands that are contained in a single file. When you "run" a script, your computer follows the commands that are contained within the script. In reality, a script is much like computer programming code, only it's what's called a "High Level" language in that it controls existing programs, rather than actually being a program itself. A script "tells" applications what to do. In fact, most scripting languages read almost like English — making them easier to learn and use.

Illustrator supports three different scripting languages:

✦ **AppleScript,** which was created by the folks at Apple and works on the Macintosh platform.

✦ **Visual Basic**, which was created by Microsoft and works on the Windows platform.

✦ **JavaScript,** which was originally developed by Netscape and is cross-platform.

Scripting versus Actions

If you've been paying attention, you remember we spoke about something called Actions back in Chapter 14. Because you're a smart person, you're probably thinking why do I need scripting if I already have Actions?

There are several big differences between Actions and Scripting.

✦ An Action is simply a recorded sequence of events that you can play over and over again, each time performing exactly the same way. A Script can contain logic and therefore perform different steps depending on the situation.

✦ An Action is a task that can only be performed completely within Illustrator. A script can involve multiple applications, not just Illustrator.

✦ An Action is easy to create right in Illustrator. A Script requires the knowledge of at least one of the Scripting languages (AppleScript, VB Script or JavaScript). So while scripts are far more powerful, they are also far more difficult to create.

For example, you can write a script to automatically create a forecast graphic by going to a weather site on the Internet, retrieving temperature information for a particular city, and draw a graphic. You can code the graphic so that temperatures below 32 degrees are colored blue, temperatures is over 90 degrees are colored red, temperatures between 75 and 85 have a smiley face with sunglasses. The script is able to bring that info into Illustrator from another application (your Web browser) and can then make decisions based on that data within Illustrator. Actions are cool, but nowhere near as cool as a Script.

It takes a lot more work to write a script than it does to record an Action, but a script can do a lot more and is more powerful than an Action is.

Note
Not everything in Illustrator is Actionable, and not everything in Illustrator is Scriptable either. There are even some things that you can do with AppleScript or VB Script that you can't do with JavaScript. With each new version of Illustrator, you can record more and more features and commands of the application as Actions or Scripted. For complete information on what you can and can't do, see the *Illustrator Scripting Guide* that's on the Illustrator application CD.

Don't let all this talk about scripting scare you. Just because a script is a necessary step in the data-driven graphics process, it doesn't mean you (the designer) have to do it. Some companies have developers on staff who know how to script and you can have them write the required scripts for you. You can also hire a developer or consultant on a freelance basis to write your scripts. Because of the potential time-savings you gain once you utilize a script, this method can also prove very economical.

Setting up a data-driven graphics template

It's beyond the scope of this book to learn how to write a script to automatically fill a template, but it's easy to set up a template and create some sample data sets, which will allow you to preview what your files will look like when they are filled with data.

1. **Using the text tool, click an empty part of the Artboard to create some point text.** The example uses the words "Good Morning". Be creative and choose a nice font and even a drop shadow if you'd like.

2. **Switch to the Select tool and select the type you just created.** For more on the Select tool, see Chapter 5.

3. **Choose Window ⇨ Variables.** This opens the Variables palette.

4. **Click the "Make Text Dynamic" button at the bottom of the palette as shown in Figure 16-53.** Alternatively, you can choose the "Make Text Dynamic" option from the Variables palette fly-out menu. Notice that a variable of type "Text" called Variable1 is created.

5. **Double click the Variable1 item in the Variables palette.** The Variable Options dialog box opens.

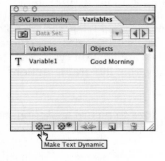

Figure 16-53: Defining a Text variable

6. **Type a name for the variable**. Change the name of the variable so that you (or a script) can readily identify it. In the example, the name is changed to "greeting."

7. **Click OK.** You can also press Enter.

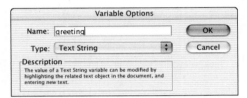

Figure 16-54: Changing the name of the variable

8. **Click the little camera, which is the Capture Data Set button in the upper left of the Variables palette.** This creates Data Set 1.

9. **Using the text tool, edit the text on your Artboard to have it read something else.** The example now reads Good Afternoon instead of Good Morning.

10. **Click the Capture Data Set button.** This creates Data Set 2.

11. **Edit the text on your Artboard to change it again.** The example was changed from Good Afternoon to Good Evening.

12. **Click the Capture Data Set button (Figure 16-55).** You now have three different data sets in your Illustrator file.

Figure 16-55: Capturing a third data set

13. **Using the left and right arrows in the Variables palette (Figure 16-56), click to step through all of the 3 data sets.** Note that as you switch between datasets, the text on your screen changes. This is extremely helpful when you create templates as it allows you, as a designer, to create a design that works

well with different data. For example a long word or name takes up more space than a short word does. Setting up several different datasets in your file allows you to preview how your design looks with different sets of data.

Figure 16-56: Stepping through data sets

Taking advantage of data-driven graphics with Adobe GoLive

Beginning with version 6, GoLive added support for working with dynamically generated content. You can also use the variable feature in Illustrator to create those graphics in GoLive yourself, and it's really easy!

1. **Start by creating a template in Illustrator.** Design your art and then assign some variables.

2. **Choose File ⇨ Save As.** Doing this opens the Save As dialog box.

3. **Choose SVG for the format** (Figure 16-57). The SVG Options dialog box appears. The reason for choosing this format is that SVG is an open standards format based on XML and can contain variable content.

4. **Click Preserve Illustrator Editing Capabilities checkbox.** Doing this allows you to reopen the SVG file in Illustrator later.

5. **Click the Advanced button.** The Advanced Options dialog box appears.

6. **Make sure the Include Extended Syntax for Variable Data check box is checked.** See Figure 16-58.

7. **Click Save.**

8. **In GoLive, open or create an HTML file.**

9. **From the Object palette in GoLive, drag an Illustrator Smart Object onto your page.**

10. **Using the point and shoot icon, load the SVG graphic that you created in Illustrator.** Because GoLive sees the variable content in the Illustrator SVG file, GoLive prompts you with a dialog box listing all of the variables, as shown in Figure 16-59. Here you can choose to replace text or change attributes of your variables.

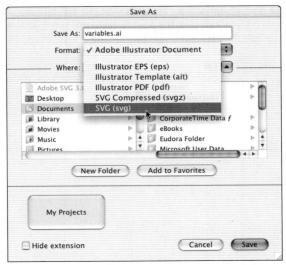

Figure 16-57: Choosing to save a file as SVG

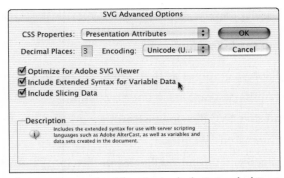

Figure 16-58: Checking the Include Extended Syntax for Variable Data option in the SVG Advanced Options dialog

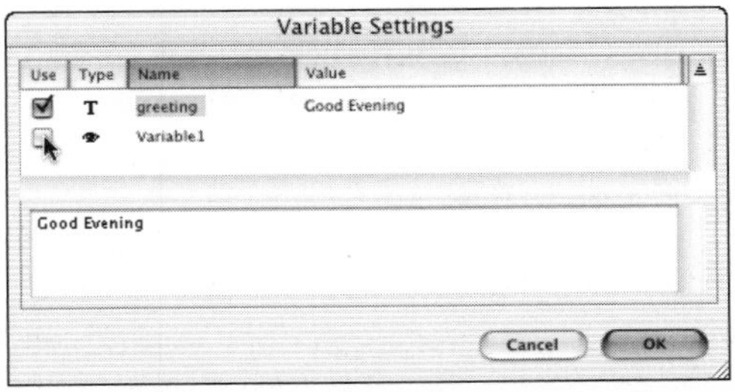

Figure 16-59: GoLive prompts you with the list of variables in the file.

11. **You can change these variables at any time in GoLive by clicking the Variables button** (Figure 16-60) **in the Inspector palette**. It's a powerful way to quickly update your graphics without even launching Illustrator!

Figure 16-60: Clicking the Variables button allows you to change the variables directly within GoLive at any time.

Summary

In this chapter, you found out the following:

✦ Pixel Preview mode displays graphics as they would appear in a Web browser.

✦ Save for Web lets you optimize graphics in one easy step.

✦ You can both open and save SVG files in Illustrator.

✦ Illustrator can export animated SWF files.

✦ You can easily bring sliced and optimized Illustrator files into Photoshop or ImageReady.

✦ Data-Driven graphics can streamline repetitive tasks and help save time.

✦ Illustrator can define four kinds of variables in the Variables palette.

✦ There are many Variables stored in XML.

✦ Illustrator supports AppleScript (Mac), VB Script (Windows), and JavaScript.

✦ Scripting is far more powerful than Actions.

✦   ✦   ✦

Appendixes

What's New in Illustrator cs

With the release of Illustrator cs, Adobe has again raised the bar in illustrating software. No wonder this product continues to blow away the competition. With the amazing new features and upgrades to existing ones, Illustrator cs has surpassed even the toughest user's expectations. Requests by Illustrator users have been answered and have contributed to some bold new features to an already strong package. This appendix summarizes the major new features of Illustrator cs.

New Features

Illustrator cs brings improvements to Illustrator in several key areas including 3D and Typography. One of the most notable new features is the support for 3D graphics. 3D are integrated into Illustrator with live previews and on the fly edits. The Typography tools are polished, giving you multiple enhancements in your type options. Another really fun addition is the new Scribble effect, which is another strong new way to enhance your graphics.

Adobe has completely overhauled the printing interface, which gives you more options to publish your images from print to cell-phone displays, broadcasting, and more. New streamlined, easy to use dialog boxes and palettes make Illustrator the strongest illustration tool in the industry.

3D

Illustrator cs has now made it easy to add three-dimensional elements to your artwork. You can create 3D effects from 2D objects by extruding or revolving them around an axis. With the extrusion option, you can add an edge effect using a bevel option (see Figure A-1). Edges add a nice crisp look to type or buttons for use on Web pages. The revolve option enables you to take a basic path and revolve it around a central axis, creating nice chess pieces, balusters, bottles, or any other rounded shapes (see Figure A-2).

Cross-Reference   You can learn to use the new 3D features in Chapter 13.

Using the 3D features, not only can you create amazing three-dimensional objects from two-dimensional art, but you can add lighting effects to them as well. Illustrator gives you four surface options: plastic, diffuse, wire frame, or no shading (see Figure A-3). To go a step further, you can map artwork onto 3D shapes (see Figure A-4). You can map any saved symbols onto a 3D shape. If you want a specific piece of artwork mapped, simply save it as a symbol and choose the Map Symbol option in the 3D dialog box.

Now, if that isn't enough, Illustrator CS takes 3D to a new level. You can edit the original 2D shape and it will automatically update the 3D shape, such as the bottle object shown in Figure A-5.

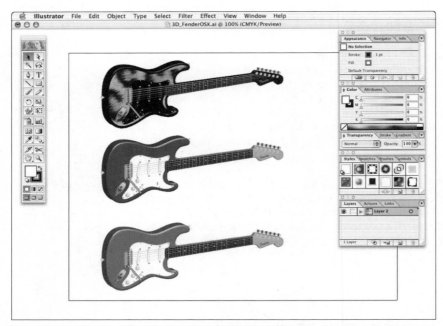

Figure A-1: The 3D Effect is shown on these guitars using the extrude feature.

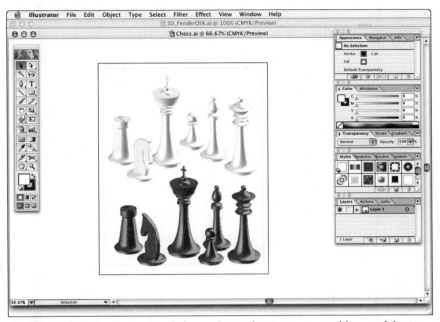

Figure A-2: Three-dimensional chess pieces that were created by revolving a simple path

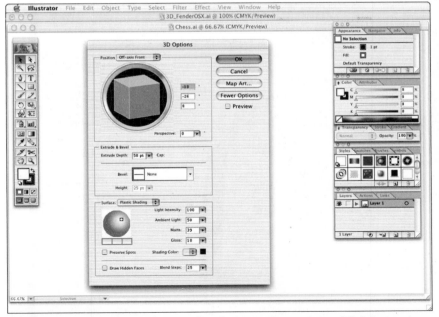

Figure A-3: The 3D Options dialog box lets you choose several lighting options.

Figure A-4: You can wrap artwork, like this image with the text, "Bubblejuice," around a 3D shape.

Figure A-5: Edits update in 3D instantly.

If you want to use the shape multiple times, you can save the shape's formatting as a graphic style and apply it to any other objects you wish.

Scribble Fill

The new Scribble Effect adds a sketchy, loose, fun effect to any artwork. Use the Scribble Effect to add a hand-drawn look to any art. Loosen up a tight design with a friendly feel of the Scribble Fill (see Figure A-6). There are 10 different presets to give you a variety of effects. In addition, you can change the settings to your preference and save those changes. Scribble Fill is a live effect like the 3D effect, so any changes you make are automatically applied instantly.

 Cross-Reference   The Scribble effect is covered along with the other effects in Chapter 13.

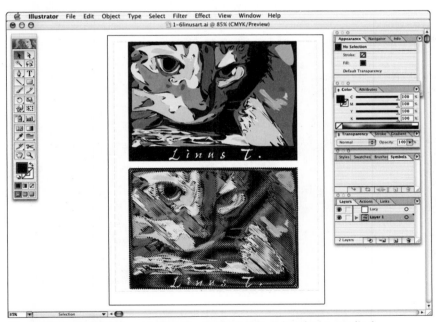

Figure A-6: Art before and after the Scribble Effect has been applied

Type Enhancements

Illustrator introduces several new type capabilities in the CS version. New to the type features is support for the Open Type font standard. OpenType fonts now work on Macintosh and Windows, making the file exchange across platforms smooth. This lets you use Open Type fonts consistently across several different systems. Along with expanded character sets for fonts, OpenType also offers richer type-character sets.

Adobe also improved many of the options found in the Character and Paragraph palettes. In addition to enhanced Character and Paragraph styles, there are more options such as faux styles, case controls, and overprinting choices (see Figure A-7). You also are offered more choices with the OpenType options with swash alternates, fractions, ligatures, and ordinals.

Cross-Reference   All the new type features are presented in Chapter 9.

Figure A-7: This text is an example of one of the new faux styles.

These new features make it even easier to pass paragraph and character attributes or styles among other workers. This increases the team's productivity and ensures accurate formatting when multiple users access a document.

Standard ligatures are automatically set using OpenType fonts. Smart Quotes and apostrophes are also automatically adjusted, showing your client that you are attentive to the smallest details. Glyphs are accessed with ease now by using the new Glyphs palette (see Figure A-8). Instead of memorizing a keyboard shortcut, you access them with a simple click.

Columns and Rows are easier controlled with specific height, width, gutter controls, and how many rows and columns will appear in a specific area. By choosing the Optical Kerning option in the Character palette, Illustrator automatically kerns text with high detail. The Optical Alignment menu option automatically lines up edges of the text at the end of a block of text (see Figure A-9). By choosing this, the type-block ends look even rather than ragged.

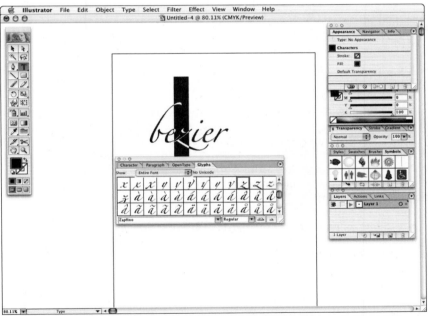

Figure A-8: The Glyph palette offers convenience in selecting specific glyphs.

Figure A-9: The Optical Alignment option is found in the Type menu.

Another new type feature in Illustrator CS is the EveryLine Composer, which gives you better control over long runs of text. Use this to set paragraphs of text. EveryLine Composer looks at each paragraph and puts in line breaks that make the paragraph look the best. Adobe uses the EveryLine Composer in Illustrator, Photoshop, InDesign, and other Adobe-specific applications. Single-Line Composer applies the same effect for one line of type. Both are found in the Paragraph palette (see Figure A-10).

Illustrator CS has new Character formatting options. Now available are Underline, Super, and Subscripts. Another wonderful addition is that Illustrator now displays fonts in the actual face under the Font menu (see Figure A-11). This makes it much easier to select fonts visually.

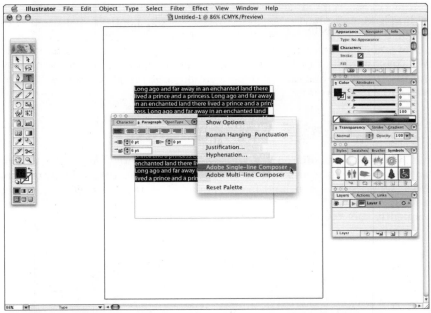

Figure A-10: The Single-Line Composer and the Multi-Line Composer are found in the Paragraph palette's pop-up menu.

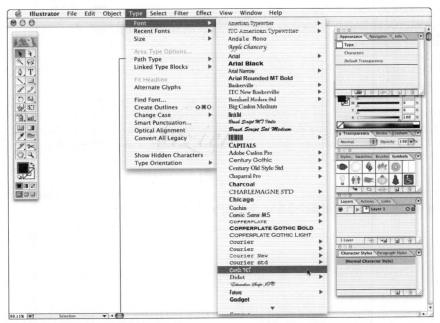

Figure A-11: The font appears in actual form under the Font menu.

Illustrator CS expands its Japanese Typography support with better mojikumi controls, Editable kinsolu shori rules, better tate-chu-yoko controls, alignment of characters, and a preference option for hiding or showing Japanese options. There are a number of embellishments added to finish off your type and make you more productive. These additions include the highlighting of missing fonts, more path-type options, improved hyphenation and justification controls, better text linking, reflow warning, and a faster-working program.

PDF 1.5 (Acrobat 6 Compatibility)

Although Illustrator has offered PDF support for a while now, with the CS version you have more options from which to choose. Now PDF is compatible with Acrobat 6.0; added security, layers, printer marks, and bleeds are supported as well (see Figure A-12). You have better viewing options and the ability to save PDF styles that you frequently use. You can also save a file as a template.

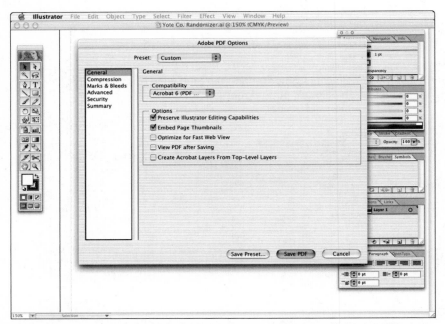

Figure A-12: PDF options dialog box gives you more control over PDF files.

Enhanced Printing Options

When checking out Illustrator CS's printing capabilities, Adobe greets you with a new, improved Print dialog box (see Figure A-13), which makes printing smoother, efficient, and more accurate. With a new, cleaner interface, you can make all of your adjustments in one dialog box. The new Print Preview shows you a small thumbnail of the art. It also shows you how your settings respond to what you have selected as output.

The Fit to Page option now automatically resizes your art to fit the paper size. This also retains the correct scaling so the width and height ration is retained. You now have the ability to save print styles so you can choose them quickly and easily the next time you output a job with the same settings. Transparency Flattener has better controls. You can also control Spot colors and how overprinting is handled. The printer's marks are customizable as well as bleed settings.

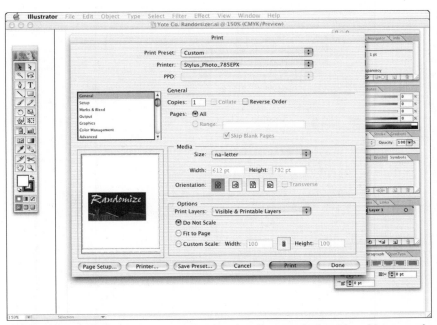

Figure A-13: The Print Options dialog box has been redesigned and improved.

Summary

In this appendix, you discovered:

✦ New 3D features in Illustrator CS are live and easily editable.

✦ The Scribble Effect adds a loose, sketchy effect to art.

✦ There are many new and updated type features that make typesetting in Illustrator much easier.

✦ Illustrator CS is compatible with Acrobat 6.

✦ The new Printing features allow you to do much more in one dialog box.

✦   ✦   ✦

Shortcuts in Illustrator cs

✦ ✦ ✦ ✦

In This Appendix

Commands

Functions

Shortcuts

✦ ✦ ✦ ✦

Illustrator has more keyboard commands, functions, and shortcuts than ever before. The tables in this appendix give you a quick reference to the commands, functions, and shortcuts for both Macintosh and Windows (as in the rest of the book, the Windows commands are in square brackets).

Caution Macintosh users should check to make sure their function keys aren't assigned to complete any system tasks. In Macintosh's Keyboard Control panel, you can set the function keys to be passed through in order to avoid any conflicts. This isn't the default value.

Menu Commands

Table B-1 The File Menu	
Command	**Shortcut**
New	⌘ (Ctrl)+N
New from Template	⌘ (Ctrl)+Shift+N
Open	⌘ (Ctrl)+O
Close	⌘ (Ctrl)+W
Save	⌘ (Ctrl)+S
Save As	⌘ (Ctrl)+Shift+S
Save a Copy	⌘ (Ctrl)+Option (Alt)+S

Continued

Table B-1 *(continued)*

Command	Shortcut
Revert	F12
Save for Web	⌘ (Ctrl)+Shift+Option (Alt)+S
Document Setup	⌘ (Ctrl)+Option (Alt)+P
Print (Print)	⌘ (Ctrl)+P
Quit (Exit) Illustrator	⌘ (Ctrl)+Q

Table B-2
The Edit Menu

Command	Shortcut
Undo	⌘ (Ctrl)+Z
Redo	⌘ (Ctrl)+Shift+Z
Cut	⌘ (Ctrl)+X
Copy	⌘ (Ctrl)+C
Paste	⌘ (Ctrl)+V
Paste in Front	⌘ (Ctrl)+Option (Alt)+V
Paste in Back	⌘ (Ctrl)+Shift+Option (Alt)+V
Find and Replace	⌘ (Ctrl)+F
Find Next	⌘ (Ctrl)+Option (Alt)+I
Color Settings	⌘ (Ctrl)+Shift+K
Keyboard Shortcuts	⌘ (Ctrl)+Shift+Option (Alt)+K
General Preferences	⌘ (Ctrl)+K (under the Illustrator menu for Mac OS X)

Table B-3
The Object Menu

Command	Shortcut
Transform ⇨ Transform Again	⌘ (Ctrl)+D
Transform ⇨ Move	⌘ (Ctrl)+Shift+M

Command	Shortcut
Transform ⇨ Transform Each	⌘ (Ctrl)+Shift+Option (Alt)+D
Bring to Front	⌘ (Ctrl)+Shift+)
Bring Forward	⌘ (Ctrl)+)
Send Backward	⌘ (Ctrl)+(
Send to Back	⌘ (Ctrl)+Shift+(
Group	⌘ (Ctrl)+G
Ungroup	⌘ (Ctrl)+Shift+G
Lock ⇨ Selection	⌘ (Ctrl)+2
Unlock All	⌘ (Ctrl)+Option (Alt)+2
Hide ⇨ Selection	⌘ (Ctrl)+3
Show All	⌘ (Ctrl)+Option (Alt)+3
Path ⇨ Join	⌘ (Ctrl)+J
Path ⇨ Average	⌘ (Ctrl)+Option (Alt)+J
Blend ⇨ Make	⌘ (Ctrl)+Option (Alt)+B
Blend ⇨ Release	⌘ (Ctrl)+Option (Alt)+Shift+B
Envelope Distort ⇨ Make with Warp	⌘ (Ctrl)+Option (Alt)+W
Envelope Distort ⇨ Make with Mesh	⌘ (Ctrl)+Option (Alt)+M
Envelope Distort ⇨ Make with Top Object	⌘ (Ctrl)+Option (Alt)+C
Envelope Distort ⇨ Edit Contents	⌘ (Ctrl)+Shift+V
Clipping Mask ⇨ Make	⌘ (Ctrl)+7
Clipping Mask ⇨ Release	⌘ (Ctrl)+Option (Alt)+7
Compound Path ⇨ Make	⌘ (Ctrl)+8
Compound Path ⇨ Release	⌘ (Ctrl)+Option (Alt)+8

Table B-4
The Type Menu

Command	Shortcut
Create Outlines	⌘ (Ctrl)+Shift+O
Show Hidden Characters	⌘ (Ctrl)+Option (Alt)+I

Table B-5
The Select Menu

Command	Shortcut
Select All	⌘ (Ctrl)+A
Deselect All	⌘ (Ctrl)+Shift+A
Reselect	⌘ (Ctrl)+6
Next Object Above	⌘ (Ctrl)+Option (Alt)+)
Next Object Below	⌘ (Ctrl)+Option (Alt)+(

Table B-6
The Filter Menu

Command	Shortcut
Apply Last Filter	⌘ (Ctrl)+E
Last Filter	⌘ (Ctrl)+Option (Alt)+E

Table B-7
The Effect Menu

Command	Shortcut
Apply Last Filter	⌘ (Ctrl)+Shift+E
Last Filter Dialog Box	⌘ (Ctrl)+Shift+Option (Alt)+E

Table B-8
The View Menu

Command	Shortcut
Outline/Preview	⌘ (Ctrl)+Y (toggle)
Overprint Preview	⌘ (Ctrl)+Shift+Option (Alt)+Y
Pixel Preview	⌘ (Ctrl)+Option (Alt)+Y
Zoom In	⌘ (Ctrl)++ (plus sign)
Zoom Out	⌘ (Ctrl)+−

Command	Shortcut
Fit in Window	⌘ (Ctrl)+0 (zero)
	Double-click Hand tool
Actual Size (100%)	⌘ (Ctrl)+1
	Double-click Zoom tool
Hide Edges	⌘ (Ctrl)+H (toggle)
Hide Template	⌘ (Ctrl)+Shift+W (toggle)
Show/Hide Rulers	⌘ (Ctrl)+R (toggle)
Show/Hide Bounding Box	⌘ (Ctrl)+Shift+B (toggle)
Show/Hide Transparency Grid	⌘ (Ctrl)+Shift+D (toggle)
Show/Hide Text Threads	⌘ (Ctrl)+Shift+Y (toggle)
Smart Guides	⌘ (Ctrl)+U
Guides ➪ Show/Hide Guides	⌘ (Ctrl)+; (toggle)
Guides ➪ Lock Guides	⌘ (Ctrl)+Option (Alt)+;
Guides ➪ Make Guides	⌘ (Ctrl)+5
Guides ➪ Release Guides	⌘ (Ctrl)+Option (Alt)+5
Show/Hide Grid	⌘ (Ctrl)+"(toggle)
Snap to Grid (Pixel)	⌘ (Ctrl)+Shift+"
Snap to Point	⌘ (Ctrl)+Option (Alt)+"

Table B-9
The Window Menu

Command	Shortcut
Show/Hide Align	Shift+F7 (toggle)
Show/Hide Appearance	Shift+F6 (toggle)
Show/Hide Attributes	F11 (toggle)
Show/Hide Brushes	F5 (toggle)
Show/Hide Color	F6 (toggle)
Show/Hide Gradient	F9 (toggle)
Show/Hide Styles	Shift+F5 (toggle)

Continued

Table B-9 *(continued)*

Command	Shortcut
Show/Hide Info	F8 (toggle)
Show/Hide Layers	F7 (toggle)
Show/Hide Pathfinder	Shift+F9 (toggle)
Show/Hide Stroke	F10 (toggle)
Show/Hide Symbols	Shift+F11 (toggle)
Show/Hide Transform	Shift+F8 (toggle)
Show/Hide Transparency	@@ Shift+F10 (toggle)
Show/Hide Character Palette	⌘ (Ctrl)+T (toggle)
Show/Hide OpenType Palette	⌘ (Ctrl)+Shift+Option (Alt)+T
Show/Hide Paragraph Palette	⌘ (Ctrl)+Option (Alt)+T
Tab Ruler Palette	⌘ (Ctrl)+Shift+T

Table B-10
The Help Menu

Command	Shortcut
Illustrator Help	F1 (Windows only)

Toolbox Commands

Table B-11
Tool Selection

Function	Shortcut
Select the next pop-up tool	Drag to the right and release on desired tool
	Option (Alt)+click on a tool
Open tool dialog box	Double click on the tool
Hide toolbox and palettes	Tab

Table B-12
Selection Tools

Tool	Shortcut
Selection tool	V
	Ctrl+Tab with Direct Selection tool, and then hold ⌘ (Ctrl)
	⌘ (Ctrl) with all other tools if Selection tool was the last tool used
Direct Selection tool	A (Mac and Windows)
	Ctrl+Tab with Selection tool, and then hold ⌘ (Ctrl)+Option (Alt) with Group Selection tool
	⌘ (Ctrl) with all other tools if Direct Selection tool was the last tool used
Group Selection tool	Option (Alt) with Direct Selection tool
	⌘ (Ctrl)+Option (Alt) with all other tools if Direct Selection tool was the last tool used
Magic Wand tool	Y
Direct Select Lasso tool	Q

Function	Procedure
Select one point	Click with Direct Selection tool
Select one segment	Click with Direct Selection tool
Select one path	Click with Group Selection tool
Select next group up	Click selected path again with Group Selection tool
Select top-level group	Click with Selection tool
Select additional	Shift+click
Select specific points	Drag with Direct Selection tool
Select specific paths	Drag with Selection tool
Deselect selected	Shift+click selected
Move selection	Drag
Duplicate selection	Option (Alt)+drag
Constrain to 45° movement	Shift+drag
Duplicate and constrain	Option (Alt)+Shift+drag

Continued

Table B-12 *(continued)*

Function	Procedure
Proportionately resize object	Shift+drag Bounding Box handle
Resize from center	Option (Alt)+drag Bounding Box handle
Resize proportionately from center	Option (Alt)+Shift+drag Bounding Box handle
Select all	⌘ (Ctrl)+A
Deselect all	⌘ (Ctrl)+Shift+A
Select all objects with similar Fill, Stroke, Opacity and/or Blending Mode	Click with Magic Wand tool
Add similar colored and stroked objects to current selection	Shift+Magic Wand tool
Subtract similar colored and stroked objects from the current selection	Option (Alt)+Magic Wand tool
Set Magic Wand options	Double click on Magic Wand tool to open the Magic Wand palette

Table B-13
Path Tools

Tool	Shortcut
Pen tool	P
Add Anchor Point tool	+ (actual the key is the equals (=) sign, not the Shift+=; the plus sign on the numeric keyboard doesn't work for this)
	Option (Alt)+Delete Anchor Point tool
	Option (Alt)+Scissors tool
Delete Anchor Point tool	−
	Option (Alt)+Add Anchor Point tool
Convert Anchor Point tool	Shift+C
	Option (Alt)+Pen tool
Pencil tool	N
Smooth tool	Option (Alt)+ Pencil tool
	Option (Alt)+ Erase tool
	Option (Alt)+ Paintbrush tool

Tool	Shortcut
Paintbrush tool	B
Scissors tool	C

Function	Procedure
Create a straight corner point	Click with Pen tool
Create a smooth point	Drag with Pen tool
Continue existing open path	Click+drag with Pen tool on end point of existing path
Close open path	While drawing, click+drag with Pen tool on the initial end point
	Click+drag with Pen tool on each end point in succession
	Select path and join (⌘ (Ctrl)+J)
Constrain new point to 45 degrees from last point	Shift+drag with Pen tool
Constrain control handles to 45 degrees	Shift while dragging handle with Pen tool
Create a path	Click+drag a succession of points with Pen tool
Add anchor points to existing path	Click with the Pen tool on path
Delete anchor points from existing path	Shift+click with Pen tool on an anchor point
Convert anchor point to smooth point existing point	Drag with Convert Direction Point tool on
Convert smooth point to corner point smooth point	Click with Convert Direction Point tool on
Convert smooth corner to combination corner	Drag one handle with Direct Selection tool back into the anchor point
Convert smooth corner to curved corner	Drag one handle with Convert Direction Point tool
Draw freestyle paths	Drag with Pencil tool
View Paintbrush options	Double-click Paintbrush tool in toolbox
Reshape a path	Select points with Direct Selection, and then drag with Reshape tool
Split path	Click with Scissors tool
Slice multiple paths	Drag with Knife tool
Constrain Knife slice to straight lines	Option(Alt)+drag with Knife tool
Constrain Knife slice to 45°	Shift+Option(Alt)+drag with Knife tool

Table B-14
Type Tools

Tool	Shortcut
Type tool	T
	Shift+Vertical Type tool
Area Type tool	Option (Alt)+Path Type tool
	Shift+Vertical Area Type tool
	Option (Alt)+Shift Vertical Path Type tool
Path Type tool	Option (Alt)+Area Type tool
	Shift+Vertical Path Type tool
	Option (Alt)+Shift+Vertical Area Type tool
Vertical Type tool	Shift+Type tool
Vertical Area Type tool	Option (Alt)+Vertical Path Type tool
	Shift+Area Type tool
	Option (Alt)+Shift+Area Type tool
Vertical Path Type tool	Option (Alt)+Vertical Area Type tool
	Shift+Path Type tool
	Option (Alt)+Shift +Area Type tool

Function	Procedure
Create point type	Click with Type tool
Create rectangle type	Drag with Type tool
Place path type on a closed path	Click path with Path Type tool
	Option (Alt)+click path with Type tool
	Option (Alt)+click path with Area Type tool
Place path type on an open path	Click path with Path Type tool
	Click path with Type tool
	Option (Alt)+click path with Area Type tool
Place area type on a closed path	Click path with Area Type tool
	Click path with Type tool
	Option(Alt)+click path with Path Type tool
Place area type on an open path	Click path with Area Type tool
	Option (Alt)+click path with Type tool
	Option (Alt)+click path with Path Type tool

Function	Procedure
Change vertical type to horizontal type	Choose Type ⇨ Type Orientation ⇨ Horizontal
Change horizontal type to vertical type	Choose Type ⇨ Type Orientation ⇨ Vertical
Select entire text block	Click text block with Selection tool
Select one character	Drag across character with any Type tool
Select one word	Double-click word with any Type tool
Select one paragraph	Triple-click paragraph with any Type tool
Select all text in text block	Click in text block with any Type tool, and then press ⌘ (Ctrl)+A
Flip type on a path	Double-click the I-bar with any selection tool or just drag it to the opposite side

Table B-15
Line Tools

Tool	Shortcut
Line Segment tool	\

Function	Procedure
Create line segments using numbers	Click with the Line Segment tool
Draw a line segment	Drag with Line Segment tool
Constrain line segments to 45 degrees	Shift+drag with Line Segment tool
Create line segment from midpoint	Option (Alt)+click with Line Segment tool using numbers
Draw line segment from midpoint	Option (Alt)+drag with Line Segment tool
Move line segment while drawing	Spacebar+drag with Line Segment tool
Create multiple line segments	~+drag with Line Segment tool
Create arc segments using numbers	Click with the Arc tool
Draw an arc segment	Drag with Arc tool
Constrain arc segments to circular sections	Shift+drag with Arc tool
Create arc segment from the center	Option (Alt)+click with Arc tool
Draw arc segment from the center	Option (Alt)+drag with Arc tool
Move arc segment while drawing	Spacebar+drag with Arc tool

Continued

Table B-15 *(continued)*

Function	Procedure
Create multiple arc segments	~+drag with Arc tool
Toggle arc between concave and convex	X+drag with Arc tool
Toggle between open and closed arcs	C+drag with Arc tool
Flip the arc	F+drag with Arc tool
Increase arc slope	↑+drag with Arc tool
Decrease arc slope	↓+drag with Arc tool
Create spiral using numbers	Click with Spiral tool
Draw spiral	Drag with Spiral tool
Constrain spiral angle	Shift+drag with Spiral tool
Move spiral while drawing	Spacebar+drag with Spiral tool
Create multiple spirals	~+drag with Spiral tool
Decrease spiral decay	⌘ (Ctrl)+drag with Spiral tool
Increase spiral length and size	Option (Alt)+drag with Spiral tool (toggle)
Increase spiral length	↑+drag with Spiral tool
Decrease spiral length	↓+drag with Spiral tool
Create a rectangular grid using numbers	Click with the Rectangular Grid tool
Draw an rectangular grid	Drag with Rectangular Grid tool
Constrain rectangular grid to a square	Shift+drag with Rectangular Grid tool
Create a square rectangular grid	Option (Alt)+click with Rectangular Grid tool
Draw rectangular grid from the center	Option (Alt)+drag with Rectangular Grid tool
Move rectangular grid while drawing	Spacebar+drag with Rectangular Grid tool
Create multiple rectangular grid	~+drag with Rectangular Grid tool
Skew horizontal dividers to the left	X+drag with Rectangular Grid tool
Skew horizontal dividers to the right	C+drag with Rectangular Grid tool
Skew vertical dividers to the top of the rectangular grid	F+drag with Rectangular Grid tool
Skew vertical dividers to the bottom of the rectangular grid	V+drag with Rectangular Grid tool
Increase vertical dividers	↑+drag with Rectangular Grid tool
Decrease vertical dividers	↓+drag with Rectangular Grid tool
Increase horizontal dividers	→+drag with Rectangular Grid tool

Function	Procedure
Decrease horizontal dividers	←+drag with Rectangular Grid tool
Create a polar grid using numbers	Click with the Polar Grid tool
Draw an polar grid	Drag with Polar Grid tool
Constrain polar grid to a circle	Shift+drag with Polar Grid tool
Create a circular polar grid	Option (Alt)+click with Polar Grid tool
Draw polar grid from the center	Option (Alt)+drag with Polar Grid tool
Move polar grid while drawing	Spacebar+drag with Polar Grid tool
Create multiple polar grid	~+drag with Polar Grid tool
Skew concentric dividers inward	X+drag with Polar Grid tool
Skew concentric dividers outward	C+drag with Polar Grid tool
Skew radial dividers counterclockwise	F+drag with Polar Grid tool
Skew radial dividers clockwise	V+drag with Polar Grid tool
Increase concentric dividers	↑+drag with Polar Grid tool
Decrease concentric dividers	↓+drag with Polar Grid tool
Increase radial dividers	→+drag with Polar Grid tool
Decrease radial dividers	←+drag with Polar Grid tool

Table B-16
Shape Tools

Tool	Shortcut
Rectangle tool	M
Ellipse tool	L

Function	Procedure
Create rectangle using numbers	Click with Rectangle tool or Rounded Rectangle tool
Draw rectangle	Drag with Rectangle tool
Draw square	Shift+drag with Rectangle tool
Create centered rectangle using numbers	Option (Alt)+click with Rectangle tool
Draw centered rectangle	Option (Alt)+drag with Rectangle tool
Draw square from center	Option (Alt)+Shift+drag with Rectangle tool

Continued

Table B-16 *(continued)*

Function	Procedure
Move rectangle while drawing	Spacebar+drag with Rectangle tool
Create multiple rectangles	~+drag with Rectangle tool
Create rounded rectangle using numbers	Click with Rounded Rectangle tool
Draw rounded rectangle	Drag with Rounded Rectangle tool
Draw square with rounded corners	Shift+drag with Rounded Rectangle tool
Create centered rounded rectangle	Option (Alt)+click with Rounded Rectangle tool
Draw centered rounded rectangle	Option (Alt)+drag with Rounded Rectangle tool
Draw square from center with rounded corners	Option (Alt)+Shift+drag with Rounded Rectangle tool
Move rounded rectangle while drawing	Spacebar+drag with Rounded Rectangle tool
Create multiple rounded rectangles	~+drag with Rounded Rectangle tool
Create ellipse using numbers	Click with Ellipse tool
Draw ellipse	Drag with Ellipse tool
Draw circle	Shift+drag with Ellipse tool
Create centered ellipse using numbers	Option (Alt)+click with Ellipse tool
Draw centered ellipse	Option (Alt)+drag with Ellipse tool
Move ellipse while drawing	Spacebar+drag with Ellipse tool
Create multiple ellipses	~+drag with Ellipse tool
Create polygon using numbers	Click with Polygon tool
Draw polygon	Drag with Polygon tool
Constrain polygon angle	Shift+drag with Polygon tool
Create centered polygon using numbers	Option (Alt)+click with Polygon tool
Draw centered polygon	Option (Alt)+drag with Polygon tool
Increase polygon sides	↑+drag with Polygon tool
Decrease polygon sides	↓+drag with Polygon tool
Move polygon while drawing	Spacebar+drag with Polygon tool
Create multiple polygons	~+drag with Polygon tool
Create star using numbers	Click with Star tool
Draw star	Drag with Star tool

Function	Procedure
Constrain star angle	Shift+drag with Star tool
Draw even-shouldered star	Option (Alt)+drag with Star tool
Move outer points only	⌘ (Ctrl)+drag with Star tool
Increase star points	↑+drag with Star tool
Decrease star points	↓+drag with Star tool
Move star while drawing	Spacebar+drag with Star tool
Create multiple stars	~+drag with Star tool

Table B-17
Transformation Tools

Tool	Shortcut
Rotate tool	R
Reflect tool	O
Scale tool	S
Free Transform tool	E

Function	Procedure
Moving objects	Drag with the Selection or Free Transform tool
Constrain movements along 45 degree axis	Shift+drag with the Selection or Free Transform tool
Rotate using numbers	Option (Alt)+click with Rotate tool
Rotate from center of selection with numbers	Double-click with Rotate tool
Free Rotate (live)	Click with Rotate to set Origin, and then drag with Rotate tool
Free Rotate around selection center	Drag with Rotate tool
Constrain rotation to 45 degrees	Shift+drag with Rotate tool
Rotate a copy	Option (Alt)+drag with Rotate tool
Rotate pattern only	~+drag with Rotate tool
Scale using numbers	Option (Alt)+click with Scale tool
Scale from center of selection with numbers	Double-click with Scale tool

Continued

Table B-17 *(continued)*

Function	Procedure
Free Scale (live)	Click with Scale to set Origin, and then drag with Scale tool
Free Scale around selection center	Drag with Scale tool
Constrain scaling to 45 degrees	Shift+drag with Scale tool
Scale a copy	Option (Alt)+drag with Scale tool
Scale pattern only	~+drag with Scale tool
Reflect using numbers	Option (Alt)+click with Reflect tool
Reflect from center of selection with numbers	Double-click with Reflect tool
Free Reflect (live)	Click with Reflect to set Origin, and then drag with Reflect tool
Free Reflect around selection center	Drag with Reflect tool
Constrain reflecting angle to 45 degrees	Shift+drag with Reflect tool
Reflect a Copy	Option (Alt)+drag with Reflect tool
Reflect Pattern only	~+drag with Reflect tool
Shear using numbers	Option (Alt)+click with Shear tool
Shear from Center of Selection with numbers	Double-click with Shear tool
Free Shear (live) with Shear	Click with Shear to set Origin, and then drag
Free Shear around selection center	Drag with Shear
Constrain shearing to 45 degrees	Shift+drag with Shear tool
Shear a copy	Option (Alt)+drag with Shear tool
Shear pattern only	~+drag with Shear tool

Table B-18
Distortion Tools

Tool	Shortcut
Wrap tool	Shift+R

Function	Procedure
Twirl using numbers	Option (Alt)+click with Rotate tool
Free Twirl (live)	Drag with Twirl tool
Reshape distortion brush Bloat, Scallop, Crystallize or Wrinkle tool	Option (Alt)+drag with Warp, Twirl, Pucker,
Constrain brush to horizontal or vertical movement	Shift+drag with Warp , Twirl, Pucker, Bloat, Scallop, Crystallize or Wrinkle tool
Set distortion options	Double click on the selected distortion tool

Table B-19 Symbol Tools	
Tool	**Shortcut**
Symbol Sprayer tool	Shift+S
Function	**Procedure**
Add a single symbol	Click+Symbol Sprayer tool
Add multiple symbols	Drag+Symbol Sprayer tool
Remove symbols from set	Option (Alt)+ Symbol Sprayer tool
Move the symbols in a set	Drag with the Symbol Shifter tool
Change the stacking order of the symbols	Option (Alt)+ Symbol Shifter tool
Scrunch the symbols closer together	Drag with the Symbol Scruncher tool
Move the symbols farther apart	Option (Alt)+ Symbol Scruncher tool
Increase the symbol size	Drag with the Symbol Sizer tool
Decrease the symbol size	Option (Alt)+ Symbol Sizer tool
Rotate the symbols	Drag with the Symbol Spinner tool
Increase the symbol's transparency	Drag with the Symbol Screener tool
Decrease the symbol's transparency	Option (Alt)+ Symbol Screener tool
Change the symbol's color	Drag with the Symbol Stainer tool
Restore the symbol's original color	Option (Alt)+ Symbol Stainer tool
Apply a style to the symbol	Drag with the Symbol Styler tool
Remove the style from a symbol	Option (Alt)+ Symbol Styler tool

Table B-20
Graph Tools

Tool	Shortcut
Column Graph tool	J

Function	Procedure
Create a Graph sized by numbers	Click with any Graph tool
Create a Graph sized by dragging	Drag with any Graph tool
Create a square or circular graph	Shift+drag with any Graph tool
Create a Graph from the center	Option (Alt)+drag with any Graph tool

Table B-21
Paint Tools

Tool	Shortcut
Gradient tool	G
Gradient Mesh tool	U
Paint Bucket tool	K
	Option(Alt)+Eyedropper tool
Eyedropper tool	I
	Option (Alt)+Paint Bucket tool

Function	Procedure
Change Linear Gradient direction and/or length	Drag with Gradient tool
Constrain Gradient Direction to 45° angles	Shift+drag with Gradient tool
Change Radial Gradient size and/or location	Drag with Gradient tool
Change Radial Gradient origin point	Click with Gradient tool
Sample color to Color palette	Click with Eyedropper tool
Sample Screen color to Color palette	Shift+click with Eyedropper tool
Change Paint Style of selected objects	Double-click with Eyedropper tool on an object with the desired style
Paint unselected objects	Click objects with the Paint Bucket tool

Function	Procedure
Measure a distance	Click the start and end location with the Measure tool
Measure a distance by 45° angles	Shift+click the start and end location with the Measure tool

Table B-22
Blend, Auto Trace and Slice Tools

Tool	Shortcut
Blend tool	W
Slice tool	Shift+K

Function	Procedure
Blend between two paths	Click corresponding selected points on each path with Blend tool
Set Blend options	Double click on the Blend tool
Auto Trace Images	Click area to be traced with Auto Trace tool
Divide artwork into slices	Drag+Slice tool
Constrain slice to a square	Option (Alt)+drag with the Slice tool
Slice selected objects	Drag+Slice Selected tool

Table B-23
Viewing Tools

Tool	Shortcut
Hand tool	H
	Spacebar (when not entering text)
Zoom tool	Z
	⌘ (Ctrl)+spacebar
Zoom Out tool	⌘ (Ctrl)+Option(Alt)+spacebar
	Option (Alt)+Zoom tool

Continued

Table B-23 *(continued)*	
Function	**Procedure**
Reposition the page	Drag with the Hand tool
Fit the page within the document window	Double click on the Hand tool
Moving page boundaries	Drag with the Page tool
Reset page boundaries	Double click on the Page tool
Zoom in	Click with the Zoom tool
	⌘ (Ctrl)++ (plus sign)
Zoom out	Option (Alt)+click with the Zoom tool
	⌘ (Ctrl)+- (hyphen)
Zoom in to a specific area	Drag with the Zoom tool
Move the Zoom Marquee while drawing	Spacebar while dragging with the Zoom tool
Draw the Zoom Marquee from its center	Ctrl+drag with the Zoom tool

Type Commands

Table B-24 **Type Shortcuts**	
Action	**Shortcut**
Copy type on a path	Option (Alt)+drag the I-bar using any selection tool. (This shortcut actually creates two paths as well as two text stories.)
Flip type on a path	Double-click the I-bar with any selection tool or just drag it to the opposite side of the path
Move insertion point to next character	→ (right arrow)
Move insertion point to previous character	← (left arrow)
Move insertion point to next line	↓ (down arrow)
Move insertion point to previous line	↑ (up arrow)
Move insertion point to next word	⌘ (Ctrl)+→
Move insertion point to previous word	⌘ (Ctrl)+←
Move insertion point to next paragraph	⌘ (Ctrl)+↓

Action	Shortcut
Move insertion point to previous paragraph	⌘ (Ctrl)+↑
Select (by highlighting) all type in story	⌘ (Ctrl)+A when the insertion point is in the story
Select all type in document	⌘ (Ctrl)+A when any tool but the Type tools are selected
Select next character	Shift+→
Select previous character	Shift+←
Select next line	Shift+↓
Select previous line	Shift+↑
Select next word	⌘ (Ctrl)+Shift+→
Select previous word	⌘ (Ctrl)+Shift+←
Select next paragraph	⌘ (Ctrl)+Shift+↓
Select previous paragraph	⌘ (Ctrl)+Shift+↑
Select word	Double-click word
Select paragraph	Triple-click paragraph
Deselect all type	⌘ (Ctrl)+Shift+A
Duplicate column outline and flow text	Option (Alt)+drag column outline with Direct Selection tool
Insert discretionary hyphen	⌘ (Ctrl)+Shift+- (hyphen)
Insert line break	Press Return (Enter) (on keypad)

Table B-25
Paragraph Formatting

Action	Shortcut
Display Paragraph palette	⌘ (Ctrl)+Shift+M
Align paragraph flush left	⌘ (Ctrl)+Shift+L
Align paragraph flush right	⌘ (Ctrl)+Shift+R
Align paragraph flush center	⌘ (Ctrl)+Shift+C
Align paragraph justified	⌘ (Ctrl)+Shift+J
Align paragraph force justified	⌘ (Ctrl)+Shift+F
Display Tab Ruler palette	⌘ (Ctrl)+Shift+T

Continued

Table B-25 *(continued)*

Action	Shortcut
Align Tab palette to selected paragraph	Click Tab palette size box
Cycle through tab stops	Option (Alt)+click tab stop
Move multiple tab stops	Shift+drag tab stops
Cycle tab measurements	Click

Table B-26
Character Formatting

Action	Shortcut
Display Character palette	⌘ (Ctrl)+T
Highlight font	⌘(Ctrl)+Option (Alt)+Shift+M
Increase type size	⌘ (Ctrl)+Shift+>
Decrease type size	⌘ (Ctrl)+Shift+<
Increase type to next size on menu	⌘ (Ctrl)+Option (Alt)+>
Decrease type to next size on menu	⌘ (Ctrl)+Option (Alt)+<
Highlight size	none
Set leading to Solid (same as pt. size)	Double-click Leading symbol in Character palette
Highlight leading	none
Increase Baseline Shift (Raise)*	Option (Alt)+Shift+↑
Decrease Baseline Shift (Lower)*	Option (Alt)+Shift+↓
Increase Baseline Shift (Raise) ×5*	⌘ (Ctrl)+Option (Alt)+Shift+↑
Decrease Baseline Shift (Lower) ×5*	⌘ (Ctrl)+Option (Alt)+Shift+↓
Reset Baseline Shift to 0	none
Highlight Baseline Shift	none
Kern/Track closer*	Option (Alt)+←
Kern/Track apart*	Option (Alt)+→
Kern/Track closer ×5*	⌘ (Ctrl)+Option (Alt)+←

Action	Shortcut
Kern/Track apart ×5*	⌘ (Ctrl)+Option (Alt)+→
Reset Kerning/Tracking to 0	⌘ (Ctrl)+Shift+Q
Highlight Kerning/Tracking	⌘ (Ctrl)+Option (Alt)+K
Reset Horizontal Scale to 100%	⌘ (Ctrl)+Shift+X

* Value/amount set in Preferences

Color Commands

Table B-27 Color Palette	
Action	**Shortcut**
Show/Hide Color palette	F6 (toggle)
	⌘ (Ctrl)+I (toggle)
Revert to default colors	D (White Fill, Black Stroke; Mac and Windows)
Toggle focus between Fill and Stroke	X
Choose current color in Color palette	, (comma)
Change paint to None	/
Apply to inactive Fill/Stroke (Fill when Stroke is active, Stroke when Fill is active)	Option (Alt)+click in color ramp on Color palette
Apply color to unselected object	Drag color swatch from Color palette to object
Apply color to selected object	Click swatch in Color palette
Copy Paint Style to unselected objects	Click unselected objects with Paint Bucket
Copy Paint Style from any (source) object to all selected objects	Click source object with Eyedropper
Tint process color	Shift+drag any Color palette slider
Cycle through Color modes	Shift+click Color Ramp (Grayscale, CMYK, RGB; Mac and Windows)

Table B-28
Swatches Palette

Action	Shortcut
Show/Hide Swatches palette	F5 (toggle)
Toggle focus between Fill and Stroke	X
Add swatch	Click the New Swatch icon
	Drag from Color or Gradient palette into swatches
Replace swatch	Option (Alt)+drag from Color or Gradient palette into swatches
Duplicate swatch	Option (Alt)+drag swatch onto New Swatch icon in Swatches palette
Delete swatch	Drag to Trash icon in Swatches palette
	Click Trash icon with swatches selected
Select contiguous swatches	Shift+click first and last swatches
Select noncontiguous swatches	⌘ (Ctrl)+click each swatch
Switch keyboard focus to Swatches palette (for selecting swatches by name as they are typed)	⌘ (Ctrl)+Option (Alt)+click in Swatches palette
Apply color to unselected object	Drag color swatch from Swatches palette to object
Apply color to selected object	Click swatch in Swatches palette

Table B-29
Gradient Palette

Action	Shortcut
Choose current gradient in Gradient palette	. (period)
Show/Hide Gradient palette	F9 (toggle)
Apply swatch to selected color stop on gradient palette	Option (Alt)+click swatch
Add new color stop	Click below gradient ramp
Duplicate color stop	Option (Alt)+drag color stop
Swap color stops	Option(Alt)+drag color stop on top of another

Action	Shortcut
"Suck" color for color stop with Eyedropper	Shift+click with Eyedropper
Reset Gradient to default Black, White	⌘ (Ctrl)+click in Gradient swatch
Apply color to unselected object	Drag color swatch from Gradient palette to object
Apply color to selected object	Click swatch in Gradient palette

<table>
<tr><th colspan="2" align="center">Table B-30
Stroke Palette</th></tr>
<tr><th>Action</th><th>Shortcut</th></tr>
<tr><td>Show/Hide Stroke palette</td><td>F10 (toggle)</td></tr>
<tr><td>Increase/decrease Stroke weight</td><td>Highlight Stroke field, use up or down arrows, press Return(Enter) when finished</td></tr>
<tr><td>Increase/decrease Miter amount</td><td>Highlight Miter field, use up or down arrows, press Return (Enter) when finished</td></tr>
</table>

Other Palettes

<table>
<tr><th colspan="2" align="center">Table B-31
Miscellaneous Palette Commands</th></tr>
<tr><th>Action</th><th>Shortcut</th></tr>
<tr><td>Collapse/display Palette</td><td>Click box in upper-right corner</td></tr>
<tr><td>Cycle through Palette views</td><td>Double-click palette tab</td></tr>
<tr><td>Apply settings</td><td>Return (Enter)</td></tr>
<tr><td>Apply settings while keeping last text field highlighted</td><td>Shift+Return (Enter)</td></tr>
<tr><td>Highlight next text field</td><td>Tab</td></tr>
<tr><td>Highlight Previous text field</td><td>Shift+Tab</td></tr>
<tr><td>Highlight any text field</td><td>Click label or double-click current value</td></tr>
</table>

Continued

Table B-31 *(continued)*

Action	Shortcut
Increase value by base increment	Highlight field, ↑
Decrease value by base increment	Highlight field, ↓
Increase value by large increment	Highlight field, Shift+↑
Decrease value by large increment	Highlight field, Shift+↓
Combine palettes	Drag palette tab within other palette
Dock palette	Drag palette tab to bottom of other palette
Separate palette	Drag palette tab from current palette

Table B-32
Transform Palette

Action	Shortcut
Show/Hide Transform palette	none
Copy object while transforming	Option (Alt)+Return (Enter)
Scale proportionately	⌘ (Ctrl)+Return (Enter)
Copy object while scaling proportionately	⌘ (Ctrl)+Option (Alt)+Return (Enter)

Table B-33
Layers Palette

Action	Shortcut
Show/Hide Layers palette	F7
New layer	Click New Layer icon
New layer with Options dialog box	Option (Alt)+click New Layer icon
New layer above active layer	⌘ (Ctrl)+Option (Alt)+click New Layer icon
New layer below active layer	⌘ (Ctrl)+click New Layer icon
Duplicate layer(s)	Drag layer(s) to New Layer icon
Change layer order	Drag layers up or down within Layer list
Select all objects on a layer	Option (Alt)+click that layer
Select all objects on several layers	Shift+Option (Alt)+click each layer
Select contiguous layers	Shift+click layers

Action	Shortcut
Select noncontiguous layers	⌘ (Ctrl)+click layers
Move objects to a different layer	Drag colored square to a different layer
Copy objects to a different layer	Option (Alt)+drag color square to a different layer
Hide/Show layer	Click Eyeball icon
View layer while hiding others	Option (Alt)+click Eyeball icon
View layer in Artwork mode	⌘ (Ctrl)+click Eyeball icon
View layer in Preview while others are artwork	⌘ (Ctrl)+Option (Alt)+click Eyeball icon
Lock/Unlock layer	Click Pencil icon
Unlock layer while locking others	Option (Alt)+click Pencil icon
Delete layer	Drag layer to Trash icon
	Select layer and click Trash icon
Delete layer without warning	Option (Alt)+drag layer to Trash icon
	Select layer and Option (Alt)+click trash icon

Miscellaneous Commands

Table B-34 Viewing Shortcuts	
Action	Shortcut
Zoom in	⌘ (Ctrl)++ (plus sign)
	Click with Zoom tool
Zoom out	⌘ (Ctrl)+- (hyphen)
	Option (Alt)+click with Zoom tool
Fit document in Window	⌘ (Ctrl)+0
	Double-click Hand tool
View at actual size (100%)	⌘ (Ctrl)+1
	Double-click Zoom tool

Continued

Table B-34 *(continued)*

Action	Shortcut
Artwork/Preview mode	⌘ (Ctrl)+Y (toggle)
Preview Selection mode	Ô (Ctrl)+P+Option (Alt)+Y
Custom View recall	⌘ (Ctrl)+Option (Alt)+Shift+1 through ⌘ (Ctrl)+Option (Alt)+Shift+0
Show/Hide edges	⌘ (Ctrl)+H (toggle)
Show/Hide guides	⌘ (Ctrl)+;
Show/Hide grid	⌘ (Ctrl)+'
Show/Hide rulers	⌘ (Ctrl)+R
Hide selected objects	⌘ (Ctrl)+3
Hide unselected objects	⌘ (Ctrl)+Option (Alt)+3
Show all hidden objects	⌘ (Ctrl)+Shift+3
Window mode (normal)	F (when in Full Screen mode in Mac or Windows)
Full Screen mode with menu	F (when in Window mode in Mac or Windows)
Full Screen mode (no menus)	F (when in Full Screen mode with menu in Mac or Windows)

Table B-35
Miscellaneous Commands

Action	Shortcut
Nudge selection*	Arrow keys
see special Status Line categories	Option (Alt)+click status bar (lower-left corner)
Cycle through units	⌘+Ctrl+U (Mac only)
Display Illustrator debug screen	⌘+Option+Ctrl+0 (zero; Mac only)
View anagrams of credits	Option (Alt)+click Illustrator click toolbox
Speed up credits in About box	Option (Alt)
Display context-sensitive menus	Ctrl+click (Right-click)
Highlight last active text field	⍺ (Ctrl)+~ (tilde)

* Value/amount set in Preferences

Generic Dialog Box Commands

Table B-36 Generic Dialog Box Commands	
Action	**Shortcut**
Cancel	Esc
OK (or dark bordered button)	Return (Enter)
Highlight next text field	Tab
Highlight previous text field	Shift+Tab
Highlight any text field	Click label or double-click current value

✦   ✦   ✦

People and Resources

This appendix contains resources for related products, services, and other information that Illustrator users may find useful. All phone numbers, addresses, and version numbers are subject to change without notice, of course.

Jennifer Alspach (jen@bezier.com)

Jennifer Alspach is the author of other books on computer-related subjects, including *Adobe Acrobat 5.0 Visual Quickstart Guide* (2001 Peachpit Press), *Teach Yourself Photoshop 5.0/5.5* (IDG Books), and *Photoshop and Illustrator Synergy Studio Secrets* (IDG Books). Her illustrations have appeared in various publications, including *Adobe Magazine*. In addition, Jennifer regularly speaks at various seminars, Macworld Expos, and user groups all over the country. Other works by Jennifer include: Co-author of *Photoshop Studio Secrets 5/e* (IDG Books); *Adobe Photoshop 5.5 and Illustrator 8.0 Advanced Classroom in a Book* (Adobe Press); *Photodeluxe Home Edition for Windows Visual Quickstart Guide* (Peachpit Press); *Photodeluxe for Windows and Macintosh Visual Quickstart Guide* (Peachpit Press); *Illustrator 7 Complete* (Hayden Books); *Illustrator Filter Finesse* (Random House); *Microsoft BOB* (Que); Illustrated for the *Macworld Illustrator Bible* (IDG Books); and the *Illustrator WOW!* books (Peachpit Press).

Joe Jones (DujaVe@aol.com)

A Denver native with a strong foundation in the fine arts, Joe Jones has been a professional illustrator and graphic artist since 1983. Since starting his successful design firm, Art Works Studio, in 1995, Joe has created award-winning illustrations and graphic design work in print, Web, and Multimedia. Although producing illustrations for clients such as Adobe Systems, Rolls Royce and performers such as Carlos Santana dominates most of Joe's time, his passion for science fiction and fantasy art remains a focus in his life. Joe finds his inspiration in real-life heroes, such as Neil Armstrong, Chuck Yeager, and the conceptual work of Ralph McQuarrie. Joe's life-long pursuit has been to combine his love of science fiction with his talent for illustration. In March of 2000 and 2001, Jones was honored as the Special Guest Artist at the 21st and 22nd International Conference on the Fantastic in the Arts. Along with winning 18 International Web design awards, Joe's work has been showcased in many prestigious books, such as Kia's *Power Tools Studio Secrets*; *Photoshop Synergy Studio Secrets and Illustrator Synergy Studio Secrets*; *Illustrator 8 F/X and Design*; *Adobe Photoshop 5.5; Illustrator 8.0 Advanced Classroom in a Book*; The *Illustrator 9 Wow* book *Photoshop 6 Studio Secrets* and the *Macworld Illustrator Bible* series, to name just a few. Committed to helping young artists, Jones takes time from his busy schedule to teach classes at The Rocky Mountain College of Art and Design. Visit him on the Web at: www.artworksstudio.com.

Cory Gray (www.thegraydomain.com)

is a commercial artist with a flare for cartoon art and has a background in traditional illustration. He strives to be a great vector artist and has created countless pieces for print production with expertise in high-end spot separation. His accomplishments include everything from silkscreen design and graphic solutions to character concepts for children's publications. Cory received his associate arts degrees from the Colorado Institute of Art and Platte College for Digital Graphics. He works at Image West Apparel and also serves as art department supervisor. Cory currently resides in Watkins, CO. His client list includes: Denver screen printers, Golden Squeegee, Graphic Elements, I.Q. Sportswear, the Alecci Foundation and many others.

Brian Warchesik (brianjudywar@earthlink.net)

Brian Warchesik is currently working as a graphic designer in Denver, Colorado. He also pursues his career as an illustrator out of his home in Littleton, Colorado, where he lives with his wife, Judy. Brian's work has been featured in publications such as the *Photoshop and Illustrator Synergy Studio Secrets* book as well as Delta's in-flight magazine, *Sky Magazine,* and has recently done some work for the Business and Marketing Association of Colorado. His paintings have been featured in gallery showings, and he continues to love working. Phone: 720-981-7722.

Todd Macadangdang (toddm@adobe.com)

An award-winning artist, instructor, and Adobe Illustrator guru, Todd shut down his design firm in 1991 to focus on a career as a freelance Illustrator. Since then, Todd has offered his services as illustrator, project manager, and creative director for numerous print, Web, and multimedia projects. Past clients include: Paramount Publishing; Simon and Schuster; Viacom; AOL; The Learning Company; Worldcom; Adobe

Systems; and Siemens. He is the current director of Illustratorworld.com and a member of the Illustrator development team at Adobe Systems in San Jose, California.

Hajime Sorayama (www.sorayama.net)

Miharu Yamamoto/Sorayama: representative Artspace Company K&Y
34 Riverside Ave.
Haverstraw, NY 10927
Phone: 212-252-9122.
Fax: 212-252-9123.

Jason McQuitty (jason@thedesignarmada.com)

Born in Colorado Springs, Colorado, Jason graduated from Rocky Mountain College of Art and Design with a bachelor in fine arts of illustration. Jason loves to work in Adobe Photoshop, Painter, and especially Adobe Illustrator. He specializes in comic book art, car illustration, and athlete illustration. Located in San Antonio, TX, you can contact Jason via his cell phone at 210-885-4742.

Martin Mendelsberg (mendelsberg@msn.com)

Martin Mendelsberg is a typographer and graphic designer. He earned his BFA degree from Minneapolis College of Art & Design and MFA degree from the University of Denver. Foreign study included Atelier 63, The Netherlands. Martin's work has been exhibited nationally and internationally. Prints from his "Holocaust Portfolio" have recently been purchased by Yale University. He has also completed Hebrew typeface designs for Masterfont Ltd. in Israel. Mr. Mendelsberg currently chairs the graphic design program at Rocky Mountain College of Art & Design in Denver, Colorado.

Shane Duerksen (duerk2@yahoo.com)

Robert Sharif (sharifr@adobe.com)

Robert has been working as a graphic designer/illustartor since May of 1996. He has created Web sites, animation presentations, illustrations, posters, and package designs for several design companies, whose clients include Cisco Systems, Sun Microsystems, Apple Computer, Espon, Hewlett Packard, Nortel Networks, and Applied Materials. For the past two and half years, Adobe Systems has employed Robert as a quality engineer (black box tester). You can contact him through Adobe Illustrator:

Robert Sharif, 2791 Lexford Ave. San Jose, CA 95124.
Work phone: 408-536-6186; home (evenings): 408-448-1015.

Trina Wai (twai@adobe.com)

Trina graduated from the Academy of Art College in San Francisco with a B.A. in Graphic Design. Contact info: Trina Wai 5027 Silver Reef Dr. Fremont, CA 94538.

Adobe Systems, Inc.

Publisher of Adobe Illustrator, Adobe Photoshop, Adobe PageMaker, Adobe Streamline, Adobe Premiere, Adobe Dimensions, and several other products.

1585 Charleston Road PO Box 7900
Mountain View, CA 94039-7900
www.adobe.com
Customer service: 800-833-6687.
Technical support (available to registered users with a valid serial number only): 206-628-3953 BBS (First Class software): 206-623-6984.

✦   ✦   ✦

Index

Continued

Continued

Continued

Continued

Continued